Richard P. Belcher has given us a commentary that is thoroughly researched, balanced, and sensitive to the needs of preaching pastors. Whether it is read by students seeking to grasp what are the issues in Ecclesiastes (and what contemporary scholars are saying about those issues), or read by ministers and teachers preparing to preach and teach the book, it will prove to be immensely beneficial.

Duane Garrett
Professor of Old Testament Interpretation

Without question, this is one of the finest commentaries I have ever read. It transformed the way I view Ecclesiastes and deeply shaped the way in which I preached the book. I give it my highest endorsement!

David Rea
Pastor, Providence Presbyterian Church (PCA), Dallas, Texas

Ecclesiastes

A Mentor Commentary

Richard P. Belcher, Jr.

MENTOR

Unless otherwise stated, Scripture quotations are from *The Holy Bible, English Standard Version*, copyright © 2001 by Crossway Bibles, a division of Good News Publishers. Used by permission. All rights reserved. ESV Text Edition: 2007.

Scripture quotations marked NIV are taken from *The Holy Bible, New International Version*®. NIV®. Copyright©1973, 1978, 1984 by International Bible Society. Used by permission of Zondervan. All rights reserved.

Scripture quotations marked RSV are taken from *The Revised Standard Version of the Bible*, copyright 1952 (2nd edition, 1971) by the Division of Christian Education of the National Council of the Churches of Christ in the United States of America. Used by permission. All rights reserved.

Scripture quotations marked NRSV are taken from *The New Revised Standard Version Bible*, copyright 1989, Division of Christian Education of the National Council of the Churches of Christ in the United States of America. Used by permission. All rights reserved.

Scripture quotations marked KJV are taken from *The King James Version*.

Scripture quotations marked NKJV are taken from *The New King James Version*. Copyright © 1982 by Thomas Nelson, Inc. Used by permission. All rights reserved.

Scripture quotations marked NASB are taken from *The New American Standard Bible*®, Copyright © 1960, 1962, 1963, 1968, 1971, 1972, 1973, 1975, 1977, 1995 by The Lockman Foundation Used by Permission. (www.Lockman.org)

Copyright © Richard P. Belcher, Jr 2017

ISBN 978-1-5271-0041-1

10 9 8 7 6 5 4 3 2 1

Published in 2017
in the Mentor Imprint
by
Christian Focus Publications,
Geanies House, Fearn, Tain,
Ross-shire, IV20 1TW, Great Britain.
www.christianfocus.com

Cover design by Daniel van Straaten

Printed and bound
by the CPI Group (UK Ltd), Croydon, CR0 4YY

All rights reserved. No part of this publication may be reproduced, stored in a retrieval system, or transmitted, in any form, by any means, electronic, mechanical, photocopying, recording or otherwise without the prior permission of the publisher or a licence permitting restricted copying. In the U.K. such licences are issued by the Copyright Licensing Agency, Saffron House, 6-10 Kirby Street, London, EC1 8TS. www.cla.co.uk

Contents

List of abbreviations 9

Preface 11

Introduction 13
   The authorship of Ecclesiastes 14
      1. The historical setting 18
      2. The Hebrew of Ecclesiastes 21
      3. The term Qohelet 25
   The Genre of Ecclesiastes 29
   Different approaches to Ecclesiastes 37
      1. The Heterodox Qohelet 38
      2. The Orthodox Qohelet 41
      3. The Struggling Qohelet 45
   Hermeneutical keys for understanding Ecclesiastes ... 51
      1. Qohelet's epistemology 51
      2. The meaning of hebel 53
      3. The phrase 'under the sun' 57
      4. The question of 'gain' and the calls to
         enjoyment 60
      5. The breakdown of the deed-consequence
         relationship 61
   The identity of Qohelet and the danger of
      speculative wisdom 63
   Preaching and teaching Ecclesiastes 67

1 **The prologue:**
   an exploration of the nature of the world (1:1-11) 71
   The superscription (1:1) 71
   The motto (1:2) 72
   The key question of the book (1:3) 75
   An introductory poem: the wonder of creation
      or the futility of effort? (1:4-11) 77
      The futility of the natural world (1:4-7) 79
      The futility of the human world (1:8-11) 82
      Homiletical Implications 86

2 **Qohelet's search for meaning under the sun**
   (1:12–2:26) 89
   The failure of wisdom (1:12-18) 90
   The failure of pleasure (2:1-11) 99
   Homiletical Implications 108
   The failure of wisdom in light of folly and
      death (2:12-17) 109
   Homiletical Implications 116
   The failure of the results of labor (2:18-23) 117
   Homiletical Implications 122
   Advice when life does not make sense
      (2:24-26) 123
   Homiletical Implications 131

3 **The search for understanding the role of human**
   beings: does God make any difference? (3:1-22) 133
   The poem on time (3:1-8) 135
   Qohelet's reflections on the poem on time:
      the frustrating work of God (3:9-15) 140
   Qohelet's reflections on injustice:
      man has no advantage over beasts
      (3:16-22) 154
   Homiletical Implications 164

4 **The frustration of unfulfilled expectations (4:1–6:9)** 167
   The frustration of loneliness met in companionship (4:1-16) 169
      Political power oppresses with no one to comfort (4:1-3) 169
      The frustrations of labor alleviated through companionship (4:4-12) 171
      The fleeting nature of political power (4:13-16) 180
      Homiletical Implications 187
   Caution in approaching God in worship? (5:1-7 [Heb. 4:17–5:6]) 189
   Corruption among government officials (5:8-9 [Heb. 5:7-8]) 202
      Homiletical Implications 208
   Unfulfilled expectations related to wealth (5:10–6:9 [Heb. 5:9–6:9]) 209
      General dissatisfaction with wealth (5:10-17 [Heb. 5:9-16]) 209
      Homiletical Implications 219
      Advice in light of the dissatisfaction of wealth: enjoy the portion (5:18-20 [Heb. 5:17-19]) 220
      The tragedy of not enjoying one's wealth (6:1-9) 224
      Homiletical Implications 235

5 **Human limitations concerning knowledge: who knows what is good? (6:10–8:17)** 239
   Human limitation: the essence of humanity (6:10-12) 240
   Proverbial sayings on 'what is good?' (7:1-14) 245
      Homiletical Implications 262
   A cautious approach to life and God (7:15-18) 263
      Homiletical Implications 270
   Searching for the sum of things (7:19-29) 271
      Homiletical Implications 286

The arbitrary nature of the world (8:1-17) 287
    The arbitrary nature of human government
    (8:1-9) 289
    The arbitrary nature of divine government
    (8:10-17) 302
    Homiletical Implications 313

6 Human limitations concerning knowledge: the uncertainty of the future (9:1–10:20) 317

    Living under the cloud of death (9:1-12) 317
    Homiletical Implications 333
    Insignificant things have grave consequences
    (9:13–10:20) 335
    Homiletical Implications 360

7 Living with the uncertainty of the future (11:1–12:8) ...363

    Take action even if the future is uncertain (11:1-6) 364
    Homiletical Implications 370
    Enjoy life before the dark days come (11:7–12:8) 371
    Homiletical Implications 402

8 The epilogue: an evaluation of Qohelet's message (12:9-14) 405

    The simple truth: fear God and keep His
    commandments (12:9-14) 406
    Homiletical Implications 422

Scripture Index 425
Subject Index 431

List of abbreviations

AB	Anchor Bible
AUSS	*Andrews University Seminary Studies*
Bib	*Biblica*
BibSac	*Bibliotheca Sacra*
BST	*The Bible Speaks Today*
BT	*The Bible Translator*
CBQ	*Catholic Biblical Quarterly*
CJT	*Canadian Journal of Theology*
EBC	*Everyman's Bible Commentary*
EQ	*Evangelical Quarterly*
FOTL	Forms of Old Testament Literature
GKC	*Gesenius' Hebrew Grammar*
HS	*Hebrew Studies*
HUCA	*Hebrew Union College Annual*
ICC	International Critical Commentary
Int	Interpretation
ITC	International Theological Commentary
ITQ	*Irish Theological Quarterly*
JNES	*Journal of Near Eastern Studies*
JNSL	*Journal of Northwest Semitic Languages*

JPSBC	The JPS Bible Commentary
JQR	*Jewish Quarterly Review*
JSOT	*Journal for the Study of the Old Testament*
JBL	*Journal of Biblical Literature*
NAC	New American Commentary
NCBC	The New Century Bible Commentary
NICOT	New International Commentary on the Old Testament
NIDOTTE	W. A. VanGemeren (ed.), *The New International Dictionary of Old Testament Theology and Exegesis*, 5 vols. (Grand Rapids: Zondervan, 1997)
NIVAC	New International Version Application Commentary
OTL	Old Testament Library
PSB	*Princeton Seminary Bulletin*
TLOT	Ernst Jenni and Claus Westermann (eds.), *Theological Lexicon of the Old Testament*, 3 vols. (Peabody, MAL Hendriksen, 1997)
TOTC	Tyndale Old Testament Commentary
TynBul	*Tyndale Bulletin*
UBS	United Bible Society
VT	*Vetus Testamentum*
WBC	Word Biblical Commentary
ZAW	*Zeitschreift für die alttestamentliche Wissenschaft*

Preface

Over the last several years there has been a lot of interest in the book of Ecclesiastes, not only academically in terms of commentaries, but also practically in terms of its message for the church. This is particularly challenging for a book like Ecclesiastes. The meaning of a text like Ecclesiastes for the church depends so much on the original meaning of the text; and as will become apparent in the Introduction to this commentary, there are a variety of different approaches to the book and its meaning. Thus the usefulness of an emphasis on modern meaning for a work is dependent on how one understands the original meaning. The distinctive approach of this commentary is that it argues for Solomonic authorship combined with a negative, 'under the sun' approach to the message of the book. These two ideas are related to each other because the book reflects the struggles of Solomon during the period of his life when his heart was turned away from the Lord (1 Kings 11:9). The purpose of the book is to warn against speculative wisdom, which is a wisdom that no longer operates from the right foundation of the fear of the Lord. The struggles of Solomon are laid out as a warning to all that even someone as wise as Solomon can operate on the wrong basis. Of course, the answer to the struggle comes at the end of the book. However, if most of the book is written from an 'under the sun' perspective, it becomes imperative for the preacher or teacher of the book to point people to the right perspective along the way. So, for major sections of the commentary there are homiletical implications that seek to move from the 'under the sun' view to an 'above the sun' perspective.

I would like to express thanks to Christian Focus for publishing this commentary on Ecclesiastes in the Mentor Series. I would like to thank the Board of Reformed Theological Seminary for a Sabbatical that was used to work on this commentary. The congregation of Christ Ridge Church, Fort Mill, SC deserves special thanks for their prayers and their willingness to listen to a sermon series on Ecclesiastes while I was their Stated Supply Pastor. I would also like to express appreciation to Rehobeth Presbyterian Church, Waxhaw, NC, for their valuable feedback when I taught Ecclesiastes to the adult Sunday School class while serving as their Stated Supply Pastor. Also, my wife, Lu, deserves many thanks for her tireless efforts on behalf of our family, especially in caring for my mom during the dark days of her alzheimers that finally took her life on September 30, 2016. I would like to dedicate this commentary to my mom and dad, Richard and Mary Anne Belcher, who helped establish a foundation for my life based on the fear of the Lord and his majestic sovereignty.

Richard P. Belcher, Jr.
Charlotte, North Carolina
May 2017

Introduction

Ecclesiastes is one of the most difficult books of the Bible. It has been called 'a baffling book,' 'alien among the other books of the Old Testament,' 'the most problematic of the whole Hebrew Bible,' and 'an embarrassment to the Old Testament.'[1] It has also provided solace for both pietists and skeptics.[2] Why are there so many different responses to the same book? One of the challenges in understanding the message of Ecclesiastes is to understand the relationship between the positive statements and the negative statements. How are the negative statements to be understood? Ecclesiastes 2:14-16 states that there is virtually no difference between the wise and the fool, Ecclesiastes 3:19-22 denies any advantage of humans over animals, and Ecclesiastes 9:1-3 denies any difference between the righteous and the wicked. However, there are also positive statements in Ecclesiastes, especially the passages known as the calls to enjoyment (2:24-26; 3:22; 5:18-20; 8:15;

---

1. George R. Castellino, 'Qohelet and His Wisdom,' *CBQ* 30 (1968): 15; James. L. Crenshaw, 'Ecclesiastes – Odd Book In,' *Bible Review* 6 (1990): 28; Pin'has Carny, 'Theodicy in the Book of Qohelet,' in Henning Graf Reventlow and Yair Hoffman (eds.), *Justice and Righteousness: Biblical Themes and Their Influence* (Sheffield: JSOT Press, 1992), 71; and James F. Armstrong, 'Ecclesiastes in Old Testament Theology,' *PSB* 4 (1983): 16.

2. Elias Bickerman, *Four Strange Books of the Bible* (New York: Schocken Books, 1967), 142.

and 9:7-10). Any serious approach to understanding this book must address how these types of passages fit together.

The authorship of Ecclesiastes

Before examining the various approaches to Ecclesiastes and the keys for understanding its message, certain introductory questions must be covered. Although there is very little consensus on the major introductory questions related to Ecclesiastes, there is almost a consensus that Solomon is not the author of the book. Only a small number of modern scholars argue that Solomon wrote the book (Gleason Archer, Duane Garrett, and Walter Kaiser).[3] Many within the Reformed and evangelical camps have denied Solomonic authorship (F. Delitzsch, E. W. Hengstenberg, H. C. Leupold, E. J. Young, R. K. Harrison, Derek Kidner, Graham Ogden, Tremper Longman, III, and Ian Provan).[4]

The major argument for Solomonic authorship is the description of the author in the book as 'the son of David, king in Jerusalem' (1:1) and 'I ... have been king over Israel in Jerusalem' (1:12).[5] Kaiser notes that Solomon was the only immediate son of David who was king over Israel, reigning in Jerusalem.[6] In fact, the phrase 'son of David' only refers

---

3. Gleason L. Archer, Jr., *A Survey of Old Testament Introduction* (Chicago: Moody Press, 1974); Duane A. Garrett, *Proverbs, Ecclesiastes, Song of Songs*, NAC (Nashville: Broadman Press, 1993); and Walter C. Kaiser, *Ecclesiastes: Total Life*, EBC (Chicago: Moody Press, 1979).

4. F. Delitzsch, 'Ecclesiastes,' in *Commentary on the Old Testament*, 10 vols. (Grand Rapids: Eerdmans, 1978 [orig. 1872]), 6:179-442; E. W. Hengstenberg, *A Commentary on Ecclesiastes* (Sovereign Grace Publishers, 1960 [orig. 1869]; H. C. Leupold, *Exposition of Ecclesiastes* (Grand Rapids: Baker Book House, 1952); E. J. Young, *An Introduction to the Old Testament* (Grand Rapids: Eerdmans, 1952); R. K. Harrison, *Introduction to the Old Testament* (Grand Rapids: Eerdmans, 1969); Derek Kidner, *The Message of Ecclesiastes: A Time to Mourn and a Time to Dance*, BST (Downers Grove, IL: InterVarsity Press, 1976); Graham Ogden, *Qoheleth*, 2nd edition (Sheffield: Phoenix Press, 2007); Tremper Longman, III, *The Book of Ecclesiastes*, NICOT (Grand Rapids: Eerdmans, 1998); and Iain Provan, *Ecclesiastes/Song of Songs*, NIVAC (Grand Rapids: Zondervan, 2001).

5. Unless otherwise noted, all translations are the author's.

6. Kaiser, *Ecclesiastes*, 25.

to a biological son of David whenever it is used in the OT.⁷ The way the author describes his search in chapter 2 sets forth opportunities and activities available to a king like Solomon: unrivaled wisdom (1:16), wealth in abundance (2:8), tremendous retinue of servants (2:7), opportunities for carnal pleasure (2:3), and extensive building activities (2:4-6).⁸

Although the text seems to point in the direction of Solomonic authorship, most have challenged this view for a variety of reasons, including the use of the perfect aspect of the verb in 1:12, the unusual statement in 1:16, and statements later in the book that do not seem to come from someone who is a king. The use of the perfect aspect of the verb 'to be' in 1:12 has been termed unusual.⁹ It seems to refer to a period in the past when Qohelet (translated 'the Preacher' by many translations) was king, with the implication that he is now no longer king (which would be translated 'I was king').¹⁰ This verb has been understood as a textual signal that the author is not Solomon but someone who is adopting a literary convention as if he was Solomon.¹¹ The statement in 1:16 reads, 'I have acquired

---

7. See Eric S. Christianson, *A Time to Tell: Narrative Strategies in Ecclesiastes* (Sheffield: Sheffield Academic Press, 1998), 129 for the evidence. Although he argues for a Solomonic guise in Ecclesiastes, he states that the phrase 'son of David' is not being used figuratively and that it makes an implicit reference to King Solomon. One could also argue for a close connection between Qohelet (translated 'the Preacher' by many translations) and Solomon based on a comparison of Proverbs 1:1 ('The proverbs of Solomon, son of David, king of Israel') and Ecclesiastes 1:1 ('The words of Qohelet, son of David, king in Jerusalem'). Doug Ingram (*Ambiguity in Ecclesiastes* [New York: T & T Clark, 2006], 80), who argues for deliberate ambiguity in Ecclesiastes, states that 'This appears to strengthen the link between Qohelet and Solomon because there were only two kings of Israel in Jerusalem, David and his son Solomon, before the southern kingdom of Judah and the northern kingdom of Israel separated.' Of course, whether this evidence is meant to identify Qohelet with Solomon or just to associate Qohelet with Solomon is the key question.

8. Archer (*Old Testament Introduction*, 478) comments that 'No other descendant of David measures up to these specifications but Solomon himself.'

9. Longman, *Ecclesiastes*, 76.

10. Delitzsch, 'Ecclesiastes,' 6:205-206.

11. Longman, *Ecclesiastes*, 5, 76; Ogden, *Qoheleth*, 39.

great wisdom, surpassing all who were over Jerusalem before me.' The problem with this statement is that there were very few before Solomon who reigned in Jerusalem to whom he could compare his surpassing wisdom. Thus the statement seems rather hollow. It is understood to be a literary device, which is meant to provide a loose association with Solomon, but not a strict identification.[12] Finally, most do not believe that the author continues to speak as a king throughout the whole book. In fact, statements are made which seem to distance the author from Solomon as king. For example, in Ecclesiastes 4:1-3 the author laments all the oppression in the world and that there is no one to comfort the oppressed. Certainly, a powerful king like Solomon could have done something to help the oppressed. Also, Ecclesiastes 5:8-9 protests against the king and policies connected with officials; and Ecclesiastes 10:20 assumes that the king is a suspicious bully. These statements seem to come from someone who is not a king. They could be made about Solomon but not by Solomon.[13] Thus the author presents himself as Solomon at the beginning of the book for the sake of the argument, but it is also clear that the author is not Solomon himself.

The foregoing reasons to reject Solomonic authorship have not gone uncontested, many times by those who themselves do not favor Solomonic authorship. R. N. Whybray calls the use of the perfect aspect of the verb in 1:12 an imaginary problem. The perfect aspect can denote an action or state that began in the past and continues into the present (which would be translated 'I have been king').[14] Also, in the self-introduction formulae of the West Semitic royal inscriptions,

---

12. Longman, *Ecclesiastes*, 57–58.

13. Longman, *Ecclesiastes*, 5–6.

14. R. N. Whybray, *Ecclesiastes*, NCBC (Grand Rapids: Eerdmans, 1989), 48. Other commentators who recognize this use of the verb in this verse include James Crenshaw, *Ecclesiastes*, OTL (Philadelphia: Westminster Press, 1987), 71; Michael V. Fox, *A Time to Tear Down & A Time to Build Up: A Rereading of Ecclesiastes* (Grand Rapids: Eerdmans, 1999), 171; and C. L. Seow, *Ecclesiastes*, AB (New York: Doubleday, 1997), 119. See also E. Kautzsch and A. E. Cowley (eds.), *Gesenius' Hebrew Grammar* (Oxford: Clarendon Press, 1910), 311 (hereinafter *GKC*).

the perfect aspect is used to refer to the present reign of the king.¹⁵ Thus 1:12 could easily have been spoken by Solomon. The statement in 1:16 may be a way to express unsurpassed wisdom. The phrase 'all who were before' is used to refer to someone who excels in something (1 Kings 14:9; 16:25, 30). In fact, it is used of Jeroboam in a negative way in 1 Kings 14:9, where it states, 'you have done evil above all who were before you.' There were not very many kings before Jeroboam with whom to compare him, so the emphasis may be on his unsurpassed wickedness in setting up the false system of worship in the northern kingdom when the kingdom divided.¹⁶ The emphasis in Ecclesiastes 1:16; 2:7; and 2:9 is on the unsurpassed wisdom and wealth of Solomon. This fits the picture of Solomon in 1 Kings 3:12, where it states something similar to Ecclesiastes 1:16: 'none like you has been before you and none like you shall arise after you.'¹⁷

An argument can be made that statements later in the book could have been spoken by a king, and thus they could have been spoken by Solomon.¹⁸ A king could certainly be aware of mismanagement and oppression within his kingdom. David

---

15. Y. V. Koh, *Royal Autobiography in the Book of Qoheleth* (Berlin: de Gruyter, 2006), 76–78.

16. Archer, *Old Testament Introduction*, 485. He points out that E. J. Young argues in his *Introduction to the Old Testament* that the phrase 'all who were before' in Ecclesiastes 1:16 could not refer to Solomon; however, in 1 Kings 14:9 Young argues that the same phrase refers to Jeroboam and that it includes elders and judges who were before him.

17. Hengstenberg, *Ecclesiastes*, 66. The view that Ecclesiastes 1:16 has in view unsurpassed wisdom is supported by taking the preposition 'before' (לפני) in a spatial sense instead of a temporal sense, so that the phrase 'before me' is not a temporal comparison to previous kings of Israel but a spatial reference to the wisest of his subjects who are in Jerusalem (see Dominic Rudman, 'Qohelet's Use of לפני,' *JNSL* 23/2 [1997]: 143–150, who argues for a spatial use of the preposition in 1:16; 2:7, 9; and 4:16). As Rudman notes, this view also coincides with the statement in Ecclesiastes 1:11 that there is no remembrance of former things.

18. Christianson (*Narrative Strategies*) and Koh (*Royal Autobiography*) argue that the Solomonic persona extends to the whole book and not just the first two chapters. If other issues regarding the date of Ecclesiastes can be answered, it is a small step from the persona of Solomon pervading the book to Solomon himself being the author.

was aware of the murderous actions of Joab (2 Sam. 3).[19] A king could also critically reflect on his own role as king and appropriate behavior in his presence.[20] The fact that no statement is made in 4:1-3 to rectify the situation of oppression could be because the focus is on observing what is taking place in the kingdom in order to draw conclusions concerning the futility of life. If the author himself is struggling with the futility of life, what difference would oppression make anyway? Plus, Solomon did mistreat his subjects as he grew older (1 Kings 12:14).[21] The fact that attention is given to appropriate behavior in the presence of a king (7:7; 8:2-9; 9:17; 10:4-7, 16-17, 20) fits the pre-exilic situation better than the post-exilic situation. During the exile few Jewish people had any contact with the distant kings of the Babylonian and Persian empires.[22]

Other reasons for the rejection of Solomonic authorship include the historical setting, the nature of the Hebrew of Ecclesiastes, and the use of the term 'Qohelet.'

1. The historical setting

Concerning the historical setting, Delitzsch argues that the book of Ecclesiastes reflects a time when things were not going well for Israel, which explains the somber mood of the book. He places the book in the Persian period of the fifth century B.C.[23] C. L. Seow also argues for a Persian setting on the basis of economic realities reflected in the book. He argues that there is evidence in Ecclesiastes of a move away from the agrarian culture of pre-exilic Judah to a more democratic use of money and commerce. There were opportunities for financial success, but also for more risk, which may explain

---

19. J. Stafford Wright, 'Ecclesiastes,' in Frank Gaebelein (ed.), *The Expositor's Bible Commentary*, 12 vols. (Grand Rapids: Zondervan, 1991), 5:1140.

20. Garrett, *Ecclesiastes*, 261.

21. Wright, 'Ecclesiastes,' 5:1140. Longman (*Ecclesiastes*, 6) makes the same point when he comments that Solomon created a heavy burden for the people that continued to the end of his reign.

22. Garrett, *Ecclesiastes*, 261.

23. Delitzsch, 'Ecclesiastes,' 6:212-215 and Hengstenberg, *Ecclesiastes*, 6–15.

the problem of the uncertainty of inheritance in Ecclesiastes.[24] Others argue that Qohelet was a Palestinian Jew of the third century B.C. who was heavily influenced by Greek thought. This would explain the more personal tone of the book and the fact that the thinking is more abstract than other wisdom literature in Scripture.[25] During this time Palestine was ruled from Egypt by the Ptolemaic dynasty, an oppressive and well-organized despotism reflected in the statement about the king in Ecclesiastes 10:20. Also, Ecclesiastes 5:8, which mentions high officials in a province, could fit this period.[26] Some argue that the social conditions of the Greek period are reflected in the book, such as the preoccupation with wealth, the isolation of the individual due to the breakdown of the family unit, and the lack of an obligation to serve others.[27] Michael Fox argues that the mention of a race in Ecclesiastes 9:11 points to a Hellenistic setting where foot-races, which originated in Greek competitions, were prominent in public athletics.[28]

None of the arguments relating Ecclesiastes to a certain historical time period are entirely conclusive. The somber tone of the book may have more to do with the outlook of the author than the particular period in which he lived.[29]

---

24. Seow, *Ecclesiastes*, 21–29.

25. Fox, *A Rereading of Ecclesiastes*, 6–8; Thomas Krüger, *Qoheleth* (Minneapolis: Fortress Press, 2004), 22; Leo G. Perdue, *Wisdom Literature: A Theological History* (Louisville: Westminster John Knox Press, 2007), 168–186; and Whybray, *Ecclesiastes*, 7–11.

26. However, R. B. Y. Scott (*Proverbs, Ecclesiastes* [New York: Doubleday, 1965], 201) comments that Ecclesiastes 5:8 could fit either the Persian period or the Ptolemaic period.

27. Whybray, *Ecclesiastes*, 6–11. Crenshaw (*Ecclesiastes*, 50–51) places the book before the Maccabean revolt, which began about 168 B.C., when the upper echelons of Jewish society experienced prosperity. Bartholomew (*Ecclesiastes*, 54–55) argues that the social setting reflects the Greek period because Qohelet is wrestling with the problems of individualism and autonomy that became prominent in the third century BC.

28. Michael Fox, *Ecclesiastes*, JPSBC (Philadelphia: The Jewish Publication Society, 2004), xiv.

29. Walter Brueggemann (*An Introduction to the Old Testament: The Canon and Christian Imagination* [Louisville: Westminster John Knox Press, 2003], 329) notes this possibility when he writes, 'The Solomonic connection

Delitzsch argues that the book reflects a period when things were not going well, but Crenshaw argues that the book reflects a period when the upper echelons of Jewish society were experiencing prosperity.[30] Ecclesiastes 5:8 and 10:20 are general enough to indicate any period in Israel's history. Although the word *medînāh* in Ecclesiastes 5:8 is commonly used for the Persian provinces, it is also used earlier to refer to the districts of Israel in the time of Ahab (1 Kings 20:14-19). The statement in Ecclesiastes 9:11, 'the race is not to the swift,' need not have originated in a competitive Greek setting. It can be understood as a general proverbial expression not tied to any time period (as is generally true for the other expressions in the verse).[31] Furthermore, the terms that Seow uses to try to establish a Persian economic setting are terms that are widespread throughout Scripture and are not limited to a Persian setting. He does recognize that silver (*kesep̄*) was used in earlier times as a medium of exchange. However, the fact that *ḥešbôn* is found in commercial documents of the Persian period does not support his argument because the word is not used in Ecclesiastes in an economic way (see Eccles. 7:25, 27, 29; 9:10).[32] The parallels between Ecclesiastes

---

in the book ... is ... secondary ... unless we can imagine that the self-indulgent Solomon by the end of his reign had come to a sad awareness of his life, a sad awareness that is reflected in the book.'

30. Delitzsch, 'Ecclesiastes,' 6:212-215 and Crenshaw, *Ecclesiastes*, 50–51.

31. George Barton (*The Book of Ecclesiastes*, ICC [Edinburgh: T & T Clark, 1971], 39–41) draws a parallel between Ecclesiastes 9:6-9 and a fragment from the Gilgamesh Epic that appears to have come from about 2000 B.C. as evidence that Ecclesiastes is Semitic in outlook and independent of Greek thinking. William P. Brown (*Ecclesiastes*, Int [Louisville: John Knox Press, 2000], 2–7) also sees parallels between the Epic of Gilgamesh and Ecclesiastes in the search for meaning before death's inescapable presence, but places Ecclesiastes at the beginning of the Persian period instead of the period of the Old Babylonian Empire.

32. Seow (*Ecclesiastes*, 260) acknowledges that *ḥešbôn* and wisdom (*ḥokmāh*) do not refer to separate ideas and that *ḥešbôn* defines wisdom more precisely. Crenshaw ('Qohelet's Understanding of Intellectual Inquiry,' in A. Schoors (ed.), *Qohelet in the Context of Wisdom* [Leuven: Leuven University Press, 1998], 208) comments that Seow's linguistic and socio-economic arguments demonstrate the difficulty of establishing the historical setting reflected in the book.

5:18–6:2 and Persian royal grants, with the uncertainty of the grants reflecting the uncertainty of a person enjoying certain benefits in life (Eccles. 6:2), lose their force without a Persian setting.[33] None of the arguments for a Persian or Greek setting are conclusive. Thus, there is no consensus on the setting of Ecclesiastes because of the ambivalent nature of the arguments that attempt to prove literary or cultural dependence.[34]

2. The Hebrew of Ecclesiastes

Many argue that Ecclesiastes must be late on the basis of the character of the Hebrew in the book. Delitzsch's statement has become quite famous: 'If the book of Koheleth were of old Solomonic origin, then there is no history of the Hebrew language.' He argues this on the basis of the use of rare words (*hapax legomena*) and words that are considered late, including Aramaisms (he lists over ninety such words). He also lists modern aspects of the Hebrew language, such as treating lamed-aleph verbs as lamed-he verbs, the use of the personal pronoun even though the person is contained in the verbal form, and the use of the demonstrative *zōh*.[35] A. Schoors argues that twenty-four linguistic features of Ecclesiastes give evidence that the language of Ecclesiastes fits best into the post-exilic period and that it shows traits of later Mishnaic Hebrew (MH).[36] Seow also argues that the language reflects the post-exilic period, but more specifically the Persian period. The high number of Aramaic expressions, including terms that appear in Official Aramaic but not in

---

33. See the article by Dominic Rudman, 'A Note on the Dating of Ecclesiastes,' *JNSL* 23/2 (1997): 143–150. He argues contra Seow that the root *šlṭ*, which occurs in Ecclesiastes 5:18 and 6:2, is not limited to the Persian period in its legal use. See also Ian Young's critical analysis of Seow in 'Late Biblical Hebrew and Hebrew Inscriptions,' in Ian Young (ed.), *Biblical Hebrew: Studies in Chronology and Typology* (New York: T & T Clark, 2003), 279, n. 4 and 285 n. 6.

34. Roland Murphy, *Ecclesiastes*, WBC (Dallas: Word Books, 1992), xlii.

35. Delitzsch, 'Ecclesiastes,' 6:190-199.

36. A. Schoors, *The Preacher Sought to Find Pleasing Words: A Study of the Language of Qoheleth* (Leuven: Peeters, 1992).

earlier inscriptions of Old Aramaic, points to a late date. Two widely recognized Persian loan words, *pardēs* ('garden' in Eccles. 2:5) and *pitgām* ('sentence' in Eccles. 8:11), plus a cluster of other economic terms occurring in fifth and fourth century documents, point to a Persian setting (no earlier than the second half of the fifth century).[37] Thus most argue that the Hebrew of Ecclesiastes does not fit the Hebrew of the pre-exilic period (usually designated Early Biblical Hebrew [EBH] or Standard Biblical Hebrew [SBH]) but is more characteristic of Hebrew after the exile (designated Late Biblical Hebrew [LBH]). The language and style of the book represent the latest stage in the development of Hebrew to be found in the Bible.[38]

The dominant view in scholarship of the development of the Hebrew language from SBH to LBH argues for a pre-exilic Hebrew that is standard or monolithic, which develops into the Hebrew after the exile.[39] Thus any Hebrew that is not in accord with standard language usage is either post-exilic or, if early, belongs to Northern Israel, so that the language of early Judah is identical with SBH.[40] Since Ecclesiastes does not match the characteristics of pre-exilic SBH, most scholars understand it to be post-exilic and representative of LBH.

The question is not whether there is a standard pre-exilic Hebrew (SBH) which can be compared with a later post-exilic Biblical Hebrew (LBH). These do exist so that one can demonstrate linguistic and grammatical developments

---

37. C. L. Seow, 'Linguistic Evidence and the Dating of Qohelet,' *JBL* 115.4 (1996): 650–654.

38. R. Gordis, *Koheleth—The Man and His World* (New York: Schocken Books, 1951), 59. Although Longman (*Ecclesiastes*, 9–10) dates the book late, he is more cautious on whether the language of the book should play a role in the dating of the book.

39. Mark F. Rooker, *Biblical Hebrew in Transition: The Language of Ezekiel* (Sheffield: Sheffield Academic Press, 1990). He argues that Ezekiel is a transitional link between the two, with SBH beginning to wane because of the influence of Aramaic and changes in LBH coming about because of dialectical differences or variations.

40. Ian Young, 'Evidence of Diversity in Pre-Exilic Judahite Hebrew,' *HS* 38 (1997): 7–20.

between the two.⁴¹ Rather, the question is whether SBH represents all that is going on in the Hebrew language before the exile. Is there evidence of more diversity within the Hebrew language before the exile? Are there other factors that may explain the language of Ecclesiastes? Bo Isaksson argues that the Hebrew of Ecclesiastes is influenced by a popular Hebrew dialect in northern Palestine and that the distinctive nature of the verb system is due to the literary genre of autobiography. He also comments that the spoken language of biblical times probably approximated to MH and that northern dialects displayed numerous features common to Aramaic, which were not common to the classical language of Jerusalem. Thus the Hebrew of Ecclesiastes seems to represent a popular Hebrew dialect.⁴² Isaksson recognizes that SBH is the classical language of Jerusalem and that there are other things going on outside the official language. Although he argues that our knowledge of Hebrew, both spoken and written, is not sufficient to allow it to be used for dating the book, his analysis of the language does not affect his dating of Ecclesiastes. He believes that an origin in the fourth century is not improbable.⁴³ Daniel Fredericks compares the language of Ecclesiastes with LBH and MH and concludes that Ecclesiastes is more closely aligned with EBH/SBH. The higher number of Aramaisms is explained by the close association of wisdom literature with the surrounding culture and the historical connections between Israel and Aram, which go back to 1000 B.C. Fredericks thus concludes that the language of Ecclesiastes is pre-exilic and that the vocabulary limits the range from the eighth to the seventh century.⁴⁴ It is interesting that Isaksson recognizes that the language of Ecclesiastes is influenced by factors *outside* SBH (dialect and

---

41. The fact that the existence of SBH is not being questioned means that Rooker's comparisons between SBH and LBH are not necessarily affected by this argument.

42. Bo Isaksson, *Studies in the Language of Qoheleth* (Stockholm: Almqvist & Wiksell International, 1987).

43. ibid., 197.

44. Daniel Fredericks, *Qohelet's Language: Re-evaluating Its Nature and Date* (Lewiston: Edwin Mellon Press, 1988).

geography), but still dates the book late, whereas Fredericks tries to fit the language of the book *within* the parameters of SBH and argues for a pre-exilic dating. As opposed to the late-date argument based on LBH, both Isaksson and Fredericks recognize that genre and dialect may provide an explanation for the nature of the language of Ecclesiastes.

Isaksson's analysis of the language of Ecclesiastes frees it from having to be compared with and fitted into SBH. This means that the typical analysis of the language of Ecclesiastes, which compares it with SBH and LBH, should no longer be the controlling factor in dating the book of Ecclesiastes. What if SBH, which represents Hebrew before the exile, is not a widespread monolithic phenomenon, but originated in the United Monarchy when a central administration was needed? Ian Young argues for a diverse linguistic situation in the development of Hebrew in the land of Canaan. A diverse group of people lived in the area and there is evidence of different languages and dialects being spoken among the people (Judg. 12:1-6). There is also evidence for the development of Akkadian as a diplomatic language for communication between the diverse groups (the Amarna letters). Young argues that Hebrew was a Canaanite dialect that began to be used as a diplomatic language and was later adopted by the Israelites. SBH, on the other hand, originated in the monarchy when the need for an administration arose; thus, it is not to be identified with any particular dialect of the area. The standard prose that developed in SBH sought to avoid Aramaic influence in order to emphasize the nationhood of Israel over against other nations who used Aramaic. However, since there was contact between Israel and Aram as early as 1100 B.C., one should expect to find Aramaic influence before the exile, which is evidenced in certain ancient forms of Biblical Hebrew and in the wisdom literature. Thus Aramaic influence alone cannot be used to argue that a text is late.[45] In light of the fact that the Philistines were from the Aegean area

---

45. Ian Young in *Diversity in Pre-exilic Hebrew* (Tübingen: J. C. B. Mohr, 1993), 63, notes that the presence of Aramaisms has no bearing on the date of a text unless there is linguistic opposition, and even linguistic opposition needs to take into consideration genre (e.g. wisdom) and dialect (e.g. Song of Songs).

and that the Assyrians had settled Iranians in Judah in the middle of the eighth century, Greek and Persian loan-words cannot be used to date a text late on that basis alone. The language of Ecclesiastes represents a local, literary dialect, exhibiting a simplified syntax which is not to be compared to the more official SBH. Thus the language of Ecclesiastes fits into the diverse language situation of the pre-exilic period.[46] If Young's analysis of diversity in pre-exilic Hebrew is correct, then the Hebrew of Ecclesiastes cannot be used to date the book late.

3. The term Qohelet

An examination of the term Qohelet also raises issues related to the authorship of Ecclesiastes. Major questions arise concerning the use of this term. Does it designate a name, an office, or a function? What does it mean and how should it be translated? Why is it used if Solomon is the author of the book? The term Qohelet (*qōhelet*) occurs in 1:1, 2, 12; 7:27; 12:8, 9, 10. Sometimes it occurs with the article (12:8 and perhaps 7:27). Most identify it as a feminine participle from the verb *qāhal*, which means 'to assemble.' However, it could designate an occupation, which would make it a noun derived from the noun *qāhal*, which means 'assembly' (as *bōqēr*, 'cowherd,' is derived from *bāqār*, 'cattle').[47] Charles Bridges argues that Qohelet is a new name given to Solomon later in his life

---

46. Young, *Diversity in Pre-Exilic Hebrew*. The basic argument concerning diversity in pre-exilic Hebrew is laid out in the first two chapters. He deals specifically with the language of Ecclesiastes on pages 140–157, where he argues that not only the language but also the content of the book, which deals with conduct before kings, fits a pre-exilic situation. For a sympathetic, yet critical review of Young's book see the review of Gary Rendsburg in *HS* 36 (1995): 135–140. See also Ian Young, 'Evidence of Diversity in Pre-Exilic Judahite Hebrew,' *HS* 38 (1997): 7–20 and Ian Young, Robert Rezetko, and Martin Ehrensvärd (eds.), *Linguistic Dating of Biblical Texts*, 2 vols. (London: Equinox, 2008). In this latter work the first volume introduces the field of linguistic dating and the second volume is a book-by-book survey of scholarship, with chapter 2 presenting a summary of the new approach to linguistic dating.

47. Many commentators identify the term Qohelet as a feminine participle. Fox (*A Rereading of Ecclesiastes*, 161) connects the term to the noun.

after his repentance.⁴⁸ There is no clear scriptural evidence that Solomon repented later in life and Ecclesiastes is not a confession of sin. The use of the article with the term seems to support the view that *qōhelet* is a name, much like the names based on the participle in Ezra 2:55 (*hassōperet*, with the article) and Nehemiah 7:57 (*sōperet*, without the article).⁴⁹ It is possible that Qohelet was a title associated with an office that has become a name.⁵⁰ Several suggestions have been offered as to how to translate Qohelet based on the meaning 'to assemble.' Seow suggests 'Gatherer' or 'Collector' as a reference to someone who gathers wisdom, wealth, or people;⁵¹ but the word is only used in the Old Testament to refer to people.⁵² The most common translation is 'Preacher,' which designates someone who gathers people into an assembly to speak to them. Others suggest 'Teacher,' which is more in line with the statement in 12:9 that Qohelet taught the people. An even better option is to leave the term untranslated as Qohelet, which will be the practice in this commentary.⁵³

But why is the name Qohelet used? An examination of that question will lead to a discussion of several issues that are important for understanding Ecclesiastes, which will bring the focus back to the issue of authorship. Although it is not clear whether the term Qohelet is an artificial name,⁵⁴ or a title, or a nickname of some sort,⁵⁵ some argue that the term Qohelet is a way for the author to distance himself from Solomon. In other words, the author adopts a Solomonic persona to demonstrate in his search for meaning that not

---

48. Charles Bridges, *Ecclesiastes*, Geneva Series (Edinburgh: The Banner of Truth Trust, 1985 [orig. 1860]), ix-x, 1.

49. Seow, *Ecclesiastes*, 96.

50. Murphy, *Ecclesiastes*, x and J. A. Loader, *Ecclesiastes: A Practical Commentary* (Grand Rapids: Eerdmans, 1986), 1.

51. Seow, *Ecclesiastes*, 97.

52. Provan, *Ecclesiastes*, 29.

53. Others who take this approach include Crenshaw, Fox, Longman, Murphy, and Ogden.

54. Michael A. Eaton, *Ecclesiastes*, TOTC (Downers Grove, IL: InterVarsity Press, 1983), 23.

55. Whybray, *Ecclesiastes*, 2 and Longman, *Ecclesiastes*, 1.

even someone like a King Solomon would have fared any better, but he makes it clear that he is really not Solomon by the use of the term Qohelet.[56] If the author wanted us to believe it was really Solomon, he would have used the name Solomon instead of Qohelet.[57] The proponents of this view argue that this is not an attempt to deceive anyone because the original readers would have understood what the author was doing.[58]

Different terminology is used to discuss the use of an assumed identity in Ecclesiastes. Recent narrative approaches to Ecclesiastes use the concept of 'literary persona,' which describes the storyteller of a literary work, who is the voice through whom the author speaks.[59] Qohelet is the voice through whom the author of the book speaks and, according to Fox, may not even be a real historical person.[60] Some use the term 'pseudonymous,' which refers to using a fictitious name and to present oneself as someone else. In other words, Qohelet presents himself as Solomon when he is not really Solomon, at least for the first several chapters. Longman uses the term 'pseudonymous' and identifies Ecclesiastes as fictional autobiography.[61] Very few scholars see this as a problem because it is assumed that the readers understand the phenomenon; so there is no intent to deceive the readers. Another significant term is 'pseudepigraphy,' but it is not

---

56. Gordis, *Koheleth*, 40 and Longman, *Ecclesiastes*, 6–7.

57. Fox, *Rereading Ecclesiastes*, 159.

58. Leupold, *Ecclesiastes*, 14.

59. For narrative approaches to Ecclesiastes see Fox (*Rereading Ecclesiastes*), Christianson (*Narrative Strategies*), and Gary D. Salyer, *Vain Rhetoric: Private Insight and Public Debate in Ecclesiastes* (Sheffield: Sheffield Academic Press, 2001).

60. Fox, *Rereading Ecclesiastes*, 371 and 'Frame-narrative and Composition in the Book of Qohelet,' *HUCA* 48 (1977): 95–96. In the latter work he uses the example of Uncle Remus, whom the author wants us to treat seriously by testifying to his reality even though he did not really exist. In this way the frame narrator is able to present a persona like Uncle Remus as a real individual.

61. Longman, *Fictional Akkadian Autobiography: A Generic and Comparative Study* (Winona Lake, IN: Eisenbrauns, 1991), 41.

often used to refer to Ecclesiastes. R. H. Charles defines this term as an author adopting another persona as an assumed identity in order for his words to be accepted.[62] It is commonly applied to works written from about 200 B.C. to A.D. 200.[63] A common assumption concerning Ecclesiastes is that it was accepted into the canon because of its association with Solomon.[64] Waltke sees the difficulty of this view when he comments that if the author claims to be the legendary Solomon but the internal evidence of the book falsifies that claim, then the book is pseudepigraphic. Such a claim would make the book fraudulent and not reliable or authoritative for the faith and practice of God's people. However, he goes on to argue that Ecclesiastes is not pseudepigraphic because the name Solomon is not used in the book.[65] Also, he does not believe it was accepted into the canon because of any associations with Solomon. He argues that Qohelet, who is portrayed as a Solomon-like figure of wisdom, is a fictitious representation of the anonymous narrator himself.[66] These questions concerning author and narrator raise issues

---

62. Charles comments that the names for the pseudepigraphic works were not chosen out of mere caprice. Enoch was chosen because he was the most appropriate author of a book which was to deal with astronomical questions because God took him into the heavens (*The Book of Enoch* [London: Society for Promoting Christian Knowledge, 1917], xvi). The parallel with Ecclesiastes would be that Solomon is chosen because he was in a position to argue that no amount of wisdom, achievements, and material possessions can give meaning to life.

63. See the definitions and discussions by R. H Charlesworth, *The Apocrypha and Pseudepigrapha of the Old Testament in English*, 2 vols. (Oxford: The Clarendon Press, 1913), 2:viii-ix; Stephen E. Robinson, 'Lying for God: The Uses of Apocrypha,' in G. Gillum and C. Criggs (eds.), *Apocryphal Writings and the Latter-Day Saints* (Provo, UT: Brigham Young University, 1986), 133-154; and Bruce Waltke, *An Old Testament Theology* (Grand Rapids: Zondervan, 2007), 947.

64. Barton, *Ecclesiastes*, 50; Brown, *Ecclesiastes*, 10; Gordis, *Koheleth*, 42; Seow, *Ecclesiastes*, 4; and Whybray, *Ecclesiastes*, 3. Loader (*Ecclesiastes*, 4) speaks in terms of Ecclesiastes being preserved in the canon because of the Solomonic connection.

65. Childs (*Introduction*, 354) makes the same point.

66. Waltke, *Old Testament Theology*, 947.

related to the structure and genre of the book, which must be addressed before definite conclusions can be drawn.

The Genre of Ecclesiastes

In a discussion of the genre of Ecclesiastes it is important to recognize that there are two different types of writing in the book. The first-person account of Qohelet (1:12–12:7) is framed by a third-person prologue (1:1-11) and a third-person epilogue (12:8-14), which is called a frame-narrative. The author introduces himself as Qohelet in 1:12, which begins the first-person discourse: 'I, Qohelet, have been king over Israel in Jerusalem.' The first person continues until 12:7, so that 1:12–12:7 encompasses the first-person narration of Qohelet. The term Qohelet also occurs in third-person sections of the book, notably 1:1-2 and 12:8, 9, 10. Thus the first-person discourse (1:12–12:7) is framed by third-person narration (1:1-11 and 12:8-14). There is even a third-person 'intrusion' in 7:27 ('says Qohelet'). One would normally expect the book to begin with the self introduction in 1:12, but someone else presents the words of Qohelet (1:1) and then comments on Qohelet's words in 12:9-14. Thus the terminology one uses to refer to the book becomes very important in order to avoid misunderstanding. In this commentary, when the term Ecclesiastes is used, both the third-person and the first-person sections are included, and when the term Qohelet is used, the first-person discourse is primarily in view (1:12–12:7).

It is important to have some idea of the type of literature one is studying in order to better understand a work. Genre discussions are based on comparisons between literature, which take into account both the similarities and the differences between texts.[67] The words of Qohelet have been compared to many texts of the ancient Near East, which demonstrates that the concepts and forms of the book reflect the ancient Near Eastern environment. A brief comparison of

---

67. For a good discussion of the comparative approach, including the relationship between biblical texts and ancient Near Eastern texts, see Longman, *Fictional Akkadian Autobiography*, 23–36, who argues for a contextual comparative approach which takes into account both similarities and differences between literature of different cultures.

Ecclesiastes with other ancient Near Eastern texts will show that although there are many similarities between these texts, there is no genre category of the ancient Near East into which Ecclesiastes neatly fits.[68]

There are conceptual connections between Ecclesiastes and the Gilgamesh Epic, which goes back to the early second millennium.[69] William Brown uses such connections to lay the groundwork for understanding Ecclesiastes because both Gilgamesh and Qohelet search for some sense of meaning before death's inescapable presence. In Gilgamesh, lessons emerge in the midst of the search for immortality. Thus the two deal with the universal themes of the dread of death, the futility of human existence, the bond of fellowship, the importance of joy, and the inscrutable will of the divine. Parallels between the two works include the proverbial advice, 'A three-ply rope cannot be cut,' a statement that all that mankind achieves is the wind, and the advice given to Gilgamesh which resembles Ecclesiastes 9:7-10:

> Let thy garments be sparkling fresh,
> Thy head be washed; bathe thou in water.
> Pay heed to the little one that holds thy hand,
> Let thy spouse delight in thy bosom!
> For this is the task of [mankind]![70]

Yet there is a clear difference in literary form as Gilgamesh is third-person epic narrative and Ecclesiastes is primarily first person.[71]

---

68. This is the conclusion of Koh (*Royal Autobiography*, 72), who has an excellent discussion of the different possibilities of the genre of Ecclesiastes, especially literature that has a royal figure. For other discussions of Ecclesiastes in the context of the ancient Near East see Murphy, *Ecclesiastes*, xli-xlv and G. A. Klingbeil, 'Ecclesiastes 2: Ancient Near Eastern Background,' in Tremper Longman III and Peter Enns (eds.), *Dictionary of the Old Testament: Wisdom, Poetry & Writings* (Downers Grove, IL: InterVarsity Press, 2008), 132–140.

69. Alexander Heidel, *The Gilgamesh Epic and Old Testament Parallels* (Chicago: University of Chicago Press, 1949) gives a full account of the sources and the story of the Gilgamesh Epic.

70. Brown, *Ecclesiastes*, 5–7.

71. Koh, *Royal Autobiography*, 123, n. 339.

Ecclesiastes has also been compared to Egyptian literature, especially the Instructions and the pessimistic, reflective discourses. In some of the Instructions the king speaks from the dead with advice for his successor. In this literature the figure of the king gives a broad sense of unity to an assorted collection of sayings. Sometimes these are called Royal Testaments and they have political objectives in mind.[72] Some compare the Royal Testaments to Qohelet, especially 1:12–2:26.[73] Qohelet, however, does not seem to have political objectives in view.[74] There do appear to be several literary similarities with Qohelet. The superscription identifies the author in third person and uses the word 'instruction.' Although the Egyptian superscriptions are more informative, there seems to be a parallel with Ecclesiastes 1:1. They appear to be pseudepigraphic and fictitious in order to gain acceptance for a work that is not official. Some would say the same thing about Ecclesiastes. There is also a prologue and an epilogue that frame a main body of work, but the prologue exhorts the reader to heed the advice, unlike Ecclesiastes, and the epilogue does not seek to guide the interpretation of the main body, which is the case in Ecclesiastes. Several themes are common to both the Egyptian Instructions and to Ecclesiastes, such as a call to enjoy life given against the background of distress, a reversal of fortune, and divine determinism and the hidden ways of God. However, the reflective style of narration is not shared by the Instructions. Egyptian works which do possess the reflective style and are pessimistic in that they express grievance over the evil condition into which Egypt has fallen, include laments, such as the Prophecies of Neferti, The Complaint of Ipuwer, and The Complaints of Khakheperresonb. Some of these have a

---

72. Murphy (*The Tree of Life: An Exploration of Biblical Wisdom* [Grand Rapids: Eerdmans, 2002], 164–165]) identifies the Instruction for King Merikare and the Instruction of King Amenemhet as Royal Testaments.

73. Gerhard von Rad (*Wisdom in Israel* [Valley Forge, PA: Trinity Press International, 1972], 227), following O. Loretz (*Qohelet und die Alte Orient* [Friburg: Herder, 1964]), applies Royal Testament to the whole book, but Crenshaw (*Ecclesiastes*, 29), like many others, limits it to 1:12–2:26.

74. Koh, *Royal Autobiography*, 125.

frame-narrative which introduces and concludes the words presented,[75] but they do not contain collections of proverbial sayings (as does Ecclesiastes). Koh notes that the Egyptian Instructions demonstrate literary creativity and fluidity, as the authors are masters of their craft. Perhaps Qohelet operates with the same creativity,[76] which makes it difficult to nail down a clear genre connection.

Qohelet has also been compared to West Semitic Royal Inscriptions, a group of eleven texts that are monumental inscriptions set up by kings as a public display and as an enduring record. Most of them date from the ninth century. Similarities to Qohelet include royal boasting of accomplishments superior to the accomplishment of predecessors and a focus on building activities. The strongest parallel is seen in their formulaic self-introduction, such as 'I am RN (royal name), king of ..., son of ...,' which uses the perfect aspect to describe the present reign of the king.[77] There are also Assyrian Royal Inscriptions, especially those of Sargon II, Sennacherib, Esarhaddon, and Assurbanipal, which display some of the same similarities, such as self-introduction, royal boasting, emphasis on treasures of kings and achievement over predecessors, and a royal wisdom theme.[78] Seow argues that Qohelet adapts this genre for rhetorical purposes and uses royal language in an ironic way

---

75. Fox, 'Frame Narrative,' 83–92. For a brief review of ancient Near Eastern literature that uses a third-person narrative to encompass a first-person discourse see Fox, *Rereading Ecclesiastes*, 367–370 and Christianson, *Narrative Strategies*, 66–69. Christianson (96) points out that the epilogue to Qohelet does not have many structural parallels to other ancient Near Eastern literature because they further the inner narrative more than Ecclesiastes 12:9-14 does.

76. Koh, *Royal Autobiography*, 143, 134. Seow ('Qohelet's Autobiography,' in A. B. Beck et al. [eds.], *Fortunate the Eyes That See: Essays in Honor of David Noel Freedman in Celebration of His Seventieth Birthday* [Grand Rapids: Eerdmans, 1995], 276) comments that apart from kingship, the general sapiential teaching of the passages, and the apparent old age of the sage-king, there is little to commend the connection between Qohelet and the Egyptian Instructions.

77. Koh, *Royal Autobiography*, 73–77.
78. ibid., 104.

to show that not even the accomplishments of a king amount to anything significant.⁷⁹ Although these inscriptions use royal self-introductory formulae and stereotypical language of boasting, they are historical narrative, which does not fit Ecclesiastes.⁸⁰ The general description of political trouble that Qohelet describes is not parallel with the large-scale military campaigns and ongoing imperial conquests of the Inscriptions.

Longman compares Qohelet with Akkadian fictional autobiographies that have a didactic ending, especially the Cuthean Legend of Naram-Sin, which circulated early in the second millennium. It is clearly autobiographical, covering a four-year period of Naram-Sin's life assessed from a later perspective. There is an 'I' that reflects upon itself and there is development and change in the personality of the narrator/subject. It is fiction: the description of the invading army and its conquest is beyond the realm of reality. It has a didactic ending with a series of admonitions or lessons drawn from the experience of the speaker. It also has a three-fold structure of first-person introduction (1–3), first-person narration (4–146), and first-person instruction (147–175).⁸¹ According to Longman, Qohelet is also autobiographical and fictional. Fictional autobiography is defined as 'a composition where the life of an individual, real or imagined, is written by a second individual under the name of the first individual at a later period of time.' Fictional autobiography is pseudonymous.⁸² Qohelet also shows a similar three-fold structure in the first-person discourse. There is a first-person introduction (1:12-18), an extended first-person narrative where Qohelet describes his quest for meaning in life (2:1–6:9), and a first-person instruction where advice is given out of personal experience (6:10–12:7).⁸³ However, the comparison between the tripartite structure of Qohelet and the Cuthean Legend is problematic because the

---

79. Seow, 'Qohelet's Autobiography,' 284–285.
80. Koh, *Royal Autobiography*, 104.
81. Longman, *Fictional Akkadian Autobiography*, 103–116.
82. ibid., 41.
83. ibid., 120–121.

comparisons are not very comparable. It has been pointed out that the endings used to separate the Akkadian texts sometimes make up 80 per cent of the inscription and many times state the main purpose of the text. The autobiographical part looks like an introduction and may comprise only a few lines.[84]

Koh argues that although there are shortcomings to Longman's analysis, he has pointed us in the right direction for comparisons to Qohelet with the subgenre 'pseudoautobiography.' There is a group of Akkadian inscriptions that describe the legendary heroic deeds of the Akkadian kings of the dynasty of Akkad in the third millennium. They are written in first-person narrative by a king describing his deeds and experiences. They are fictional literary compositions that are not afraid to describe the weaknesses of the king as a reason for the misfortune described in the text. They are meant to provide lessons for future rulers. Texts included in this category include the Cuthean Legend of Naram-Sin, the text of a King of Isin, and two Sargon texts (a Sargon Autobiography and a Sargon Legend). The similarities with Qohelet include a great king recording experiences during his rule, the pseudepigraphic nature of the texts even though they purport to be genuine royal inscriptions, the first-person style of autobiography, and the didactic nature of the texts.[85]

The similarities between the words of Qohelet and other ancient Near Eastern literature demonstrate that Qohelet reflects the ancient Near Eastern environment. However, it is hard to point to a body of literature and confidently say that Qohelet fits a particular genre because of the many differences between Ecclesiastes and the other texts. The Akkadian

---

84. Koh, *Royal Autobiography*, 106–112. See also William Farber's review of Longman, *Fictional Akkadian Autobiography*, in *JNES* 56.3 (1997): 228–230. Craig Bartholomew (*Reading Ecclesiastes: Old Testament and Hermeneutical Theory* [Rome: Editrice Pontificio Istituto Biblico, 1998], 152–153]) points out that Longman's analysis does not take into account the whole book of Ecclesiastes in his genre discussion because he limits his comparisons to the first-person discourse. He comments that this points to the limits of the comparative approach and that the nature of Ecclesiastes must be argued primarily from the text itself.

85. Koh, *Royal Autobiography*, 120–121.

INTRODUCTION   35

literature, which some argue has the most similarities, is very early in light of the fact that most date Qohelet late. The Akkadian literature comes from the third millennium, and most date Qohelet to the fourth or third centuries of the first millennium. Although many works share themes similar to Qohelet's, the differences are compelling. The Gilgamesh Epic is a third-person mythological account and the Western Semitic Royal Inscriptions are historical in nature. Some of the Egyptian literature is too political in nature (the Royal Testaments) or does not exhibit the reflective nature of Qohelet (the Instructions). In the end, there is no consensus concerning the genre of Ecclesiastes.[86] Thus it is hard to avoid the conclusion that there is no clear genre category of the ancient Near East to which the book of Ecclesiastes is analogous.[87]

One term that is prominent in discussing the words of Qohelet is the term 'autobiography.' Although some doubt whether 'autobiography' is an apt description,[88] many have recognized the appropriate nature of that term to describe the words of Qohelet. Longman defines autobiography as 'an account of the life (or part thereof) of an individual written by the individual himself.' It must be written in the first person and include reminiscences of the past life of the individual.[89] Isaksson examines what he calls the 'autobiographical thread' of Qohelet, which includes every first common singular perfect (suffixing conjugation, abbreviated SC) verbs. He demonstrates that this thread runs through the whole first-person discourse.

---

86. Bartholomew, *Reading Ecclesiastes*, 147.

87. Roland E. Murphy, *Wisdom Literature: Job, Proverbs, Ruth, Canticles, Ecclesiastes, Esther*, FOTL (Grand Rapids: Eerdmans, 1981), 131 and Koh, *Royal Autobiography*, 72. Brown (*Ecclesiastes*, 17) comments that Ecclesiastes is sui generis, a messy mixture of autobiographical references, theological reflections, philosophical musings, and proverbial instructions.

88. There is some discussion whether 'autobiography' is too modern a term that only became significant when the uniqueness of the individual emerged in the eighteenth century, but Longman argues that this definition of autobiography is too narrow (*Akkadian Fictional Autobiography*, 41–42). Murphy wants to be sure that autobiography is not used to derive personal data concerning the life or psychological history of the author (*Ecclesiastes*, xx).

89. Longman, *Akkadian Fictional Autobiography*, 40–41.

The dominance of SC forms in the thread may suggest a 'looser' kind of narration that relates points of interest in the life of an author rather than telling a story of connected events.[90] Koh argues for royal autobiography by arguing that the royal voice is dominant throughout the book. This voice is a coherent personality which gives unity to the work. The fact that the book contains two sections which are a collection of proverbs does not challenge the autobiographical nature of the work because the proverbs are used by Qohelet to investigate wisdom.[91] Ecclesiastes as a whole can be identified as autobiography cast in a narrative frame, that is, a framed autobiography.[92]

The fact that the words of Qohelet, which are first person, are framed by third person with a third-person intrusion in 7:27, raises significant questions that affect the interpretation of the book. How many hands are involved in the book itself? What is the relationship between the first-person autobiography (1:12–12:7) and the third-person frame (1:1-11; 12:8-14)? Some have argued that there are several hands involved in the book, which reflect several different viewpoints expressed in the book (see below for a brief discussion of this view). A few have argued that the author of the epilogue (12:8-14) is also responsible for the first-person discourse, so that one person is responsible for the whole work. Delitzsch argues that the epilogue is a postscript added by the author of the book, because the spirit of the book and the epilogue are the same. In the book itself the author puts on the mask of Qohelet-Solomon and then in the epilogue he speaks only of Qohelet.[93] Garrett argues that there are three levels of discourse in the book: the first level is the level of the frame narrator, the second level is the level of wisdom (the

---

90. Isaksson, *Language of Qohelet*, 43, 48.

91. Koh, *Royal Autobiography*, 147, 154–155, 162.

92. Bartholomew, *Reading Ecclesiastes*, 157. This is also Longman's view (*Ecclesiastes*, 17). However, Bartholomew does not agree with Longman's comparison of Qohelet with the Cuthean Legend because he thinks his genre analysis is based more on a description of the text than on comparisons with other literature of the ancient Near East.

93. Delitzsch, 'Ecclesiastes,' 6:429-430.

authoritative teaching of proverbial wisdom), and the third level is the first-person meditations of Qohelet. These levels flow together and are part of the single perspective of one author.[94] In this view Qohelet in the epilogue is commenting on his own words in the first-person discourse.

It is better to understand the third-person frame to be from a different hand. This view is supported by the shift from first person to third person in the epilogue and by the fact that the epilogue comments on the words of Qohelet. Although it is possible that someone could comment on his own work and speak about himself in the third person, it is not likely that one would do so in the middle of a first-person sentence, as in 7:27.[95] Thus it seems that someone is responsible for setting forth the words of Qohelet and then offering an appraisal of his words. Fox argues that this editor is an active editor because he is involved in sentence composition, as he has joined two halves of a sentence in 7:27. Thus he becomes the transmitter of Qohelet's words.[96]

Different approaches to Ecclesiastes

The fact that an editor is presenting the words of Qohelet raises the question of the purpose behind such a presentation. No doubt there is a didactic purpose, for the epilogue is addressed to 'my son,' which reminds one of the instructions in the book of Proverbs (Prov. 1:8; 2:1; 3:1; 5:1; 6:1; 7:1). But there is debate concerning whether the editor is agreeing with the words of Qohelet or warning his son about the words of Qohelet. The best way to answer this question is through an exegesis of the epilogue, but it is helpful to lay out the different approaches to the book of Ecclesiastes to get an idea of some of the questions involved. One of the difficulties of understanding the words of Qohelet is how to relate the positive and the negative statements of the book, or, more specifically, how to handle what seem to be contradictions in the book. For example, in 8:10-15 Qohelet goes back and

---

94. Garrett, *Ecclesiastes*, 262–263.
95. Fox, 'Frame Narrative,' 84.
96. Fox, *Rereading Ecclesiastes*, 365.

forth over whether the righteous and the wicked get their just rewards.⁹⁷ In 8:10 there is an observation concerning the burial of the wicked, which is followed in 8:11 by the conclusion that evil increases when the sentence against an evil deed is not executed speedily. In 8:12a Qohelet recognizes that sinners do evil and live long lives, but then he states the opposite in 8:12b-13: it will not be well with the wicked and his days will not be prolonged. Then in 8:14 Qohelet notes that the righteous are not rewarded for their righteousness and the wicked are not rewarded for their wickedness, but the exact opposite occurs. The righteous get what the wicked deserve and the wicked get what the righteous deserve. This is followed by a call to enjoyment in 8:15. The way in which commentators handle the tension in these verses is a window into how they understand Qohelet and his relationship to the epilogue.

1. *The Heterodox Qohelet*

Some argue that Qohelet deviated from orthodox wisdom teaching and rejected the claim that wisdom could secure one's existence.⁹⁸ The positive statements in the book are dogmatic corrections made by another hand in order to try to bring the message of Qohelet more in line with traditional wisdom thinking. Thus there are several editors and viewpoints represented in the book. The first editor, or redactor (R1), admired the thinking of Qohelet and so did not change anything. He was responsible for 1:1; 1:2; 7:27; 12:8; and 12:9-12. The second redactor (R2) was disturbed by the

---

97. The relationship between a person's deeds and the consequences of those deeds is called divine retribution. Normally one expects that if good deeds are done good consequences will follow and if bad deeds are done bad consequences will follow. The good consequences from good deeds can be seen as reward and the bad consequences from bad deeds can be seen as punishment from God. Qohelet struggles with the breakdown of the relationship between deeds and consequences, which makes it appear that the wicked do not get what they deserve. This raises questions concerning God's justice. For further discussion see Richard P. Belcher, Jr., 'Divine Retribution in Ecclesiastes' (Ph.D. diss., Westminster Theological Seminary, 2000).

98. Aare Lauha, *Kohelet* (NeuKirchen-Vluyn: Neukirchener Verlag, 1978), 7 and Crenshaw, *Ecclesiastes*, 28.

thinking of Qohelet because it did not support traditional wisdom thinking. He set out to make dogmatic corrections to the work. Barton identifies R2 as someone whose philosophy was Pharisaic. Concerning 8:11-14, 8:12b-13 are a dogmatic correction stating the validity of the deed-consequence relationship, which is denied by verses 11 and 14. Thus 8:12b-13 states a viewpoint that is the opposite of Qohelet's view, as does 12:13-14 in the epilogue, which is also from the hand of R2.[99] In arguing that Qohelet has denied the views of traditional wisdom, Qohelet's relationship with God is also called into question.[100]

The view that there are redactors at work in Ecclesiastes who insert glosses to the text to correct Qohelet's thinking is not as prominent today as it was in the past. Part of the reason is that source criticism is not as dominant in Old Testament studies because the emphasis has moved toward understanding the final form of the text.[101] Furthermore, the corrective glosses do not really fulfill their intended purpose, because the pessimistic statements still dominant the passages. For example, in 8:11-14, the corrective gloss (8:12b-13) is surrounded by the opposite viewpoint so that a denial of retribution (the deed-consequence relationship) is the last word in these verses. One wonders why the glossators copied the book to begin with instead of suppressing it altogether.[102]

Others argue for some kind of dialogue in the book between Qohelet and traditional wisdom. Qohelet denies the principle of the deed-consequence relationship in 8:11 and 14 over against traditional wisdom thinking represented in Proverbs and Ecclesiastes 8:12b-13. Robert Gordis explains the dialogue between the tensions in the book by means of quotations. He defines a quotation as words which do not reflect the present

---

99. Barton, *Ecclesiastes*, 45–46.

100. Barton (*Ecclesiastes*, 48) comments that God is no longer a warm personality to Qohelet and Lauha (*Kohelet*, 159) states that a personal relationship with God is missing.

101. Bartholomew, *Reading Ecclesiastes*, 93–94.

102. Fox, *Rereading Ecclesiastes*, 18–19.

sentiments of the author of the literary composition in which they are found, but have been introduced to convey the standpoint of another person or situation. Thus 8:12b-13 are a quotation of traditional wisdom from which Qohelet dissents in 8:14-15. He is an unconventional sage, parting company with Proverbs on the issue of reward and punishment; thus, he can be called heterodox.[103] Although Murphy does not see 8:12b-13 as a quotation, he does affirm that Gordis' analysis is basically correct and stresses the importance of dialogue in understanding the book of Ecclesiastes. In his view 8:12b-13 introduces Qohelet's awareness of the orthodox claim concerning divine retribution, which he then denies.[104] Both Murphy and Gordis see some tension between the epilogue and the views of Qohelet. Gordis argues that since the epilogue is from another hand the contradiction between 12:13-14 and the rest of the book does not have to be reconciled.[105] Murphy comments that the epilogue is an oversimplification of the book's message because the statements in 12:13-14 go beyond what Qohelet has said.[106]

One problem with the quotation view is that clear criteria for identifying quotations have not been developed. It is hard to identify a quotation unless there is some introductory statement, such as, 'the sages say.'[107] Whybray develops formal criteria to identify quotations which emphasize forms and themes that are consistent with proverbs.[108] But Fox wonders how one distinguishes a quotation from a statement

---

103. Gordis, *Koheleth*, 95–96, 101–108, 287, 28 and 'Quotations in Wisdom Literature,' *JQR* 30 (1939–40): 123–147.

104. Murphy, *Ecclesiastes*, lxvi, 85–87.

105. Gordis, *Koheleth*, 339–340. He seems to qualify this statement when he later acknowledges that although the editor has not done full justice to Qohelet's thought, the concepts of fear of God and obedience to commands are part of Qohelet's view if he is allowed to define them in his own way (341).

106. Murphy, *Ecclesiastes*, lxv, 126.

107. Fox, *Rereading Ecclesiastes*, 20. See also Fox, 'The Identification of Quotations in Biblical Literature,' *ZAW* 92 (1980): 416–431.

108. R. N. Whybray, 'The Identification and Use of Quotations in Ecclesiastes,' in J. Emerton (ed.), *Congress Volume. Vienna 1980* (Leiden: E. J. Brill, 1981), 435–481.

that Qohelet himself might have composed because, according to the epilogue (12:9), he composed proverbs. Quotes which express the author's viewpoint do not need to be marked, but those that are contrary to the viewpoint of the author need to be marked in some way. Ecclesiastes 8:12b-13 is not listed in Whybray's clear examples of quotations in Ecclesiastes,[109] and Gordis' definition that a quotation does not express the sentiments of the author is too general to be useful.[110] These views allow one side of the equation (the denial of retribution in 8:11 and 14) to dominate over the other side (the working of retribution in 8:12b-13) so that they conclude that Qohelet is heterodox in that he has abandoned the principle of retribution.

2. *The Orthodox Qohelet*

This approach argues that the views of Qohelet are in full agreement with views expressed in the book of Proverbs and that the statement in the epilogue, 'fear God and keep his commandments' (12:13), is the message of Qohelet himself. In this approach the positive statements take precedence over the negative statements. Early commentators on Ecclesiastes, both patristic and Jewish, took this view. The Targum of Qohelet teaches the importance of Torah study, repentance, and prayer through a periphrastic translation of the text. In Ecclesiastes 8:11-15 the perspective of 'the world to come' is added, introducing a concept that is not in the original.[111] Gregory Thaumaturgos, who lived in the second

---

109. Whybray ('Quotations in Ecclesiastes,' 438) confines himself to sayings which are in every respect indistinguishable in character from those in Proverbs. He lists eight clear examples: 2:14a; 4:5; 4:6; 7:5; 7:6a; 9:17; 10:2; 10:12.

110. Fox, *Rereading Ecclesiastes*, 21–22 and 'The Identification of Quotations,' 417. Whether or not there is dialogue between Ecclesiastes and Proverbs and the wisdom tradition will be dealt with later.

111. Peter S. Knobel, *The Targum of Qoheleth*, The Aramaic Bible, edited by Martin McNamara (Collegeville, MN: Liturgical, 1991), 14–15. Targums were Aramaic translations of the Hebrew text read in the synagogue alongside the reading of the Hebrew for people who no longer understood Hebrew. Some of these translations were very loose. For example, Ecclesiastes 8:12b reads, '*For it was revealed to me by the holy spirit* and I know that it

century A.D., offers the earliest full treatment of Ecclesiastes among Christian interpreters. The statement in 8:14, which denies the principle of retribution (the deed-consequence relationship), is introduced as 'a false opinion among human beings.'[112] Thus Qohelet is made orthodox by introducing other concepts or by rejecting as error certain statements that Qohelet makes.

R. N. Whybray has called Qohelet a preacher of joy.[113] He sees the crucial question to be whether the negative statements of the book dominate Qohelet's world-view or whether they are a foil for some other positive assessment of the human situation. He tries to steer a course between pessimism and optimism by calling Qohelet a realist. Qohelet affirms the traditional view of divine retribution because what he argues has a long Old Testament tradition, which includes a denial of a fixed relationship between cause and effect, a frustration with the prosperity of the wicked, and an affirmation of the freedom and sovereignty of God.[114] In Ecclesiastes 8:11-15 there are two opposing viewpoints which stand side by side. In an article published in 1982, Whybray argues that 8:12b-13 is the answer to the problem stated in 8:11,[115] but in his later commentary he is more cautious. He argues that it is uncertain whether Qohelet totally disagrees with 8:12b-13, or whether he regards the traditional view as generally valid, but recognizes that there are lamentable exceptions. In the final analysis, Whybray understands that Qohelet does not entirely abandon the traditional belief that justice will prevail.[116] The epilogist builds on views that Qohelet frequently advocates and

---

will be well *in the world to come for those who fear the Lord who fear Him and do His will*' (italics original, denoting words not specifically in the Hebrew text; Knobel, *Targum of Qohelet*, 43).

112. John Jarick, *Gregory Thaumaturgos' Paraphrase of Ecclesiastes* (Atlanta: Scholars Press, 1990), 3–4, 214–217.

113. R. N. Whybray, 'Qoheleth, Preacher of Joy,' *JSOT* 23 (1982): 87–98.

114. Whybray, *Ecclesiastes*, 27–29.

115. Whybray, 'Preacher of Joy,' 90.

116. Whybray, *Ecclesiastes*, 137.

states them in ways that make it clear that Qohelet is an orthodox wisdom teacher.[117]

Graham Ogden also understands the message of Ecclesiastes to be positive. The key to the meaning of the book is *hebel* (1:2). Since most commentators take it as representing the conclusion or thesis which Qohelet is arguing, they have concluded that the meaning of the book is negative. However, *hebel* does not signify 'meaningless,' but identifies the enigmatic in life. It suggests that life is not fully comprehensible. The term *hebel* does function as an answer to the question of 1:3, but it is not his main conclusion or advice, which is found in the calls to enjoyment (such as 2:24-26; 3:12; 3:22; 5:18-20; 8:15; and 9:7-10). These positive statements represent the theological affirmations of faith in a just and loving God, despite many signs to the contrary. The person of faith is aware of the mysteries of life (*hebel*), but the person of faith moves forward to positively enjoy life.[118] In Ecclesiastes 8:11-15 Ogden sees Qohelet as supporting the traditional view of the deed-consequence relationship, but he also raises serious questions that need to be faced. By putting the anomaly (8:14) alongside the tradition (8:12b-13), he demands that his readers come to terms with how things are in the real, but less than ideal, world. The purpose of the epilogue is not to correct Qohelet's views but to commend them to others.[119]

Michael Eaton calls Ecclesiastes an essay in apologetics, which 'defends the life of faith in a generous God by pointing to the grimness of the alternatives.' God is left out of the picture for much of the argument, which leads to a very

---

117. Whybray, *Ecclesiastes*, 173. In a later article Whybray calls Qohelet a defender of the Jewish faith ('Qoheleth as a Theologian,' in A. Schoors (ed.), *Qohelet in the Context of Wisdom* [Leuven: Leuven University Press, 1998], 245). Although he recognizes that Qohelet's theology is in some sense unorthodox, the purpose of Qohelet's writing was to show young, adult males how to maintain their faith in the Hellenistic context that militated against it.

118. Ogden, *Qoheleth*, 14–18, 26. See also Ogden and Lynell Zogbo, *A Handbook on Ecclesiastes*, UBS Handbook Series (New York: United Bible Societies, 1997).

119. Ogden, *Qoheleth*, 148–149, 229–231.

pessimistic view of life. A major part of the book is an exploration of the barrenness of life without a practical faith in God. However, suddenly God is introduced and the pessimism gives way to joy and purpose. Instead of beginning with the premise of the fear of the Lord, Qohelet argues as a humanist or secularist in order to show that such a starting point leads one to the meaninglessness of life. The audience is then in a position to hear the good news revealed at the end of the book. The contradictions in the book draw our attention to the viewpoint of faith, and so Qohelet is revealed as a man of faith.[120] The statement of Ecclesiastes 8:12b-13 is the answer of faith. Having shown the bankruptcy of the secularist approach, Qohelet allows the heavenly perspective to shine through in 8:12b-13. These verses are a declaration of Qohelet's faith that the vindication of the righteous is only a matter of time. The epilogue summarizes the message of Qohelet and points out the implications of the life of faith.[121]

Bruce Waltke does not see Ecclesiastes as an intentional apologetic against secularism leading to a positive assessment of faith, but as a debate by Qohelet between skepticism and faith, with the latter winning out. It is an agonizing struggle of an honest man wrestling with his absurd existence. Although Waltke acknowledges that Qohelet does not fall back on faith to save the day, he does agree that the orthodox statements are the key to the book. Ecclesiastes 8:11-13 is a confession of faith against the contrary evidence. 8:12b-13 states what his heart knows over against a world that seems to go against such affirmations. The epilogue confirms what Qohelet knows in his heart, for the narrator understands Qohelet's sayings as upright, true, and reliable.[122]

---

120. Eaton, *Ecclesiastes*, 44–45.
121. Eaton, *Ecclesiastes*, 122–123, 156.
122. Waltke, *Old Testament Theology*, 951, 954–955. Andrew G. Shead could also be included here as he argues that the epilogue is the key to the book. The inner frame of the book consists of 1:2 and 12:8 with the message of vanity and the outer frame consists of 1:1 and 12:9-14 with the message of the fear of God. The outer frame is the controlling frame and it offers the last word by synthesizing the two frames of vanity and fear in 12:13-14. Life can be called vain only if God can be acknowledged as a God worthy of fear. But

The main problem with the view that the message of Qohelet is positive is that the positive statements in the book are given precedence over the negative statements even when the text seems to indicate otherwise. Although the calls to enjoyment are positive exhortations which increase in their urgency as one reads through the book, it is debatable whether they should be seen as theological affirmations of faith. The target of Qohelet is not secularism, as in the apologetic view, but the failure of wisdom itself to produce what is promised. Qohelet is not starting on a secular basis to show where such a basis will lead, but is in a real struggle trying to understand what he observes in life. There is a tendency for commentators to give the final word to the positive statements when, in reality, the text moves in the other direction. For example, in discussing 8:11-15, it is hard to understand 8:12b-13 as winning the day when they are followed by 8:14. The negative statements that the righteous are not rewarded occur in 8:11 and 14, while the positive statement of the reward of the righteous occurs in 8:12b-13. Qohelet could have written the text differently, but he gave the negative statements the final word. It is hard to see how 8:12b-13 could be the answer of faith for Qohelet.[123]

3. *The Struggling Qohelet*

The positions set forth above believe that Qohelet takes a definite position concerning the subject of the reward of the righteous and the wicked, either rejecting it or affirming it. The views considered here allow the tensions in the thought of Qohelet to stand without trying to resolve them. The tensions are evidence of the honest struggle that Qohelet is

---

it is difficult to see how 'fear God and keep his commandments' is a synthesis of 'all is vanity' and 'fear God.' Perhaps the one frame might drive a person to the other frame, but that is different from a synthesis. Even Shead acknowledges that his view would be a surprise to the average first-time reader of the book (see 'Ecclesiastes From the Outside In,' *Reformed Theological Review* 55 (1996): 24–37 and 'Reading Ecclesiastes "Epilogically,"' *TynBul* 48 (1997): 67–91).

123. Although Waltke (*Old Testament Theology*, 961) recognizes the honest struggle that Qohelet is going through, he quotes Ecclesiastes 8:11-13, omitting verse 14, and declares that Qohelet confesses faith against contrary evidence.

experiencing. A major question is whether one side of the tension ultimately wins out in 1:12–12:7.

Hans Wilhelm Hertzberg employs a 'yes-but' principle to explain the tensions. Qohelet will often set forth the opposite of what he has discovered in his investigations (the 'yes fact'), and then he will set forth the other side (the 'but fact'). The 'but fact' qualifies the 'yes fact' and represents his own viewpoint. In Ecclesiastes 8:11-15, 8:12b-13 represents the 'yes fact,' which is followed in 8:14 by the 'but fact.' Although Qohelet does not completely deny 8:12b-13, they do not stand up to the reality of life as he has observed it. They are certainly not a solution to the problems of life. The 'yes fact' is thus pushed to the periphery and the 'but fact' is emphasized and highlighted.[124] Hertzberg argues that there are three hands involved in the epilogue. The first hand (12:9-11) praises Qohelet, the second hand (12:12) is a warning and correction of 12:9-11, and the third hand adds a concluding word by giving direction for the practical use of the book with an edifying ending.[125]

Craig Bartholomew examines Ecclesiastes from a narrative standpoint. He argues that the juxtaposition of *hebel* and joy (the calls to enjoyment), which are contradictory answers given by Qohelet in his search, creates a gap that needs to be filled.[126] He notes that the two sides of this tension make it difficult to assess the true meaning of the book, for usually one side of the tension is made dominant. Qohelet is seen as either a skeptic or as a person of faith, with the latter view understanding the calls to enjoyment as the answer to the problem. Allowing the tension to remain creates a gap that

---

124. Hans Wilhelm Hertzberg, *Der Prediger* (Gütersloh: Gütersloher Verlagshaus Gerd Mohn, 1963), 29–39. Although Fox (*Rereading Ecclesiastes*, 16–17) correctly points out that the approach of Hertzberg can be used to harmonize contradictory statements by relating them to different points of view, Hertzberg does allow the tensions to remain in many cases.

125. Hertzberg, *Prediger*, 220–221.

126. Bartholomew, *Reading Ecclesiastes*, 238 and *Ecclesiastes* (Grand Rapids: Baker, 2009), 79–82. He is dependent on Meir Sternberg, *The Poetics of Biblical Narrative* (Bloomington: Indiana University Press, 1987) for his narrative discussion of literary gaps.

needs to be filled. Ecclesiastes 8:11-14 juxtaposes the positive statements of 8:12b-13, that sinners will be punished and not live long lives, with the negative statements of 8:11-12a and 14, that sinners will not be punished and will live long lives, creating a gap that needs to be filled. The gap is ultimately filled with 12:13-14, which makes the epilogue an integral part of the book itself and necessary for understanding the book. Bartholomew argues that the narrator reads Qohelet positively and at least arrives at a point of agreement with Qohelet in the statement 'fear God and keep his commands.' He also believes that 12:1 ('Remember also your Creator in the days of your youth') is a bridge to the filling of the gap in 12:13-14. In 11:7–12:7 the more positive element comes before the enigmatic, dark element, which shapes the last section toward the possibility of integration and resolution. Thus in 11:7–12:7 life under the sun is assessed positively.[127]

Tremper Longman III understands Qohelet to be a wisdom teacher who struggles with the normative traditions of his people represented in Proverbs. Pessimism permeates the book because Qohelet takes an 'under the sun' approach, a limited perspective which does not take into account heavenly realities. In Ecclesiastes 8:11-14 Qohelet contradicts in 8:13 what he stated in 8:12a. In 8:12b-13 the traditional view of divine retribution is stated, which Qohelet does not affirm, for he clearly questions that view in 8:14. Qohelet displays a quandary of doubt concerning the issue. He is a confused wise man whose thoughts are filled with tensions and contradictions as he struggles with traditional wisdom thinking. The epilogue sets forth a view contrary to Qohelet as the epilogist evaluates the teaching of Qohelet, shows the dangers of speculative wisdom, and reinforces the normative teaching of the Old Testament.[128]

Finally, Michael Fox argues that one must recognize the contradictions in the thought of Qohelet in order to bring into focus the book's central concern: the problem of the meaning of life. The contradictions which Qohelet observes

---

127. Bartholomew, *Reading Ecclesiastes*, 248–254, 170.
128. Longman, *Ecclesiastes*, 32–39.

in the world must be allowed to stand because they state the problems encountered in life, which once recognized can pave the way for a more constructive approach to life. Thus one should not try to eliminate or harmonize the contradictory statements but must let them have their place. In Ecclesiastes 8:11-14 Qohelet states both sides without resolving them. He knows the principle of retribution (8:12b-13) and does not deny it, but he also knows there are situations which violate the principle (8:11, 14). Qohelet does not subordinate the violations of the principle to his belief that God is judge. He could have abandoned belief in God's justice or he could have subordinated injustice to a larger theological perspective, but he does neither, allowing both to stand. He calls Qohelet a man of faith who trusts in God and His justice, but he also calls him a man of doubt who knows the realities that violate his belief.[129] The frame narrator keeps a respectful distance from Qohelet. The advice to 'fear God and keep his commandments' echoes certain elements of Qohelet's teaching and states standard religious teaching with a dogmatic certainty that is in contrast with the uncertainty of all knowledge in Qohelet. This conclusion is a call to tolerate the expression of unorthodox opinion, which allows everything to be heard as long as one reaches a proper conclusion. Objections to the book are blunted by the implication that the frame narrator is just reporting what Qohelet said without rejecting the latter's ideas. A reader can align himself with the editor so as not to reject the book, even if he rejects the views of Qohelet.[130]

---

129. Fox, *Rereading Ecclesiastes*, 3, 51, 55–56, 134. Although one may appreciate the approach of Fox, who seeks to allow both sides of the issue to stand without resolving them, it is hard to accept his assertions that Qohelet is both a man of faith who trusts in God (134) and a man who fears God but does not love God or have any feelings of warmth or fellowship with God (136–137). Longman's idea that Qohelet is wrestling with the issues works better.

130. Fox, 'Frame Narrative,' 103–104. F. Delitzsch and C. L. Seow could also be placed in this category. Although Delitzsch ('Ecclesiastes,' 6:180-184) calls Ecclesiastes 'The Song of the Fear of God,' he also acknowledges that there are self-contradictions and 'the most dissonant and confused impressions of the present world' in the book. He understands Ecclesiastes 8:12b-13 as Qohelet's own conviction of a righteous requital which is contradicted

These views attempt to allow the tensions in the thought of Qohelet to remain without resolving them. There is always a tendency to move toward one pole or the other to bring some resolution to the tension, which is why there are a variety of approaches to the book. Although allowing the tensions to remain in the thought of Qohelet is the best approach to the book, an analysis of the views that advocate this approach brings further clarification to the issues involved. Bartholomew's approach—that Qohelet juxtaposes two contradictory views, creating a gap that needs to be filled—allows both sides of the tension to be stated. It also gives a rationale for the epilogue to the book as the filler of the gap created by the tension. Although this may work on a broad scale for Ecclesiastes, it is not as clear how it works for individual passages.[131] For example, in Ecclesiastes 8:11-15 the juxtaposition is between the view that sinners will be punished and not live long lives and the view that sinners will not be punished and will live long lives. One could argue that the gap between those two is filled with 8:15, the call to enjoyment (see below for an analysis of how the calls to enjoyment function in the book). Or when Qohelet

by appearances. Qohelet affirms the judgment of God, but it is only an abstract postulate of faith not powerful enough to raise a person above the miseries of this life. Qohelet sets forth a dark view of the world, a darkness that is broken only by scattered gleams of light. Seow (*Ecclesiastes*, 41–42, 288) believes that Qohelet is in a debate with himself, which is a reflection of his inner struggles, where the inconsistencies and outright contradictions in the world cannot be explained. It is the intention of the author that the reader wrestles with these contradictions. Qohelet accepts the orthodox doctrine of retribution (8:12b-13), but sees that it is contradicted in reality (8:11, 14). However, Seow does not believe that the major message of Ecclesiastes is that everything is meaningless or futile, but that people cannot comprehend what is happening or control their own destiny.

131. It is amazingly difficult to find clear statements in Bartholomew on how the gaps are to be filled because when he talks about gaps he rarely specifies how the gap is to be filled (*Ecclesiastes*, 81–82). It becomes clear how the gaps are to be filled in his passing comments and then in a few places where he specifically states that the resolution comes in 12:13-14 (*Ecclesiastes*, 119 and *Reading Ecclesiastes*, 253–254). After having read *Reading Ecclesiastes* one expects that in his commentary on Ecclesiastes there would be an application of this method to the book, but only in a few places is the role of gaps discussed.

juxtaposes wickedness in 3:16 with God's judgment in 3:17, the gap may be filled by the negative assertions that humans are no different from beasts in 3:18-21. In other words, why does one have to wait until 12:13-14, or 12:1, for the gap to be filled? Perhaps the gap is filled in individual passages with the negative conclusions of Qohelet. It seems in most passages that the negative assertions get the last word (as in 8:11-14). Also, his view that 11:7–12:7 is a positive assessment leading toward a resolution does not take into account the concluding *hebel* statement in 12:8, which does not just balance 11:7 and 12:1, but frames the whole work.[132] In other words the final word is *hebel*, not joy. Longman's pessimistic view of Qohelet, on the other hand, understands that the final word is *hebel* and that the calls to enjoyment are resigned conclusions in light of the meaninglessness of life. However, he does not believe that Qohelet affirms the positive side of the tension, at least in terms of the traditional doctrine of retribution in 8:12b-13. Fox allows both sides of the tension to stand and recognizes this as a key aspect of the thought of Qohelet. In the final analysis, the best approach is to understand that Qohelet does not subordinate the anomalies of life and the breakdown of the principle of retribution to a higher principle in order to bring a resolution to the problem. Although it is true that Qohelet does not use the traditional view to explain the anomalies of life, he does subordinate the traditional view to the anomalies of life. Although he may not completely deny the traditional view, he does not affirm it. The troubles of life dominate his thinking so that he calls into question the traditional understanding of the deed-consequence relationship. Reasons why Qohelet operates this way will be explored below. The epilogist, on the other hand, does allow one side of the tension to win the day when he brings in the commandments of God and the secret judgment of God (12:13-14). This raises the question as to why the epilogist would transmit the words of Qohelet in

---

132. Bartholomew, *Reading Ecclesiastes*, 252. Brown (*Ecclesiastes*, 22) argues that *hebel* is part and parcel of the structure of life, that it engulfs both the universal and the individual.

the first place. This question will be addressed below, which will raise again the issue of the identity of Qohelet, but first it is important to try to understand why Qohelet struggles with the tensions in life without being able to come to a resolution of those tensions.

Hermeneutical keys for understanding Ecclesiastes

1. *Qohelet's epistemology*

There are several important exegetical decisions with which an interpreter of Ecclesiastes is faced; these decisions determine how one understands the book. Several of the major problem areas will be covered here. The first deals with the methodology behind the search of Qohelet, which can be called his epistemology. In other words, on what basis does Qohelet draw conclusions about life? What role does experience play in drawing those conclusions? There is no doubt that in Proverbs and Ecclesiastes observation and reflection are presented as playing a role in drawing conclusions about life. In Proverbs 24:30-34 observations are made concerning a vineyard that was not kept, followed by reflection and then instruction (24:32; see also 7:6-23). However, as Fox points out, observation in Proverbs is not presented as the source of new knowledge, but is used as an occasion for reflection and the reinforcement of known principles. Observation is used to confirm knowledge already accepted. Many of the statements in Proverbs concerning justice are statements of faith based on divine revelation.[133] In other words, the sages do not observe creation from a neutral standpoint but rather stand on the foundation of divine

---

133. Fox, 'The Epistemology of the Book of Proverbs,' *JBL* 126.4 (2007): 670–673, 683 and Fox, *Rereading Ecclesiastes*, 80–81. Fox argues that the sages in Proverbs operated according to a coherence theory of truth where the truth of any true proposition coheres with a specified set of propositions. Crenshaw, on the other hand, argues that at the early stages the sages in Proverbs were operating primarily by experience ('Qoheleth's Understanding of Intellectual Inquiry,' in A. Schoors [ed.], *Qohelet in the Context of Wisdom* [Leuven: University Press, 1998], 214).

revelation and the fear of Yahweh.[134] The question 'how do you know?' is answered 'because I learned it.'[135] Observation, reflection, and conclusions conform to what the sages believe concerning God and His ways in the world.

Qohelet seems to have a different approach as he stresses more than Proverbs does the role of experience and the use of independent rational intelligence to draw his conclusions about life. The first common singular form of the Hebrew verb 'to see' (*rā'āh*) is used about nineteen times in Ecclesiastes. Six times it is used with the word 'all' (1:14; 4:1; 4:4; 7:15; 8:9; 8:17), which emphasizes the comprehensive nature of the observations. Four times it is used with 'under the sun' (5:18; 6:1; 9:13; 10:5). It is also used in the context of the calls to enjoyment (2:24; 3:10; 3:22; 5:18; 8:17; only 9:7-10 is omitted). It occurs in contexts dealing with divine retribution (3:16; 6:1; 7:15; 8:10). The whole process of investigation used by Qohelet, including his conclusions, is based on observation. Experience is his primary source of knowledge as he observes, reflects, and draws conclusions.[136] Although there are statements in the book concerning God and justice that are not based on experience (3:17; 8:12b-13), these statements are not used by Qohelet to alter his conclusions based on experience. There is no body of truth, not even the teachings of the sages, to which Qohelet is willing to submit his empirical conclusions. The question 'how do you know?' would be answered 'because I saw it.'[137] On this basis Bartholomew argues that Qohelet's epistemology is best described as autonomous and that Qohelet's use of wisdom to investigate the world means he will use his powers of reason in light of his experience and observations to understand the world. One cannot assume that wisdom, as used by Qohelet, means the same thing as in the book of Proverbs. Rather,

---

134. Bruce Waltke, *The Book of Proverbs: Chapters 1–31*, 2 vols. (Grand Rapids: Eerdmans, 2004, 2005), 1:55.

135. Fox, *Rereading Ecclesiastes*, 85.

136. Waltke, *Old Testament Theology*, 959 and Fox, *Rereading Ecclesiastes*, 76–77.

137. Fox, *Rereading Ecclesiastes*, 85.

Qohelet's use of wisdom is ironic because one expects wisdom to be rooted in the fear of Yahweh but it turns out that the wisdom in Qohelet refers to a quest for knowledge based on experience and observation.[138] If Qohelet's wisdom is not rooted in the fear of Yahweh, then one would expect that his use of 'fear God' would not necessarily follow the traditional view in Proverbs.

2. The meaning of hebel

Qohelet's 'empirical' epistemology is a limiting factor of Qohelet's thinking that undermines confidence in knowledge (8:17). This is supported by his main conclusion about life: *hebel*. This word is used more than any other word in the book, occurring some thirty-eight times.[139] It occurs in a superlative sense in the motto of the book that frames the book (1:2; 12:8). The superlative indicates something complete, absolute, and unqualified.[140] It is also the word that Qohelet keeps coming back to as he examines various aspects of life. But what does Qohelet mean by *hebel*?

The basic meaning of *hebel* is 'breath,' as seen in its use in Isaiah 57:13, where it parallels 'wind' (*rûaḥ*). Most of the time it is used metaphorically, either on the temporal level or the level of meaning. On the temporal level it stresses the idea that something is fleeting or transient. Fredericks argues for this view in Ecclesiastes because the emphasis on death reinforces the brevity of life.[141]

It is also possible to understand *hebel* in the realm of meaning rather than the temporal realm, which may have several different nuances. Some understand *hebel* to mean 'incomprehensible,' which stresses that life is hard to understand. Life can be incomprehensible in the sense that humans are unable to fully grasp the meaning of God's ways in the world, which may

---

138. Bartholomew, *Ecclesiastes*, 269–277. Bartholomew has one of the best discussions of Qohelet's epistemology.

139. Ogden, *Qoheleth*, 21.

140. Whybray, *Ecclesiastes*, 34–35.

141. Daniel C. Fredericks, *Coping with Transience* (Sheffield: JSOT Press, 1993), 30.

lead to frustration at human limitations.¹⁴² In this sense *hebel* is translated as 'mystery' or 'enigma.'¹⁴³ Another nuance of *hebel* in the sense of 'incomprehensible' is not just that life is hard to understand, but that life is not able to be understood, even by the wise men who are supposed to understand life. Here the idea of *hebel* is 'vanity' (in the sense of futile or purposeless), or 'meaningless,' or as Fox argues, 'absurd.' He does not think that *hebel* connotes 'incomprehensible,' in the sense of enigmatic, because it does not necessarily refer to what is contrary to reason. Qohelet, however, uses *hebel* to refer to scenarios where there is a disparity between rational expectations and the actual consequences. Thus *hebel* refers to what is contrary to reason, which is best designated in Fox's view as 'absurd.'¹⁴⁴

The view that *hebel* connotes 'futility' is an old view, which has the support of some ancient versions (the Septuagint and the Vulgate), as well as many English translations (KJV, NKJV, NASB, NIV, NRSV, ESV). Christianson closely examines the use of *hebel* outside Ecclesiastes, which occurs about thirty-two times. He lists eight different connotations: breath/vapor (Pss. 39:5, 11; 62:9; 94:11; 144:4; Prov. 21:6; Isa. 57:13), idols (Deut. 32:21; 1 Kings 16:13, 26; Ps. 31:6; Jer. 8:19; 10:8; 14:22; Jonah 2:6), worthless/false (Jer. 16:19; 23:16; 1 Kings 16:13; 2 Kings 17:15; Jer. 2:5), no purpose/useless (Job 27:12; Isa. 49:4; Jer. 10:3, 15; Lam. 4:17; Zech. 10:2), futile (Job 9:29; Pss. 62:10; 78:33; Isa. 30:7), nothing/empty (Job 21:34; 35:16; Prov. 13:11), fleeting (Job 7:16), and deceptive in appearance (Prov. 31:30). In all these occurrences something obviously false, futile, or empty is likened to or named *hebel*.¹⁴⁵ Longman also examines *hebel* outside Ecclesiastes and argues for the meaning 'uselessness' or 'meaninglessness,' not that which is transitory,

---

142. David A. Hubbard, *Ecclesiastes, Song of Solomon*, The Communicator's Commentary (Dallas: Word Books, 1991), 21–22.

143. W. E. Staples, 'Vanity of Vanities,' *CJT* 1 (1955): 143 translates *hebel* as 'mystery' and Ogden, *Qoheleth*, 17 uses 'enigmatic' in the sense that life is not fully comprehensible (see also Ogden, '"Vanity" It Certainly Is Not,' *BT* 38 [1987]: 307).

144. Fox, *Rereading Ecclesiastes*, 36–42 (see also Fox, 'The Meaning of Hebel for Qohelet,' *JBL* 105 [1986]: 413).

145. Christianson, *Narrative Strategies*, 79–80.

as evidenced by its use in parallel with 'false' (*šqr*) in Jeremiah 16:19 and 'worthless' (*šw'*) in Zechariah 10:2. In some passages *hebel* may mean 'temporary' or 'fleeting' (Pss. 144:4; 39:4-5, 11; Job 7:16; Prov. 31:30), but even in these passages the connotation of 'meaningless' is not out of the question.[146]

The primary way to understand *hebel* in Ecclesiastes is in the sense of futile or senseless.[147] Its use in the superlative sense in 1:2 and 12:8, and its fairly constant use throughout the book (it occurs thirty-eight times in Ecclesiastes), shows that it is the major theme of the book (contra Ogden). It is the main concept to which Qohelet keeps coming back. It is used as a negative judgment of evaluation in relationship to different situations in life. Its use with 'all' or 'everything' (*kōl*) implies that there is a meaning common to the various occurrences of the term so that, for the most part, the term should be translated by the same word throughout the book.[148]

The phrase *re'ût rûaḥ* (many times translated as 'chasing the wind') is used in conjunction with *hebel* and is thus important for understanding *hebel*. There are actually two phrases in the book (*re'ût rûaḥ* occurs in 1:14; 2:11, 17, 26; 4:4, 6; 6:9 and *ra'yôn rûaḥ* occurs in 1:17 and 4:16), which virtually mean the same thing.[149] The understanding of these phrases depends on the nuance of the root of the

---

146. Longman, *Ecclesiastes*, 62–64.

147. Martin A. Shields (*The End of Wisdom: A Reappraisal of the Historical and Canonical Function of Ecclesiastes* [Winona Lake, Ind.: Eisenbrauns, 2006], 113) notes that the meaning 'vanity' for *hebel* is somewhat problematic because its connotation has shifted from 'empty' to 'self-pride.' Also, the problem with the translation 'absurd' is that in English it is shifting to mean 'ludicrous' or 'laughable,' meanings which Fox rejects. Fox himself recognizes this and acknowledges that for a popular translation the connotation 'senseless' might be better (*Rereading Ecclesiastes*, 31–32), which is adopted in this commentary.

148. Fox, *Rereading Ecclesiastes*, 36 and Christianson, *Narrative Strategies*, 90. Although it is possible that in a few passages later in the book as Qohelet speaks of the period of youth before the coming of death, *hebel* may have the connotation of fleeting (11:8, 10), even in those passages the point seems to be that the period of youth is futile.

149. Fox (*Rereading Ecclesiastes*, 42–43) notes that there is no discernible difference in the way Qohelet uses them.

words *reʿût* and *raʿyôn* and the meaning of the word *rûaḥ* (spirit, wind, breath).¹⁵⁰ Usually one's understanding of *hebel* affects how one understands these two phrases. For example, Fredericks understands the phrase *reʿût rûaḥ* to support his view that *hebel* means temporary. The word *reʿût* means 'choosing' or 'desire,' with the translation 'desiring the wind.' This meaning of the phrase connotes the brevity of life and its experiences, which are like the wind's desire that constantly changes direction, and so is fleeting.¹⁵¹ Hubbard, who takes *hebel* as enigmatic, translates the phrase as 'grasping for the wind,' understood as puzzlement at the workings of life and our human strivings to make sense of them.¹⁵² Ogden follows the translation 'striving after the wind' and connects it with a shepherd attempting to herd the wind as he would herd sheep. He explains the phrase as referring to someone who is attempting something beyond his power to control, which means certain things are beyond our power to understand them as fully as we may wish. This view also fits his understanding of *hebel* as 'enigmatic.'¹⁵³ Longman, who understands *hebel* as 'meaningless,' understands *reʿût rûaḥ* to be reinforcing the meaninglessness of life, which is seen in the translation 'chasing the wind.' He appeals to Hosea 12:1, where the phrase 'feeds on the wind' (*rō ʿeh rûaḥ*, which uses the root *rʿh*) is used in parallel with 'pursues the east wind' (*rōdep̄ qādîm*). This supports the translation 'chasing the wind,' which describes life on earth as futile and frustrating and reinforces the meaning of *hebel* as meaningless. Life is not mysterious or enigmatic, but is

---

150. Fox (*Rereading Ecclesiastes*, 43) points out that there are several roots that sound identical but that have different meanings or spellings (homophonic), which leads to different understandings of the root *rʿh*.

151. This meaning is supported by the Septuagint (*proairesis* can mean 'deliberate choice'). Fredericks (*Transience*, 30) argues that the phrase *reʿût rûaḥ* could either be taken as a subjective, possessive genitive ('the desire of the wind') or as an objective genitive ('desiring the wind'). He thinks that both support the idea of transience.

152. Hubbard, *Ecclesiastes*, 44.

153. Ogden, *Qoheleth*, 40.

as futile as attempts to control the course of the wind.[154] Fox argues that most of the phenomena and experiences described by *reʿût rûaḥ* are not pursuits and that some of the activities covered by the phrase do attain their immediate goal. Thus he argues that 'chasing the wind,' in the sense of futility, is not the best rendering of the phrase. He connects *reʿût* with the root *rʿʿ* ('break'), or perhaps *rāʿāh* ('bad'), which is etymologically from *rʿʿ*. The idea of 'breaking of the spirit' or 'badness of the spirit' refers to someone who is conflicted and unhappy, whose soul is afflicted by various thoughts. Thus the phrase could be translated 'affliction of the spirit' or 'vexation of the spirit.' Fox emphasizes that in Aramaic the root *rʿy* (*rʿh* in Hebrew) produces verbs for both thinking and wishing, and understands the meaning of *reʿût* as 'senseless thoughts.' The full phrase (*reʿût rûaḥ*) means 'thoughts of wind' or 'windy thoughts,' which implies chaotic, aimless thoughts. Thus *rûaḥ* refers to a senselessness that comes from either an internal perspective (a person's senseless, irritating thoughts) or from an external perspective (a phenomenon that strikes the observer as senseless).[155] It is difficult to nail down the precise translation of these terms,[156] but the phrase *reʿût rûaḥ* does support the view that *hebel* refers to what is futile, meaningless, or senseless. The translation followed in this commentary will be 'chasing the wind.'

3. The phrase 'under the sun'

The phrase 'under the sun' is an important phrase as it occurs twenty-nine times in the book. Parallel expressions include 'under heaven' (1:13; 2:3; 3:1) and 'upon the earth' (8:14-16; 11:2), which occur less frequently.[157] A similar expression also

---

154. Longman, *Ecclesiastes*, 81–82 and Shields, *The End of Wisdom*, 115.

155. Fox, *Rereading Ecclesiastes*, 42–45. Fox consistently translates *reʿût rûaḥ* as 'senseless.'

156. Waltke (*Old Testament Theology*, 957) understands the phrase *reʿût rûaḥ* as a double entendre meaning both 'chasing after the wind' and 'a vexation of spirit.'

157. Although there is some debate whether the meaning of 'under heaven' is identical to 'under the sun,' the majority of commentators see

occurs in ancient Near Eastern inscriptions in imprecations protecting the monuments of kings. The earliest occurrence is in a twelfth-century inscription, but it also occurs twice in fifth-century Phoenician inscriptions. In the twelfth-century inscription there is an imprecation against anyone who would destroy the monument of the Elamite king Untashgal ('May his seed not prosper under the sun'). In the fifth century the imprecations are offered against anyone who would desecrate the tombs of King Tabnit and his son Eshmunazor, with the malediction that tomb robbers would have no progeny 'among the living under the sun.'[158] There is an emphasis on this world, the world of the living, over against the realm of the dead. This is also the meaning of the phrase in Ecclesiastes. The phrase 'under the sun' focuses attention on this world over against both the realm of the dead and the heavenly realm, which is God's domain.[159] It is commonly used with the Hebrew concepts ʿāsāh (stressing what is done or human deeds) and ʿāmāl ('work, toil'), along with the verb rāʾāh ('to see'), indicating the world people experience while they are alive, the observable world of work and other human activity.[160]

There is debate concerning whether 'under the sun' has a universal or a restrictive meaning. The universal meaning underscores the fact that Qohelet's observations include the entire world, not just a part of the world. The human condition and human experience described by Qohelet are universal.[161] There seems to be little doubt that Qohelet would affirm that his observations about life are universal in relationship to this world. The restrictive meaning of the phrase 'under the

---

them as virtually identical (see the discussion in Ingram, *Ambiguity in Ecclesiastes*, 253–261).

158. For a list of the use of 'under the sun' in inscriptions see Seow, *Ecclesiastes*, 105. The use of this phrase in early inscriptions means that there is no necessary Greek connection with this phrase.

159. Fox, *Rereading Ecclesiastes*, p. 165 and Tomas Frydrych, *Living Under the Sun: Examination of Proverbs and Qohelet* (Leiden: Brill, 2002), 45.

160. Ingram, *Ambiguity in Ecclesiastes*, 257.

161. Fox, *Rereading Ecclesiastes*, 165; Crenshaw, *Ecclesiastes*, 59; and Whybray, *Ecclesiastes*, 38.

INTRODUCTION 59

sun' can be understood in two ways. Some restrict Qohelet's observations to 'under the sun' as a way of holding out for the possibility of a different scenario somewhere else. Kathleen A. Farmer argues that the phrase 'under the sun' opens up the possibility that there is a distinction between what happens on the earth and what happens elsewhere, particularly in the afterlife.[162] Ogden notes that since there is no lasting benefit on this earth, Qohelet may be suggesting that there is one beyond this life.[163] But understanding 'under the sun' in a restrictive sense does not have to point to a situation other than in this life. Fox comments that since most of the facts that Qohelet observes under the sun can hardly be imagined to exist in any other domain but human life, there is no need for him to exclude other domains of reality.[164] It will become clear that a resolution of the problem in another realm is not a part of Qohelet's approach. Instead, 'under the sun' as a restrictive concept means that Qohelet's thinking is limited to this earthly life and the horizons of an earthly perspective without recourse to divine revelation. God is never brought in as a solution to the problems that plague Qohelet, even when there is a clear opportunity to do so in 9:1-2.[165] Leupold comments that this is like drawing a horizontal line between the earthly and heavenly realities and leaving out of consideration everything above the line.[166] In the final analysis, the universal view and the second way of understanding the restrictive view of 'under the sun' virtually mean the same thing. Qohelet thus offers a realistic portrayal of a world that suffers under the curse apart from God.[167] This view of 'under the sun' reinforces the empirical epistemology of Qohelet.

---

162. Kathleen A. Farmer, *Who Knows What Is Good? A Commentary on the Books of Proverbs and Ecclesiastes*, ITC (Grand Rapids: Eerdmans, 1991), 150.

163. Ogden and Zogbo, *Handbook on Ecclesiastes*, 24; see also Eaton, *Ecclesiastes*, 45.

164. Fox, *Rereading Ecclesiastes*, 35, 165.

165. Longman, *Ecclesiastes*, 66.

166. Leupold, *Ecclesiastes*, 28.

167. Longman, *Ecclesiastes*, 39 and Loader, *Ecclesiastes*, 15.

4. The question of 'gain' and the calls to enjoyment

The key question of the book comes in 1:3: 'What profit is there for a person in all his labour which he labours under the sun?' The question is repeated in some form in 2:22; 3:9; and 5:16. The term for 'profit' (*yitrôn*) is a commercial term which refers to a surplus or gain, but it has a wider meaning in Ecclesiastes as it is used in reference to wisdom (2:13).[168] When two things are compared, it refers to an advantage one thing might have over another thing (2:13; 3:19; 5:9; 6:8, 11; 7:11, 12; 10:10, 11). When *yitrôn* is used by itself it refers to any net gain that allows one to get ahead in life,[169] or to a desired result produced by effort or labor. The term for 'labour' (*'āmāl*) also has a broad use, for it can refer specifically to labor or toil, to any activity that requires effort (8:17), or to the product of an activity (2:18).[170] The basic answer to the question of 1:3 comes in 2:11 where Qohelet considers all his activities and concludes that there is no profit (*yitrôn*) under the sun. This is not just a 'temperamental overreaction' or 'temporary disillusionment'[171] but is the answer Qohelet gives to the question throughout the book. In other words, his answer does not change in the course of his argument. However, he will recognize that some things under the sun have a relative advantage over other things. For example, in 2:13-17 he argues that wisdom has an advantage (*yitrôn*) over folly, but in the long run it does not matter whether you are wise or a fool because there is no ultimate difference between them. Anything that may seem to provide a net gain or a desired result (labor, wisdom, wealth) always falls short. This includes the enjoyment that does come from labor expressed in the 'calls to enjoyment' (2:24-26; 3:12; 3:22; 5:18-20; 9:7-10). The calls to enjoyment are gifts from God (2:24; 3:13), but they are not the answer to the question of 1:3.[172] Rather, they are

---

168. Seow, *Ecclesiastes*, 103.
169. Fox, *Rereading Ecclesiastes*, 112.
170. ibid., 54–55.
171. Fredericks, *Transience*, 52–53.
172. Both Fredericks (*Transience*, 51) and Ogden (*Qoheleth*, 32–33) argue that the calls to enjoyment are the answer to the question of 1:3.

a recognition that this is all one can expect in a world where there is no lasting benefit. Most of them end on a negative note, which emphasizes that they do not provide a net gain or a desired result. Instead of using the term *yiṯrôn*, some of the calls to enjoyment employ the term *ḥēleq*, which means 'portion' or 'lot' (3:22; 5:19; 7:9). The difference between 'profit' (*yiṯrôn*) and 'portion' (*ḥēleq*) is not necessarily that the former refers to a lasting gain and the latter to a temporary gain. There are some passages where the concept 'temporary' does not work well (9:6), and in some passages the 'portion' may endure throughout life itself (9:9). As Fox notes, there is no point in complaining that there is no enduring profit in life when man himself does not endure.[173] The 'portion' refers to all that one can expect in a world where human activity and effort do not achieve the desired results. Thus, even though there is no profit to labor, one should enjoy the portion that does come from labor.

5. The breakdown of the deed-consequence relationship

The reason that human activity and labor do not achieve a net gain or the desired result is that the connections between wisdom and the blessings that should result from it, and foolishness and the negative consequences that should result from it, do not work out in the world, at least not consistently enough so that one can count on it. This is a problem that Qohelet keeps coming back to in one way or another (2:15-16; 2:26; 3:16-21; 6:1-2; 7:15-18; 8:10-14; 9:1-6). There is no difference between the wise person and the fool because they suffer the same fate (2:15-16). Humans have no advantage over the animals because they also suffer the same fate (3:16-22). There is very little difference between the righteous and the wicked because being in the hand of God makes no difference to what people experience in life, for they too suffer the same fate (9:1-6).[174]

---

173. Fox, *Rereading Ecclesiastes*, 110.

174. For a discussion of the role of the deed-consequence relationship in Ecclesiastes see Richard P. Belcher, Jr., 'Divine Retribution in Ecclesiastes' (Ph.D. diss., Westminster Theological Seminary, 2000).

The same fate that befalls both the righteous and the wicked in these verses is death itself, especially the manner of death, the timing of death, and the outcome of death. Although the subject of death in the Old Testament is a complex subject[175] and death is always considered an enemy, the Old Testament does distinguish between a good death and a bad death. In Numbers 23:10 Balaam exclaims, 'Let me die the death of the upright.' Such a death would be similar to the death of Abraham, who died in good old age, a man full of years (Gen. 25:8). Long life is seen as a great blessing from God (Pss. 21:4; 61:6; 91:16) and a benefit of wisdom (Prov. 3:16). Thus death at the end of a long life does not raise questions. But there is also a bad death described in the Old Testament, which could include impending violent death, as in the case of Joab or Saul, or a sudden, premature death, as in the case of the wicked. It is premature death, or dying while one is still young, that raises questions.[176] The blessing of long life and the avoidance of premature death is represented in Proverbs as coming from wisdom (9:10) and from the fear of Yahweh (10:27; 14:27). Although life in Proverbs includes life beyond this earthly life,[177] death is discussed as a part of the deed-consequence relationship (Prov. 6:12-15; 8:34-36; 10:21, 27; 11:19; 21:16). The concept of premature death cannot be ruled out of the discussion in the book of Proverbs. For Qohelet there is little difference between the death of the wise and the fool, the righteous and the wicked, the human and the animal. As he states in 2:16: 'How the wise dies just like the fool!' What is more, one cannot even be sure that humans and animals end up in different places after they die (3:19-21). In sum, the fact that the righteous do not receive the promised blessings in life and the wicked do not receive

---

175. The difficult nature of the subject of death in the Old Testament is attributed to the fact that the material is divergent, brief, sporadic, and often bound to a particular historical context (see L. R. Bailey, 'Death as a Theological Problem in the Old Testament,' *Pastoral Psychology* 22 [1971]: 22).

176. James L. Crenshaw, 'Introduction: The Shift from Theodicy to Anthropodicy,' in James L. Crenshaw (ed.), *Theodicy in the Old Testament* (Philadelphia: Fortress Press, 1983), 4.

177. Waltke, *Proverbs*, 1:104-107.

the expected negative consequences in life is a major reason Qohelet concludes that there is no net gain or desired result from human activity under the sun.

The identity of Qohelet and the danger of speculative wisdom

If the first-person discourse (1:12–12:7) is written from an 'under the sun' perspective and the third-person epilogue (12:8-14) provides the answer to Qohelet's quest (12:13-14), why would someone present the words of Qohelet for others to read since his perspective seems so different? Waltke asks whether it is plausible that the narrator would create a fictitious figure (Qohelet) to mouth sayings with which he disagrees.[178] Eaton observes that there is no other example of a wisdom document that exists in two recensions with opposite theologies.[179] The relationship of the epilogue to the rest of the book raises a host of issues, partly centered on how one understands 12:11-12,[180] but the focus here is on how 12:13-14 relates to 1:12–12:7. Although Qohelet may make statements that affirm God's judgment (3:17) and the deed-consequence relationship (8:12b-13), he does not allow those statements to solve the problems with which he is wrestling. Such statements stand side by side with the problems he observes in life. Instead of allowing the theological affirmations to explain the anomalies in life, the problems Qohelet observes take center stage without a resolution to those problems. In fact, one could argue that the problems get the last word since many times the problems frame the theological statements (8:11-14). Plus, the full *hebel* statement frames much of the book (1:2; 12:8). The epilogue, however, affirms the theological affirmations made by Qohelet and makes them the foundation of the answer to Qohelet's search.[181] The epilogue does not allow

---

178. Waltke, *Old Testament Theology*, 950.
179. Eaton, *Ecclesiastes*, 41.
180. See the discussion of these verses in the commentary.
181. There is debate concerning the relationship between the views of the epilogist and the views of Qohelet. Some argue that the epilogist is

the problems observed by Qohelet to trump the theological affirmations. However, the epilogue goes beyond the words of Qohelet once the commandments and the fear of God are mentioned (12:13-14). The commandments of God are never mentioned by Qohelet, but the commandments mentioned in the epilogue make clear that the fear of God speaks of a reverence for God that is willing to submit to God's ways no matter what problems one encounters in life. Also, the judgment mentioned in 12:14 includes secret elements which clearly push the judgment beyond this earthly life.[182]

The reason someone would present the struggles of Qohelet and then offer a simple explanation to that struggle is that the struggle of Qohelet is a common struggle in the Old Testament. The problem of the prosperity of the wicked or the suffering of the righteous is not an isolated problem. The prophets Jeremiah and Habakkuk wrestled with it, the whole discussion of Job with his friends centers around it, and certain psalms explore it (37; 49; 73). The warning in Ecclesiastes 12:12 may be against a speculative wisdom that allows the problems of life to dominate. It is possible that someone can lose the very foundation of wisdom itself in trying to explain those problems. The book of Proverbs lays out the foundation of wisdom as the fear of Yahweh (1:7). The short proverbial sayings in Proverbs

---

in agreement with Qohelet, and that he even supports and confirms his teachings (Bartholomew, *Reading Ecclesiastes*, 170; Farmer, *Ecclesiastes*, 197; Garrett, *Ecclesiastes*, 345; Hengstenberg, *Ecclesiastes*, 257; Provan, *Ecclesiastes*, 33; and Shead, 'Reading Ecclesiastes Epilogically,' 70). Others argue that the epilogist disagrees with the views of Qohelet and that he offers a corrective to Qohelet's teaching (Crenshaw, *Ecclesiastes*, 190; Longman, *Ecclesiastes*, 37–39; and Shields, 'Ecclesiastes and the End of Wisdom,' *TynBul* 50:1 (1999): 137–139). The approach of this commentary is that the epilogist affirms and builds on the theological affirmations made by Qohelet, but then he goes beyond Qohelet's *hebel* judgment by allowing those theological affirmations to be foundational for one's approach to life. The difficulty of this question is seen in the different ways commentators speak of the relationship between the epilogist and Qohelet. Fox (*Rereading Ecclesiastes*, 372) argues that the epilogist supports Qohelet but also distances himself from him. Murphy (*Ecclesiastes*, 126) comments that in relationship to judgment the epilogist goes beyond Qohelet. Seow (*Ecclesiastes*, 394) sees two editors at work, one who praises Qohelet (12:9-12) and one who goes beyond Qohelet (12:13-14).

182. Longman, *Ecclesiastes*, 283.

can easily be misunderstood if one assumes a mechanical connection between deed and consequence.[183] For example, Proverbs 12:21 states, 'No ill befalls the righteous, but the wicked are filled with trouble.' One misunderstands this proverb if he uses it to mean that no harm ever comes to the righteous and that if someone is experiencing harm, then he must not be righteous.[184] This was the problem of Job's friends, who saw his suffering and concluded that he must have committed some sin for this suffering to come into his life. Psalm 73 also struggles with trying to explain the problems of life. The struggle in this psalm is a microcosm of Qohelet's struggle. Psalm 73 begins with a theological affirmation that God is good to Israel and to the pure in heart; but then the psalmist acknowledges that he almost stumbled because of the prosperity of the wicked (vv. 2-3). He goes on to describe the security and prosperity of the wicked (vv. 3-12). He then lays out some of the implications of his struggle. In many ways, these struggles parallel Qohelet's struggle. He wonders whether it has been useless to live a life of purity before God (v. 13). He talks about the anguish and the wearisome task of trying to understand this problem (v. 16). He specifically states that if he had continued down this path and had taught

---

183. Many also argue that the longer instructions in Proverbs 1–9 are in some way a preparation for understanding or receiving the shorter sayings of Proverbs 10 and following. Childs (*Introduction*, 354–355) comments that they provide a theological context of wisdom in creation, from which the whole book is to be read, Waltke (*Proverbs*, 1:11) notes that the beginning lectures prepare the youth's heart to receive the proverbs and sayings in the rest of the book, and Longman (*Proverbs* [Grand Rapids: Baker, 2006], 61) argues that Proverbs 1–9 is the hermeneutical prism through which the shorter sayings are to be understood.

184. The problem with misunderstanding the shorter proverbs in some kind of a mechanical deed-consequence relationship is not that the book of Proverbs misrepresents them or sets forth a faulty teaching. There is clear recognition in the book that wealth has only relative, not absolute value (Prov. 17:1; 19:1), that there are extenuating circumstances in life that must be taken into account (13:23; 14:31), and that God is sovereign over the events in life, including the deed-consequence connection (16:9; 19:21; 21:30-31). For a discussion of this issue see Raymond C. Van Leeuwen, 'Wealth and Poverty: System and Contradiction in Proverbs,' *HS* 33 (1992): 25–36; Longman, *Proverbs*, 61–62; and Waltke, *Proverbs*, 1:107-109.

such things he would have betrayed God's people (v. 15). Here is the danger of speculative, doubting wisdom where the experiences and problems of life can so dominate a person's thinking that they move away from the foundation of wisdom itself. We see a glimpse in Psalm 73 of the struggle that Qohelet is going through in Ecclesiastes. In Psalm 73 the change comes when the psalmist goes into the temple and from that renewed perspective sees the true end of the wicked. In Ecclesiastes we are pointed back to the true foundation of wisdom in 12:13-14. Such a problem was not just an OT problem; it is a human problem (see also John 9:2). For example, Rabbi Harold Kushner lost his son to leukemia and through that struggle came to the conclusion that God cannot be both all-powerful and good because if He were both all-powerful and good then such tragedies in life would not happen. He concluded that we must choose either a God who is all-powerful and not good, or a God who is good, but not all-powerful. Kushner chose to believe that God is good but not all-powerful.[185] The book of Ecclesiastes sets forth Qohelet's 'under the sun' struggle to show the danger of speculative, doubting wisdom and to remind God's people of the true foundation of wisdom: a reverent trust in God and His revelation.

After all this discussion the question still remains: 'Who is Qohelet?' The use of the term 'Qohelet' does seem to distance him from Solomon, unless there is an historical connection with Solomon in the use of Qohelet that has been lost. Such distance from Solomon has been explained as a literary persona or a Solomonic guise in order to present Qohelet as Solomon, although he is not really Solomon. However, the phrase 'son of David, king in Jerusalem' in the superscription of the book (1:1) and Qohelet's own identification of himself as 'king over Israel in Jerusalem' (1:12) have more in view than just a literary persona or a Solomonic guise.[186] The fact

---

185. Harold S. Kushner, *When Bad Things Happen to Good People* (New York: Avon Books, 1983).

186. See the earlier discussion, where it was pointed out that every time 'son of David' occurs in the Old Testament it refers to a biological son of David (Christianson, *Narrative Strategies,* 129) and where the parallels between Proverbs 1:1 and Ecclesiastes 1:1 show an association between

that such an identification occurs in the superscription of the book calls into question limiting the Solomonic guise as king to the first couple of chapters. If the author is a king who is responsible for all of the first-person discourse,[187] then the Solomonic guise has actually given way to Solomon himself. One must also accept that the language situation before the exile is diverse and that Ecclesiastes is not a part of SBH, but represents one of the local dialects.[188] If the author really is Solomon, what better example is there of the danger of speculative wisdom, of a wisdom that loses the proper foundation? Solomon had more wisdom than anyone and he was tremendously blessed by God (1 Kings 3:10-14), but his heart was turned away from God to the worship of foreign gods by wives who did not believe in Yahweh (1 Kings 11:4-8). How does one explain what happened to Solomon? He moved away from the true foundation of wisdom and was distracted by other things. If the words of Qohelet are part of Solomon's struggle in moving away from the true foundation of wisdom, then one understands why this struggle was preserved and presented to God's people. If Solomon, who had more wisdom than anyone, fell prey to this problem, it could happen to anyone. Perhaps the name Qohelet is used to preserve the name 'Solomon' from being only identified with an embarrassing fall after such a promising rise.

Preaching and teaching Ecclesiastes

In order to preach or teach from Ecclesiastes, certain exegetical decisions have to be made on a number of issues, many of which have been covered in this Introduction. If one comes to accept the premise that Qohelet is operating from an 'under the sun' perspective throughout the first-person discourse (1:12–12:7), then preaching from the book becomes more difficult. In preaching on specific passages week by week, the solution is not given in those particular passages; rather,

---

Solomon and Qohelet (Ingram, *Ambiguity in Ecclesiastes*, 79–80).

187. Koh, *Royal Autobiography*, 18–19 and Christianson, *Narrative Strategies*, 134, 147.

188. Young, *Diversity in Pre-Exilic Hebrew*, 140–157.

one is left with the dark, under the sun view. Thus it becomes important that the major concepts developed in a passage are connected with an 'above the sun' perspective. This can be done by relating such concepts to the epilogue of the book, to other Old Testament passages, or to New Testament passages. Thus each week God's people are not left with just an analysis of the problems of life but are pointed to the solution from other parts of Scripture. This is basically a redemptive-historical approach that regularly makes connections from the Old Testament to other parts of Scripture, especially to the New Testament. Such connections will be explored in the commentary in sections entitled Homiletical Implications.

Several factors come into play when considering how to preach through a book of the Bible, including how many weeks there are to cover the book. If there are no time constraints, there is more freedom to divide the text into preaching passages. If a preacher has only a few weeks, perhaps only key passages can be preached. In dividing a book into preaching passages it is important that complete passages are chosen. Of course, with Ecclesiastes, there are a variety of opinions as to its structure.[189] G. A. Wright argues that the book is well-organized, based on key phrases used throughout the book and numerical patterns he thinks he finds in the book.[190] On the other hand, Delitzsch despairs of finding any overall plan in the book and does not find any progress of thought in the book.[191] Others, like Fox, recognize that the book does not

---

189. See Crenshaw (*Ecclesiastes*, 38–48) for a review of the various approaches to the structure of Ecclesiastes.

190. George Addison Wright, 'The Riddle of the Sphinx: The Structure of the Book of Qoheleth,' *CBQ* 30 (1968): 313–34, 'The Riddle of the Sphinx Revisited: Numerical Patterns in the Book of Qoheleth,' *CBQ* 42 (1980): 35–51, and 'Additional Numerical Patterns in Qoheleth,' *CBQ* 45 (1983): 32–43. Some of the numerical patterns he observes are that the book is divided into two parts with 111 verses in each part (with the division at 6:9/10); the numerical value of *hebel* is 37, of which 111 is a multiple; *hebel* occurs 37 times in the book; and the numerical value of 'vanity of vanities, all is vanity' in the Hebrew is 216, with 1:12–12:8 containing 216 verses. Murphy generally follows Wright's analysis, if not all of his numerical patterns. See Fox (*Rereading Ecclesiastes*, 148–149) for analysis and criticism of Wright's work.

191. Delitzsch, 'Ecclesiastes,' 6:189.

progress in an orderly fashion but that it does establish one basic proposition—'everything is *hebel*'—which gives the book its organization.[192] Some argue that Ecclesiastes 6:10-12 acts as a transition between the first part (1:12–6:9) and the second part (6:13–12:7) of the first-person discourse. The first part is seen as an evaluation of Qohelet's search and the second part is seen as Qohelet's advice based on what he found in the first part.[193] Although there are more imperatives in the second part of the first-person discourse, there also continues to occur the evaluative declaration of *hebel* in the second part; so a hard and fast division between evaluation and advice is not absolute.[194] It is better to see Qohelet offering advice throughout the first-person discourse in the calls to enjoyment and in the imperatives he uses. Wright may be correct that the first part of the book deals primarily with the vanity of human activity and the second part with the inability to understand the work of God in the world, but even this is not a hard-and-fast division, for the inability to understand what God is doing is mentioned already in 3:11. Appropriate text divisions occur wherever Qohelet makes an evaluative *hebel* judgment or issues a call to enjoyment. However, as Fox points out, many times Qohelet maintains continuity from one topic to the next, so that sometimes divisions are a matter of exegetical preference. For example, Ecclesiastes 2:1-26 could

---

192. Fox, *Rereading Ecclesiastes*, 150. Fox notes the difficulty of nailing down a structure for Qohelet's thoughts because it is the report of a journey of consciousness over the landscape of experience.

193. Not every commentator who understands 6:10-12 to be transitional argues for a distinct difference between the first part of Qohelet's autobiography and the second part, including Brown, Crenshaw, and Longman. Fox (*Rereading Ecclesiastes*, 147 n. 1) doubts whether 6:10-12 is transitional, but then he acknowledges that the division of the book into two parts designated 'Doctrinal' and 'Admonitory' does characterize the emphasis of each half of the book fairly well.

194. Christianson (*Narrative Strategies*, 244) shows in a graph the relationship between first person and second person in Qohelet's autobiography, with second person dominating in chapters 10–12, which he uses to argue that there is a shift from experience to advice in the latter half of the book. It does seem that 11:1–12:7 is more advice oriented, but that advice is not given apart from the *hebel* evaluation (11:8, 10) and the assertion of human ignorance (11:5-6).

be considered a single unit or it could be divided into three units (2:1-11, 12-17, 18-26).[195] Although such decisions are exegetically based, there is some flexibility in determining preaching texts. To access the different ways that Ecclesiastes may be divided one need only examine the commentaries. The outline of Ecclesiastes followed in this commentary is given in the Contents section. The following division is based on the author's actual sermon series on Ecclesiastes and is given only as a possibility, and with the understanding that there are many ways one can preach through a book of the Bible, especially a book like Ecclesiastes:

Ecclesiastes 1:1-11	When life does not make sense
Ecclesiastes 1:12–2:11	Having it all: the search for meaning
Ecclesiastes 2:12-26	The uncertainty of the future
Ecclesiastes 3:1-22	God's incomprehensible world: are we no different from the animals?
Ecclesiastes 4:1-16	Loneliness: it is all about me!
Ecclesiastes 5:1-7	Disappointment with God: unfulfilled expectations
Ecclesiastes 5:10–6:9	Wealth: at least enjoy what you have
Ecclesiastes 6:10–7:14	Who knows what is good?
Ecclesiastes 7:15-29	When life is all messed up
Ecclesiastes 8:1-17	No solutions: when the foundations of knowledge evaporate
Ecclesiastes 9:1-12	Living under the cloud of death
Ecclesiastes 9:13–10:20	It only takes one
Ecclesiastes 11:1–12:8	Make use of every opportunity
Ecclesiastes 12:9-14	When all is said and done: can it be that simple?

---

195. Fox, *Rereading Ecclesiastes*, 151.

1.
The prologue: an exploration of the nature of the world (1:1-11)

Before Qohelet introduces himself (1:12) in his first-person discourse (1:12–12:7) he is presented to us in a prologue which is part of the third-person frame (1:1-11; 12:8-14). The prologue consists of the superscription of the book (1:1), the motto of the book (1:2), the key question of the book (1:3), and an introductory poem (1:4-11) which reinforces the motto of the book. The purpose of the prologue is not only to introduce Qohelet but also to prepare the reader for Qohelet's message.

The superscription (Eccles. 1:1)

1:1 *The words of Qohelet, the son of David, king in Jerusalem.*[1]

The superscription introduces the one who will be speaking in 1:12–12:7. It parallels other superscriptions, such as Proverbs 30:1 ('The words of Agur'), Proverbs 31:1 ('The words of King Lemuel'), Jeremiah 1:1 ('The words of Jeremiah') and Amos 1:1 ('The words of Amos'), and is similar to Proverbs 1:1 ('The proverbs of Solomon, son of David, king of Israel'). The identity of '*Qohelet*' was discussed in the Introduction. The majority of commentators argue for an association between Qohelet and Solomon but not an identification between the two,[2] but

---

1. Translations are the author's own translation unless otherwise noted.
2. Longman (*Ecclesiastes*, 57) uses the phrase 'near identity' to describe the relationship between Qohelet and Solomon, and Norbert Lohfink

the superscription makes the connection more concrete. The parallels between the superscription of Ecclesiastes 1:1 and the other superscriptions demonstrate that more than just an association is in view. Although the term 'son' can refer to a distant descendant,[3] the phrase '*son of David*' always refers to a biological descendant of David when it is used in the OT.[4] The phrase '*king in Jerusalem*' refers to Qohelet as the king, and not to David as the king, based on the statement of Ecclesiastes 1:12.[5] If the royal identity is only for the sake of the argument in Ecclesiastes 2 and is not pertinent for the whole book, it is strange to identify Qohelet as the king in the superscription.[6] Thus the superscription is identifying Qohelet with Solomon and not just making an association with Solomon.

The motto (Eccles. 1:2)

1:2 *'Utterly Senseless!' says Qohelet, 'Utterly Senseless! Everything is senseless.'*

Several questions arise from the motto of the book. One major issue is the meaning of *hebel* and how it should be translated. In the Introduction it was argued that the best

---

(*Qoheleth: A Continental Commentary* [Minneapolis: Fortress Press, 2003], 35), among others, uses the term 'association' to describe the relationship between Qohelet and Solomon.

3. This meaning of '*son*' is pointed out by several commentators, including Hubbard (*Ecclesiastes*, 43) and Seow (*Ecclesiastes*, 97), although Seow recognizes that the phrase '*son of David*' always refers to a literal son of David, particularly, but not exclusively, Solomon. Thus Ogden's comment that the phrase 'son of David' is a flexible term including generations of descendants is incorrect (*Qoheleth*, 27).

4. Seow, *Ecclesiastes*, 97 and Christianson, *Narrative Strategies*, 129.

5. Ogden and Zogbo, *Handbook on Ecclesiastes*, 21. Although some try to redefine *melek* ('*king*') as 'property owner' or 'counsellor' (see Whybray, *Ecclesiastes*, 34 for bibliography), these proposals have not commended themselves to interpreters (Crenshaw, *Ecclesiastes*, 29). Whybray also points out that the activities in 2:4-11 are hardly credible of any private person.

6. Longman, *Ecclesiastes*, 5–6; Crenshaw, *Ecclesiastes*, 29; and others argue that the royal identity is dropped after Ecclesiastes 2. Murphy (*Ecclesiastes*, 2) raises the interesting point that a king fiction seems like a weak justification for the royal pretense if it does not go beyond chapter 2. It was not necessary for Qohelet to be described as king in the superscription for the sake of Ecclesiastes 2.

understanding of *hebel* is not on the level of time (fleeting, transience) but on the level of meaning. Within the context of meaning, *hebel* could describe situations that are difficult to understand (enigmatic, mysterious) or situations that cannot be understood because life does not make sense. Various translations are possible within this understanding of *hebel*, including vanity (NKJV; NASB; NRSV; ESV; Delitzsch), futility (NJPS; Crenshaw), meaningless (NIV; Longman), and absurd (Fox). Each term has its limitations. The meaning of the term 'vanity' has shifted from that which is empty, futile, or without effect to self-pride, an excessive regard for one's self, beauty, or possessions (as in the phrase 'you're so vain').[7] Fox argues that the terms 'futile' and 'meaningless' are not broad enough to encompass everything that *hebel* covers. In Ecclesiastes 8:14 *hebel* includes the fate of the wicked and that they receive what the righteous deserve, which does not imply any futility in their actions. Rather, *hebel* describes a situation where an action does not yield the expected result. He prefers the term 'absurd,' which describes what is an affront to reason, which includes the disjunction between effort and result.[8] The term 'absurd' is a modern term used in existentialism, but it has also changed meaning from that which is irrational, or an affront to reason, to that which is laughable or ludicrous.[9] Fox suggests that for a popular translation the concept 'senseless' might work best.[10] For the most part *hebel* is applied to situations where an action does not yield the expected results, so that these situations are not just incomprehensible or mysterious, but they do not make sense. Thus *'senseless'* would be a good translation, but so would 'futile' or 'meaningless' if one keeps in mind that although some efforts may achieve some benefit in life, ultimately those efforts fail to achieve the desired results

---

7. Shields, *The End of Wisdom*, 113.
8. Fox, *Rereading Ecclesiastes*, 30–31.
9. Shields, *The End of Wisdom*, 113. Longman (*Ecclesiastes*, 63) thinks that the term 'absurd' is too modern to use to translate *hebel*.
10. Fox makes this suggestion in *Ecclesiastes*, 3 and it is the term this commentary uses to translate *hebel*.

(see the discussion of wisdom in 2:12-17). Even though there may be some things in life that can be enjoyed, ultimately life does not make sense because the order of life has broken down, leaving only disconnected occurrences, which are meaningless from a human perspective.[11]

The motto is a summary statement of Qohelet's thought stated in an emphatic way and meant to be taken as comprehensive.[12] The translation 'utterly senseless' is a superlative (*hăḇēl hăḇālîm*), which stresses that this statement is complete, absolute, and unqualified.[13] It represents the ultimate conclusion of Qohelet concerning life.[14] An almost identical statement also occurs in 12:8, which forms an inclusio between 1:2 and 12:8. Everything in between these two verses takes on the character of *hebel*, which is demonstrated by how many times *hebel* is used in the body of the book to pass judgment on an activity within human experience.[15]

The comprehensive nature of the summary is brought out in the statement '*everything is senseless.*' There is some debate on how comprehensive the term '*everything*' (*kōl*) is. Lohfink, followed by Seow, wants to limit 'everything' to the question raised in 1:3, the realm of humans and their labor.[16] Others want to give 'everything' a universal meaning, encompassing all that exists 'under the sun' (1:3), with only the world of the dead and heaven excluded.[17] Fox notes that there are some things 'under the sun' which in themselves are not *hebel* (he lists 3:17; 7:11; 9:13-15), so that 'everything' must refer to events in their totality or to what happens in life taken as a

---

11. Fox, *Rereading Ecclesiastes*, 48.

12. Although Whybray (*Ecclesiastes*, 34–35) calls Ecclesiastes 1:2 a summary of Qohelet's thought, he also argues that it is a misunderstanding of Qohelet's thought written by the editor. Such a view is not tenable.

13. ibid., 34.

14. Longman, *Ecclesiastes*, 61.

15. Frydrych, *Living Under the Sun*, 50.

16. N. Lohfink, 'Koh 1,2 "alles is Windhauch" — universale oder anthropologische Aussage?' in R. Mosis and L. Ruppert (eds.), *Der Weg zum Menschen: Für Alfons Deissler* (Freiburg: Herder, 1989), 204, 207–210, and Seow, *Ecclesiastes*, 103.

17. Crenshaw, *Ecclesiastes*, 58–59; Delitzsch, 'Ecclesiastes,' 6:219; and Eaton, *Ecclesiastes*, 56–57.

whole.[18] This view fits in with the fact that there may be some things in this life that have limited value (wisdom in 2:12-17), and there may be some things in life that can be recommended (the calls to enjoyment), but ultimately even these things fall short so that Qohelet concludes that *'everything is senseless.'*

If 'everything' is limited to this world then it would seem to follow that God is exempted. Although God Himself may not be in view in the expression 'everything is senseless,' certainly His works are included because His works are manifested in this world (3:11).[19] One of the later emphases of the book is the inability of human beings to understand what God is doing (the works of God) 'under the sun' (6:12; 8:1, 17). Thus creation (1:4-8), history (1:9-11), and the order of the world, including the deed-consequence relationship, falls under the verdict 'everything is senseless.'

The key question of the book (Eccles. 1:3)

1:3 *What profit is there for a person[20] in all his labour at which he labours under the sun?*

The question in 1:3 is the programmatic question of the book, which sets out the fundamental problem that Qohelet sets out to answer.[21] The question also occurs later in the book at 2:22; 3:9; and 5:11. There are several key concepts in the question

---

18. Fox, *Rereading Ecclesiastes*, 40–41. He also notes that the emphatic statement of *hebel* in 1:2 and 12:8 gives justification for translating *hebel* with one word throughout the book.

19. There is no reason to include God by implication in the verdict *'everything is senseless,'* as Christianson (*Narrative Strategies*, 89) does, because God Himself understands how everything fits together (3:11), even if His works cannot be understood by mankind.

20. The phrase *'for a person'* (*lā'ādām*) uses *'ādām* in a generic sense referring to human beings. It includes the definite article, but Qohelet's use of the article is 'without consequence' and its syntactical significance seems to diverge from classical prose (Isaksson, *Language of Qohelet*, 145), so that there is little exegetical significance in Qohelet's use of the article (Shields, *The End of Wisdom*, 123, n. 32). The lamed expresses to whose advantage or disadvantage something is done (Paul Joüon, *A Grammar of Biblical Hebrew*, 2 vols. [Roma: Editrice Pontificio Istituto Biblico, 1991], 2:488).

21. Ogden and Zogbo, *Handbook on Ecclesiastes*, 23 and Frydrych, *Living Under the Sun*, 44.

which affect the meaning and tone of the question. The term for *'profit'* (*yiṯrôn*) is a commercial term which refers to a surplus or gain, but it has a wider meaning in Ecclesiastes, as it is used in reference to wisdom (2:13).[22] When two things are compared it refers to an advantage one thing might have over another thing (2:13; 3:19; 5:8; 6:8, 11; 7:11, 12; 10:10, 11). When *yiṯrôn* is used by itself it refers to any net gain that allows one to get ahead in life,[23] or to a desired result produced by effort or labor. The term for *'labour'* (*'āmāl*) has strong negative connotations. It is used in the Old Testament with terms that are extremely negative, such as 'trouble' (Num. 23:21; Job 4:8; Prov. 24:2), 'wrong' (Hab. 1:13) and 'toil' (Jer. 20:18 in parallel with 'sorrow'). Thus *'āmāl* is not just work but it is hard labor.[24] It is also clear in Ecclesiastes that *'āmāl* is not limited to work, but can refer to any activity that requires effort (8:17), or to the product of an activity (2:18).[25] Finally, the focus of the question concerns human activity *'under the sun.'* This phrase limits the search for *'profit'* to the realm of human activity. It also functions as a limiting concept keeping Qohelet's search for meaning within the horizons of this earthly life, which means he does not use the theological affirmations he makes concerning God to solve the problems with which he is wrestling (see the discussion of 'under the sun' in the Introduction). Human beings work hard in life and Qohelet wonders whether any human effort, as strenuous as it may be, leads to a desired result or a net gain that allows one to get ahead in life.

The question of Ecclesiastes 1:3 is not only a key question for the book of Ecclesiastes, but it is also an important question in the wisdom literature, especially the book of Proverbs (12:11; 14:23).[26] It is interesting to compare Ecclesiastes 1:3

---

22. Seow, *Ecclesiastes*, 103. The Septuagint renders *yiṯrôn* as 'surplus' (*perriseia*).

23. Fox, *Rereading Ecclesiastes*, 112.

24. Seow, *Ecclesiastes*, 104. Some translate *'āmāl* with toil to bring out the negative reality of the word (Longman, Murphy).

25. Fox, *Rereading Ecclesiastes*, 54–55.

26. D. Michel, *Untersuchungen zur Eigenart des Buches Qohelet* (Berlin: Walter de Gruyter, 1989), 3.

THE PROLOGUE: AN EXPLORATION OF THE NATURE OF THE WORLD 77

with Proverbs 14:23. The first part of the proverb reads, 'In all labour (*'eṣeḇ*) there is profit (*môṭār*).' Both passages use the concept of 'profit' with 'labour.' Concerning 'profit,' there is a linguistic connection between *yiṯrôn* (1:3) and *môṭār* (Prov. 14:23) because both come from *yṯr*. Also, the terms for labor are similar in meaning, for they both have in view the difficult aspect of labor. The term *'āmāl* (1:3) refers to arduous and strained effort (Deut. 26:7; Ps. 107:12). The term *'eṣeḇ* (Prov. 14:23) can refer to both physical pain (Gen. 3:16; 1 Chron. 4:9-10) and mental pain (Gen. 6:6; 1 Sam. 20:3; Isa. 63:10; Ps. 78:40), and it is used in Isaiah 14:3 in a series of words, including 'hard service' (*hā'ăḇōḏāh haqqāšāh*). Thus, Proverbs 14:23 uses a word that stresses the difficult aspect of labor to say that even though work is difficult, there is profit to it. Qohelet also uses a word that stresses the difficult aspect of labor, but he questions whether such labor produces any proft. It will become clear that he does not answer this question the same way that Proverbs 14:23 answers the question, which supports the idea that Qohelet is wrestling with traditional wisdom teaching in light of his experience.

An introductory poem: the wonder of creation or the futility of effort? (Eccles. 1:4-11)

Not everyone agrees that this section is poetry. Longman denies that it is poetry because it lacks the heightened presence of traits that define Hebrew poetry, such as parallelism, terseness, and word plays.[27] Krüger, on the other hand, calls these verses 'poetically stylized' because he sees parallelism at work.[28] Murphy divides this section into poetry (1:4-7) with a prose commentary (1:8-11).[29] Although not everyone will agree on the relationship between prose and poetry because

---

27. Longman, *Ecclesiastes*, 59.
28. Thomas Krüger, *Qoheleth: A Commentary*, Hermeneia (Minneapolis: Fortress Press, 2004), 48.
29. Murphy, *Ecclesiastes*, 7.

the relationship between the two is fluid,[30] most designate this section as poetry.[31]

There is also debate concerning the meaning of the description of the world in this section. Whybray calls 1:5-7 'the wonders of nature' and Lohfink understands the poem as expressing praise to the cosmos as splendid and eternal.[32] Whybray argues that the point of 1:5-7 is not the futility of the actions but the regularity of the actions.[33] The point of 1:9 is that these cycles are self-contained.[34] Others argue that the point of the poem is to show the transitory nature of all things on the earth, which is usually contrasted with the permanence of the earth itself.[35]

A negative view of Ecclesiastes 1:4-11 sees the description of nature in 1:5-7 as describing the futility of the endless actions of the natural phenomena: a constant movement with no discernible purpose.[36] The concept is not just repetition, because 1:8 describes the realm of human activity as not achieving its purpose. The mouth, eyes, and ears do not just repeat their actions, but fail in their actions.[37] History itself is going nowhere (1:9-11). The futility of events in this world fits with the view expressed in the motto (1:2) and the key question (1:3) of the book. Whybray's positive assessment is partly

---

30. The main elements that identify poetry are terseness, parallelism, and imagery. Although these elements are found in prose, a text can be identified as poetry when these characteristics are prominent in a text (see Tremper Longman III, *How To Read the Psalms* [Downers Grove, IL: InterVarsity Press, 1988], 94).

31. Crenshaw, *Ecclesiastes*, 61; Hubbard, *Ecclesiastes*, 49; Lohfink, *Qoheleth*, 40; Ogden, *Qohelet*, 34.

32. R. N. Whybray, 'Ecclesiastes 1.5-7 and the Wonders of Nature,' *JSOT* 41 (1988): 105–12 and Lohfink, *Qoheleth*, 40.

33. Whybray, 'Ecclesiastes 1.5-7,' 105.

34. Whybray, *Ecclesiastes*, 39.

35. Farmer, *Ecclesiastes*, 153 and Christian D. Ginsburg, *The Song of Songs and Coheleth* (New York: KTAV Publishing House, 1970 [orig. 1861]), 260.

36. Crenshaw, *Ecclesiastes*, 62.

37. D. Michel, *Untersuchungen zur Eigenart des Buches Qohelet* (Berlin: Walter de Gruyter, 1989), 5.

based on his view that 1:4-8 is unconnected to 1:2-3, which he sees as an attempt by the editor to summarize Qohelet's teaching. It is better to see a connection between these verses. The motto (1:2) is a summary statement of Qohelet's thought: everything is senseless or futile. The key question (1:3) raises the issue of whether or not there is any profit to human labor. The answer to the question becomes apparent in the opening poem which describes the futility of events under the sun, including the actions connected to creation, humans, and history. If the mighty efforts of nature can achieve nothing new, surely human labor is also futile. Fox states, 'After 1:2, 1:4-7 cannot be a celebration of the glorious stability of the natural order.'[38] Thus the opening poem reinforces the theme of the whole book.

The futility of the natural world (Eccles. 1:4-7)

1:4 A generation goes and a generation comes but[39] the earth remains forever.

1:5 The sun rises,[40] and the sun sets and it pants toward its place. There it rises again.

1:6 Going to the south and circling to the north, round and round goes the wind; the wind continues its circling around.

---

38. Fox, *Rereading Ecclesiastes*, 163, 169–170.

39. Although Murphy (*Ecclesiastes*, 6) argues that the *waw* is best translated 'while,' signifying the permanence of the earth as the background for the succession of the generations, there seems to be some kind of contrast intended (Crenshaw, *Ecclesiastes*, 63).

40. The verb at the beginning of this clause is a perfect waw consecutive (*wĕzāraḥ*), but many believe it should be emended to a participle, based on switching the *waw* and the *zayin* (*zôrēaḥ*). The reasons for this emendation are that the conjunction *waw* does not occur elsewhere in 1:4-8 and participles dominate this section (Murphy, *Ecclesiastes*, 7). However, as Seow (*Ecclesiastes*, 106) points out, the Hebrew manuscripts support the perfect waw consecutive; also, the presence of the *waw* at the beginning of 1:5 may deliberately link the activities of humanity in 1:4 with the movements of the natural elements in 1:5.

1:7 All the streams flow to the sea but the sea is never full. To the place where the streams flow, they continue to flow.

This section emphasizes the cyclical nature of events on the earth in order to demonstrate the futility of those cyclical processes. The word *'generation'* (*dôr*) refers to human generations in other parts of Scripture (Gen. 9:12; 15:16; 17:7; Exod. 3:15). Although *dôr* can refer to periods of time without any reference to human life,[41] in this passage the focus is on the going and coming of human generations, which are contrasted with the permanence of *'the earth.'*[42] Although the fleeting nature of these generations in contrast with the permanence of the earth is part of the meaning of 1:4, the emphasis in the whole section is on the contrast between the cyclical movement of events on the earth and the permanence of the earth.[43] The participles of 1:4 stress repeated activity. Thus 1:4 presents the cyclical, repeating pattern of generations going and coming in contrast to the permanence of the earth.

In 1:5-7 the focus shifts from human generations to natural phenomena (1:5 speaks of the sun, 1:6 of the wind, and 1:7 of the streams). Not only do participles dominate these verses, but the participles *hôlēk* and *bô'* are common, stressing the continuous nature of the activities. Also, the futility of the repeating, cyclical processes becomes apparent in these verses. 1:5 describes the continual rising and setting of the sun. The meaning of the verb *'pants'* (*šô'ēp*), which describes the sun's movement, is debated. It can have the positive meaning of longing or desire (Ps. 119:131; Job 7:2), which would mean that the sun eagerly moves toward its

---

41. Whybray (*Ecclesiastes*, 40) lists Isaiah 41:4; 51:9; and Psalm 72:5 as passages where *dôr* is not used of human life.

42. Seow (*Ecclesiastes*, 106) points out that the participle *hôlēk* (*'going'*) is used by Qohelet to speak of death (3:20; 5:15-16; 6:6; 7:2; 9:10; 12:5).

43. Fox (*Rereading Ecclesiastes*, 166) understands *'the earth'* in 1:4 to mean humanity as a whole. The meaning is not the transience of human generations in contrast to the permanence of the earth, but that the movement of generations does not change the face of humanity.

next appearance.⁴⁴ However, this verb can also have the connotation of a weary panting (Isa. 42:14; Jer. 2:24). Then the idea would be that the sun has a monotonous, exhausting task to complete, which entails a strenuous panting to reach its destination.⁴⁵ One's decision will be determined by how one understands this passage as a whole, but the negative idea is supported by the Septuagint ('drags,' $helkō$) and the Targum ('crawls,' $styp̄$).⁴⁶

1:6 describes the blowing of the wind, as it goes round and round and round. Several things in this verse emphasize the monotonous nature of this activity. The use of participles stresses the continuous, round and round nature of the blowing of the wind. These participles use a long 'o' vowel, the repetition of which gives the verse a howling or mournful effect.⁴⁷ Also, the subject of 1:6 is delayed. In 1:4 the subject stands first, in 1:5 it stands second, but in 1:6 it does not come until after five participles. The effect of withholding the subject and the use of the participles ($sōḇēḇ$ occurs three times, twice in a row) makes the verse deliberately drawn-out and monotonous, which reinforces the impression of weariness.⁴⁸ The movement of the wind in circles also gives the impression of much action with little consequence.⁴⁹

1:7 describes the continual flowing of the streams into the sea. Whybray comments that the cyclical movement of the water is not futile: the constant flow and redistribution of the water over the earth is a wonderful and beneficial phenomenon.⁵⁰ However, nothing is said about what is accomplished by the flowing of the streams into the sea. 1:7 only mentions that the continual flowing of the streams

---

44. Whybray, *Ecclesiastes*, 41.
45. Crenshaw, *Ecclesiastes*, 63.
46. Longman, *Ecclesiastes*, 69.
47. Whybray, *Ecclesiastes*, 41–42. Although Whybray recognizes this rhetorical device, he does not think it gives the verse a negative meaning.
48. Crenshaw, *Ecclesiastes*, 64 and Delitzsch, 'Ecclesiastes,' 6:221.
49. Longman, *Ecclesiastes*, 69.
50. Whybray, *Ecclesiastes*, 43.

into the sea does not have any effect because the sea is not full.[51] Thus the activity is futile because it does not produce anything. No advantage is gained.[52]

The futility of the activity of the natural world in 1:4-7 can be seen when it is compared with other passages of Scripture which speak of the purposeful nature of these activities. In Psalm 19:5 the sun goes forth as a strong man running a race, full of vigor, reflecting the glory of God. But in Ecclesiastes 1:5 the sun *'pants'* along, tired and weary. In Psalm 104:3-4 God rides on the wings of the wind as He directs the wind as His messenger to accomplish His purposes. But in Ecclesiastes 1:6 the wind goes round and round and round in monotonous repetition with no purpose stated. In Psalm 104:10-11 the rivers are sent forth with the purpose of giving drink to the animals and causing the grass to grow for the cattle. But in Ecclesiastes 1:7 the rivers are on a futile run as they flow into the sea but the sea is not full. Thus Ecclesiastes 1:4-7 is a demonstration of the motto that everything is futile.

The futility of the human world (Eccles. 1:8-11)

1:8   *All things are weary.*
      No one[53] is able to express it.
      No eye is satisfied with seeing.
      No ear is fulfilled from hearing.

---

51. There is debate whether 1:7 describes the streams as *continuing to flow* into the sea with no lasting effect (NASB, NRSV, ESV), or whether the streams are presented as *returning* to the source of the stream in order to flow again (NKJV, NIV). Murphy, Delitzsch, Crenshaw, and Eaton argue the former and Ginsburg, Ogden, and Whybray argue the latter. As Longman (*Ecclesiastes*, 70–71) points out, either meaning does not change the principle that is being taught: all this activity does nothing significant.

52. Murphy, *Ecclesiastes*, 8 and Seow, *Ecclesiastes*, 115.

53. The use of the word 'man' (*'îš*) with the negative (*lō'*) can be translated *'no one'* (E. Kautzsch [ed.], *Gesenius' Hebrew Grammar* [hereinafter GKC], 2nd edition [Oxford: Clarendon Press, 1910], §139, d). Because the three clauses in 1:8 dealing with speaking, seeing, and hearing are parallel in structure (a negative, an imperfect verb, a noun as subject, an infinitive that complements the verb), the translation has tried to reflect that parallel.

1:9   Whatever⁵⁴ has been is what will be
      and whatever has been done is what will be done.
      There is nothing new under the sun.

1:10 Suppose⁵⁵ there is something about which someone says,
      'See this is new.'
      It already existed in ancient times
      which were before us.

1:11 There is no remembrance of former things,
      nor also of later things which will come.
      There will be no memory for these things
      among⁵⁶ those who will come afterward.

In Ecclesiastes 1:8 the natural world is left behind in order to focus on the human world. The first statement in 1:8, *'all things are weary,'* is a transitional statement. Although the phrase *'all things'* could be translated 'all words,'⁵⁷ it is better to understand the phrase as summarizing what has gone before and anticipating the emphasis on speaking in the next clause. This also leaves three parallel clauses for the rest of the verse, which deal with speaking, seeing, and hearing.

Some commentators understand 1:8 to be very positive. Whybray explains the verse as expressing the overwhelming effect of the ceaseless activity of natural phenomena on the observer; that is, they leave him speechless. The eye and the

---

54. Although the Septuagint understands *māh* to be interrogative, that translation does not coincide with the way *māh-š* is used in the rest of Ecclesiastes (1:9; 3:15, 22; 6:10; 7:24; 8:7), where it indicates an indefinite *'whatever'* (Murphy, *Ecclesiastes*, 8).

55. The particle *yēš* can be used in a conditional sense (Murphy, *Ecclesiastes*, 6; Gordis, *Koheleth*, 225; and Isaksson, *Language of Qohelet*, 172). Delitzsch ('Ecclesiastes,' 6:225) takes it here as having the force of a hypothetical antecedent; thus the translation *'suppose.'*

56. The preposition *'im* can mean *'among'* (Gen. 23:4; Lev. 25:6), as noted by Seow (*Ecclesiastes*, 111).

57. The term *dāḇār* in the plural can mean 'words' or 'things.' Although Murphy (*Ecclesiastes*, 6) argues for the meaning of words based on the emphasis on speech in 1:8, the meaning of *dāḇār* as 'thing' also occurs in 1:10. Most English translations translate the phrase as *'all things'* (NKJV, NASB, NIV, NRSV, ESV).

ear are not able to take in what they perceive.[58] Hubbard sees 1:8 to be describing the mystery inherent in creation: a person cannot describe it in words, an eye cannot see it clearly enough to be satisfied, and an ear cannot be filled with hearing about it.[59]

An important word in 1:8 is the adjective translated '*weary*' (*yĕgē'îm*). Ogden comments that apart from the translation of this word with the connotation of weariness, there is no reason to take these verses as expressing a negative view of futility.[60] The adjective is related to the root *yḡ'*, which can mean 'labour' (Josh. 24:13; Prov. 23:4) or 'weary' (2 Sam. 23:10; Ps. 6:6; Isa. 43:22). Although it is possible that 1:8 may be expressing the labor or *exertion* of '*all things*' in the sense of ceaseless activity,[61] the burden of proof falls on those who would omit the aspect of weariness from this adjective. The other uses of this adjective mean 'weary' (Deut. 25:18; 2 Sam. 7:12), and the related word *yĕgēa'* (12:12) is understood by many to express the idea of that which is 'weary.'[62]

If one understands 1:8 to refer to ceaseless repetition in nature, then the assertions concerning speaking, seeing, and hearing refer to the fact that these activities are also endless. Just as the sea is never full, the eye always sees things, the ear always hears things, the mouth continues to speak. They are never full.[63] However, the context and the meaning of *yĕgēa'* as '*weary*' points to the futility of these activities. In describing the continuous, futile activity of the natural world in 1:4-7, only one negative was used (1:7). However, in describing the human world of experience in 1:8, three negatives are used. In relationship to speech, no one is able to express the true condition of futility and weariness that characterizes the world.

---

58. Whybray, *Ecclesiastes*, 44.
59. Hubbard, *Ecclesiastes*, 51.
60. Ogden, *Qoheleth*, 39.
61. Ogden and Zogbo, *Handbook on Ecclesiastes*, 32.
62. Commentators who take *yĕgēa'* as '*weary*' in Ecclesiastes 12:12 include Murphy, Hubbard, Farmer, Whybray, Ginsburg, Gordis, Fox, Longman, Barton, and Delitzsch.
63. Ogden and Zogbo, *Handbook on Ecclesiastes*, 32.

In light of the rest of the book of Ecclesiastes, the idea is that no one is able to speak meaningfully about the world (8:17); in other words, human words never achieve their purpose.[64] The same idea is expressed in relationship to the eyes and ears. The eyes and the ears never achieve a final goal or result.[65] The eye would be satisfied if it had no desire to see more and the ear would be filled if it had no desire to hear more, which would be a result of being satisfied with one's interaction with the world of experience. As Qohelet will argue later in the book, there is no real answer to the futilities of life. Thus 1:8 seems to be a judgment on the empirical possibilities of human knowledge, which are limited and always fall short.[66]

Natural phenomena and the human experience of speech, sight, and sound have been examined, and in 1:9-11 history comes into view. The keynote of these verses is that *'there is nothing new under the sun.'* Some try to understand this expression in a positive way. Whybray argues that the parallel between nature and human life is an indication of the limitations with which people must live their lives 'as an integral part of the whole "work of God."'[67] Lohfink takes *'new'* (*ḥādāš*) as a negative word. In a world of unending duration and return, what is 'new' could only be worse than what exists; it may even describe what is wicked. Thus the statement 'there is nothing new under the sun' is a negative formulation of a universal triumph.[68]

---

64. Murphy, *Ecclesiastes*, 8 and Garrett, *Ecclesiastes*, 287.

65. Crenshaw, *Ecclesiastes*, 66. Krüger (*Qoheleth*, 51) points out that the verb *ykl* ('to be able') can be used in the sense of 'to be able to do something successfully,' or 'to be able to grasp or understand something.' This fits the meaning of 1:8, where *ykl* is used with a negative.

66. Krüger, *Qoheleth*, 51.

67. Whybray, *Ecclesiastes*, 45.

68. N. Lohfink, 'Der Bibel skeptische Hintertür. Versuch, den Ort des Buches Kohelet neu zu bestimmen,' *Stimmen der Zeit* 198 (1980): 22. Even many who understand the message of Ecclesiastes to be positive recognize the unorthodox nature of 1:9. Eaton explains the negative nature of this section as due to the 'under the sun' approach which leaves God out of the picture (*Ecclesiastes*, 60). Ogden comments that it is not appropriate to look for 'profit' and something new under the sun (*Qohelet*, 33). Hubbard sees this section as describing the depths of the spiritual crisis in Qohelet's day, which Qohelet

However, it is difficult to give the expression 'there is nothing new under the sun' a positive meaning. The emphasis in 1:9-11 is on 'a paralyzing repetition of the past.' The twofold repetition of *'whatever'* in 1:9 reinforces the claim of recurrent phenomena.[69] The use of *'already,' 'ancient times,'* and the double use of the verb 'to be' (translated *'has been'*) in 1:10, in response to the possibility that something is new, stresses the entrenchment of the past and the impossibility of something new occurring in the future. The fact that something seems new is due to the faulty faculties of human *'memory'* (1:11). Thus history is going nowhere and individuals are destined to live lives that never achieve fulfillment.[70] Such a view contrasts with other teaching in the OT, where history is seen as controlled by God and moving toward a goal.[71] The word 'memory' is used to mark memorable events in Israel's history (Exod. 12:14; Josh. 4:7). If there is no memory, then the anchor of the past is lost.[72] The possibility of something new is seen in the exhortations to sing a new song (Ps. 96:1), the possibility of a new covenant (Jer. 31:31), and the prospect of a new heavens and a new earth (Isa. 65:17).[73] To say 'there is nothing new under the sun' negates these possibilities and demonstrates an 'under the sun' perspective, which stands in sharp contrast to the flow of redemptive history in the OT.

Homiletical Implications

One of the key words of Ecclesiastes, *hebel*, is translated in the Septuagint as *mataiotēs*, which is the term used in Romans 8:20

---

had to take into consideration to help the people keep a steady course (*Ecclesiastes*, 53). Leupold understands this section to be a fact of common observation, not a resigned assertion. It is an indirect way of pointing to higher values which makes everything take on a different outlook (*Ecclesiastes*, 50).

69. Crenshaw, *Ecclesiastes*, 65–67. Fox (*Rereading Ecclesiastes*, 168) explains these phenomena not as specific, unique occurrences, such as World War II, the book of Ecclesiastes, or the death of Lincoln, but as the realization of archetypes, such as war, a book, and an assassination.

70. Longman, *Ecclesiastes*, 72 and Crenshaw, *Ecclesiastes*, 67.

71. Eaton, *Ecclesiastes*, 60.

72. Hubbard, *Ecclesiastes*, 53.

73. Longman, *Ecclesiastes*, 72.

to describe the subjection of creation to futility. The creation groans as it waits to be set free from the bondage of decay. Ecclesiastes 1:1-11 sets forth a similar viewpoint. Qohelet gives a true assessment of the world from an 'under the sun' perspective without the hope expressed in Romans 8. There is no doubt that he describes a world struggling under the effects of the curse, but his limited earthly perspective keeps him from affirming various answers that other Scriptures offer. Thus his view of the activities of creation (sun, wind, streams) and his view of history is very different from the rest of Scripture. Qohelet sounds very modern because he describes the despair of a world that has no purpose and is going nowhere. However, the futility to which creation has been subjected can be overcome. Creation itself is eagerly awaiting freedom from bondage, just as the sons of God, although groaning inwardly, are eagerly waiting for the redemption of their bodies (Rom. 8:18-25). Futility will not have the last word because Jesus has taken upon Himself our sin, the curse, and the futility of life.[74] We have seen the power of the new creation in the resurrection of Jesus from the dead and have experienced what it is to be a new creature through the first-fruits of the Spirit. We are able to see beyond the earthly horizon of this world to the light of the glory of the new heavens and the new earth. When that day comes the former things, which in context refers to the troubles of life, will not be remembered (Isa. 65:16-17).

---

74. ibid., 39–40.

2.
Qohelet's search for meaning under the sun (1:12–2:26)

Although this section can be divided into smaller units, it is appropriate to look at it as a whole. Ecclesiastes 1:12 begins the first-person discourse, which clearly sets it off from the prologue, which is third person. Ecclesiastes 2:24-26 is the first call to enjoyment, which acts as a conclusion to this section. Chapter 3 begins the next section with a poem on time. Thus 1:12–2:26 can be seen as a unit that sets forth Qohelet's search for meaning under the sun. This search is a response to the question of whether there is any profit to labor in 1:3,[1] which he will answer in 2:11. Each division of this section focuses on an aspect of his search. Wisdom is the focus in 1:12-18. Pleasure, including the efforts to produce pleasure, is the emphasis in 2:1-11. Wisdom and folly are compared in 2:12-17 after both have been mentioned earlier as objects of Qohelet's search (1:16-18). Labor and the results from labor are in view in 2:18-23. Finally, the conclusion is given in the call to enjoyment in 2:24-26. Each section includes a *hebel* statement, many times at the end of the unit, including the end of the call to enjoyment (2:26).

---

1. Ogden and Zogbo, *Handbook on Ecclesiastes*, 38.

The failure of wisdom (Eccles. 1:12-18)

1:12 *I am Qohelet. I have been² king over Israel in Jerusalem.*

1:13 *I devoted myself to seek and to explore by wisdom all that is done under heaven.*
It is a grievous task God has given to human beings to occupy³ them.

1:14 *I have seen all the works which are done under the sun. Look,⁴ all is senseless and chasing after the wind.*

1:15 *What is crooked cannot be straightened,⁵*
What is missing cannot be counted.

---

2. For the justification of translating the perfect in this verse as 'have been,' and its significance for Solomonic authorship, see the discussion of this verse in the Introduction.

3. The noun 'task' (*'inyan*) and the verb 'to occupy' (*'nh*) may be related. The noun only occurs in Ecclesiastes and is used in later rabbinic materials to mean 'task, situation, occupation, affair' (Longman, *Ecclesiastes*, 80). Four Hebrew verbs have the root consonants *'nh*, with the possible meanings of 'to answer,' 'to afflict,' 'to be busy or concerned with,' or 'to sing' (see Crenshaw, *Ecclesiastes*, 72–73 and Longman, *Ecclesiastes*, 80). Although Gordis (*Koheleth*, 200) thinks the evidence for the meaning 'to be busy' is weak, and so prefers 'to afflict,' the use of this verb in 5:19 favors 'to be busy' or 'occupy.'

4. The Hebrew word translated 'look' (*hinnēh*) is used in some places (Ps. 121:4; Gen. 12:11) to reinforce affirmation (Joüon, *Grammar*, 2:616-617), and so could be translated 'surely.' However, Fox (*Rereading Ecclesiastes*, 176) points out that hinnēh at the beginning of a clause can indicate participant perspective, which includes a sense of discovery. In this use it has a focusing effect that tends to subordinate a preceding verb of perception. He translates it with 'I realized.' The translation 'look' also brings out the focusing effect.

5. There is no need to emend the verb *liṭqōn* (qal infinitive construct) to a passive (pual) to correspond to the nifal of the second clause ('be counted'), as argued by Whybray (*Ecclesiastes*, 50), because *liṭqōn* can be understood as an intransitive qal, 'to be or become straight' (Murphy, *Ecclesiastes*, 12).

1:16 *I[6] said to myself, 'I[7] have greatly surpassed in wisdom all who were over Jerusalem before me. I experienced[8] much wisdom and knowledge.*

1:17 *I devoted myself to understand wisdom, and to understand maddening folly.[9] I discovered that this also is a chasing after wind.'*

1:18 *For with much wisdom comes much vexation, whoever increases knowledge increases sorrow.*

---

6. It is a characteristic of Qohelet to use the personal pronoun 'I' (*'ănî*) when it is not necessary because it is included in the verbal form. There is debate concerning its function. A common use is for emphasis, but Seow (*Ecclesiastes*, 123) argues that it does not emphasize the person but the thought, and is used when a conclusion is drawn or when a new thought is introduced. Many times it is not translated.

7. This clause is introduced by *hinnēh*, and when it is used with the verb 'to say' (*'āmar*) it serves to introduce direct speech and need not be translated (see Bill T. Arnold and John H. Choi, *A Guide to Biblical Hebrew Syntax* [Cambridge: Cambridge University Press, 2003], 4.5.1). Also, two hifil perfect verbs translate the phrase 'I have surpassed' (*gādal* ['to become great'] and *yāsap* ['to add or increase']). When there is a coordination of complementary verbal ideas the two verbs can be translated together (GKC §120.d).

8. The Hebrew clause literally reads, 'my heart sees.' Since the heart can refer to the center of one's being, it is appropriate to tranlsate the phrase 'my heart' as 'I.' The Hebrew verb 'to see' (*rā'āh*) can refer to what one experiences (Eaton, *Ecclesiastes*, 64), hence the translation 'I experienced.'

9. This translation follows the Masoretic Text, which takes *wĕda'at* as an infinitive construct, so that there are two infinitive constructs; the first has the object 'wisdom,' and the second has the object 'maddening folly.' The phrase 'maddening folly' is actually two nouns, 'madness' and 'folly,' joined by the conjuction, which function as a single concept (called a hendiadys). Longman (*Ecclesiastes*, 77) follows the Septuagint, which has only one infinitive followed by four nouns, which is translated, 'to know wisdom and knowledge, madness and folly.' Gordis (*Koheleth*, 138, 203) offers the translation, 'to know that wisdom and knowledge are madness and folly,' but his suggestion has not been followed by many. There is also no need to take 'maddening folly' as a gloss because it is an intrusion to the context and breaks the thread of the argument which focuses on wisdom (Fox, *Rereading Ecclesiastes*, 173; Ginsburg, Coheleth, 274). Rather, it anticipates the following section of 2:1-11 (Whybray, *Ecclesiastes*, 51; Eaton, *Ecclesiastes*, 64).

These verses can be divided into two parallel sections that follow a similar pattern (1:12-15 and 1:16-18).[10] There is a royal statement (1:12, 16), then a statement on the search itself (1:13, 17a), followed by a conclusion (1:14, 17b), and then a proverbial saying that supports the conclusion (1:15, 18). Wisdom is mentioned in both sections. In 1:12-15 wisdom is the instrument by which the search is carried out (1:13). In 1:16-18 wisdom itself is the field of investigation as Qohelet searches wisdom to see what profit it brings.

Qohelet begins his autobiography with a self-introduction in verse 12. Although most English translations and commentators translate the personal pronoun 'I' in apposition to the personal name Qohelet ('I, Qohelet, was or have been king'),[11] there are good reasons to translate the beginning of verse 12 as '*I am Qohelet. I have been king.*' Fox points out that it is appropriate for Qohelet to introduce himself at the beginning of the first-person discourse before he identifies his office.[12] This translation also fits the way the Masoretic scribes understood the verse, as indicated by their accents.[13] Furthermore, it parallels the self-introductions of various inscriptions of the ancient Near East, which begin with 'I am PN.'[14]

In 1:13 Qohelet states several things concerning his search for meaning '*under heaven.*' The serious nature of his search is seen in the statement '*I devoted myself,*' which literally reads 'I gave my heart.' Although 'heart' could be a synonym for a person's understanding,[15] it may here refer to the core of a person's being that directs the understanding, the will, and the emotions.[16] Either way it shows the determination

---

10. Ogden and Zogbo, *Handbook on Ecclesiastes*, 40.

11. English translations include the NKJV, NASB, NIV, NRSV, and ESV; commentators include Delitzsch, Ginsburg, Gordis Longman, and Murphy.

12. Fox, *Rereading Ecclesiastes*, 170.

13. Krüger, *Qoheleth*, 56.

14. PN stands for 'personal name' of the king who is writing. For examples see Fox and Seow.

15. Gordis, *Koheleth*, 199.

16. Longman, *Ecclesiastes*, 78. Alex Luc (לֵב, in NIDOTTE, 2:749) defines 'heart' as referring to 'the centre of human psychical and spiritual life, to the entire inner life of a person.'

of Qohelet in his search: it is a focused, deeply personal, disciplined pursuit.[17] He is totally committed to it.

Qohelet's search is also thorough, as demonstrated in the statement *'all that is done under heaven.'* This is a comprehensive statement and should not be limited to the human world by omitting events in the natural world.[18] Rather, it refers to all that happens in life, which includes not only human deeds but also things that happen to people in life. Although God is not an object of the search, his works that occur on earth do come into view. The work of God is identified with the work that is done under the sun in 8:17.[19] In 1:13 God is the one who has given to *'human beings'* that *'grievous task ... to occupy them.'* Some try to understand this statement in a positive way by referring to the pride of a person's heart which looks out for his own happiness,[20] or by viewing the task as a discipline from God for apostasy,[21] or as a result of the Fall.[22] But Qohelet does not revert here to the Fall or to the pride of heart to explain the *'grievous task'* God has given to human beings. The adjective *'grievous'* (*ra'*) can refer to what is evil in a moral sense, which is the way the Septuagint translates the adjective. Shields also argues for the meaning 'evil' in the sense that the task is pointless and has no redeeming value because no solution is found after much hard work.[23] Others avoid the connotation of 'evil' and see the *'task'* described as difficult or burdensome.[24] The reason why the *'task'* is *'grievous'* will be answered later, but it will relate to the inability of human beings to understand God's work in the world (3:11).

---

17. Longman, *Ecclesiastes*, 78.

18. As does Delitzsch ('Ecclesiastes,' 6:227) and Ogden (*Qoheleth*, 34–35).

19. Fox, *Rereading Ecclesiastes*, 175.

20. Ginsburg, *Coheleth*, 269.

21. Bridges, *Ecclesiastes*, 19.

22. Kidner, *Ecclesiastes*, 29.

23. Shields, *The End of Wisdom*, 130. See also Longman, *Ecclesiastes*, 77.

24. Provan, *Ecclesiastes*, 68. Others who avoid the connotation 'evil' include Barton, Delitzsch, Fox, Hubbard, and others.

Finally, Qohelet's search is carried out *'by wisdom.'* Although some argue that *'wisdom'* here is the object of the search,²⁵ it is better to understand the preposition *bet* in an instrumental sense, which yields the translation *'by.'* Seow points out that when the preposition *bet* is used with *'wisdom'* in Ecclesiastes, it is always used in the sense of agent or instrument and not as the object of the verb (2:3; 7:23; 9:15).²⁶ The object of the investigation in this verse is not wisdom but *'all that is done under heaven.'*²⁷ The way the investigation is carried out is through the methods and insights of *'wisdom.'* The phrase *'by wisdom'* emphasizes the methodology Qohelet is going to use to carry out his search. The term 'wisdom' connects the approach to other wisdom literature, such as Proverbs, but Qohelet's quest will turn out to be different from Proverbs because his approach does not start with the presupposition of the fear of the LORD (see the discussion of Qohelet's epistemology in the Introduction).²⁸

In 1:14-15 Qohelet offers a preliminary conclusion that sums up his investigation.²⁹ After stating that his search is a comprehensive search based on observation, he concludes that *'all is senseless and chasing after the wind.'* In other words, Qohelet's attempt to make sense out of life is as fruitful as *'chasing after the wind.'* He is unable to make sense out of life (for a discussion of the word *hebel*, translated *'senseless,'* and

---

25. Ginsburg, Lauha, and Lohfink argue this point.

26. Seow, *Ecclesiastes*, 120. Others who take it this way include Gordis, Delitzsch, Fox, and Crenshaw.

27. Seow, *Ecclesiastes*, 120.

28. Bartholomew (*Ecclesiastes*, 269–277) has an excellent discussion of Qohelet's epistemology and how it compares with Proverbs. He calls Qohelet's use of wisdom ironic because one assumes similarity with Proverbs but it turns out to be so much different from Proverbs. He also argues that autonomous is a better description of Qohelet's epistemology than empirical.

29. Hubbard, *Ecclesiastes*, 61. Ogden (*Qoheleth*, 40) understands the conclusion in 1:14-15 as a temporary or interim conclusion, which is not the final conclusion. However, it is better to understand these verses as a preliminary conclusion in the sense that he gives his conclusion before he lays out his experimental investigation in 2:1-11. The preliminary conclusion is, in reality, the final conclusion of Qohelet.

the phrase *'chasing after the wind,'* see the Introduction). The proverb of 1:15 reinforces the conclusion of 1:14; thus, it also is a comment on Qohelet's search. Ogden takes the proverb in a neutral sense, which means that certain facts about life cannot be altered, and so they must be accepted. The result is that humans must work within certain limitations.[30] But the proverb goes deeper in light of the statement of 1:14: the world does not make sense and it is impossible to change the situation. The proverb is a comment on the hopelessness of Qohelet's intellectual pursuit. If something is *'crooked'* it *'cannot be straightened.'* The verb translated *'straightened'* (*tqn*) can have the idea of 'set in order,' which may refer to the futility of trying to find order in the world.[31] Certain problems cannot be solved because there is information that is *'missing.'*[32] The fact that God is the subject of the verb *'crooked'* in 7:13 reinforces the impossibility of solving the problems of life.[33]

Such a conclusion is counter to the sentiments of wisdom literature in general. The prologue to the book of Proverbs sets forth the goal of receiving instruction as being able to deal wisely in righteousness, justice, and equity (1:3). Not only do youth receive knowledge and discretion through wisdom, but also the wise increase in learning (1:4-5). Through the

---

30. Ogden, *Qoheleth*, 40–41.

31. Whybray, *Ecclesiastes*, 50.

32. Garrett, *Ecclesiastes*, 289–290. Although Fox (*Rereading Ecclesiastes*, 172) thinks 1:15b is a pointless truism, which he uses as justification to emend the text, there is no support for his emendation. Longman (*Ecclesiastes*, 83) notes that the truism makes the flawed nature of the world self-evident and beyond dispute.

33. The fact that God is the subject of the verb ʿ*wt* ('crooked') in 7:13 also raises the moral question of God's relationship to a crooked world. Longman (*Ecclesiastes*, 82) prefers the translation 'bent' to avoid any moral connotation in relationship to God. The verb is used in Ecclesiastes 12:3 in the physical sense of bending over which comes as a result of old age. But everywhere else this verb is used in Scripture it has a moral connotation (Job 8:3; 19:6; 34:12; Pss. 119:78; 146:9). Job struggles with the justice of God in relationship to his innocent suffering. Whereas Bildad and Elihu deny that God perverts justice (Job 8:3; 34:12), Job at one point in his struggle (19:6) exclaims, 'then know that God has wronged me' (NIV). Qohelet himself is going to struggle with God's justice and how it is or is not worked out in the world.

wisdom of a father's instruction the son gains insight (4:1). Thus wisdom brings understanding in the living of life, which includes choosing the right paths (2:9). There is no hint of such success in Qohelet's search. Seow calls attention to an Egyptian proverb that says the opposite of Qohelet's conclusion. In the *Instruction of Anii* it is asserted that even a crooked stick can be straightened, while a straight stick can be bent. This proverb stresses the effectiveness of the teaching of the wise to straighten out the crooked. But Qohelet concludes that it is impossible to straighten out the world because of its crooked nature. As will become clear, such a view undermines confidence in wisdom.[34]

It was argued above that 1:16-18 parallel 1:13-15. Thus both 1:13 and 1:16 comment on the search itself. The serious nature of the search is emphasized in 1:13, but in 1:16 the capability of Qohelet to carry out the search is the focus. Qohelet describes himself as a man of great wisdom. Although some understand his remarks as sounding presumptuous,[35] his description of himself fits the way Solomon is presented in 1 Kings 3:12, where God tells Solomon, 'I give you a wise and discerning mind [Hebrew "heart"], so that none like you have been before you and none like you shall arise after you' (see also 1 Kings 4:29-34; 10:23-24).[36] Qohelet reassures the reader that he has the capability to carry out this search.

The preliminary conclusion to the search is given in both 1:14 and 1:17, but 1:17 adds an interesting comment on an aspect of the search before the conclusion is given. Qohelet seeks to *'understand wisdom.'* The verb *'understand'* is the Hebrew verb 'to know' (*yāda'*), which can mean to know by experience.[37] Qohelet wants to investigate how wisdom works in life and the consequences that come from wisdom. Wisdom is not only the instrument through which Qohelet carries out his search (1:13), but wisdom also becomes the object of the investigation. But Qohelet takes his investigation a step further. He not only wants

---

34. Seow, *Ecclesiastes*, 122, 147–148.
35. Longman, *Ecclesiastes*, 83.
36. For a discussion of the difficulties of Ecclesiastes 1:16 in relationship to Solomonic authorship see the Introduction.
37. Ogden and Zogbo, *Handbook on Ecclesiastes*, 47.

to *'understand wisdom,'* he also seeks to *'understand maddening folly.'* In other words, he seeks to investigate by experience how *'maddening folly'* operates in life and the consequences that come from it. Kidner points out that this phrase refers to moral perversity rather than to mental oddity.[38] The phrase occurs in 2:12; 7:25; 9:3; 10:13 and is associated with wickedness (7:25; 9:3; 10:13). Hubbard concludes that the phrase refers to behaving badly, wildly, or irresponsibly.[39] Thus Qohelet's search for meaning in life is again represented as truly comprehensive.

A preliminary conclusion is stated at the end of 1:17, which parallels 1:14. Qohelet *'discovered'* that the attempt to understand how *'wisdom,'* on the one hand, but also *'maddening folly,'* on the other hand, work out in life is a futile endeavor; it is a *'chasing after wind.'* This conclusion is supported by the proverb of 1:18. *'Wisdom'* and *'knowledge'* do not solve the problems of life but bring with them *'vexation'* and *'sorrow.'* The Hebrew word *'vexation'* (*kaʿas*) is in some contexts translated 'grief' (Pss. 6:7; 31:9; Eccles. 7:3), but here it seems to refer to anger produced because of some kind of distress (Ps. 112:10; Prov. 12:16; 21:19; 27:3).[40] It may also include frustation over things which do not turn out the way one hopes (2:23; 5:16), which would fit the way Qohelet describes wisdom (2:12-17). The Hebrew word *'sorrow'* (*makʾōb*) can refer to both mental and physical pain. Although it only occurs twice in Ecclesiastes (1:18; 2:23), Longman argues that the emphasis is more on mental anguish than bodily pain.[41] The proverb of 1:18 is clear that *'wisdom'* and *'knowledge'* are not the answer to the search for meaning, but demonstrate how impossible it is to find meaning in this life. More *'wisdom'* and *'knowledge'* do not help in the search; rather, they only increase the level of frustration and mental anguish because one sees better the problems of life and how impossible it is to solve them.[42]

---

38. Kidner, *Ecclesiastes*, 31.
39. Hubbard, *Ecclesiastes*, 64.
40. Fox (*Rereading Ecclesiastes*, 170) translates the Hebrew word *kaʿas* with 'irritation.'
41. Longman, *Ecclesiastes*, 85.
42. Delitzsch, 'Ecclesiastes,' 6:232.

The fact that wisdom, whether as an instrument in the search for meaning (1:13-15) or as the object of the search for meaning (1:16-18), does not help people live a long and blessed life is a bold conclusion that goes against the perspective of the book of Proverbs. In Proverbs 2:10 wisdom and knowledge are pleasant to the one who possesses them. In Proverbs 3:13-18 the blessings which come with wisdom are laid out. The more one has wisdom and knowledge the better (16:16, 22). Qohelet, however, sees none of these benefits connected to wisdom. This fact raises the question of the definition of wisdom, as used by Qohelet, in comparison with wisdom in Proverbs. The wisdom of Qohelet is defined in many ways. It is called secular wisdom,[43] human wisdom,[44] or the best thinking that a person can do on their own.[45] Although there is some truth in these assertions, how the issue is discussed is important. Qohelet does not adopt secular wisdom as an apologetic method to show where secular wisdom ends up (see the discussion of the different approaches to Ecclesiastes in the Introduction). He is a wise man who is connected to the wisdom tradition and is having trouble understanding that tradition in light of the problems of life.[46] However, the foundation of wisdom as set forth in Proverbs has begun to crack, so that Qohelet has been willing to put wisdom itself under investigation. In other words, instead of starting from the sure foundation of wisdom, as presented in Proverbs, and allowing that perspective to help him answer the questions and problems of life, he has questioned wisdom itself. Thus, he has not privileged the position of wisdom, but has placed wisdom on the same level as madness and folly.[47] Instead of starting from the standpoint that there are two ways of life and that one way is correct (as in Proverbs and Psalm 1), he has

---

43. ibid.
44. Whybray, *Ecclesiastes*, 49.
45. Kidner, *Ecclesiastes*, 31.
46. Longman, *Ecclesiastes*, 79–80.
47. Although Qohelet recognizes that wisdom is better in some ways than folly, wisdom ultimately does not make any difference when it comes to death and enduring remembrance (see the discussion in Eccles. 2:12-18).

started from the standpoint that both ways need investigating to see whether either way is beneficial (see also 7:15-18). Such a position is evidence that even though Qohelet stands in the wisdom tradition and is called a wise man (12:9), he no longer operates with the same foundation of wisdom as in the book of Proverbs; otherwise, he would privilege the position of wisdom and would allow the theological affirmations he makes to explain the problems and tragedies of life.[48] Herein lies the danger of speculative wisdom.

The failure of pleasure (Eccles. 2:1-11)

2:1 *I thought to myself,[49] 'Come now, I will make you experience pleasure.[50] Enjoy the good life.' But look,[51] this is also senseless.*

2:2 *I said of laughter, 'It is madness,' and of pleasure, 'What does this accomplish?'*

2:3 *I explored with my heart[52] pleasure[53] by giving my body up*

---

48. See Ecclesiastes 5:1-7 for a discussion of what fearing God means when used by Qohelet.

49. Jerome A. Lund (אמר, NIDOTTE, 1:446) points out that when ʾāmar ('to say') is used with the word heart (lēḇ), which is introduced by an appropriate preposition, the meaning is 'to think' or 'to suppose.' Longman (*Ecclesiastes*, 83) notes that such expressions refer to inner dialogue.

50. The translation of this phrase is a little awkward with the piel verb nāsāh and a 2ms suffix. This verb means 'to test' or 'to try,' but Seow points out that when it is used with verbs of hearing, seeing, knowing, and learning it means to experience something, with the object indicated by the preposition bet. This fits the meaning of the piel as expressing causation with a passive nuance in the sense of causing a state (see the discussion in Arnold and Choi, *Biblical Hebrew Syntax*, 41-43). Thus the object of the search is pleasure (simḥāh), which is introduced by the preposition bet.

51. For a discussion of the translation of hinnēh, see the comments on 1:14.

52. Although the word 'heart' (lēḇ) can be translated 'mind,' which stresses the intellectual nature of the investigation (Murphy, Longman, Delitzsch, Gordis, Ogden, Barton, and others mention this aspect), one should not draw the conclusion that Qohelet did not participate in the activities listed. The translation 'heart' brings out the idea that he explores with his whole being.

53. The word 'pleasure' is in roman because it does not occur in the verse, but it has been added because pleasure is the object of the investigation.

to wine[54] *and by grabbing hold of folly, my heart guiding me by wisdom, until I might see what is good for people to do under heaven during the few days of their lives.*

2:4 *I accomplished great achievements. I built for myself houses and I planted for myself vineyards.*

2:5 *I made for myself gardens and parks,*[55] *and I planted in them every kind of fruit tree.*

2:6 *I made for myself pools of water from which to water the forest of growing trees.*

2:7 *I purchased male and female servants, and I had*[56] *servants born in the house. I also greatly increased livestock, both herds and flocks,*[57] *more than any who were before me in Jerusalem.*

2:8 *I also accumulated for myself silver and gold, and the treasure of kings and provinces. I acquired for myself male*

Two infinitive clauses will follow to explain the focus of his exploration of pleasure.

54. This is the first of two infinitive clauses. The second clause is easy to translate ('by grabbing hold of folly'), but the first clause is difficult to translate. In whatever way the first clause is translated, it should focus on the exploration of 'pleasure' and it should parallel in some way the second infinitive clause. The phrase 'by giving up' has been translated a number of ways, including 'to refresh' (Murphy), 'to cheer' (Longman), 'to induce' (Seow), 'to stimulate' (Gordis, Barton), and 'to sustain' (Crenshaw). The verb *māšak* means 'to draw or pull' and is used in Hosea 11:4 in the sense of drawing someone with the cords of love. On this basis Fox (*Rereading Ecclesiastes*, 174) translates this clause in Ecclesiastes as 'drawing my body with wine,' which he takes to mean that Qohelet is leading his body by means of wine. The meaning seems to be that Qohelet grabs hold of folly and gives his body over to wine.

55. The word 'parks' (*pardēs*) is considered to be a Persian loan word, which is taken as evidence that the Hebrew of Ecclesiastes is late. However, see the Introduction for a discussion of the language of Ecclesiastes, and the counter-arguments by Fredericks (*Qohelet's Language*, 242–245) and Young (*Diversity in Pre-Exilic Hebrew*, 161–162) concerning *pardēs*.

56. The expression *hāyāh lî* (literally 'there was to me') expresses possession in past time (Mark D. Futato, *Beginning Biblical Hebrew* [Winona Lake: Eisenbrauns, 2003], 143).

57. The phrase 'herds and flocks' is an accusative of specification, further defining what the term 'livestock' entails (Seow, *Ecclesiastes*, 118).

> *and female singers, and many concubines, the delight of men.*[58]

2:9 *So I became great and I surpassed all who were before me in Jerusalem. In addition, my wisdom remained with me.*

2:10 *Whatever my eyes desired I did not keep from them. I did not hold back my heart from any pleasure because my heart received enjoyment from all my labour. This was my portion from all my labour.*

2:11 *Then I considered all my works which my hands had accomplished and the labour that I had laboured to do. Surely,*[59] *all is senseless and chasing the wind, and there is no profit under the sun.*

The focus of Qohelet's search in 2:1-11 is *'pleasure'* and the activities in life which bring *'pleasure.'* The activities described involve the kinds of things in which kings would be involved, and they are termed *'labour'* (*'āmāl*), which connects these activities to the question of 1:3. The Hebrew word translated *'pleasure'* (*śimḥāh*) can have the connotation 'joy,' but its use in 2:1-11 is more in line with the idea of *'pleasure'* or enjoyment. It is used in parallel with *'laughter'* in 2:2, and it is the result of activities that would normally bring *'pleasure'* or enjoyment to people (wine, gardens, parks, great possessions, singers, and concubines). The section begins with a statement of the object of the investigation and another preliminary conclusion (2:1-2). There follows an account of all the activities in which Qohelet tried to find *'pleasure'* (2:3-8), followed by a summary of his findings (2:9-11). The summary includes a restatement of the search for pleasure (2:9-10c), an immediate judgment that pleasure was the portion he received from his labor (2:10d),

---

58. Although most of the time in Ecclesiastes the phrase 'children of men' (*benê hā'āḏām*) refers to people in general (3:18, 19, 21; 8:11; 9:3, 12), in light of the context it refers to males in 2:8 (Crenshaw, *Ecclesiastes*, 81).

59. The Hebrew word *hinnēh* has been translated as 'look' in 1:14 and 2:1 because at the beginning of a clause it can indicate participant perspective, which includes a sense of discovery. Its use in 2:11 comes in the context of his conclusion, which is used to reinforce affirmation, and so is translated 'surely' (Joüon, *Grammar*, 2:616-617).

and an ultimate judgment that there is no profit from his labor (2:11). Thus pleasure and activities that would produce pleasure, including *'labour,'* are deemed *'senseless'* (*hebel*). Qohelet urges himself to *'experience pleasure'* and *'enjoy the good life'* (2:1) as a part of his search for meaning in this life. The phrase *'enjoy the good life'* literally reads 'to see good.' The Hebrew verb 'to see' (*rā'āh*) can mean to experience something; for example, 'to see death' would mean 'to experience death' (Ps. 89:48). Many times the verb *rā'āh* is used with *'good'* (*ṭôḇ*) with the connotation to experience good (Ps. 34:12; Job 7:7).[60] The Hebrew word *'good'* refers here to that which is pleasant and pleasurable.[61] The translation *'the good life'*[62] reflects the pleasurable activities that Qohelet experiences in 2:3-8. He had everything at his fingertips to enjoy to his heart's content. But before he lays out his list of pleasurable activities he offers his conclusion. He gives the customary *hebel* judgment at the end of 2:1 (*'this is also senseless'*), but then he goes on to explain the basis of this judgment in 2:2, where he comments on *'pleasure'* (*śimḥāh*) and *'laughter'* (*śeḥôq*). The latter term refers to the good time that results from the investigation of pleasure described in 2:3-8. Some would translate it *'merriment'* or *'merrymaking.'*[63] Concerning *'laughter'* the verdict is *'madness'* (*hll*).[64] This is the same root as the word in 1:17 (*hôlēlāh*), where it was the object of Qohelet's search for meaning. Here a form of the word is used to evaluate the search. Perhaps the idea is that *'laughter,'* including the good time that comes from the activities in 2:3-8, turns out to be delusional, a false premise, if one thinks

---

60. Seow, *Ecclesiastes*, 126.
61. Fox, *Rereading Ecclesiastes*, 116.
62. This is Longman's translation (*Ecclesiastes*, 86).
63. Seow (*Ecclesiastes*, 118) translates it 'merriment' and Fox (*Ecclesiastes*, 12) 'merrymaking.'
64. Instead of 'madness,' some translate this word as 'folly' (Ogden, *Qoheleth*, 43; Krüger, *Qoheleth*, 56; Whybray, *Ecclesiastes*, 52). Seow (*Ecclesiastes*, 126) suggests that the consonants of the poal participle *mĕhôlal* should be divided differently, yielding *mh hwll*, which would be a question paralleling the question in the next clause. He translates the question, ' does it boast?'

it will bring meaning to life. The verdict on pleasure comes in the form of a rhetorical question: '*what does this accomplish?*' No doubt this question expects a negative answer. At the end of the day, neither pleasure nor the good time that comes from pleasurable activities achieves anything.[65]

Some parameters of Qohelet's search are laid out in 2:3, which is difficult to translate. The main verb ('*I explored*') is followed by two infinitive clauses, which surround a participial clause (main verb, infinitive clause, participial clause, infinitive clause). All three clauses describe how Qohelet conducted his exploration of pleasure, with the two infinitive clauses pointing out the focus of the investigation, and the participial clause pointing out the way the investigation will be evaluated. The focus of the investigation (the two infinitive clauses) includes '*giving my body up to wine*' and '*grabbing hold of folly.*' The reference to '*wine*' includes drinking in general, but it also includes activities that accompany the drinking of wine, such as banqueting and feasting.[66] The mention of '*folly*' shows that Qohelet seeks to be more than just a connoisseur of fine wines,[67] but is willing to explore activities that would be called 'foolish.' Instead of rejecting outright the way of folly, Qohelet is willing to explore whether such activities might bring meaning to life. In fact, the purpose of his investigation is to '*see what is good for people to do.*' The Hebrew word '*good*' ($\underline{tôb}$) refers to what is beneficial in terms of the question of 1:3.[68] An answer is forthcoming in 2:10-11.

The participial phrase, '*my heart guiding me by wisdom,*' shows that he will not get so involved in the investigation of pleasure as not to be able to weigh the significance of what is happening.[69] There is a rational component to the investigation so that Qohelet will indulge in pleasure without being consumed by it.[70] It is rather jarring to imagine Qohelet

---

65. Fox, *Ecclesiastes*, 12.
66. Ginsburg (*Coheleth*, 278) notes Proverbs 9:2 and Song 8:2.
67. Longman, *Ecclesiastes*, 90.
68. Ogden, *Qoheleth*, 44 and Fox, *Rereading Ecclesiastes*, 116.
69. Longman, *Ecclesiastes*, 89.
70. Garrett, *Ecclesiastes*, 291.

participating in activities that can be designated *'folly'* while at the same time having *'wisdom'* guide the process! It seems that *'wisdom'* refers here to the methodology of the sages, which includes observation, reflection, and the drawing of conclusions.[71] But the fact that Qohelet is willing to examine *'folly'* shows that his perspective is not the same as the sages in Proverbs, who operate with the doctrine of the two ways, which seeks to avoid folly at all costs.[72]

Qohelet gives an account of the activities he pursued in his search for meaning in pleasure in 2:4-8. He sets forth his *'great achievements,'* which fit the 'résumé of a king.'[73] Kings were known for their building activities. The building of *'houses'* (2:4) is described in 1 Kings 7:1-12, where there is not only the list of what Solomon built, but a description of the extravagance that went into the building projects (1 Kings 7:9-11). Kings also *'planted vineyards,'* which produced the large amount of wine needed for the daily provisions of the king's table (1 Kings 10:5). The *'gardens and parks,'* with *'pools of water'* and *'every kind of fruit tree,'* were a great source of delight in the hot, dry climate of the ancient Near East.[74] Large property holdings required many *servants* and Qohelet acquired them by buying them and by having them *'born'* to the *'servants'* he had already acquired. The wealth of kings was seen in their *'livestock,'* which were needed for the provision of food for the king's administration (1 Kings 10:5 refers to 'the food of his table'), and also in their accumulation of *'silver and gold'* (see the description of Solomon's wealth in 1 Kings 10:14-27). It is possible that the phrase *'the treasure of kings and provinces'* refers to the source

---

71. Ogden and Zogbo, *Handbook on Ecclesiastes*, 53.

72. Bartholomew (*Ecclesiastes*, 131) specifically highlights that Qohelet's use of wisdom is contrary to wisdom in Proverbs. In discussing the wise and the fool, Waltke (*Proverbs*, 1:93) comments that there is not a third category between the two.

73. Seow, *Ecclesiastes*, 128.

74. See Ginsburg (*Coheleth*, 280) for a description of the refreshing quality of these 'gardens and parks' in the hot climate of the ancient Near East. King Nebuchadnezzar was known for his Palace Gardens.

of the wealth in foreign tribute and in taxation.[75] Finally, Qohelet mentions entertainment, in the form of *'male and female singers'* (1 Kings 10:12), and sensual pleasure, in the form of *'many concubines.'* There is debate concerning the meaning of the phrase *'many concubines'* (*šiddāh wĕšiddôṯ*). The same two feminine nouns are joined together by the conjunction. The first noun is singular and the second noun is plural, which could be taken to mean 'a multitude,'[76] although Seow points out that this exact construction does not occur anywhere else in the Old Testament.[77] The meaning of the word *šiddāh* is unclear. The Septuagint understands it to be a reference to male and female wine stewards. The Vulgate and the Targums are close to the Septuagint in understanding the word to be referring to a 'goblet.'[78] The New King James Version translates the word as 'musical instrument.'[79] Seow thinks the term refers to chests for silver and gold. He also understands the word *'delight'* (*taʿănûḡ*) to refer to delightful and fine things (Prov. 19:10; Micah 1:16; 2:9), which he does not believe has any sexual connotation, as it does in Song 7:6. He translates the phrase, 'along with humanity's treasures in chests.'[80] However, the majority of commentators understand the phrase *šiddāh wĕšiddôṯ* to refer to many concubines.[81] In this view the word 'delight'

---

75. Longman, *Ecclesiastes*, 91. The word 'treasure' (*sĕḡullāh*) can refer to one's own personal possessions (1 Chron. 29:3), and it is used of Israel (Exod. 19:5 as chosen by God as His own unique possession (סְגֻלָּה, Eugene Carpenter, NIDOTTE, 3:224).

76. Ginsburg, *Coheleth*, 285 and Delitzsch, 'Ecclesiastes,' 6:239.

77. Seow, *Ecclesiastes*, 131.

78. In this view the root of the word *šiddāh* would be from the Aramaic *šdy*, which means 'to pour out' (Longman, *Ecclesiastes*, 87).

79. Here the root seems to be *šdd*, ('to spoil, to ravish'), which could refer to a musical instrument that ravishes the heart (Ginsburg, *Coheleth*, 285).

80. Seow (*Ecclesiastes*, 130) takes the word *šiddāh* to be related to the Akkadian *šaddu*, a term that refers to chests of silver and gold.

81. Longman (*Ecclesiastes*, 92) points out that some take the word *šiddāh* as from the root *šdd* ('to seize,' referring to women seized in battle) or from *šd* ('breast'). Murphy (*Ecclesiastes*, 18) notes possible connections to an Akkadian word, *šaditum*, or a Ugaritic word, *št*, which means 'mistress' or

has erotic connotations, as it does in Song 7:6, and fits the description of Solomon's harem in 1 Kings 11:3 (700 wives and 300 concubines). In a description of a search for meaning in pleasure, where nothing is held back from the search (2:10), it would be a strange omission if the search did not include this part of pleasure, especially in light of what is known about Solomon in this area (1 Kings 11). Thus the best translation of *šiddāh wěšiddôt* is many concubines.

Qohelet offers a summary of his findings in 2:9-11. He states again the comprehensive nature of his search for pleasure by pointing out that he did not hold his heart back from '*any pleasure*' that he saw and desired: '*whatever my eyes desired I did not keep from them.*' Such statements seem to go against the command in Numbers 15:39, which specifically states that the people were not to seek after the desires of their hearts and their eyes.[82] One also thinks of the statement in Psalm 119:37: 'Turn my eyes from looking at worthless things.' But once Qohelet decided to include folly in his search for meaning (1:17; 2:3), the door was opened for pursuing pleasure. But how far did he go in his pursuit of pleasure, or as one might say, in his pursuit of wine, women, and song? There are two kinds of statements in 2:1-11. There are statements that emphasize that the search for meaning in pleasure was comprehensive, unrestrained, and self-indulged. The phrase '*for myself*' (*lî*) occurs eight times in nine verses. All the activities described in 2:4-8 are done for himself and his own pleasure. These statements make it hard to draw lines concerning appropriate behavior. But there are also statements that remind the reader that Qohelet's search for meaning is not a complete abandonment to pleasure. Twice he mentions that wisdom remains a guiding factor in his pursuit of pleasure (2:3, 9). The mention of '*wisdom*' is taken to mean that Qohelet did not abandon good sense,[83] that he did

---

'lady.' Eaton (*Ecclesiastes*, 67) points to the word *šiddâ*, a Canaanite gloss of an Egyptian word for concubine in a letter from Pharaoh Amenophis II to Melkilu, prince of Gezer.

82. Crenshaw, *Ecclesiastes*, 81–82. The verb 'to explore' (*tûr*) occurs in Numbers 15:39 and Ecclesiastes 1:13.

83. Fox, *Rereading Ecclesiastes*, 180.

not fall to the level of mindless stupor,[84] and that he remained in control of the experiment.[85] It is interesting that the wisdom in 2:9 is identified as *'my wisdom,'* which supports the idea that the foundation of wisdom has shifted to a more human, speculative wisdom. But the fact that wisdom accompanied him in his search suggests that he kept his mind alert so that he could evaluate the possible benefits of his pursuit of pleasure.[86]

The evaluation of the search for meaning in pleasure comes in two parts. There is an immediate evaluation that focuses on the limited benefit that derives from all the activities in which Qohelet participated, which are called his *'labour'* (*'āmāl*). In fact, some form of the term *'āmāl* occurs four times in 2:10-11. Qohelet's search for meaning in pleasure cannot be separated from the activity of his labor. In fact, the activities described in 2:4-8 are the kinds of activities in which kings are typically involved. The immediate evaluation is that Qohelet received *'enjoyment'* from all his labor. In the pursuit of pleasure through all the activities described in 2:4-8, Qohelet did enjoy himself in those activities. He labels this enjoyment his *'portion'* (*ḥēleq*). The meaning of this term will be filled out in its other occurrences in Ecclesiastes (2:21; 3:22; 5:18, 19; 9:6, 9; 11:2), but in this verse *'portion'* refers to the limited benefit of *'enjoyment'* that comes from *'labour.'* Although Qohelet will encourage people to enjoy this portion, it does not attain to the level of *'profit'* (*yitrôn*). Qohelet's ultimate judgment in 2:11, where he reflects on his labor and its results, is that there is no profit to labor. This is his answer to the question of 1:3, which is confirmed by the statement, *'all is senseless and chasing the wind, and there is no profit (yitrôn) under the sun.'* Qohelet affirms that *'labour,'* and the product of labor, is not worth the effort because it all comes under the judgment of *'senseless'* (*hebel*). Although *'enjoyment'* is a by-product of labor, and is the *'portion'* one can expect from *labor*, it also is inadequate.[87] The portion is something that

---

84. Crenshaw, *Ecclesiastes*, 81.
85. Provan, *Ecclesiastes*, 73.
86. Longman, *Ecclesiastes*, 93.
87. Fox, *Ecclesiastes*, 15.

will be encouraged to be enjoyed, but it will also come under the *hebel* judgment. The reason for this evaluation by Qohelet is not because Qohelet distinguishes between the pursuit of pleasure in itself, which is *hebel*, and the pursuit of pleasure accepted as a divine gift, which is not *hebel*.[88] It will become clear that the gift of enjoyment will also have its problems (2:24-26; 5:19-20). The problem is that labor itself does not produce what one expects; therefore, the conclusion is that *'there is no profit under the sun.'*

Homiletical Implications

The pursuit of pleasure or enjoyment in life is something with which everyone can identify because people operate with the assumption that having more things will bring meaning and satisfaction in life. It is easy to look at someone like Bill Gates and think that he has it made because he is wealthy and can enjoy all the benefits that wealth brings. People would also look at Solomon and draw the same conclusions. Not only was he king, but he was a very wealthy man who had everything he could want at his fingertips. If someone like Solomon could not find meaning in the pursuit of pleasure, there is little hope that anyone else could. However, people are constantly trying to find meaning in the pursuit of things, perhaps not on the same scale as Solomon, but in many smaller ways. The temptation is there all the time and it is easy to fall into it. Solomon had it all and he did not find meaning in anything under the sun, not even in the little amount of enjoyment he received from his labor, which he identifies as his portion. One could contrast Solomon's situation with Jesus, who really did have it all at His fingertips, but gave it all up to enter this sinful world to deliver people from the bondage of sin and the attitude of thinking that having it all brings fulfillment. As followers of Jesus, who will one day truly have it all when Jesus returns, we should be willing to give it all up now for the sake of Christ's kingdom and His glory. Only Christ can restore what was lost in the Garden of Eden, and one day in the

---

88. Whybray, *Ecclesiastes*, 55.

future He will restore a paradise where having it all and full satisfaction will exist without fail.[89]

The failure of wisdom in light of folly and death (Eccles. 2:12-17)

2:12 *So I turned to examine wisdom and maddening folly,[90] for what is the person who comes after the king if he has already accomplished it?*

2:13 *Then I observed that wisdom has an advantage over folly as the light has an advantage over darkness.*

2:14 *The wise man's eyes are in his head but the fool walks in darkness. Yet I also perceived[91] that the same fate happens to both of them.*

2:15 *Then I thought to myself, 'Even I will meet the same fate as the fool. So why then have I become very wise?' So I concluded[92] that this also is senseless.*

2:16 *For there is no lasting remembrance for the wise as well as[93] the fool, inasmuch as in the coming days both are soon forgotten. How will the wise die? Like the fool!*

---

89. It is possible that there is an allusion to the Garden of Eden in Ecclesiastes 2:4-8, especially in the word 'parks' (which many connect to the old Persian word *paridaida*, which is attested later as Greek *paradeisos* [Seow, *Ecclesiastes*, 128]) and the mentioning of 'every kind of fruit tree' in 2:5 (A. Verheij, 'Paradise Retried: On Qohelet 2:4-6,' JSOT 50 [1991]: 113–115). If there is an allusion then Qohelet fails in recreating paradise.

90. The phrase 'maddening folly' occurs also in 1:17. Literally it reads 'madness and folly,' and it is clear in this section that it is a hendiadys (two nouns joined by a conjunction that express a single concept) because in these verses Qohelet compares two things, wisdom and folly (Fox, *Rereading Ecclesiastes*, 182).

91. The verb 'perceived' (*yāda'*) is the basic Hebrew word for 'know' and here refers to what Qohelet came to realize on the basis of further reflection on his observations (Delitzsch, 'Ecclesiastes,' 6:247).

92. The verb *dābar* ('to speak, to declare') is translated 'concluded' because it introduces the hebel clause, which functions as a regular conclusion concerning many different issues throughout the book.

93. The preposition *'im* is used here and at the end of the verse in a comparative sense (Bruce K. Waltke and M. O'Connor, *An Introduction to Biblical Hebrew Syntax* [Winona Lake: Eisenbrauns, 1990], 220).

2:17 *So I hated life because the work which is done under the sun is grievous to me, for everything is senseless and chasing after the wind.*

This section is marked off by the *hebel* judgments in 2:11 and 2:17,[94] with 2:12 introducing the next stage of the investigation with the phrase '*I turned to examine.*'[95] Having concluded that there is no profit from labor under the sun, Qohelet now addresses whether wisdom has any advantage over folly.[96] One would think that if meaning was to be found anywhere, it would be found in wisdom as distinguished from folly.[97]

The second part of 2:12 is extraordinarily difficult to translate and interpret. Literally it could be translated, 'for what is the person who comes after the king? That he has already done.'[98] There are numerous issues that present difficulties in understanding this verse. For example, what is the relationship of 2:12b to 2:12a, which raises the question of how *kî* should be translated ('for,' 'because,' 'indeed'). Does the word *māh* introduce a rhetorical question, or is the question answered by the verse itself (as in the literal translation above)? How is the phrase *'eṯ 'ăšer*, which introduces the last part of 2:12, to be understood? How should the last verb, which is a plural verb with a singular suffix, be handled? Various proposals have been offered.[99] Garrett takes 'man' (*'āḏām*) to refer to Adam, the first king, and the phrase 'whom they already have made' at the end of the verse as a reference to the divine creation of Adam. The meaning is that there is little chance that humans will behave with greater wisdom than their first ancestor, Adam, who came directly from the

---

94. Murphy, *Ecclesiastes*, 21.
95. Whybray, *Ecclesiastes*, 56 and Hubbard, *Ecclesiastes*, p. 82.
96. Murphy, *Ecclesiastes*, 21.
97. Longman, *Ecclesiastes*, 94.
98. This is Longman's literal translation (*Ecclesiastes*, 96).
99. The Septuagint seems to get off on the wrong foot when it takes the word for 'king' (*meleḵ*) as the word 'counsel' (see Murphy, *Ecclesiastes*, 20 and Longman, *Ecclesiastes*, 96 for a discussion of the Septuagint and other early versions).

hand of God.[100] However, the noun *'āḏām* always refers to human beings in Ecclesiastes, and a reference to Adam at this point in the discussion seems intrusive and forced. Fox takes the word for king (*hammelek*) and makes it into the participle *hammōlēk* ('to rule'), and translates the phrase, 'who will come after me who will rule over what I earned earlier.' Here the focus is on the successor to the king who will have control of what the king has amassed, which foreshadows the subject of 2:18-23.[101] A weakness of this view is that the verb 'rule' expects the prep *ʿal* ('over') to follow it, which is not the case here. A common approach is to add the verb 'to do' (*ʿāśāh*) in 2:12b, yielding the translation, 'what can the man do who comes after the king?'[102] The answer is 'Only what has already been done' (ESV). The meaning could be that the future king will fall in line with the routine established by his predecessors,[103] which might indicate that subsequent royal figures will also pursue the quest for life's meaning as Qohelet has done.[104] Another possible meaning could be that if Qohelet, the king, cannot find meaning in his search, then no one else who comes after him will be able to do so.[105] This view has much to commend it. The *kî* ('*for*') gives the reason for the investigation of '*wisdom and maddening folly*': a king has everything at his disposal to conduct such a search.[106] The question introduced by *māh* with *'āḏām* ('man') is used in other places in the OT to explore the value or standing of human beings (Pss. 8:4; 144:3), and the question in Ecclesiastes 2:12b may also question the value or standing of anyone who

---

100. Garrett, *Ecclesiastes*, 294.

101. Fox, *Rereading Ecclesiastes*, 182–183. Seow (*Ecclesiastes*, 118, 134) takes a similar view.

102. The justification for the addition of *ʿāśāh* ('to do') is explained by Longman (*Ecclesiastes*, 96) as either homoioteleuton (it has accidentally been omitted through a scribal error) or aposiopes (the suppression of the verb).

103. Murphy, *Ecclesiastes*, 21.

104. Ogden, *Qoheleth*, 48.

105. Longman, *Ecclesiastes*, 96.

106. Delitzsch, 'Ecclesiastes,' 6:245; Ogden and Zogbo, *Handbook on Ecclesiastes*, 65; and Fox, *Ecclesiastes*, 15.

would come after Qohelet to carry out the search for meaning that he has carried out.[107] The end of the verse, introduced by 'ēṯ 'ăšer, stresses that nothing beyond what Qohelet has done can be accomplished.[108] This view fits the comments of Qohelet (1:16; 2:7, 9), and the statements concerning Solomon (1 Kings 4:29-30; 10:23-25) that his position and wisdom is unique. Thus 2:12b is translated, *'for what is the person who comes after the king if he has already accomplished it.'*[109] The *'he'* refers back to the king. This view emphasizes that Qohelet's search is unique and cannot be surpassed.

In 2:13-14a Qohelet makes an observation concerning the relationship between wisdom and folly.[110] Wisdom clearly has *'an advantage over folly.'* The word for *'advantage'* is the word used earlier in 1:3 and 2:11 for *'profit'* (*yiṯrôn*). In the earlier verses it is used in an absolute sense, whereas in 2:13 it is used in a comparison, which yields the translation *'advantage.'* Qohelet observes that wisdom yields a 'profit' when compared with folly. In other words, wisdom is superior to folly. To demonstrate this statement Qohelet compares wisdom to light and folly to darkness. It is fairly clear how light is superior to darkness, but Qohelet goes on to explain that *'the wise man's eyes are in his head but the fool walks in darkness.'* In other words, the wise person is able to

---

107. Some point out that *māh* may focus on value (Ginsburg, *Coheleth*, 288 and Gordis, *Koheleth*, 140) or the quality of something (Fox, *Rereading Ecclesiastes*, 182).

108. Eaton (*Ecclesiastes*, 68, n. 2) takes the 'ēṯ as the 'ēṯ of specification ('concerning') and the plural verb at the end of the verse in an impersonal sense. K. A. D. Smelik ('A Reinterpretation of Ecclesiastes 2,12b,' in A. Schoors [ed.], *Qohelet in the Context of Wisdom* [Leuven: Leuven University Press, 1998], 385–389) takes the phrase 'ēṯ 'ăšer as introducing a conditional clause, which is justified if one compares 1 Kings 8:31 with 2 Chron. 6:22. Smelik's view is followed in the translation above.

109. This view does not need to insert '*āśāh* ('to do') near the beginning of 2:12b. It also takes the verb at the end of the verse as a singular verb, which has support of sixty-eight Hebrew manuscripts (Smelik, 'Ecclesiastes 2,12b,' 385), and understands the question as a rhetorical question.

110. Fox (*Rereading Ecclesiastes*, 183) notes that when the verb 'to see' (*rā'āh*) is used with a 'that' (*šĕ*) clause it introduces a proposition that the speaker believes is true. Qohelet will affirm the value of wisdom even if it is a limited value.

see where he is going, but the fool is not able to see where he is going. The fool goes through life as if he is walking in the dark. He keeps stumbling over obstacles in life.[111] This view is reminiscent of Proverbs 22:3, 'The prudent sees danger and hides himself, but the simple go on and suffer for it.' Wisdom allows a person to see the obstacles in life and to avoid them, which helps him to succeed in life.

However, Qohelet *'also perceived'* that the absolute contrast[112] between wisdom and folly, as expressed in the comparison between light and darkness, ultimately breaks down. The distinction between the wise and the fool breaks down in light of the fact *'that the same fate happens to both of them.'* The word *'fate'* (*miqreh*) describes what happens to a person as opposed to what a person does to himself. A person has no control over certain events, which may appear to occur without rhyme or reason.[113] From a human perspective, it appears that something may happen 'by chance,' but this does not necessarily rule out divine determination.[114] In 2:15 Qohelet acknowledges that the *'fate'* that comes to the fool will *'even'* overtake him. It is clear from 2:16 that this fate is death itself. Thus it is death that destroys the distinction between the wise and the fool and makes the advantage that wisdom has over folly to be a relative advantage. Wisdom fails to give the wise person any ultimate advantage over the fool because death wipes out the distinction between the two.

---

111. Longman, *Ecclesiastes*, 97; Garrett, *Ecclesiastes*, 294; and Hengstenberg, *Ecclesiastes*, 82.

112. Ogden and Zogbo (*Handbook on Ecclesiastes*, 66) use the phrase 'absolute contrast.'

113. Many commentators agree on this understanding of 'fate' (*miqreh*) in Ecclesiastes, including Longman, Fox, Seow, Ogden, Krüger, Eaton, and Whybray.

114. Fox, *Rereading Ecclesiastes*, 183. Many times 'fate' (*miqreh*) refers to what takes place from a human standpoint, which appears to be random or by chance, when in reality God's sovereignty is directing events (see Ruth 2, where Ruth does not know where she will end up that day, but God does know as Boaz is introduced at the beginning of the chapter). It is significant that the Septuagint translates *miqreh* with *sunantāmaos* ('meeting') and not *tukā* ('fate, chance'), which means that Qohelet's notion is Semitic and is not to be identified with the Greek concept (Seow, *Ecclesiastes*, 135).

Thus Qohelet wonders, '*So why then have I become very wise?*' The problem is not excessive wisdom, as if the right amount of wisdom would have supplied the meaning to life, but the problem is wisdom itself (1:18). Qohelet questions why he has devoted so much time to becoming wise when wisdom falls short of what one expects. The value of wisdom and the absolute contrast between the wise and the fool found in, for example, Proverbs 10 is denied by Qohelet in light of death.

If wisdom fails in light of death and death destroys the distinction between the wise and the fool, it is important to ask what it is about death that brings about this state of affairs. Qohelet comments on this question in 2:16, where he explains why there is no ultimate difference between the wise and the fool in death (*kî* here gives the reason, '*for*'). He notes that there is '*no lasting remembrance*' for either '*the wise*' or '*the fool*' in light of the fact that '*in the coming days both are forgotten.*' Qohelet could be referring to the problem that no one remembers the fool or the wise after they die.[115] In other words, death brings an end to whatever fame or achievements one accomplished in life because when a person is gone none of those things are remembered any longer (similar to 1:11). There also may be a sense that death brings extinction to both the wise and the fool (9:10), which destroys any distinctions between them.[116] The issue of death is a fact of life which the OT and wisdom literature were able to incorporate into their worldview (see the discussion in the Introduction), but that death destroys the difference between the wise and the fool is something that Qohelet has observed in contrast to the teaching of the Old Testament. Both Proverbs 10:7 and Psalm 112:6 promise that the righteous will be remembered, with the former contrasting the memory of the righteous with the wicked: 'The memory of the righteous is a blessing, but the name of the wicked will rot.' On the basis of his observations Qohelet clearly calls this teaching into question. Wisdom fails because it does not guarantee an enduring legacy.

Qohelet laments this fact with an exclamatory question at the end of 2:16: '*How will the wise die? Like the fool!*' This

---

115. Ogden and Zogbo, *Handbook on Ecclesiastes*, 69.

116. Kidner, *Ecclesiastes*, 34.

question not only reinforces that there is no distinction between the wise and the fool when it comes to death, it also raises the question of the manner of death. Although the word *'How'* can express emotions such as horror and amazement, and may even indicate a lament, it is also asking a true question (as in 4:11).[117] One of the benefits of wisdom is long life (Prov. 3:16-18; 13:14; 14:27), which entails not just long life on this earth, but also life after death (Prov. 14:32; 15:24).[118] Qohelet denies both possibilities. The denial of life after death fits into his denial of any distinction between the wise and the fool in their death (see also 9:10). The denial that the wise necessarily live long is seen in the fact that the manner of death is the same for the wise and the fool.[119] In other words, both the wise and the fool die without regard to how they have lived their life, something Qohelet will develop later in the book (8:11-14; 9:1-6). Thus Qohelet is bothered because death seems random in that it comes to the wise and the fool in the same way without differentiating between them.

Qohelet brings this section to a close with a statement that shows his deep sense of frustration[120] at the way things work in this world *'under the sun'*: *'I hated life.'* Qohelet's hatred for life comes from what he observes in life concerning the lack of distinction between the wise and the fool. What he sees is a great burden to him: *'the work done under the sun is grievous to me.'* The word *'grievous'* (*ra'*) can have the connotation 'evil,' which is not too far from the way Qohelet views the world, but it can also have the idea of 'burdensome,' which seems to

---

117. As noted by Waltke and O'Connor (*Hebrew Syntax*, 328–329), the particle *'êk* can ask a true question of circumstance (Gen. 26:9; 2 Sam. 1:5; 1 Kings 12:6) or it can express an exclamatory question (2 Sam. 1:19). Many commentators see a lament aspect here as well (Whybray, *Ecclesiastes*, 59; Hubbard, *Ecclesiastes*, 87, among others).

118. Waltke, *Proverbs 1–15*, 634.

119. David laments in 2 Samuel 3:33 that Abner had died as a fool dies, which is a reference to his premature and violent death (Philip S. Johnston, *Shades of Sheol: Death and Afterlife in the Old Testament* [Downers Grove, IL: InterVarsity Press, 2002], 27).

120. Ogden and Zogbo, *Handbook on Ecclesiastes*, 70.

fit here better.¹²¹ Instead of embracing life (Prov. 8:35; 3:16), Qohelet has an aversion to life based on his observations concerning the way the world operates. The problem in this section is the failure of wisdom to produce any lasting difference between the wise and the fool. Although wisdom is better than folly and may bring some advantage to a person, when it really counts, in the face of death, it makes no difference. Thus death relativizes the value of wisdom and makes everything '*senseless.*' Since death ends all and Qohelet does not offer a resolution in this life or the afterlife, *hebel* cannot be referring to what is fleeting or mysterious.

Homiletical Implications

The failure of wisdom is rooted in Qohelet's limited perspective. In this section he continues to operate on the basis of observation (2:13-14) and the limited horizon of an earthly, under the sun, perspective (2:17). Thus the events of life do not make sense to him, especially the destiny of the wise and the fool in light of death. Wisdom is not able to solve this problem because Qohelet is not able to bring in a different perspective. The statements by Qohelet which go against the views expressed in Proverbs demonstrate that Qohelet's view of wisdom may not necessarily be the same as the view of wisdom in Proverbs. Ogden is correct when he notes that 'profit' or 'advantage' (*yitrôn*) is not to be found before or at death, but he goes beyond Qohelet's view when he argues that Qohelet pushes us to seek it beyond death.¹²² For Qohelet, there is nothing beyond death. Thus the events of this life are tragic because he has no broader perspective with which to explain why the death of the wise is no different than the death of the fool.

True wisdom is not limited to the horizons of this world. On April 12, 2001, Sarah Ann Longstreet left her home in the morning to attend high school, but she never made it because she was killed in an automobile accident. She was

---

121. The use of the preposition '*al* ('upon') supports the idea that *ra'* means 'grievous' in this verse (Ginsburg, *Coheleth*, 294).

122. Ogden, *Qoheleth*, 50.

young, talented, a strong believer in Jesus Christ, with her whole life in front of her, and yet in one instant she was gone. Qohelet would understand this accident as a quirk of fate or a grievous burden because how Miss Longstreet lived made no difference in how long she lived. However, her parents saw things differently. They could have appealed to certain proverbs that give the hope of life to God's people beyond this life (Prov. 3:18; 14:32; 15:24), but they found their consolation in the One who is the fullness of wisdom, Jesus Christ Himself (1 Cor. 1:24; Col. 2:2-3). Here is a portion of her obituary:

> While most would call the car accident that took Sarah's life a 'tragedy' her family knows that it was the case of God calling one of His children home. Certainly unexpected, but an indication that Sarah's work on earth was complete. For those who read of Sarah's accident and feel that a young life has been cut short, the Longstreets believe that Sarah would want them to know what the Bible says, 'for me to live is Christ, and to die is gain.' And she would challenge you to consider where you will spend eternity.

The Longstreets were able to place the loss of their child within a worldview that included the sovereignty of a loving God, who is working out His purposes for their lives even in the midst of the 'tragedies' of life. Such is true wisdom.

The failure of the results of labor (Eccles. 2:18-23)

2:18 *Then I hated all the results of my labour for which I laboured under the sun because I must leave them to the one who comes after me.*

2:19 *And who knows whether he will be wise or a fool, yet he will control all the results of my labour for which I had laboured and for which I had become wise under the sun. This is also senseless.*

2:20 *So I became full of despair[123] over all the results of labour for which I had laboured under the sun.*

---

123. The opening phrase of 2:20 is difficult. It could be translated in a literal sense as, 'I turned to cause my heart to despair' or 'I turned to despair

2:21 Indeed,[124] there is a person who labours with wisdom, knowledge, and success, but he must leave his portion to someone who did not labour for it. This too is senseless and a great burden.

2:22 For[125] what comes to a person in all his labour and in the striving of his heart with which he labours under the sun?

2:23 For[126] during all his days[127] his work is full of pain and frustration. Even in the night his heart does not rest. This also is senseless.

In this section Qohelet examines the results of labor in his search for meaning 'under the sun.' Some form of the word for 'labour' ('āmāl) occurs nine times in this section. This word can refer either to the work itself or the results of the work,

---

with my heart.' The phrase 'I turned to despair' seems to refer to a change of heart towards the fruits of his labor (Ogden and Zogbo, *Handbook on Ecclesiastes*, 74). Thus Longman (*Ecclesiastes*, 103) translates it 'I began to despair.' Murphy (*Ecclesiastes*, 24) seeks to bring out the mention of the heart with 'I turned to heartfelt despair.' The translation 'I became full of despair' seeks to bring out both the idea of the change of heart and the depth to which he felt the despair.

124. There is debate concerning how the *kî* that begins 2:21 should be understood. Ginsburg (*Coheleth*, 297) takes it as causal, which is giving a reason for the despair. Whybray (*Ecclesiastes*, 61), on the other hand, argues that it introduces a general statement and that it does not function as an explanation for his own situation. Thus it should be translated with 'indeed.' Although 2:21 introduces a general example that demonstrates the futility of the results of labor, it also relates to Qohelet and what he is trying to establish. The translation 'indeed' focuses the attention on the example that follows.

125. Ogden and Zogbo (*Handbook on Ecclesiastes*, 77) argue that the *kî* should be translated 'indeed' because it draws attention to the question. They do not think it is causal because it is not giving a motive for an action of Qohelet. Fox (*Ecclesiastes*, 186) understands the *kî* as introducing a question which will give a reason for the evaluation at the end of 2:22: 'this too is senseless and a great burden.'

126. This is the third verse in a row that has begun with the particle *kî*. Longman (*Ecclesiastes*, 105) argues that it gives a rationale for the answer to the question in 2:22.

127. The phrase *kol- yāmāyw* is understood as an accusative of time (Gordis, *Koheleth*, 215).

which is the focus of this section.¹²⁸ In 1:3 the question was raised whether there was any profit to labor, and in 2:11 the question was answered: 'there is no profit [to labor] under the sun.' However, there was a portion that resulted from labor, which included the enjoyment that comes from labor (2:10). Thus labor produces other results, called a portion, which includes material possessions and property and can be passed on to someone else (2:21). Perhaps meaning can be found in the portion that comes from labor. Is it possible that the enjoyment that comes from labor and the possessions that one obtains from labor give meaning to life?

Qohelet wastes no time in giving his conclusion: *'then I hated all the results of my labour.'* What brought about such a negative conclusion? Qohelet gives the reason for this negative conclusion in 2:18b-19,[129] where he examines what happens to the goods and possessions that result from labor when someone dies: *'I must leave them to the one who comes after me.'* The problem is not just that a person works hard, dies, and then loses control over his goods and possessions,[130] which is bad enough, but the problem also has to do with *'the one who comes after me.'* Qohelet points out two things about his successor that cause him to hate the results of his labor. First, in 2:19, he asks the question, *'Who knows whether he will be wise or a fool?'* The character of his successor bothers him because there is no way to tell whether the one who takes control of his possessions will be a wise person or a fool.[131] The problem is that Qohelet may work hard and he may work

---

128. Fox (*Rereading Ecclesiastes*, 186) shows that 'labour' (*'āmāl*) in this passage must refer to the results of labor because of the suffix on the verb 'leave' translated 'them.' It is only the results of labor that someone can leave to his successor.

129. Many recognize that the particle *šě* has a causal force, 'because' (Murphy, *Ecclesiastes*, 24; Longman, *Ecclesiastes*, 102; Ogden and Zogbo, *Handbook on Ecclesiastes*, 72).

130. Longman, *Ecclesiastes*, 102.

131. Crenshaw (*Ecclesiastes*, 87) shows that although the use of the question 'who knows' in other parts of the Old Testament is an open-ended question giving the object of knowledge freedom to act unexpectedly (2 Sam. 12:22; Joel 2:14; Jonah 3:9; Ps. 90:11; Esther 4:14; Prov. 24:22), in Ecclesiastes the question expresses utter skepticism: no one really knows.

in a wise manner to obtain goods and possessions, but then he must leave them to someone who may be a fool. How quickly a fool can destroy what a person has worked a lifetime to achieve![132] This prospect throws into question whether working hard is worth the effort and brings about the verdict: *'this is also senseless.'*

The second thing that Qohelet says about his successor comes in 2:21. When Qohelet realized what would happen to the results of his labor at death his reaction was: *'So I became full of despair'* (2:20). Fox understands this difficult phrase to refer to the fact that Qohelet is giving up the illusion of the profitability of labor. Whybray argues that it refers to his resigned acceptance of a situation that cannot be helped. Both comment that he has given up hope.[133] He no longer sees any value to labor and what it produces. This is confirmed by 2:21, where he sets forth a general example[134] with an added comment concerning the successor. The example is of a person who works in a way that leads to success, but then he must leave behind what he has worked for, called his *'portion,' 'to someone who did not labour for it.'* All the hard work and success which results from labor is passed on to someone who did not lift a finger to help produce what he receives. Not only does this not make sense to Qohelet (the *hebel* verdict), but it also greatly troubles him, for he calls it *'a great burden.'*[135]

---

132. It is impossible to know whether Qohelet/Solomon is referring to his own successor, Rehoboam, because he speaks in very general terms (*'āḏām* in 2:18), but Rehoboam would aptly illustrate the point that is being made in terms of someone destroying something that has been given to them (1 Kings 12).

133. Fox, *Rereading Ecclesiastes*, 188 and Whybray, *Ecclesiastes*, 61. Although Whybray thinks 'despair' is too emotive a reading, the whole passage is full of emotion.

134. The Hebrew *yēš* introduces a particular instance (stated by Murphy, *Ecclesiastes*, 24, although he takes it in a conditional sense).

135. The word translated 'burden' (*rā'āh*) can also have the connotation 'evil.' Many take it this way in 2:21 (Murphy, Longman, Delitzsch, Gordis, and Crenshaw). It is hard to know whether Qohelet has in view the idea of 'evil' in connection to his struggles at this point. As the issue of injustice becomes more prominent in the book, the connotation of 'evil' becomes more likely.

In light of his conclusions concerning what happens to the results of labor at death, Qohelet raises in 2:22 a variation of the question he had asked in 1:3: *'What comes to a person in all his labour and in the striving of his heart with which he labours under the sun?'* The addition of *'the striving of his heart'* reinforces the difficult nature of labor associated with the word ʿ*āmāl*. The accumulation of goods does not come easily, but involves tremendous human effort, which includes anxiety and frustration.[136] It is significant that the term *'profit'* (*yiṯrôn*) is not used in this question as in 1:3. Qohelet has already answered the question related to the *'profit'* of labor (2:11). In 2:21 the term *'portion'* (*ḥēleq*) is used, which had already occurred in 2:10 as referring to the limited amount of benefit from labor. The portion in 2:10 is the enjoyment of labor and the portion in 2:21 is the goods and possessions one will pass on to a successor at death. The question of 2:22 does not use profit because the focus is on the portion. If there is no profit to labor, perhaps some benefit can be found in the portion that does come from labor. The answer in 2:23 takes away any hope that the portion will provide any real meaning to life. His answer is that *'during all his days his work is full of pain and frustration.'* Ogden argues that the phrase *'all his days'* is referring to the daily experience of labor in contrast to the *'night'* that is mentioned in the next sentence.[137] While that may be true, the emphasis on death in this section means that one cannot disregard the idea that a person's whole life is in view. Qohelet's answer covers every day, all day, all throughout a person's life. The statement, *'Even at night his heart does not rest,'* shows how extensive is the all-consuming nature of labor. Even the enjoyment, which is identified with the portion in 2:10, seems to be gone in light of the prospect of what happens at death to the results of labor. This is not just something

---

136. Longman (*Ecclesiastes*, 105) understands the phrase 'the striving of his heart' as referring to anxiety and Murphy (*Ecclesiastes*, 26) understands it as referring to frustration.

137. Ogden and Zogbo, *Handbook on Ecclesiastes*, 77–78.

that is mysterious or unexplainable, but it makes labor to be unprofitable, meaningless, and *'senseless.'*

Homiletical Implications

Qohelet emphasizes the difficult nature of labor. Work is hard in every respect. It involves both physical exertion and mental anguish. A person may work long and hard and then be frustrated because all the efforts put into the work do not pay off in a way that someone expects. For Qohelet, that includes the prospect of leaving all that you work hard for to someone who did not work for it at all. It is even worse if that person is a fool. It seems clear that Qohelet's view of labor fits in with the concept of the Fall and the effects of the curse on labor as it is described in Genesis 3:17-19.[138] However, what Qohelet does not stress in his view of labor is that labor is a divine vocation given by God (Gen. 1:26-28; 2:15). Even though the Fall made it more difficult to carry out that mandate, the Fall did not remove the mandate. The hope of overcoming the curse does not seem to be a part of Qohelet's worldview. He does not say that God ensures real profit to labor so that there is meaning to work. Nor does he say that it does not matter if you leave the results of your hard work behind to someone else because there is a reward in heaven. He does not have that broader perspective. The 'above the sun' view would affirm that when labor is hard and frustrating, and things do not go the way you would hope, there is a broader principle to live by (Rom. 8:28). The drudgery and futility of work is overcome by seeing work as a divine vocation that is itself redeemed by the work of Christ. After a lengthy chapter on the importance of the resurrection of Christ and a statement of thanksgiving for the victory of Christ's resurrection, Paul exhorts the people of God with these words, 'Therefore, my beloved brothers, be steadfast, immovable, always abounding in the work of the Lord, knowing that in the Lord your labour is not in vain' (1 Cor. 15:58).

---

138. See William H. U. Anderson, 'The Curse of Work in Qoheleth: An Exposé of Genesis 3:17-19 in Ecclesiastes,' *EQ* 70.2 (1998): 99–113.

Advice when life does not make sense (Eccles. 2:24-26)

2:24 *There is nothing better*[139] *for a person*[140] *than that he should eat and drink and find enjoyment in his labour. Also,*[141] *I have seen that this is from the hand of God.*

2:25 *For who can eat and who can worry*[142] *apart from him?*[143]

---

139. The word *ṭôḇ* ('good') at the beginning of 2:24 is translated with a comparative sense, 'better,' even though there is not a comparative mem. Some commentators supply a mem which may have dropped out due to haplography with the final mem on *'āḏām*, making 2:24 more like 3:22, which has a comparative mem (Crenshaw, *Ecclesiastes*, 89; Delitzsch, 'Ecclesiastes,' 6:251-252; Fox, *Rereading Ecclesiastes*, 189; Longman, *Ecclesiastes*, 107; Murphy, *Ecclesiastes*, 24; Whybray, *Ecclesiastes*, 63). Seow notes that Qohelet expresses the calls to enjoyment in a variety of ways by comparing 3:12; 8:15; and 3:22. He translates 2:24 without the comparative mem: 'there is no good among humanity (except) that they should eat' (*Ecclesiastes*, 139). It seems clear in comparing the *'ên ṭôḇ* statements (2:24; 3:12; 3:22; and 8:15) that Qohelet is not consistent in the use of the form. Ogden ('Qoheleth's Use of the "nothing is better" form,' JBL 98 [1979]: 339-340) notes that 5:18 and 9:7-10 express the same sentiment without the use of the *'ên ṭôḇ* form. Most agree that Qohelet is encouraging the activities mentioned in 2:24. Thus, Leupold's understanding that Qohelet says it is not a good thing to eat because satisfaction from these things comes from a higher source is to be rejected (*Ecclesiastes*, 75-76).

140. Ginsburg (*Coheleth*, 300) notes that the bet on *'āḏām* has the same signification as the lamed in Ecclesiastes 6:12 and 8:15 and is similar to the bet in 10:17, which denotes the object of the action, and is equivalent to the idea 'for.' It is also possible that the bet expresses the idea 'among human beings' (the spatial sense according to Arnold and Choi, *Biblical Hebrew Syntax*, 103), which Crenshaw (*Ecclesiastes*, 89) believes generalizes the statement.

141. Although Delitzsch ('Ecclesiastes,' 6:252) takes *gam* as adversative, 'but,' and Gordis (*Koheleth*, 142) takes it as emphatic, 'indeed,' most translations translate *gam* as 'also' (NKJV, NASB, NIV, ESV). The *gam* may connect 2:24 back to 1:13 in terms of what God gives.

142. There has been a lot of debate over the meaning of the verb *ḥwš*. See the discussion in the commentary for the various views.

143. The Hebrew has *mimmemmî* ('from me'), which is also attested by the Targum and the Vulgate. The 1cs suffix could either refer to Solomon's own exceptional opportunities for enjoyment, not typical of the human situation (Lohfink, *Qoheleth*, 56), or it could be seen as a quotation of God Himself (cited by Whybray, *Ecclesiastes*, 64). On the other hand, some Hebrew manuscripts, the Septuagint, the Syriac, and Jerome support *mi*

2:26 *For to a person who is good before him God has given wisdom, knowledge, and pleasure, but to the sinner he has given the task of gathering wealth[144] to give to the one who is good before God. This also is senseless and chasing the wind.*

There is general agreement that 2:24-26 functions as some kind of conclusion, summary, or advice based on the argument up to this point. The change of subject in Ecclesiastes 3:1, the full *hebel* statement at the end of 2:26, and the 'nothing is better' formula in 2:24 all point to the fact that 2:24-26 is a reflection on what has gone before and is not the start of a new section.[145] There is considerable disagreement, however, whether this section should be understood as positive advice or as a negative, resigned conclusion.

A positive understanding of the advice in 2:24-26 takes a number of different approaches. D. Lys argues that a new dimenion of dependence on God is introduced in this section, which the horizontal search of Qohelet was not able to discover.[146] Whybray differentiates between different kinds of pleasure or enjoyment. Instead of deceptive pleasure achieved by self-indulgence, Qohelet sets forth in 2:24-26 the idea that unsought pleasure given by God is good.[147]

---

mmennû ('from him'). The 3ms suffix as a reference to God fits the context better since God is referred to in both 2:24 and 2:25. A reference to Solomon seems intrusive at this point and God never speaks in Ecclesiastes (Seow, *Ecclesiastes*, 140–141). Dahood ('Qoheleth and Recent Discoveries,' 306) suggests that *mimmemmî* might represent the Phoenician spelling of 'from him,' but he is cautious because of how easy it is to confuse yod and waw in the original Hebrew.

144. The phrase 'gathering wealth' is a translation of two verbs, 'to gather and to collect,' which is taken as a hendiadys (two verbs stressing one concept). Eaton (*Ecclesiastes*, 75) comments that the two verbs have no object, which gives the impression of an all-embracing enquiry.

145. Only a few argue that 2:24 begins a new section (2:24–3:22), including Leupold (*Ecclesiastes*, 74) and Eaton (*Ecclesiastes*, 72–73). Eaton argues that God becomes more prominent in the next section, wisdom is viewed as God's gift, and the argument becomes more positive with the 'under the sun' limitations set aside.

146. D. Lys, *L'Ecclésiaste ou Que Vaut la Vie?* (Paris: Letouzey et Ane, 1977), 286, 288.

147. Whybray, *Ecclesiastes*, 63.

Fredericks sees these verses as a direct answer to the main question of 1:3 so that Qohelet's search is now somewhat satisfied.[148] And finally, Ogden argues that these verses are a response to the question of 1:3 and 2:22, as well as a response to the negative answers in 2:11. He argues that Qohelet moves from the problem to the solution and lays out the attitude that leads to profit.[149] The positive view of the advice in 2:24-26 emphasizes that the good things in life come from the *'hand of God'* (2:24), Who is the real source of the blessings of life as they are His gift. How 2:26 is understood in relationship to the concluding *hebel* judgment is also an important question (see below).

Bartholomew understands 2:24-26 as celebrating creaturely human life. This is a refreshing vision of life after the despair of 2:1-13. In fact, it presents an alternative view of life which is set in contradictory juxtaposition to the despair of 2:1-23 and the *hebel* verdict in 2:26. This juxtaposition creates a gap that waits to be filled with the statements in 12:13-14.[150]

Others argue that the advice in 2:24-26 is a resigned conclusion in light of the inability of pleasure, wisdom, or work to give meaning to life.[151] Longman understands 2:24 as advising that one should not wait for tomorrow but should get all the enjoyment that is possible in the present. In other words, what is encouraged in 2:24 is all one can expect in a world of futility. Some view God's actions in these verses as random or arbitrary.[152] In order to understand the advice of 2:24-26 several questions need to be addressed. How does this section relate to what has gone before? The advice of Qohelet is related to God, but what does God give in these verses? What is the meaning and function of 2:26, which seems to be a statement of traditional divine retribution, which is the way

---

148. Fredericks, *Transience*, 47.
149. Ogden, *Qoheleth*, 47–48.
150. Bartholomew, *Ecclesiastes*, 152–153. For a critique of Bartholomew's approach see the Introduction and the discussion of Ecclesiastes 8:12-15.
151. Murphy, *Ecclesiastes*, 26.
152. Longman, *Ecclesiastes*, 106.

life is supposed to work? And finally, how extensive is the final *hebel* judgment of verse 26?

The best understanding of Qohelet's advice in this section is that it is a resigned conclusion based on the futility of life. This view fits the context of the argument better than other views. In 1:3 the question was asked concerning whether there was any profit (*yitrôn*) to labor. After a review of all his activities (2:1-9) Qohelet concludes in 2:11 that there is no profit to labor under the sun. Nothing that Qohelet says in 2:12–2:26 overturns the answer of 2:11. In Qohelet's view nothing under the sun leads to profit. However, Qohelet has stated that even though there is no profit to labor, there is a portion (*ḥēleq*), which in 2:10 is identified with the enjoyment that comes from labor. In 2:21 the word 'portion' is used again, but this time it refers to the results of labor, such as goods and possessions, that are passed on to someone who did not work hard for them. In 2:22 he raises a similar question to the one raised in 1:3, except that this time the word 'profit' does not occur because he has in view the portion of 2:21. In light of the fact that the portion must be passed on at death to someone who did not work for it, he reflects that the only thing left is the hard work, the pain, and the frustration that accompanies work (2:23). Yet his advice in 2:24 is to enjoy what does come from labor.[153] So it seems that he contradicts himself because he says that the only thing one has from labor is pain and frustration (2:23), but then he encourages the limited enjoyment that comes from labor (2:10, 24). However, the focus of 2:18-23 is what happens to the portion at death. If one must leave it to someone who has not worked for it then one is left with pain and frustration in relationship to labor. This does not take away the immediate enjoyment that one can get from labor, which is the focus of 2:10 and 2:24.[154] If this enjoyment is the immediate benefit from labor, then it

---

153. It is signficant that the word 'portion' is used in the context of the calls to enjoyment to refer to both the enjoyment that comes from labor (3:22; 9:9) and the results from labor, including eating and drinking (5:18), wealth and possessions (5:19).

154. Hengstenberg (*Ecclesiastes*, 84) comments that the focus in 2:24 is on living for the present moment.

is not necessarily lasting, especially in light of death and the senselessness of the world. Thus the phrase *'there is nothing better than'* is not a rousing endorsement or the answer to the search for meaning, but it is all one can expect from labor in a world that is characterized by *hebel* and a chasing after the wind. One might as well enjoy the present, limited benefit that comes from labor, because that is all one has left.

But does not the fact that things come *'from the hand of God'* put the matter in a more positive light? Qohelet's view of God will unfold as more passages are covered, but this is the second time Qohelet mentions God. The first time God is mentioned is in 1:13, where He gives to people a grievous task to occupy them. Even if the term 'grievous' (*raʿ*) does not have the connotation 'evil' in 1:13, it is not a positive term. God gives to human beings a task that is hard and burdensome. What God gives in 2:24 is more positive because the focus is on the limited results from labor: '*eat, drink, and find enjoyment in his labour.*' However, it is possible that 2:25 also states that something negative comes from God, but the meaning of the verse is disputed. Discussions concerning the meaning of the verb *ḥwš* go all the way back to the Greek versions. One option is to translate the verb with a positive meaning, such as 'drink' or 'enjoy,' which makes both verbs of 2:25 positive.[155] Some argue that the meaning of the verb in 2:25 should be related to the two examples of 2:26, which sets forth a positive and a negative example. Gordis takes the verb in 2:26 to mean 'refrain' (that is, refrain from enjoyment) because 2:26 speaks of the enjoyment and the failure to enjoy the results of labor. Both come from the hand of God.[156] Seow understands the verb to mean 'gather' or 'collect' because in 2:26 a contrast is made between those who are able to eat heartily and those who must gather and collect in order to give it to someone

---

155. Some early Greek manuscripts (such as Theodotion) have *pivō*, 'to drink.' Many English translations translate the verb with 'enjoy' (NKJV, NASB, NIV, ESV), which may be supported by the Ugaritic *ḥšt* (Dahood, 'Qohelet and Recent Discoveries,' Bib 39 [1958]: 308).

156. Gordis (*Koheleth*, 217) supports the meaning 'refrain' based on an Arabic root. Aquila and Symmachus also have this meaning with the translation *pheidomai*.

else. He sees two cases set forth in 2:25-26. On the one side is one who eats, is favored, and has wisdom, knowledge, and pleasure and, on the other side, is the one who gleans, who is an offender, and who gathers, accumulates, and gives what he has gathered. Not only does God give the ability to eat (2:25a), but God also gives the ability to gather together (2:25b); but what is gathered is then given to someone else (2:26b).[157] Although Seow's view has much to commend it, the gathering together of goods still leaves open the possibility of presently enjoying them, which is not necessarily negative. Another option is to start with the common meaning of the verb $ḥwš$ in the O.T., which is 'to hurry' (Deut. 32:35; Judg. 20:37; 1 Sam. 20:38; Job 31:5; among others). The King James Version translates verse 25 with this idea: 'who can eat, or who else can hasten hereunto.'[158] There are two passages where this verb refers to an inward disturbance (Isa. 28:16; Job 20:2). F. Ellermeier connects $ḥwš$ to the Akkadian word $ḥâšu$, which means 'to worry.'[159] Although one cannot be completely certain, it is possible to see a semantic relationship between 'hurry' and some kind of inward disturbance like panic or '*worry*.'[160] In this view Qohelet would be saying that two things come from the hand of God, one positive and one negative: '*for who can eat and who can worry apart from him?*' The eating would be positive and the '*worry*' would be negative. It is precisely these two things that Qohelet has discovered in his work: the anxiety that one has because there is no profit in labor and the limited enjoyment that comes from labor. Thus 2:25 explains what is from the hand of God.[161] The rhetorical

---

157. Seow (*Ecclesiastes*, 140) relates the verb $ḥwš$ to the Arabic $ḥâša$, 'to gather,' and translates it 'who will glean.'

158. Hengstenberg (*Ecclesiastes*, 85), who understands the meaning of the verb $ḥwš$ as 'hurry,' explains 2:25 this way: 'The avaricious man does not hasten to eat, for his eye is looking into the uncertain future, but he delays therein and stores up his pleasures against another day.'

159. F. Ellermeier, 'Das Verbum חוש in Koh 2,25: Eine exegetische auslegungsgeschichtliche und semasiologische Untersuchung,' *ZAW* 75 (1963): 197–217.

160. Fox (*Ecclesiastes*, 189) and Longman (*Ecclesiastes*, 108).

161. 2:25 begins with a causal *kî*.

question '*who?*' expects a negative answer so that God is the One who determines whether one finds enjoyment or not (see 5:18–6:2).[162]

In 2:26 Qohelet sets forth the example of two types of people who parallel the two things stated in 2:25. The one '*who can eat*' in 2:25 parallels the '*one who is good* (*ṭôḇ*) *before God*' in 2:26, and the one '*who can worry*' in 2:25 parallels the '*sinner*' (*ḥôṭēʾ*) in 2:26. However, there is debate concerning the meaning of the words *ṭôḇ* and *ḥôṭēʾ*, which affects how one understands 2:26. One view is that the words *ṭôḇ* and *ḥôṭēʾ* have moral connotations ('*good*' and '*sinner*') and that 2:26 is stating the traditional view of divine retribution: God gives certain gifts to the good, and all that the sinner works for ends up in the hands of those who are good. This is very similar to the teaching in Proverbs 13:22 and 28:8, which Qohelet affirms in 2:26.[163] In this view, the grievous task of 1:13 is now seen to be the work of the sinner,[164] whose efforts lead nowhere, and the final *hebel* statement refers only to the frustrating work of the sinner.[165] Qohelet's advice is seen as very positive. Others argue that the terms *ṭôḇ* and *ḥôṭēʾ* do not have any moral connotation in this passage because in the context Qohelet denies any distinction between such groups of people.[166] He has just said that the fortunate recipient may be a fool (2:19) and that the unfortunate man may toil in wisdom (2:21).[167] So why would Qohelet think it *hebel* if good things happen to

---

162. Crenshaw, *Ecclesiastes*, 90. Fox (*Ecclesiastes*, 185, 189) understands the phrase 'apart from him' in the sense of 'except as he determines,' which means unless God wills it.

163. Whybray, *Ecclesiastes*, 64–65. Lauha (*Kohelet*, 58) also affirms that the terms of 2:26 have a moral connotation and that 2:26 is affirming the traditional view of divine retribution, but he believes it is a dogmatic correction of a redactor. Not everyone who argues that Qohelet affirms the teaching of 2:26 believes that the words *ṭôḇ* and *ḥôṭēʾ* have moral connotation (see Ogden and Zogbo, *Handbook on Ecclesiastes*, 82–83).

164. Provan, *Ecclesiastes*, 77.

165. Wright, 'Ecclesiastes,' 5:1159. Others who limit the final *hebel* statement in 2:26 to the work of the 'sinner' (*ḥôṭēʾ*) include Eaton, Garrett, and Hengstenberg.

166. Murphy, *Ecclesiastes*, 26.

167. Fox, *Ecclesiastes*, 189.

good people and bad things happen to bad people (2:26)?[168] In this view the ḥôṭēʾ is not a sinner in terms of breaking a law, but is one who is offensive in some way and has incurred God's disfavor. Fox notes that just as someone can irritate a king and bring disfavor to himself, so one can irritate God (1 Kings 1:21; 8:31; Gen. 40:1; Prov. 20:2; Eccles. 10:4).[169] Seow defines ḥôṭēʾ as one who bungles things all the time and cannot do anything right (Prov. 13:22; 14:21; 19:2).[170] Crenshaw defines the ṭôḇ and the ḥôṭēʾ as the fortunate and the unfortunate or the lucky and the unlucky.[171] Murphy defines the one *'who is good before God'* as the one who does not come under God's disfavor but is the one who pleases Him.[172] The meaning of 2:26 in this view is that a person may work hard in gathering goods but God is the One who disposes of those goods in an arbitrary way apart from a person's conduct. It is the disconnection between the effort and the result that makes the whole scenario *hebel*, not just the actions of the ḥôṭēʾ.[173]

Although the terms ṭôḇ and ḥôṭēʾ may at times lack a clear moral connotation in Ecclesiastes (9:18; 10:4), Fox recognizes that such uses occur when the terms are used with other humans.[174] However, when the terms are used with God, it is hard to omit the moral connotation, even in Ecclesiastes (7:20, 26; 8:12-13; 9:2).[175] If such is the case, then 2:26 reflects the teaching of Proverbs 13:22: 'the sinner's (ḥôṭēʾ) wealth is laid up for the righteous.' Qohelet states such a teaching not because he agrees with it, but because it does not work as he has observed the world. Thus in 2:24 Qohelet states his resigned conclusion that one might as well enjoy what comes from labor, which is from the hand of God. Then 2:25 explains

---

168. Longman, *Ecclesiastes*, 110.
169. Fox, *Ecclesiastes*, 189.
170. Seow, *Ecclesiastes*, 141.
171. Crenshaw, *Ecclesiastes*, 90.
172. Murphy, *Ecclesiastes*, 26.
173. Fox, *Ecclesiastes*, 186, 191.
174. Fox, *Ecclesiastes*, 190.
175. Fox (*Ecclesiastes*, 190) acknowledges that there is a moral aspect in 7:20; 8:12; and 9:2, so that the translation 'sinner' is correct in these verses.

what it is that comes from the hand of God. Not only the enjoyment of labor comes from the hand of God, but also the worry and frustration related to work comes from the hand of God. Further explanation of what God gives comes in 2:26. He gives to the good person wisdom, knowledge, and pleasure, but to the sinner he gives the task of gathering wealth, which is only going to go to the one who is good. This scenario is what one would hope would happen because then the good person would be rewarded and the sinner would end up in frustration by having their goods given to the righteous. Although this view of 2:26 stands against what Qohelet has argued in 2:18-23, it gives a glimpse of hope for what could happen. Things could turn out right, but that hope is dashed at the end of 2:26: '*this also is senseless and chasing after the wind.*' Such a statement is not limited to the work of the sinner, but in light of the context of 2:18-23 includes the whole scenario of work and the enjoyment of the results of labor. Ultimately, one cannot be sure whether enjoyment or worry will come from the hand of God.

Homiletical Implications

Qohelet's advice in 2:24-26 is his resigned conclusion in a world that does not work out the way one would hope 'under the sun.' This advice is not an exhortation toward hedonism because he recognizes that in some respects wisdom is better than folly (2:12-17). Later in the book he will show that a foolish person can do much damage. So it is not as if one should throw off all restraints and pursue a life devoted to pleasure (see 7:15-18). Such a life can lead to negative consequences that are harmful and painful. On the other hand, eating, drinking, and enjoying the benefit from labor is not the answer to life's problems. Although these are gifts from God, the disjunction between the effort put forth in labor and the outcome of labor falls short of what one would expect. Instead of affirming that the results of the labor of the sinner will eventually go to the righteous (Prov. 13:22), Qohelet denies that outcome, which only leaves the enjoyment of the fruits of one's own labor now while that enjoyment is possible. There is no encouragement by Qohelet to eat, drink, and find enjoyment in the results of labor to the glory of God (1 Cor. 10:31). Such a perspective would have required Qohelet to look beyond the horizons of this world to the judgment that is coming.

3.
The search for understanding the role of human beings: does God make any difference? (3:1-22)

Ecclesiastes 3 is connected to what has gone before in many ways. After the introductory poem (3:1-8),[1] the question concerning labor is asked again (3:9), a question found in the prologue to the book (1:3) and in the first major section of the book (2:10-11, 22). Also, 3:10 reflects 1:13, 3:14-15 reflects 1:9, and 3:12 and 22 reflects 2:24-26. Thus 3:1-22 carries on the search begun in the first section of the book. However, there is a different emphasis in 3:1-22. Up to this point in the book God (Elohim) is mentioned only four times. Two of the four times occur in a statement that expresses an orthodox understanding of how things should work in terms of the results of labor (2:26). In chapter 3, however, God is more prominent in that He is mentioned eight times. The question concerning profit to labor is broadened to include the proper role and function of human beings within the world in relation to God.[2] Does God

---

1. Most commentators call Ecclesiastes 3:1-8 a poem, but Whybray (*Ecclesiastes*, 66) sees it as a list (onomastica) similar to the numerical sayings in Proverbs 30:7-31.

2. Ogden (*Qoheleth*, 55) comments that in Ecclesiastes 3 the emphasis moves to what God does and to humanity's place in God's world. Lohfink (*Qoheleth*, 59) also sees a change of focus in Ecclesiastes 3: what was spoken in worldly terms before is now spoken with reference to God.

133

make any difference to the questions raised and the answers given concerning labor and the results of labor? Some answer this question in a very positive way. For example, Eaton titles 3:1-15 as 'The Providence of God' and sees it as contributing to the solution to the problem of the vanity of life.[3] Others assert that now we see life from God's point of view, an 'above the sun' perspective, instead of being limited to the earth-bound perspective of the previous section.[4] God is shown to be at work in our lives accomplishing His will, and if human beings cooperate with God's timing life will not be meaningless.[5] However, an examination of chapter 3 will show that although God is more prominent in this section, He does not provide for Qohelet an answer to his questions. Frustration related to labor and its results are still prevalent and at the end of the chapter the role and place of humanity within creation is not settled because the future is uncertain.

There is general agreement that 3:1 begins a new section. Not only does 2:24-26 conclude the previous section (1:12–2:26), but the beginning of chapter 3 changes literary style and content with the poem on time (3:1-8). However, there is not agreement concerning where the section ends. Murphy argues that section divisions should be guided by the refrain of *hebel* and 'chasing after the wind' so he takes 3:1–4:6 as a section.[6] Crenshaw divides the text into 3:1-15 and 3:16–4:3, with the latter held together by the theme of divine retribution.[7] It is better to take chapter 3 as a major section that deals with the role and function of human beings in light of what is said about God. Thus chapter 3 has a vertical dimension. However,

---

3. Eaton, *Ecclesiastes*, 78. Kaiser (*Ecclesiastes*, 60) understands 3:1-8 as setting forth the eternal and comprehenive plan of God which gives comfort to God's people.

4. Stuart Olyott, *A Life Worth Living and a Lord Worth Loving* (Durham: Evangelical Press, 1983), 27 and Jim Winter, *Opening Up Ecclesiastes* (Leominster: Day One Publications, 2005), 50.

5. Warren W. Wiersbe, 'Time and Toil: Ecclesiastes 3,' in Roy B. Zuck (ed.), *Reflecting with Solomon: Selected Studies on the Book of Ecclesiastes* (Grand Rapids: Eerdmans, 1994), 264.

6. Murphy, *Ecclesiastes*, 31–32.

7. Crenshaw, *Ecclesiastes*, 91–92.

God is not mentioned in chapter 4, where the emphasis is on horizontal relationships among human beings. Although it is possible to take 4:1-3 as continuing the theme of injustice from chapter 3, the focus on human relationships makes it a good fit with the rest of chapter 4. God will be brought back into the picture at the beginning of chapter 5.

It is common to divide chapter 3 into two sections. Ecclesiastes 3:16-22 reflects on the issue of injustice, which raises the issues of God as judge and the relationship of human beings to animals. Ecclesiastes 3:1-15 sets forth a poem on time (3:1-8) and then reflects on the question of labor in light of God's involvement with human beings and the world (3:9-15). First, a translation of 3:1-8 is offered, followed by a discussion of the meaning of the poem, and then 3:9-15 will be examined.

The poem on time (Eccles. 3:1-8)

3:1 *For everything there is a season, a time for every activity under heaven.*

3:2 *A time to be born[8] and a time to die,*
A time to plant and a time to uproot what is planted.

3:3 *A time to kill and a time to heal,*
A time to tear down and a time to build up.

---

8. Commentators are divided over how *lāleḏeṯ* (a qal active infinitive construct of *yālaḏ*) is to be translated. There are strong arguments on both sides of the question. Some argue that the active infinitive should be translated 'to give birth.' If the verb was passive ('to be born') it would use the nifal *hiwwālēḏ*, which occurs in Ecclesiastes 7:1. The active sense is also supported by the ancient versions, except the Vulgate (Murphy, *Ecclesiastes*, 29). Crenshaw (*Ecclesiastes*, 93) argues that 'to give birth' provides a better parallel with 'to plant.' Joseph Blenkinsopp ('Ecclesiastes 3:1-15: Another Interpretation,' *JSOT* 66 [1995]: 56–57) takes the unusual step of arguing from the translation 'to give birth' that the parallel term should be translated 'to put an end to one's life' (suicide) because all the rest of the actions of the poem are under human control. There are also good reasons to translate *lāleḏeṯ* as 'to be born.' One argument is that the comparison with 'to die' supports the translation 'to be born' because the perspective of both would be from the same person's point of view (Delitzsch, 'Ecclesiastes,' 6:256), which is not the view of the parents (Whybray, *Ecclesiastes*, 70). Fox (*Ecclesiastes*, 207) argues that the parallel of 'to give birth' would be 'to kill,' not 'to die.' There are also other places where an active infinitive is used with passive force, such as Jeremiah 25:34 (Delitzsch, 'Ecclesiastes,' 6:256).

3:4 *A time to weep and a time to laugh,*
A time to mourn and a time to dance.

3:5 *A time to throw stones, and a time to gather stones,*
A time to embrace and a time to refrain from embracing.

3:6 *A time to seek and a time to give up as lost,*[9]
A time to keep and a time to throw away.

3:7 *A time to tear apart and a time to sew,*
A time to be silent and a time to speak.

3:8 *A time to love and a time to hate,*
A time for war and a time for peace.[10]

There is much discussion concerning the meaning of the poem on time (3:1-8) in light of the comments that follow (3:9-15). There is a tendency to let one's view of one section affect how one views the other section. For example, some understand the poem to be a positive statement concerning God's providence, which is followed by Qohelet's comments, which reinforce the positive message of the poem.[11] On the other hand, a number of commentators understand the message of the poem to reflect a divine determinism in life which has a negative effect on the human condition, which is further developed in Qohelet's comments in 3:9-15. For example, Gordis argues that 3:9-15 is the key for understanding the poem on time, which expresses that all human actions are determined by God.[12] The flaw in these two approaches is

---

9. The phrase *'to give up as lost'* is a piel infinitive with the piel having a declarative sense (Murphy, *Ecclesiastes*, 29; Longman, *Ecclesiastes*, 112, n. 4). Fox (*Ecclesiastes*, 208) disputes that the piel is declarative and translates the phrase as 'a time to lose,' which may refer to losses that are fortuitous.

10. The last two pairs of the poem (love, hate, and war, peace) are chiastically arranged (A, B, B′, A′), with the final two pairs using nouns instead of the qal infinitive. This seems to bring closure to the poem (Whybray, *Ecclesiastes*, 72 and Delitzsch, 'Ecclesiastes,' 6:259). Also, hate does not necessarily imply something that is sinful, which is clear in its use in Deuteronomy 12:31 (Bartholomew, *Ecclesiastes*, 165).

11. Ogden, *Ecclesiastes*, 55–58 (see also Eaton, *Ecclesiastes*, 77–83 and Leupold, *Ecclesiastes*, 79–93).

12. Gordis, *Koheleth*, 144 (see also Crenshaw, *Ecclesiastes*, 101; Murphy, *Ecclesiastes*, 39; Ginsburg, *Coheleth*, 303; and Delitzsch, 'Ecclesiastes,' 6:254-255).

that the former reads the positive nature of the poem into the comments of Qohelet which follow, and the latter reads the negative comments of Qohelet which follow the poem back into the poem itself. It is better to let the poem stand on its own and then to see the progression of thought that develops in Qohelet's comments in 3:9-15.

It is hard to avoid the beauty of the balance and the rhythm of the poem on time as there are fourteen pairs of opposites, with each pair beginning with the word *'time'* (*'ēṯ*). However, that the focus of the poem is on divine determination that makes human action fruitless is not obvious. God is not even mentioned in the poem.[13] Plus, all the times listed, except for the first pair (*'a time to be born and a time to die'*) speak of times that require human action to do something.[14] For example, there may be *'a time to plant,'* but if people do not act to plant at the right time, the opportunity is lost. Thus the poem is setting forth the traditional view that wisdom includes not only knowing the right time to act, but also acting according to the right time. Proverbs 15:23 uses the word *'time'* (*'ēṯ*) to refer to how good a word is when spoken at the right time (*'in its time,'* see also Prov. 25:11). Proverbs 10:4-5 speaks of the importance of gathering during harvest time and 20:18 mentions waging war *'by wise guidance,'* which emphasizes thoughtful preparation for action.[15] Thus the purpose of the poem is to set forth a positive picture of the world in accordance with traditional wisdom teaching. It is a world which is purposeful and which people can understand in order to make wise decisions.

This understanding of the poem is reinforced by an analysis of the meaning of the words *'time'* (*'ēṯ*) and *'season'* (*zĕmān*). Both can refer to a point in time or a period of time in which an event occurs.[16] Fox argues that these words do

---

13. Ogden and Zogbo, *Handbook on Ecclesiastes*, 88 and W. Sibley Towner, 'The Book of Ecclesiastes,' in *The New Interpreter's* Bible, 12 vols. (Nashville: Abingdon Press, 1997), 5:305.

14. However, even *'a time to be born'* could be understood from the perspective of human action because Hosea 13:13 speaks of the wisdom of the timing of birth from the *child's* standpoint.

15. Longman, *Proverbs*, 382.

16. See the discussions by Anthony Tomasino concerning 'זמן (*zmn*),'

not refer to a specific time or date, such as the date on which World War II started, but to occasions or situations in which something might occur, such as the conditions that brought about the start of World War II. Thus the times described in the poem are typical and not specific. Every type of event has a set of circumstances in which it is appropriate for that event to take place. Such a set of circumstances may be unique, such as the circumstances that brought about World War II, or they may be periodic, such as the times for planting and uprooting. The poem, then, speaks about the right times, the circumstances when something should be done, not the times when things will inevitably occur.[17] When the time is right, human action is required.

A few comments on the structure of the poem and the meaning of some of the pairs are in order. Some go out of their way to try to find some relationship among the pairs. For example, Loader labels each item in the pairs as desirable and undesirable, and finds an intricate structure of chiasms within chiasms.[18] Perhaps the most that can be said is that the pairings usually have a negative and a positive component, which means that even the negative, destructive events have their right time; however, to see some larger pattern is not necessarily fruitful.[19] Others seem to over-interpret the poem by going into lengthy explanations of what each of the times means, even trying to explain each pair in relationship to what has gone before or what comes after.[20] But Whybray argues

---

in *NIDOTTE*, 1:1114-1115 and 'עֵת (*'ēṭ*),' in *NIDOTTE*, 3:563-567, as well as Ernst Jenni, '*ta 'ēṭ time*,' in *TLOT*, 2:951-961. Both Longman (*Ecclesiastes*, 113) and Murphy (*Ecclesiastes*, 29) note that it is difficult to draw a clear distinction between these two words.

17. Fox (*Rereading Ecclesiastes*, 194–206) has the best discussion of the concept of '*time*' in Ecclesiastes 3:1-8.

18. J. A. Loader, 'Qohelet 3, 2–8: A "Sonnet" in the Old Testament,' *ZAW* 81 (1969): 240–242.

19. See Fox's simple chart of a plus or a minus placed next to each item (*Rereading Ecclesiastes*, 193). See also the criticisms of Loader's analysis by Seow, *Ecclesiastes*, 170–171.

20. See Hengstenburg (*Ecclesiastes*, 93–103) for an overanalysis of the pairs in the poem and Delitzsch ('Ecclesiastes,' 6:254-258) for seeing some kind of meaning in the relationship between the pairs in the poem.

THE SEARCH FOR UNDERSTANDING THE ROLE OF HUMAN BEINGS   139

that although there may be a thematic relationship within the pairs, one should not try to see thematic relationships between pairs on a larger scale within the poem.[21] There does not seem to be a meaningful relationship between the pairs in 3:7. It also may be fruitless to try to nail down a specific meaning to each pair[22] because there may be multiple possibilities depending on the context in which a phrase is used. For example, there is much discussion concerning the meaning of the phrase *'a time to uproot what is planted'* (3:2). Ginsburg argues that it refers to the harvest and not to the destruction of an enemy's field.[23] Fox, on the other hand, does not believe it is referring to the harvest, but to the deliberate destruction of vegetation, as when clearing a field for new cultivation or as an act of war. He does not see it as a seasonal chore but as a sporadic act of destruction.[24] Whybray argues that the phrase refers to when a fruit tree or vine needs to be destroyed because it is no longer bearing fruit.[25] It may be better not to nail down the meaning of the phrase because all three possibilities could work depending on the context. Life context is important for making decisions, which is evident when one compares Proverbs 26:4-5. The wise person will know what kind of fool one is dealing with and will respond appropriately. The most disputed pair is in 3:5a: *'a time to throw stones and a time to gather stones.'* The Jewish rabbis understood this as a reference to sexual intercourse. When the wife is clean (menstrually) it is time to throw stones and when the wife is unclean it is time to gather stones.[26] Although a few commentators take this view,[27] there is little evidence that

---

21. Whybray, *Ecclesiastes*, 70.

22. Ogden (*Qoheleth*, 57) notes that in trying to ascertain the meaning of the poem as a whole it is not necessary to assign a meaning to every element.

23. Ginsburg, *Coheleth*, 305.

24. Fox, *Ecclesiastes*, 20–21.

25. Whybray, *Ecclesiastes*, 70.

26. See the explanation in Longman, *Ecclesiastes*, 116 and Murphy, *Ecclesiastes*, 33.

27. Towner, 'Ecclesiastes,' 5:305 and Loader, 'The Grip of Time: Ecclesiastes 3:1-8,' in Roy B. Zuck (ed.), *Reflecting with Solomon: Selective Studies on the Book of Ecclesiastes* (Grand Rapids: Baker, 1994), 260. Athalya Brenner ('M Text Authority in Biblical Love Lyrics: The Case of Qoheleth 3:1-9 and

throwing stones refers to a sexual relationship. The parallel with *'a time to embrace'* does not necessarily support a sexual reference because there are many ways of showing affection, such as greetings, welcomes, and separations.[28] Other possibilities for the meaning of this pair include the demolishing of a building and then the preparation for rebuilding,[29] the accumulation and distribution of wealth in the gathering of precious stones,[30] the clearing of a field for agricultural use (Isa. 5:2) and, by contrast, the ruining of an enemy's field (2 Kings 3:19, 25).[31]

Qohelet's reflections on the poem on time: the frustrating work of God (Eccles. 3:9-15)

3:9 *What profit does the worker have from his toil?*

3:10 *I have seen the task which God has given to human beings to occupy them.*[32]

3:11 *He has made everything appropriate in its*[33] *time. He has also*[34] *put a sense of totality into their hearts except that*

---

its Textual Relatives,' in Athalya Brenner and Fokkelien Van DijkHemmes [eds.], *On Gendering Texts: Female and Male Voices in the Hebrew Bible* [Leiden: Köln, 1993], 133–164) not only understands 3:5 to express a sexual meaning, she sees it as the central stanza and reinterprets the whole poem to express the fluidity of love and sexual desire from a male perspective.

28. Longman, *Ecclesiastes*, 115.

29. The Targum takes this view, as do Ginsburg (*Cohelet*, 306) and Wright ('Ecclesiastes,' 5:1161).

30. Provan, *Ecclesiastes*, 88.

31. Delitzsch, 'Ecclesiastes,' 6:257; Longman, *Ecclesiastes*, 116; Fox, *Rereading Ecclesiastes*, 208; and Whybray, *Ecclesiastes*, 71.

32. For justification of the translation *'to occupy them'* see the discussion of the translation of 1:13 and 5:20.

33. Although Crenshaw (*Ecclesiastes*, 97) comments that it is impossible to determine whether the 3ms suffix refers to God ('his time') or to the abstract idea of time ('its time'), there is a better option. The $‘\bar{e}t$ of the phrase $b\check{e}‘itt\hat{o}$ refers back to the times of the poem in 3:1-8, which is not the abstract idea of time but a reference to the appropriate times delineated there, which supports the translation *'in its time.'*

34. How one translates *gam* ('also') depends on how one conceives the

> *people cannot discover the work that God does*[35] *from beginning to end.*
>
> 3:12 *I perceived that there is nothing better*[36] *for them*[37] *but to be glad and to enjoy themselves*[38] *during their*[39] *lives.*

relationship between 3:11a and 3:11b. If the relationship is adversative, with the meaning 'however' or 'yet' (Seow, *Ecclesiastes*, 162), then 3:11b is a qualification of the statement in 3:11a. If, however, the *gam* is a simple addition, translated '*also*,' then 3:11a and 3:11b are parallel and complementary (Whybray, *Ecclesiastes*, 73). The qualification would then come in the clause beginning with '*except that*' (*mibbĕlî 'ăšer*), which is the approach followed in this commentary. See the commentary for discussion of the relationship between 3:11a and 3:11b.

35. The use of the perfect verbs in this passage expresses a general truth and thus should be rendered by the present tense (Whybray, *Ecclesiastes*, 72).

36. A literal translation of the beginning of 3:12 would be 'I know there is nothing good among them except ...' (Seow, *Ecclesiastes*, 158). Ogden ('The "Nothing is Better" Form,' 339–340) argues that in comparing the *'ên ṭôḇ* statements in 2:24; 3:12; 3:22; and 8:15 Qohelet is not consistent in his use of the form (also, 5:18 and 9:7-10 express the same sentiments without the use of the form). Thus the best translation is '*there is nothing better.*' However, the meaning of the verse is not much different even with a literal translation of 3:12. See the discussion of Seow (*Ecclesiastes*, 173) and Barton (*Ecclesiastes*, 101–102), who translate 3:12 with a literal meaning but understand the verse to be affirming that humans are to live life fully in the present.

37. Contrary to Gordis (*Koheleth*, 222), the prepositional phrase *bām* ('*for them*') should not be deleted due to dittography (a scribal error involving the duplication of consonants) because it parallels *bā'āḏām* in 2:24. The proposed emendation in the Hebrew text (*Biblia Hebraica Stuttgartensia*) of changing *bām* to *bā'āḏām* is not necessary. As Murphy (*Ecclesiastes*, p. 35) points out, the plural suffix refers back to the collective *'āḏām* ('people') in 3:11.

38. The phrase *la'ăśôṯ ṭôḇ* literally reads 'to do good' and is understood by some to have a moral meaning because it has a moral meaning in other places in Biblical Hebrew (Num. 24:14; Pss. 37:3, 27; Ps. 119:65) and also in Ecclesiastes 7:20 (Fredericks, *Qohelet's Language*, 247). However, most commentators do not find a moral connotation in this phrase here because the phrase *la'ăśôṯ ṭôḇ* parallels the phrase *rā'āh ṭôḇ* (literally 'see good' but translated 'find enjoyment') in 3:13a (Delitzsch, 'Ecclesiastes,' 6:262; Ginsburg, *Coheleth*, 311; Longman, *Ecclesiastes*, 122; Murphy, *Ecclesiastes*, 30; Seow, *Ecclesiastes*, 164; and Whybray, *Ecclesiastes*, 74).

39. Crenshaw (*Ecclesiastes*, 98) notes that the 3ms suffix is collective referring back to the 3mp suffix in the phrase *bām* ('*for them*').

3:13 And also,[40] *every person who eats and drinks and finds enjoyment in all his labour*[41] — *that is a gift of God.*

3:14 *I perceived that everything which God does will be forever. Nothing can be added to it and nothing can be taken from it.*[42] *God acts*[43] *in order that they will fear*[44] *him.*

3:15 *Whatever is has already been, and whatever will be has already been. And*[45] *God seeks what has been sought.*

These verses are Qohelet's comments in light of the poem on time. The question concerning profit from labor is followed

---

40. As Barton (*Ecclesiastes*, 102) points out, the word '*also*' (*gam*) continues and completes the thought of 3:12 and is dependent on the verb '*I perceived*' (*yāḏaʿtî*) in 3:12.

41. The syntax of this verse is difficult because the first part of the verse is not a complete sentence, but the thought is broken off (called anacoluthon) and is followed by a short, independent sentence (Longman, *Ecclesiastes*, 122). There is no need to supply the conditional particle *kî* after *gam* so that *mattaṯ* ('*gift*') forms an apodosis (Ginsburg, *Coheleth*, 312).

42. Deuteronomy 4:1-2 and 12:32 use the same verbs to refer to the prohibition of adding or subtracting from the laws of God. Longman (*Ecclesiastes*, 123) points out that it is not unusual to find such a proverbial statement used in other contexts. There is a slight difference between the two passages. The Deuteronomy passages stress prohibition and deal with the divine *word*, but Ecclesiastes stresses the impossibility of changing the divine *deeds* (Murphy, *Ecclesiastes*, 35).

43. Some translations add a direct object to the verb; for example, the ESV translates the clause as 'God has done it' (see also the KJV and the NIV). However, there is no direct object in the Hebrew and one is not needed because the focus is on God's activity (Longman, *Ecclesiastes*, 123). Although the verb ʿāśāh is in the perfect aspect, which has the connotation of completed action ('God acted'), it is translated '*acts*' because God's activity is not just in the past but continues in the present (the proverbial use of the perfect which denotes actions that are considered to be general truths [Arnold and Choi, *Biblical Hebrew Syntax*, 56]).

44. Ogden (*Qohelet*, 62) argues that the verb is not *yārēh* ('fear') but is *rāʾāh* ('see'). He translates it with the sense that God has done this so that they might see what proceeds from Him, which he thinks fits the context better where the emphasis is on what humanity can or cannot discover concerning the divine activity. However, no one else follows Ogden in this view, and this view is not mentioned in the *Handbook on Ecclesiastes* by Ogden and Zogbo.

45. It is possible that the *waw* on Elohim ('*God*') should be understood as causal, with the function of assigning a reason for the previous assertion (Ginsburg, *Coheleth*, 313).

by an observation concerning God's works in this world (3:10-11), and two conclusions (3:12-13 and 14-15). The role and meaning of the question in 3:9 is an important issue. Some take 3:9 to be a negative conclusion to the poem itself, which reinforces the idea that human effort has no profit because the times are determined by God.[46] But this reads a negative, divine determinism, supposedly expressed in the poem on time, into the question of 3:9. It is not only doubtful that the poem expresses a divine determinism that negatively impacts human activity (see the discussion in the previous section), but it is also better to understand 3:9 to be a rhetorical question that begins Qohelet's comments on the poem on time. The question of 3:9 restates the question that was asked at the beginning of the book in 1:3 and was restated in 2:22. The question of 1:3 was answered in 2:10-11: although there can be a portion (*ḥēleq*) one can enjoy from labor, there is no profit (*yitrôn*) to labor. In 2:22 the question of the benefit to labor is raised again to show that even the portion from labor does not bring meaning to life, although it is to be enjoyed (2:24-26). So why does Qohelet repeat the question in 3:9 following the poem on time? The poem on time has set forth the view that there are appropriate times for humans to take action. Wise people are able to understand the times and make good decisions (Prov. 15:23; 25:11). Surely in such a world there would be a profit to human activity. Thus Qohelet sets forth a view of the world in line with traditional wisdom thinking and then asks the rhetorical question concerning *'profit'* to see whether his negative conclusions still stand. He also adapts the question in 3:9 to the poem on time. The question in 1:3 used the generic term for humanity (*'āḏām*), but the question in 3:9 uses the term *'worker'* (*'ôśeh*). This term is broader than the idea of one who labors and includes any type of human

---

46. Fox (*Rereading Ecclesiastes*, 192) and Hubbard (*Ecclesiastes*, 104) state that the conclusion of 3:9 shows that there is no profit in toiling. Murphy (*Ecclesiastes*, 29) calls 3:9 a conclusion that leaps ahead of the data and is explained by 3:10-15. Others, such as Delitzsch, Ginsburg, Barton, and Crenshaw, do not call 3:9 a conclusion to the poem, but understand 3:9 in a negative way because of the view that the poem sets forth divine determinism.

activity.⁴⁷ Although labor is still in view because of the use of the term toil (*'āmāl*), the general term for human acitivity brings into view all the human acitivities stated in the poem on time. Thus the question becomes whether there is any profit to human activities which are accomplished in their appropriate times. Does such a positive view of the times change his negative conclusions concerning profit to human labor and activity?

Qohelet makes an empirical observation in 3:10-11 (*'I have seen,' rā'îtî*) in response to the question of 3:9.⁴⁸ The statement of 3:10 is very similar to the statement in 1:13, as both refer to the task that God has given to people to occupy them. In 1:13 the statement is in the context of Qohelet's preliminary conclusions before he gives an account of his search for meaning 'under the sun' to see if there is profit in labor. The task of humans is broad, as it entails all the activities Qohelet discusses in 1:12–2:26. The task in 3:10, in light of the times in the poem of 3:1-8, involves knowing when to act at the right time, which would produce profit. However, in 3:11 it becomes clear that it is impossible to act at the right time, which implicitly means that one should not expect profit from labor. Although Qohelet does not specifically state in this section that there is no profit from labor, there are enough parallels with previous statements in 1:12–2:26 that such a conclusion is inevitable. Thus, even though God is brought into the picture in a more prominent way, Qohelet's conclusions do not change.

There are several important issues raised in 3:11 as God's role in the task He has given to people is emphasized, with implications then drawn as to what impact this has on people. The first part of 3:11 states that God '*has made everything appropriate in its time.*' The word translated '*appropriate*' can mean 'beautiful' when it refers to something physical, like human appearance (Gen. 39:6), but when referring to actions

---

47. Seow, *Ecclesiastes*, 162 and Whybray, *Ecclesiastes*, 72.
48. Bartholomew, *Reading Ecclesiastes*, 243. Qohelet's empirical observation assumes certain things about God, but his focus is on the task of human beings in this world and the limitations of human knowledge concerning God's activities in this world.

as those listed in 3:1-8, the translation 'appropriate' expresses the meaning better.⁴⁹ It becomes clear that although the times in 3:1-8 are times in which humans need to take action (see the discussion of the poem above), God is the One orchestrating the times. Although many find connections in 3:11 to the creation of the world in Genesis 1,⁵⁰ Fox makes a strong case that *'everything'* in 3:11 goes back to the 'everything' in 3:1. Thus 3:11 refers primarily to the range of events and activities in human life, which are delineated in 3:1-8, and not the major constitutents of creation.⁵¹ However, the times in 3:1-8 cannot totally be separated from God's work of creation because the times reflect the order which God established at creation. The point is that the times and activities in the poem reflect an ordered world, established by God, Who knows how everything fits together in its proper time.

The next statement in 3:11 concerning God's activity has produced a volume of discussion: *'he has put a sense of totality into their hearts.'* The Hebrew text has the word ʻ*ôlām* (traditionally translated 'eternity'), which is handled a number of different ways. One option is to emend ʻ*ôlām* to ʻ*elem* (a change of vowels but not consonants), which means 'darkness' or 'ignorance,' so that 3:11 would read that God put ignorance into the heart of people. This view looks to the Ugaritic word *ģlm* ('to be dark') for support, as well as to Ecclesiastes 12:14 and Job 28:21; 42:3, which use a verbal form of the word. It also fits in with the rest of 3:11, which states that human beings cannot find out what God has done.⁵² Another view, argued by Gordis, is that the word ʻ*ôlām* means

---

49. Longman, *Ecclesiastes*, 112, n. 6. Fox (*Rereading Ecclesiastes*, 209) also notes that *yāpeh* does not have aesthetic value in this context.

50. Possible allusions to Genesis 1 include a connection between '*appropriate*' (*yāpeh*) and 'good' (*ṭôḇ*), as both imply a judgment concerning the suitability of an object (H. J. Stroebe, 'טוב,' *TLOT*, 2:487), and a connection between ʻ*ôlām* ('eternity,' '*a sense of totality*') and humans made in the image of God. Longman (*Ecclesiastes*, 120) comments that it is hard to assess the significance of these allusions.

51. Fox, *Rereading Ecclesiastes*, 209; see also Hubbard, *Ecclesiastes*, 106.

52. Barton, *Ecclesiastes*, 105; also, Whybray (*Ecclesiastes*, 74) leans toward this view.

'world' or 'love of the world,'[53] a meaning that is attested in later Hebrew, but not in Biblical Hebrew.[54] Fox wants to emend ʿôlām to the word ʿāmāl ('toil'), which would mean that this toil is in the heart and so should be understood as a mental labor, which becomes an arduous task to attempt to understand what God has brought to pass.[55] Although one can see how the switching of two Hebrew consonants could take place, there is no manuscript evidence for this emendation of the text. Another common option is to understand ʿôlām to have a temporal meaning, which could have a couple of different nuances. Some argue for the meaning 'eternity' in the sense of that which transcends time.[56] This concept seems to be the predominant meaning of ʿôlām in Ecclesiastes (1:4, 10; 2:16; 3:14; 9:6), including its use just three verses away in 3:14. Ogden takes this meaning in a positive direction to argue that Qohelet wants us to think beyond this temporal life to the life beyond.[57] But as Fox points out, Qohelet has little interest in the life beyond this life (Eccles. 9:10).[58] Also, many who translate ʿôlām with 'eternity' explain the concept in terms of having a desire to move beyond the fragmentary knowledge of our immediate situation in order to know the character and purpose of the events in the world.[59] In other words, Qohelet is not emphasizing life beyond this earthly life, but he is asserting that humans have a desire to see the whole picture of how events fit together in this life so that wise decisions can be made. Several things support this view. Qohelet has been operating with an 'under the sun' perspective, and a temporal meaning that is limited to the totality of life in this world

---

53. Gordis, *Koheleth*, 146.
54. Seow, *Ecclesiastes*, 163.
55. Fox, *Rereading Ecclesiastes*, 211.
56. Seow, *Ecclesiastes*, 164 and Longman, *Ecclesiastes*, 120–121.
57. Ogden and Zogbo, *Handbook on Ecclesiastes*, 100.
58. Fox, *Rereading Ecclesiastes*, 210.
59. Longman, *Ecclesiastes*, 121; Bartholomew, *Reading Ecclesiastes*, 243; Bridges, *Ecclesiastes*, 68; Kaiser, *Ecclesiastes*, 66, and Crenshaw, 'The Eternal Gospel (Eccles. 3:11),' in James L. Crenshaw and J. T. Willis (eds.), *Essays in Old Testament Ethics* (New York: KTAV Publishing House, 1974), 23–55, among others.

would fit that perspective. The knowledge of God or things eternal are never used by Qohelet to solve the problems with which he is wrestling. To understand ʿôlām as a sense of totality would contrast the use of ʾēṯ in the poem, which refer to definite points in time or to periods of time. This meaning is also supported by the concept of everything (hakkōl, 3:1, 11), which is another way of expressing the concept of totality, and by the phrase 'from beginning to end' at the end of 3:11. Thus ʿôlām has been translated in 3:11 as 'a sense of totality.' In conclusion, Ecclesiastes 3:11a asserts that God has made everything appropriate in its time and He has given people the deep-seated desire to understand the character of the world and how everything fits together.

The meaning of 3:11b is not disputed, but its relationship to 3:11a is debated because of the different ways the phrase mibbĕlî ʾăšer is understood. Ecclesiastes 3:11b states that 'people cannot discover the work that God does from beginning to end.' Although mibbĕlî usually has a disjunctive meaning, some opt to translate the phrase 'without which.'[60] Such a rendering could mean that without ʿôlām in their hearts people would not be able to find out the work of God, which makes discovering the work of God a possibility for people. However, if mibbĕlî is taken in a disjunctive sense, there are two common ways it is understood. It could be a purpose clause with the idea that God has deliberately made it impossible for people to discover what He does from end to beginning[61] Or it could be taken as a result clause referring to the limitations of human knowledge without indicating that God deliberately sets up this tension in human experience. In this view the phrase simply introduces a fact that qualifies the preceding clause.[62] The idea is that even though God has put into people's hearts a desire to comprehend how everything fits together, it is an impossible task because people are not

---

60. Deltitzsch, 'Ecclesiastes,' 6:260 and Anthony Tomasino, 'עֹלָם,' NIDOTTE, 3:350.

61. Seow (Ecclesiastes, 172) calls it a purpose or final clause. Isaiah 5:13 and Ezekiel 14:15 would be examples of such usage.

62. Bartholomew, Ecclesiastes, 166–167.

able to understand what God is doing in the world. The problem is not that people cannot discover the work of God in its entirety[63] because, as Fox points out, it would be trivial to hope for absolute knowledge.[64] Rather, it is the limitation of human knowledge that makes the task enigmatic.[65] The problem is that people cannot understand what God is doing in the world as He makes everything appropriate in its time. This makes it difficult for people to make proper decisions at the appropriate times. The desire to understand the world in conjunction with the inability to understand what God is doing leads to frustration. Thus the wisdom teaching of acting at the right time to ensure a profit is thwarted.

Qohelet draws two conclusions based on his observations in 3:10-11. Both conclusions are introduced by the 1cs form of the verb 'to know' (*yāḏa'tî*), translated '*I perceived*' (3:12, 14). The content of 3:12-13 parallels the content of 2:24, Qohelet's conclusion based on his search for meaning, which supports the idea that Qohelet in this section is drawing conclusions based on his observations. He is not setting forth a premise or an additional piece of information,[66] nor is he offering some kind of confession that is more traditional in nature, which is not based on his observations but is in tension with them.[67] The only times (*yāḏa'tî* is used in Ecclesiastes are in 1:17; 2:14; 3:12; and 3:14. It is clear in 1:17 and 2:14 that Qohelet is setting forth something he has discovered or come to realize in his observations and search for meaning. The same is true for 3:12 and 3:14, as these are conclusions he has realized based on his observations.[68] It is easier to see this in 3:12, which parallels 2:24, but even in 3:14 the statements concerning God are not

---

63. As Eaton argues (*Ecclesiastes*, 81).
64. Fox, *Rereading Ecclesiastes*, 212.
65. Bartholomew, *Reading Ecclesiastes*, 243.
66. Garrett, *Ecclesiastes*, 299.
67. Bartholomew, *Reading Ecclesiastes*, 244. Bartholomew (*Ecclesiastes*, 168) comments that the two 'I know' responses in this section are more of a confessional nature.
68. Those who see 3:12 and 3:14 as a conclusion include Ginsburg (*Coheleth*, 311), Murphy (*Ecclesiastes*, 35), Longman (*Ecclesiastes*, 121), and Ogden and Zogbo (*Handbook on Ecclesiastes*, 102).

THE SEARCH FOR UNDERSTANDING THE ROLE OF HUMAN BEINGS   149

positive, which one would expect in a confessional statement. Plus, the ideas in 3:14-15 reflect the argument in 1:9-10. Qohelet draws his first conclusion in 3:12-13, which deals with the proper human response to the observation of 3:10-11. The parallels between this conclusion and the conclusion in 2:24 include the following: both come in response to the question concerning profit (*yitrôn*) in relationship to human activity, both include the concepts of eating, drinking, and finding enjoyment in life, and both recognize that if one is able to enjoy these basic pleasures that is a gift from the hand of God. Thus the conclusion of 2:24 still stands even after Qohelet presents the poem of appropriate times. There is no profit from human activity because people cannot understand what God is doing in the world (3:11b), and so they are unable to make the appropriate decisions at the proper times. Thus, the best response is to enjoy life, which is not a positive conclusion,[69] but like 2:24 is the best that someone can do in light of the frustration of not being able to understand what God is doing in the world.

Qohelet draws a second conclusion in 3:14-15 based on his observation in 3:10-11. This conclusion is also introduced by the 1cs of the verb 'to know' (*yāda'tî*), translated '*I perceived*' ('I came to know or realize'). The first conclusion in 3:12-13 focused on the proper human response to the fact that people cannot discover the work of God (3:11b). The second conclusion focuses on God's activities and explains why people will never be able to understand God's work in the world: '*everything which God does will be forever*.' The idea here is that God's activity takes on the character of '*ôlām* ('*forever*'), which has important implications for our inability to understand God's work.[70] Characterizing God's work as

---

69. Contra Leupold, *Ecclesiastes*, 91; Ogden and Zogbo, *Handbook on Ecclesiastes*, 102; and Whybray, *Ecclesiastes*, 74. Eaton (*Ecclesiastes*, 82) even comments that in this section Qohelet moves from secularism to theism, pessimism to optimism, and human autonomy to human faith; however, the parallels between 3:12-13 and 2:24 show that Qohelet's conclusions have not changed even though God has a more prominent place in the discussion.

70. Seow (*Ecclesiastes*, 174) comments that the idea in 3:15 is not that everything God does will last forever in the sense of duration, which is irrelevant to Qohelet, but that whatever God does is not confined by time.

'ôlām sets his activity beyond the structure of time ('ēṭ) set forth in the times of 3:1-8, which define human activity, and places them in the permanent and unchangeable realm.[71] What God does is not bound by the times in which humans must act within this world. Thus, although humans have a desire to understand God's work, the fact that its character is 'ôlām places His work beyond human comprehension.[72] Human inability to change the situation is emphasized in the fact that 'Nothing can be added to it and nothing can be taken from it.'[73] 3:15 reinforces the permanent, unchangeable nature of God's works. Anything that exists now has already been in existence. And anything that will exist in the future has already been in existence. This is another way for Qohelet to state that 'there is nothing new under the sun' (1:9). Thus Fox comments that 3:15a uses 1:9a to restate 3:14 to show that what is in view in 3:14-15 is the eternal recurrence of the same class of events.[74] What was not clearly stated in 1:9 now becomes clear in 3:15: God is the One who stands behind the repetitive nature of events in that there is nothing new under the sun.

The last clause of 3:15 is a problem clause because there is uncertainty as to its meaning. Whybray notes that perhaps it is a quotation of a popular saying that Qohelet appropriates for his own use, but that the meaning is no longer clear to modern readers.[75] The key factor is the meaning of the participle at the end of the verse, which comes from the verb rāḏap ('to pursue'). One explanation is that it refers to the persecuted, which is followed by most of the ancient

---

71. Murphy, *Ecclesiastes*, 35.

72. The 'ôlām that God has set within the heart of humanity in 3:11 and the 'ôlām that is a part of God's work are no doubt related to each other. Humans are created with a sense of God and with a sense of what transcends time, but are unable, according to Qohelet, to penetrate that realm and so are left without an understanding of God's works in this world.

73. Longman, *Ecclesiastes*, 123. Ginsburg (*Coheleth*, 312) notes that the negative 'ēn before an infinitive with *lamed* denotes inability or impossibility.

74. Fox, *Rereading Ecclesiastes*, 213.

75. Whybray, *Ecclesiastes*, 76.

versions, except the Vulgate.[76] One problem with this view is that it does not seem to fit the context, which deals with events and not persons.[77] However, Garrett connects this clause with 3:16 and sees it as a proleptic introduction to the topic of injustice. He also refers to the use of the verb *rāḏap* in Lamentations 5:5, where the prophet seeks justice for the persecuted.[78] However, the clause at the end of 3:15 goes better with 3:15. Such a transition at the end of 3:15 is abrupt and 3:16 begins a new section. Another suggestion is to take the idea of 'pursue' as a reference to what we as humans are to pursue. In other words, God seeks that we should pursue the task of determining the appropriate times for action, or that we should pursue the gifts of enjoyment and pleasure. This view, which is argued by Ogden,[79] fits his positive understanding of this section of Ecclesiastes. Seow, on the other hand, argues that what is pursued is what people seek in vain. He sees the verb *rāḏap* as a near synonym of *rʿh*, used in the phrase 'pursuit of the wind.' Thus God looks after what people seek in vain in the sense that God takes care of all those matters that are beyond the human grasp. Thus humans should not concern themselves with these matters.[80] However, this view does not reflect the frustration that human beings experience in not being able to discover or understand the work of God. A different nuance of the view that *rāḏap* refers to what man seeks is that only God can pursue what humans seek in the sense that all human attempts to discover the work of God in the world are frustrated.[81] Yet it is significant that the majority of commentators understand the verb *rāḏap* as that which God pursues or seeks, a reference to events in the past which

---

76. See Murphy's discussion (*Ecclesiastes*, 29), where he also lays out the grammatical difficulties with the final clause in 3:15.
77. Murphy, *Ecclesiastes*, 30.
78. Garrett, *Ecclesiastes*, 301.
79. Ogden and Zogbo, *Handbook on Ecclesiastes*, 108.
80. Seow, *Ecclesiastes*, 174.
81. D. Michel, *Untersuchungen zur Eigenart des Buches Qohelet* (Berlin: Walter de Gruyter, 1989), 78.

God pursues in order to call them back into existence. Thus God seeks to do things He has already done.[82] Longman paraphrases the clause as God makes things to happen over and over again.[83] This view fits the immediate context best and reinforces the idea that nothing related to the work of God changes. There is nothing new under the sun because God stands behind the repetitive nature of events in the world.[84]

The last phrase to examine in 3:14-15 is the phrase '*they will fear him.*' The concept of the fear of God is an important concept in Ecclesiastes, but its exact nuance is not always easy to grasp. There is a tendency to assume that the fear of God in Ecclesiastes communicates the same idea as the fear of Yahweh in the book of Proverbs. Hubbard comments that the fear of God is evidence of Qohelet's deep piety and is a call to worship and obedience.[85] Whybray also understands it to refer to a proper attitude of reverence toward God.[86] On the other hand, Crenshaw understands the fear of God as terror before an unpredictable despot, a cold terror because one is in mortal danger when dealing with God.[87] There may be some ambiguity to Qohelet's concept of the fear of God at this point in the book because this is the first time the concept is used. However, the argument of the book of Ecclesiastes must be taken into account in order to grasp

---

82. Fox, *Rereading Ecclesiastes*, 213–214.

83. Longman, *Ecclesiastes*, 113.

84. Bartholomew (*Ecclesiastes*, 169) comments that 3:15 also refers to the order that God has put into creation, which is sustained by Him so that there is always a fitting time and a place for things and activities. This is true, but the problem is that human beings are not able to figure out the fitting time and place to make appropriate decisions. Thus, contra to Bartholomew, 3:12-15 are not a positive answer to 3:9, which are juxtaposed to a negative answer in 3:10-11. The call to enjoyment (3:12-13) is a resigned conclusion because there is no hope that things will change (3:14-15).

85. Hubbard, *Ecclesiastes*, 109.

86. Whybray, *Ecclesiastes*, 74–75.

87. Crenshaw, *Ecclesiastes*, 99–100. Longman (*Ecclesiastes*, 123) comments that God acts the way He does to frighten people into submission, not to arouse respectful awe.

Qohelet's understanding of the fear of God, which leads one to question the identification of the fear of God in the first-person discourse with the fear of Yahweh in Proverbs. In the book of Proverbs the fear of Yahweh is connected to wisdom and the knowledge of God (Prov. 2:5; 9:10). The benefits of wisdom have already been called into question in Ecclesiastes 2:12-17 and in Ecclesiastes 3:11 it is stated that the knowledge of God's works is not available to humanity.[88] Rather, the fear of God is the intended response that God wants people to have in light of the nature of His indiscernible work in the world.[89] Because people are unable to discover what God is doing in this world, there is no assurance that an action will lead to an expected result, which means that people are directionless in their own lives for making decisions. As a result, there is no profit to human labor in this world, but people are left in a state of uncertainty when it comes to God's works in the world.[90] This is not the fear of God that leads to wisdom in knowing how to live and how to make right decisions, but is the fear that results from understanding the distance between humans and God. The apparent inability of people to understand the right time and to act upon it is thwarted by God Himself, who stands behind the unchanging, continually repetitive world.[91] There is nothing here of

---

88. Qohelet does not speak about the knowledge of God in terms of His character but only speaks about God in terms of His position and His activity in the world.

89. The clause which begins with the particle *šĕ* can express purpose (Murphy, *Ecclesiastes*, 29–30) or result (Ogden and Zogbo, *Handbook on Ecclesiastes*, 106). If it expresses purpose (*'in order that'*), God's intention is more strongly stated. If it expresses result (*'so that'*), God's intention is not as strongly connected to the result. Fox (*Rereading Ecclesiastes*, 212–213) takes it as a purpose clause but he then states that God does not impose that fear.

90. This point is specifically brought out in Ecclesiastes 9:1.

91. The fear of Yahweh is the beginning of wisdom in Proverbs, which is the starting point from which everything else flows, including the exploration of knowledge, but in Ecclesiastes such knowledge is not open to humans. Thus the fear of God in Ecclesiastes cannot be the starting point, but comes in response to human inability to understand God's work in the world.

revelation or the law of God, but just a world 'as is' under the sun.

Qohelet's reflections on injustice: man has no advantage over beasts (Eccles. 3:16-22)

3:16 *And again, I observed under the sun: in the place*[92] *of justice there was wickedness, and in the place of righteousness there was wickedness.*

3:17 *I said to myself, 'God will judge the righteous and the wicked because there is a time for every activity and for every work too.'*[93]

---

92. Although the Septuagint and the Vulgate take *'place'* (*māqôm*) to be the direct object of the verb *'I observed,'* most modern commentators take seriously the Hebrew accent which separates the two clauses — an athnach pause occurs under *'sun'* (Crenshaw, *Ecclesiastes*, 101; Murphy, *Ecclesiastes*, 30; and Seow, *Ecclesiastes*, 166).

93. Much has been written to explain the word *šām* at the end of 3:17. Some want to emend it to *šîm*, with God presupposed as the subject, 'for God has set a time' (Barton, *Ecclesiastes*, 111; Crenshaw, *Ecclesiastes*, 102). Although Crenshaw mentions the fact that Qohelet sometimes holds the verb until the end, Gordis (*Koheleth*, 255) argues that its position at the end of the verse goes against identifying *šām* as a verb. He also points out that there is no testimony from the versions for this meaning. Seow (*Ecclesiastes*, 167) wants to repoint the word as a noun from *śym/śwm*, which could refer to the determination of events (2 Sam. 13:32) or the setting of a date (Exod. 9:5; Job 34:23). Gordis (*Koheleth*, 255) translates *šām* as 'over there,' a reference to the other world with satirical intent. Fox (*Rereading Ecclesiastes*, p. 215) connects *šām* to the word *šāmāh* in 3:16 and understands it to be a reference to the place where judgment will occur, which in context would be the courts. If, however, the reason given in 3:17b for the statement that God will bring the righteous and the wicked to judgment is referring to 3:1, then the *'time for every activity'* in 3:17 would be broader than the law court. Two options seem to make the best sense. Eaton (*Ecclesiastes*, 84) argues that *šām* has a weak sense without local force (as in Isa. 48:16), with the idea 'there is a time for every activity in reference to those events.' C. F. Whitley ('Has the Particle שׁם an Asseverative Force?' *Bib* 55 [1974], 395–397) argues on the basis of Hosea 6:10; Zephaniah 1:14; and Jeremiah 5:15 for the meaning *'too.'* He argues that *šām* must function in an affirming relationship with *kî 'ēṯ* (*'because there is a time'*) at the beginning of the clause.

3:18 *I said to myself concerning*[94] *human beings, 'God is testing them*[95] *so that they might see*[96] *that they are really animals.'*[97]

3:19 *For the fate*[98] *of human beings and the fate of animals is the same fate. As one dies so the other dies. Both have the same breath. So human beings have no advantage over the animals for*[99] *everything is senseless.*

---

94. The phrase ʿ*al-diḇraṯ* also occurs in Ecclesiastes 7:14 with the meaning 'so that.' A similar phrase, ʿ*al-dĕḇar*, occurs in Genesis 20:11, 18 and Deuteronomy 4:21 with the meaning 'because of' or '*concerning*' (Murphy, *Ecclesiastes*, 30), which is adopted here.

95. There is debate concerning the meaning and the identification of the form *lĕḇārām*. One option is to take it as a qal infinitive from *brr* with a 3mp suffix. Another option is to take *brr* as a finite verb with an emphatic *lamed* (Gordis, *Koheleth*, 226 and Seow, *Ecclesiastes*, 167). Longman (*Ecclesiastes*, 128) notes that the sense of *brr* is not changed if it is an infinitive or a finite verb. For the meaning of the verb see the discussion in the commentary.

96. The Hebrew text points the verb *rāʾāh* as a qal infinitive. It seems better to take human beings as the subject of the verb rather than God (Longman, *Ecclesiastes*, 129; Whybray, *Ecclesiastes*, 78). Some of the versions (Septuagint, Syriac, Vulgate) and many of the commentators repoint this infinitive to a hifil (with the loss of the *he* performative), which would mean 'to show' (Ginsburg, *Coheleth*, 316; Murphy, *Ecclesiastes*, 29; and Seow, *Ecclesiastes*, 168). The meaning 'show' fits well the parallel of God as the subject of two infinitives, but ultimately the meaning of the verse is not affected.

97. The last clause of 3:18 is difficult. Some argue that the word *hēmmāh* is added due to a copyist's error from the preceding word *bĕhēmāh* (Fox, *Rereading Ecclesiastes*, 216 and Seow, *Ecclesiastes*, 168). This particular error is called dittography. Garrett (*Ecclesiastes*, 305) argues that one should be cautious in emending the text in view of the chiastic, rhyming structure of the phrase. The alliteration of the phrase could account for the strange syntax. The phrase makes sense without emendation if the *hēmāh* is taken as a copula and the *lamed* on *lāhem* is taken as a dative of means, which could be literally translated, 'they are beasts, they themselves' (Crenshaw, *Ecclesiastes*, 103 and Murphy, *Ecclesiastes*, 30).

98. Although *miqreh* is translated as if it is in the construct state ('*fate of*'), the Masoretic Text points it as an absolute, which could be translated 'for man is mere chance, and the beast is mere chance, and they are both subject to the same chances' (translation of Ginsburg, *Coheleth*, 317–318). To change *miqreh* into a construct only takes a vowel change. Murphy suggests (*Ecclesiastes*, 30) that the Hebrew scribes may have taken it as an absolute to avoid the implications of Qohelet's statement concerning the relationship of human beings and animals.

99. Ogden and Zogbo (*Handbook on Ecclesiastes*, 115) understand the *kî* to be introducing a concluding comment, so they translate it as 'indeed.'

3:20 Both[100] are going to the same place. Both are from the dust. Both return to the dust.

3:21 Who knows whether[101] the human breath of life[102] ascends upward or whether the breath of life of animals descends to the earth?

3:22 So I perceived that there is nothing better than that a person should enjoy his activities because this is his portion. For who can bring him to see what will happen after him?

The beginning of 3:16, 'And again, I observed' (wĕʻôḏ rāʼîtî), sets this section apart from the previous section, so commentators can speak of a new section that deals with the topic of injustice.[103] Some argue for a loose connection between 3:1-15 and 3:16-22 based on the phrase in 3:17 that states 'there is a

---

They argue that the kî should not be taken as a motive clause to explain the difference between humans and animals because the logic does not follow that humans have no advantage over animals because all is vanity. However, the *hebel* judgment introduced by kî does not function as a concluding statement because 3:20 further comments on the similarity of humans and animals.

100. The Hebrew word kōl is translated 'both' instead of 'all' because two things are primarily in view, humans and animals.

101. There is debate as to whether the participles have the definite article or the interrogative *he*. A translation of the verse with the article would assert that there is no distinction between the spirit of people and animals (Kaiser, *Ecclesiastes*, 71; Eaton, *Ecclesiastes*, 88–89; see the NKJV translation). However, there are reasons for understanding the *he* as the interrogative. It has the support of the ancient versions (Septuagint, Vulgate, and the Targums). Gordis (*Koheleth*, 228) argues that the interrogative and the article may be very similar in some forms so that it is not impossible to read the Hebrew text with the interrogative (interrogatives before gutterals may take a patach vowel [*GKC* §100.m]). The interrogative also fits the context better for the question 'who knows' at the beginning of the verse sets the stage for the verse to be seen as a question which expects a negative answer (Murphy, *Ecclesiastes*, 37; Crenshaw, *Ecclesiastes*, 104).

102. The term *rûaḥ* is used in both 3:19 and 3:21. It is translated 'breath of life' in 3:21 to show the connection with the translation 'breath' in 3:19. Longman (*Ecclesiastes*, 130) argues for a slight distinction between the concepts in 3:19 and 3:21, with 3:21 stressing more the concept of life in the sense of 'spirit.'

103. Longman, *Ecclesiastes*, 125; Ogden and Zogbo, *Handbook on Ecclesiastes*, 109; and Whybray, *Ecclesiastes*, 76.

time for every activity,' which closely follows 3:1.[104] It is not as clear where the section ends because Ecclesiastes 4 seems to continue the topic of injustice by describing oppression. Thus Crenshaw ends this section of the text with 4:3 (3:16–4:3).[105] However, the familiar 'better than' saying in 3:22 acts as a conclusion to 3:16-22, and chapter 4 begins with a phrase that seems to set it apart from what has gone before ('then I turned and I observed').

In 3:16-22 Qohelet moves from a discussion of the inability of people to discover what God is doing in the world to the fact of injustice in the world. Such injustice is part of the reason that people cannot figure out what God is doing in the world, because it hinders people from understanding the plan of God. Qohelet sets forth an observation of personal experience in 3:16 (*'I observed,' rā'îtî*). He follows his observation with two reflections in 3:17 and 3:18-21. Both begin with *'I said to myself'* and both include a motive clause that explains the reflection (3:17b; 3:19).[106] The section concludes with a final observation in 3:22 ('I perceived,' *rā'îtî*), which includes the well-known 'there is nothing better' formula.

Qohelet presents another observation in 3:16 based on his experience of the world *'under the sun.'*[107] The problem that Qohelet observes is that wherever one would expect to find justice one discovers only wickedness. The place of justice and righteousness refers to any place where proper judgment should occur, including the law courts and the city gates.[108]

---

104. Murphy, *Ecclesiastes*, 32 and Barton, *Ecclesiastes*, 108.

105. Crenshaw, *Ecclesiastes*, 101. Others see 3:16–4:16 as a unit. Hubbard (*Ecclesiastes*, 113) sees the whole section dealing with the distortion of justice, with five instances of injustice set forth. Kaiser (*Ecclesiastes*, 69) understands 3:16–4:16 to be setting forth six facts that might appear to negate the thesis that God has an overall plan (3:1-15).

106. Ogden, *Qoheleth*, 63.

107. Although some understand the word *wĕ'ôd* to be used in an adverbial sense with the meaning 'continually' (noted by Murphy, *Ecclesiastes*, 30), Whybray (*Ecclesiastes*, 77) notes that evidence for such usage is slight. The word *wĕ'ôd* is better understood as referring to the observation in 3:10. Thus *wĕ'ôd* has been translated *'again.'*

108. Ogden and Zogbo, *Handbook on Ecclesiastes*, 110.

The problem that Qohelet observes is that the very places where the innocent should be cleared of wrongdoing and the wicked should be declared guilty, with the appropriate punishment, have become places of wickedness because justice is not carried out. The observation of injustice in places where justice should be carried out would seem to question the orderly view of the world set forth in the poem in 3:1-8. In response to his observation of injustice Qohelet offers two reflections in 3:17 and 3:18, which both begin with '*I said to myself*' (literally, 'I said in my heart'). The first reflection is a theological statement about God's justice. Qohelet reminds himself that God will judge the righteous and the wicked, which would re-establish the relationship between deed and consequence.[109] The basis for this statement of judgment ('*because,*' *kî*) goes back to the poem of 3:1-8 by not only picking up the key word '*time*' ('*ēt*), but also the whole phrase from 3:1: '*a time for every activity.*' There is a time for every activity so there must be a time for God's judgment. However, commentators are divided as to what this judgment refers to. Some think the judgment refers to eschatological judgment because of the use of the imperfect of the verb ('*God will judge*') or the use of *šām* at the end of 3:17. Garrett points out that *šām* is used in Psalm 14:5a to refer to eschatological judgment and so argues that the word *šām* is shorthand for eschatological judgment.[110] However, the use of *šām* in the context of Ecclesiastes is determinative for its meaning (see the note on this word in the translation), and there are good reasons for arguing that the focus of Qohelet is not eschatological judgment. The reason given at the end of 3:17 for the statement of God's judgment uses the phrase from 3:1, '*a time for every activity.*' This phrase is followed in 3:1 by another phrase that limits the focus to '*under heaven.*' Also, all the events in the poem of 3:1-8 have their time in this life. Since God's judgment is included in the '*time for every activity*' (3:17), it seems likely that Qohelet is thinking of judgment in

---

109. Franz Josef Backhaus, 'Denn Zeit und Zufall trifft sie alle': Zu Komposition und Gottesbild im Buch Qohelet (Frankfurt: Hain, 1993), 133.

110. Garrett, *Ecclesiastes*, 302.

this life.¹¹¹ This view also fits with Qohelet's later statement in this section concerning uncertainty at death (3:19-21). Even if God's judgment is limited to this world, 3:17 can appropriately be seen as a statement that is in agreement with traditional wisdom thinking;¹¹² perhaps, it can even be called a confessional statement.¹¹³ However, the way the verse functions in this context is a very important question which cannot be examined until the second reflection in 3:18-21 is discussed.

Qohelet's second reflection concerning injustice occurs in 3:18-21, but this time the focus is on human beings. God's role related to human beings is debated because the meaning of the verb *bārar* in 3:18 is not absolutely clear. Some argue for 'separate' or 'choose,' but that meaning does not make good sense in the context because the next verse goes on to specify that human beings are on the level of animals. Seow avoids this problem by opting for irony: God chose them to show that they are no better than animals because they are mortals.¹¹⁴ Whybray understands the verse to mean that God separates or sets apart people to show them that they are not like God but are like the animals. This is understood to mean that both the righteous and the wicked in their death equally experience God's ultimate hidden judgment, which demonstrates the lowly status of human beings and their dependence on God.¹¹⁵ However, the concept of a hidden judgment at death seems foreign to the context. Some argue that *bārar* here means 'purify' (Dan. 11:35; 12:10). Provan understands the verse to mean that purity of heart leads to a clarity of perception so that people are able to see the truth of

---

111. Others who argue that the judgment of 3:17 is not necessarily eschatological judgment but judgment that occurs in this life include Seow, Whybray, and Hubbard.

112. Although the book of Proverbs includes the idea of judgment beyond this life (Waltke, *Proverbs*, 1:104-106), some proverbs focus on the outworking of God's judgment on the wicked in this life (Prov. 11:31), which includes the outworking of the deed-consequence relationship on the wicked.

113. Bartholomew, *Reading Ecclesiastes*, 245.

114. Seow, *Ecclesiastes*, 175.

115. Whybray, *Ecclesiastes*, 79.

their mortality without any illusions.[116] Hengstenberg argues that God's people are visited with temporal misfortune in order to purify them of their pride, with the result that they would see that they are animals.[117] These views do not take into account the strong negative conclusion in this passage that humans are really no different from animals. In other words, Qohelet has more in view than just the idea that humans and animals are subject to death (mortality), but he argues in 3:19-21 that humans are like animals in that death ends life's existence. A related concept to the idea of 'purify' is the idea of 'sifting' or 'testing.' Although this is not an attested meaning for *bārar*, it is the way the Vulgate and the Targum translate the verb and it fits the context well.[118] Hubbard understands the testing in a positive sense, with the purpose of showing humans the need to trust in God because life is too short for ultimate justice to be carried out here.[119] Longman understands the testing to lead to the negative conclusion that humans are no different from the animals because death signals the end for both. Nothing comes after death.[120]

Although the meaning of the verb *bārar* is debated, the key to Qohelet's thought is what he means when he says at the end of 3:18 that human beings are *'really animals.'* He explains what he means in 3:19-21. The reason (*kî*) Qohelet gives for this statement is that *'the same fate'* awaits both humans and animals. It is obvious that this fate is death, for Qohelet goes on to specify the things that human beings and animals have in common in relationship to death. Both have the same breath (*rûaḥ*), which is lost to them at death. Both go to *'the same place,'* which probably refers to some kind of burial because they *'return to the dust'* from which they came. Other Old Testament passages of Scripture argue similar things (Gen. 2:7; Ps. 104:29-30; Gen. 2:19; 3:19; Ps. 90:3). However, Qohelet's views do not line up with other Old Testament passages

---

116. Provan, *Ecclesiastes*, 93.
117. Hengstenberg, *Ecclesiastes*, 114–115.
118. Longman, *Ecclesiastes*, 128.
119. Hubbard, *Ecclesiastes*, 115–116.
120. Longman, *Ecclesiastes*, 128.

because he does not see any distinction between human beings and animals. He specifically says that because of death *'human beings have no advantage over the animals.'* The word for *'advantage'* (*môṭar*) is related to the term for profit (*yiṭrôn*), from which it derives its meaning.[121] Qohelet has already argued that there is no profit from labor (1:3; 2:10-11) and that even though wisdom has an advantage (*yiṭrôn*) over folly, the fact of death destroys the distinction between the wise and the fool (2:12-17). In 3:19 Qohelet boldly states without qualification that humans have no advantage over the animals because of death. Although Ogden and Zogbo argue that the manner of death is not in view,[122] Qohelet does make a comparison between humans and animals in terms of how they die (*'as ... so'*). In light of the context of injustice in 3:16, Qohelet would seem to have in view the fact that the way someone lives their life has no bearing on their manner of death (premature or after a long life). Thus the blessing of long life connected to wisdom (Prov. 3:2, 16; 4:10; 9:11) is called into question.

Qohelet also calls into question any distinctions between human beings and animals at death by the question in 3:21: *'Who knows?'* Although the question 'who knows?' in some places of Scripture is a question that remains open to possible response for human good (Joel 2:14; Jonah 3:9), the question 'who knows?' in Ecclesiastes is a closed question with the implied answer that no one really knows the answer.[123] Thus no one really knows whether there is a difference at death between the breath or spirit (*rûaḥ*) of human beings and the breath or spirit (*rûaḥ*) of animals in terms of their destination. Not only does injustice plague life on this earth (3:16), there is no confidence that at death things will be made right.[124] One

---

121. ibid., 129.

122. Ogden and Zogbo, *Handbook on Ecclesiastes*, 114.

123. James Crenshaw, 'The Expression *mî yōdea'* in the Hebrew Bible,' *VT* 36 (1986): 274–288.

124. Whybray's explanation (*Ecclesiastes*, 79) that Qohelet reinterprets traditional wisdom thinking, cited in 3:17, to show that it is in the death of humans, which they share with animals, that the righteous and wicked experience the hidden judgment of God runs counter to the skepticism in this passage concerning the future destiny of humans.

is not surprised to find in the midst of this discussion another *hebel* judgment in 3:19: *'everything is senseless.'*

The fact that the strong theological affirmation of God's judgment in 3:17 is placed next to such strong denials of any difference between human beings and animals in relationship to death has raised questions concerning the function of these verses in this section of Ecclesiastes. Some see an affirmation of God's judgment to be so out of harmony with the context that they argue that 3:17 has been added by someone else[125] (see the Introduction, where this view is discussed). Others who allow the two statements to stand side by side argue for a positive message because they think the theological statement of 3:17 trumps the negative statements of 3:19-21. In other words, the affirmation of God's judgment in 3:17 is an answer to the charge of 3:16, which sustains Qohelet in his perplexity.[126] Ogden, in a similar vein, sees 3:17, as a faith statement that Qohelet affirms, over against the anomaly of human existence that Qohelet also recognizes.[127]

Bartholomew argues that 3:18-19 are juxtaposed to 3:17 in a contradictory way, each representing radically opposed responses to the problem. He argues that 3:20-21 mediates between the *hebel* conclusion of 3:19 and the positive 'nothing better' saying in 3:22. Because of the proximity of 3:12-15, he understands 3:22 as a positive, shalomic appropriation of the human task in creation, which recognizes the portion (*ḥēleq*) God has assigned humans. However, 3:22 is not necessarily the answer to the problem of injustice because there is still tension between the enjoyment of work (3:22) and the possibility of being dragged unjustly into the law courts (3:16). Bartholomew raises the question concerning whether Qohelet's observations in 3:19-21 deconstruct the confession of 3:17. He ultimately denies this approach because of his view of 3:22. Although he recognizes that the juxtapositions of this text leave gaps to be filled, he ultimately allows the theological affirmation of 3:17 to control the negative

---

125. Barton, *Ecclesiastes*, 108 and Lauha, *Koheleth*, 75.
126. Kaiser, *Ecclesiastes*, 69.
127. Ogden, *Qoheleth*, 64.

statements in 3:19-21 because he places the question of 'who knows' in 3:21 under God's control.[128]

There is no doubt that Qohelet places next to each other a theological reflection on God's justice and an anthropological reflection on the relationship between human beings and animals; however, he does not allow the theological reflection of God's judgment to override the negative anthropological reflection that there is no difference between humans and animals. Qohelet does not resolve the difference between humans and animials by appealing to God's justice, either in this life or in the life to come. In fact, 3:19-21 ends in a rhetorical question that is not answered in a positive way. If the 'who knows' questions in Ecclesiastes really mean 'no one knows,' then there is an implied answer which is negative. Although there is a theological reflection on God's justice, the way the text is structured leaves the negative anthropological reflection and the rhetorical question in 3:21, with an implied negative answer, as the last word.

The 'nothing is better' statement in 3:22 supports this interpretation because it sets the enjoyment of the present in light of the uncertainty of the future. In light of the fact that there is no difference between humans and animals in their death, Qohelet observes that the best a person can do is to *'enjoy his activities.'* This limited enjoyment is his 'portion' (*ḥēleq*). Qohelet supports this observation with another question concerning the inability of people to know the future. This question also expects a negative answer so that no one can bring someone to see what will come in the future. It is possible that the Hebrew for *'after him'* (*'aḥărāyw*) is a 'frozen form' which would mean 'afterwards.'[129] It could then refer to a person's earthly future: since no one can be sure of justice in this life, the best option is to enjoy the present. However, in light of the question in 3:21, the question in 3:22

---

128. Bartholomew, *Reading Ecclesiastes*, 245–246 and *Ecclesiastes*, 177–178.

129. Gordis, *Koheleth*, 228. A 'frozen form' would mean that the suffix at the end of the form would not be stressed and that the word regularly appears in this form.

would also seem to have death in view.[130] Since no one knows what is coming at death, and whether their *'life-breath'* will rise or descend,[131] the best option is to enjoy one's activities now. There is no profit (*yiṯrôn*), so one should enjoy their portion (*ḥēleq*).

Homiletical Implications

Although some argue that Qohelet in this section finally gives an 'above the sun' perspective because God is more prominent in this section, he is still limited by an 'under the sun' view of life. The statement of an ordered world (3:1-8) does not change Qohelet's basic conclusions about life. Although God is very much involved with the order of the world in that He has made everything appropriate for its time, human beings are left in the dark because we cannot figure out what God's activity in the world means. Thus the world appears very messy from a human standpoint because injustice seems more prominent than justice. Although Qohelet acknowledges that God will judge the righteous and the wicked (3:17), he does not allow that theological statement to explain the messiness of life, but goes on to assert that human beings are no different from animals because they both experience the same fate of death. No one can be sure what happens at death. Thus death renders justice uncertain because there is no assurance of anything different after this life. Thus one is left with the limited enjoyment of the present.

---

130. Fox, *Rereading Ecclesiastes*, 217; Longman, *Ecclesiastes*, 131; Seow, *Ecclesiastes*, 168; Ogden and Zogbo, *Handbook on Ecclesiastes*, 119; Crenshaw, *Ecclesiastes*, 105; and others.

131. The relationship between 3:21 and 12:7 is debated since 12:7 seems to contradict 3:21. Frederick (*Transience*, 47) argues that 12:7 is an answer to the question of 3:21. Others contend that 12:7 is merely affirming a return to a pre-life situation (Crenshaw, *Ecclesiastes*, 105; Longman, *Ecclesiastes*, 273). Fox (*Rereading Ecclesiastes*, 332) comments that 12:7 is really more pessimistic than 3:21 because 3:21 grants the possibility that the spirit's ascent to God would redeem humanity from absurdity; however, 12:7 assumes that the spirit ascends but there is still no escape from death's obliterating power. The concluding refrain of 12:8 certainly precludes understanding 12:7 in too positive a light.

The ordered world in which we live makes science possible. The regularity of the 'laws of nature' allows scientists to perform experiments and put forth hypotheses. Yet many of those scientists operate with a view of the world that denies the very order that makes their experiments possible. A naturalistic evolutionist view of the world argues that evolution is driven by random mutations apart from any divine guidance. Human beings are the product of chance and many would argue that human beings are really no different from animals. Some in the environmental movement argue that human beings should have no privileged position in nature. Peter Singer, moral philosopher at Princeton University, argues that there is not one species that is higher or better than another. Without God, human beings lose their dignity. Without God being brought in as a solution to the problems and injustice of life, life is a total mess without hope either in this life or the life to come.

Other passages in the Old Testament sound very similar to Qohelet's struggle. In Psalm 73 the psalmist almost slipped because of the prosperity of the wicked. It is amazing how many parallels there are between the struggles of the psalmist and the struggles of Qohelet. Both become very wearied in trying to understand the inequities of the world (Pss. 73:14, 16; Eccles. 12:12). Both wonder whether their efforts to live a life for God have been in vain. The psalmist wonders why he has kept his heart pure (73:13) and Qohelet wonders why he has pursued wisdom (2:15) and righteousness (7:16). The psalmist recognizes that if he had taught the things he was contemplating, he would have betrayed the next generation (73:15). Qohelet makes statements that go against other Old Testament teaching when he denies any difference between human beings and animals (3:16-21). The breakthrough to a broader horizon comes for the psalmist when he enters the temple of God and comes to see clearly again the end of the wicked. A renewed vision of God helps him break free of his struggle with the prosperity of the wicked. In the first part of the psalm, the wicked are secure and the psalmist is on slippery ground, but in the second part of the psalm, the psalmist is secure and the wicked are on slippery ground. In Ecclesiastes the broader vision comes through at the end

(12:13-14), where the fear of God is mentioned along with the commandments of God, and the judgment of God includes secret things, whether good or evil.

Psalm 49 sounds very much like Ecclesiastes 3:16-22. It is a wisdom psalm that deals with the prosperity of the wicked. They boast in their abundance, trust in their wealth, and seem to triumph over the psalmist (vv. 5-6). Similarities with Ecclesiastes include the statement that 'even the wise die' along with the fool and the stupid (v. 10) and that man is like the beasts that perish (vv. 12, 20). Also, the psalmist has experienced 'days of evil' that have produced a deep-seated anxiety about the meaning and destiny of life that can derail a person's faith in God (v. 5). Yet Psalm 49 approaches the subject with a different perspective from Qohelet. The 'riddle' (v. 4) of the prosperity of the wicked is explained. The question 'why should I fear' is answered by showing that wealth cannot deliver from death (vv. 7-9). The psalmist answers the 'why' question of verse 5 with verse 16, 'Be not afraid when a man becomes rich.' The basis for this admonition is given in verse 15, which is a strong confession of faith and is the answer to the riddle: only God is able to ransom a life from death. The final statement of verse 15 makes an allusion to the translation of Enoch (Gen. 5:24) and Elijah (2 Kings 2:1, 9), who were taken into the presence of God apart from death.[132] The examples of Enoch and Elijah would give God's people hope for life beyond death. Psalm 49 reinforces this hope by connecting the examples of Enoch and Elijah to the power of God to redeem from death. Death does not have the final word for those who trust in God. Although Qohelet and the psalmist use similar terminology to describe the problem they are examining, the psalmist is not limited to an 'under the sun' perspective, but he allows what he knows about God to help solve the problem of the wicked. Only mankind in his pomp, who does not understand the true nature of wealth, is like the beasts (v. 20). The wise and the fool may both die, but the psalmist is assured that 'God will ransom my soul from the power of Sheol' (v. 15).

---

132. The allusion is found in the verb *lāqaḥ* ('to take'), used in Psalm 49 and in reference to Enoch and Elijah.

4.
The frustration of unfulfilled expectations (4:1–6:9)

It is not always easy to determine where one section ends and another section begins in the book of Ecclesiastes. In 3:16 Qohelet introduces the subject of injustice, which also seems to be the focus of 4:1-3, so that a connection between chapter 4 and chapter 3 is possible. For example, Crenshaw takes 3:16–4:3 to be a major section entitled 'The Tears of the Oppressed.'[1] Others deal with individual sections in chapter 4 without trying to connect them together. Whybray covers chapter 4 in small units that are not necessarily related to each other (4:1-3, 4-6, 7-8, 9-12, 13-16).[2] A more common approach is to see some connection between the smaller sections of chapter 4. Fox understands chapter 4 to consist of thematic clusters of five sections which comment on desirable or undesirable patterns in human relationships, with each section linked thematically to the next.[3] Usually chapter 5 is broken down into smaller sections (5:1-7, 8-9) with 5:10–6:9 understood to be a unit dealing with wealth. Thus some justification must be given for the broad division of 4:1–6:9.

The beginning of chapter 4 is an observation, much like 3:16, but the observation in 4:1 is introduced differently from the observation of 3:16. In 3:16 the phrase *'and again, I observed'*

---

1. Crenshaw, *Ecclesiastes*, 101; see also Gordis, *Koheleth*, 148–149. Murphy (*Ecclesiastes*, 28) divides the text at 4:6.

2. Whybray, *Ecclesiastes*, 81–91; see also Longman.

3. Fox, *Rereading Ecclesiastes*, 218–219.

is used but in 4:1 the more emphatic phrase '*then I turned and I observed*' sets it apart from what has gone before. Qohelet had not dealt with oppression earlier in the book, so the topic itself signals a new section.[4] The same phrase occurs in 4:7, which reinforces the idea that 4:1 introduces chapter 4 rather than concluding the observations of injustice in chapter 3. Also, thematically, 4:1-3 fits in well with the rest of chapter 4, which focuses on human relationships.

If 4:1 begins the section, where does the section end? Ecclesiastes 6:10-12 plays an important role in the book. Most take it either as a transition passage (Longman, Crenshaw), or as the introduction (Murphy) or the beginning (Seow) of the second half of the book. Fox sees it as a conclusion to 5:10–6:9 and a pivot unit between sections.[5] If 6:10-12 is a transition passage, it can go with either what comes before or what comes after it. There is also the recognition that 5:10–6:9 is a unit that deals with wealth.[6] Thus the larger unit of 4:1–6:12 can be broken down according to the following topics: (a) political power (4:1-3, 13-16; 5:8-9); (b) relationships connected to labor (4:4-12); (c) God (5:1-7); (d) money (5:10–6:9); and (e) transition to the second part of the book (6:10-12). An overarching theme of 4:1–6:12 is the frustration that comes with unfulfilled expectations in connection with relationships and wealth. Not only does money not satisfy (5:10–6:9), but various relationships in life do not satisfy either (4:1–5:9). These relationships include labor, political power, and God. Political power not only frames chapter 4 (4:1-3, 13-16) but political power frames the whole section that focuses on relationships (4:1-3; 5:8-9). Interspersed are sections dealing with relationships connected with labor (4:4-12) and one's relationship with God (5:1-7). The whole section can be divided into the following segments: political power (4:1-3), relationships connected with labor (4:4-12), political power

---

4. Longman, *Ecclesiastes*, 133. Fox (*Rereading Ecclesiastes*, 219) also notes that the verb *šûḇ* points to another in a series of actions or events.

5. Fox, *Rereading Ecclesiastes*, 235, 247.

6. Fox, *Rereading Ecclesiastes*; Longman, *Ecclesiastes*; and Crenshaw, *Ecclesiastes*. Some, such as Seow and Barton, include 5:8-9 in the section (5:8–6:9).

(4:13-16), one's relationship to God (5:1-7), and political power (5:8-9). It is clear that political power and labor do not escape the theme of frustration from unfulfilled expectations, and that same theme sets the tone for how the section on God should be understood. In fact, one of the most positive sections in the book comes in the discussion of companionship in relationship to labor (4:9-12) and not in the discussion of the relationship with God. Thus one can conclude that the best relationship in a world characterized by the frustration of unfulfilled expectations is the relationship of a companion.

Ecclesiastes 5:1-7 is such an important passage, because it deals with Qohelet's concept of God, that any teaching or preaching through Ecclesiastes will have to give it special attention. Thus one way to divide the text for preaching or teaching purposes is 4:1-16; 5:1-9; and 5:10–6:9. Because 6:10-12 is a transition section, it can be covered with either 5:10–6:9 or 7:1-14.

The frustration of loneliness met in companionship (Eccles. 4:1-16)

Political power oppresses with no one to comfort (Eccles. 4:1-3)

4:1 *Then I turned and I observed all the oppression that occurs under the sun, and look—the tears of the oppressed but there is no one to comfort them, and on the side of their oppressors was power, but there was no one to comfort them.*

4:2 *So I praised*[7] *the dead who had already died more than the living who are still alive.*

4:3 *But better than both of them*[8] *is the one who does not yet*

---

7. The verb *śabēaḥ* is an infinitive absolute standing in place of a finite verb. The fact that it is followed by an explicit subject is unusual but not unprecedented (Waltke and O'Connor, *Hebrew Syntax*, 596, n. 60).

8. There is much discussion concerning the function of *ʾet ʾăšer* in this verse (the *ʾet* normally designates the direct object of a verb). Some argue that the phrase is governed by the verb 'I praised' in 4:2 (which might be translated 'still more than both of them I count fortunate' [see Krüger, *Qoheleth*, 82]). The

exist because[9] *he has not seen the evil work that is done under the sun.*

At the beginning of chapter 4 Qohelet observes the effects of oppression on those who are oppressed. The topic of these three verses is broader than the topic of 3:16, which focused on the administration of justice.[10] Opression can include injustice in the law courts, but it also includes any misuse of *power* by those who have the authority to exercise it. The phrase '*all the oppression*' can be understood to mean all kinds of oppression '*that occurs under the sun.*'[11] But the focus is on the effect of the oppression with the repetition of '*there was no one to comfort them.*' This '*comfort*' probably refers to more than just soothing words in the face of oppression, but also refers to active help and assistance to deal with the oppression.[12] The repetition of the phrase '*there was no one to comfort them*' seems to express despair and hopelessness.[13] Although some think that such hopelessness is evidence that Qohelet is not a king, because a king would have the power to assist the oppressed,[14] if such a king was struggling with the meaninglessness of life he would not have the motivation to get involved. It also fits his detached observations of the problems of life. What is more surprising is that Qohelet does not mention that God is on the side of the oppressed (Pss. 103:6; 146:7),[15] and he does not encourage the oppressed to call out to God for help.

Septuagint and the Syriac take the phrase in a nominative sense as the subject of an independent clause, with the word *ṭôḇ* ('*better*') as predicate (Gordis, *Koheleth*, 229). This is common among English translations and is followed here. But as Whybray (*Ecclesiastes*, 83) points out, the general sense is not affected either way.

9. Although not many commentators or translations take *'ăšer* as causal, it makes sense in this verse as introducing the reason that it is better that some have never existed (suggested by Fox, *Rereading Ecclesiastes*, 218–219 and Krüger, *Qoheleth*, 82).

10. Murphy, *Ecclesiastes*, 37.

11. Seow, *Ecclesiastes*, 177.

12. Whybray, *Ecclesiastes*, 81.

13. Longman, *Ecclesiastes*, 134 and Fox, *Ecclesiastes*, 27. In *Rereading Ecclesiastes* (219) Fox sets forth the unlikely view that Qohelet is expressing how unfortunate *he is* because he must observe such evils.

14. Longman, *Ecclesiastes*, 133.

15. Shields, *The End of Wisdom*, 150.

In 4:2-3 Qohelet gives his response to the observation of the effects of oppression. In 4:2 Qohelet *'praised the dead who had already died'* as better off than *'the living who are still alive.'* The use of the word *'praise'* (*šābaḥ*) is ironic, because normally life is preferable to death.[16] Plus, this verb is used in the Psalms to express admiration for God (Pss. 63:4; 106:47).[17] Here the dead are praised because they no longer have to experience oppression, but the living are still subject to it. But there is a condition that is even *'better'* than *'both of them'* (the dead and the living) and that is the condition of having never lived. The person who has not been born is better off *'because he has not seen the evil work that is done under the sun.'* Job and Jeremiah expressed a similar sentiment that it would have been better for them not to have been born so that they could have escaped their suffering (Job 3:11-19; Jer. 20:14-18). Qohelet observes the suffering of those who have no one to comfort them and concludes that death is better than to be alive, but that it is even better never to have been born. There is no hope of justice after death held out to the oppressed.[18] Thus, to face oppression without the help of a companion is unbearable.

The frustrations of labor alleviated through companionship (Eccles. 4:4-12)

4:4 *And I observed that all labour and all the success[19] of labour comes from a person's envy of his neighbour. This is also senseless and a chasing after wind.*

4:5 *The fool folds his hands and consumes his own flesh.*

---

16. Murphy, *Ecclesiastes*, 38.
17. Longman, *Ecclesiastes*, 134.
18. Shields, *The End of Wisdom*, 150.
19. There is a minor debate concerning whether *kišrôn* means 'skill' or 'success.' Fox (*Rereading Ecclesiastes*, 220) argues for skill in work because the context deals with the reasonableness of the effort rather than the outcome of the effort. He understands 'skilled work' as a form of wisdom. Longman (*Ecclesiastes*, 136, n. 20), on the other hand, argues for success based on the use of *kišrôn* in Ecclesiastes 5:10, where he thinks it must mean success. This is a hard call to make because the two ideas are not that far apart. Skill is needed to get ahead and success is what puts one ahead, so maybe there is not that much difference between them.

4:6 *Better is a handful with quietness than two handfuls with labour and chasing after the wind.*

4:7 *And I turned and I saw* an example of[20] *senselessness under the sun.*

4:8 *There is a person without a companion.*[21] *He has neither son nor brother, yet there is no end to all his labour, and also his eyes*[22] *are never satisfied with riches.* But he never asks,[23] *'For whom do I labour and deprive myself of pleasure.' This also is senseless and a grievous task.*

4:9 *Two are better than one because they have a good reward for their labour.*

4:10 *For if one of them falls,*[24] *the other can lift up his companion, but too bad to the one who falls and there is no one to lift him up.*

4:11 *Also, if two lie down together, they can keep warm, but how can one keep warm alone?*

---

20. The noun *hebel* is translated as *'an example of senselessness'* because the next verse begins with the particle of existence *yēš* ('there is'), which presents the example (Longman, *Ecclesiastes*, 139).

21. The Hebrew literally reads 'there is one and not a second,' with the word 'second' (*šēnî*) being a form of the key word 'two' in this section.

22. What is written in the text (Ketiv) is *'his eyes,'* but the Qere (what is read) is 'his eye.' The ancient versions read the Qere but Seow (*Ecclesiastes*, 181) argues that the plural noun with the singular verb is the more difficult reading. Ginsburg (*Coheleth*, 326–327), however, notes that this noun in the plural regularly takes a singular feminine verb after it (1 Sam. 4:15; Micah 4:11).

23. The first-person question intrudes into a third-person text, which leads to the addition of *'But he never asks.'* Fox (*Rereading Ecclesiastes*, 222) argues that the additional words are not necessary because he understands the first-person question as Qohelet speaking out of his own experience, which would need no introductory statement. However, it is not obvious that Qohelet is interjecting his own experience here. Also, it does not really matter whether the question was one the man in the story actually asked ('and he says') or whether it was a question that the man in the story ought to have asked (*'but he never asks'*) because the point of the question remains the same (Shields, *The End of Wisdom*, 152 gives the above options).

24. Although the verb is 3mp, it can be translated as *'one of them.'* Murphy (*Ecclesiastes*, 41) calls this the distributive use of the plural (Gen. 11:3; Judg. 6:29). Gordis (*Koheleth*, 232) terms it a partitive plural ('if either of them falls') and Gesenius (*GKC*, 124o) notes that the plural is used to denote an indefinite singular.

4:12 *And though someone may overpower the one,*[25] *two may*[26] *withstand him. A three-fold cord does not quickly snap.*

The common subject of Ecclesiastes 4:4-12 is labor (*'āmāl*), which occurs in verses 4, 6, 8, and 9. Qohelet begins this section with another observation. The focus of his observation is the motivation behind '*labour and all the success of labour,*' which he identifies as '*envy of his neighbour.*' Ogden and Zogbo seek to give '*envy*' a positive meaning as a stimulus that encourages a person to greater effort when confronted with a challenge.[27] But Longman points out that a positive view of envy only occurs in relationships which require exclusivity, such as the divine-human relationship and the marriage relationship.[28] Otherwise, '*envy*' is a dangerous attitude which leads to self-destructive behavior, as Proverbs 14:30 states: 'envy makes the bones rot.'[29] Qohelet calls this selfish motivation '*senseless and a chasing after the wind.*' Envy is a motive that cannot be satisfied, which leads to ceaseless work and 'the mad rush to gain.'[30] As someone has commented, 'Whenever a friend succeeds, a little something in me dies.'[31] Thus envy sets people over against one another.

If envy is the motivation behind labor and its success, then one might draw the conclusion that a person should forego all labor and opt for a life of ease. However, Qohelet follows

---

25. The word '*the one*' (*hā'ehād*) functions as the object of the verb '*overpower,*' which itself has a 3ms pronominal suffix that anticipates the object ('he may overpower him, the one'). A suffix on a verb that anticipates an object is also found in Exodus 2:6, 'she saw him, the child' (see the discussion in Seow, *Ecclesiastes*, 183).

26. Shields (*The End of Wisdom*, 153) points out that to translate this verb as an indicative ('two *will* withstand him') brings too much certainty into the verse, which is better seen as a hypothetical statement of an irreal mode. Two may not always prevail against an attacker, but two stand a better chance of prevailing than one.

27. Ogden and Zogbo, *Handbook on Ecclesiastes*, 129.

28. Longman, *Ecclesiastes*, 137.

29. Seow (*Ecclesiastes*, 179) comments that in wisdom literature envy (*qin'āh*) is always the cause of self-destructive behavior.

30. The last phrase comes from Provan, *Ecclesiastes*, 104.

31. The quotation is from Gore Vidal and occurs in Winter, *Ecclesiastes*, 62.

his comments about the motivation behind labor in 4:4 with a proverb in 4:5 which speaks against laziness: *'the fool folds his hands and consumes his own flesh.'*[32] This proverb is similar to proverbs against laziness in the book of Proverbs (10:4; 19:15; 20:13; 21:25). The fact that a *'fool folds his hands'* is a statement of inactivity (Prov. 6:10) that leads to the result that he *'consumes his own flesh.'* In other words, people who refuse to work end up devouring themselves.[33] The laziness of the fool leads to his self-destruction and ruin.

Instead of pursuing the success of labor, which is motivated by envy, or the path of laziness, which leads to destruction, Qohelet advocates a way of moderation in a 'better-than' saying in 4:6. A contrast is drawn between *'one handful'* and *'two handfuls'* and between *'quietness'* and *'labour.'* There is debate concerning whether the Hebrew expresses a construct relationship (one handful of quietness and two handfuls of labor)[34] or whether the nouns are adverbial accusatives (one handful with rest and two handfuls with labor). The best option seems to be to take the nouns as adverbial accusatives. The construct relationship in the phrase 'two handfuls' of labor would require an emendation of the text.[35] Seow also notes that

---

32. The proverb of 4:5 has been understood by some in a positive sense. Gordis (*Koheleth*, 150) argues that Qohelet is teaching that the only sensible course is to take one's ease, especially if one does not have family ties or responsibilities to others. However, to make this view work he must add 'some men teach' before 4:5 and 'but I declare' before 4:6. Lohfink (*Qoheleth*, 69) and Crenshaw (*Ecclesiastes*, 109) entertain the possibility that *'his flesh'* refers to the meat of the fool, with the proverb expressing the meaning that even though the fool does nothing, he is still able to eat well. But Seow (*Ecclesiastes*, 179) points out that the word *'flesh'* (*bāśār*) occurs four times in Ecclesiastes (2:3; 5:6; 11:10; and 12:12) and in each case it refers to the human body, and that when it is used with a pronominal suffix it never refers to a portion of food.

33. Longman, *Ecclesiastes*, 138 and Seow, *Ecclesiastes*, 179.

34. Krüger (*Qohelet*, 97) prefers this option because 4:6 does not contain any verbs.

35. Longman (*Ecclesiastes*, 136, n. 2) notes that the final mem on *'two handfuls'* (*ḥopnayim*) would have to be taken as an enclitic mem (a mem attached to the end of a word whose function is uncertain) instead of the absolute dual form.

the comparison is not between one handful of rest over against two handfuls of labor, but between one handful of anything with rest over against two handfuls of anything with labor. In this view *'quietness'* (*naḥaṯ*) does not refer to idleness or laziness but to rest or peace.[36] The word *'labour'* (*'āmāl*) refers to the difficult aspect of work, plus Qohelet adds the futility of the effort with the phrase *'chasing the wind.'* The point of the proverb is that having a little with *'quietness'* is better than having more, because the more is accompanied with the strenuousness of *'labour.'* Behind it all is the motivation of envy (4:4). Although the term 'portion' (*ḥēleq*) is not used, the 'better-than' saying of 4:6 fits in with Qohelet's encouragement to enjoy the portion that comes from labor, even though there is no profit (*yiṯrôn*) from it.

Qohelet moves to another topic in 4:7 (*'and I turned and I saw'*), although it is not a completely new topic because a situation of labor is in view that takes on the character of *hebel* (*'senseless'*). The key word for 4:7-12 is a form of the word 'two,' which occurs in 4:8, 9, 10, 11, and 12.[37] The focus is on the benefit of a companion. The *'senseless'* situation that Qohelet describes in 4:7-8 is a person who labors without a companion. The term *'eḥāḏ* (the number one) refers to a single person and in the context refers to a loner or a solitary person.[38] Whybray calls him the lonely miser because he is all alone without brother or son, the two closest male relatives who might help in the labor or benefit from the inheritance.[39] This lonely laborer is described as working all the time (*'there is no end to his labour'*), and as *'never'* being *'satisfied with riches,'* the results of his labor. He is also not very self-conscious about his situation because he does not step back and analyze the purpose of his endless labor that does not bring satisfaction. In verse 8 there is an abrupt intervention of first-person into

---

36. Seow, *Ecclesiastes*, 180.

37. The word 'second' also occurs in 4:15 (literally 'the second youth'), but that section deals with government and forms an inclusio with 4:1-3. Murphy (*Ecclesiastes*, 41) notes that the connection of 4:13-16 with 4:4-12 is a loose one.

38. Seow, *Ecclesiastes*, 180.

39. Whybray, *Ecclesiastes*, 86 and Longman, *Ecclesiastes*, 140.

a third-person text: *'for whom do I labour and deprive myself of pleasure?'* There are various ways the first-person question is understood. It could be that Qohelet uses it in the mouth of the miser to tell the moral tale and that it is not a biographical statement concerning Qohelet himself.[40] Others draw a closer connection between the miser and Qohelet. Either Qohelet closely identifies with the plight of the lonely miser or he puts himself in the place of the miser.[41] It is not obvious that Qohelet is interjecting his own experience here and it does not ultimately affect the meaning of the example. The point is that there is no use toiling and depriving oneself of pleasure if there is no one with whom to share the benefits in the present or the future.[42]

Qohelet responds in 4:9-12 to the senseless situation of the lonely individual laborer in 4:7-8 by showing the benefits of companionship. He offers a proverb in 4:9 that sets forth the principle of the benefits of companionship. He gives a general reason for the truth of the proverb in 4:9, and then he gives several examples that illustrate the proverb in 4:10-12. The section ends with another proverb in 4:12.

The proverb in 4:9 states: *'two are better than one.'* The justification (causal *'ăšer, 'because'*) for this proverb is that *'they have a good reward for their labour.'* The word *'reward'* (*śāḵār*) can have the connotation of wages for work done.[43] Although some of the illustrations in 4:10-12 could result in financial difficulty, they are not limited to that aspect. In other words, the focus is not so much on *'riches,'* which even the lonely laborer accrues (4:8), but the focus is on the benefits that come from having someone to help you.[44]

---

40. Whybray, *Ecclesiastes*, 86.

41. Longman (*Ecclesiastes*, 140) argues the former and Delitzsch ('Ecclesiastes,' 276) argues the latter.

42. Longman, *Ecclesiastes*, 140 and Seow, *Ecclesiastes*, 188.

43. Cornelius van Dam, שכר, *NIDOTTE*, 3:1244-1245.

44. Gordis (*Koheleth*, 151) understands these verses to be commenting sarcastically on the alleged benefits of family companionship, which do not justify hard and unremitting toil. The benefits of family companionship are mostly physical and thus he sees them as exaggerated benefits. Gordis seems to asssume that the lonely laborer is one extreme and the physical

Each illustration is introduced by the word '*if*' ('*im*) followed by an imperfect verb, which shows that these are typical examples of what might occur.[45] All three seem to deal with situations that could arise as someone would travel[46] and so some limit the focus to a business venture and the benefits that come when someone has a business partner.[47] This understanding would fit the emphasis on labor in 4:7-9. However, Fox argues that the word for '*labour*' ('*āmāl*) in 4:9 can also refer to life's activities in general, and so the illustrations must refer to any trouble or difficulty in life.[48] If there is a connection between 4:7-8 and 4:9-12,[49] the emphasis would be on labor, but that does not preclude taking the principles involved and applying them to other life situations.

The first illustration of the benefits of companionship shows the mutual support of a companion if there is an accident (4:10). It envisions some kind of serious fall that would require the help of the companion to avoid being left

---

benefits of family companionship are the other extreme, with the right view somewhere in the middle. Although Fox (*Rereading Ecclesiastes*, 222) also downplays the benefits listed in this passage, calling them cheerless benefits because they do not include the emotional blessings of fellowship, the benefits are real benefits, the absence of which has disastrous consequences for the one who does not experience them because he is alone. Bartholomew (*Ecclesiastes*, 189) notes that, far from the writer being sarcastic concerning family life, the lack of community may be the cause for the experiences in life that are described.

45. Ogden and Zogbo (*Handbook on Ecclesiastes*, 139) call these examples hypothetical possibilities to consider. The conjunction '*im* can introduce a situation that has the potential of being fulfilled, which is called a real conditional clause (Arnold and Choi, *Biblical Hebrew Syntax*, 173).

46. Krüger, *Qoheleth*, 98.

47. Lohfink, *Qoheleth*, 71.

48. Fox, *Rereading Ecclesiastes*, 223. However, the passages he references (Micah 7:8; Ps. 145:14) do not speak about a physical fall but more about a metaphorical fall (a fall before enemies in Micah 7:8); but even then there is the need to be helped up, even if it is by God and not a physical companion (Ps. 145:14).

49. Although Whybray (*Ecclesiastes*, 86) acknowledges a progression of one, two, and three from 4:7 to 4:12, he does not see any thematic continuity between 4:7-8 and 4:9-12.

alone. The implication is that the result would be serious, for such a situation is described as *'too bad for the one who falls and there is no one to lift him up.'*⁵⁰ The fall could refer to someone falling into a pit (Prov. 26:27; 28:10), but it includes any serious fall that would leave someone injured enough to be unable to get up on their own. The second illustration in verse 11 (*'also'*; *gam*) highlights the benefit of a companion on a cold night: *'if two lie down together, they can keep warm, but how can one keep warm alone?'* Whenever the verb *'lie down'* (*šāḵaḇ*) is used in sexual situations it is followed by the preposition 'with' (*'ēṯ*),⁵¹ but here the preposition is not used because a sexual situation is not in view. The verb is also used to refer to sleep (Gen. 28:11), which is the meaning here.⁵² If a person is alone on a cold night, it is hard to get warm, but if there is another person, then the two people are able to share body heat to keep warm.⁵³ Although the companion could be a marriage partner, the context points more toward a business partner, so the companion should not be limited to a spouse.⁵⁴ The third illustration, in 4:12, deals with dangers that can arise on a journey. If someone is traveling alone, it is easier for another person to *'overpower the one.'* A single individual traveling alone is vulnerable to being robbed, *'but two may withstand him,'* that is, the robber or attacker. Thus there is security in traveling with a companion to avoid the dangers of traveling alone.

---

50. The translation *'too bad'* is literally 'woe to him' (*'îlô*). Murphy (*Ecclesiastes*, p. 41) understands the interjection *'î* as a later form of *'ôy* ('woe'), which describes an unfortunate circumstance (Ogden and Zogbo, *Ecclesiastes*, 139). Longman (*Ecclesiastes*, 141) translates it as 'pity.'

51. William C. Williams, שׁכב, in *NIDOTTE*, 4:102.

52. Longman, *Ecclesiastes*, 141.

53. A modern day example would be getting stuck on an interstate highway on a cold winter night because of weather or an accident. It would not be a good idea to keep the engine idling for fear of running out of petrol. If one is traveling with a companion, sitting together under a blanket in the back seat is an excellent way to keep warm.

54. Bartholomew, *Ecclesiastes*, 190. Longman (*Ecclesiastes*, 142) notes that the dominant opinion today is that the two are not a married couple.

A proverb brings this section to a climactic conclusion: '*a three-fold cord does not quickly snap.*'[55] Although the number two has been dominant, the number three would not be unusual in a numerical proverb (one, two, three) and it does function to conclude the section on the benefits of companionship by emphasizing strength in numbers.[56] The number three, however, should not be over-interpreted, for the point is not that two is better but that three is best, but that there is safety in numbers.[57] Thus the proverb is a fitting conclusion to the statement that '*two are better than one*' (4:9).

It is significant that a proverb concludes 4:9-12 and not a *hebel* statement ('this too is senseless'), which makes these verses some of the most positive verses in the book. Companionship brings true benefit to a person's life. It is possible that this principle should be applied to what comes earlier in chapter 4.[58] A companion could bring true comfort in the midst of oppression (4:1), or even better, the strength that comes in numbers could stand against oppression. Companionship would curtail the envy that motivates labor (4:4), would broaden the perspective of the lonely laborer (4:7-8), and would provide the other benefits listed in 4:9-12. However, companionship is not the answer to the problems of life with which Qohelet is wrestling, but brings only a

---

55. This may be a common proverb in the ancient Near East. It also occurs in the Gilgamesh Epic in a similar context of the protection a traveling companion brings to another person on a long journey (see Seow, *Ecclesiastes*, 189 and Fox, *Rereading Ecclesiastes*, 223, who quotes the significant section from the Gilgamesh Epic).

56. Longman, *Ecclesiastes*, 143–144. Crenshaw (*Ecclesiastes*, 112) comments that the x/x + 1 pattern signifies fullness or completion.

57. Seow, *Ecclesiastes*, 189. There is a tendency to make the number three significant in some way. Gordis (*Koheleht*, 233) thinks it refers to the added strength a son would bring, Kidner (*Ecclesiastes*, 51) that it may refer to children or God, and Ambrose took it to refer to Christ as the One who lifts up His companion (noted by Longman, *Ecclesiastes*, 143). Jerome saw a reference to the Trinity in the number three, and others have connected the three to faith, hope, and love (also noted by Longman). But Kidner is correct when he comments that these suggestions are probably more specific than what Qohelet intends by his use of the proverb.

58. Krüger, *Qoheleth*, 99.

relative advantage.⁵⁹ Although there is strength in numbers, the next section will demonstrate that ultimately numbers cannot be counted on as a sure thing.

The fleeting nature of political power (Eccles. 4:13-16)

4:13 *A poor but⁶⁰ wise youth is better than an old but foolish king who no longer has regard for⁶¹ advice.⁶²*

4:14 *For⁶³ he went from prison⁶⁴ to rule as king even though he was born poor in his kingdom.*

---

59. Seow, *Ecclesiastes*, 190; Bartholomew, *Ecclesiastes*, 190; and Shields, *The End of Wisdom*, 153.

60. Although a simple *waw* conjunction is used to connect '*poor*' and '*wise*' in relationship to the '*youth*,' and '*old*' and '*foolish*' in relationship to the king, Longman (*Ecclesiastes*, 144, n. 61) notes that the surprising connection between poverty and wisdom in relationship to the youth requires the translation '*but*.' Fox (*Rereading Ecclesiastes*, 224) notes that the translation 'old and foolish king' gives the impression that age was the cause of the king's folly (Whybray's view), but age is not normally associated with folly, so a better translation is '*old but foolish king*.'

61. The Hebrew word for 'know' (*yāḏaʿ*) is used with the meaning '*has regard for*' as it is used in Genesis 39:6; Deuteronomy 33:9; Job 9:21 (Seow, *Ecclesiastes*, 190).

62. The best way to understand the nifal infinitive verb *zāhar* is in the sense of 'to be warned, instructed, or advised' instead of 'can no longer take care of himself,' which is the translation of Gordis (*Koheleth*, 152). Crenshaw (*Ecclesiastes*, 113) comments that the latter meaning robs the statement of its sting.

63. There is debate as to how to understand the two *kî* clauses in this verse. Seow (*Ecclesiastes*, 104) takes the first *kî* clause to refer to the destiny of the youth and the second to refer to the fate of the old king. Fox (*Rereading Ecclesiastes*, 225) understands the first clause to refer to the youth of 4:13 and the second clause to refer to a second youth. In this view the second *kî* clause (*kî gam*) is taken in the adversative sense, setting forth the consequences of the rise of the youth: 'even under his rule another poor child is born' (Krüger, *Qoheleth*, 104). Another view, followed in the translation above, takes all of 4:14 to refer to the youth of 4:13. The first *kî* clause assigns a reason for the preference of the youth, and the second clause (*kî gam*) is taken in a concessive sense, translated '*even though*,' which explains the background of the youth. For further discussion, see the comments on this text.

64. Many commentators (Murphy and Longman, among others, including the Septuagint) point out that the word *hāsûrîm* is missing an

4:15 *I saw all the living who are walking about[65] under the sun on the side of[66] the second youth[67] who stood in place of him.[68]*

4:16 *There was no end to all the people, to all whom he led,[69]*

---

aleph (*hāʾăsûrîm*), so that the word refers to *'prison'* and not 'the house of rebellion,' which Barton (*Ecclesiastes*, 119–120) takes in a political sense to refer to the Ptolemaic dynasty.

65. Ogden and Zogbo (*Handbook on Ecclesiastes*, 147) take this phrase to refer to people who are going about the daily activities of their lives.

66. The preposition *ʾim* can mean 'with' in the sense of *'on the side of'* (Ginsburg, *Coheleth*, 333).

67. This is a key phrase because the omission of this phrase, as in the RSV, makes the story about two characters, the king and the youth, instead of three characters, the king and two youths (although see the view of Fox below, who argues for three youths). However, there is no textual evidence to support its omission and it is found in all the ancient versions. Gordis (*Koheleth*, 235) takes 'second' in apposition to the youth, 'the youth, the second one,' and understands it as a reference to the old man's successor, which would support a two-character view of the story. He sees a parallel with Hosea 2:7, where the the use of 'first husband' does not imply that there are other husbands. The term 'second' would then simply mean 'next,' so that the youth of 4:15 is the youth of 4:13-14 (Bartholomew, *Ecclesiastes*, 192 also takes this position). Whybray (*Ecclesiastes*, 90) states the view that 'second' could refer to place of command, a possible heir, but he notes that it is not likely that the heir would be a nobody just released from prison. Ginsburg (*Coheleth*, 333) sets forth the unusual idea that 'second' has in view the fact that the youth is willing to associate with people in a sociable way in contrast to the solitary individual in 4:7-8.

68. The reference of the 3ms suffix depends on how many characters one sees in this story. The three-character view takes it as referring to the first youth, who has been replaced by a second youth. Seow (*Ecclesiastes*, 185) notes that the verb *'stood'* (*ʿāmad*) can be used of people taking office (Ezra 2:63; 10:14).

69. The phrase *'to all whom he led'* (*lĕkōl ʾăšer-hāyāh lipnêhem*, literally 'to all whom he was before them') is difficult because it is uncertain what is the subject of the singular verb and to what the 3mp suffix on *lipnêhem* refers. Most of the ancient versions (Septuagint, Syriac, and Vulgate) take the subject of the singular verb *hāyāh* to be the people: 'to all [the people] who were before them [the kings].' However, Seow (*Ecclesiastes*, 185) notes that kings are typically described as going before their subjects (1 Sam. 18:16; 2 Chron. 1:10) rather than the other way around. Others (Murphy, Longman, and Seow) take the subject of the verb *hāyāh* to be the youth who goes before the vast multitudes who acknowledge their allegiance.

yet⁷⁰ *those who came later were not happy⁷¹ with him.
Surely⁷² this also is senseless and chasing the wind.*

The story in this section is a 'tantalizing tale'⁷³ that raises many questions. As will become evident in the discussion that follows, the details of the story are obscure because there is ambiguity concerning how many characters there are in the story. In general, the story recounts how someone from a lowly social position becomes king through wisdom, and gathers to himself a large following through popularity; but this popularity is not permanent, because it is easily lost. There is a strong tendency among some commentators to try to relate the events of the story to a particular historical situation. The suggestions are almost endless, depending on when a commentator believes the book of Ecclesiastes was written.⁷⁴ A modest proposal is argued by Ogden, who sees the Joseph story in the background of 4:14a (the rise from prison) and the David story in the background of 4:14b (the rise from poverty).⁷⁵ However, the connections are too general and none of the suggested historical examples really fit well the account in 4:13-16. For example, Ogden has to take *limlôk*, an infinitive construct meaning 'to reign,' in the sense of 'royal advisor' to

---

70. The *gam* is best taken in an adversative sense to bring out the contrast between the following of the youth in 4:16a and the lack of following in 4:16b.

71. The verb is *śāmaḥ*, which means 'rejoice.' Seow (*Ecclesiastes*, 192) points out that this verb can mean acceptance of a king's rule (Judg. 9:19; Pss. 97:12; 32:11).

72. The *kî* here is emphatic stressing how senseless is the fickleness of popularity.

73. A phrase used by Seow, *Ecclesiastes*, 190.

74. For lists of possibilities see Murphy, *Ecclesiastes*, 42; Seow, *Ecclesiastes*, 190; and especially Barton, *Ecclesiastes*, 120.

75. G. S. Ogden, 'Historical Allusion in Qoheleth iv 13–16?,' *VT* 30 (1980): 309–15. The Joseph connection is based on the parallels between Joseph and the poor but wise youth in the story in Ecclesiastes 4:13-14. The David connection is based on the word 'poor,' which is also used in the story of David (1 Sam. 18:23), who protests to Saul that he is too poor to be eligible to marry the king's daughter. This word is used six times outside the wisdom tradition, and three of them are used in relationship to David (see Ogden and Zogbo, *Handbook on Ecclesiastes*, 144–145).

make it fit the Joseph story, because Joseph did not go from prison to the kingship.[76] It is better to understand the story as a typical story that Qohelet tells to make his point.[77]

It is helpful to discuss briefly the details of the story and the various ways the story has been understood. The main difficulty comes in 4:14, where '*he*' is used without a clear indication to whom it refers. In other words, does 4:14 refer to the '*old but foolish king*' or does it refer to the '*poor but wise youth*'? Are there just two characters involved in the story, or are there more than two characters? Two characters are introduced in 4:13, the '*poor but wise youth*' and the '*old but foolish king*.' A few argue that these are the only two characters of the story. In this view, the subject of 4:14 is the old but foolish king, who also had been born in poverty and had even been in prison before coming to the throne; but now he is no longer open to advice and so is cut off from political reality. The old but foolish king is supplanted by the poor but wise youth, which is what 4:15 relates.[78] Although the nearest antecedent of '*he*' in the phrase '*he went from prison*' is the '*old but foolish king*,' the contrast between the '*king*' and the '*youth*' in 4:13 in terms of social status leads many to understand the poor youth as the subject of 4:14.[79] Fox argues for four characters in the story. The old but foolish king is supplanted by youth number 1, who was wise and rose from prison to the throne (4:13-14a). Youth number 2 is described in 4:14b; he is also born poor, but during the reign of youth number 1. Then youth number 3 is introduced in 4:15 as the one who comes next in line. Fox argues that youth number 1 has already been introduced as poor in 4:13, so 4:14b becomes redundant if it is speaking of youth number 1.[80] Many

---

76. Ogden and Zogbo, *Handbook on Ecclesiastes*, 145. Although Ogden appeals to the use of *mālak* in Nehemiah 5:7 for the meaning of 'royal advisor,' the verb in Nehemiah 5:7 is in the nifal and not the qal, as in Ecclesiastes 4:14.

77. Murphy, *Ecclesiastes*, 42.

78. Garrett, *Ecclesiastes*, 309; Hengstenberg, *Ecclesiastes*, 130–132; and Kidner, *Ecclesiastes*, 51–52.

79. Shields, *The End of Wisdom*, 154.

80. Fox, *Rereading Ecclesiastes*, 224. Krüger, *Qoheleth*, 104 and Shields, *The End of* Wisdom, 155 also take this view.

others see three characters in the story, with a second youth introduced in 4:15. Seow argues that 4:14 sets forth the cases of both the *'old but foolish king'* and the *'poor but wise youth,'* each introduced by a *kî* clause. Thus 4:14a refers to the youth, who went from prison to the throne, and 4:14b refers to the fate of the king, translated 'though born into his kingship, is impoverished.'[81] Others take 4:14 to refer to the poor but wise youth introduced in 4:13, with *'his kingdom'* either referring to the kingdom over which the youth became ruler (his own kingdom)[82] or to the kingdom of the old but foolish king.[83] In the final analysis the main point of the story is not greatly affected by which scenario is accepted, because 4:16 seems to be the conclusion toward which the story is moving.

The contrast between the two characters sets up the story. There is a contrast in social status, for the king enjoys all the privileges that come with being king, and the youth is poor.[84] There is a contrast in age, for the king is old and the youth is young, relatively speaking. The term *'youth'* (*yeled*) is a broad term, in that it designates a wide span of ages, from a child who has not reached maturity, to Joseph at seventeen years of age (Gen. 37:30; 42:22), and even to the advisors of Rehoboam who are over forty (1 Kings 12:8).[85] There is also a contrast in terms of knowledge, with the youth being called wise and the king being called foolish. The 'better than' saying in 4:13 reverses the audience's expectations, because normally age is associated with wisdom and youth with foolishness. The foolishness of the king is described as *'no longer'* having *'regard for advice,'* which goes against the wisdom of taking counsel

---

81. Seow, *Ecclesiastes*, 184. Shields (*The End of Wisdom*, 155) points out that Seow's view is based on taking the word for *'poor'* (*rāś*) as a perfect, instead of a participle or adjective, which is an unattested use of the verb. It does occur in Ps. 34:10 in the perfect, but with a stative meaning.

82. Bartholomew, *Ecclesiastes*, 190.

83. Crenshaw, *Ecclesiastes*, 113 and Whybray, *Ecclesiastes*, 89.

84. The word for *'poor'* may be a loan word from Akkadian (*muškēnu/maškēnu*), which may not focus so much on poverty, but on social status, that is, someone of a dependent class contrasted with royalty and nobility (Seow, *Ecclesiastes*, 190).

85. Longman, *Ecclesiastes*, 145 and Seow, *Ecclesiastes*, 190.

The frustrations of unfulfilled expectations 185

from others (Prov. 11:14; 15:22; 20:18; 24:6). Even though the youth faced the obstacles of being young and poor, wisdom helped him to achieve a very high position in society, for he went from prison *'to rule as king.'* As Seow points out, prison in the ancient Near East was not for criminals or for the purpose of rehabilitation, but was for those who could not pay their debts or who were seen as a political threat.[86] In light of what is said about the youth, the former is probably the case in this story. The point is that the old king becomes foolish for lack of wisdom and the poor youth achieves great success in becoming king through wisdom.

The success of wisdom, however, is short-lived, because wisdom is not able to secure the throne for very long. In 4:15 a *'second youth'* is introduced who replaces the first youth (*'who stood in place of him'*). The reason for the rise of the *'second youth'* is not attributed to wisdom but to his popularity with the people, who are on his *'side.'* In fact, 4:16a highlights that he has the acclaim of the multitude in that *'there was no end to all the people.'* The phrase *'no end'* stresses numbers beyond measure.[87] However, this enormous popularity did not last long because *'those who came after him were not happy with him.'* The popularity of the multitudes seemed endless but it faded quickly, which Qohelet evaluates as *'senseless and a chasing after the wind.'*

Although there is debate concerning some of the details of the story and the number of characters, the general flow of the story is that someone supplants an old but foolish king by overcoming the obstacles of youth and poverty through wisdom. Such a person achieved great popularity with the multitudes over whom he ruled, but this popularity was easily lost because the multitudes quickly changed their allegiance to someone else. The point of the story is generally clear. The story begins with a 'better than' saying showing the benefits of wisdom, but in the long run the benefit of wisdom is relative because it cannot produce anything lasting. Through wisdom a poor youth comes to the throne,

---

86. Seow, *Ecclesiastes*, 191.
87. Ogden and Zogbo, *Handbook on Ecclesiastes*, 148.

but he cannot maintain his position of power. Longman notes that wisdom can bring temporary success but it cannot guarantee what a king really desires, a long reign and a hereditary successor.[88] The reason that wisdom fails is that the popularity of the multitudes is fickle and ever changing toward someone else. Thus even when the people have a wise ruler, there is no guarantee that they will follow that ruler.[89] The point is not just that the benefits of wisdom are relative, a point already established by Qohelet (2:13-17), but that people follow their leaders on the basis of something other than wisdom. Popularity trumps wisdom, and popularity is fleeting because the people are fickle. If the glory of a king is having a multitude of people (Prov. 14:28), how quickly that glory can be lost.

The connection of the story with the context is not obvious. Krüger argues that the point of 4:13-16 is a critique of monarchical rule because within this system the problem of poverty will not be eliminated. The hope for a new king does not go far enough to bring about improvement. Instead of focusing on improvement of conditions from above it is better to focus on improvement of conditions from below with one's fellow human beings. The emphasis on fellow human beings connects to the view of companionship that is set forth in 4:7-12. However, it does not take into account that one's fellow human beings are the multitudes in 4:13-16 who are fickle and so cannot be counted upon. Eaton connects this story with the theme of isolation found in 4:7-8 and sees the unwillingness of the king to heed advice as another example of isolation. Yet isolation is not the main theme of the story. If the main theme of the story is the relative value of wisdom because of the fickleness of the multitudes, then other connections with chapter 4 become apparent. Over against the power of rulers to oppress and the lack of anyone to comfort the oppressors (4:1-3), one should not put one's hope in a multitude of people whose allegiances are fickle (4:13-16). Both 4:1-3 and 4:13-16 question political power

---

88. Longman, *Ecclesiastes*, 147.
89. Bartholomew, *Ecclesiastes*, 199.

itself. The first shows the misuse of political power and the second shows the fleeting nature of political power. In the context of the benefits of companionship (4:7-12), the story in 4:13-16 at least raises some questions related to that topic. A key word in 4:7-12 has been the word 'second,' which has reinforced the benefits of having a companion in labor. The word 'second' is also used in 4:15, but the focus is not on companionship but on being left behind when the crowd changes its allegiance. This key word is at least neutralized in 4:13-16, which raises questions concerning the benefits of 'the second' in 4:7-12. Also, if there is benefit to having two or three companions (4:12), one might draw the conclusion that there is safety in numbers, but 4:13-16 shows that this is not the right conclusion to draw because numbers do not ensure stability. The multitudes may not recognize wisdom and may easily change their allegiance.

Homiletical Implications

There are several ways one can approach Ecclesiastes 4. One could combine 4:1-3 and 4:13-16, along with 5:8-9, and deal with political power. It is also possible to cover chapter 4 under the general theme of loneliness, companionship, and self-interest. It is the misuse of political power that ends in oppression, which leads to the loneliness of not having anyone to comfort those who are suffering. The situation is so bad that it is better never to have been born than to experience the evil deeds that are done under the sun (4:1-3). The fact that envy is the motivation for labor (4:4) highlights the problem of self-interest that is implicit in parts of chapter 4. The lonely laborer (4:7-8) is never satisfied and does not ask the key question concerning the goal of labor. Such a lack of self-awareness, driven by self-interest, leads to loneliness. On the other hand, quietness over against laziness is a proper response to the motivation of envy that drives labor. Plus, companionship is a proper response to the problem of loneliness that can result from self-absorbed labor (4:7-12). However, numbers are no guarantee against loneliness because the multitudes are fickle. A ruler can quickly be left behind for the next ruler who comes along. Such a switch of allegiance is also driven by self-interest, the self-interest of the crowds who think the next ruler will be better for them.

The statements on quietness (4:5-6) and the benefit of companionship (4:7-12) are good but limited answers to the problems described. The statements on quietness sound much like the exhortations to enjoy what comes from our labor (the calls to enjoyment). Companionship has tremendous benefits, but just the fact of numbers does not solve every problem because of injustice and self-interest. Even Proverbs 18:24 recognizes the difficulty of many companions: 'A man of companions may come to ruin, but there is one who loves who clings more than a brother.' The contrast in this verse is between 'companions' and the 'one who loves.' Since the 'one who loves' is presented as sticking by a person more than a brother, the emphasis is on the faithfulness of such a one no matter what trials may come into a person's life. Such a 'one who loves' is there no matter what. The contrast is between the faithfulness of the one and the unreliability of the companions.[90] Here the number of companions is not important, but what is important is having just one who will never forsake the other. In the context of Ecclesiastes 4, this companion would be there to comfort in the injustice of oppression, would not be driven by envy in the relationship, would not be self-centered in laboring only for riches to satisfy themselves, would be the one who gives help in facing the dangers of the journey, and would not abandon someone when others shift their loyalty to another. Such a companion is willing to face injustice, to abandon riches, to stand against the fickle crowds, and even to face the danger of death for the sake of another. The ultimate companion who fits this description is Jesus Christ. He renounced His own self-interest, put aside the wealth of His glory, faced the injustice of a mock trial, experienced the fickle crowds who one minute acclaimed Him and the next wanted to crucify Him, and went willingly to the cross in demonstration of His love. Upon His ascension He sent His

---

90. Waltke, *Proverbs*, 2:87 translates 'companions' as 'unreliable companions.'

Holy Spirit, who will never abandon the one who trusts in Jesus. As Qohelet recognizes, a human companion is a great blessing, but even greater is the One whose presence can never be taken away.

Caution in approaching God in worship? (Eccles. 5:1-7 [Heb. 4:17–5:6])

5:1 [4:18][91] *Watch your step*[92] *whenever*[93] *you go to the house of God.*[94] *It is more acceptable*[95] *to listen*

---

[91]. The Hebrew and English versification is off by one verse from 5:1-20 (4:17–5:19 in Hebrew). In the translation section the English verse comes first followed by the Hebrew in brackets. In the commentary itself, the reference will be to the English versification. Any verse in brackets is the Hebrew verse.

[92]. The Hebrew attests both the singular 'step' (the Ketiv, or what is written in the text) and the plural 'steps' (the Qere, or what is read). The ancient versions support the singular (Murphy, *Ecclesiastes*, 45), but ultimately it does not make any difference for the meaning whether one reads the singular or the plural.

[93]. The verb form following *ka'ăšer* is an imperfect, which conveys the habitual activity of going to the temple, and is best expressed by translating *ka'ăšer* as *'whenever'* (Ogden and Zogbo, *Handbook on Ecclesiastes*, 151).

[94]. The *'house of God'* refers to the temple rather than the synagogue in light of the emphasis on vows in 4:4-7. Most commentators believe it refers to the second temple because they date the book of Ecclesiastes late and because the phrase 'house of God' occurs in later literature (Ezra 3:8; 6:22; 8:36; 10:1, 6, 9). However, the phrase 'house of God' also occurs in Genesis 28:17 (in reference to Jacob's meeting with God), Judges 18:31 (in reference to the ark at Shiloh, which is also called the house of the LORD in 1 Sam. 1), and Psalms 42:4; 52:8; 55:14. The phrase 'house of God' by itself cannot be used as an indication of date.

[95]. The verb *qārôḇ* is an infinitive absolute and can be taken a number of ways. It could be taken as the subject of the sentence, which usually means the ellipsis of *ṭôḇ* ('better'): 'to come near to listen is better' (mentioned by Longman, *Ecclesiastes*, 149, n. 5). Or, the infinitve absolute can be understood as an imperative in parallel with 'guard' (Longman, *Ecclesiastes*, 149, n. 5). It is also possible to take it as an adjective meaning *'acceptable,'* used with the comparative *min* (Seow, *Ecclesiastes*, 194), which is the way it is translated above. The basic meaning is not really affected whichever way *qārôḇ* is understood.

than[96] *for the fools to offer a sacrifice,*[97] *for they do not recognize they are doing wrong.*[98]

5:2 [1] *Do not be quick* to speak *with your mouth and let not your heart be in a hurry to utter a word before God, because God is in heaven and you are on the earth; therefore, let your words be few.*

5:3 [2] *For a dream*[99] *comes with much activity and a voice of a fool with many words.*

5:4 [3] *Whenever you make a vow to God do not delay to fulfil it for there is no delight in fools. Fulfil whatever you vow.*

5:5 [4] *It is better that you never make a vow than that you make a vow but never fulfil it.*

---

96. For those who take *qārôḇ* as a verb, the *min* is explained as the pregnant use (*GKC* 133e) in which the attributive idea must be supplied from the context (Longman, *Ecclesiastes*, 149, n. 6). For those who take *qārôḇ* as an adjective, the *min* functions as a comparative *min*.

97. This phrase is difficult because the word '*fools*' is plural with the article, the verb is an infinitive construct, and the word '*sacrifice*' is a singular absolute. Longman (*Ecclesiastes*, 149, n. 7) translates it 'offer the sacrifice of fools' and notes that his translation involves the transposition of the word 'fools' and 'sacrifice.' The translation offered above is a literal translation of the phrase.

98. The final phrase in this verse has been understood in a number of ways. Some argue that it should be translated as 'they do not know how to do wrong,' either taken as a sarcastic comment (Murphy, *Ecclesiastes*, 46) or as a contemptible comment concerning fools because they lack the brains to do evil (Gordis, *Koheleth*, 238). Fox (*Rereading Ecclesiastes*, 231) translates the phrase literally ('they do not know how to do wrong') without understanding its point! Delitzsch ('Ecclesiastes,' 6:283-284) understands the phrase to refer to the fool's lack of knowledge, with the idea that the lack of knowledge leads them to do evil. The idea that fools do not know how to do wrong seems strange because fools do know how to do wrong. Seow (*Ecclesiastes*, 195) argues that the key to understanding this phrase is to take the verb *yāḏaʿ* ('to know') followed by the *lamed* preposition to mean 'to know of' in the sense of 'recognize' or 'acknowledge' (Ps. 69:5; Deut. 33:9; Jer. 3:13). Thus the idea is that fools do not recognize that they are doing wrong (see also Bartholomew, *Ecclesiastes*, 201).

99. The word '*dream*' in the Hebrew has the definite article, which could be designated as the generic use of the article (Crenshaw, *Ecclesiastes*, 116), which denotes a class of persons or things (Arnold and Choi, *Biblical Hebrew Syntax*, 31). Most commentators translate the word as '*a dream*' or 'dreams.'

5:6 [5] Do not let[100] your mouth cause you[101] to sin. Do not say before the messenger[102] that it was a mistake. Why should God be angry with your words and destroy the work of your hands?

5:7 [6] For when dreams multiply so do many senseless words.[103] Instead,[104] fear God.

In this section Qohelet focuses on the way one should approach God in worship. It is clear that Ecclesiastes 5:1 begins a new section. The previous section ended in a *hebel* judgment (4:16) and this section exhibits not only a change in subject matter but also a change in the way the subject is

---

100. The verb 'give' (*nātan*) can have the connotation of 'allow' or 'permit' in some contexts, as evidenced in Genesis 20:6 and Exodus 3:19 (C. F. Whitely, *Koeheleth: His Language and Thought* [Berlin: Walter de Gruyter, 1979], 48).

101. The word '*you*' literally reads 'your flesh,' which probably stands for the whole person (Murphy, *Ecclesiastes*, 46).

102. Instead of '*messenger*' (*mal'āk*) the Septuagint and the Syriac read 'God,' which is explained as an attempt to soften the anthropomorphism (Whitley, *Koheleth*, 48–49); however, there is no attempt to soften the same phrase with God in 5:2 in the Septuagint and the Syriac. There is also debate concerning the meaning of 'messenger.' Some take it as referring to an angel presiding over the altar (Ginsburg, *Coheleth*, 340), but more likely it is a reference to a priest, as in Malachi 2:7 (Seow, *Ecclesiastes*, 196). Some further explain this 'messenger' as the person responsible for making the collection for the temple, such as a 'cultic functionary' (Ogden, *Qohelet*, 83) or 'a kind of religious bill collector' (Longman, *Ecclesiastes*, 154).

103. The syntax of this verse is difficult as there are three *waws* that join together three nouns (dreams, senseless [*hebel*], and words). The relationship of the nouns to each other is not clear. The solution is not found in emendation, such as removing the *waw* before '*words*' (proposed by Lauha, *Koheleth*, 96 and Fox, *Rereading Ecclesiastes*, 233), because the versions do not reflect a better souce text (Murphy, *Ecclesiastes*, 44). The solution must be found in the meaning and relationship of the nouns and *waws*. Whitley (*Koheleth*, 50) translates all three nouns separately and takes the second *waw* as emphatic, 'For in a multitude of dreams and vanities there are indeed many words.' Seow (*Ecclesiastes*, 193, 197) takes the first two nouns ('dreams and *hebel*') to be a hendiadys and translates, 'for vacuous dreams are in abundance, and there are words aplenty.' Longman (*Ecclesiastes*, 156) takes the second two nouns (*hebel* and 'words') as a hendiadys, with the translation 'meaningless words,' which is adopted in the translation above.

104. The *kî* is adversative (Longman, *Ecclesiastes*, 156).

presented.¹⁰⁵ Qohelet moves from reflections about life based on his observations to admonitions based on imperatives, which are commands directed toward an individual (the imperatives are 2ms). Qohelet offers instruction concerning the proper behavior in worship. The end of the section is not as clear. Ecclesiastes 5:8-9 continues the use of the second person, but imperatives are not as prominent, and 5:10 reverts to third person.¹⁰⁶ However, Ecclesiastes 5:1-7 is framed by imperatives, which sets it apart from other sections. Also, the subject matter of 5:8-9 changes to government officials, and 5:10 begins a section on wealth. Thus the following division seems appropriate: 5:1-7 (worship), 5:8-9 (government officials), and 5:10–6:9 (wealth).

The main issue in this passage is how one should understand the intent of Qohelet's admonitions. Qohelet seems very conventional in the content of this section and the way the content is presented.¹⁰⁷ The concept of the fear of God appears in 5:6 and there seems to be a reference to Deuteronomy 23:21-23 in the discussion of vows in 5:5. For the first time Qohelet uses imperatives, which is a form of admonition common in the book of Proverbs.¹⁰⁸ Thus it is no surprise that commentators have understood this passage as a positive exhortation toward worship. For example, Eaton understands the passage to be pointing people to greater companionship with God that is needed in light of the isolation and injustice of 4:1-16. Although one should approach the temple with caution because of the majesty of God ('*God is in heaven*'), one should also come ready to obey the law as it comes from the instructions of the priests. The concept of the fear of God nails down the proper attitude of worship.¹⁰⁹ Thus Qohelet is warning his readers not to badger God with superfluous talk, which anticipates Jesus' words in Matthew 6:7-8.¹¹⁰ On

---

105. Lohfink, *Qoheleth*, 74.
106. J. A. Loader, *Ecclesiastes* (Grand Rapids: Eerdmans, 1986), 57.
107. Fox, *Rereading Ecclesiastes*, 229.
108. Seow, *Ecclesiastes*, 197.
109. Eaton, *Ecclesiastes*, 97 and Bartholomew, *Ecclesiastes*, 205.
110. Murphy, *Ecclesiastes*, 50.

the other hand, others understand this passage as teaching something negative concerning God. Lauha calls Qohelet's God a distant despot. Prayer is an activity that is useless and not worth the effort and the admonition to fear God is in line with Israelite belief that it is dangerous to approach God (Exod. 19:12). Thus one must be careful in coming before God, which puts a damper on the activity of prayer.[111]

It is difficult to solve this issue because the tone of Qohelet is ambiguous and one's assumptions concerning the rest of the book are a factor in how one understands this passage. Although the view that Qohelet's God is a distant despot and that prayer is a useless activity may go too far in the negative assessment of the passage, an argument can be made that the basic attitude expressed toward God here, and in other places of the book, is caution before God because it is impossible to figure out what God is doing in the world. The implication is that one cannot be sure how God will respond (see 9:1-2). Although God is the One who gives the gift of enjoying 'the portion' that comes from labor (2:24-26), it is not a sure thing that God will give this to everyone (see 5:18–6:6). Plus, even the *hebel* judgment of senselessness is associated with the 'calls to enjoyment' (2:26), or other negative statements temper them (3:14-15; 3:22; 5:20; 9:10). God is the One who has given to humanity a grievous task and God is the One who is behind the unchangeableness of the world (3:14-15). The one positive theological affirmation concerning God (3:17) is mitigated by the negative anthropological statements that follow (3:18-22). Qohelet does not allow the statement in 3:17 to solve the problems with which he is wrestling. Plus, the context of Ecclesiastes 5 supports the idea of a cautious approach to God because it emphasizes unfulfilled expectations toward political power (4:1-3, 13-16, 5:8-9) and wealth (5:10ff). Thus, one should not necessarily be predisposed to see Qohelet's view of God in 5:1-7 in a totally positive way.

There is also debate concerning how many subjects Qohelet deals with in these verses. Fox argues that the central theme

---

111. Lauha, *Koheleth*, 98–99 and Loader, *Ecclesiastes*, 58–69.

is vows and that remarks concerning sacrifice and speech are subordinate to the theme of vows.[112] Others argue that three topics are in view, which include sacrifice, prayer, and vows.[113] Perhaps it is better to see two major topics because of the structure of the passage. A proverb on dreams concludes both sections (5:3, 7), which naturally divides the passage into two parts, with the first part dealing with speech before God (prayer) and the second part dealing with vows.

Caution before God is expressed by the first admonition in verse 1: *'Watch your step whenever you go to the house of God.'* Although the concept *'step'* is used in Proverbs as a figure for human conduct in general (Prov. 1:15-16; 4:27),[114] the focus in Ecclesiastes 5:1-3 is on the attitude with which one approaches the temple, particularly one's attitude toward prayer. The point is driven home by a comparison with fools. The contrast is between listening and offering a sacrifice, with listening being *'more acceptable ... than for fools to offer a sacrifice.'* The attitude of caution before God is represented by listening[115] and the lack of caution is represented by the sacrifice a fool offers. Although it is possible that the sacrifice of a fool is a literal sacrifice that is rashly offered, it is also possible that this sacrifice is referring to the foolish verbosity that comes from a fool's mouth,[116] because the emphasis in 5:1-3 is on the mouth and words. Whichever view one adopts concerning sacrifice does not affect the motive clause explaining the activity of fools: *'for they do not recognize they are doing wrong.'* In other words, fools do not recognize that the sacrifices they offer are unacceptable. They lack caution before God that would include a quiet, self-conscious attitude to their activity in the temple. Perhaps it refers to the fact that their lives are hypocritical, which makes their worship unacceptable, or that

---

112. Fox, *Rereading Ecclesistes*, 229.

113. Longman, *Ecclesiastes*, 148.

114. Seow, *Ecclesiastes*, 197.

115. The Hebrew verb 'listen' (šāmaʿ) can have the connotation of 'obey.' The primary meaning in Ecclesiastes 5:1 is 'listen,' although the concept of 'obey' cannot be completely ruled out.

116. Farmer, *Ecclesiastes*, 167.

they follow ritual without understanding the true meaning of their worship.[117]

Qohelet reinforces the idea of caution before God in 5:2 by emphasizing restraint in speech before God, which goes along with the encouragement to listen to God in 5:1. It is difficult to listen if one is always talking. Qohelet gets across his point with two admonitions, a motive clause, and a concluding admonition, followed by a proverbial statement. Both admonitions stress that one should not be in a hurry to speak when in the presence of God. Qohelet first deals with the *'mouth'* as the organ of speech which is the instrument with which one speaks to God, but he also deals with the *'heart,'* which directs the mouth to speak. If one is in a *'hurry'* in the presence of God there is a tendency to say something inappropriate, such as uttering wild promises, making unguarded comments, and speaking vain repetitions.[118] There is also a tendency to become self-absorbed and forget to whom One is talking. Thus, the motive clause gives the reason why someone should show caution before God in their prayers: *'God is in heaven and you are on the earth.'* There is a vast gulf between God and the one who is praying which can never be forgotten when one approaches God in prayer. The fact that God is transcendent can be understood to refer to His sovereign majesty, much like Psalm 115, or it can be understood to refer to His distance and otherness. Part of the reason for taking Qohelet's remarks as stressing the distance of God is not only what he says about God in other places of the book, but also that one does not see any passion in Qohelet's approach to God. The Psalms, which also are prayers, are full of passion as the psalmist pours out his heart to God with the use of questions, complaints, and pleadings. Even Psalm 115 shows some intensity toward God. The psalmist addresses God with the question, 'Why should the nations say, "Where is their God?"' The answer is that God is in the heavens and He does whatever pleases Him (vv. 2-3). The inability of the idols is contrasted with God's sovereign power, followed by the exhortation to Israel to

---

117. Ogden and Zogbo, *Handbook on Ecclesiastes*, 152.
118. Hubbard, *Ecclesiastes*, 132.

trust in the Lord (vv. 4-9). There is also confidence expressed that God will bless the people (vv. 12-13). The atmosphere in Ecclesiastes 5:1-7 is different because caution before God is the emphasis without the corresponding side of passion and confidence before God. Thus Qohelet concludes verse 2 with another admonition: '*therefore, let your words be few.*' Although restraint of speech can be a mark of wisdom in some situations (Prov. 10:19; 21:23), in prayer one should be able to pour out their heart to God (Ps. 62:8).

Qohelet adds in 5:3 a comment concerning dreams and the speech of fools in the form of a proverb.[119] The verse begins with an explanatory *kî* ('*for*'), which connects it to the previous verse as an explanation (a motive clause) for using few words when one approaches God in prayer.[120] The main problems with understanding the verse are the meaning of the word '*dream,*' the meaning of the phrase '*a dream comes with much activity,*' and the relationship of the first half of the verse to the second. There is general agreement on the meaning of the second half of the verse and that it is the punchline: '*a voice of a fool*' comes '*with many words.*' It is unlikely that '*dream*' refers to a revelation from God, as it does in some places in Scripture (Num. 12:6).[121] Seow argues that the idea of dream in this verse does not refer to a literal dream, but is used figuratively to refer to something unreal, an illusion, which he believes approximates the idea of *hebel*. The point is that much preoccupation with something amounts to nothing more than an illusion.[122] The idea that a dream refers to something that is unreal makes further definition of a dream unnecessary,

---

119. Longman, *Ecclesiastes*, 152. Murphy (*Ecclesiastes*, 50) notes that the verse has the air of a wisdom saying. It is difficult to tell whether this is a proverb that Qohelet made up or whether it was already in existence and he is using it here to make his point.

120. Longman, *Ecclesiastes*, 152.

121. Lohfink (*Qoheleth*, 75) connects dreams to the popular religion of the day, which would include oracles, ecstatic utterances, prophecies, and perhaps apocalyptic things. Others connect dreams to the temple; however, Longman (*Ecclesiastes*, 152) points out that dream revelations by a cultic official are not well-attested in Israel as a normal part of Israelite worship.

122. Seow, *Ecclesiastes*, 200.

because such a definition can refer either to that activity which takes place when someone is sleeping,[123] or to false hopes someone might have for the future.[124] Such a view supports the parallel in 5:3 between a dream and '*a voice of a fool*' because neither of them leads to anything substantial. But what, then, does the first part of 5:3 mean? It could mean that whenever someone is involved '*with much activity*' (perhaps a reference to overwork), then dreams, or that which is unreal, accompany such busyness.[125] Or 5:3a could be saying that dreams, in the sense of unreal hopes for the future, are associated with much activity, but that activity is as meaningless as the '*many words*' that come from a fool's mouth. Either way, the idea that a dream is unreal fits the meaning.

Fox understands a dream to be that activity that takes place when someone is sleeping, but argues for a different relationship between a dream and the idea of 'much activity.' Instead of seeing 'much activity,' or busyness, as that which provokes dreams, one should understand dreams as the source for busyness, with the idea that busyness ('*inyān*) refers to the meaningless stream of thoughts that accompany dreams. This understanding fits the second half of the verse where '*many words*' should not be seen as the source of '*a voice of a fool*,' but '*a voice of a fool*' should be seen as the source of '*many words*.'[126] However, Fox sees the notion of causality at

---

123. Longman, *Ecclesiastes*, 153; Murphy, *Ecclesiastes*, 50; Crenshaw, *Ecclesiastes*, 116; Whybray, *Ecclesiastes*, 94; Ogden, *Qoheleth*, 52; and Bartholomew, *Ecclesiastes*, 206.

124. Although this meaning of dream may not be well-attested in the OT, Garrett (*Ecclesiastes*, 311) references Psalm 126:1. Also, the basic idea certainly occurs in relationship to the fool. For example, Proverbs 17:24 talks about the eyes of the fool being on the ends of the earth, which stresses that the fool is always looking to what will take place in the future and is not able to deal with the present. In other words, a fool always talks about his dreams for the future but is not able to deal with the concerns of the present, so his hopes for the future remain only an illusion (a dream).

125. This view is argued by the following who take 'dream' to be the actitivy that takes place when someone is sleeping: Longman, *Ecclesiastes*, 153; Murphy, *Ecclesiastes*, 50; Crenshaw, *Ecclesiastes*, 116; Whybray, *Ecclesiastes*, 94; Ogden, *Qoheleth*, 52; and Bartholomew, *Ecclesiastes*, 206.

126. Fox, *Rereading Ecclesiastes*, 231.

work in the verse, which is not necessary for understanding the meaning of the verse. The preposition *bet* (*'with'*) may just be making an association between two things.[127] In other words, whenever one has dreams there is the likelihood that a person is involved with 'much activity,' and whenever one is involved in 'much activity,' one is not surprised that one has dreams. The same would be true for the second half of the verse: whenever one hears a voice of a fool one will also hear many words, and whenver one hears many words, one is not surprised to hear a voice of a fool. Regardless of how one understands 5:3a, the point of the proverb is to give a reason for the concluding clause in 5:2: *'therefore let your words be few.'* Many words are bad because they are evidence that one is a fool. Thus 5:3 supports the idea of caution before God in relationship to prayer to keep one from acting like a fool.

The topic of vows is addressed in 5:4-7 with the same emphasis of being cautious before God.[128] A vow is a promise that someone would make to God, particularly when a person is in a difficult situation and they are seeking God to help them in the situation. Examples would include Jacob when he had to flee from his brother (Gen. 28:18-22), Hannah in her barrenness (1 Sam. 1), and Jonah as he is sinking in the sea (Jonah 2:9). If God delivered someone from the situation of distress, then that person would fulfill the vow by making a

---

127. Although the *bet* can signify the cause (Delitzsch, 'Ecclesiastes,' 6:286), Krüger (*Qoheleth*, 108, n. 8) points out that it is difficult to tell whether dreams come through much occupation (occupation is the source of dreams) or whether they are accompanied by much occupation. The interpretation in this commentary understands the *bet* in the latter sense.

128. Some argue that careless speech is in view in 5:6. If a vow is in view, then Qohelet is seen as pointlessly repeating what he had just said (Whybray, *Ecclesiastes*, 95). Plus, the word 'mistake' (*šigāgāh*) is not used in reference to vows (Krüger, *Qoheleth*, 109), and the word recalls Leviticus 5:1-4, where unintentional sins are in view, such as careless speech (Hertzberg, *Prediger*, 122). Thus, the first admonition is not to commit a willful sin and the second admonition is not to compound guilt by lying about it (Leo Perdue, *Wisdom and Cult* [Missoula, Montana: Scholars Press, 1977], 186). However, most commentators see in 5:6 a continuation of the discussion of vows. Thus 5:6 is a further explanation of what it means to delay fulfilling a vow and the results that will come when someone gives such an excuse to explain the delay of the vow.

sacrificial offering to God at the temple (Jonah 2:9), or fulfill whatever promise was made to God (1 Sam. 1). The point of this passage is that if someone does *'make a vow to God'* they must *'not delay to fulfil it.'* In fact, no one is under any obligation to make a vow, so *'it is better that you never make a vow than that you make a vow but never fulfil it.'* Qohelet's advice concerning vows sounds very much like Deuteronomy 23:22; in fact, he may be referring to it because of the close similarity of the two passages.

Deuteronomy 23:21a [22a] *kî tidōr neḏer layhwh 'ĕlōhêḵā lō' tĕ'aḥēr lĕšallĕmô*

Ecclesiastes 5:4 [3] *ka'ăšer tidōr neḏer lē'lōhîm 'al tĕ'aḥēr lĕšallĕmô*

Nothing is gained in trying to distance Qohelet from an acquaintance of the law of vows in Deuteronomy.[129] The main point of both passages is the same. It is a serious matter to make a vow to God and not to fulfill it (see also Prov. 20:25).[130] Both passages lay out the negative consequences of not fulfilling a vow. Deuteronomy 23:21 [22] declares such a person guilty of sin (*ḥēṭĕ'*) without specifying the results of such sinful behavior. Ecclesiastes 5:4 warns against making excuses for a vow that one cannot fulfill by calling it a *'mistake'* (*šĕḡāḡāh*), with the specific possibility that *'God'* would *'be angry with your words and destroy the work of your hands.'* Although some have seen a tension in Qohelet's thoughts between God's distant non-involvement in the world (5:2; 9:2) and the statement that He might intervene to bring destruction into a person's life,[131] there is really no tension if one recognizes that the

---

129. Shields (*End of Wisdom*, 162) seeks to distance Qohelet from the law in Deuteronomy because such a connection has been used to argue that Qohelet encourages the commandments from God; however, there is little doubt that Qohelet knew the law, but his views are limited by his 'under the sun' perspective, which affects his view of God's involvement in the world.

130. Longman (*Ecclesiastes*, 153) notes that Qohelet's views concerning vows are the same as the rest of the canon.

131. Loader, *Ecclesiastes*, 60 and Farmer, *Ecclesiastes*, 168.

issue is that one can never be certain what God is going to do. The prospect of judgment in this life is not denied by Qohelet, but there is no guarantee that the wicked will get what they deserve and that the righteous will get what they deserve. In fact, the opposite seems to be the case too many times (8:11-14; 9:2). Thus there is always the possibility that God will become angry with a superficial excuse and destroy someone's work. This possibility, and the fact that no one really knows what God is going to do (3:11; 8:1, 17), reinforces the attitude of caution before God.

This section on vows also contains a statement on dreams and words giving a final reason (*kî*) for caution before God in the temple (5:7). Thus 5:7 is parallel with 5:3, which also mentions dreams, and it supports the idea that dreams are a reference to what is unreal or illusory. There is a parallel between the multiplication (*rōḇ*) of '*dreams*' and the multiplication (*rāḇāh*) of '*words*,' and because the focus of the passage is on '*words*' before God in the temple, it is better to take '*senseless*' (*hebel*) with words: '*when dreams multiply so do many senseless words.*' The idea is that the dreams of a fool are the cause of the senseless rash vows that he speaks, which make God angry and may lead to his destruction.

This section ends with an admonition in the form of an imperative introduced by an adversative *kî*: '*instead, fear God.*' Of course, the million-dollar question is: how does Qohelet understand the concept '*fear God*'? Is Qohelet's understanding of the fear of God the same as that of the book of Proverbs, which expresses a deep reverence for God reflecting awe at what is sacred?[132] Or is Qohelet's understanding of the fear of God more on the negative side of being afraid of God, either because He is more distant, or because His actions are inscrutable from a human standpoint? In the context of Qohelet's thinking,

---

132. Ogden and Zogbo, *Handbook on Ecclesiastes*, 162. Kaiser (*Ecclesiastes*, 75) defines the fear of God here as true piety and Bartholomew (*Ecclesiastes*, 207) as a holy reverence before God with an openness to being instructed by Him.

the fear of God is not the positive reverential awe that is the foundation of wisdom in Proverbs. This is apparent for several reasons. First of all, the immediate context stresses unfulfilled expectations in reference to labor (4:7-12), political power (4:1-3, 13-16; 5:8-9), and wealth (5:10–6:9). It would make sense that 5:1-7 would also deal with unfulfilled expectations in relationship to God. Secondly, Qohelet does not display any passion toward God in his discussion of prayer, which is very different from what one sees in the Psalms. For example, Psalm 73:23-28 talks about how good it is to be near God because God is the psalmist's refuge and strength, and says that there is nothing else on earth that the psalmist desires besides God. Such sentiments are never expressed by Qohelet.[133] Third, the concepts associated with the fear of Yahweh in Proverbs are expressly questioned by Qohelet. For example, in Proverbs 2:5 the fear of Yahweh is associated with finding the knowledge of God. Qohelet denies that humans can understand what God is doing in the world (3:11; 8:1, 17) because His works are inscrutable. In Proverbs 10:27 the fear of Yahweh prolongs life, but Qohelet questions whether the life of the righteous is prolonged (8:11-14; 9:1-6). In Proverbs 14:26 the fear of Yahweh is associated with a strong confidence, but instead of confidence before God Qohelet stresses caution before God. Fourth, caution before God may explain why Qohelet uses the name Elohim for God instead of the name Yahweh. Yahweh is the covenant name for God that stresses God's covenant faithfulness and His willingness to fight for His people. It is used in Genesis 2 when God prepared the garden for Adam and Eve and provided all they needed, including fellowship with Him. This name became prominent at the Exodus event where God delivered His people. Although the name Yahweh is prominent in Proverbs, it is not used once in Ecclesiastes.[134] In light of Qohelet's

---

133. Perdue (*Wisdom and Cult*, 187) comments that the divine beneficence of the cult is not mentioned by Qohelet.

134. It is also interesting that the name Elohim is only used four times in Proverbs.

statements concerning God up to this point in the book (1:13; 2:24-26; 3:11, 14-15), it is not a stretch to understand Qohelet's view of God as more distant, partly because humans cannot figure out God's activity in this world. Thus one should not assume that *fear God* in 5:7 has the positive meaning that is found in the book of Proverbs.[135]

Corruption among government officials (Eccles. 5:8-9 [Heb. 5:7-8])

5:8 [7] If you see oppression of the poor and violation of justice and righteousness in the province,[136] do not be surprised concerning the matter, for one high official watches out for another high official, and high officials[137] are over them.

---

135. See the discussion of Qohelet's epistemology in the Introduction, where it is argued that Qohelet's use of wisdom is different from the concept in the book of Proverbs, which leads to the conclusion that his use of the fear of God would also be different from Proverbs.

136. The word 'province' (*mĕdînāh*) is seen as evidence of the late date of Ecclesiastes because it is thought to be an Aramaism and because it is thought to reflect a government system reflected in the Persian period (Murphy, *Ecclesiastes*, 46) or Greek period (Krüger, *Qoheleth*, 114; Fox, *Rereading Ecclesiastes*, 234). Lohfink (*Qoheleth*, 80) relates the events of the verse to the Ptolemaic policy of turning much cultivated land into royal land. However, the word *mĕdînāh* occurs in 1 Kings 20 in reference to administrative government districts during Ahab's reign (the ninth century B.C.). Thus this word cannot be used to argue for a late date of Ecclesiastes (see Fredericks, *Qoheleth's Language*, 230).

137. Normally the word 'official' (*gāḇōah*) is an adjective that means 'high,' but in this verse it seems to be used as a noun meaning 'high official' (Longman, *Ecclesiastes*, 157, n. 52). It also means 'haughty' in 1 Samuel 2:3 and Psalm 10:4, which is the way Seow (*Ecclesiastes*, 204) translates it (following J. Kugel, 'Qohelet and Money,' *CBQ* 51 [1989], 32–49). But Seow must understand 5:8 to refer to ambitious people (see the discussion above in the Commentary). Some take the plural of '*officials*' as a plural of majesty that refers to God (Hengstenberg, *Ecclesiastes*, 140–141), who is the highest judge of all (Kaiser, *Ecclesiastes*, 76). But this view has little evidence to support it.

5:9 [8] And the profit of a land is taken by all officials,[138] a king is for[139] cultivated fields.[140]

---

138. The syntax of this verse is notoriously difficult. The phrase *bakkōl* is followed either by a feminine singular form of the pronoun (*hî*ʾ), which is what is written in the text (Ketiv), or it is followed by a masculine singular form of the pronoun (*hû*ʾ), which is what is read (Qere). Supposedly, the feminine singular would refer back to the land (*ʾereṣ*), and the masculine singular would refer back to profit (*yitrôn*). It is probably best to go with the masculine singular form and take it as referring back to profit (Bartholomew, *Ecclesiastes*, 214 n. 5). The phrase *bakkōl* is also difficult, and can be understood as a general statement, such as 'in all things' (Delitzsch, 'Eccleiastes,' 6:293-294) or 'in every respect' (Crenshaw, *Ecclesiastes*, 119). Others take the 'all' as referring to all the people with the idea that the profit of the land is for everyone (Eaton, *Ecclesiastes*, 101; Ogden and Zogbo, *Handbook on Ecclesiastes*, 168), which is usually accompanied by a positive view of the king who is mentioned in the next clause. Seow (*Ecclesiastes*, 201, 204) redivides the Hebrew consonants to give what he believes is a smoother reading of a text he thinks is hopelessly corrupt. Instead of *bakkōl hûʾ melek* he suggests *bĕkîlāh wĕʾim lekîl*, which omits any reference to a king. He translates the verse, 'But the advantage of the land is in its provision, that is, if the field is cultivated for provision.' This means that the land should not be cultivated for its own sake but for what it produces. This is an encouragement to the ambitious (the arrogant of 5:7) not to abandon agriculture as a way of life in their quest for success. However, if one takes the 'all' of *bakkōl* as referring to the 'officials,' who are the immediate antecedent, then the profit of the land is related to the officials, which in context means it is taken by the officials (see Longman, *Ecclesiastes*, 159 for a similar view).

139. The *lamed* preposition ('*for*') is understood in a number of ways, depending on one's view of the passage as a whole. It can mean 'for' in the sense that the king delights in the cultivated fields; that is, he takes pride in the promotion of the welfare of the people (Delitzsch, 'Ecclesiastes,' 6:294-295). Another view is that the king is 'subject to' the soil, which is supposed to mean that the king is not an absolute authority but is dependent upon the industry of the people (Ginsburg, *Coheleth*, 346–347; Gordis, *Koheleth*, 240). Another way to take 'for' is that the king is committed to the cultivation of the fields, which is understood to mean that a just king ensures that the profit is not for a select few but is for everyone (Bartholomew, *Ecclesiastes*, 217–218). A negative view would stress that the king is committed to cultivated fields because of the profit it brings for himself and his officials (Longman, *Ecclesiastes*, 158–159; Brown, *Ecclesiastes*, 59).

140. Although it is possible that '*cultivated*' (*neʿĕbad*) may refer to the king, with the idea that the 'king is served by the fields' (Targum, Vulgate, and discussed by Murphy, *Ecclesiastes*, 46), it is better to take the verb with 'field,' which is in line with the other uses of the nifal verb, such as in Deuteronomy 21:4 and Ezekiel 36:9, 34 (Longman, *Ecclesiastes*, 159).

These two verses present numerous difficulties, especially 5:9, which has been called 'an insuperable crux.'[141] The emphasis on *'officials'* in 5:8 seems to resume the theme of problems with political power, but whether 5:9 reinforces that idea or is a corrective to it is debated. The relationship of these two verses to the context is also debated. Whybray argues that these two verses are completely independent of their context and thus unrelated thematically to what precedes and what follows.[142] Seow argues for a strong connection between 5:8-9 and what follows, based on content and structure. The movement of thought in 5:8–6:9 is similar to the movement of thought earlier in the book from injustice to contentment and enjoyment of life (3:16-22). Just as 4:1-7 begins a new section by emphasizing lack of contentment and people's inability to enjoy life, so 5:8-9 begins the next section by using the same idioms. The coherence of the section is seen in the structure of this passage, which Seow believes is demonstrated in the following chiasm:[143]

A People who cannot be satisfied (5:8-12)
  B People who cannot enjoy (5:13-17)
    C What is good (5:18-19)
      D Enjoy the Moment (5:20)
    C' What is bad (6:1-2)
  B' People who cannot enjoy (6:3-6)
A' People who cannot be satisfied (6:7-9)

The whole passage deals with the problem of human insatiability and the lack of contentment, finding resolution in 5:20.[144] However, for the chiasm to work, 5:8-9 cannot deal with the corruption of government officials, but instead has in view economic injustices carried out by ambitious people who think

---

141. Gordis, *Koheleth*, 240.
142. Whybray, *Ecclesiastes*, 97.
143. Seow's chiasm is based on the work of Daniel Fredericks, 'Chiasm and Parallel Structure in Qoheleth 5:9–6:9,' *JBL* 108/1 (1989): 17–35. However, Fredericks' chiasm keeps together 5:18-20 as a unit which is parallel with 6:1-2 as C and C' and does not include 5:8-9 in the chiasm as Seow does.
144. Seow, *Ecclesiastes*, 216–217.

that they can achieve anything at anyone else's expense. This view is based on understanding *gāḇōah* to mean 'arrogant one' instead of *'official,'* with reference to haughty people trying to climb the economic ladder who are not content until they get to the next rung. But Bartholomew questions the chiastic structure because it separates 5:20 from its integral connection to 5:18-19.[145] Also, the use of the word *'province'* (*mĕḏînāh*) points to some kind of government administration.[146] Plus, grammatically, 5:8-9 is separated from 5:10–6:9. Ecclesiastes 5:8 continues the pattern of second person prohibition followed by a motive clause found in 5:1-7, whereas 5:9 changes to third person and sets forth the first of three wisdom sayings (5:9-11).[147] The focus broadens, however, from what takes place at the temple to things which occur in the province.[148]

It is better to understand 5:8-9 as a separate section that has a loose connection with its context. Delitzsch sees a connection between the admonition to fear God (5:7) and the statement about the king (5:9), which he thinks is similar to Proverbs 24:21.[149] Murphy sees 5:8-9 as a transition to the topic of human desires covered in the next section.[150] Fox sees a loose connection between the topic of injustice in 5:8-9 and the topic of greed in the following section.[151] Although there may be loose connections with the immediate context, Ecclesiastes 5:8-9 has more in common with 4:1-3 and 4:13-16 than it does with 5:1-7 or 5:10–6:9. These three passages deal with political power: its oppressive nature (4:1-3), its fleeting nature (4:13-16), and its corrupting nature (5:8-9).

The corruption of government officials is highlighted in 5:8 in Qohelet's description of how *'officials'* operate in a *'province.'*

---

145. Bartholomew, *Ecclesiastes,* 217. He also argues against the chiasm based on his view that Qohelet juxtaposes different views next to each other. These criticisms would not apply as much to Fredericks' chiasm.
146. Shields, *End of Wisdom,* 164.
147. Murphy, *Wisdom Literature,* 138.
148. Krûger, *Qoheleth,* 113.
149. Delitzsch, 'Ecclesiastes,' 6:291.
150. Murphy, *Wisdom Literature,* 139.
151. Fox, *Rereading Ecclesiastes,* 234.

If one happens to *'see oppression of the poor and violation of justice and righteousness,'* one should *'not be surprised'* at what is taking place. The reason (*kî*) is that *'one high official watches out for another high official, and high officials are over them.'* The verb *'watches out for'* (*šāmar*) is a key factor concerning how this verse is understood. Although a few understand the verse to be stressing that the power of injustice is limited by higher officials who watch out for the injustice of lower officials in order to stop it, which is meant to bring comfort to the readers,[152] most understand the verse to be teaching something negative about the officials. Delitzsch understands the verb *šāmar* as a hostile watching (1 Sam. 19:11; 2 Sam. 11:16), where higher officials spy on lower officials, seeking their own advantage and the downfall of the other officials.[153] Eaton understands the verb to mean that officials look after the interests of each other, with the result of an oppressive bureacracy which crushes the concerns of the poor. Justice is lost between the tiers of the hierarchy.[154] Although it is possible that bureacracy is in view, the emphasis is on officials who are more concerned about maintaining their own position, and the position of their colleagues, than they are about justice and righteousness. Thus the corruption of the government officials stems from their self-interest, which takes precedence over justice. The fact that more than one official is involved shows that injustice is a structural problem[155] and thus not easy to correct.

There are numerous problems with 5:9, not only concerning its translation but also its relationship to 5:8. A review of the different ways 5:9 is understood is helpful. Gordis argues that the verse extols agriculture as the basis for national prosperity because 'even a king is subject to the soil.'[156] Ginsburg, who understands 5:8 as asserting that the power of injustice is limited, argues that 5:9 teaches that even the

---

152. Ginsburg, *Coheleth*, 344–345 and Ogden, *Qoheleth*, 114.
153. Delitzsch, 'Ecclesiastes,' 6:293.
154. Eaton, *Ecclesiastes*, 101.
155. Provan, *Ecclesiastes*, 126.
156. Gordis, *Koheleth*, 156, 240.

monarch himself is subject to law and is dependent on the industry of the people. He translates 5:8 as, 'the advantage for the people is, that it extendeth to all; even the king is subject to the field.'[157] Eaton argues that 5:9 is a positive counterpart to the oppression of 5:8 in that the king is able to check the oppression of officials. He translates, 'but an advantage to a land for everyone is: a king over cultivated land.'[158] Delitzsch understands the verse to be praising the patriarchal form of government based on agriculture where the king takes pride in the promotion of the welfare of the people, with the translation, 'but the advantage of a country consists always in a king given to the arable land.'[159] Ogden and Zogbo take a similar view in arguing that the benefits of the land should be shared by all members of the society and it is the king's responsibility to make sure this happens.[160] These views understand 5:8 in a negative way, with 5:9 offering the solution to the problem, which is a king who will ensure that everyone profits from the land and not just a select few.[161] Others understand 5:9 as reinforcing the negative teaching of 5:8, which is reflected in the following translation: '*and the profit of a land is taken by all officials, a king is for cultivated fields.*' The word '*all*' in the phrase *bakkōl* ('by all') refers to the officials in 5:8, who are the immediate antecedents, with the idea that the '*profit of the land*' is '*taken by*' the officials mentioned in 5:8 (see the translation note). The '*king*' himself is a part of this corruption as he is also '*for cultivated fields,*' that is, he also benefits from the produce of the fields.[162] The negative view of the officials and the king fits with the way political power has been presented by Qohelet in previous passages (4:1-3, 13-16).[163]

---

157. Ginsburg, *Coheleth*, 346–347.
158. Eaton, *Ecclesiastes*, 101.
159. Delitzsch, 'Ecclesiastes,' 6:293-294.
160. Ogden and Zogbo, *Handbook on Ecclesiastes*, 168.
161. Bartholomew, *Ecclesiastes*, 118.
162. The following understand 5:9 as implicating the king in the corruption: Longman, Brown, Farmer, and Hubbard.
163. Longman, *Ecclesiastes*, 159.

Homiletical Implications

There are a variety of ways that this section of Ecclesiastes could be divided for preaching purposes. One could take a thematic approach and cover the three texts that deal with political power in one sermon, with each text functioning as a main point for the sermon. A sermon that deals with the problems of political power could cover its oppressive nature (4:1-3), its fleeting nature (4:13-16), and its corrupting nature (5:8-9). The passage about caution before God (5:1-7) is such an important text that a single sermon should be devoted to it. If one takes a negative view of this passage, there are more hurdles to overcome in the sermon because God's people do not normally think about their relationship with God in this way. If the preacher has been emphasizing week by week the 'under the sun' perspective of Qohelet, then one is not surprised to find that same perspective in this text. The context also supports the idea of caution before God because of the theme of unfulfilled expectations related to political power (4:1-3, 13-16; 5:7-8) and wealth (5:9–6:10). Thus, it makes sense in context to find the same emphasis in the topic of a person's relationship to God, especially when it becomes apparent that there is no passion for God in this text.

The question still remains concerning how caution before God is to be understood and applied. The following questions might help. How does a person respond if they believe that their expectations concerning God are not fulfilled? How does a person act toward God if they believe God has let them down? What does a person do if they are disappointed with God? For example, what if something happens in a person's life, such as some kind of tragedy, which results in a person no longer believing that God has their best interests in view? When people lose confidence in God there may be several responses. Some drop out of church and no longer worship God regularly. When they do worship they come cautiously. Some become bitter and angry toward God because they believe that God is no longer on their side or that they have experienced the disfavor of God. Some people live their lives without thinking about God on a daily basis, but when they do think about God they fear Him because they are afraid that they have done something wrong. Thus, they are cautious toward God. They do not want to abandon God because they may experience His displeasure. On the other hand, they have no desire to commit their lives to God or have Him involved in their daily life. God is at a distance, held at arms length because they do not believe that God has their best interest in view.

There is no way to know from the scriptural account how Solomon ended his life, but he should have known from his earlier experience that God is not a distant God who does not have the best interests of His people in view. At the dedication of the temple Solomon declared, 'The LORD our God be with us, as he was with our fathers' (1 Kings 8:57). When the ark of the covenant was brought into the temple, the glory of God filled the temple so that the priests could no longer stand in the temple to minister to the LORD. The temple represented the dwelling of God with His people. God is not a distant God; rather, He is near to His people. A more powerful demonstration of God's presence came near to us in Jesus Christ, the Word made flesh, Who tabernacled among His people and displayed the glory of God's presence (John 1:14). God is not a distant God, because Jesus is Immanuel, God with us. It is because of the work of Jesus that a person never has to worry whether God has their best interests in view. God has demonstrated that He is on our side by sending His Son to deliver us from our sin. Jesus' work ensures that nothing can ever separate us from the love of God: 'He who did not spare his own Son but gave him up for us all, how will he not also with him graciously give us all things?' (Rom. 8:32). Thus we do not draw near cautiously but boldly to the throne of grace.

Unfulfilled expectations related to wealth (Eccles. 5:10–6:9 [Heb. 5:9–6:9])

General dissatisfaction with wealth (Eccles. 5:10-17 [Heb. 5:9-16])

> 5:10 [9]   Whoever loves money will not be satisfied with money

nor whoever loves wealth[164] with its yield.[165] This is also senseless.

5:11 [10] Whenever goods increase those who consume them increase. What benefit[166] comes to their owner[167] but to see[168] them with his eyes?

5:12 [11] Pleasant is the sleep of the labourer whether he eats little or much, but the abundance of the rich does not allow him to sleep.

5:13 [12] There is a sickening tragedy I have seen under the sun: wealth guarded by[169] its owner to his own harm;

---

164. Although there are questions concerning the second clause of this verse, the meaning is fairly certain. It seems that the verb 'satisfy' (*śbʿ*) from the first clause should be carried over into the second clause, although the verse can be translated without repeating the verb. Also, many take the *bet* preposition on the noun 'riches' (*hāmôn*) to be a result of dittography from the previous verb 'love' (*ʾāhaḇ*) because the bet preposition does not ever follow this verb (Murphy, *Ecclesiastes*, 46; Longman, *Ecclesiastes*, 160, n. 69; Fox, *Rereading Ecclesiastes*, 235). However, Seow (*Ecclesiastes*, 204–205) points out that the *bet* preposition has the support of all the Hebrew manuscripts and believes *ʾāhaḇ* is analogous to other verbs followed by bet, such as *bāṭaḥ* and *śāmaḥ*.

165. Seow (*Ecclesiastes*, 205) notes that 'yield' can refer to the yield of land (Ps. 107:37; 2 Chron. 31:5) or to income in general (Prov. 3:14; 10:16; 15:6; 16:8).

166. Although Seow (*Ecclesiastes*, 205) argues that *kišrôn* ('benefit') is virtually identical to *yiṯrôn* ('profit'), the concept *yiṯrôn* has a special use in Ecclesiastes, so it is better to translate *kišrôn* with a different word. Gordis (*Koheleth*, 241) argues that the two should not be equated.

167. The word 'owner' (*baʿal*) is in the plural, which some have understood as a plural of power (Ginsburg, *Coheleth*, 349) or an abstract plural emphasizing 'lordship' (Henstenburg, *Ecclesiastes*, 146). However, Longman (*Ecclesiastes*, 160, n. 73) argues that the plural can have a singular force with some nouns, including *baʿal* (see also GKC 124i). Seow (*Ecclesiastes*, 205) notes that the 3ms suffix on 'eyes' supports the singular meaning of 'owner.'

168. The word 'see' comes either from *rěʾyyaṯ*, which is the Ketiv, or *rěʾûṯ*, which is the Qere. Both are nominal forms which are found nowhere else in the Hebrew Bible. Thus, some suggest emending the text to the infinitive construct (*rěʾôṯ*), which has the support of a few manuscripts (Longman, *Ecclesiastes*, 160, n. 74).

169. Gordis (*Koheleth*, 242) and Ginsburg (*Coheleth*, 351) argue that the *lamed* on the phrase 'by its owner' (*liḇʿālāyw*) should be translated as 'for its

5:14 [13] that is,[170] that wealth was lost in a bad situation. Though he fathers a son there is nothing in his[171] hand.[172]

5:15 [14] Just as he came out of his mother's womb—naked—so he will also depart as he came. Nothing will he take from[173] his labour that he is able to bring into his hand.[174]

---

owner' and is a reference to the heir of the wealth. However, the *lamed* is best understood here as expressing agency (Seow, *Ecclesiastes*, 206), as in Genesis 14:19.

170. The *waw* at the beginning of this verse explains the harm that comes to the owner of the wealth in the preceding clause. It is called a *waw explicativum* (GKC 154a, note b; Murphy, *Ecclesiastes*, 47; Seow, *Ecclesiastes*, 206).

171. It is uncertain if the pronoun 'his' should refer to the father or the son. If it refers to the father, then the father has nothing left to pass on to the son (Murphy, *Ecclesiastes*, 47; Gordis, *Koheleth*, 243: 'there is nothing for him'). If it refers to the son, then the son does not inherit anything from the father's estate (Longman, *Ecclesiastes*, 161, n. 80; Ginsburg, *Coheleth*, 352). Seow (*Ecclesiastes*, 221) thinks the pronoun points backward to the father's loss but also may point forward to the son's plight. Fox (*Rereading Ecclesiastes*, 238) argues that the primary reference is to the father, because the main problem is not that some people die poor but that some people, like the father, dissipate their lives on useless toil. Because v. 15 mentions labor, it is best to see the father primarily in view even if one takes the last clause of 5:14 to refer to the son. Ogden and Zogbo (*Handbook on Ecclesiastes*, 177) understand 5:14b-15 to be an illustrative aside that is not directly related to the situation of the father, who is picked up again in 5:16, inserted to make a point concerning wealth. The point about wealth is made no matter how the details of the passage are understood.

172. Lohfink (*Qoheleth*, 83) understands the phrase '*in his hand*' (*bĕyādô*) to be a business term that refers to what is in an account which is lost through bad business dealings. However, Seow (*Ecclesiastes*, 221) examines the texts Lohfink uses (Elephantine and Qumran) and concludes that the phrase does not have this technical meaning. Rather, a similar phrase is used in Scripture (Gen. 39:23; Deut. 13:17; 1 Sam. 12:5) to mean 'nothing in the possession of.'

173. The meaning of *bet* as '*from*' is attested in Ugaritic and Phoenician (Garrett, *Ecclesiastes*, 314).

174. The last phrase of 5:15 seems to refer to what is acquired from labor, which cannot be taken with a person at death.

5:16 [15] *This indeed*[175] *is a sickening tragedy: just as*[176] *he came so also he departs. So what is the profit to him who labours for the wind?*

5:17 [16] *Moreover, all his days he eats in darkness with much vexation, sickness, and frustration.*[177]

There is a general recognition that 5:10–6:9 forms a single unit.[178] The beginning (5:10-12) and the end of the section

---

175. There seems to be ambiguity in the word *gam* in this verse. Although Longman (*Ecclesiastes*, 161, n. 86) is correct that 5:16 emphasizes by repetition the tragedy of the previous verse so that the right translation of *gam* should be '*indeed*,' it is also possible to see in 5:16 a second sickening tragedy added to the first stated in 5:13, so that a translation of 'also' would be appropriate. Whybray (*Ecclesiastes*, 101) comments that there is part repetition and part expansion of the previous ideas. Because 5:16 repeats what was stated in 5:15, the translation '*indeed*' is used here.

176. There is much discussion surrounding the phrase *kol-ʿummat še*, which is translated '*just as.*' Longman (*Ecclesiastes*, 161, n. 87) notes that this phrase is unattested in Biblical Hebrew and so it becomes a proving ground for the theories of scholars. Gordis (*Koheleth*, 244) takes the phrase to mean 'exactly.' GKC 161b states that the phrase expresses the exact coincidence of two facts. Since ʿ*mt* is normally joined to a *lamed*, some argue for a misreading of the phrase. For example, the Septuagint has *ōsper gar*, which may read the Hebrew *ky lᵉmt* (Murphy, *Ecclesiastes*, 47). Seow (*Ecclesiastes*, 207) thinks the Hebrew reads *kilʿummat*, which also means 'exactly.' However the phrase is understood, the sense does not seem to be affected.

177. Longman (*Ecclesiastes*, 162) notes that the syntax of the second clause of 5:17 is awkward. Barton (*Ecclesiastes*, 133) thinks that the text is hopelessly corrupt. There are problems with the verse, but it is not necessarily hopeless. The problems include whether the clause begins with a verb or a noun and whether the noun '*sickness*' should have the pronominal suffix ('his sickness'). Gordis (*Koheleth*, 245) translates the clause 'he is greatly vexed and he has illness and anger.' The phrase 'he has illness' understands the suffix as 'to him' (Ginsburg, *Coheleth*, 354). Others take the verb as a noun (the change of a vowel) and omit the suffix on '*sickness*' as a textual error, which is supported by the Septuagint. This leaves four nouns without a verb, which could be an example of a noun clause shortened in an unusual manner because of strong emotion (GKC 147e, noted by Longman, *Ecclesiastes*, 162). Many argue that the *bet* on '*darkness*' in the first clause is carried over into the second clause (Murphy, *Ecclesiastes*, 47; Longman, *Ecclesiastes*, 162). However, this is not necessary if the *waw* at the beginning of the second clause is translated as '*with*' (Williams, *Hebrew Syntax*, 71).

178. Whybray (*Ecclesiastes*, 98) questions whether 5:10–6:9 is a unit and argues that 5:10-20 is a section with 5:18-20 concluding the unit.

(6:7-9) deal with the topic of man's insatiable desires.[179] Two example stories occur in 5:13-17 and 6:1-6 that surround the center of the passage (5:18-20), which is Qohelet's advice in another call to enjoyment. Everything revolves around the theme of unfulfilled expectations related to wealth.

The first section (5:10-12) highlights that wealth does not really satisfy by using three wisdom sayings.[180] The first wisdom saying in 5:10 focuses on one's attitude toward wealth. If someone *'loves money'* or *'wealth'* they *'will not be satisfied'* with it or its *'yield.'* This saying lays bare the attitude of greed. If someone pursues *'money'* or *'wealth,'* that person *'will not be satisfied,'* because there is no end to such a pursuit. The more a person has, the more a person wants.[181] Qohelet adds a *hebel* statement (*'this is also senseless'*) because the love of money does not reach the goal of being satisfied. It is not unusual for Qohelet to add such a statement near the beginning of a section to show where the conclusion of his argument is heading (see 1:14; 2:1).[182] It is hard to understand *hebel* here as 'enigmatic' or 'hard to understand.'[183] It is not enigmatic or hard to understand that the pursuit of wealth does not satisfy, because it happens over and over again. Rather, the pursuit of wealth as a way to gain satisfaction is futile, *'senseless,'* or meaningless. It is an activity that does not lead to the desired result.

Although the statement *'whoever loves money'* (5:10) focuses on greed, the statements concerning wealth in 5:11-12 are broader than greed because they deal with problems that come with wealth itself, whether or not greed is involved. The saying in 5:11 asserts that an increase of wealth means an *'increase'* of *'goods,'* which brings with it an *'increase'* of *'those*

---

179. Murphy, *Ecclesiastes*, 139. Fredericks ('Chiasm and Structure,' 20) entitles this section 'Limitations to Satisfaction.'

180. Murphy, *Ecclesiastes*, 138.

181. Murphy, *Ecclesiastes*, 51; Longman, *Ecclesiastes*, 160; Ogden and Zogby, *Handbook on Ecclesiastes*, 169; and Whybray, *Ecclesiastes*, 98.

182. Shields, *End of Wisdom*, 167.

183. Ogden (*Qoheleth*, 87) comments that it is enigmatic given the deep human longing for the security which wealth appears to offer.

who consume' the goods. Although there is some discussion concerning the identity of those who consume the goods, the basic point of the verse is not affected; namely, the one who has wealth seldom has opportunity to enjoy that wealth.[184] An increase of goods does not mean an increase of enjoyment but rather an increase of hassle, especially if those who consume the wealth are 'hangers-on,' relatives, or new found friends.[185] Or, an increase of goods could mean an increase of responsibility, especially if those who consume the wealth are servants needed to manage the wealth.[186] In other words, when goods increase, so do expenses. The verse ends with a rhetorical question: *'what benefit comes to their owner but to see them with his eyes?'* There is some debate in this verse concerning the meaning of *'to see.'* Seow argues that it means 'to enjoy,' with the meaning that there is no benefit to an increase of goods except to enjoy those goods. In other words, wealth is good only when enjoyed in the present and satisfaction should not be postponed in anticipation of a greater benefit in the future.[187] Fredericks also argues for the meaning of 'enjoy,' but the enjoyment entails the 'mere purview of one's wealth' in the sense that just to see one's wealth brings enjoyment.[188] Delitzsch adds the idea that the wealthy look on all they have accomplished with proud self-sufficiency.[189] Others move away from the idea of enjoyment and stress the idea of seeing wealth. Longman's understanding is that the wealthy have no pleasure in their riches except to see them pass through their hands.[190] Gordis and Ogden argue that the wealthy see

---

184. Longman, *Ecclesiastes*, 165.

185. Whybray, *Ecclesiastes*, 98. Seow (*Ecclesiastes*, 220) lists the options and then argues that the most likely view is that the consumers of the wealth are the greedy, wealthy ones themselves.

186. Murphy, *Ecclesiastes*, 46 and Delitzsch, 'Ecclesiastes,' 6:297.

187. Seow, *Ecclesiastes*, 220.

188. Fredericks, 'Chiasm and Structure,' 21. Although the verb *'to see'* (*rā'āh*) can mean 'enjoy' when used with 'good' (*ṭôḇ*), that is not the construction in 5:11, so Fredericks' rationale for taking 'see' in this verse to mean enjoy is not absolutely established.

189. Delitzsch, 'Ecclesiastes,' 6:297.

190. Longman, *Ecclesiastes*, 165.

their wealth but do not really enjoy it,[191] perhaps because they look on as others consume their possessions.[192] The point is either that the enjoyment of wealth is fleeting and limited, or that there is very little enjoyment in wealth. Whichever way one understands the verb *'see,'* the result is a negative view toward wealth which emphasizes that wealth brings with it unfulfilled expectations.

In 5:12 another reason is given to support the idea that wealth does not satisfy. Qoheleth contrasts *'the sleep of the labourer'*[193] with the inability of *'the rich to sleep.'* The *'sleep of the labourer'* is called *'pleasant'* (*mĕṭûqāh*), which some describe as a calm and peaceful sleep,[194] and it comes regardless of whether *'the labourer'* has a full or empty stomach. The hard work of labor tires one out so that sleep is not a problem. However, *'the abundance*[195] *of the rich does not allow him to sleep,'* which probably means that abundance brings with it cares and worries which make it difficult for the rich to sleep. Having less leads to less worry and stress. Thus, wealth does not bring the satisfaction one might expect, but brings with it troubles that disrupt one's wellbeing.

The troubles that come with wealth are further demonstrated in an example story (5:13-17). The phrase *'sickening tragedy'* is used twice (5:13, 16) to comment on two aspects of the

---

191. Gordis, *Koheleth*, 241 and Ogden and Zogbo, *Handbook on Ecclesiastes*, 172.

192. Ginsburg, *Coheleth*, 349 and Krüger, *Qoheleth*, 120.

193. Fox (*Rereading Ecclesiastes*, 236) argues that the concept of 'slave,' supported by the Septuagint, is better than the concept 'worker/labourer' in the Masoretic Text because it provides a better contrast. The rich also work hard, as does the laborer, but slaves own very little, which is the contrast being drawn in the verse. However, Crenshaw (*Ecclesiastes*, 122) argues that the evidence for reading 'slave' is weak. Plus, it is clear in the context that the laborer has very little. in contrast with the rich, because there is the real possibility he may go to bed without eating very much.

194. Ogden and Zogbo, *Handbook on Ecclesiastes*, 173.

195. Although some follow Gordis (*Koheleth*, 242), who argues that the word *'abundance'* (*śābāʿ*) refers to the full stomach of the rich (Prov. 25:16), meaning that the rich do not sleep because of overeating (Whybray, *Ecclesiastes*, 99 and Kidner, *Ecclesiastes*, 56), the focus of the passage is on an overabundance of things the rich possess, not just food.

disappointment that comes with wealth, which revolve around the main idea of the futility of wealth.[196] This phrase describes something that is deeply hurtful and very painful to observe.[197] It shows how much Qohelet is bothered by the unfulfilled expectations that accompany wealth. The first *'sickening tragedy'* he describes is when *'wealth is guarded by its owner to his own harm.'* It is possible that *'guarded'* (*šāmār*) means 'to hoard,' which would express the idea that the wealthy person in this situation is acting out of greed and is hoarding his wealth for his own benefit rather than using wealth for the benefit of others.[198] However, another scenario could be possible. The wealthy might guard their wealth in the sense of watching over it carefully[199] and being cautious in how the wealth is used, which might not be done out of greed as much as out of careful business planning. Either way, wealth disappoints because it brings *'harm'* to the *'owner.'* This harm might refer to the anxiety and care that comes from guarding the wealth,[200] or it could refer to the agitation and self-deprivation that the wealthy person experiences.[201] If, however, the conjunction *waw* (many times translated 'and') at the beginning of 5:14 is an explanation of the preceding clause (see the translation notes), then 5:14a is also an explanation of the *'harm'* done to the *'owner'*: *'that is, that wealth was lost in a bad situation.'* The *'bad situation'* refers to something disagreeable, but the details of the situation are not given.[202] It could refer to a bad or risky business venture[203] or some misfortune[204] that has wiped out all

---

196. Longman, *Ecclesiastes*, 166. Murphy (*Ecclesiastes*, 166) sees the main idea to be the loss of riches, which is part of what is being argued, but the main idea is broader than the loss of riches.

197. Delitzsch, 'Ecclesiastes,' 6:298 and Ogden and Zogbo, *Handbook on Ecclesiastes*, 175.

198. Seow, *Ecclesiastes*, 221.

199. Ogden and Zogbo, *Handbook on Ecclesiastes*, 175.

200. Longman, *Ecclesiastes*, 166; and Gordis, *Koheleth*, 242.

201. Fox, *Rereading Ecclesiastes*, 237.

202. Murphy, *Ecclesiastes*, 47.

203. Crenshaw, *Ecclesiastes*, 122.

204. Longman, *Ecclesiastes*, 166.

the wealth of the father. The point is that wealth disappoints. It provides no advantage to the person who possesses it because it can be lost so easily.

Qohelet reflects in the middle of 5:14 on the implications that wealth can be lost so easily, and in the process further underscores the disappointing nature of wealth. The *'harm'* of losing wealth in a *'bad situation'* is compounded by the fact that the father has nothing to pass on to his son (5:14b). An inheritance is considered a good thing (Prov. 13:22), but because wealth is easily lost both the father and the son are left destitute. However, one should not be surprised at this turn of events because this is the way life works on a broader scale (5:15). Just as a person comes into the world with nothing, that is, *'naked,'* so shall a person *'depart'* this world with *'nothing.'*[205] Even if a person is able to *'bring into his hand'* material possessions *'from his labour,'* he will not be able to take anything with him when he dies. This fact further underscores the disappointing nature of wealth. Not only can wealth be lost in this life, but any wealth acquired through labor in this life must remain in this life; and thus, wealth is no benefit to a person when this life is over.

The disappointing nature of wealth leads Qohelet to reflect on the advantage of wealth in 5:16-17, which will be followed by his advice in another call to enjoyment in 5:18-20. He asserts again the fact that you cannot take wealth with you at death and calls this *'a sickening tragedy.'* The fact that you cannot take it with you was the conclusion he came to after showing that wealth can be lost, leaving nothing to pass on to the heir. In 5:16 Qohelet reasserts the fact that you cannot take it with you at death—*'just as he came so also he departs'*—which leads to the question: *'So what is the profit to him who labours for the wind?'* The key word *'profit'* (*yiṯrôn*) is used, which was the word used in the question that began the book in 1:3. Qohelet answered that question in 2:11-12 by asserting that there is no profit to labor. Nothing he has said in the book has changed that conclusion, which is reinforced

---

205. Ogden and Zogbo (*Handbook on Ecclesiastes*, 179) point out that *hālaḵ* ('going') and *bô'* ('coming') refer to dying and being born.

by the question in this verse. It is clear again that there is no profit to labor. For one thing, the rhetorical question expects a negative answer; also, the question is asked in a way that prejudices the answer toward a negative response. The phrase *'who labours for the wind'* is a negative phrase. Fox points out that it refers to that which is fleeting because it is not easily held onto. It does not refer to something that is unattainable, because the wealth was attained, but was subsequently lost.[206] The fact that the rewards to labor evaporate would also fit the idea of futility or senselessness. Thus the phrase *'labours for the wind'* supports the view that *'chasing the wind'* stresses futility or senselessness, and not that which is mysterious or enigmatic.[207] Although wealth may be a product of labor, the fact that wealth is so easily lost leads to the conclusion that all a person's labor to acquire material possessions is for nothing. But even worse, not only is wealth lost at death, but the life lived on this earth is full of sorrow and misery: *'all his days he eats in darkness with much vexation, sickness, and frustration.'* The idea of eating *'in darkness'* could refer to literal darkness, in the sense that the laborer works long hours and eats alone, or that he is too poor or stingy to light a lamp. Or it could be figurative expressing the idea of loneliness and misery.[208] Wealth does not satisfy; rather, it makes life very miserable. The misery in life that comes with wealth is expressed in the words *'vexation, sickness, and frustration.'* Two of the terms (vexation and frustration) refer to the inward, mental distress and agitation that can accompany wealth. The term *'sickness'* may also refer to inward agitation, perhaps torment,[209] but it may also have in view an illness of some sort (1 Kings 17:17; 2 Kings 1:2). Thus it is clear that not only

---

206. Fox, *Rereading Ecclesiastes*, 238.

207. Bartholomew (*Ecclesiastes*, 219) takes the phrase *'labours for the wind'* to mean that everything is enigmatic.

208. Seow (*Ecclesiastes*, 222) discusses both possibilities and argues for the figurative understanding of darkness. Brown (*Ecclesiastes*, 61) notes that darkness in Ecclesiastes is associated with either death or misery (2:14; 6:4; 12:2).

209. William L. Holliday, *A Concise Hebrew and Aramaic Lexicon of the Old Testament* (Grand Rapids: Eerdmans, 1988), 105 lists Jer. 6:7 and 10:19 with this meaning.

is wealth disappointing at death, but wealth does not fulfill expectations related to it during this life.

Homiletical Implications

The frustrating nature of wealth is the focus of 5:10-17. Many people who do not have wealth believe that wealth will solve their problems, so the unfulfilled expecations surrounding wealth may need to be highlighted. The distinction between the love of wealth and the frustrating nature of wealth itself may also need to be emphasized. The love of wealth is a problem in this text because the love of money is mentioned in 5:10. It is also possible that the 'guarding' of wealth in 5:13 refers to the hoarding of wealth. The negative effect of money is a common biblical theme (Deut. 6:10-15; Matt. 6:19-21, 24; 1 Tim. 6:10). The love of money is problematic for God's people because it is idolatry. However, more than the love of money seems to be in view in this text. It is not just the love of wealth that leads to problems, but wealth itself is examined and found wanting. Qohelet does *not* acknowledge the blessings that come with wealth (Prov. 3:9-10; 8:18-21), but focuses on the failure of wealth to bring into a person's life what would be expected. Some of the problems associated with wealth include an increase of worry, which may lead to a lack of sleep (5:11-12), the fleeting nature of wealth in the sense that it can be easily lost (5:13), and that its usefulness is limited only to this life (5:15). But even in this life wealth disappoints. An heir can be left with nothing (5:14) and the accumulation and maintenance of wealth can lead to a life of misery (5:17).

Howard Hughes would be a good example to illustrate this. At one point the richest man in America, he died alone on an aeroplane en route from Mexico to Houston. He had become a recluse, addicted to drugs so that at the time of his death he was unrecognizable. His hair, beard, fingernails, and toenails had grown grossly long. His once strapping 6' 4" frame weighed a mere 90 lbs. The FBI had to resort to fingerprints to identify the body. He had developed in his life obsessive-compulsive behaviors. He stored his urine in jars, once wore Kleenex boxes as shoes, and picked up objects with paper towels to insulate himself from germs. He was obsessed with avoiding taxes, so he would live in a hotel penthouse for a period of time before moving to another. He was full of worry and distress, he did not trust anyone, he was paranoid, he was sick, and he was all alone. His money did not bring him any semblance of happiness as his life came to an end.[210] Obviously, not everyone who is wealthy dies this way, but the point is that money does not live up to its expectations. It brings much more trouble and worry than anyone can ever imagine.

Advice in light of the dissatisfaction of wealth: enjoy the portion (Eccles. 5:18-20 [Heb. 5:17-19])

> 5:18 [17] Here is what I have observed to be good: it is appropriate[211] to eat, to drink and to enjoy good in all the labour in which one labours under the sun the few days[212] of one's life which God gives to him because that is one's portion.
>
> 5:19 [18] Furthermore,[213] everyone to whom[214] God gives riches

---

210. *Time Magazine* (December 13, 1976) has a picture of Howard Hughes on its cover that depicts his woeful condition just before his death, as well as coverage of his death.

211. It is difficult to know how to relate the two clauses which begin with *ʾăšer* in 5:18 [17]. The first *ʾăšer* clause is followed by 'I have seen good,' which is followed by *ʾăšer yāp̄eh*. It is possible to take the second *ʾăšer* as a conjunction instead of a relative pronoun and translate it 'what I have seen is good (is) that it is appropriate' or 'it is good because it is appropriate' (suggested by Murphy, *Ecclesiastes*, 47, who uses 'beautiful' instead of *'appropriate'*). Others take 'good' to be the object of the verb '*I have observed*' and the second *ʾăšer* as nominalizing the following clause, which means that it acts like a colon (Longman, *Ecclesiastes*, 162, n. 92; Fox, *Rereading Ecclesiastes*, 239; see Williams, *Hebrew Syntax*, 76). Either way, the sense is not greatly affected.

212. The phrase '*the few days of one's life*' could be translated 'the number of the days of one's life,' which Ogden and Zogbo (*Handbook on Ecclesiastes*, 185) understand as a general statement, such as 'throughout life' rather than as a statement asserting the few days of life. However, the word *mispār* can mean '*few*,' which fits the 'under the sun' perspective of Qohelet where death hangs over this life.

213. Murphy (*Ecclesiastes*, 47) notes that *gam* introduces a second observation that is good.

214. How one understands *ʾăšer* affects the translation of this verse, but it does not really affect the meaning. If *ʾăšer* is a relative clause, then the main clause is without a verb and the thought is left incomplete, which

> *and wealth and the power to consume them and to accept one's portion and to find enjoyment in one's labour—this is a gift of God.*
>
> 5:20 [19] *For*[215] *one will not greatly ponder the days of his life because God keeps him occupied*[216] *with the enjoyment of his heart.*

Qohelet offers his advice in light of the inability of wealth to fulfill expectations related to it. This advice is based on what Qohelet has observed to be good (*tôḇ*) and appropriate (*yāp̄eh*). Although the characteristic phrase 'there is nothing better than' is not used in this passage, there is little doubt

---

explains the dash before the phrase '*this is a gift of God*' (followed by Murphy, Longman, Fox, Whybray, Delitzsch). Seow (*Ecclesiastes*, 202, 223) understands *ʾăšer* as a conjunction functioning in a similar way to 5:18, and translates the phrase 'to all people God has given wealth and assets and he has authorized them to partake of them.' However, Ecclesiastes 6:2 would seem to argue against Seow's view because it asserts that God has not given to all people the power to enjoy wealth.

215. There are two clauses that begin with *kî* in 5:20. The first one, translated '*for*,' gives the reason why God has given the gift of enjoyment to people. God gives enjoyment so that people will not reflect on the days of their lives. The second clause beginning with *kî*, translated '*because*,' gives the reason people will not reflect on the days of their lives: the joy that comes from God's gifts keeps them occupied.

216. The hifil participle *maʿăneh* is either from ʿ*nh* (I), which means 'answer,' or from ʿ*nh* (II), which means 'occupy.' Usually the qal means 'answer' and the hifil 'occupy,' but Murphy (*Ecclesiastes*, 47–48) notes that the hifil form with a first gutteral may be analogous to the qal form, and so it could have the meaning 'answer.' Clearly in Proverbs 29:19 the hifil participle means 'answer.' Delitzsch ('Ecclesiastes,' 6:303-304) argues that the lack of a suffix on *maʿăneh* supports the idea of 'occupy,' not 'answer.' The meaning is that God answers, not in the sense of answering a request, but in the sense of assenting to the joys of the heart. With this understanding a suffix is not needed. Lohfink ('Qohelet 5:17-19 — Revelation by Joy,' *CBQ* 52 [1990], 625–35) argues for the meaning of 'answer' based on the use of the word in the book of Ecclesiastes, especially 3:10-15. In response to the fact that people cannot know what God is doing (3:11), God answers by revealing Himself in the joy of the heart. However, in favor of '*occupy*' is that the Septuagint (*perispaō*) and the Vulgate (*occupet*) attest this meaning (Murphy, *Ecclesiastes*, 47). These versions do translate the verb with a suffix, which is probably supplied for clarification, so that emendation is not necessary (Longman, *Ecclesiastes*, 163, n. 95; Seow, *Ecclesiastes*, 209).

that Ecclesiastes 5:18-20 is a call to enjoyment because the concepts are basically the same as in 2:24-26; 3:12-13; and 3:22.[217] Ecclesiastes 2:24; 3:22; and 5:18 use '*I have observed*' (*rā'îtî*). Ecclesiastes 2:24; 3:13; and 5:18 specifically refer to eating, drinking, and enjoying the good that comes from labor. In fact, the word '*labour*' ('*āmāl*) occurs in 2:24; 3:13; and 5:18, while '*activity*' (*ma'ăśeh*) occurs in 3:22. The word '*portion*' (*ḥēleq*) is found in 3:22 and 5:18. The fact that enjoyment comes from God is expressed in 2:24 and 5:19, with 3:13 and 5:19 using the phrase '*gift of God.*' Thus Qohelet's advice here is in line with the former passages in terms of its basic emphasis, even if he may add a twist to the advice offered in Ecclesiastes 5:18-20.

There is debate, however, concerning whether the advice is a resolution and an answer to the problems that have been presented, or whether the advice is only expressing a resigned, limited enjoyment that is available to people. Those who argue that the passage sets forth a resolution to the problem stress the contrast between Ecclesiastes 5:13-17 and 5:18-20. What is good and appropriate in 5:18 is contrasted with the sickening tragedy in 5:14.[218] Wealth is described in 5:13-17 as being loved and kept by the owner of the wealth, which results in laboring for the wind, but in 5:18-20 wealth is the gift of God.[219] This view asserts that the attitude toward wealth is different in 5:18 because the focus is on wealth as God's gift. Also, the fact that the enjoyment of wealth is called '*appropriate*' (*yāp̄eh*) connects this passage with 3:11, where the term is used of God.[220] Thus Qohelet affirms what is good

---

217. Bartholomew (*Ecclesiastes*, 224) argues that the 'nothing is better than' formula is omitted because 5:18 is in a mediating position in the structure of this passage. Longman (*Ecclesiastes*, 168) argues that Qohelet is being more assertive in this passage than he was in earlier passages. It is also possible that there is some flexibility in Qohelet's use of the 'nothing is better than' formula, which is recognized by Ogden even though he argues that in 5:18 the difference stems from a different functional task of the form ('Qohelet's Use of the "nothing is better" form,' 342).

218. Seow, *Ecclesiastes*, 223.

219. Winter, *Ecclesiastes*, 80–82.

220. Seow, *Ecclesiastes*, 223. Bartholomew (*Ecclesiastes*, 224) argues that

and fitting in life for people.[221] If one can accept and enjoy what God gives, one can live a blessed life that is favored by God and can find true contentment in life.[222] Such a person is so preoccupied with joy that the brevity of life is forgotten (5:20).[223] Some would argue that 5:20 specifically states that joy is the answer from God, a revelation from God in the joy of the heart.[224]

Although there is a contrast between 5:13-17 and 5:18-20, and although Qohelet encourages people to enjoy the results of one's labor because it is the gift of God, it is short-sighted to see 5:18-20 as a resolution or an answer to the problems that Qohelet has set forth in relationship to wealth. The word 'portion' (*ḥēleq*) is used in 2:10-11 over against 'profit' (*yiṯrôn*). There is no profit to labor, but a person should receive the limited benefit that comes from labor, which can be identified with the enjoyment of what labor produces (2:10; 3:22). This *'portion'* is called *'good'* and *'appropriate'* because it is given by God and includes eating, drinking, and finding enjoyment in labor itself (5:18). Truly this is good and is God's gift. However, the twist comes in 5:20 in light of what Qohelet identifies as the reason for this enjoyment.

It is true that God's role is highlighted in 5:18-20. God is directly involved in what a person receives in life. God gives to a person *'the few days of life'* on this earth (5:18), *'God gives riches and wealth'* (5:19), God gives *'the power to enjoy'* riches and wealth (5:19), God gives a person the ability

---

the concentration of the name of God in 3:10-15; 4:17–5:6, and in this passage make them the three main theological passages in the book. However, Qohelet never brings God into the picture to solve the problems with which he is wrestling.

221. Bartholomew (*Ecclesiastes*, 227) understands Qohelet's advice to agree with Proverbs 3:9-10, which speaks of the overflowing of abundance when God is honored with a person's wealth.

222. Whybray, *Ecclesiastes*, 102; Eaton, *Ecclesiastes*, 103; Ogden, *Ecclesiastes*, 91; Hubbard, *Ecclesiastes*, 149; and Fredericks, 'Chiasm and Structure,' 26. Bartholomew (*Ecclesiastes*, 228) calls 5:18-20 a marvelous vision of what life could be.

223. Eaton, *Ecclesiastes*, 104 and Farmer, *Ecclesiastes*, 170. Ogden (*Qohelet*, 91) speaks of Qohelet's boundless optimism.

224. Lohfink, *Qoheleth*, 85.

'*to accept one's portion*' (5:19), but then 5:20 provides the rationale (*kî*) for all that God gives. These gifts of God are given so that a person '*will not greatly ponder the days of his life.*' Instead of expressing satisfaction or contentment, this statement expresses the notion of distraction. The second part of 5:20 gives the reason (*kî*) why a person will not '*ponder the days of his life*' in the statement '*for God keeps him occupied with the pleasures of his heart.*' There is much discussion concerning whether *ma'ăneh* means 'occupy' or 'answer' (see the translation note), but the best meaning is 'occupy.' Thus, the purpose of the gift of God, which includes the ability to eat, to drink, and to enjoy good in labor, is to keep people distracted so that they will not reflect on the miserable nature of life under the sun which never works out the way one hopes. Wealth is full of unfulfilled expectations so that there is nothing left but present enjoyment of what wealth does produce. Although this enjoyment is dependent upon God, it is meant to distract people from the futility of life.[225] Instead of boundless optimism, Qohelet offers the advice of a resigned conclusion in line with the other calls to enjoyment (2:24-26; 3:12-13; 3:22).[226]

The tragedy of not enjoying one's wealth (Eccles. 6:1-9)

> 6:1 There is a tragedy I have observed under the sun and it weighs heavily[227] upon people.

---

225. Longman, *Ecclesiastes*, 168. Fox (*Rereading Ecclesiastes*, 239) argues that people are distracted by pleasures which dull the pain of consciousness.

226. Ogden (*Qoheleth*, 91) argues for 'boundless optimism.' The negative view of Ecclesiastes 5:18-20 will be supported by the chiastic structure of this passage, where 5:18-20 parallels 6:1-2 (see the discussion of this passage).

227. The Hebrew *rabbāh* ('much, great') could express the idea of quantity in the sense of something that occurs frequently. The NKJV translates the phrase 'it is common among men' and the NASB 'prevalent among men' (see also Longman, *Ecclesiastes*, 163 and Ogden, *Qoheleth*, 96). On the other hand, this Hebrew word could express quality, with the idea of weighing heavily upon humanity (NIV; ESV; and many commentators, including Crenshaw, Delitzsch, Eaton, Ginsburg, and Murphy). The parallel passage of Ecclesiastes 8:6 and the preposition *'al* ('upon') support the idea of '*weighs heavily upon.*'

6:2 *There is a man to whom God gives riches, wealth, and honour*[228] *so that he lacks nothing for himself among all that he desires, yet God does not give him the power to consume*[229] *them, but a stranger*[230] *consumes them. This is senseless and a sickening tragedy.*

6:3 *If*[231] *a man fathers a hundred children and if he lives many years, however*[232] *many are the days of his years, but he*[233] *is*

---

228. Many translate *kābôd* as another term for riches (Ginsburg, *Coheleth*, 358; Ogden, *Qoheleth*, 96, and Seow, *Ecclesiastes*, 202). Although R. B. Salters questions how one can 'eat' or even 'enjoy' honor ('Notes on the Interpretation of Qoh 6:2,' *ZAW* 91 [1979]: 282–289), Longman (*Ecclesiastes*, 163, n. 99) correctly points out that honor, which comes with certain privileges and preferential treatment, can be enjoyed. It is interesting that the exact phrase 'riches, wealth, and honour' occurs in 2 Chronicles 1:11-12 to refer to what God gave Solomon in response to his request for wisdom.

229. Many see in the verb '*consume*' the idea of the enjoyment of wealth (Fox, *Rereading Ecclesiastes*, 241; Whybray, *Ecclesiastes*, 104; and Barton, *Ecclesiastes*, 134).

230. Although *nokrî* can refer to a foreigner in the sense of a non-Jew (Deut. 17:15; Ezra 10:2), in this context it is best to take it as a Jewish person outside the family, not known to the person (Crenshaw, *Ecclesiastes*, 126; Longman, *Ecclesiastes*, 163; Murphy, *Ecclesiastes*, 53; and others).

231. Murphy (*Ecclesiastes*, 48) notes that the Hebrew ʿ*im* ('*if*') governs all the clauses down to the main verb, which is ʾ*āmartî* ('*I say*'), except that he takes the phrase concerning a lack of burial to refer to the stillborn child, which results in placing the conjunction '*then*' before that phrase (see the discussion on this phrase in the translation). The word '*if*' should be taken with the first two clauses (Gordis, *Koheleth*, 248) that recount the blessings the man possesses (long life and many children), which are separated from the next two clauses by a contrasting '*but*' (no enjoyment of the good things and no burial). The conclusion, introduced by '*then I say*,' completes the verse.

232. This phrase is awkward. Seow (*Ecclesiastes*, 202, 211) amends the text from *weraḇ* ('and many') to *werāḇ* (from the verb *rîḇ*, 'to complain') and translates it 'but he complains that the days of his years will come to pass and his appetite is not satisfied with bounty and also he has no burial site.' Many understand the phrase as a parenthetical, concessive clause (Gordis, *Koheleth*, 248; Longman, *Ecclesiastes*, 163; Muphy, *Ecclesiastes*, 48), which no doubt it is, but it also emphasizes the length of this man's life (Ogden and Zogbo, *Handbook on Ecclesiastes*, 195). The phrase is redundant, but it fits in with the hyperbolic expression of this man's possession of the good things of life. Delitzsch ('Ecclesiastes,' 6:305) notes that to designate long life in an emphatic way the author expresses the years particularly in days.

233. The Hebrew has *napšô*, which could mean 'his appetite' (Seow, *Ecclesiastes*, 202), or it could be translated 'his soul' (ESV; NKJV). The translation

> not satisfied by[234] the good things of life, and he also[235] has no burial, then I say that the stillborn child is better off than he,
>
> 6:4 though it comes in futility and it goes in darkness and its name is covered in darkness;
>
> 6:5 Also, though it does not see the sun and it does not know anything,[236] yet this one has more rest than the other one.[237]
>
> 6:6 Even if he[238] should live a thousand years twice over and not enjoy the good things of life—do not both go to one place?[239]

'appetite' seems too narrow because the verse has in view the man's whole life (Bartholomew, *Ecclesiastes*, 235). The translation 'soul' suffers from the same problem, because it communicates to people today that the man's spiritual life is in view. The word *nepeš* communicates that the whole person is in view. The simple translation '*he*' is used in the translation of this verse.

234. In a few places the preposition *min* can express means ('*by*'), as in Genesis 9:11 (see Williams, *Hebrew Syntax*, 56).

235. A few commentators understand the *wegam* ('and also') as anticipatory, with *lô* referring to the stillborn child, so that the phrase on proper burial refers to the stillborn child who was not given a proper burial (see Murphy, *Ecclesiastes*, 48 and Crenshaw, *Ecclesiastes*, 120). Longman (*Ecclesiastes*, 170) sees this as possible, but not likely, and Bartholomew (*Ecclesiastes*, 233) argues that it is more natural to take the clause as referring to the rich man.

236. The verb '*know*' (*yāda'*) does not have a direct object and some argue that the sun is the direct object of the verb, with the translation 'did not know the sun' (Ogden and Zogbo, *Handbook on Ecclesiastes*, 199). However, the verb *yāda'* can be used without a direct object with the meaning 'have knowledge' (Isa. 44:9; 45:20) and the phrase 'see the sun' is not attested anywhere else in the Hebrew Bible (Seow, *Ecclesiastes*, 212). This reinforces the first clause of the verse, that the stillborn does not experience anything in life (Longman, *Ecclesiastes*, 171), for to '*see the sun*' is to be alive (Murphy, *Ecclesiastes*, 48).

237. The last clause of 6:5 uses *zeh* ('this') twice with a comparative *min*. The comparison is between the stillborn and the rich man. Murphy (*Ecclesiastes*, 45) translates the phrase 'it has more rest than he.' The translation above follows Seow's literal translation of the phrase (*Ecclesiastes*, 213).

238. Longman (*Ecclesiastes*, 164) takes 6:6 as an impersonal, general reference that is not connected to the situation in 6:5. Thus, he translates the subject as 'someone' and believes this justifies the translation of *kōl* as 'all' instead of '*both*.' However, it is also possible to take the subject of 6:6 to refer back to the last mentioned person in 6:5, who is the rich man.

239. The sentence in 6:6 is incomplete. The verse begins with a protasis (an 'if clause'), but instead of an expected apodosis (a 'then clause') Qohelet breaks off his thought with a question to which a negative answer is expected (Gordis, *Koheleth*, 250).

6:7 All the labour of mankind is for his mouth[240] and yet[241] his appetite is never satisfied.

6:8 For[242] what advantage is there to the wise man over the fool? What advantage is there to the poor man who knows how to walk before the living?

6:9 Better is the sight of the eyes than the wandering of the appetite. Even this is senseless and a chasing after wind.

In the structure of 5:10–6:9, the section of 6:1-9 parallels earlier passages. The beginning of the section (5:10-12) and the end of the section (6:7-9) deal with the topic of man's insatiable desires. Two inner sections specifically deal with the lack of enjoyment of wealth (5:13-17 and 6:3-6). This leaves 5:18-20 to parallel 6:1-2, but in a contrasting way. The scenario in 5:18 is called '*good*' but the scenario in 6:1 is called bad or evil in the sense of a '*tragedy*' or a disastrous event. In both situations God gives wealth and possessions; however, in 5:18-19 God gives '*the power to consume them*'; but in 6:1-2 '*God does not give the power to consume them.*' In 5:19 the scenario of the partaking of the enjoyment of wealth is called '*the gift of God*,' but in 6:2 the scenario of not enjoying the partaking of wealth is called '*a sickening tragedy.*'[243] It is clear that 5:18-19 is not the answer

---

240. Murphy (*Ecclesiastes*, 48) comments that the suffix on '*mouth*' does not need to be expressed if the reference is to human beings. He translates the phrase 'all human toil is for the mouth.' However, M. J. Dahood ('Hebrew-Ugaritic Lexicography,' *Bib* 49 [1968]: 368) takes 'mouth' as a reference to Sheol, which was alluded to in 6:6. A reference to Sheol is problematic for a number of reasons. The nearest antecedent is human beings (Longman, *Ecclesiastes*, 173) and the idea of Sheol consuming human toil is peculiar (Murphy, *Ecclesiastes*, 48).

241. The translation '*and yet*' takes the *wegam* as adversative (Seow, *Ecclesiastes*, 213).

242. The *kî* at the beginning of this verse is taken as either a causal use, translated '*for*' (Ginsburg, *Coheleth*, 363), or an asseverative use, translated 'indeed' (Seow, *Ecclesiastes*, 202; Ogden, *Qoheleth*, 101). Whichever way one understands its use does not seem to affect the meaning. Murphy (*Ecclesiastes*, 48) notes that the *kî* introduces a question that is equivalent to a denial.

243. Seow (*Ecclesiastes*, 225) gives other contrasts between 5:18-20 and 6:1-2, including the fact that the former is positive and the latter negative, the former is universal and the latter is a particular case, and the former is the rule and the latter the exception. However, 6:1-2 should not be seen as

to the problem of wealth, because 5:20 states that the reason that God gives wealth and its enjoyment is to distract people from the futility of life. Now in 6:1-2 it is further evident that 5:18-19 is not the answer to the problem of wealth because God does not always '*give the power to consume*' wealth.

The inability '*to consume*' the wealth that one possesses, which includes not being able to enjoy that wealth, is introduced in 6:1 as '*a tragedy*' that Qohelet has '*observed*' that '*weighs heavily upon people.*' Although the term '*tragedy*' (rāʿāh) can refer to moral evil, the term can also refer to anything in life that is detrimental to life and its fullness.[244] The inability to consume wealth is not a moral problem, because the reason that the rich person does not consume his wealth is not attributed to anything he has done, and God is not morally obliged to provide anyone with '*the power to consume*' wealth. However, Qohelet is greatly disturbed by this situation, as is demonstrated by the phrase at the end of 6:2: '*this is senseless and a sickening tragedy.*' It certainly '*weighs heavily*' upon him.

The reason why a rich person is unable to consume his wealth is attributed directly to God in 6:2. Not only are '*riches, wealth, and honour*' from God, but the ability to consume the riches that one has also comes from God. A person is described in 6:2 as not lacking anything '*that he desires,*' so that the bounty of life is before him. However, God does not give him the power to consume the bounty of life. Although some commentators suggest reasons why a rich person might not consume his wealth, such as war, sickness, or injustice,[245] the cause goes directly back to God Himself: '*God does not give him the power to consume them.*' Whatever situation brought this condition, the end result is that '*a stranger consumes them.*' The '*stranger*' (nokrî) is not necessarily a non-Jew, although that is a common meaning of the term, but in this context is any person beside the rich person himself or his family who

---

the exception in light of the fact that this whole section emphasizes unfulfilled expectations in relationship to wealth.

244. David Baker, 'רעע,' *NIDOTTE*, 3:1154.

245. Kidner, *Ecclesiastes*, 59. Kidner does not mention God's role in the lack of the consumption of wealth.

'*consumes*' the '*wealth.*'[246] This is another example of unfulfilled expectations related to wealth, for even the rich person who has all that he desires may not be able to enjoy his wealth. Thus wealth does not bring the blessings one would expect (Prov. 3:16; 8:18), but proves to be ultimately valueless.[247] The failure to enjoy one's possessions is still the problem in 6:3-6. Here it is not the abundance of riches that is highlighted, but other joys of life come into view.[248] Qohelet sets forth a hypothetical example of a man who experiences the good things of life but does not enjoy those good things. The specific good things that Qohelet has in view are having many children and living a long life, which are recognized in other Scriptures as divine blessings (Gen. 24:60; Pss. 127:3, 5; Prov. 3:16; 4:10; 28:16). There is an emphasis on these blessings as the man '*fathers a hundred children,*' a statement of hyperbole, and two statements on the '*many years*' of his life. There is no doubt that this man has experienced the blessings of life. However, two clauses express that this man does not enjoy the blessings he has received. First, '*he is not satisfied by the good things of life.*' This man is not fulfilled by the things in life which should bring fulfillment. The second clause moves beyond this life to the man's life after death: '*and he also has no burial.*'[249] Not only is this man unfulfilled in life, but he also experiences a dishonorable death, so that his miserable life ends in a bad death.[250] Although Qohelet does not call this situation a sickening tragedy, the way he describes the situation expresses a similar thought. He compares the man who is not able to

---

246. Crenshaw, *Ecclesiastes*, 126; Longman, *Ecclesiastes*, 163; and Murphy, *Ecclesiastes*, 53.

247. Whybray, *Ecclesiastes*, 104.

248. Murphy, *Ecclesiastes*, 53 and Longman, *Ecclesiastes*, 170. Seow (*Ecclesiastes*, 217) shows the comparisons between 5:13-17 and 6:3-6.

249. Seow (*Ecclesiastes*, 211) argues that the term '*burial*' ($qĕbûrāh$) refers to a burial site rather than the act of being buried based on its use in Western Semitic inscriptions, but this understanding fits his view that the clause describes the rich man complaining about not having a burial site rather than describing what happens to the rich man at death. Others argue that the word can also mean a proper burial (Gordis, *Koheleth*, 361).

250. Provan, *Ecclesiastes*, 129.

enjoy *'the good things of life,'* and then is not given a proper burial, with a *'stillborn child.'* It is better to be a *'stillborn child'* than to have *'the good things of life'* but not enjoy them. In other words, it is better to miscarry at birth than to miscarry in life. If one cannot enjoy life, it is better not to enter life at all.[251]

Qohelet gives the reason why the stillborn child is better off than the rich man in 6:4-6. It seems that 6:4-5a states the negative condition of the stillborn child in order to contrast that negative condition with the reason that the stillborn child is better off than the rich man.[252] Thus the *kî* at the beginning of 6:4 should be translated as a concessive (*'though'*). The *gam* at the beginning of 6:5 continues a description of the negative condition of the stillborn, and can be translated as *'also,'* which carries forward the concessive idea *'though.'*[253] The condition of the stillborn is described in a number of ways. First, *'it comes in futility'* (*hebel*). Although some try to understand *hebel* here as enigmatic,[254] that meaning does not work well. The point is not that the birth of the stillborn is enigmatic or mysterious, because Qohelet goes on to describe explicitly the condition of the stillborn, a condition which does not fulfill any purpose. The coming and going of the stillborn is futile because at birth the child has no life. Thus its birth is pointless because even at the moment of birth is the *'darkness'* of death. The child is born dead and is thus covered in darkness from the beginning, so

---

251. The first statement comes from Eaton, *Ecclesiastes*, 106 and the second statement from Ogden, *Qoheleth*, 98.

252. Fox (*Rereading Ecclesiastes*, 243) argues that 6:4 is not describing the stillborn but is describing the rich man. He tries to explain the phrases in 6:4 in relationship to the rich man and does not believe a description of the stillborn would be relevant. However, the phrases do not fit the description of the rich man (see the explanation in the commentary) and a comparison with the stillborn is relevant to the point Qohelet is making, especially if one understands 6:4-5a as concessive.

253. Ginsburg (*Coheleth*, 361) argues that the *gam* intensifies what has already been said.

254. Ogden and Zogbo (*Handbook on Ecclesiastes*, 197) argue that *hebel* means enigmatic, stating that inexplicably the stillborn denies its parents the joy of parenthood. However, this idea is completely foreign to the context. Even the idea of fleeting (Seow, *Ecclesiastes*, 212) does not seem to fit well, because the child is dead at birth.

there is no opportunity for the child to develop a character or reputation, which seems to be the point of the clause, '*its name is covered in darkness.*'[255] The potential of what the child could become is cut off at birth because the child is already dead. 6:5a continues the description of the condition of the stillborn child: '*it does not see the sun and it does not know anything.*' The stillborn child does not experience life and is not consciously aware of anything because at the moment of birth it is shrouded in the darkness of death. However, even though the stillborn child is dead at birth and has no opportunity to experience life itself, Qohelet concludes that the stillborn child is better off than the rich man because the stillborn child is experiencing '*rest.*' This '*rest*' describes the lack of conscious awareness of life that death brings. Thus the stillborn child who experiences nothing of this life is better off than the rich man who has been blessed with experiencing the good things of life but is not able to enjoy them. Qohelet drives home this point in 6:6 by focusing on one of the blessings of life in a hyperbolic way: '*even if he should life a thousand years twice over and not enjoy the good things of life.*' Here the blessing of long life is used as an example. What does it matter if a rich person lives for two thousand years if that person does not enjoy the good things of life? Such a life itself is futile, not only because there is no enjoyment of life but because eventually such a person will end up where the stillborn child ended up: '*do not both go to one place?*' Since death trumps everything it is better to reach death quickly, like the stillborn, than to live a very long time without the enjoyment of life, and then to experience death. Perhaps Qohelet is saying that one death is better than two deaths with one of those deaths being a living death without the enjoyment of life. Thus it is better to have no experience of life than to have a joyless life.[256]

---

255. Murphy (*Ecclesiastes*, 54) takes the phrase as idiomatic for non-existence or death and Seow (*Ecclesiastes*, 212) that the memory of the stillborn will be buried with it. The point seems to be a lack of identity (Longman, *Ecclesiastes*, 171). The word '*name*' could refer to memory (Whybray, *Ecclesiastes*, 106) or it could refer to personality or reputation (Ogden and Zogbo, *Handbook on Ecclesiastes*, 197 and Eaton, *Ecclesiastes*, 106).

256. Delitzsch, 'Ecclesiastes,' 6:307.

Ecclesiastes 6:7-9 closes the section of 5:10–6:9 by dealing with the general topic of man's insatiable desires, which are also covered in 5:10-12. In Ecclesiastes 5:10-12 Qohelet shows how money does not satisfy (*śāḇaʿ*) and in 6:7-9 Qohelet raises some questions related to the fact that the appetites of human beings are never satisfied (*mālēʾ*).[257] In 6:7 Qohelet states that '*all the labour of mankind is for his mouth and yet his appetite is never satisfied.*' This verse focuses on the daily physical needs that people must meet. People work to satisfy the basic physical need of food, which is an ongoing concern because even if there is enough food for one day, the next day will bring more hunger pains that need to be met. Thus the '*appetite is never satisfied.*'[258] In 6:7 Qohelet states the basic principle, but the focus should not be limited to physical needs. The word '*appetite*' (*nep̄eš*) has the broader meaning of 'desire,' and people work for much more than their daily physical needs. Thus, not only food, but shelter, clothing, and other desires can be the goal of human labor. The broader idea is that the life of the person as a whole is unfulfilled.[259]

The broader aspect of the desires of life is evident in 6:8. Part of the difficulty of 6:8 is that it does not seem to be connected to the previous verse or to the section as a whole.[260] There is a general connection between the concept of 'benefit' (*kišrôn*) in 5:11 and the concept of '*advantage*' (*yôṯēr*) in 6:8, in that both occur in the context of the inability of wealth to satisfy human desires. The owner of wealth has no real benefit over others not only because wealth does not satisfy but also because wealth brings worry which does not allow

---

257. Although the terms used in 5:10-12 and 6:7-9 are different, the basic ideas are the same. The parallel concepts include being satisfied (*śāḇaʿ*) in 5:10 and being filled (*mālēʾ*) in 6:7, the yield (*teḇûʾāh*) from wealth in 5:10 and the concept of labor (*ʿāmāl*) in 6:7, and the idea of benefit (*kišrôn*) in 5:11 and advantage (*yôṯēr*) in 6:8.

258. One should not limit the problem to greedy people (Seow, *Ecclesiastes*, 226), because everyone faces the challenge of meeting daily physical needs.

259. Bartholomew, *Ecclesiastes*, 233, n. 13.

260. Whybray (*Ecclesiastes*, 108) argues that 6:8 is totally unrelated to what precedes or follows.

the owner to sleep (5:11-12). In 6:7-8 Qohelet moves from the acquisition of wealth through labor to the skills that are needed to accumulate wealth.[261] Such skills are commonly associated with wisdom, which can enable a person to acquire riches (Prov. 3:16; 22:4). If the *'appetite is never satisfied,'* then what use are the skills that come with wisdom? Qohelet thus returns to a question that he raised earlier in the book (2:13-16): *'what advantage is there to the wise man over the fool?'* If the skills associated with wisdom that enable one to acquire material goods ultimately do not lead to satisfaction because *'the appetite is never satisfied,'* then the *'wise'* do not have any *'advantage'* over the *'fool'* in quenching the appetite.[262] The same can be said for the *'poor man'* who learns how to conduct himself *'before the living.'*[263] He also has no advantage because the skills he uses to act appropriately in various situations of life do not lead to a satisfied life. In both cases there is no satisfaction. The wise are not satisfied with the material wealth that may accompany wise living and the poor are not satisfied when the basic needs of life are met. Whether one is wealthy or poor, the basic thesis remains: the *'appetite is never satisfied.'*

Two conclusions are drawn in 6:9 in light of the thesis that the appetite is never satisfied. The first conclusion is a relative conclusion, which is followed by an ultimate conclusion. The relative conclusion states, *'Better is the sight of the eyes than the wandering of the appetite.'* There is some debate concerning whether *'the sight of the eyes'* refers to the action of seeing or to the object which is seen, but perhaps both are in view.[264] The contrast is between *'the sight of the*

---

261. Shields, *End of Wisdom*, 172.

262. Longman, *Ecclesiastes*, 173; Seow, *Ecclesiastes*, 214.

263. The phrase 'to walk before the living' refers to appropriate conduct before others (Ogden and Zogbo, *Handbook on Ecclesiastes*, 205; Fox, *Rereading Ecclesiastes*, 246; and Crenshaw, *Ecclesiastes*, 129).

264. Seow (*Ecclesiastes*, 214) comments that normally the term *mar'eh* refers to the ability to see but that here it refers to what one has, that is, the experiencing of what the eyes see. Murphy (*Ecclesiastes*, 54), on the other hand, opts for the straightforward action of seeing because the comparison is not between objects but between the actions of seeing and desiring, with

eyes' and *'the wandering of the appetite.'*²⁶⁵ The phrase *'sight of the eyes'* includes not only what one can see with their eyes, but also what one possesses. The latter idea is supported by the parallel with 5:11, where the concept of 'seeing' is used of the owner of goods. Thus the sight of the eyes refers to what one has in their possession, or possibly what one can attain. On the other hand, the *'wandering of the appetite'* refers to things that a person desires to have but which are beyond his possession. Thus Qohelet's relative conclusion states that what a person has in their possession is better than what a person desires but does not have. If the appetite can never be satisfied, then what one already possesses is better than what one desires but does not possess. The implicit advice is to rest content with what one possesses. The modern proverb, 'A bird in the hand is worth two in the bush,' would express a similar idea.²⁶⁶ However, this conclusion is only a relative conclusion because Qohelet goes on to render a judgment on what he has stated to be *'better'*: *'Even this is senseless and a chasing after wind.'* Although this concluding phrase brings to a close the whole section,²⁶⁷ it is also particularly connected with the previous statement in 6:9a by the *gam zeh* (*'even this'*). Not even what one possesses can give satisfaction. Thus the basic thesis of 6:7-9 is established: *'the appetite is never satisfied.'*

---

the former being superior. However, the reason Murphy offers to argue that the action of seeing is superior is that seeing implies some kind of possession. Thus it seems appropriate to see both seeing objects and possession of those objects in view.

265. Seow (*Ecclesiastes*, 202, 215) argues that the phrase *mĕhălăk-năpeš* refers to death and should be translated 'the passing of life.' He argues that Qohelet uses the verb *hălăk* to refer to death and that the metaphor of a wandering appetite is somewhat forced. The idea being expressed would be that the pleasure of the moment is better than the departing of life (see also Whybray, *Ecclesiastes*, 109 and Bartholomew, *Ecclesiastes*, 233, n. 17). However, Longman (*Ecclesiastes*, 174) points out that this would require a translation of *nepeš* that is different from the one two verses before. Thus the context favors the concept of *'appetite.'*

266. Several commentators mention this proverb, including Murphy (*Ecclesiastes*, 48) and Longman (*Ecclesiastes*, 175).

267. Ogden and Zogbo (*Handbook on Ecclesiastes*, 206) specifically comment that *'this'* has in view issues raised in these verses and not just the proverb itself.

But the general thesis of the whole unit is also established, for *'this is senseless and a chasing after wind'* is a fitting conclusion to a section that stresses the inability of wealth to satisfy. Part of the dissatisfaction relates to what comes with wealth (5:10-12), but part of the dissatisfaction relates to the human craving for more. In some instances God Himself withholds the power to enjoy what one has (5:18-20).

Homiletical Implications

This section clearly shows that money does not satisfy, which clearly fits the context which emphasizes unfulfilled expectations. Such a theme is always valid, but especially in a Western culture that has an abundance of things. Many people live their lives in a way that seems to exemplify the belief that money and material goods would satisfy if only people could get enough of them. As a dear brother in a former church used to ask periodically, 'How much money is needed to make someone happy?' And he would always answer with a twinkle in his eye, 'Just one more dollar, just one more dollar.' Qohelet clearly shows that money and material goods do not satisfy. It is important to note that the problem is not money itself, but as the apostle Paul reminds us it is the love of money that is the root of all kinds of evil (1 Tim. 6:10). It is the craving for more that is identified as the problem in both 1 Timothy 6:10 and in Ecclesiastes 5:10 and 6:9. Thus part of the problem relates to the human desire for more, which affects both the wise and the fool. But wealth itself is also part of the problem in the sense that wealth brings with it worries that those who are poor do not have, because life becomes more complex with the accumulation of wealth. One particular problem that Qohelet mentions is that many times the wealthy have a hard time sleeping (5:12). Another particular worry is that whatever one gains in this life can be lost in a bad venture, with the result that one has nothing to leave as an inheritance (5:15). Plus, whatever one gains in this life is forfeited at death because it cannot be taken to the next life (5:16). Thus there is nothing permanent about wealth.

Qohelet's basic conclusion is that one must seek to enjoy what one has in their possession. In 5:18 this is called a person's *'portion'* (*ḥēlĕq*), which falls short of 'profit' (*yitrôn*) but is available for a person's enjoyment even though there is no profit in labor (2:10-11). This portion is also called a gift of God, but it is clear that this portion is not an answer to the issues with which Qohelet is struggling. There are several things that demonstrate the shortcoming of this portion that comes from God. First, God gives this portion to keep people occupied so that they will not reflect on the meaninglessness of their lives (5:20). Second, God does not give everyone the power to enjoy this portion (6:1-2). This fact calls into question all the benefits that normally come with wisdom, because one can experience all those benefits but not enjoy them. Qohelet calls this *'a sickening tragedy'* (6:2) and concludes that a stillborn child who has never experienced anything in life is better off than the person who is not able to enjoy the good things in life (6:3-6). Thus Qohelet questions again whether the wise person has any advantage over the fool (6:8), with the implied answer that the wise have no advantage over the fool, which fits earlier conclusions in the book (2:13-16). Finally, Qohelet acknowledges that what one possesses is better than what one desires, but then concludes that even this is senseless and a chasing after wind. Thus the problem with wealth relates to the insatiability of human desires, the burdens that come with the accumulation of wealth, and the fact that God does not always allow a person to enjoy wealth's benefits.

Qohelet is ultimately limited by his earthly, 'under the sun,' perspective so that he is not able to argue that wealth and its benefits are to be used for the glory of God (1 Cor. 10:31). It is appropriate for believers to enjoy the blessings of this life, which come from the hand of God, for everything created by God is good and is to be received with thanksgiving. Things in this life are made holy by the word of God and prayer (1 Tim. 4:4-5). The enjoyment of God's good gifts should come from a heart of thanksgiving. We are not looking for an escape from the troubles of life but we look to use what good gifts God has given us for our benefit and His glory. We understand that there is more to life than what we experience in this life, which dramatically affects our attitude and perspective on the good things of this world. Our 'above the sun' view puts into proper perspective the riches of this world. We know that one day we will be rich, so we are free to use the wealth of this world for the glory of God. We are not concerned about taking it with us because we realize that what we will receive in the next life is far greater than anything we can receive in this life. Without this 'above the sun' view people are stuck in seeking to find fulfillment in the things of this life. Even Qohelet acknowledges that such an approach will not work.

5.
Human limitations concerning knowledge: who knows what is good? (Eccles. 6:10–8:17)

Ecclesiastes 6:10-12 plays a key role in the book by acting as a transition from the first part to the second part of the book. Connections to the first part of the book include the cyclical and determined nature of the world (6:10a with 1:9-10), the nature of humanity (6:10b with 3:11), and the nature of God (6:10c with 3:14-15, 18).[1] The two questions in 6:12 introduce the second part of the book. The first question, 'Who knows what is good?' is addressed in 7:1–8:17. The second question, 'Who can tell what will come in the future?' is addressed in 9:1–10:20. Salyer makes the interesting argument that Qohelet moves from pessimism in the first part of the book to skepticism in the second part of the book, which is demonstrated by the different overriding questions that dominate the two parts of the book. In the first part of the book the dominant question is the 'what profit' question, but in the second part of the book the dominant question is 'who knows?' The quest for meaning takes a back seat in the second part of the book and more philosophical issues become prominent.[2] Qohelet

---

1. Salyer, *Vain Rhetoric*, 332–333.

2. Salyer, *Vain Rhetoric*, 326–328. He defines pessimism as referring to attitudes about the relative evil or goodness of the world or of people's experience of the world. He defines skepticism as expressing grave doubts about the ability of humans to know adequately in any absolute and certain sense, which questions the sufficiency of the faculties of knowing.

begins to question the ability of human beings to understand the world in which they live, which is a challenge to the ability and achievement of wisdom.[3]

The theme of 'Who knows what is good?' dominates 7:1–8:17. The question is immediately addressed in 7:1-14, which is composed of proverbial sayings (7:1-12) followed by a conclusion (7:13-14). In the conclusion (7:14), the question is presented in terms of human beings not being able to find out what they are seeking. The theme of trying to 'find out' also occurs in 7:24, 29, and 8:17. At the end of chapter 7 Qohelet specifically takes up the topic of trying to know the scheme of things, which he admits he has not found (7:28). Then the question 'who knows?' frames chapter 8, which ends with the negative statement that even the wise man does not know.

Human limitation: the essence of humanity (Eccles. 6:10-12)

6:10 Whatever exists[4] has already been named and it is known what mankind is[5] and he is unable to dispute with one stronger than he.

---

3. Longman (*Ecclesiastes*, 176) states this in a more general way when he notes that Qohelet leaves his explicit search for meaning and focuses on advice and commentary about the future.

4. The Hebrew phrase *mah-šĕhāyāh* is understood in two ways. Seow (*Ecclesiastes*, 230) argues that it refers to current events or states of affairs with an emphasis on what has been done in the universe. This view fits in well with the emphasis in Ecclesiastes on what takes place under the sun (1:9-11; 3:14-15). Ogden and Zogbo (*Handbook on Ecclesiastes*, 208) argue that the focus in this text is broader than events but that it includes all that exists in this world. This seems to be one of those situations where it may not be either/or but both/and. This section makes explicit connections to creation (naming and the use of *'āḏām*), which would support the view that everything that exists is in view, although this would include activities and events. Thus the phrase is translated with the broader idea of '*whatever exists.*'

5. This meaning of the phrase *'ašer hû' 'āḏām* is debated. The Hebrew literally reads 'it is known that he is human,' and the Septuagint reads 'it is known what the human is.' Seow (*Ecclesiastes*, 231–232) finds the Hebrew awkward and the Greek hardly possible. He notes that *'ašer* can mean 'what' as a relative pronoun but not as an answer to a question; rather, after verbs of perception it means 'that,' which throws doubt on the Septuagint

6:11 *If*[6] *there are many words senselessness increases. What profit is there to mankind?*

6:12 *For who knows what is good for mankind during the few days of his senseless life? He makes them*[7] *as a shadow so*[8] *who can tell mankind what will be after him under the sun?*

---

understanding. Seow wants to connect *'ăšer* to an Arabic noun, *'atar*, which means a course or a path that one follows, which he relates to the Hebrew word *'ašûr*. The meaning of the phrase is 'the course of human beings is known,' which parallels the previous phrase that whatever happens is designated. Bartholomew (*Ecclesiastes*, 234, n. 19), on the other hand, accepts 'what' as the translation of *'ăšer* on the basis that the relative pronoun can be translated 'that which' when used in a statement. Either way one translates the phrase, the point of human limitation is still the issue, whether what is known is what a human being is or the course of a human life. Some commentators disregard the Hebrew accents and take *'āḏām* with the following phrase: 'it is known that man cannot contend with one mightier than himself' (Gordis, *Koheleth*, 162; Fox, *Rereading Ecclesiastes*, 247–248), but such a change must also overlook the pronoun *hû'* and the *waw* conjunction on the following clause.

6. Many take the *kî* as causal, which gives a reason for 6:10c (Longman, Delitzsch, Ogden, and Zogbo). This leads to the translation, 'For there are many words that increase senselessness.' But as Fox (*Rereading Ecclesiastes*, 248) notes, this translation does not fit the context for it seems to exempt some words from being senseless. He suggests translating the *kî* as '*if*,' which is followed above (for the conditional meaning of *kî* see Gen. 4:24; Exod. 12:48). This view fits in well with what was said about words earlier in the book (5:7). There may still be a causal relationship between 6:11a and 6:10 based on the juxtaposition of the two verses.

7. The meaning of '*āśāh* in the phrase *wĕyaʿăśēm* ('*he makes them*') is debated. Murphy (*Ecclesiastes*, 57) takes the *waw* plus the verb as functioning like a relative clause, with the meaning of '*āśāh* as 'pass through.' Gordis (*Koheleth*, 254) and Seow (*Ecclesiastes*, 233) understand the verb '*āśāh* to mean 'spend time,' which is a meaning of this verb in Rabbinic Hebrew. The phrase refers to human beings who spend their life like a shadow. Both of the views above appeal to Ruth 2:19 as justification for the meaning of '*āśāh*. However, Crenshaw (*Ecclesiastes*, 132) points out that in Ruth 2:19 the verb means 'work.' If one follows this meaning of the verb and makes God the subject, then the idea is that God makes human beings like a shadow (Longman, *Ecclesiastes*, 178). Since God is implied in the passive verbs of 6:10-11, it is not impossible that He could be the subject here; plus, this seems to make the best sense of the phrase in context.

8. The meaning of *'ăšer* ('*so*') is not absolutely clear, but both Longman (*Ecclesiastes*, 176) and Bartholomew (*Ecclesiastes*, 234, n. 22) take it as expressing a result.

There is some debate concerning whether 6:10-12 concludes the previous section or introduces the following section. A few commentators understand these verses as concluding the previous section on riches, which affects the interpretation of the verses. For example, Ginsburg understands these verses as stating that the reason why riches fail to secure solid happiness is that everything's nature and fate is predetermined.[9] However, it is better to understand 6:10-12 as a transition section that makes connections with the first part of the book but introduces the second part of the book.

The major theme of 6:10-12 is human limitation in relationship to God and the world in which humans live. There is a clear connection to the creation account in 6:10 with the reference to naming and the use of the term *'āḏām* ('*mankind*'). For someone to name something or another person means that the person doing the naming has knowledge of what is named and exercises some authority over what is named.[10] For example, Adam named the animals in Genesis 2:19-20, which demonstrates his knowledge and authority over them. The focus in 6:10, however, is not primarily on the activity of human beings, but on the activity of God, Who is the implied subject of the passive verb '*been named*' and is the One who is '*stronger*' at the end of the verse.

Human limitation is stressed in three ways in 6:10-11. First, everything that exists has already been determined by God: '*whatever exists has already been named*' (6:10a). Earlier in Ecclesiastes the idea that everything is already determined has been the basis for the idea that the world is the way it is and that human beings have no power to change it (1:9-11; 3:14-15). Second, the nature of mankind also highlights human limitation. The phrase '*it is known what mankind is*' is a debated phrase (see the translation note), but it supports the notion of human limitation. This clause narrows the focus to human beings, who have already been named and

---

9. Ginsburg, *Coheleth*, 366; see also Kaiser, *Ecclesiastes*, 81. In this view the '*many words*' (*dĕḇār'm*) are 'many things' (6:11), which is a reference to wealth.

10. Longman, *Ecclesiastes*, 177.

whose name shows their true identity and destiny. The term *'mankind'* (*'āḏām*) is related to the term for ground (*'āḏāmāh*), which binds human beings to the earth and dust, from which they came and to which they will return (Gen. 2:7; 3:19).[11] Thus mankind's nature is limited by human frailty and weakness. The third clause in 6:10 explicitly states the limitation of *'mankind'* when it states, *'he is unable to dispute with one stronger than he.'* This is an example of what is known about the human condition[12] and seems to be a reference to God, Who is clearly stronger than human beings.[13] The verb *'dispute'* (*dîn*) regularly refers to the legal tasks of maintaining order through governing and judging. It is the responsibility of kings (Ps. 72:2) and judges (Ezra 7:25) to defend the cause of the weak members of society through the administration of justice. It is possible that *'dispute'* in 6:10 refers to the administration of a legal dispute,[14] but it is more likely that this word is used here in a non-administrative sense with the idea of defending one's rights against one who is stronger.[15] One is reminded of Job's dispute with God concerning his situation of suffering (Job 40:2).[16] Qohelet asserts that it is impossible to win a dispute with someone who is in a *'stronger,'* or possibly higher, position.[17] No doubt the one in the stronger position has the advantage. Qohelet explains in 6:11 why it is impossible to win a dispute with someone who

---

11. Krüger, *Qoheleth*, 132 and Provan, *Ecclesiastes*, 130–131.

12. Ogden and Zogbo, *Handbook on Ecclesiastes*, 208.

13. Many point out that the passive verbs are the basis for understanding 6:10 to be a reference to God (Seow, *Ecclesiastes*, 241). However, it is also possible that the king, as one who rules under God, is also being alluded to on the basis that kings also name things (Prov. 25:2; 1 Kings 4:33-34) and administer disputes from a position of strength. This would foreshadow what Qohelet will say in Eccles. 8:2-9.

14. G. Liedke, דין *dîn* to judge, *TLOT*, 1:336.

15. Richard Schultz, דין, *NIDOTTE*, 1:939-940.

16. Although *rîḇ* is used in Job 40:2, there is an overlap of meaning between *dîn* and *rîḇ* (Liedke, דין *dîn* to judge, *TLOT*, 1:336). Both are used in Job.

17. Fox (*Ecclesiastes*, 42) notes that Qohelet differs from Job in that he does not expect a change in the situation or an explanation for the situation.

is stronger: *'if there are many words senselessness increases.'* This reason shows that the dispute in 6:10 is a verbal dispute and that it is fruitless to try to win an argument with someone who is stronger. The result of such an attempt is senseless (*hebel*), because the tendency is to keep talking (*'many words'*) when the argument is not going anywhere. If God is the stronger party, then it is futile to question His work, which flows from the determination of all events (6:10a).[18] Thus it is impossible for human beings to escape their limitations and to change the basic character of life.[19]

The second part of 6:11 uses the key word *'profit'* (*yôṯēr*), which was used in the key question of the book in 1:3 (*yi ṯrôn*): *'what profit is there to mankind?'* This question seems to function in two ways at this point of the book. First, it relates to the argument of 6:10-11a. There is no profit for human beings in arguing with One who is stronger. Thus the question reinforces the statement of 6:11a that words increase senselessness and do not lead to any advantage. Secondly, the question of profit connects with the first part of the book (1:3) and reminds the reader that there is no profit for human beings in their search for meaning in this world under the sun. One is reminded of this conclusion before the transition to the second part of the book in 6:12.

The two questions of 6:12 transition to the argument of the second part of the book. The first question, *'Who knows what is good?'* will be addressed in 7:1–8:17. The second question, *'Who can tell mankind what will be after him under the sun?'* will be addressed in 9:1–10:20.[20] Normally, the question *'who knows'* in Ecclesiastes expects the negative answer 'no one knows,'[21] but the function of the questions in 6:12 is to

---

18. Murphy, *Ecclesiastes*, 58.

19. Eaton, *Ecclesiastes*, 107.

20. Murphy (*Ecclesiastes*, 69) explains the questions in 6:12 in relationship to each other in the sense that humans do not know what is good because they do not know how things will turn out. Although such a connection may not be totally out of place, the functions of the questions in 6:12 support the view that the questions are not related in the way Murphy argues.

21. Crenshaw, *'mî yōḏea'* in the Hebrew Bible,' 274–288.

introduce the topics of the second part of the book. However, negative answers are anticipated by the way the questions are asked. The question '*Who knows what is good?*' is limited by the statement '*during the few days of his senseless life.*' Thus what is good is to be found in the limited horizon of human life, which is characterized as fleeting and senseless (*hebel*). The second question seeks knowledge of the future in '*what will be after him under the sun?*' The quest for knowledge of the future is also limited to the horizon of this life '*under the sun,*' which means the future '*after him*' is a future limited to what will happen on the earth.[22] Ogden and Zogbo's attempt to give these questions a positive slant by extending the future to life beyond death and to suggest that '*shadow*' may refer to shade or protection fails in light of the context of human limitations.[23] The limitations of 6:10-11 continue into 6:12, which includes the frailty of humans in a transient and senseless life. These limits will affect the answer to the questions in the following sections.

Proverbial sayings on 'what is good?' (Eccles. 7:1-14)

7:1 *Better[24] is a good name than good oil and the day of death is better than the day of one's birth.*

7:2 *It is better to go to the house of mourning than to go to the house of feasting because[25] it is the end of all mankind, and the living should take it to heart.[26]*

---

22. Longman, *Ecclesiastes*, 178; Fox, *Rereading Ecclesiastes*, 248–249; and Whybray, *Ecclesiastes*, 111.

23. Ogden and Zogbo, *Handbook on Ecclesiastes*, 211–212.

24. The word 'good' (*ṭôḇ*) is a predicate adjective used with a comparative *min*, translated '*better is a good name.*' The first clause is also a chiasm that uses alliteration: *ṭôḇ šēm miššemen ṭôḇ* (Murphy, *Ecclesiastes*, 63).

25. Although Joüon (*Grammar*, 640) notes that the meaning of *baʾăšer* as '*because*' is rare, it does occur with this meaning in Genesis 39:9, 23 and Ecclesiastes 7:2; 8:4.

26. Longman (*Ecclesiastes*, 62) notes that the phrase 'give to his heart' is an idiomatic phrase for taking it to heart, which is followed by the majority of commentators.

7:3 Vexation[27] is better than laughter for a sad face[28] is good for the heart.[29]

7:4 The heart of the wise is in the house of mourning but the heart of fools is in the house of pleasure.[30]

7:5 It is better to hear the rebuke of the wise than for a person[31] to hear the song of fools.

7:6 For as the sound of thorns under a pot[32] so is the laughter of fools. This is also senseless.

---

27. Many English translations translate *kaʿas* as 'sorrow' (ESV, NIV, NKJV). Ogden and Zogbo (*Handbook on Ecclesiastes*, 221) argue for 'sorrow' based on the context of mourning the death of a neighbor. Some translate *kaʿas* as 'sorrow' to harmonize this text with Ecclesiastes 5:17, where *kaʿas* is described in negative terms (following Luther, also Delitzsch, and Ogden). But as Bartholomew (*Ecclesiastes*, 221) points out, there is no philological justification for the meaning 'sorrow.' Also, the predominant meaning of *kaʿas* in Ecclesiastes is *'vexation'* or 'frustration' (1:18; 2:23; 5:17; for its meaning in 7:9 see the discussion there). In this context it refers to being distressed because the person is in the house of mourning.

28. The use of *'face' (pānîm)* with *rōaʿ* refers to a sad countenance in Gen. 40:7 and Neh. 2:2.

29. The Hebrew reads 'by' or 'in sadness of face a heart is good.' Some translate the verb *'good' (ytb)* as 'merry' or 'joyful' (Murphy) based on its use in Ruth 3:7; Judg. 19: 6, 9; and 1 Kings 21:7, but in these passages the verb is used with eating and drinking, which makes the heart merry, joyful, or content. Some translate the verb 'good' with the sense of 'improve' (Ginsburg, Gordis, and Ogden) or 'heal' (Bartholomew, Eaton); however, this seems to over-interpret the proverb. The point is not that the heart is improved or made well, but that some things are better than other things. The reason vexation is better than laughter (Eccles. 7:3a) is that a sad face is good for the heart. In context, a sad face helps one reflect on the negative aspects of life, which helps one face the realities of life.

30. The term *simḥāh* is translated *'pleasure'* here, which fits the context in chapter 7 and in the book itself (2:1-2). The term 'joy' can give the idea of a divine aspect to the term. Seow (*Ecclesiastes*, 246) notes that there is no real difference between the terms 'house of feasting' (7:2) and *'house of pleasure'* (7:4).

31. Several commentators point out that the addition of the word *'person'* (*'îš*) in the second part of the proverb distinguishes the individual who hears the song of fools from the person who hears the rebuke of the wise, which puts the emphasis on mocking the lighthearted song of fools (see especially Crenshaw, *Ecclesiastes*, 135).

32. There is a word play in this clause, which can be represented as, 'like the sound of *sîrîm* under the *sîr*' (Eaton, *Ecclesiastes*, 110). This is hard

7:7 For[33] *oppression makes a fool of the wise and a gift corrupts*[34] *the heart.*

7:8 *Better is the end of a thing than its beginning, better is a patient spirit than a proud spirit.*

7:9 *Do not be quick in your spirit to become angry because anger*[35] *resides*[36] *in the bosom of fools.*

7:10 *Do not say, 'Why were the former days better than these?' For you do not ask this from*[37] *wisdom.*

7:11 *Wisdom is good with*[38] *an inheritance, an advantage to those who see the sun.*

---

to produce in an English translation, but Ginsburg (*Coheleth*, 372) suggests 'the crackling of nettles under the kettle.'

33. For the justification of the causal use of *kî* at the beginning of 7:7 and its relationship to the *hebel* verdict at the end of 7:6, see the discussion in the Commentary. Commentators have struggled with the connection between 7:6 and 7:7. Delitzsch ('Ecclesiastes,' 316–317) argues that something has been lost at the beginning of 7:7 and he suggests adding Prov. 16:8. It is interesting that in the Qumran text (4QQoh^a) there is a blank space of 15–20 letters after 7:7, but the versions do not support an addition at the beginning of 7:7 (Longman, *Ecclesiastes*, 186).

34. Longman (*Ecclesiastes*, 187) points out that the most common meaning of the verb *ʾābad* in the piel is 'to destroy,' but in the context of extortions and bribes the word '*corrupt*' expresses the idea better. There is no need to emend the text as Seow suggests (see *Ecclesiastes*, 238).

35. The verb and the noun in 7:9, translated as '*angry*' is *kaʿas*, the same word as in 7:3, where it is translated 'vexation.' It has a similar idea here and so 7:9 could have been translated 'to become vexed because vexation resides in the bosom of fools.' The connection is that something that is distressing can provoke a person to a certain action or feeling, such as irritation, frustration, or anger.

36. The word translated '*resides*' is the verb *nûaḥ*, which means 'to rest or settle.' Longman (*Ecclesiastes*, 181, n. 23) notes that it may have been chosen because of its similarity in sound to the word 'spirit' (*rûaḥ*).

37. The Masoretic Text has the preposition *min* ('*from*'), but the Septuagint and the Syriac read the preposition *bet* ('in wisdom'), which Fox (*Rereading Ecclesiastes*, 249) translates as 'wisely,' indicating the manner of how the question is asked. He supports the Septuagint because '*from wisdom*' deals more with the source or motive of the question, which he does not see as relevant in this context. Seow (*Ecclesiastes*, 248), on the other hand, argues that *min* is common after verbs of speaking and that the Septuagint is a contextual translation and not evidence of a different reading.

38. There are two major ways that the preposition *ʿim* is understood.

7:12 *For to be in the shadow of wisdom is to be in the shadow of money[39] and[40] the advantage of knowledge is that wisdom preserves the life of its possessor.*

7:13 *Consider the work of God, for[41] who is able to straighten what he has made crooked?*

7:14 *On a good day enjoy the good but on a bad day consider that God has made the one as well as the other so that a person may not find out anything that is after him.*

Although Ecclesiastes 7:1-14 is connected to the question in 6:12 concerning 'What is good?,' 7:1 begins a new section,

---

Some take it in the sense of 'as' or 'like' (Murphy, Seow, Ogden, Ginsburg), which draws a comparison between wisdom and an inheritance. The preposition is used in this way in Ecclesiastes 2:16. Some, like Murphy (*Ecclesiastes*, 65), argue this view because they think Qohelet is praising wisdom. On the other hand, the preposition ʿ*im* can mean 'with,' which is the most common use of the preposition and is followed by all major ancient versions, except the Peshitta, which has major problems of its own in this verse (see Longman, *Ecclesiastes*, 189, n. 62). Some reject this view because they believe it denigrates wisdom, but it will be shown that whether Qohelet is praising or denigrating wisdom is not ultimately based on how this preposition is translated.

39. This is a difficult phrase in the Hebrew, which literally reads 'in the shadow of wisdom, in the shadow of money.' Some kind of comparison is being drawn between wisdom and money, which the versions (Septuagint, Vulgate, and Syriac) bring out in their translations by the use of the word 'as.' Ginsburg (*Coheleth*, 376) and Barton (*Ecclesiastes*, 143) suggest that the preposition *bet* ('in') should be emended to the preposition *kaph* ('as'), but others argue for a particular use of the *bet* called the *beth essentiae* (*GKC* 119.i; Murphy, *Ecclesiastes*, 61). The translation above reads the *bet* as 'in' and supplies the verb 'to be' to bring out the relationship between wisdom and wealth (Longman, *Ecclesiastes*, 190).

40. Ogden and Zogbo (*Handbook on Ecclesiastes*, 238) translate the *waw* with 'but' because they argue that Qohelet is setting forth wisdom as more valuable than money. But even if these verses are very positive toward wisdom, wisdom only gives a relative advantage over money (see the discussion of this verse). Plus, if 7:12a is a comment on 7:11a and 7:12b is a comment on 7:11b, as Ogden and Zogbo argue, then it makes sense to translate the *waw* with '*and*' because of the parallelism between the two verses.

41. It is possible that *kî* should be understood in an emphatic sense, translated as 'indeed' (Ogden and Zogbo, *Handbook on Ecclesiastes*, 241), but it also makes sense to understand 7:13b as a reason for why a person should consider the work of God.

which is evident in the shift to proverbial sayings in 7:1-12. These proverbs take up the concept of *'good'* (*ṭôḇ*), which occurs eleven times in these verses, many times in the comparative sense of *'better.'* It is common to understand 7:13-14 to be the conclusion to this section, which is framed by the words *'good'* and *'day'* in verses 1 and 14.[42] There is debate concerning the relationship of the proverbs to each other. One view is that the proverbs in 7:7-12 challenge the proverbs in 7:1-6,[43] but this assumes that Qohelet finds an answer to the question of what is good, which seems to be denied by 7:14, as well as by the general inability of human beings to know or understand how this world works (7:28; 8:17). Krüger argues that 7:1-12 and 7:13-14 set forth different and contradictory attitudes toward life, but that in these verses Qohelet does claim to know what is good.[44] However, it is by no means certain that 7:1-12 or 7:13-14 set forth a unified argument, and it is even more questionable that Qohelet finds an answer to what is good. Thus, it is better to see a loose relationship between the proverbs in Ecclesiastes 7, which are connected by key words and literary form.[45] There is a high concentration of 'better than' sayings among these proverbs, which is related to the message of the proverbs.[46] It has already been demonstrated by Qohelet that there are certain things in life that have relative value. Wisdom is better than foolishness, but it is only a relative value because the wise dies just like the fool (2:12-16). The

---

42. Murphy, *Wisdom Literature*, 140 and Longman, *Ecclesiastes*, 180. Ogden (*Qohelet*, 107) is one of the few who argue that 7:13 begins a new unit; however, Ogden and Zogbo (*Handbook on Ecclesiastes*, 214) take 7:1-14 as a unit which attempts to answer the questions of 6:12.

43. This is noted by Murphy, *Ecclesiastes*, 62.

44. Krüger (*Qoheleth*, 135) argues that in 7:1-12 Qohelet sets forth the view that a person's present behavior is determined by future expectations, but in 7:13-14 advice is given to live entirely with one's eyes on the present.

45. Longman (*Ecclesiastes*, 180) argues for unity based on word repetition: the word 'good' is used eleven times, 'wise, wisdom' is used six times, 'heart' is used five times, 'fool' is used four times, and 'sorrow, anger' is used three times.

46. Salyer, *Vain Rhetoric*, 335.

key question of the book concerning whether there is profit to labor (1:3) is answered in 2:11. Even though there is no profit to labor, there is some limited benefit to labor (2:10), which is what is encouraged in the calls to enjoyment. These calls to enjoyment are introduced by 'better than' sayings (2:24; 3:12, 22).[47] Thus the proverbs in 7:1-12 are setting forth things which do not have absolute value, but which do have relative value.[48] Such a view fits in with the argument of this section that no one really knows what is good.

Qohelet presents a collection of proverbs in Ecclesiastes 7. Proverbs are commonly used among the wise and so are normally seen as illustrative of the instruction of wisdom.[49] However, it will become clear that many of the proverbs in this chapter are shocking and go against normal expectations.[50] The first clause of the proverb in 7:1 reads, *'Better is a good name than good oil.'* This proverb sounds very much like Proverbs 22:1, which compares a good name to great riches. A *'good name'* refers to a person's good reputation. The *'good oil'* refers to an expensive item that is used as ointment or perfume (2 Kings 20:13; Song 1:3).[51] Thus the proverb in 7:1a states that it is better to have a good reputation than to possess expensive ointment or perfume. This is in line with Proverbs 22:1, where a good name is better than riches. However, the second half of 7:1 is very different from the second half of Proverbs 22:1. The second half of Proverbs 22:1 is similar to the proverb in the first half: 'and favour is better than silver

---

47. For a discussion of the 'better than' saying see the note in connection with the translation of 2:24.

48. Longman, *Ecclesiastes*, 180. Views which understand the 'better than' sayings as expressing something positive (Kidner, *Ecclesiastes*, 65), or which see this section as expressing the instruction of suffering related to whether the life of faith will survive hard and troublesome times (Eaton, *Ecclesiastes*, 108), do not coincide with the more negative message of this passage.

49. Seow, *Ecclesiastes*, 235. For discussions on how to interpret proverbs see Raymond C. van Leeuwen, 'Wealth and Poverty: System and Contradiction in Proverbs,' *HS* 33 (1992): 25–36 and Longman, *Proverbs*, 29–33.

50. Ogden and Zogbo, *Handbook on Ecclesiastes*, 214.

51. Longman, *Ecclesiastes*, 181 and Murphy, *Ecclesiastes*, 63.

or gold' (ESV). In Proverbs 22:1 a good name (v. 1a) and favor (v. 1b) correspond to each other, as do riches (v. 1a) and silver and gold (v. 1b). In Ecclesiastes 7:1 the second half (v. 1b) does not correspond to the proverb in the first half of the verse: *'the day of death is better than the day of one's birth.'* This proverb produces discord with the first proverb, for normally *'the day of death'* is not considered *'better than the day of one's birth.'* Some try to interpret this proverb in light of the first proverb in the sense that a person's good reputation is not made known until the day of death,[52] but that is not what Qohelet means. The statement in 7:1b is very rare in Hebrew wisdom literature,[53] and when a person does express the view that the day of death is better than the day of one's birth, such a person is going through a very difficult time of suffering (Job 3; Jer. 20). Thus the second proverb is 'rather shocking' in relationship to the first proverb because it prefers death over life.[54]

Qohelet explains further what he means with another proverb in 7:2. If *'the day of death is better than the day of one's birth,'* then there are certain things in this life that would help someone to see that truth. The proverb in 7:2 gives an example: *'it is better to go the house of mourning than to go to the house of feasting.'* The *'house of mourning'* refers to a house where mourners for a dead person would gather. The *'house of feasting'* refers to a place of joy and festivity, such as a wedding feast or some other celebration. Thus Qohelet is saying that it is better to go to a funeral than to go to a party, or it is better to go to a wake than to a wedding.[55] He offers a reason for this

---

52. Gordis, *Koheleth*, 257. Attempts which seek to connect the oil to the anointing at death or its use at birth are not necessary if the two proverbs are not meant to be interpreted in light of each other.

53. Shields, *End of Wisdom*, 176. He may overstate the case when he says that the proverb in Ecclesiastes 7:1b is unparalleled in Hebrew wisdom literature. At least the idea occurs in Job and Jeremiah.

54. Bartholomew (*Ecclesiastes*, 246) notes that 7:1b deconstructs 7:1a. If death is all that awaits people then what is the value of life and a good reputation?

55. Longman (*Ecclesiastes*, 182) states the first one and Seow (*Ecclesiastes*, 245) states the second one.

assertion in the statement *'because it is the end of all mankind.'* The pronoun *'it'* (*hû'*) probably refers back to *'death'* in 7:1.[56] When someone goes to a festival event they are not reminded of *'death,'* but when someone goes to mourn the death of a person, they are very much reminded of *'death'* as *'the end of all mankind.'* A funeral causes one to reflect on the possibility of their own death, which can help to put the fleeting nature of this mortal life into perspective;[57] which is what Qohelet stresses at the end of 7:2 in the statement *'the living should take it to heart.'* Death helps one to reflect seriously on this life.

When 7:1-2 is placed into the context of other statements of Qohelet it is hard to give these words a positive meaning. It is difficult to conceive of Qohelet confirming the enduring nature of a good reputation after death when he has emphasized that there is no enduring remembrance and that everything will be forgotten (1:11; 2:16). Such statements occur even in the comparison of the wise and the fool. Death is better than life because it enables one to escape the suffering and frustrations of life (4:2-3; 6:3). From an 'under the sun' perspective, there is no assurance that there is anything beyond this life (9:10). Thus the *'end (sôp) of all mankind'* could refer not just to the destination of all human beings, but it could also refer to the termination of the life of all human beings. If death ends everything, then enjoying the relative good in this life is even more important because that is all that there is.[58]

The proverb of 7:3 fits well into the argument of the passage. Qohelet has been arguing that the negative things in life are better than the happier things in life, which is also the point of 7:3: *'vexation is better than laughter.'* Here is another 'better than' saying where a negative aspect of life is better than something that is more positive. In context, the *'laughter'* is

---

56. Ginsburg, *Coheleth*, 370. Even if it refers back to going to the house of mourning, death is what is ultimately in view.

57. Seow, *Ecclesiastes*, 246.

58. Qohelet's counsel here is not necessarily inconsistent with his calls to enjoy life earlier in the book if one recognizes that the absolute good escapes human beings, which leaves only the relative good. Since no one knows what is absolutely good for human beings, it is appropriate to pursue what is relatively good in this life.

naturally connected to the *'house of feasting'* in 7:2. The term *'vexation'* refers to an experience that is irritating or frustrating. It describes the reaction people have to the difficulties of life which cause pain and misery. If someone is experiencing *'vexation'* it is evidence that they are not avoiding the difficulties of life by masking them in *'laughter'* and merrymaking. The reason (*kî*) *'vexation is better than laughter'* is given in 7:3b: *'for a sad face is good for the heart.'* The idea is not that *'a sad face'* makes the heart well or improves the heart (see the translation note), but that *'a sad face'* demonstrates that a person is facing up to the reality of the difficulty of life, which is *'good for the heart'* because the person is not living in a false world of merriment.[59]

The proverb in 7:4 is very similar to the proverb at the beginning of 7:2, except that there is a transition in 7:4 to the relationship between the *'wise'* and the *'fool,'* which continues through 7:7. The use of the word *'heart'* (*lēḇ*) connects 7:4 to 7:3, and brings to mind the basic orientation and direction of the wise and the fool.[60] The *'wise'* are associated with *'the house of mourning'* because the wise recognize the troubles of life. The fools are associated with *'the house of pleasure'* because they do not live in recognition of the troubles of life. This view fits with the emphasis in Proverbs on the prudence of the wise, who are able to see the obstacles in life and either avoid them or meet them, in contrast to the fool who does not see the obstacles of life and runs right into them (Prov. 14:8, 15; 22:3; 27:12). In this way Qohelet would argue that there is a relative advantage to wisdom over foolishness, for *'the wise person has eyes in his head but the fool walks in darkness'* (2:14).

---

59. There is not necessarily a contradiction between 7:3 and 5:17 concerning vexation. In 5:17 Qohelet describes a sickening evil where a person labors for nothing and eats in darkness with much vexation. In 7:3 a proverb affirms that vexation is better than laughter. But both passages are negative toward life. The statement in 5:17 comes after an acknowledgment of the difficulty of life. The proverb of 7:3 is trying to get someone to see that life is full of trouble so that they do not live in a false world of merriment. Thus both passages affirm that life is full of trouble and never works out the way you want.

60. Whybray (*Ecclesiastes*, 114) comments that 7:4 sharpens the tone of 7:2 with the use of an antithetical proverb rather than a 'better than' saying and the contrast of the wise and the fool.

Qohelet goes on to show with another proverb in 7:5 that the perspective of the wise is much better than the perspective of the fool: *'it is better to hear the rebuke of the wise than for a person to hear the song of fools.'* If the wise live in such a way that they face reality and so understand the troubles of life, then *'the rebuke of the wise'* will be more advantageous for a person than *'the song of fools.'* A rebuke is a verbal warning directed toward someone's attitude or behavior, which seeks to correct something that can have negative consequences in a person's life. Although a rebuke can be difficult to hear, it is highly valued in the book of Proverbs (12:1; 13:1, 18; 17:10; 19:25; 27:5; 29:15). The *'song of fools'* can either refer to songs of frivolity,[61] which are found in the house of pleasure, or to songs of insincere praise and flattery,[62] in contrast to the rebuke of the wise. These songs do not deal with the difficult realities of life and so they have no value in instructing people. The reason (*kî*) for the proverb in 7:5 is given in 7:6, where *'the laughter of fools'* is compared to *'the sound of thorns under a pot.'* Qohelet describes what happens when *'thorns'* are used for fuel. The fire flames up quickly and makes a lot of noise, but then dies down very quickly; or, as Crenshaw notes, 'quick flames, little heat, and a lot of unpleasant noise.'[63] In other words, there is the appearance of a good fire, but the reality is that no heat is produced. Such is *'the laughter of fools.'* It gives the impression of real joy, but it is really empty, a lot of noise with nothing real behind it. This explains why the *'rebuke of the wise,'* which is rooted in reality, is better than *'the laughter of fools.'*

7:6 ends with a *hebel* verdict: *'this is also senseless.'*[64] There is debate concerning the role of this statement in the context of 7:6-7. Murphy takes the *hebel* verdict with 7:7 as a comment on the weakness of the wise, so that verse 7 gives a reason for the

---

61. Murphy, *Ecclesiastes*, 64. Eaton (*Ecclesiastes*, 110) argues that *'song'* always refers to literal songs.

62. Seow, *Ecclesiastes*, 236. Towner (*Ecclesiastes*, 326) refers to Ps. 145:1 and Isa. 42:10 to support this meaning. However, Whybray (*Ecclesiastes*, 115) denies this meaning.

63. Crenshaw, *Ecclesiastes*, 135.

64. The meaning 'enigmatic' does not work well here for *hebel*. The advice in these proverbs is not enigmatic, but it is senseless in light of the movement in this text from the advantage of wisdom to its vulnerability.

hebel verdict of 7:6.⁶⁵ Normally, the *hebel* verdict concludes a section and is a statement on what has gone before. In this line of thinking, Ogden limits the *hebel* verdict to the laughter of the fools.⁶⁶ However, others widen its scope to be a comment on the benefit of the rebuke of the wise in 7:5, which would also be considered *'senseless.'*⁶⁷ This view seems to fit the context better in light of the vulnerability of wisdom in 7:7. The *hebel* verdict functions as a statement on what has gone before, but it is then elaborated on in 7:7.⁶⁸ Thus there is a general movement in this passage from the advantages of wisdom to its weakness, which reflects the same movement as in 2:13-15.⁶⁹

The problem with wisdom is expressed in 7:7. The advantage of wisdom over folly has been directly stated in the proverb of 7:5. The advantage of wisdom also comes out subtly in 7:5 in the contrast between the word for *'wise,'* which is singular, and the word for *'fools,'* which is plural.⁷⁰ The wisdom of one wise person is so much more beneficial than the laughter of many fools. The problem, however, is that a wise person can become corrupted by certain circumstances of life. For example, Qohelet notes that *'oppression makes a fool of the wise.'* The word *'oppression'* (*'ōšeq*) is the same word used in Ecclesiastes 4:1 and it can legitimately be understood as 'extortion' based on the parallel of 7:7b and its use in Leviticus 6:4.⁷¹ Some debate whether the wise are victims of extortion or whether they engage in extortion themselves.⁷² The second

---

65. Murphy, *Ecclesiastes*, 64.
66. Ogden and Zogbo, *Handbook on Ecclesiastes*, 226.
67. Longman, *Ecclesiastes*, 185 and Seow, *Ecclesiastes*, 247.
68. Shields, *End of Wisdom*, 177.
69. Murphy, *Ecclesiastes*, 64.
70. Ogden, *Qoheleth*, 112.
71. Longman, *Ecclesiastes*, 186.
72. Murphy, *Ecclesiastes*, 64 and Ogden, *Qoheleth*, 113–114. Eaton (*Ecclesiastes*, 110–111) argues that the wise are suffering the oppression and that the point of the passage is to show the less beneficial aspects of the trials of life. In this way he avoids the negative view toward the wise in the passage. Ogden (*Qoheleth*, 113–114) also avoids a negative view of wisdom by arguing that oppression makes it easier for people to disregard the words of the wise and to prefer the flattering words of fools.

half of 7:7 seems to favor the latter: *'a gift corrupts the heart.'* Clearly the word *'gift'* (*mattānāh*) refers to a bribe (Prov. 15:27) which negatively affects a person's *'heart.'* The Hebrew word for *'heart'* (*lēḇ*) can refer to the mind, which is appropriate here, but the idea of the heart pushes one back to the core of a person which directs the mind, will, and emotions. Thus the idea is that the whole person is corrupted by the bribe. The weakness of wisdom is that a wise person can be corrupted by extortion or a bribe, which means that their advice is not based on wisdom but on other factors which may negatively affect their judgment. This possibility supports the *hebel* verdict of 7:6. If a wise person can be corrupted so that their advice becomes suspect, the proverb of 7:5 is called into question. Just as the advantage of wisdom was negated by a lack of distinction between the wise and the fool in death (2:13-17), so the advantage of wisdom is negated by the fact that the wise may not be that different from a fool in that the wise can also be corrupted by certain circumstances of life.

There is discussion concerning how 7:8 fits into the rest of the proverbs of chapter 7. Some connect *'the end of a thing'* in 7:8 to the assertion in 7:1 that 'the day of death is better than the day of one's birth.' Longman takes both statements in 7:8 as specifically referring to the day of death.[73] Fox understands the statements to generally mean that one should wait patiently for the end to see how things turn out.[74] Seow understands the 'better than' sayings in chapter 7 to be thematically linked, with 7:8 as the climax which confirms the assumption of 7:5-6 that the end (the result of rebuke) is more important than the beginning (the initial hurt of rebuke).[75] Some take 7:8 to be the beginning of the next section, which either ends at 7:12 or 7:13.[76] It is important to understand that Qohelet does not present a tightly organized argument in

---

73. Longman, *Ecclesiastes*, 187.

74. Fox, *Rereading Ecclesiastes*, 254.

75. Seow, *Ecclesiastes*, 247. A connection between 7:8 and the rebuke of the wise in 7:5 leads some to understand *dāḇār* in 7:8 as 'word' instead of 'thing' (see Ginsburg, *Coheleth*, 373–374).

76. Murphy (*Wisdom Literature*, 140) ends the section at 7:12 and Ogden and Zogbo (*Handbook on Ecclesiastes*, 229) at 7:13.

chapter 7; rather, there are loose connections between verses based on structure or key words. The argument does not go in a straight line and may at times be circular. For example, having demonstrated that wisdom has advantages over folly, he shows that wisdom is vulnerable to extortion, which calls into question its advantage (7:5-7). Qoehelet then states again the advantage of wisdom in 7:11. Thus it seems best to take 7:8-10 as a section with a 'better than' saying in 7:8 followed by two prohibitions serving as motivations in 7:9-10.[77]

The proverb of 7:8 clearly states, *'better is the end of a thing than its beginning.'* Although it may be profitable to connect this proverb to the broader context of the chapter, it should primarily be understood in the context of 7:8-10. The second half of 7:8 has another 'better than' saying: *'better is a patient spirit than a proud spirit.'* If these two are taken together, the idea is that patience is needed to reach *'the end of a thing,'* whereas a *'proud spirit'* is not humble enough to wait for *'the end.'*[78] Both proverbs in 7:9-10 begin with a prohibition which is followed by a causal clause that explains the prohibition. The two prohibitions explain the 'better than' proverbs of 7:8. The prohibition of 7:9 elaborates on the proverb of 7:8b and the prohibition of 7:10 elaborates on the proverb of 7:8a. The proverb of 7:9 further explains why *'a patient spirit'* is *'better'* than a *'proud spirit'* (7:8b) as it admonishes a person not to *'be quick in your spirit to become angry.'* The verb translated *'to become angry,'* and the noun that follows, are both from *kaʿas*, which is translated in 7:3 as 'vexation.' Vexation means to suffer distress, affliction, or frustration over something and to *'become angry'* (7:9) is the reaction to the situation that is causing the distress. Although some argue that Qohelet contradicts himself in verses 3 and 9, verse 3 has in mind the situation that causes the distress and verse 9 has in view the reaction to whatever is causing the distress.[79] Qohelet goes on

---

77. Murphy, *Wisdom Literature*, 130.
78. Seow, *Ecclesiastes*, 247.
79. Longman (*Ecclesiastes*, 188) understands 7:9 to be a direct contradiction of 7:3. Others understand the word in 7:9 to have a different nuance from 7:3. The most common suggestion is that in 7:3 the meaning is 'sorrow' (Murphy, *Ecclesiastes*, 65), but see the comments in this commentary in 7:3

to give the reason one is not to become angry quickly: *'because anger resides in the bosom of fools.'* The word *'bosom'* (*ḥêq*) is the place where one holds on to what is cherished, such as one's beloved children.[80] The fact that anger resides in the bosom of fools shows how deep-seated and passionate is the anger of fools.[81] They are quick to express anger, which demonstrates impatience (7:8b), because anger is not a passing reaction. Anger has become a permanent state of mind and is thus uncontrollable. So fools are known by how they react to situations (Prov. 12:16). In this way a patient spirit is better than a proud spirit because a quick reaction of anger shows everyone that a person is a fool.[82]

The prohibition of 7:10 elaborates on the 'better than' saying of 7:8a, which states that the end of a thing is better than its beginning. The prohibition in 7:10 is an exhortation not to say, *'Why were the former days better than these?'* This may be a question Qohelet had heard many times and it is hard to be precise as to its specific meaning. Some see this as a criticism of traditional wisdom, which held up the ideal of the patient sage who cultivated the teaching of the past. If this is a criticism of traditional wisdom, then the tradition of the past is seen as a dead weight.[83] However, the question may just refer to the tendency of every age to glorify the past and to live with a nostalgic view of the past. Such a view

---

that argues against this meaning. Others argue that the anger of 7:3 is different from the anger of 7:9. For example, Gordis (*Kohelet*, 262) understands 7:3 as dealing with a serious disposition and the anger of 7:9 as dealing with an uncontrollable bad temper. Fox (*Rereading Ecclesiastes*, 254) understands the difference to be in the application of the anger, with 7:3 directed against reproof and 7:9 directed against one's own misfortunes.

80. Longman, *Ecclesiastes*, 181, n. 24.

81. Ogden and Zogbo, *Handbook on Ecclesiastes*, 232.

82. Seow (*Ecclesiastes*, 248) argues that 7:9 undermines what is said in 7:8 about patience based on his understanding of 7:9b that fools are patient by nurturing their anger in secret, so patience is not always better. But just because anger 'rests' in the bosom of fools does not mean they are patient. Bartholomew (*Ecclesiastes*, 249) argues that 7:8 is undermined by 7:9 because 7:9 shows that patience is no help when it comes to vexation; however, that would be true only for the fool.

83. Murphy, *Ecclesiastes*, 65 and Seow, *Ecclesiastes*, 247.

does not come *'from wisdom'* in the sense that it goes against the 'better than' saying of 7:8. If the end of a thing is better than its beginning, then it does not make sense to glorify the past as better than today. Such a view may be evidence of an impatient spirit that does not want to deal with the challenges of today. The relative advantage of wisdom over foolishness is demonstrated here, but ultimately Qohelet's view will be that even this relative advantage will fall short because there is really no difference between the past, the present, and the future. There is nothing new under the sun (1:9) and that which is today has already taken place (3:15), so that the past, present, and the future are all the same.

It seems that 7:11-12 is a subunit focusing on wisdom.[84] The major question concerns how Qohelet is presenting wisdom in these two verses. Those who argue for a positive view of wisdom would point out several things. First, the comparison of *'wisdom'* to an *'inheritance'* (7:11) and to *'money'* (7:12) is meant to enhance the value of wisdom. The idea is that just as precious things are passed along in an inheritance, so precious things are passed along in wisdom. The idea of *'shadow'* in 7:12 means that wisdom and money act as a protection to a person (Pss. 17:8; 91:1). But secondly, wisdom is presented as more valuable than money in 7:12b, where wisdom gives life to those who *'possess'* it. The noun 'possessor' (*baʿal*) also means 'master,' so the idea is that wisdom gives life to those who are masters of wisdom. This explains what is meant by saying that wisdom and knowledge are an *'advantage'* to people. The advantage (*yitrôn* in 7:11 and *yōtēr* in 7:12) is that wisdom brings lasting benefit to a person, a benefit that goes beyond this life.[85]

Others argue that 7:11-12 is not setting forth a positive view of wisdom but a negative view of wisdom. Seow comments that the sudden praise of wisdom seems out of place in this section of the book. The point of 7:11 is that wisdom is only as good as an inheritance. Qohelet has already been negative toward

---

84. Ogden and Zogbo, *Handbook on Ecclesiastes*, 235.

85. Ogden and Zogbo, *Handbook on Ecclesiastes*, 238–239. Hubbard (*Ecclesiastes*, 165) also takes a positive view of wisdom, but sees the advantage of wisdom only limited to this life.

material possessions in Ecclesiastes 5:10–6:9, so his point is that both an inheritance and wisdom are insubstantial and fleeting. Qohelet does not assert clearly that wisdom is better than money, which is a common assertion in Proverbs (3:14; 8:11,19; 16:16). Also, the metaphor of shadow in 7:12 underscores the idea of the insubstantial nature of wisdom because a shadow only gives temporary relief and so is unreliable (Pss. 102:11; 109:23). The advantage that comes from wisdom is that wisdom allows a person to live, which is understood in the sense of 'to survive.' Wisdom helps a person to cope with the difficulties of life, but it does not give people control over their lives. Thus the advantage of wisdom is only a relative advantage.[86]

It is clear from the context of this section and from the context of the discourse of Qohelet that wisdom only gives a person a relative advantage. In a limited way one can acknowledge that *'wisdom is good with an inheritance'* and that wisdom and money do act as protection against certain things in life. Wisdom gives people the ability to see obstacles in the way and to avoid them (2:13-14). Money is a protection from hunger and poverty. Even if wisdom is understood in a positive way, the advantages of wisdom do not solve the issues with which Qohelet is wrestling and do not provide a person with any kind of permanent benefit that goes beyond this life.[87] Qohelet has already argued for the relative advantage of wisdom in 2:13-16, where wisdom ultimately fails in the matter of how a person dies. Although Qohelet can affirm that 'wisdom is good with an inheritance,' he is not sure that a person can really know what is good (6:12). In fact, the use of 'shadow' in 6:12 in reference to the few days of our senseless life, gives support for taking the word *'shadow'* in 7:12 in a negative way.

The view that wisdom only provides a relative advantage is supported by 7:13-14. These verses are a conclusion to 7:1-14 and a partial response to 6:10-12.[88] Twice Qohelet uses

---

86. Seow, *Ecclesiastes*, 249–250.

87. Contra Ogden and Zogbo. Longman (*Ecclesiastes*, 190–191) argues for a positive view of wisdom in that it can protect from the harsh realities of life, but he also sees this advantage of wisdom as only a relative advantage.

88. Seow, *Ecclesiastes*, 251. Horne (*Ecclesiastes*, 473) points out that the imperative of 7:13 sets these verses apart from the preceding.

an imperative to exhort his readers to *'consider'* the activity of God in the world. He is asking his readers to observe carefully and to reflect on what is observed.[89] In 7:13 he focuses on the activity of God in general: *'consider the work of God, for who is able to straighten what he has made crooked?'* This statement is very similar to Ecclesiastes 1:15, but it is clear in 7:13 that God is the One who has made things crooked. In 1:15 the emphasis was on the inability to solve the problems of life. Many times the word *'crooked'* is used in contexts where people are struggling with the justice of God (Job 8:3; 19:6; 34:12; Pss. 119:78; 146:9), which is going to be the topic of 7:15-18.[90] At this point of the argument, the fact that things are made crooked by God prohibits someone from being able to know 'what is good for mankind' (6:12). In 7:14 the work of God is made up of good days and bad days. If one is experiencing a *'good day,'* the response should be to *'enjoy the good.'* On the other hand, if one is experiencing a *'bad day,'* the response should be to *'consider'* the relationship of the good and bad days to the activity of God. Qohelet asserts that *'God has made'* both with the result that *'a person may not find out anything that is after him.'* The fact that good days and bad days come from God is not foreign to other passages of Scripture (Amos 3:6; Isa. 45:7), but if bad days come from God Qohelet thinks it is difficult to define what is good.[91] There is also no guarantee that the wise will experience the good in the future; in fact, it is impossible to *'find out anything'* that will come in the future. Thus a person should enjoy the good days when they come

---

89. Ogden and Zogbo, *Handbook on Ecclesiastes*, 240.

90. Ogden and Zogbo (*Handbook on Ecclesiastes*, 241) argue that *'crooked'* should be understood in a positive way as simply the way things are in the world. It is a description of how God has fashioned the world. But this seems far-fetched in light of the connection of 'crooked' with injustice in other places of the Old Testament. Plus, God's declaration of creation in Genesis 1 is that it is good. Qohelet cannot see the creation in that way because of his 'under the sun' perspective.

91. Murphy (*Ecclesiastes*, 66) comments that God is keeping humans off-balance by an erratic performance. Longman (*Ecclesiastes*, 192) notes that God purposely designed life in this way in order to hide the future even from the wise.

because the future is uncertain.[92] A person should also accept life as it is, because there is no way that it can be changed.[93]

Homiletical Implications

It is difficult to preach on a passage that is a collection of proverbs. A proverb is a short saying that is full of meaning. They are also meant to be used in life (Prov. 22:17-18), which means that in some cases they are dependent on the life situation. A comparison of Proverbs 26:4 and 5 shows that whether one answers a fool depends on the kind of fool with whom one is confronted. One common abuse of a proverb is to make it a general statement that is absolute. For example, Proverbs 10:22 states that 'The blessing of the LORD makes rich' (ESV), which some have used to teach the health and wealth gospel. For example, they argue that if you are not rich you must not be experiencing the blessing of the LORD. Qohelet, on the other hand, absolutizes the problems of life because very little in life works the way one would hope. The proverbs in Ecclesiastes 7 must be understood in the context of Ecclesiastes 6:10-12, which questions whether someone can really know what is good. This fits the perspective of Ecclesiastes 2:13-16, where wisdom has only a relative advantage over foolishness. Thus Qohelet asserts some things that are relatively good in chapter 7, such as a good name, the rebuke of the wise that keeps one from foolishness, patience, living in the present, an inheritance, and protection that wisdom brings. But there are also things which question the good things in life, such as the inability of humans to straighten what God has made crooked and the inability of humans to discover what awaits them in the future (7:13-14). Thus major questions in 6:10-12 and 7:13-14 frame the

---

92. Although Ogden and Zogbo (*Handbook on Ecclesiastes*, 244) understand '*after him*' to include things that take place in a life after death, it is not clear that Qohelet affirms life after death in his 'under the sun' approach (9:10). Qohelet thus has in view what will take place in a person's experience in this life before death.

93. Qohelet does not encourage a life of dependence on God (Ginsburg, *Coheleth*, 377) or faith in God's sovereignty (Eaton, *Ecclesiastes*, 113) because of the uncertainty of the future.

proverbial statements in 7:1-12. Certain things may be good in a relative sense and they may even help a person cope with certain things in life, but humans are not able to know for sure what is really good. This perspective fits Qohelet's 'under the sun' view, which can lead to hopelessness and despair.

An 'above the sun' view is able to affirm that there are things in this life that are absolutely good based on God's revelation. Human beings can know what is good. God is good and He pronounced His creation good when He created it. Although sin marred God's creation, God is at work to restore His creation. Qohelet absolutizes the problems of life so that he is not able to see what is good, but an 'above the sun' view recognizes that even in the problems of life God is able to accomplish His good purposes (Rom. 8:28). God's good purposes will triumph even in situations where life does not work out the way one would hope. Although we cannot know what the future may bring, we know the God of the future and His good purposes will triumph. There is even coming a day when it will be appropriate to generalize a proverb such as Proverbs 10:22, because when the purposes of God triumph the blessing of the LORD will make every one of His people rich. When Jesus comes again we will have everything we need. We will be rich. Thus despair should not take root in our lives. God is good and all things will in some way turn out for good to those who love Him. This is our confession. This is our hope.

A cautious approach to life and God (Eccles. 7:15-18)

7:15 *I have seen both*[94] *in my senseless*[95] *days: there is a righteous*

---

94. The phrase *'eṭ-hakkōl*, translated *'both,'* appears first in the verse for emphasis. Although it can be translated as 'everything' (NKJV; NASB; ESV; and Murphy, *Ecclesiastes*, 68), Qohelet describes two situations in 7:15-18, so it is appropriate to translate the phrase as 'both' (NIV; Longman, *Ecclesiastes*, 192; Seow, *Ecclesiastes*, 251; Fox, *Rereading Ecclesiastes*, 257).

95. Although the use of *hebel* with *yôm* leads some to understand the meaning of *hebel* here as 'fleeting' (Crenshaw, *Ecclesiastes*, 140 and Seow, *Ecclesiastes*, 252), the breakdown of the deed-consequence relationship described in this passage strongly supports the idea of *'senseless.'*

> *person who perishes in spite of*[96] *his righteousness and there is a wicked person who lives long in spite of his evil.*
>
> 7:16 *Do not be very righteous and do not be so very wise. Why should you ruin yourself?*
>
> 7:17 *Do not be very wicked and do not be a fool. Why should you die when it is not your time?*
>
> 7:18 *It is good*[97] *that you seize the one and that you also not let go of the other, for the one who fears God will go forth*[98] *with both of them.*[99]

There is general agreement that Ecclesiastes 7:15 begins a new section, but it is not clear where the section ends. Some end the section at 7:22 because both 7:15 and 7:23 begin with a first-person verb.[100] Murphy ends the section at 7:24 based on the phrase 'who can find.'[101] Part of the difficulty is that some

---

96. Although Hertzberg (*Prediger*, 153) translates the preposition *bet* as 'because of' due to his view that 7:16-17 sets forth an exaggerated righteousness and wickedness, it is better to translate the *bet* as either 'in' or '*in spite of*' (Deut. 1:32; Murphy, *Ecclesiastes*, 68; and Fox, *Rereading Ecclesiastes*, 259), which highlights the incongruity between righteousness and perishing, on the one hand, and wickedness and long life, on the other hand. Bartholmew (*Ecclesiastes*, 253, n. 4) comments that there is little difference between 'in' and 'in spite of.'

97. Although Ogden calls this verse a 'better than' saying (*Qoheleth*, 124), Longman (*Ecclesiastes*, 197) is correct to note that since there is no comparative *min*, this is not a 'better than' saying.

98. The meaning of the verb '*go forth*' (*yāṣā'*) is understood in a number of ways. The NIV and NKJV translates the verb as 'escape,' a meaning that is consistent with its use in Genesis 44:4. However, 'escape' does not fit the context since the admonition in the first part of the verse is to hold on to the one and not let go of the other (Seow, *Ecclesiastes*, 255). The meaning 'go forth' makes the best sense (attested by the Septuagint and the Targum), especially if *'et* is taken as the preposition '*with*' and not the direct object marker. Longman (*Ecclesiastes*, 193) captures the idea with 'will follow both of them.'

99. The most likely reference of the 3mp suffix of *kullām* ('*both of them*') is the double use of the demonstrative *zeh* in the first part of the verse (Seow, *Ecclesiastes*, 255).

100. Barton, *Ecclesiastes*, 143; Longman, *Ecclesiastes*, 192; Seow, *Ecclesiastes*, 266; Crenshaw, *Ecclesiastes*, 140.

101. Murphy, *Ecclesiastes*, 68–69. Some divide this section differently. For example, Ogden (*Qohelet*, 118–119) understands 7:13-29 to be a section

verses can stand alone, and these verses set forth concepts that may refer to both the preceding and following sections. It is apparent that vv. 15-18 go together based on the subject matter and that the word *'both'* (*kōl*) acts as an *inclusio* setting the section apart.[102] There follow several proverbs in 7:19-22 which seem to be independent proverbs, but which deal with the general topic of the failure of righteousness. There then follows a statement by Qohelet in 7:23-24 concerning his test of wisdom, which may be the beginning of the next section, or it may be a transition to the next section where Qohelet speaks of his search to find the scheme of things.[103]

Part of the reason no one knows what is good (6:12) is related to the activity of God in the world. Having stated in 7:14 that God makes the good day and the bad day to keep people from knowing anything about their future, Qohelet puts forth an observation in 7:15 that explains why no one can figure out the work of God and why no one knows what the future holds for them. It is the age-old question of why the wicked prosper put in the context of long life and premature death. This question is also discussed in connection with the deed-consequence relationship (also called divine retribution), which sees a relationship between the way a person lives their life and the consequences they experience in life. Job's friends saw a mechanical relationship between the deed and the consequence, so they concluded that Job must have been sinful because he was suffering so greatly. This is a common way that certain proverbs are misunderstood.[104] Qohelet struggles with the breakdown

---

with 7:13-14 introducing the section. Kaiser (*Ecclesiastes*, 78) sees 7:15 as closing the section 6:1–7:15, which deals with a proper evaluation of outward fortunes as a way to explain the inequalities of divine providence. The next section is 7:16-29, which deals with a proper evaluation of a person's character as a way to explain the inequalities of divine providence. Whybray (*Ecclesiastes*, 119–120) understands 7:15 to be a short saying that is not related to what precedes or follows.

102. Ogden, *Qohelet*, 121.
103. Murphy, *Ecclesiastes*, 68–69.
104. The book of Proverbs is nuanced in the way it presents individual proverbs and does not teach a mechanical view of the deed-consequence

of the deed-consequence relationship because he does not see life working according to the general principles of that relationship.[105] In other words, people are not reaping what they have sown. Thus he has observed '*a righteous person who perishes in spite of his righteousness*' and '*a wicked person who lives long in spite of his evil.*' The incongruity of putting together righteous with perishing and wicked with long life stands out as wholly untraditional[106] and contrasts with passages that speak of a long life for the wise (Prov. 3:2, 16; 4:10; 10:2; 11:4; 12:21) and an early death for the wicked (Prov. 7:24-27; 10:27; 11:5). However, this is the way the world operates according to Qohelet's empirical observations.

The advice in 7:16-18 is based on the observation of 7:15. In other words, Qohelet exhorts people how they should live in light of the fact that the righteous die premature deaths and the wicked live long lives. However, there is no agreement concerning what Qohelet is encouraging people to avoid in these exhortations. Some argue that Qohelet has in view self-righteousness. Thus he exhorts people to avoid self-righteousness and intellectualism in 7:16, and he exhorts people to be careful not to abandon themselves to folly and wickedness in 7:17. Whybray argues that Qohelet has self-righteousness in view for two reasons. First, he argues that the more complex form of the verb in 7:16 (*'al-tĕhî ṣaddîq*) instead of the simpler form (*'al ṣiddōq*) suggests the meaning 'Do not claim to be righteous.' He believes that this meaning is supported by the parallel verb in 7:16, which uses the hitpael of the verb 'to be wise,' which he understands as 'pretend to be wise' (see the use of the hitpael in 2 Sam. 13:5, which means 'pretend to be ill'). This view of 7:16 would be in line with Proverbs 16:18. Secondly, he argues that the use of the adverb 'very' (*harbēh*)

---

relationship (see Raymond C. Van Leeuwen, 'Wealth and Poverty: System and Contradiction in Proverbs,' *HS* 33 [1992]: 25–36).

105. For the role of the deed-consequence relationship in the book of Ecclesiastes see Richard P. Belcher, Jr., *Divine Retribution in Ecclesiastes: An Analysis of the Deed-Consquence Relationship with Implications for the Interpretation of the Book*, PhD. diss, Westminster Theological Seminary, 2000.

106. Crenshaw, *Ecclesiastes*, 140.

supports the view of self-righteousness because it recognizes the tendency in human nature toward self-righteousness. Thus the exhortation means, 'Do not allow righteousness to become your dominating characteristic.' This is not a golden mean, a moderate course between righteousness and wickedness, but a warning that takes account of human weakness.[107] According to this view, 7:18 becomes an exhortation to true wisdom, with different views of what the two things that must be grasped are in that verse. Perhaps the two things refer to true wisdom and the avoidance of foolishness, or the teachings of wisdom and the true enjoyment of the good things in life, but both are rooted in the fear of God.[108] Thus the purpose of 7:18 is to advocate wise conduct, which has its rewards.

There are problems with understanding Qohelet to be exhorting people to avoid self-righteousness and a pretense to wisdom. The syntactical similarity between 7:16 and 17 argues against it. The parallel to 7:16a ('*do not be very righteous*') is 7:17a ('*do not be very wicked*'). The parallel to 7:16b ('*do not be so very wise*') is 7:17b ('*do not be a fool*'). It is clear that 7:17a is not a pretense to being wicked and 7:17b is not a pretense to being a fool. If 7:17 does not have pretense in mind, then it is unlikely that 7:16 has pretense or self-righteousness in mind.[109] Also, the only other use of '*wise*' (*ḥākam*) in the hitpael in the Old Testament is Exodus 1:10, which also does not support the idea of pretense. The passage refers to Pharaoh's plan against the Israelites, which in his view is not a pretense to a wise plan because he really thinks he has a wise plan.[110]

---

107. R. N. Whybray, 'Qoheleth the Immoralist? (Qoh 7:16-17),' in J. G. Gammie et al. (eds.), *Israelite Wisdom: Theological and Literary Essays in Honor of Samuel Terrien* (Missoula, MT: Scholars Press, 1978), 195–197.

108. George R. Castellino ('Qohelet and His Wisdom,' *CBQ* 30 [1968]: 24) argues for the first pair and Garrett (*Ecclesiastes*, 324) argues for the second pair.

109. Krüger (*Ecclesiastes*, 140 n. 4) points out the awkward imbalance between a warning not to pretend to be something (7:16a) and a warning not to be something (7:17a). Plus, pretension to wisdom in Proverbs is expressed by the phrase 'to be wise in one's own eyes' (Prov. 3:7; 26:12; 28:11).

110. Fox, *Rereading Ecclesiastes*, 261. He understands the verb '*wise*' in the hitpael to mean 'becoming wise' and refers to its use in Sirach 6:32 and 10:26 to refer to genuine wisdom.

Another possible way to take the advice in 7:16-18 is to understand that Qohelet is warning against the pursuit of an exaggerated righteousness, a warning against trying to become the wisest person on the earth. Perhaps he is warning against being a 'super sage.'[111] Some argue that in light of 7:20 Qohelet is warning against over-confidence in human ability and about the impossibility of perfection. Since no one can achieve full justice and avoid sinning, the prudent path is to be realistic and not try to deceive oneself.[112] In 7:17 he would be warning against turning to immorality or acting like a fool. In this view 7:18 is positive toward wisdom. Although wisdom has its limitations, one should not let go of wisdom because both wickedness and foolishness lead to disaster. Righteousness and wisdom, on the other hand, are achieved through the fear of God.[113]

But is Qohelet really warning against becoming a 'super sage'? Is Qohelet's problem that no one can be perfect? It is not necessary to understand the adverbs *'very'* (*harbēh*) and *'so very'* (*yôṯēr*) as indicating an exaggerated pursuit of righteousness and wisdom. The adverb *yôṯēr* primarily occurs in Ecclesiastes. In 2:15, where Qohelet recognizes that the same fate happens to the wise and the fool, he does not have in mind an exaggerated wisdom when he declares 'why then have I become very wise?' The other adverb, *harbēh*, can mean 'exceedingly' or 'abundantly,' but then it is used with *mĕ'ōḏ* to bring out the idea of a great amount (Gen. 15:1; 41:49; 1 Sam. 16:21; 2 Sam. 8:8; 1 Kings 10:10). Without *mĕ'ōḏ* the adverb *harbēh* generally means 'much' or 'many' (2 Sam. 1:4; 2 Kings 10:18; Hag. 1:6, 9). Nowhere in Ecclesiastes is *mĕ'ōḏ* used with *harbēh*. Thus Qohelet does not have in mind trying to become a 'super sage' or trying to attain perfection.

The best way to understand Qohelet's advice is as a warning against the pursuit of wisdom and righteousness because they do not produce the benefits in life that they promise. Qohelet

---

111. E. Glasser, *Le Procès du Bonheur par Qohelet* (Paris: Cerf, 1970), 116.

112. Crenshaw, *Ecclesiastes*, 143 and Seow, *Ecclesiastes*, 268–269.

113. W. A. Brindle, 'Righteousness and Wickedness in Ecclesiastes 7:15-18,' *AUSS* 23 (1985): 256–257.

observes in 7:15 that the righteous die prematurely and the wicked live a long life. On that basis he gives the advice, '*Do not be very righteous and do not be so very wise.*' Wisdom and righteousness fail to deliver on their promises, so there is no use seeking to be a very righteous person or a very wise person. The question at the end of 7:16 shows that the effort is not worth it: '*Why should you ruin yourself?*' This question makes sense if all that Qohelet observes in life concerning the hope of wisdom and righteousness is dashed by premature death. Why become so invested in something if it continually disappoints? On the other hand, one might think that if Qohelet sees the wicked living long lives, he would advise people to pursue wickedness and foolishness. But that is not his advice; rather, he exhorts people in 7:17, '*Do not be very wicked and do not be a fool.*' Qohelet recognizes that the connection between how people live their lives and the consequences that they experience based on how they live their lives is not a strong one. Thus he can argue that wisdom is better than foolishness (2:13-16), but wisdom ultimately fails, as is seen in the observation of 7:15. Qohelet also recognizes a weak connection between wickedness and long life. Although he sees many wicked people living long lives, he also knows that wickedness and foolishness can bring very negative consequences into a person's life, which is shown in the question at the end of 7:17: '*Why should you die when it is not your time?*'[114] The problem is that one cannot be sure which consequences will come into a person's life based on how they live their life. A life lived in the pursuit of wickedness and foolishness can be a disaster, which a person would want to avoid at all costs.

The ambiguity in the deed-consequence relationship leads Qohelet to set forth what he believes to be good in such a tenuous situation: '*It is good that you seize the one and that you also not let go of the other.*' The two things that Qohelet refers to here are the two sides of the equation laid out in 7:16-17. A person should grab hold of both righteousness and wisdom, on the

---

114. The use of the preposition *bet* ('*when*') is temporal (Longman, *Ecclesiastes*, 192, n. 70). It is translated by many translations as 'before your time' (NKJV, NIV, NASB, and ESV).

one hand, and also not let go of wickedness and foolishness, on the other hand. Qohelet then says that the person '*who fears God will go forth with both of them.*' The concept of fearing God has led people to understand this verse and this passage in a positive way.[115] However, there are good reasons for understanding the fear of God here not in the sense of reverence for God, as in the book of Proverbs, but as caution before God. This is the meaning that fits best in other places of Ecclesiastes (see the discussion at 5:7). The idea of caution before God also fits this context. The fear of God arises out of the incongruity between the fact that the righteous die prematurely and the wicked live long lives. God is the One who has made the world crooked (7:13).[116] Thus the best approach before God is to be cautious, because a person cannot be sure that righteousness will lead to long life. The inability to know what God will do in response to righteousness or wickedness makes one hesitant to pursue either one with much enthusiasm. One should not waste effort in pursuing either one very strongly, which also supports Qohelet's cautious approach to life and to God.

Homiletical Implications

A possible theme for these verses could be that it is difficult to understand the meaning of life because life is easily messed up. It is rather shocking in 7:15-18 that Qohelet does not set out a clear path for one to follow and that he connects the ambiguity of the consequences of righteousness and wickedness with the fear of God. In contrast, other places of Scripture clearly set out two ways. In Psalm 1 two ways are set forth. The way of the righteous leads to fruitfulness and blessing and the way of wickedness leads to instability and death. The same view is set forth in Proverbs, where two radically different alternatives

---

115. Whybray, *Ecclesiastes*, 201. Ogden and Zogbo (*Handbook to Ecclesiastes*, 252) argue that 7:18 means that a wise person will be able to cope with the situation that is described in 7:15-17, which means that a person will shun pretensions to righteousness and also keep free from evil.

116. Bartholomew (*Ecclesiastes*, 256) comments that the reference to the fear of God in 7:18 is ironic because of 7:13. Shields (*End of Wisdom*, 182) argues that fear refers to the dread a person experiences when they understand that there is no reliable way of determining how God will act in a given situation.

are laid out with two radically different consequences. There is a clear choice because the results are explicitly laid out. Qohelet, on the other hand, on the basis of his 'under the sun' perspective, does not set forth two distinct ways of living because he does not see the consequences of each clearly lived out in life. Qohelet views life as messed up. If ruin can come to the righteous, then why should someone be righteous? On the other hand, there are dangers to wickedness, so one should be careful not to pursue wickedness. Such a scenario describes a person who may want to trust in God and do what is right, but they are not sure that such a life will really produce what they desire in life. They are hesitant to fully pursue God and His way. The prospect of a few pleasures of wickedness pulls them toward the way of wickedness, but not too far. They have their life under control. They hold on to a few pleasures of life, perhaps partying a little too hard a couple of times a year. They are not committed to wickedness, but they are not committed to living a righteous life either. They have no passion for God's righteous ways; and thus, they have no passion for God. They take a non-committal approach to life which leads to a cautious approach toward God.

Searching for the sum of things (Eccles. 7:19-29)

7:19 *Wisdom makes the wise person stronger*[117] *than ten rulers who are in the city.*

7:20 *Surely among human beings*[118] *there is no one righteous on earth who does good and never sins.*

---

117. The verb 'strong' (*'āzaz*) is translated without a direct object (intransitive), as is its normal use, instead of with a direct object (transitive). Some, however, follow the latter (Gordis, *Koheleth*, 269). Such a translation would be 'Wisdom gives strength to the wise more than ten rulers in the city.' Either way, the meaning is not affected.

118. It is difficult to know how to translate the initial phrase *kî 'āḏām* of 7:20. If one sees a direct relationship with 7:19, then a causal meaning of *kî* is proposed. If one understands the proverbs of 7:19 and 20 as independent of each other, then an asseverative meaning of *kî* ('*surely*') is used (see the discussion in Longman, *Ecclesiastes*, 198 for these options). Most translations do not translate *'āḏām* as a separate term, but it is set apart from what

7:21 Moreover,[119] do not take to your heart all the things people say[120] so that you do not hear your servant cursing you.

7:22 For your heart also knows that many times even[121] you yourself have cursed others.

7:23 All this I have tested by wisdom; I said, 'I will be wise!'[122] but it was far from me.

7:24 Whatever happens[123] is far off, and deep, very deep.[124] Who can find it?

---

follows by a Hebrew accent (literally 'for/surely humanity'). It is tempting to translate the *kî* with an adversative sense ('but') to show a more direct connection with 7:19 (Seow, *Ecclesiastes*, 258). However, 'surely' has been used because the proverb is an independent saying even though its meaning is affected by its juxtaposition with 7:19.

119. It is hard to know how to understand *gam* at the beginning of 7:21. It seems to connect 7:21 with 7:20 in some way (contra Ogden [*Qoheleth*, 127], who understands 7:21 as introducing a new section separate from 7:19-20). Murphy (*Ecclesiastes*, 68–69) leaves it untranslated. Seow (*Ecclesiastes*, 258) takes it as rhetorical and translates it 'Yes' (see Willliams, *Hebrew Syntax*, 63). Bridges (*Ecclesiastes*, 171) is correct when he comments that *gam* points to an admonition suggested by the statement of 7:20 of the universal corruption of humanity. It seems to have the sense of 'for example.' The translation *'moreover'* (Longman, *Ecclesiastes*, 193) tries to bring out this connection.

120. The verb literally reads 'they say.' The subject is an indefinite subject, which is often introduced by third person forms (*GKC* 165b), so the translation *'people say'* is appropriate.

121. The first *gam* in 7:22 expresses the idea of addition (*'also'*) and the second *gam* expresses an emphatic idea (*'even'*), which is reinforced by the use of the independent personal pronoun with the verb.

122. The verb used here is a cohortative, which shows the determination of Qohelet to become wise. This determination is expressed in the translation by the exclamation point (Longman, *Ecclesiastes*, 200).

123. The phrase *mah-ššehāyāh* is used several times in Ecclesiastes and the context is a key factor for how it is translated. In 1:9 it is used in a clause that looks to the past and to the future, and it is parallel to a passive verb in the next clause and so is translated 'whatever has been.' In 3:15 the phrase refers to the present in contrast to other clauses that refer to the past and the future, and so it is translated 'whatever is.' In 7:24 the focus is to try to explain the events of life and so it is translated *'whatever happens'* (see also Fox and Seow). For the translation of this phrase in 6:10 see the note there.

124. The word for *'deep'* (*'āmōq*) is repeated, which expresses the superlative idea (GKC, 133k).

7:25 *I fully dedicated myself to know and to search out and to seek wisdom and the sum of things, and to know the wickedness of folly and foolishness that is madness.*[125]

7:26 *I am finding more bitter than death the woman who is a snare and her heart a net and her hands fetters. The one who is good before God will escape from her but the sinner will be taken by her.*

7:27 *'Look! This I have found,' says Qohelet, 'by adding one to one to find the sum of things—*

7:28 *which my soul has sought repeatedly but I have not found—I have found one man among a thousand but a woman among all these I have not found.*

7:29 *Only look! This I have found, that God has made mankind upright but they have sought out many schemes.'*

The relationship of 7:19-24 with the preceding section is a major question that affects how one understands these verses. The proverb on wisdom in 7:19 begins a series of proverbs (7:19-22) that sets these verses apart from what has gone before. In fact, the relationship of 7:19 to the preceding section seems very tenuous to many.[126] However, the subject matter

---

125. The four nouns at the end of 7:25 (wickedness, folly, foolishness, and madness) are hard to translate because the relationship between the nouns is not clear. Gordis (*Koheleth*, 271) understands them to be a double accusative after a verb of cognition (*GKC* 117ii) and supplies the verb 'to be' to get the translation, 'to know wickedness is folly and foolishness is madness.' Fox (*Rereading Ecclesiastes*, 267–268) argues against this because he sees it as expressing a tautology and it leaves the last clause detached from the context. Fox takes all four nouns as direct objects of the verb 'know,' which yields the translation 'to know wickedness, stupidity, and folly, madness.' However, to make this work at least one *waw* ('and') must be added to the text. Others (Longman, *Ecclesiastes*, 201) translate the four nouns as two construct chains, but the first nouns in the chain are not in the construct state. The first noun in the first chain ('wickedness') is not a problem because it only requires a change of vowels, which yields the translation the '*wickedness of folly*.' But the other noun that stands first in the second clause ('foolishness') has the definite article so that it is more difficult to take it as a construct noun. It is best taken as an absolute noun, followed by a word in apposition, which yields the translation '*foolishness that is madness*' (ESV).

126. Murphy, *Ecclesiastes*, 71. Fox (*Rereading Ecclesiastes*, 256–257) believes that 7:19 is irrelevant to the context and interrupts the relationship

of the proverbs in 7:19-22 is related to 7:15-18 in the emphasis on wisdom and righteousness.[127] A person's understanding of 7:15-18 determines how one understands 7:19-22. Those who understand 7:15-18 as a warning against an extreme righteousness, or some kind of exaggerated righteousness, see 7:19-22 enforcing that teaching by showing that such righteousness is beyond the reach of human beings.[128] Some take a reserved view of wisdom, arguing that the point of these verses is not to praise wisdom but to warn against overconfidence in what wisdom can do.[129] Others take a more positive view of wisdom as a way to help the wise avoid the pitfalls of 7:16-17.[130] However, if the point of 7:16-17 is the failure of righteousness and wisdom itself, as Qohelet observes in 7:15, then 7:19-22 continues that theme. Wisdom may have great value (7:19), but the value of wisdom is easily undermined by sin (7:20-22), which throws into question wisdom itself (7:23-24). Even the sin of the righteous can hinder the benefits of wisdom.

The proverb of 7:19 is very positive towards wisdom and sounds very much like a conventional wisdom saying extolling the benefits of wisdom: *'Wisdom makes the wise person stronger than ten rulers who are in the city.'* This sounds very much like Proverbs 24:5-6. One wise person's wisdom can be more beneficial to a city than ten rulers. Normally, rulers are considered important because they have power and authority, but this proverb states that wisdom is more valuable than the power and authority of ten rulers.[131] The value of wisdom is

---

between 7:18 and 20. He places 7:19 after 7:12 because he believes that it continues the teaching of wisdom's advantage over wealth. This dislocation could have happened accidentally, but as Longman (*Ecclesiastes*, 197) points out, there is no textual evidence for moving 7:19.

127. Ogden and Zogbo, *Handbook on Ecclesiastes*, 254.

128. Seow, *Ecclesiastes*, 257.

129. ibid., 268–269.

130. Hubbard, *Ecclesiastes*, 171; Eaton, *Ecclesiastes*, 115.

131. Longman, *Ecclesiastes*, 197. Seow (*Ecclesiastes*, 252, 256–257) does not believe that a comparison of wisdom to ten rulers makes sense. Why would wisdom be stronger for the wise than for anyone else? It makes better sense to him to compare wisdom to wealth and to understand *'rulers'* not

not specified in the proverb of 7:19, but its benefit is laid out in Proverbs 24:5-6 and the example story in Ecclesiastes 9:13-15. Another proverb follows in 7:20, which is illustrated in 7:21-22. The proverb in 7:20 begins with *kî*, which raises questions concerning its relationship to the previous proverb in 7:19. A more direct relationship with 7:19 would translate *kî* as adversative ('but') or causal ('for').[132] Some who see a causal relationship between the two verses understand the meaning to be that wise men are necessary in human society because human sin is universal.[133] The translation of *kî* as '*surely*' understands 7:20 to be either an independent saying or a saying that is a counterbalance to 7:19.[134] Qohelet puts forth the positive value of wisdom in 7:19 and then raises questions about wisdom by emphatically stating that '*Surely among human beings there is no one righteous on earth who does good and never sins.*' The point is not that righteous people do not exist, otherwise 7:15 would not make sense, but the point is that even the righteous can mess things up.[135] Qohelet then demonstrates in 7:21-22 how easy it is to mess things up in terms of what people say. 7:21 begins with an admonition: '*do not take to your heart all the things people say.*' Qohelet advises the reader not to pay too close attention to all the things people say. He sets forth the negative result if the admonition is not heeded: '*so that you do not hear your servant cursing you.*' If

---

as a political term but as a socio-economic term describing someone who has authority over property. However, the idea 'wealth' is not attested for this text, and a comparison of wisdom with ten rulers does make sense in light of Proverbs 24:5-6.

132. Seow (*Ecclesiastes*, 258) argues for the adversative sense even though the adversative meaning usually comes after a preceding negative.

133. Garrett, *Ecclesiastes*, 324.

134. Longman (*Ecclesiastes*, 198–199) takes it as a counterbalance. He also raises the possibility that 7:20 is a motivation for 7:16 in the sense that since no one can be consistently righteous, why try for it to the point of frustration?

135. However, Krüger (*Qoheleth*, 141) argues that 7:19-20 relativizes the distinctions in 7:15-18 so that humanity can no longer be neatly divided into the categories of the righteous and the wicked, which are presupposed in 7:15. Yet Qohelet continues to use the categories righteous and wicked; he just shows that even the righteous can mess things up.

someone is overly concerned with what people are saying the likelihood increases that they will hear something negative said about them, even from someone who is fairly close to them. Such talk could lead to trouble and strife. However, Qohelet seeks to defuse such a situation in 7:22 by reminding the reader that deep down you know '*that many times even you yourself have cursed others.*' If one is guilty of such negative talk themselves toward others, they should not get upset when others speak of them in this way. The point in the context is to show how easy it is to say something negative about someone else. Everyone can identify with this tendency, which means that everyone realizes how easy it is for even the righteous to stumble in this regard. The overall point is that life is easily messed up, even by the righteous, so that even the righteous can hinder the benefits of wisdom.

The problem with wisdom is continued in 7:23-24, which acts as a transition unit that looks both backward and forward. These verses look forward to 7:24-29 by the use of 'wisdom' and the verb 'to find.'[136] 7:23-24 also looks backward, not only to the immediately preceding sayings of 7:1-22, but also to Qohelet's original statement concerning his search for wisdom (1:13; 2:3). This backward look includes 7:25, as there are many connections between 7:23-25 and the earlier statements of Qohelet's search for meaning. In each case the search is carried out '*by wisdom,*' with the exact phrase being used in 1:13 and 2:3. The total involvement of Qohelet in the search is brought out by the use of the word '*heart*' (1:13; 2:3). The seriousness of the search is seen in the piling up of infinitives in 7:25, which uses a key infinitive for the search from 1:13 (*lātûr*). The focus of the search includes not only '*wisdom*' itself but also '*wickedness,*' '*folly,*' and '*madness*' (1:17; 7:25). The use of '*whatever*' (*mah-ššehāyāh*) recalls statements where it is used earlier in the book. It is used in 1:9, where the argument is made that there is nothing new under the sun, and it is also used in 3:14-15, where God is the One behind the unchanging

---

136. Longman (*Ecclesiastes*, 200) mentions the word '*find*' and Murphy (*Ecclesiastes*, 71) mentions the word '*wisdom*' as elements that look forward to the next section. Both Longman and Murphy also make connections to what has gone before, especially to Ecclesiastes 1:13.

nature of whatever exists. Finally, the desire for Qohelet to become wise and the failure of wisdom is also a theme of both sections (2:14-16; 7:23). These comparisons demonstrate that Qohelet's comments in 7:23-29 are a further reflection on what he has discovered in his search for meaning 'under the sun.' Qohelet moves from the proverbial statements of 7:19-22 to a summary statement in 7:23: *'all this I have tested by wisdom.'* No doubt *'all this'* refers to what has immediately gone before in 7:1-22,[137] so that 7:23-29 can be seen as a comment on the question of 6:12 concerning whether anyone knows what is good for human beings. However, in light of the comparisons noted above between this section and Qohelet's original search, 'all this' also includes all that Qohelet has examined between 1:13 and 7:23.[138] Thus these verses are commenting further on all that has been investigated up to this point in the book.

In the summary statement of 7:23 wisdom is both an instrument by which Qohelet conducts his search and the object of his search, which agrees with the use of wisdom in 1:12-18. He seeks to be wise through wisdom but fails in the endeavor. This use of wisdom has raised questions concerning whether Qohelet is speaking of two different kinds of wisdom, such as a practical wisdom versus an ideal wisdom.[139] It is not so much that Qohelet is using two different kinds of wisdom, but that wisdom as an instrument refers to the methodology of his search, which has as its object

---

137. Murphy, *Ecclesiastes*, 68–69. Ogden and Zogbo (*Handbook on Ecclesiastes*, 260) limit the reference of 'all things' to 7:19-22 and see 7:23-24 as a conclusion to those verses.

138. Bartholomew, *Ecclesiastes*, 264.

139. Ginsburg, *Coheleth*, 384 and Gordis, *Koheleth*, 270. Fox (*Rereading Ecclesiastes*, 263) notes that this is a distinction Israel would not have recognized. Ogden (*Qoheleth*, 128) argues that it is a special wisdom that is beyond human reach, a wisdom that transcends all limits and lifts the sage above the boundaries of human thought and experience. However, Qohelet does not have in view a special wisdom, but the traditional wisdom associated with the book of Proverbs, which is limited in his 'under the sun' perspective. Bartholomew (*Ecclesiastes*, 264) understands 'by wisdom' as referring to Qohelet's epistemological approach, which is different from Proverbs. Although this is true, the wisdom that is the object of the search in Qohelet is the wisdom set forth in Proverbs.

wisdom itself.[140] The search for wisdom includes seeking to become wise through an understanding of how the world works. This understanding is what has evaded Qohelet so that he comments, '*it was far from me.*' The pronoun '*it*' refers to the attempt to become wise, expressed in a determined way in the previous clause: '*I will become wise!*' In 7:24 Qohelet continues the thought of the inaccessibility of wisdom in several ways. First, he uses the term '*far off*' (*rāḥôq*), a word that occurred at the end of 7:23. But in 7:24 this word occurs in the emphatic position at the beginning of the verse before the phrase '*deep, very deep.*' Second, he repeats the adjective '*deep*' ('*āmōq*), which intensifies the idea of the unattainability of wisdom. Finally, Qohelet ends the verse with the rhetorical question, '*Who can find it?*', which expects the negative answer 'no one can find it.' Thus wisdom is inaccessible because it is far off and exceedingly deep.[141]

In 7:25 Qohelet begins his conclusion concerning the findings of his search. He begins with a statement of the search. The failure of the search is not because of a lack of effort on his part. Qohelet asserts '*I fully dedicated myself,*' which literally reads 'I and my heart turned.' The use of 'heart' not only shows the personal nature of the search, but also that his whole being was engaged in the search.[142] Also, the stringing together of three infinitives in a row ('*to know and to search out and to seek*') emphasizes the serious nature of

---

140. See the discussion in the Introduction and in Ecclesiastes 1:12-18 concerning Qohelet's use of wisdom as the methodology of his search. It is argued that Qohelet's approach is more of an autonomous approach because he does not begin with the starting point of the fear of the LORD, as the book of Proverbs does.

141. Although this passage sounds like Job 28, where the inaccessibility of wisdom is also emphasized, in Job 28 the fear of the LORD is set forth as the foundation of wisdom, which is accessible to human beings. In the quest for wisdom in the first-person discourse, Qohelet does not come to the same conclusion because of his 'under the sun' perspective. The book itself, however, does come to that conclusion (Eccles. 12:13-14).

142. Bartholomew, *Ecclesiastes*, 263. Crenshaw (*Ecclesiastes*, 145) notes that the verb 'turned' (*sābab*) is the verb used in 1:6 to refer to the useless circling of the wind, and that here it may thus refer to Qohelet's vain effort to discover an answer to his search.

the search. Qohelet completely gave himself to this effort. It is also clear that the focus of the search is comprehensive: '*to seek wisdom and the sum of things, and to know the wickedness of folly and foolishness that is madness.*' Not only is '*wisdom*' the object of his search, but also '*the sum of things*' (*ḥeśbôn*). This word means 'calculation' or 'give an accounting' and is translated in a variety of ways, such as 'the scheme of things' (ESV, NIV), 'the reason of things' (NASB, NKJV), 'answer' (Murphy), and 'solutions' (Fox). The idea is not that Qohelet is seeking a comprehensive understanding of life, in the sense that he must explain everything, but rather that he is seeking an explanation for how the world works.[143] The focus of his search has been 'what is good for mankind' (6:12), which has raised the question of wisdom, the work of God in the world (7:13), and how this affects the righteous and the wicked (7:15-18). Thus part of the focus of his search has been to try to explain why the wicked live long and the righteous die prematurely. In this way his search has been comprehensive because it has included 'wickedness' and 'foolishness' (which were also in view in 1:17 and 2:1). It becomes clear again that the two ways laid out in Proverbs do not form the starting point for Qohelet's search. In other words, he does not prejudice his search toward wisdom and righteousness, nor does he make his starting point the fear of the LORD, but he places wisdom and righteousness on the same level as wickedness and foolishness in his investigation of the meaning of life. Up to this point Qohelet has concluded that wisdom is inaccessible (7:23-24), and in 7:25 he begins his conclusion of what he has found by reasserting the serious and comprehensive nature of the search itself.

What Qohelet has discovered in his search becomes clear in 7:26-29. However, there are major questions related to the way Qohelet sets forth his argument,[144] and specifically what he has in view in his discussion of 'woman.' It is clear that Qohelet is setting forth what he has '*found*' or '*not*

---

143. Longman, *Ecclesiastes*, 202; Seow, *Ecclesiastes*, 261; Fox, *Rereading Ecclesiastes*, 265.

144. Murphy (*Ecclesiastes*, 75) comments that Qohelet's verbose style makes it difficult to grasp what he is saying.

found' (*māṣā'*), because this verb occurs five times in these four verses, but the presentation of his argument is rather convoluted. He begins in 7:26 by setting forth something he has discovered. He uses the participle of the verb 'to find' ('*I am finding*') and talks about '*a woman.*' Then in 7:27 he calls attention to what he has found with the use of '*Look!*' and uses the form of the verb that stresses completed action, '*I have found.*' Qohelet mentions at the end of 7:27 the process of his investigation: '*adding one thing to another to find the sum of things.*' But then he breaks off the argument and does not immediately state what he has found; rather, he further comments on the investigation by asserting that '*my soul has sought repeatedly but I have not found.*' Then at the end of 7:28 and in 7:29 he states what he has found. There are also major questions concerning what he has found which will be taken up in the following exposition.

In 7:26 Qohelet states something that he has found with the use of the participle: '*I am finding more bitter than death the woman who is a snare and her heart a net and her hands fetters.*' There is much discussion concerning how this woman should be understood. A common view is that Qohelet is not referring to all women but that he has in mind a particular kind of woman. Not all women are '*more bitter than death*' but only the type of woman who is a snare. Such language recalls the adulterous woman of the book of Proverbs who seeks to snare young men (Prov. 6:26).[145] Some understand Qohelet to be referring to women in general because in 7:28 he contrasts '*man*' (*'āḏām*) with '*woman*' (*'iššāh*), which demonstrates that he does not have a particular woman in mind in 7:27 but that all women are in view.[146] Others identify the woman as a personification of foolishness, as found in the book of Proverbs. In other words, this woman is not a literal woman, but represents Dame Folly, who is presented in Proverbs 9:13-18. The context is supposed to support this view with its

---

145. Murphy, *Ecclesiastes*, 75; Ogden and Zogbo, *Handbook on Ecclesiastes*, 268.

146. Longman, *Ecclesiastes*, 204; Fox, *Rereading Ecclesiastes*, 268–268; Ginsburg, *Coheleth*, 387.

emphasis on wisdom. Also, the definite article on 'woman' in 7:26 has as its immediate antecedent folly in 7:25.[147] The problem with this view is that every time Qohelet mentions men or women in this context he has in view literal men and women (7:28-29). It seems forced to introduce the figure of Dame Folly at this point. Also, the description of the woman in 7:26 fits so well the description of the adulterous woman in the book of Proverbs that one immediately thinks of that connection (Prov. 5:4; 7:23). Although it is true that 7:28 has women in general in view, the two women of 7:26 and 7:28 should not be identified, because there is a development of the argument between 7:26 and 7:28.

In 7:26 Qohelet sets forth what he has found in the process of his investigation, which is why he uses a participle,[148] but it is not the final statement of his discovery, which comes in 7:28-29, where he uses the aspect of the verb that stresses completed action ('*I have found*'). He sets forth a view that is in line with traditional wisdom concerning the adulterous woman who entraps men. This view is supported by the last clause of 7:26: '*the one who is good before God will escape from her but the sinner will be taken by her.*' This statement also supports traditional wisdom teaching (Prov. 6:23-24; 7:4-5).[149] Thus Qohelet starts his conclusion with something he has found that agrees with the sentiments of Proverbs, but it is not the final statement of his discovery. In fact, this sentiment will be undermined by 7:28-29. Although most attention has been paid to a discussion concerning the meaning of '*woman*' in 7:26, the key statement for Qohelet might be the statement concerning '*the one who is good*' and '*the sinner.*' In light of 7:29 one can argue that such a distinction no longer holds.

---

147. Seow, *Ecclesiastes*, 262; Bartholomew, *Ecclesiastes*, 266. Although both Seow and Bartholomew argue that Dame Folly is called bitter in Prov. 5:4, that verse has in view the forbidden, adulterous woman. No one follows the view of Ogden (*Qoheleth*, 130) that the woman in Ecclesiastes 7:26 is a figure for untimely death.

148. The participle might also denote that this conclusion is the result of repeated experience (Longman, *Ecclesiastes*, 203).

149. For the view that the terms '*good*' and '*sinner*' are moral terms see the discussion at 2:26 and Bartholomew, *Ecclesiastes*, 266.

Much like the statement in 2:26 that is undermined by the concluding *hebel* judgment, the finding of 7:26 is undermined by Qohelet's statement of his final discovery in 7:28-29. In 7:27 Qohelet begins to focus on the conclusion of his investigation by calling attention to what he has found. He uses the imperative '*Look!*,' and asserts '*I have found.*'[150] Before he relates what he has found he indicates the method of his investigation: '*by adding one to one to find the sum of things.*' Although the phrase '*by adding*' is an addition to the text, it is justified because the phrase '*one to one*' and the term *ḥešbôn* ('*the sum of things*') are words used in accounting.[151] Qohelet's investigation includes a careful analysis of the evidence. His goal has been to accumulate the information and to assemble the facts together in order to provide an explanation of things.[152] One then expects to read what it is that Qohelet has found, but instead Qohelet breaks off the argument in 7:28a and comments further on his investigation. 7:28 begins with the relative pronoun *ʾăšer*, which refers back to '*the sum of things*' (*ḥešbôn*).[153] Qohelet emphasizes

---

150. For a discussion of the third person statement, '*says Qohelet*,' see the Introduction. Bartholomew (*Ecclesiastes*, 265) understands the phrase to signify a highly important point of reflection in Qohelet's journey. There is also discussion of whether the verb is feminine (with a final *he*), or whether Qohelet has the article (an initial *he*). Ginsburg (*Coheleth*, 388) follows the Hebrew text (feminine verb) because he argues that Qohelet here is the personification of wisdom. Murphy (*Ecclesiastes*, 74) and Seow (*Ecclesiastes*, 265) believe that Qohelet has the article with a masuline verb because in Ecclesiastes 1:12 and 12:8 the verb is already understood as masculine and this is in agreement with the Septuagint.

151. Seow (*Ecclesiastes*, 265) translates the phrase 'one by one to find an accounting' and explains the phrase as someone checking the ledger item by item.

152. Longman, *Ecclesiastes*, 205 and Ogden and Zogbo, *Handbook on Ecclesiastes*, 271.

153. Some argue that *ʾăšer* is not referring back to '*the sum of things*' in 7:27 but is introducing a new statement that further defines what he has found. The clause would then be translated, 'what my soul has always sought without finding (is this).' In this view Qohelet is actually denying the truth of the proposition that follows, which states that only one man has been found but not one woman has been found (see Murphy, *Ecclesiastes*, 75 and Ogden and Zogbo, *Handbook on Ecclesiastes*, 272). Seow (*Ecclesiastes*,

his complete investment in the search by emphasizing his personal involvement in the investigation ('*my soul*') and his continual involvement in the investigation ('*sought repeatedly*'). He concludes this digression with '*but I have not found.*' This digression shows that Qohelet is exasperated because he has not been able to discover the sum of things. Although he has been personally involved and has continually sought the sum of things, he has not been able to find it. In context this means that Qohelet has not been able to find an explanation of how the world works. He has not been able to determine what is good (6:12). He has not been able to access wisdom to help him in his search (7:23-24). He is not able to explain the events of this world (7:15-18). Thus there is no rationale for the events of the world, which means that there is no explanation for why the wicked live long and the righteous die early.

After the digression in 7:28a Qohelet states what he has found in 7:28b-29. Although he has not been able to discover the sum of things, he asserts what he has found: '*I have found one man among a thousand but a woman among all these I have not found.*' Since Qohelet does not specify the kind of man or woman he has in view, the context becomes signficant for understanding what kind of man or woman Qohelet may have in mind. In 7:29 Qohelet states the final conclusion of his investigation, the ultimate discovery from his search, which is important for understanding this whole section. He highlights his discovery by the opening phrase, '*Only look!*'[154]

---

264) denies the validity of this view because it goes against the usage of 'find' and 'seek' in the rest of the passage. However, he argues that 7:28b is secondary because the use of *ʾāḏām* as 'male' instead of 'humanity' goes against its usage in every other place in the book. This is a weak argument and is somewhat dependent on his view that 'woman' is Lady Wisdom. Fox (*Rereading Ecclesiastes*, 270) wants to emend *ʾăšer* ('*which*') to *ʾiššāh* ('woman') and translate the clause, 'a woman I sought continually,' but there is no evidence for this emendation.

154. Longman (*Ecclesiastes*, 202, n. 121) notes that 7:29 is the only place in the OT where '*only*' (*leḇaḏ*) is used absolutely. Although some take it with the phrase '*this I have found,*' it begins the verse and is separated from '*this*' so that it goes with '*Look!*' Ogden and Zogbo (*Handbook on Ecclesiastes*, 273) point out that *leḇaḏ* draws attention to what follows as the single conclusion Qohelet was able to make.

Qohelet then states his discovery: '*This I have found, that God has made mankind upright but they have sought out many schemes.*' Qohelet uses the generic term '*mankind*,' so he has in view men and women. He also uses the word '*schemes*' (*ḥiššābôn*), which seems related to the term 'sum of things' (*ḥešbôn*).[155] A few try to give a positive meaning to the idea of 'schemes' by understanding it as 'great solutions' or a healthy search for the meaning of life. The former view, argued by Fox, understands this as a flaw because he thinks that Qohelet is contrasting intellectual simplicity with seeking after great solutions.[156] But to make this work the term '*upright*,' which also means 'straight,' has to be understood as intellectual directness or simplicity. Ogden and Zogbo understand 7:29 as positive. Qohelet's single discovery is that the job of human beings is to search to understand the sum of things.[157] However, such a discovery seems rather anticlimactic and does not really offer any kind of closure for his search. It is better to understand 'schemes' as human invention and planning which is wrong, ineffective, and evil. It is a deliberate pun on Qohelet's search for the sum of things. Instead of an answer to his search for the sum of things Qohelet discovered many schemes, which actually hinder the search for an explanation.[158] There also may be an allusion to Genesis 6:5, which describes the great wickedness of mankind on the earth before the flood and notes that 'every intention of the thoughts (*maḥăšābāh*) of his heart was only evil continually.' The 'thoughts' of human beings are full of evil invention and planning. Thus Qohelet's discovery agrees with the first several chapters of Genesis. In Genesis 1:31 God declared everything that He had made good. God created '*mankind upright*' and provided for them everything they needed, but Adam and Eve rejected God's authority and sought to establish their own moral autonomy.

---

155. Whybray (*Ecclesiastes*, 127) sees the connection between the two terms in the common reference to the results of human ingenuity.

156. Fox, *Rereading Ecclesiastes*, 265 and 272.

157. Ogden and Zogbo, *Handbook on Ecclesiastes*, 274.

158. Bartholomew, *Ecclesiastes*, 268.

The early history of mankind shows how they *'sought out many schemes'* (Gen. 6:5).

The discovery of Qohelet in 7:29 puts some issues in perspective. It confirms that no one really knows what is good for humanity (Eccles. 6:12). It also confirms the statement of 7:20 concerning righteous people and sin. In fact, things are worse than that proverb states. It is not just that there is not a righteous person who never sins (7:20), but that there are very few righteous men in existence. In light of 7:29 the statement in 7:28b concerning the discovery of one man among a thousand but no discovery of a woman should be understood as referring to men and women who are upright. Qohelet could find only a few upright men but he could not find any upright women. Although this is a negative statement about women, it is also a negative statement about men.[159] Humanity in general is basically corrupt, with very few who can be considered righteous. The problem is not the universal corruption of humanity, but the problem is that very few are righteous. Such a view undermines the doctrine of the two ways by denying that many righteous exist. It also helps explain why Qohelet muddles the distinction between the way of the righteous and the way of the wicked in 7:15-18. Furthermore, the traditional wisdom statement of 7:26 is also undermined. Not only are there very few who please God and so escape the adulterous woman, but most women fall into the category of the adulterous woman who traps men with her snares. If there are no upright women then the positive

---

159. There is much discussion concerning whether Qohelet is a misogynist (someone who dislikes women) in this passage. Those who argue that 7:26 refers to women in general normally view Qohelet as negative toward all women (Longman), but those who see a particular woman in view (Ogden and Zogbo) or argue that Lady Wisdom is the focus tend to deny that Qohelet is a misogynist (Seow, Bartholomew). Some attribute Qohelet's negative view of women to the many women in his harem (Barton, Wright). The view argued in this commentary is that 7:26 has in view a particular type of woman, but that this traditional wisdom saying is undermined by 7:28b, where all women are placed in a negative light. However, Qohelet is also very negative toward men, so that both men and women are seen in a bad light. He does encourage the enjoyment of one's wife in Ecclesiastes 9:10.

statements about women in the book of Proverbs are called into question (Prov. 18:22; 31:10).[160]

Homiletical Implications

Qohelet wrestles with how he can explain the events of life and it becomes clear that an explanation is far from him. Life's experiences do not always add up.[161] Qohelet's final discovery is that human beings plan and scheme to do what is wrong. Although this explains why Qohelet has had trouble trying to discover an answer to the sum of things, it is only part of the problem that Qohelet has pinpointed. The other problem that Qohelet has stated several times relates to the work of God (3:14-15; 7:13). He specifically asks in 7:13 concerning the work of God, 'who can make straight what he has made crooked?' So how should one understand the many schemes of human beings in relationship to the crookedness of the work of God? The source of the wickedness of human beings is clear in Genesis 3 and the chapters that follow. God created human beings upright, but they have rejected God and have gone their own wicked way. However, the crookedness of the work of God does not refer to God's creation of the world because He created the world good (Gen. 1:31). The work of God in Ecclesiastes is identified with events that take place in the world which cannot be changed and which Qohelet is not able to explain. God's work is associated with both the day of prosperity and the day of adversity because God has made both (7:14). It includes what Qohelet observes taking place on the earth, such as the wicked living long and the righteous dying prematurely (7:15-18). The work of God is the sovereignty of God over the activities that take place in the world. God's work is crooked not because His works are evil but because His works are impossible to explain. Qohelet lacks a theological framework to put the crooked ways of God's works and the evil schemes of human beings together

---

160. Although Proverbs 31:10 states that an excellent wife is hard to find, there is plenty of evidence in Proverbs of good women. Qohelet does not see them as rare or hard to find, but as non-existent (Barton, *Ecclesiastes*, 147).

161. This is a phrase used by Ogden and Zogbo, *Handbook on Ecclesiastes*, 271.

in order to make sense out of life because he is operating from an 'under the sun' perspective. An 'above the sun' perspective is presented by the apostle Paul when he describes the trials and sufferings of his life. He gives an account of those trials in 2 Corinthians 11:24-28, including whippings, beatings, a stoning, being shipwrecked and adrift at sea, and dangers from many quarters, such as dangers on his journeys and dangers from robbers, from Jews, Gentiles, and false brothers. Paul also experienced sleepless nights, hunger and thirst, cold and exposure. These hardships are not evidence of Paul's failure as an apostle; rather, Paul is able to give a theological analysis of his troubles because he saw these hardships as part of his work as an apostle, as a way for the power of Christ to be manifest, and for the name of Christ to be exalted (2 Cor. 12:9-10). Although it would be inappropriate to expect Qohelet to have the same kingdom perspective as the apostle Paul, it is not inappropriate to expect Qohelet to be able to give a theological explanation of the tragedies of life. The book of Proverbs recognizes that there are exceptions to the benefits of wisdom when it recognizes that wealth is not an absolute benefit but only a relative benefit (Prov. 11:4, 28; 16:8, 19); that there is injustice in the world, so poverty is not always a result of laziness (Prov. 13:23; 14:31); and that there is mystery connected to what happens in the world because ultimately God is sovereign (Prov. 19:21; 21:30-31). The purpose of suffering also becomes clearer in light of the suffering of Jesus Christ. His suffering was the avenue through which God was redeeming His people and it was the path to His glory. God is able to work out His purposes through suffering. The Christian life is presented as a spiritual battle, but there is a way of righteousness that will one day lead to glory.

The arbitrary nature of the world (Eccles. 8:1-17)

There is debate as to whether 8:1 closes 7:25-29 or begins 8:1-17. Several different options have been set forth. Fox argues that 8:1a closes the previous section and 8:1b begins the next section. He contends that 8:1a implies that the wise man knows the meaning of the saying that follows, but 8:1b is a rhetorical question implying that no one knows the saying. Thus the two should be separated.[162] Few have followed his suggestion and Krüger argues that the common theme in 8:1a and 8:1b suggests that they should not be separated.[163] Others argue that 8:1 closes the previous section because of the prominent use of wisdom terminology. Thus the use of 'wise' (*ḥāḵām*) in 8:1 is reflecting on the pessimistic conclusion of 7:29. The attempt to discover the sum of things has failed.[164] The next section begins in 8:2 with its series of imperatives.

There are also good reasons for understanding 8:1 to be the beginning of the next section. The word 'matter' (*dāḇār*) is a catchword linking 8:1a to 8:3 and 8:5 (*dāḇār* as thing) and 8:4 (*dāḇār* as word). Plus, the question 'who knows' is repeated in 8:7 and 8:17, which means that the term 'wise man' and the verb 'know' frame chapter 8.[165] In fact, the question of 8:1a is answered in 8:17.

Perhaps the best solution is to see 8:1 as a transitional or pivotal verse.[166] The connections of 8:1 to 8:17 show that chapter 8 is a distinct unit, but the topic of chapter 8 is related to what has gone before; in fact, the topic of chapter 8 goes all the way back to Ecclesiastes 6:12. In the discussion of that passage it was argued that 6:12 introduces the next two major sections of Ecclesiastes. The question, 'Who knows what is good?' is addressed in 7:1–8:17 and the question, 'Who can tell what will come in the future?' is addressed in 9:1–10:20. Thus 8:1-17 is still dealing with the general question of 'Who knows what is good?' with particular focus on whether the wise man can answer this question. Qohelet has not been able to answer this question (7:25-29), and so it is appropriate to reflect on

---

162. Fox, *Ecclesiastes*, 53.

163. Krüger, *Qoheleth*, 151.

164. Whybray, *Ecclesiastes*, 128; Towner, *Ecclesiastes*, 332; and Eaton, *Ecclesiastes*, 117, who understands the next section to be 8:2–9:10.

165. Seow, *Ecclesiastes*, 290 and Ogden and Zogbo, *Handbook on Ecclesiastes*, 275.

166. Garrett (*Ecclesiastes*, 325) uses the word 'transition' and Ogden and Zogbo (*Handbook on Ecclesiastes*, 274) use the word 'pivot.'

whether a wise man could give an answer to the question of what is good. The answer Qohelet comes to is that a wise man is not able to answer this question (8:17). The reasons for his conclusion are laid out in chapter 8. The chapter can be divided into the following sections: the arbitrary nature of human government (8:1-9), the arbitrary nature of divine government (8:10-15), and the answer to the question raised in 8:1 (8:16-17).

The arbitrary nature of human government (Eccles. 8:1-9)

8:1 *Who is like the wise man? And who knows the explanation of a matter? A man's wisdom makes his face shine and the hardness of his face is changed.*

8:2 *I say,*[167] *'Obey the command of the king even*[168] *according to the manner of*[169] *the oath of God.'*

8:3 *Do not be rash*[170] *that you depart from his presence. Do not stand with a bad cause because all that he desires he will do.*

---

167. This verse begins with a textual difficulty. The word 'I' (*'ănî*) stands alone and so its connection to the rest of the verse is debated. Murphy (*Ecclesiastes*, 80) briefly lays out most of the options, which include changing the pronoun *'ănî* to the direct object marker (*'ēṯ*), adding the verb '*say*' (*'āmar*), and redividing the consonants to read 'in the presence of the king.' Seow (*Ecclesiastes*, 279) understands the pronoun to be a corruption of a suffix that was on the previous verb. No solution is completely free of difficulty.

168. The *waw* at the beginning of this phrase is difficult; in fact, Seow (*Ecclesiastes*, 279) retains it as the more difficult reading and explains it as having an emphatic function ('*even*').

169. There is much discussion concerning the phrase '*al diḇraṯ*. Many understand it in a causal sense, but there is debate whether '*the oath of God*' is a subjective or objective genitive. If it is an objective genitive, then the reason one should obey the command of the king is because of the oath of fidelity a person has made to the king before God, as expressed in 1 Kings 2:43 (Delitzsch, 'Ecclesiastes,' 6:340; Gordis, *Koheleth*, 278). If it is a subjective genitive, then the reason to obey the king is that God has taken an oath in support of the king (Ogden and Zogbo, *Handbook on Ecclesiastes*, 280). It is also possible to take '*al diḇraṯ* in a modal sense, '*according to the manner of*' (Ps. 110:4), with the meaning that one must keep the command of the king in the same manner that one would keep an oath sworn to God (Seow, *Ecclesiastes*, 279). Whichever way the verse is understood, it is clear that obeying the king is a serious matter and is not to be taken lightly.

170. Several issues surround the first imperative phrase in this verse.

8:4 For the word of the king is power, and who will say to him, 'What are you doing?'

8:5 Whoever keeps a command will not experience a bad situation and the heart of the wise man[171] should know the proper time and the right action.

8:6 Indeed, to every activity there is a proper time and a right action; however, the misfortune of mankind is great upon him.

8:7 For he does not know what will happen because who can tell him when[172] it will happen?

8:8 No one has power over the wind to retain the wind; no one has power over the day of death; there is no discharge during the battle; and wickedness[173] will not deliver those who practise it.[174]

8:9 All this I observed and gave my heart to every activity which

---

Some argue that it goes with the preceding verse, which yields the translation 'do not rush into a vow to God. You should leave his presence ...' (Longman, *Ecclesiastes*, 209–210 argues this on the basis that otherwise 8:3 advises the reader against leaving the king's presence in 8:3a and then advises in favor of it in 8:3b; see also the RSV). The approach in this commentary is to take the two imperatives in 8:3 as stating opposite things, and to translate the first imperative in line with the way the verb has already been used in Ecclesiastes 5:2 and 7:9, which favors '*rash*' or 'be in a hurry' (Ogden and Zogbo, *Handbook on Ecclesiastes*, 281–281) over 'terrified' or 'stupefied' (Seow, *Ecclesiastes*, 279).

171. Although it is possible to take *lēḇ ḥāḵām* as 'a wise heart' based on the lack of the article on *ḥāḵām* (Longman, *Ecclesiastes*, 210) and the passage in 1 Kings 3:12 (Seow, *Ecclesiastes*, 281), the article in Ecclesiastes is not consistently used and Prov. 16:23 supports taking *lēḇ ḥāḵām* as a construct chain. The emphasis in this section of Ecclesiastes is on the wise man, so *ḥāḵām* is translated that way.

172. Barton (*Ecclesiastes*, 150) points out that *kaʾăšer* always means '*when*' in Ecclesiastes (5:1 [Heb. 4:17]; 5:4 [Heb. 5:3]; 8:16).

173. Some emend the word '*wickedness*' (*ršʿ*) to read 'wealth' (*ʿšr*), which is supposed to make better sense in the context (Fox, *Rereading Ecclesiastes*, 281). The same consonants are used in these two words but in a different order. However, there is no textual evidence for reading 'wealth' (Murphy, *Ecclesiastes*, 84).

174. The phrase '*those who practise it*' (*bĕʿālāw*) literally reads 'its owners.'

is done under the sun when[175] a person has power over another person to their harm.[176]

Qohelet has concluded in 7:25-29 that he has not been able to explain the sum of things. He also laid out what he did discover in the process of his search (7:29). If Qohelet could not discover the sum of things, one wonders if anyone else can discover it. So attention is directed toward those who were supposed to be able to answer such questions. Qohelet raises the question of the wise man in 8:1 and will analyze what the wise man is able to discover or find in 8:17. The verb 'discover' or 'find' (*māṣā'*) was prominent in 7:25-29 as a description of Qohelet's search, so it is appropriate that Qohelet would use this verb again in his answer to whether the wise man is able to find an answer.

Qohelet raises two questions in 8:1 that focus on the wise man's wisdom. The first question, '*Who is like the wise man?*,' sets the wise man apart from everyone else because the wise man is very involved with wisdom.[177] Although a different

---

175. The word '*ēṯ* ('time') in the phrase '*ēṯ* '*ašer* is an accusative of time which can be translated '*when*' (Murphy, *Ecclesiastes*, 80 cites GKC 118i).

176. There is some discussion whether '*harm*' refers to the harm done to the oppressor or the harm done to the one who is oppressed. Some think both are in view (Seow, *Ecclesiastes*, 284, who understands *šlṭ* as a legal economic term referring to economic oppression; Ogden and Zogbo, *Handbook on Ecclesiastes*, 292). However, if oppression harms the oppressor, then the arbitrary use of power is not much of a problem.

177. Although Longman (*Ecclesiastes*, 209) takes the answer to this verse to be that no one is wise, if one translates the verse, as he does, in relation to the wise man (he uses 'person'), then a 'no' answer would mean that no one is like the wise person. This answer places the wise man in a category separate from others, not in a category just like others who do not have wisdom. Ginsburg (*Coheleth*, 391) recognizes the question as an emphatic negation that states that no one can be compared to the wise man. On the other hand, Delitzsch ('Ecclesiastes,' 6:337) understands Ecclesiastes 8:1a as asserting the incomparable superiority of the wise man. He does not recognize that the second question ('who knows the interpretation of a matter?') expects a negative answer and he understands 8:1b to refer to the intellectual and ethical transformation of the countenance of the wise man in the sense that wisdom makes things clear to him (see also Hubbard, *Ecclesiastes*, 177-178 and Kaiser, *Ecclesiastes*, 88 for very positive approaches to the possibilities of wisdom).

division of the Hebrew consonants leads to the translation, 'Who is so wise?,' which is followed by the Septuagint,[178] the Hebrew text as it stands makes good sense.[179] The role of the wise man is important for the book of Ecclesiastes (12:9-11). 1 Kings 4:29-34 speaks of the great wisdom of Solomon, which must have been a great impetus for the development of a professional class of wise men who were distinguished from the priests and the prophets (Jer. 8:9; 18:18). This first question expects the answer that no one is like the wise man.

The second question that Qohelet asks deals with the wisdom of the wise man: *who knows the explanation of a matter?*' On the one hand, in light of the first question and the way the wise man is presented in Proverbs, one might expect a positive answer to this question. The preamble to the book of Proverbs states that the purpose of the book is that people would 'know wisdom and instruction, to understand words of insight.' Proverbs is for both the wise and the simple youth (Prov. 1:2-6). There are proverbs that emphasize the role of knowledge in relationship to the wise (Prov. 14:6; 15:7). It is presumed that the wise man would be able to use knowledge to explain matters related to life. Thus in the context of Proverbs one would expect a positive answer to the second question in Ecclesiastes 8:1. One would certainly not expect a totally negative answer, for even if the wise man cannot explain every matter, he is able to explain many matters related to life. However, the question *'who knows?'* in other parts of Ecclesiastes has been a closed question with the expected answer 'no one knows.' Thus there is tension in 8:1 between the fact that there is no one like the wise man and the expected answer that no one knows the explanation

---

178. Instead of reading *mî kĕhehākām*, as in the Hebrew text ('who is like the wise man?'), the Septuagint reads *mî kōh hākām* ('who is so wise?'), which is also followed by Seow (*Ecclesiastes*, 277).

179. The problem some see with the Hebrew text (*mî kĕhehākām*) is that the preposition *kaph* does not displace the article on the word *hākām*. However, there are other examples of this in the Hebrew text (Ezek. 40:25; 47:22; 2 Chron. 10:7), so a different division of Hebrew consonants is not necessary (see Gordis, *Koheleth*, 276).

of a matter.[180] One would expect a wise man to know the explanation of a matter, but one is not sure at this point how Qohelet is going to answer this question.

The second part of 8:1 continues this tension by setting forth a benefit of wisdom: '*A man's wisdom makes his face shine and the hardness of his face is changed.*' In fact, there may be a twofold benefit of wisdom set forth in this verse. Wisdom is able to brighten up a person's face, which probably refers to a pleasant and cheerful demeanor.[181] Thus wisdom has a positive effect on people. Furthermore, wisdom is even able to change a face that is hard. The word that is translated '*hardness*' is the word for 'strength' ('ōz) and in some contexts it may have the connotation 'bold' or 'brazen' (as in the ESV and the NIV in Prov. 7:13), or 'fierce,' 'hard' (as in the ESV and the NIV in Deut. 28:50). Commentators understand this word in Ecclesiastes 8:1 to mean 'hardness,' 'stern,' 'impudent,' 'boldness,' and 'an angry look.'[182] It has a negative connotation and the point is that wisdom is able to change a harsh or stern demeanor. Thus the beneficial effects of wisdom can be seen in a person's life. Wisdom is able to change a negative facial expression to a positive, cheerful expression. How this is done is not explicitly said in Ecclesiastes 8:1, but it may be through the explanation of a matter.[183] When wisdom is able to solve a problem, there is relief and gladness. An example of this would be the situation of Pharaoh and Joseph. Pharaoh had some dreams that troubled him greatly. Genesis 41:8 states that 'his spirit was disturbed' because no one could explain the dreams to him. Joseph, however, was able to interpret the dreams of Pharaoh through the wisdom of God (Gen. 41:25).

---

180. Murphy (*Ecclesiastes*, 82) states that the questions in 8:1 are exclamatory and they suggest the exalted task of the sage and the impossibility of that task (7:25-29).

181. Fox, *Rereading Ecclesiastes*, 276 and Brown, *Ecclesiastes*, 86.

182. See Murphy, Longman, Seow, Delitzsch, and Whybray.

183. Although the proverbial saying in 8:1b has implications for the section on behavior before the king (8:2-9), some commentators jump ahead and interpret the saying of 8:1b solely or primarily in reference to behavior before the king (Seow, *Ecclesiastes*, 291; Gordis, *Koheleth*, 277; Crenshaw, *Ecclesiastes*, 149; Provan, *Ecclesiastes*, 163).

Joseph's interpretation of Pharaoh's dreams and his proposal 'pleased Pharaoh' (ESV), which literally reads 'the word was good in his eyes.' One can assume that the change of Pharaoh from having a troubled spirit to being pleased with Joseph's interpretation and proposal brought about a change in his outward demeanor, which is evidenced in the way he treats Joseph (Gen. 41:37-45). This positive benefit of wisdom reminds the reader that Qohelet has already set forth the relative value of wisdom (2:12-17), but that wisdom has not been able to solve the problems with which Qohelet has been wrestling (7:25-29). The argument of chapter 8 will determine whether wisdom and the wise man are able to solve the problems of life.

In 8:2-4 Qohelet turns more directly to the subject of the king. How does wisdom work in the presence of a king? Working at the royal court must have had its challenges, and part of the purpose of wisdom is to help someone know how to conduct themselves before the king (Prov. 14:35; 16:14; 24:21; 25:6). Qohelet is seeking to answer the question concerning the explanation of a matter (8:1a) and whether wisdom can have the beneficial effect stated in 8:1b. What better place to test this than in the presence of the king? He begins with the exhortation, '*Obey the command of the king even according to the manner of the oath to God.*' The serious nature of these words is emphasized in a number of ways. The use of the imperative ('*obey*') shows that this advice is not to be taken lightly. The object of what is to be obeyed, '*the command of the king,*' has a distinct parallel to the phrase 'the command of Yahweh' (Num. 14:41; 22:18; 24:13).[184] Both phrases use the word *peh*, which literally means 'mouth,' to express the idea of command. This parallel places the command of the king on the same level as the command of Yahweh. Finally, the seriousness of this command is seen in the way in which obedience is to be carried out ('*according to the manner of the oath of God*'). Although there is much discussion concerning the meaning of the last phrase (see the translation notes), it is possible to understand a parallel between the command

---

184. Seow, *Ecclesiastes*, 279.

of a king and an oath made to God. Just as a person would seriously carry out an oath made to God, so a person should take seriously the command of a king by obeying it. Implications concerning the importance of obeying the command of a king are laid out in 8:3-4. Both verses emphasize that the king will do *'all that he desires'* to do. The principle is stated in 8:4: *'the word of the king is power.'* There is no higher earthly authority than the king and his commands. Because his word is supreme, no one *'will say to him, "What are you doing?"'* It is clear that the way one reacts to the authority of the king is very important, which is highlighted in 8:3 with two contrasting examples. Both examples use negative imperatives, but they advise different responses. The first imperative, *'Do not be rash,'* warns against a hasty, ill-conceived action whereby one *'departs from'* the presence of the king.[185] Such an action could signify that a person is leaving his post or that he is disagreeing with the king.[186] The second imperative, *'Do not stand with a bad cause,'* warns against persisting to push for something that the king has rejected, which makes it a *'bad cause.'*[187] These two imperatives warn against contrasting behavior in the presence of the king. It is not good to react in a rash way so that a person leaves the presence of the king and it is not good to push a matter that the king has rejected. Although this advice represents wise behavior in the presence of the king, it ultimately falls short because the king is both unlimited and arbitrary. The king will do whatever he desires to do regardless of what the wise man says. Wisdom may have some relative benefits, but it is ineffective before the power of a king. This seems to contradict the proverb that a wise man can appease the king's wrath (Prov. 16:14). It is also interesting that there is no prophetic word that calls the king's actions to account as in Samuel's relationship to Saul (1 Sam. 13) or Nathan's

---

185. Ogden and Zogbo, *Handbook on Ecclesiastes*, 281.
186. Gordis, *Koheleth*, 278.
187. Ogden and Zogbo (*Handbook on Ecclesiastes*, 281) argue that there is evidence from Akkadian and Ugaritic that such language may refer to a plot against the king or rebellion against the king.

relationship to David (2 Sam. 12). There is nothing in the first-person discourse concerning God's commands. Thus the king's word is both powerful and arbitrary, which nullifies the effectiveness of wisdom. Wisdom has little chance to change the king who will do all that he desires. The only option one has is to *'keep'* the *'command'* of the king[188] in order to avoid a *'bad situation'* (8:5a). The *'bad cause'* of 8:3 and the *'bad situation'* of 8:5 both translate the phrase *dāḇār rāʿ*. The emphasis in 8:3 is on something that the king has rejected, which makes it a bad cause and thus detrimental to someone who persists in it. The emphasis in 8:5 is on the negative consequences that would come to someone who does not keep a command of the king.[189] Although there is overlap between the two verses, the *dāḇār rāʿ* in 8:5 is broader than 8:3; thus, the two phrases have been translated a little differently.[190]

The emphasis in 8:5 shifts from the warnings of how not to act in the presence of the king to the benefits of wise behavior in the presence of the king. Not only will wise behavior in keeping a command of the king avoid negative consequences, the basis of wise behavior is stated at the end of 8:5: *'and the heart of the wise man should know the proper time and the right action.'* The use of the word *'time'* (*ʿēṯ*) in 8:5 and *'activity'* (*ḥēp̄eṣ*) in 8:6 remind the reader of the poem on time in 3:1-8. The times listed in that poem referred to activities that required human action to accomplish something. Wisdom understands when the time is right so that the appropriate action can be taken (Prov. 10:4-5). The term *'right action'* (*mišpāṭ*) is used in Ecclesiastes 3:16 and 5:8 in the sense of justice. Human judgment that is right leads to justice, which

---

188. Although the phrase *'What are you doing?'* (8:4) is a question asked about God in Job 9:12, the context (8:2, 5) limits the command to the command of the king and so does not have in view divine commands, which are absent from the first-person discourse (Murphy, *Ecclesiastes*, 79; contra Hengstenberg, *Ecclesiastes*, 188).

189. The lack of a suffix on *'command'* is no reason to take this as referring to a divine command (Bartholomew, *Ecclesiastes*, 282).

190. Fox (*Rereading Ecclesiastes*, 278) distinguishes the *dāḇār rāʿ* of 8:3 and 8:5 by noting that in 8:3 the phrase refers to an action that angers the king, but in 8:5 it refers to something the king may do when angry.

Qohelet does not observe taking place in 3:16. In Ecclesiastes 5:8, oppression is defined as the violation of justice. Thus *mišpāṭ* refers to justice in the sense that right action is being taken. This emphasis fits the meaning of 8:5b, where the '*wise man should know*' both '*the proper time*' for action and '*the right action*'[191] to take at the proper time. The verb '*know*' is translated '*should know*' (imperfect aspect) because both chapter 3 and the following verses (8:6-9) question the ability of the wise man to know the proper time and the right action. No sooner has Qohelet mentioned the basis of wise behavior than he starts showing the problems with it.

The beginning of 8:6 affirms the statement at the end of 8:5 that '*to every activity there is a proper time and a right action*' with an emphatic use of *kî*, translated '*indeed.*' This statement is not causal, supplying the reason for the previous verse or giving justification to the previous verse, but is affirming the statement of 8:5b.[192] A good question is, why would Qohelet restate the assertion concerning proper time and right action in 8:5b? The statement in 8:5b asserts that the wise man should know the proper time and right action, but in the context of chapter 8, such knowledge is going to be called into question. The statement in 8:6a affirms that there is a proper time and right action to every activity. In this way it agrees with the poem on time in 3:1-11 that God has made everything appropriate in its time. The question is not whether proper time and right action exist, but whether a wise man really knows the proper time and the right action. Qohelet reaffirms in 8:6a that such time and action do exist, but this is followed by three statements in 8:6b-7, each introduced by *kî*, which question whether a wise man can really know the proper time and the right action. The second *kî* should be understood as adversative, which can be translated as 'but' or '*however.*'

---

191. Some understand *mišpāṭ* to mean 'custom' in the sense of the proper manner or procedure (Longman, *Ecclesiastes*, 213 and Gordis, *Koheleth*, 279). The meaning 'divine judgment' (Ogden and Zogbo, *Handbook on Ecclesiastes*, 28) does not fit the use of the term in Ecclesiastes 3:16 or 8:5-9.

192. Longman (*Ecclesiastes*, 213) takes *kî* as causal and Ogden and Zogbo (*Handbook on Ecclesiastes*, 286) take it as giving justification to the previous verse.

The problem in knowing the proper time and right action is that *'the misfortune of mankind is great upon him.'* The word *'misfortune'* (*rāʿāh*) can either mean 'evil' or 'trouble' and it has both meanings in Ecclesiastes. Seow understands the meaning in 8:6 as 'evil' because the exact phrase *rāʿat hāʾāḏām*, along with the word *rabbāh* (*'great'*), occurs in Genesis 6:5 with the meaning 'evil.' According to this view Qohelet expresses the idea that there is a time and judgment against people because of terrible evil.[193] However, the issue in the context of Ecclesiastes is not mankind's sin but his ignorance (8:7).[194] Thus the best way to translate *rāʿāh* is 'trouble' or *'misfortune.'*[195] Knowing the right time and proper action is made difficult because life is full of tragedy and trouble. The misfortunes of life cloud the ability of people to know and make it impossible for people to discern the right time and proper action in different situations in life.

In 8:7-8 Qohelet further explains the statement in 8:6b that *'the misfortune of mankind is great upon him'* by focusing on the lack of knowledge (8:7) and the lack of power (8:8). In 8:7 there are two more statements that begin with *kî*, which should be understood as giving a reason for the previous statement. The beginning of 8:7 states *'for he does not know what will happen.'* This explains why the *'misfortune of mankind is great upon him.'* Misfortune brings into life uncertainty concerning how events will really turn out. Thus a person does *'not'* really *'know what will happen'* in life. This statement is further explained in the next clause of 8:7: *'because who can tell him when it will happen?'* The reason a person does not know what will happen in life is that no one knows when events in life will occur. In the context of the proper time and

---

193. Seow, *Ecclesiastes*, 281–282. Crenshaw (*Ecclesiastes*, 152) also takes this word as 'evil' with the meaning that human evil burdens the mind, making it incapable of knowing the right time for action.

194. Longman, *Ecclesiastes*, 214 and Fox, *Rereading Ecclesiastes*, 279.

195. Ogden and Zogbo (*Handbook on Ecclesiastes*, 286) understand the meaning of *rāʿāh* in this passage to be the difficulties of life, but they give the passage a positive meaning. People will face difficulties in life despite knowing when it is appropriate to act. Kaiser (*Ecclesiastes*, 89) sees this passage as praising the discernment of wise men.

the right action these events refer to the kinds of activities listed in 3:1-8, where people must make decisions at the right time. Thus the ability to know the proper time and right action is hindered because of the uncertainty of the events of life itself. The misfortunes of life so dominate the thinking of Qohelet that it is impossible to be able to discern the proper time and the right action. Life is too uncertain to know what will happen and when it will happen. The uncertainty of the unknown overshadows too much the certainty of what is known. The arbitrary nature of the events of life makes it virtually impossible to live according to wisdom.[196]

In 8:8 Qohelet sets forth the lack of human power over certain things in life which have an effect on the ability of people to know the proper time and the right action. The first example is ambiguous because *rûaḥ* can mean either 'wind' or 'life-breath.' Some favor 'life-breath' because the next clause deals with the day of death. In other places in Ecclesiastes the life-breath is understood as unpredictable (3:19, 21; 11:5; 12:7), and the idea here would be that no one is able to prevent the life-breath from leaving the human being.[197] In other words, no one can prevent the day of death.[198] Although many commentators argue for 'life-breath' on the basis of the following clause, which mentions the day of death, this understanding means that the first two clauses in 8:8 basically say the same thing. Thus it is better to understand *rûaḥ* as *'wind,'* with the translation, *'no one has power over the wind to retain the wind.'* This statement agrees with the refrain 'chasing the wind,' which Qohelet has used in the book to emphasize the senselessness of life (1:14; 2:11, 17, 26). The meaning is that humans have no ability to control the wind.[199] The second example of human impotence deals with the day of death: *'no*

---

196. Some take a positive view of these verses. Delitzsch ('Ecclesiastes,' 6:342-343) understands the uncertainty to refer to the judgment of God upon the wicked which will unexpectedly overwhelm them.

197. Gordis, *Koheleth*, 208. Seow (*Ecclesiastes*, 282) argues for the double meaning of *'wind'* and 'life-breath.'

198. Ogden and Zogbo, *Handbook on Ecclesiastes*, 143.

199. Longman (*Ecclesiastes*, 210) is one of the few who argues for the meaning *'wind.'*

one has power over the day of death.' The inability to know when the '*day of death*' is coming is not necessarily a problem, unless the death in view is premature. Then it becomes a part of the misfortunes of life that weigh heavily on people (8:6b) because the future is so uncertain (8:7). The third example of human powerlessness deals with war: '*there is no discharge during the battle.*' Some compare this statement to Deuteronomy 20:5-7, which gives reasons why someone could be released from war, and conclude that the verse in Ecclesiastes must deal with something other than release from war.[200] Seow argues that this statement refers to the common practice among the wealthy in the Persian period of sending a substitute to war on their behalf.[201] Others argue more generally that the idea is that people cannot escape from the usual evils of war, such as pillaging, capture, and even death.[202] Some argue that death is the dominant note of 8:8, with the idea that everyone must face their own personal death.[203] The best approach is to recognize that the '*discharge*' in view does not refer to release from the battle before the battle starts, but that it refers to a discharge from the battle after the battle has begun. The force of the preposition *bet* would be 'in' the battle or '*during the battle.*'[204] Thus there is no contradiction with Deuteronomy 20, which deals with release before the battle starts. Once the battle starts there is no possibility of discharge. Thus a bad decision concerning whether a battle should be fought can be disastrous if the wrong decision is reached.

The first three examples are introduced by *ʾên* ('there is no'), but the last example is introduced by the common negative '*not*' (*lōʾ*). Whybray argues that this stylistic variation ends the series of examples of human powerlessness.[205] The

---

200. Fox (*Rereading Ecclesiastes*, 281) argues that Deuteronomy 20 contradicts this verse in Ecclesiastes.

201. Seow, *Ecclesiastes*, 282. His view is based on the Septuagint's translation ('dispatch') and the historical context of the Persian period.

202. Murphy, *Ecclesiastes*, 84.

203. Seow, *Ecclesiastes*, 283.

204. Longman, *Ecclesiastes*, 215.

205. Whybray, *Ecclesiastes*, 133.

fourth example states: '*wickedness cannot deliver those who practise it.*' Here the powerlessness of human wickedness is emphasized. Human wickedness may boast concerning certain benefits it offers, such as wealth (Prov. 1:11-13) and pleasure (Prov. 7:13-20), but it is powerless to deliver those who are given over to it. It is possible that death is in view, which would mean that wickedness is not able to deliver from the day of death. It is also possible that in view of the emphasis on misfortune in the context (8:6b), Qohelet is further commenting on the bad day (7:14) and the response one should have in light of the wicked living a long life and the righteous dying early (7:15-18). Qohelet's comment in 8:8 concerning the inability of wickedness to deliver those who practice it would support his advice in 7:17 not to be very wicked, which itself can lead to an early death. Qohelet does not affirm the favor of righteousness or the benefit of wisdom in 8:6b-8, but he shows how difficult it is for a wise man really to know the right time and the proper action. The problem is a lack of knowledge concerning the way the world works (8:6b-7) and a lack of power to control or change things (8:8).

Qohelet brings this section to a close in 8:9. Although some commentators argue that 8:9 is the beginning of a new reflection on injustice (8:9-15),[206] it is better to take it as a summary statement concluding the previous section.[207] The word '*power*' (a form of *šlṭ*) binds together verses 4, 8, and 9 and also shows the development of thought in this passage. Qohelet begins with the necessity of obeying the word of the king because the king's power is arbitrary (8:3-4). In 8:5-6 the discussion is broadened to reflect on the issue of the proper time and the right action. Although the context is still generally related to the king, the examples of the lack of human power in 8:8 are broader than how one should act before the king. However, 8:9 brings the reader back to the

---

206. Murphy, *Ecclesiastes*, 84. Seow (*Ecclesiastes*, 293) points out that the root for '*what is done*' ('*śh*) occurs throughout 8:9-17.

207. Longman, *Ecclesiastes*, 215; Ogden and Zogbo, *Handbook on Ecclesiastes*, 292; and Gordis, *Koheleth*, 282; among others. Seow (*Ecclesiastes*, 293) argues that 8:9 may function both to recall the previous section and to introduce the next section.

isssue of the arbitrary nature of human power. It is interesting that in 8:9 the word for 'king' (*melek̲*) is not used, but the word for 'mankind' (*'ād̲ām*) is used. The problem is that not just kings use their power in an arbitrary manner, but anyone who *'has power over another person'* uses that power to *'harm'* the other person. The principle is that people with any kind of authority generally abuse that power.

The broadening of the perspective from kingly power (8:3-4) to the reflection on the proper time and right action (8:5-8), and then the conclusion which focuses on general human authority and power (8:9) is significant. The chapter begins with the focus on the wise man and whether the wise man can give an explanation of the way the world works. This question will be answered in 8:17, but here we get a glimpse of the answer. Wisdom should help someone know how to act before the king and to determine the proper time and the right action; however, not even the wise man can succeed in these things. The only response before the arbitrary nature of the king's power is to obey. The proper time and the right action are not even accessible to a wise man because of the limitations of human power. The problem the wise man has to deal with is not just arbitrary kingly power, but the misuse of power of anyone who exercises power over another. Thus it is possible to see the wise man in focus in these verses. It is the wise man who feels the burden of misfortune that occurs in this life because he does not know what will happen and when it will happen (8:7b). If the wise man does not know these things, there is little hope for the common person to be able to live according to wisdom.

The arbitrary nature of divine government (Eccles. 8:10-17)

8:10 *And then I saw the wicked buried*[208] *and they used to come*

---

208. There are numerous difficulties with the translation of 8:10 (see the discussion in the commentary). The Hebrew reads, *'then I saw the wicked buried.'* The difficulty with this translation is how to understand the following verb 'to go, enter' (*bô'*) in relationship to being buried. Some suggest a minor emendation of the text (the transposition of two consonants from *qāb̲ar* to *qārab̲*), which would yield the progression 'approach-enter-go out' in relationship to the holy place. This makes excellent sense in the context,

and go from the holy place and they were praised[209] in the city where they had done so.[210] This is also senseless.

8:11 Because[211] the sentence of an evil deed is not carried out quickly, therefore, the heart of people is filled with evildoing.

but there is no evidence of this emendation in the Hebrew manuscripts or the versions (J. J. Serrano, 'I Saw the Wicked Buried [Eccl 8,10],' *CBQ* 16 [1954]: 169–170). The Septuagint may read 'tomb' (*qeḇer*) instead of 'buried' (*qěḇurîm*), which Gordis (*Koheleth*, 285) favors. One can make sense of the Hebrew text if one understands the verb 'to enter' in reference to the holy place and translates it in the sense of 'they used to enter' or '*they used to come*' to the holy place.

209. The Hebrew uses the verb 'forgotten' (*šākaḥ*), which is the reason why many understand this to refer to the righteous who are treated differently from the wicked. Seow (*Ecclesiastes*, 286) understands the verb to mean 'discarded' based on its parallel use with 'abandon' (*ʿāzaḇ*), as in Jeremiah 30:14; Job 19:14; Isaiah 49:14; 65:11. The idea would be that the righteous, in contrast to the wicked, are not given a decent burial, which is one of the worst curses one can receive (Deut. 28:26; 1 Kings 14:11; 21:23-24; Jer. 7:33). However, a number of Hebrew manuscripts read *'praise'* (*šāḇaḥ*), which is also the reading of the Septuagint, and is adopted here.

210. The meaning of the phrase *ʾăšer kēn-ʿāśû* depends on how one interprets the rest of the verse. If there is a contrast between the righteous and the wicked, then it refers to the just acts of the righteous. This view takes *kēn* as an adverb meaning 'justly' and *ʾăšer* as a relative pronoun referring to the righteous. However, the most common meaning of the word *kēn* is 'thus' or 'so.' Plus, there is no clear indication in 8:10 that the righteous are in view. When the wicked are discussed in opposition to other people, Qohelet always defines who the other party is (Panc Beentjes, '"Who is Like the Wise?" Some Notes on Qohelet 8,1–15,' in A. Schoors [ed.], *Qohelet in the Context of Wisdom* [Leuven: Leuven University Press, 1998], 311). If the wicked are the subject throughout the verse, which is the better way to understand this verse, then *ʾăšer kēn-ʿāśû* refers to their activities, with *kēn* meaning 'thus' or 'so' and *ʾăšer* used as a relative pronoun meaning *'where'* (Gordis, *Koheleth*, 174).

211. The conjunction *ʾăšer* occurs nine times in 8:11-15. It is the initial word in both 8:11 and 8:12, with a *'therefore'* (*ʿal-kēn*) in between in 8:11. Although this is a little unusual, it is not without parallel (Jer. 44:23). Fox (*Rereading Ecclesiastes*, 284–285) argues that the *hebel* judgment at the end of 8:10 introduces the situation of 8:11. He takes the conjunction *ʾăšer* as a nominalizing particle that means 'namely.' It could be translated with a colon. The problem with taking the *hebel* judgment as introducing 8:11 is that it usually ends a verse or section. The *hebel* at the beginning of 8:14 is different because it contains the word *yēš*. Both conjunctions are understood here as causal, with 'therefore' in 8:11 introducing the main clause of 8:11 (Longman, *Ecclesiastes*, 216, n. 39).

8:12 For[212] *a sinner does evil a hundred times*[213] *and his days are long—although I know that it will be well for those who fear God because they fear him.*

8:13 *But it will not be well for the wicked, and their days like a shadow will not be long because they do not fear God.*

8:14 *This is an example of senselessness that occurs on the earth: there are righteous people who are treated according to the deeds of the wicked. And there are wicked people who are treated according to the deeds of the righteous. I say that this is also senseless.*

8:15 *So I commended pleasure, for there is nothing better for human beings under the sun except to eat and to drink and to have pleasure. It should accompany them in their labour the days of their life which God gives to them under the sun.*

8:16 *When I devoted myself to know wisdom and to examine the task done on the earth, even though*[214] *by day and by night there is no sleep in the eyes of the one who examines;*

8:17 *Then I observed all the work of God; indeed, a person is not able to discover all the work which is done under the sun. However much a person may labour to seek it he will not discover it. And even if the wise man claims to know, he is not able to discover it.*

Qohelet moves from an analysis of human government to an examination of how God governs the world. He focuses

---

212. Because 8:12 is giving a reason for 8:11, the *ʾăšer* should be translated in a causal sense (Longman, *Ecclesiastes*, 217; Whybray, *Ecclesiastes*, 137) and not as a concessive ('although'), as in the NKJV, NIV, NASB, and ESV (also argued by Barton, *Ecclesiastes*, 153).

213. The word *mĕʾaṯ* ('one hundred') in the construct state has generated a lot of discussion. Gordis (*Kohelet*, 287) suggests the possibility of an archaic absolute that goes with '*evil*,' giving the translation 'a hundred of evils.' The ancient versions had trouble with this word. The Septuagint has 'from then' (*apo tote*, reading *mʿz* for *mʾt*). Other Greek versions, such as Aquila, Symmachus, and Theodotion, read 'hence' (*apethanen*, reading *mt*). The Syriac and the Targum support the Masoretic text. Many argue that the word *paʿam* is implied, giving the translation '*a hundred times,*' which is followed here (Longman, *Ecclesiastes*, 217; Murphy, *Ecclesiastes*, 81).

214. Every time that *kî gam* occurs in Ecclesiastes it is used in a concessive sense (4:14; 8:12).

on the relationship between the righteous and the wicked (8:10-15) to see whether he can understand the activity of God in the world, on which he will comment in his conclusion in 8:16-17. Just as human government uses power in an arbitrary way, so God's governing of the world is also arbitrary because of what happens to the wicked and the righteous. Based on the arbitrary nature of God's rule Qohelet will offer another 'call to enjoyment' (8:15).

Qohelet states his observation in 8:10, which is a verse that is much debated. In fact, this may be the most difficult verse in the book in trying to decide how certain phrases should be translated.[215] A straightforward reading of the Hebrew has its own problems. For example, a fairly literal rendering would read: 'Then I saw the wicked buried. And they used to enter and walk about the holy place and they were forgotten in the city where they had done so. This is also senseless.' For the wicked to be forgotten would be a positive thing, which does not fit in with the final *hebel* phrase.[216] A few argue that the wicked end up dead, buried, and forgotten. This could mean that they escaped judgment while they were on this earth and now they are not even remembered for what they were really like.[217] Or the point could be to show that it is a waste of time to live a wicked life because the wicked are forgotten, which would explain the *hebel* clause of 8:10.[218] However, the whole tenor of this passage is to show the senselessness of the relationship between the righteous and the wicked because the wicked do not get what they deserve but are treated like the righteous (8:14). Some argue that in 8:10 there must be a contrast between the righteous and the wicked, with the righteous being the ones forgotten, which would explain the *hebel* judgment.[219] But the phrase upon which this view is based (*'ăšer kēn-'āśû*) cannot support this argument (see

---

215. Longman, *Ecclesiastes*, 218.
216. Hubbard, *Ecclesiastes*, 192.
217. Bartholomew, *Ecclesiastes*, 289.
218. Olyott, *A Life Worth Living*, 52.
219. Seow, *Ecclesiastes*, 285; Hubbard, *Ecclesiastes*, 192; and Fox, *Rereading Ecclesiastes*, 282.

the translation notes). It is better to see the wicked as the subject throughout 8:10. What seems to be clear is that there is some kind of relationship between the wicked and the holy place, which yields the verdict '*this is also senseless*.'[220] Qohelet presents his observation of the burial of '*the wicked*,' who are described as being regular worshippers at '*the holy place*.' Even though they practiced wickedness while they were alive, they are '*praised*.' Thus the wicked not only get away with their wickedness, but they are also praised even though they are wicked. Such a scenario is truly '*senseless*,' because the wicked are not getting what they deserve.

Qohelet sets forth in 8:11 the reason why wickedness flourishes and is praised. Whenever there is a delay of justice, as when '*the sentence of an evil deed is not carried out quickly*,' people conclude that the pursuit of wickedness is worth the risk. When the wicked are not dealt with in a timely manner, '*the heart of people is filled with evildoing*.' The heart being full of something may imply desire or intention, which could be translated 'the heart is set on doing evil.'[221] The '*sentence*' (*pitgām*)[222] refers to a legal decision to punish evil. It is used in Esther 1:20 to refer to the decision of the king. Although it is possible that a human sentence of a king or a judge is in view here, the context of this section supports a reference to a divine sentence. Qohelet clearly mentions in 8:17 the work of God and the relationship between the righteous and the wicked in 8:11-14 revolves around the fear of God. Swift action shows people the negative consequences of wickedness, but when justice is delayed the door is opened for people's wickedness to flourish.

Qohelet offers an example of the flourishing of the wicked in 8:12a, which he interrupts in 8:12b-13 to state the opposite point of view, but then in 8:14 he affirms what was stated in

---

220. Longman, *Ecclesiastes*, 218–219.

221. Fox (*Rereading Ecclesiastes*, 285) argues the former and Murphy (*Ecclesiastes*, 81) offers the translation.

222. This Hebrew word has been understood as a Persianism and used as evidence for the lateness of the language of Qohelet; however, see the discussion in Fredericks, *Qoheleth's Language*, 242–244 and Young, 'Late Biblical Hebrew and Hebrew Inscriptions,' 284–285.

8:12a. The flow of thought in these verses is significant and the way commentators solve the contradiction between 8:12a and 8:13b is an indication of their understanding of the thought of Qohelet (see the Introduction). In 8:12 Qohelet begins to explain the principle stated in 8:11 that wickedness benefits when it is not quickly stopped: *'for a sinner does evil a hundred times and his days are long.'*[223] Long life should be a blessing for the righteous and the wise, not for the wicked. But then in the middle of his thought he breaks off and declares the opposite idea in 8:12b-13. He introduces these verses with a concessive clause that affirms wellbeing for the righteous: *'although I know that it will be well for those who fear God.'* Then in 8:13 he states the opposite for the wicked: *'But it will not be well for the wicked, and their days like a shadow will not be long because they do not fear God.'* This affirms that the wicked will get what they deserve because they do not fear God. The tension, or contradiction, can be seen by a comparison of 8:12a and 8:13b. 8:12a affirms that a sinner's *'days are long,'* but 8:13 affirms that the days of the wicked *'will not be long.'* The same Hebrew verb (*'rk*) is used in both phrases. In explaining the prosperity of the wicked Qohelet stops and seems to affirm the opposite point of view. What is the best way to understand this tension?

It is clear that 8:12b-13 set forth the traditional view of the deed-consequence relationship.[224] Some argue that these verses set forth what Qohelet believes in spite of the evidence he oberves. In other words, although he observes the prosperity of the wicked, he affirms that both the wicked and the righteous will receive what is appropriate, so it will not go well with the wicked but it will go well with the righteous.

---

223. Because the word 'day' (*yôm*) is not used in 8:12a, the Septuagint understands the phrase to refer to a postponement of punishment rather than long days for the wicked (Whybray, *Ecclesiastes*, 137). Such a view does not affect the meaning of the phrase, unless one is reading the whole passage in a positive way. For example, Hubbard (*Ecclesiastes*, 193–194) argues that divine slowness in punishing the wicked should not dampen the hopes of the faithful for their own reward. Such a view goes against the development of Qohelet's argument.

224. It is good to remember that the book of Proverbs does not teach a mechanical view of the deed-consequence relationship (see van Leeuwen, 'System and Contradiction in Proverbs', 25–26).

The basis for this affirmation is related to the fear of God. In this view 8:12b-13 represents the confessional statement of Qohelet, which is the answer to the problem of the prosperity of the wicked. He affirms here his faith in God's justice.[225] However, if this is the answer to the problem of the prosperity of the wicked, why does Qohelet frame his answer with the view that the wicked and the righteous do not get what is appropriate to them? In 8:12a Qohelet sets forth the view of the prosperity of the wicked, which is interrupted by the orthodox statement concerning the righteous and the wicked in 8:12b-13. But then Qohelet comes back in 8:14 to the problem of the treatment of the wicked. The wicked do not get what they deserve but are rewarded with what the righteous should receive. And the righteous receive what the wicked really deserve. This breakdown in the deed-consequence relationship trumps the statement in 8:12b-13. If Qohelet had stated the problem of the prosperity of the wicked and then ended the section with 8:12b-13, one could argue that these verses represent the answer to the problem. But that is not how the argument unfolds. The treatment of the wicked gets the last word before the call to enjoyment in 8:15.

There are other ways to understand the relationship of 8:12b-13 to the context which allow for the tension in Qohelet's thinking to stand. Bartholomew understands 8:12b-13 to be a confession of what Qohelet knows about God's justice (8:12b-13), which he places next to the problem of what he has observed concerning the long life of the wicked (8:12a, 14) in order to draw the reader's attention to the contradiction. The juxtaposition of these two views leaves a gap which is left unfilled and not resolved.[226] Bartholomew does not specify in his discussion of these verses how the gap is filled in, but he writes elsewhere that the gap is filled in by Ecclesiastes 12:13-14.[227] However, it is also possible that the gap is filled

---

225. Whybray, 'Preacher of Joy,' 90. Eaton (*Ecclesiastes*, 123) calls this the answer of faith and Kidner (*Ecclesiastes*, 77) asserts that Qohelet drops the veil of secularism for a statement of his own faith.

226. Bartholomew, *Ecclesiastes*, 291.

227. It is amazingly difficult to find clear statements in Bartholomew on how the gaps are to be filled because when he talks about gaps he rarely

in with the call to enjoyment in 8:15 as the only response to a world that does not work the way it should work.²²⁸

Fox argues that 8:12b-13 state the view of Qohelet. He translates 8:12 as 'It is a fact that ... and I also know that ...' Thus Qohelet knows the principle expressed in 8:12b-13 and nowhere denies that it will be well with the righteous. However, he also knows that there are cases that violate the rule. He allows both to stand without resolving them.²²⁹ Although it is true that Qohelet states both sides of the argument and allows the contradiction to stand, the development of the argument in 8:12-14 subordinates the 'confessional' statement of 8:12b-13 to the contrary observations in 8:12a and 8:14. 8:12b-13 is introduced with a concessive clause which functions as a subordinate clause.²³⁰ It is also interesting that the verb '*know*' in 8:12b is a participle. Qohelet uses the perfect aspect of 'know' in the first-person to state his conclusions, which are based on his observations (1:17; 2:14; 3:12, 14). Fox argues that the participle stresses the present nature of the knowledge,²³¹ but an examination of the use of the participle 'know' in Ecclesiastes shows that it is used predominantly in situations where the knowledge being discussed is not being affirmed but rather is being questioned or is on shaky ground. For example, the participle is used in the question 'who knows' (2:19; 3:21; 6:12; 8:1), which is a

---

specifies how the gap is to be filled (*Ecclesiastes*, 81–82). It becomes clear how the gaps are to be filled in his passing comments and then in a few places where he specifically states that the resolution comes in 12:13-14 (*Ecclesiastes*, 119 and *Reading Ecclesiastes*, 253–254). After having read *Reading Ecclesiastes* one expects that in his commentary on Ecclesiastes there would be an application of this method to the book, but only in a few places is the role of gaps discussed.

228. Bartholomew (*Ecclesiastes*, 81) understands the calls to enjoyment as a positive, confessional response to life. For a discussion of the role of the calls to enjoyment see the Introduction to this commentary. Bartholomew also sees a gap between 8:14 and 8:15, and one begins to wonder if there are too many gaps in Qohelet's thinking that need to be filled.

229. Fox, *Rereading Ecclesiastes*, 26.
230. Murphy, *Ecclesiastes*, 85.
231. Fox, *Rereading Ecclesiastes*, 27.

rhetorical question meant to affirm that no one knows.[232] In some passages the participle is used when a person, such as a fool, does not really know what they are doing (5:1) or when a person is ignorant of something (8:7; 9:1; 11:6). It is also used of a poor man in a question that asks what advantage he has even though he knows how to conduct himself (6:8). In 9:5 the knowledge that the living have is not positive, and the knowledge of the dead is non-existent. It is possible that Qohelet uses the participle in situations where the knowledge is not certain. If that is the case, the use of the participle in 8:12b is not used to make an affirmation of what Qohelet confesses, but is used to present the traditional view which Qohelet has observed does not explain the way life works. Whatever one's view of the verb 'know,' the development of the argument in 8:12-14 shows that the traditional statement in 8:12b-13 is subordinated to the statements that deny the traditional view (8:12a, 14). Qohelet may not completely deny the view expressed in 8:12b-13, but he does not affirm it either. The problems of life dominate his thinking so that the last word is that the wicked prosper and live long lives.

To summarize the argument, Qohelet offers an example of the flourishing of the wicked in 8:12a to support the statement in 8:11. Midway through his statement that *'a sinner does evil a hundred times and his days are long,'* he breaks off the discussion to acknowledge that he knows the standard, traditional view of the deed-consequence relationship (8:12b-13).[233] The traditional view is that it *'will be well for those who fear God'* but *'it will not be well for the wicked'* whose *'days'* are not *'long because they do not fear God.'* Instead of affirming or giving reasons for why this is the correct view, Qohelet goes on in 8:14 to show that the traditional view of 8:12b-13 does not really explain how life works. He offers *'an example of senselessness that occurs on the earth'* where *'righteous people are treated according to the deeds of the wicked'* and *'wicked people are treated according to the deeds of the righteous.'* In

---

232. Crenshaw, 'The Expression *mî yôdeaʿ* in the Hebrew Bible,' *VT* 36 (1986): 274–88.

233. Murphy, *Ecclesiastes*, 85.

other words, the wicked do not get what their wickedness deserves but they receive the blessings the righteous should receive, and the righteous do not receive the blessings of their righteousness but they experience the negative consequences that should come to the wicked. Qohelet is not just setting forth 'inexplicable exceptions' to the traditional view;[234] in fact, the use of *'senseless'* (*hebel*) twice in 8:14, at the beginning and the end of the verse, emphasizes that this is the regular state of things in this world. Thus Qohelet demonstrates that the traditional view does not work.

In light of the breakdown of the deed-consequence relationship, Qohelet offers another call to enjoyment in 8:15, which begins with *'So I commended pleasure.'* This is a strong recommendation because the verb 'commend' can have the meaning 'praise.' The *'pleasure'* Qohelet has in mind is further delineated in the familiar statement, *'for there is nothing better for human beings under the sun except to eat and to drink and to have pleasure.'* Similar advice occurs in 2:24-26; 3:12; 3:22; and 5:18. In each case the advice is the only possible response in a world that does not work out the way one would hope. If the wicked do not experience the negative consequences of their wickedness and the righteous do not experience the blessings of their righteousness, then one should at least enjoy the pleasure that life does afford. This pleasure has been identified earlier in the book with the portion (*ḥēleq*) that comes from labor (2:10; 3:22) even though there is no profit (*yitrôn*) to labor (2:11).[235] Qohelet notes that this pleasure *'should accompany them in their labour the days of their life which God gives to them under the sun.'* The verb *'accompany'* is in the imperfect aspect and is translated *'should'* because there is no guarantee that this pleasure will accompany labor, as Qohelet had observed in 5:18–6:6. But Qohelet hopes that people will be able to enjoy this benefit that comes from labor.

---

234. Whybray, *Ecclesiastes*, 137–138. The comment by Hubbard (*Ecclesiastes*, 194) that 8:14 is the exception and that 8:12b-13 is normative goes against the development of the argument in this passage.

235. There is no contradiction between Qohelet's negative statements about pleasure in 2:2, which occur in his search for meaning, and the pleasure advocated here in 8:15, which is identified with the portion.

Qohelet brings his argument to a close in 8:16-17 with a summarizing, concluding statement.[236] The argument is presented with a protasis (an 'if' or *'when'* statement) in 8:16 followed by the apodosis (the *'then'* statement) in 8:17.[237] Qohelet reviews in 8:16 the goal and the intensity of his search, which he had also laid out in 1:13-18. Thus there are concepts and ideas that these passages have in common. For example, in 8:16 Qohelet sought *'to know wisdom'* and *'to examine the task done on the earth.'* The word *'task'* (*'inyān*) is the same word used in 1:13, where Qohelet sets out the goal of his search and then comments, 'it is a grievous task God has given to human beings.' The phrase *'to know wisdom'* also occurs in 1:17 in another statement concerning Qohelet's search. In 8:16 Qohelet also talks about the intensity of his search. For example, he literally says, 'I gave my heart,' which is translated *'I devoted myself,'* a phrase that also occurs in 1:13 and 1:17. The amount of devotion the search has taken is emphasized in the phrase *'even though by day and by night there is no sleep in the eyes of the one who examines.'*[238] The connections between this section and 1:12-18 shows that Qohelet is drawing conclusions concerning his original search. Concepts in 8:17 will also relate to the question raised in 6:12 concerning who knows what is good and the question in 8:1 concerning who knows the interpretation of a thing.

After laying out in 8:16 the goal and intensity of his search, in 8:17 Qohelet gives his conclusion concerning his observation of *'all the work of God.'* This phrase brings to mind 3:11, which states that people are not able to find out what God

---

236. Many commentators argue that a new unit begins with 8:16. For example Ogden and Zogbo (*Handbook on Ecclesiastes*, 309) and Fox (*Rereading Ecclesiastes*, 288) take 8:16–9:10 as a unit dealing with the limits of wisdom. However, it is better to see these verses as closing a section based on the concepts 'not know' and 'cannot find' (Murphy, *Ecclesiastes*, 81).

237. Murphy (*Ecclesiastes*, 81) and Longman (*Ecclesiastes*, 222) understand the structure of these verses as protasis and apodosis.

238. Some take this clause as a parenthesis (Delitzsch, 'Ecclesiastes,' 6:352; Barton, *Ecclesiastes*, 157). Seow (*Ecclesiastes*, 209) argues that this clause is disruptive and difficult to interpret in its present context, so he transposes the line to 8:17 after the phrase 'all the work that is done under the sun.' There is no evidence for this move.

has done from beginning to end. Qohelet's conclusion here is the same: '*a person is not able to discover all the work which is done under the sun.*' It does not matter how much effort a person may put into the search. Although he '*may labour to seek it, he will not discover it.*' This conclusion affirms that human beings are not able to make sense of the events that take place on earth. God's government of the world is inexplicable because it appears to be arbitrary, as is demonstrated in how the righteous and the wicked are treated (8:12-14). But what is even more stunning is that Qohelet states that '*even if the wise man claims*[239] *to know, he is not able to discover it.*' The very ones who would be expected to explain how the world works are not able to provide an explanation. Not even the wise man knows.

The conclusion in 8:17 answers the question raised in 8:1: 'who knows the explanation of a matter?' The answer is that no one knows, not even the wise man. 8:17 also answers the question raised in 6:12: 'who knows what is good for mankind during the few days of his senseless life?' Again, the answer is that no one knows how to define what is good for people during their life on this earth, an answer which was anticipated in the proverbs of chapter 7. Finally, 8:17 also agrees with the conclusions Qohelet has drawn throughout the first-person discourse up to this point. There is no answer to his search. Not even the wise man can figure out how the world works (3:11; 7:28).

Homiletical Implications

There are times in life when God's government of the world seems arbitrary. There are things in this world that we cannot understand. People react strongly when there are clear instances of injustice. In 1985 Willie 'Pete' Williams

---

239. The use of the verb 'to say' (*'āmar*) followed by an infinitive can have the meaning 'think,' 'plan,' or 'intend.' Fox (*Rereading Ecclesiastes*, 289) argues that the best translation is that the wise man 'intends to know' (as in Exod. 21:14; 2 Chron. 13:8; 2 Sam. 21:16). Such a meaning would work well here. However, because the context stresses the inability of anyone, including the wise man, to know or discover the work of God, the translation '*claims to know*' is used (Ogden and Zogbo, *Handbook on Ecclesiastes*, 313).

was accused of aggravated sodomy, kidnapping, and rape. Despite his repeated claims of innocence, he was convicted of the crimes and sentenced to forty-five years behind bars. For twenty-two years Mr Williams slept on hard bunks, ate prison hash, and could only wonder about what his life would be like if he was not in prison. He did not give up hope of being found innocent. A re-examination of his case, including the DNA evidence, showed that he was innocent. Falsely accused, falsely convicted, an innocent man spent twenty-two years behind bars. Qohelet would see such a situation as fully without explanation and as evidence that no one can really understand or explain how the world works. What happened to Mr Williams is a picture of how life works. He wasted twenty-two years in jail. Existentialist philosopher Jean Paul Sartre wrote a novel in which he gave a powerful and moving description of a world devoid of meaning. He describes the overpowering consciousness of the nothingness within man and in the world around him. Existence is meaningless, a whirl of purposeless activity. What is the title of the novel? *Nausea.* That is the feeling that man has living in this meaningless world – nausea, angst, despair. Despair is the way of life and there is no escape.

Qohelet's advice to Mr Williams as he sat in jail, and his advice to all of us caught in this nauseating life, would be to at least enjoy the little that life offers. At least enjoy the food they serve you in jail. This is the 'under the sun' perspective. Qohelet is caught in the maze of life and it appears that life is hopeless. But there is an 'above the sun' perspective. There is Someone who sees and knows the end from the beginning. There is Someone who can affirm that the troubles of life will not have the last word. Even the troubles in life can serve God's purposes. We can even rejoice in the tribulations of life (James 1:2-4), because God can use those troubles for His purposes. Mr Williams had an 'above the sun' perspective. Even though he was falsely labeled a sex offender and unjustly held for twenty-two years, when he was released from prison he sang a few lines of 'Amazing Grace' and walked away a free man. His faith in Christ gave him the broader perspective he needed. Sometimes life in this world looks like the back of a knitted rug. It is messy and there is no clear picture. Everything seems confused. But if you turn the rug over everything becomes clear. The picture can be seen and it is understood. That is the broader perspective given by God. By faith we believe that life is in His hands and that the trials of life do have a purpose. We may not be able to explain everything in life, but we trust in the revelation of God, which affirms what is good for us in life in this world.

6.
Human limitations concerning knowledge: the uncertainty of the future (Eccles. 9:1–10:20)

This section of Ecclesiastes takes up the second question of 6:12. The first question, 'who knows what is good?' was answered in 7:1–8:17. Now the second question, 'who can tell what will be in the future?' is addressed in 9:1–10:20. There are two major topics dealt with in this section. Both raise the question of the uncertainty of the future. The first is death (9:1-12), which clouds the future of life on earth and brings uncertainty into people's lives. Death ends earthly existence and there is little hope for any life after death. The second topic is the great damage that one sinner can do (9:18), which also makes the future uncertain (9:13–10:20).

Living under the cloud of death (Eccles. 9:1-12)

9:1 *Indeed, I devoted myself to all this, even to explain all this, that the righteous and the wise, and their works, are in the hand of God. Whether love or hate, no one knows all that is before them.*[1]

---

1. Because the context refers to the uncertainty of the future, it is best to take the phrase *'before them'* as a temporal phrase (see the discussion in Longman, Murphy, and Whybray). Longman (*Ecclesiastes*, 224) points out that an idiomatic translation of the phrase would be 'awaits them.'

9:2 *Everything is the same for everybody.*² *There is one fate for the righteous and the wicked,*³ *for the clean and the unclean, for those who sacrifice and for those who do not sacrifice; as it is for the good, so also for the sinner; as it is for the one who swears an oath, so also for the one who fears an oath.*⁴

9:3 *This is evil in all that is done under the sun that there is one fate for all. And furthermore, the heart of people is full of evil and madness is in their hearts during their lives, and afterwards*⁵—*to the dead.*

---

2. The opening phrase *hakkōl ka'ăšer lakkōl* literally reads 'all (is) as to all' (Murphy, *Ecclesiastes*, 89). Fox follows the Septuagint, which reads the first word *hakkōl* as *hebel*, leading to the translation 'everything is *hebel*,' but there is no evidence that this translation should be followed.

3. The single phrase 'for the good' (*laṭṭôḇ*) stands alone in the Hebrew text in a series of pairs, which makes it a problem text (Longman, *Ecclesiastes*, 255, n. 7). Aside from translating the phrase as it stands, there seem to be two choices. The Septuagint adds the term 'evil' to make a pair, which is followed by Fox (*Rereading Ecclesiastes*, 292), who argues the Septuagint of Ecclesiastes is too literalistic to have added a word for literary balance, and Seow (*Ecclesiastes*, 299), who argues for the inadvertent omission of letters based on homoioarcton (a scribal error caused by similarities at the beginning of words). In light of 'as the good' (*kaṭṭôḇ*) later in the verse, it is possible that *laṭṭôḇ* is an intrusion and so should be omitted (followed by Longman, *Ecclesiastes*, 225, n. 7 and Ogden, *Qoheleth*, 158–159).

4. As Longman (*Ecclesiastes*, 227) notes, it is difficult to tell in the contrasting phrases about the oath which term is negative and which is positive. Is it good or bad to be afraid to swear an oath? In the previous contrasting pairs, the positive term comes first, which could mean that the second term is the negative term. Eaton (*Ecclesiastes*, 125) understands the second term concerning the oath to mean shunning loyalty to the covenant. Others take the first term as the negative term; for example, Seow (*Ecclesiastes*, 299) understands the first term to refer to a perjurer who does not respect the seriousness of the oath. If the negative term comes first, then it could be a climactic reversal of the good-bad pattern in the earlier pairs (Longman, *Ecclesiastes*, 227).

5. The 3ms suffix on this word (*'aḥărāyw*), which would literally read 'after it,' has caused much discussion. Some of the versions (Septuagint, Syriac) reflect another form ('after them'). Delitzsch ('Ecclesiastes,' 6:358) understands the suffix to refer to human beings, Gordis (*Koheleth*, 291) understands it to refer to life, and Bartholomew (*Ecclesiastes*, 302) takes it as referring to the madness of human life as a whole. Others take it in an adverbial sense, translated *'afterwards,'* which is followed here (see Longman, *Ecclesiastes*, 225; Murphy, *Ecclesiastes*, 89). It is possible that the ending is an archaic ending (Crenshaw, *Ecclesiastes*, 160).

9:4   Indeed, there is hope for whoever is joined to all the living, for a living dog is better than a dead lion.

9:5   For the living know that they will die, but the dead do not know anything. There is no longer for them a reward because the memory of them is forgotten.

9:6   Their love, their hate, their envy have already perished. They will never again have a portion in anything that is done under the sun.

9:7   Go, eat your bread with pleasure and drink your wine with a merry heart because God has already approved your works.

9:8   Let your garments be white all the time, and let not the oil upon your head be lacking.

9:9   Enjoy life with the wife whom you love all the days of your senseless life which he has given to you under the sun all your senseless days, because it is your portion in life and in your labour which you labour under the sun.

9:10 Whatever your hand finds to do, do it with your might because there is no work, or planning, or knowledge, or wisdom in Sheol to which you are going.

9:11 I turned and I observed under the sun that the race does not belong to[6] the swift, nor the battle to the strong. So also food does not belong to the wise, nor wealth to those who are perceptive, nor favour to those who have knowledge, for a time of misfortune happens to all of them.

9:12 For indeed,[7] people do not know their time. Like fish caught in a cruel net and like birds caught in a snare, so[8]

---

6. Delitzsch ('Ecclesiastes,' 6:365) notes that the *lamed* ('*belong to*') can refer to someone having power over the object to be able to freely dispose of it.

7. Although *kî gam* (translated here as '*for indeed*') is translated in Ecclesiastes 8:12 as 'although,' such a meaning does not fit this passage, where the phrase introduces an additional reason for the situation Qohelet is describing (Whybray, *Ecclesiastes*, 146).

8. The Hebrew *kāhēm* can be translated literally 'as these.' Some argue the *mem* should go with the following verb, which is without the *mem* of the participle, leaving the word *kōh*, which is translated '*so*,' which is followed here (see the discussions in Murphy, Longman, and Seow).

people are ensnared in an evil time when[9] *it falls suddenly upon them.*

There is no agreement concerning the division of chapter 9. Many take 9:1-10 as a distinct unit, with 9:11-12 starting a separate section.[10] However, the theme of 9:1-9 continues into 9:11-12, with 9:13-18 turning to the topic of wisdom.[11] Thus 9:1-12 deals with the general topic of death and its significance for living life. Qohelet establishes in 9:1-6 that death is the common fate of everyone. There is then a lengthy call to enjoyment in 9:7-10, which is followed by further reflections on how death, represented by time and chance, affects what happens in life.

This section begins in 9:1 with a *kî*, which some translate as 'for' because they see a connection with what has gone before.[12] However, it is better to see 9:1 as starting a new section, even if there are connections with chapter 8, and translating the *kî* as '*indeed.*'[13] Qohelet examines the impact of death on people's lives and in the development of the argument several key facts concerning death will become apparent. The devotion of Qohelet to this quest is seen in the statement, '*I devoted myself to all this.*' The goal of his quest is shown in the statement '*even to explain all this.*' He begins by affirming '*that the righteous and the wise, and their works, are in the hand of God.*' In other

---

9. The translation '*when*' represents the temporal use of *kî* (Williams, *Hebrew Syntax*, 47).

10. Longman (*Ecclesiastes*, 224), Seow (*Ecclesiastes*, 302), and Whybray (*Ecclesiastes*, 139), among others, take 9:1-10 as a distinct unit. Longman and Whybray deal with 9:11-12 as a separate unit, with Whybray calling these verses an independent piece. Seow connects these verses to the next section (9:11–10:15).

11. Bartholomew, *Ecclesiastes*, 313.

12. For example, Fox (*Rereading Ecclesiastes,* 290) divides the section into 8:16–9:6. Others do not see a causal connection between 9:1 and the preceding section, but some kind of continuation of thought. Eaton (*Ecclesiastes*, 124) translates the *kî* as 'now' and divides the text into 8:16–9:1, and Ogden and Zogbo (*Ecclesiastes*, 309) translate the *kî* with 'but' and divide the text into 8:16–9:10. Bartholomew (*Ecclesiastes*, 296) translates the *kî* as 'for,' but argues that 9:1 both starts a new section and has connections to chapter 8.

13. Murphy, *Ecclesiastes*, 90; Longman, *Ecclesiastes*, 224; Whybray, *Ecclesiastes*, 139.

places of the Old Testament the phrase '*in the hand of God*' refers to the protection of divine power (Ps. 10:12; Isa. 50:2). It is a comforting thought to be in the hand of God because God has the power to protect someone from all evil. Perhaps someone may think that Qohelet is going to offer consolation to his readers,[14] but that is not the case because he goes on to affirm that being in the hand of God does not bring the protection and the consolation one would expect. Not even the righteous and the wise '*know*' the future, '*whether love or hate*' awaits them. Although some argue that love and hate in 9:1 refer to human activities, it is better to understand love and hate to refer to divine activities. These words in 9:1 do not have a suffix[15] and the hand of God in the previous clause refers to divine power. On the other hand, in 9:6 where love and hate do refer to human activities, the words have suffixes and the context favors a reference to human activities. Also, the emphasis in 9:2 is that no matter how one lives their life they will suffer the same fate as everyone else, which comes from the hand of God. Thus the focus is on God in 9:1-2, and only in 9:3 does the focus shift to people. It is not human psychology that is incomprehensible to Qohelet, but divine psychology.[16] Bartholomew points out that the word '*hate*' is a strong word that refers to God's wrath and judgment. This statement by Qohelet goes against the way love and hate are normally seen to operate; for example, Proverbs 3:33 states, 'The Lord's curse is on the house of the wicked, but he blesses the dwelling of the righteous.'[17] But according to Qohelet a person who is in the hand of God cannot be sure whether God's favor or displeasure awaits them.[18] There is no way to

---

14. Some understand these verses in a very positive way. For example, Ogden (*Qoheleth*, 156–157) understands the statement that the future lies in God's hands as a statement of faith contrary to the context. For other positive views of these verses see Kaiser, *Ecclesiastes*, 94–95 and Winter, *Ecclesiastes*, 119.

15. Gordis, *Koheleth*, 289.

16. Fox, *Rereading Ecclesiastes*, 291.

17. Bartholomew, *Ecclesiastes*, 299–300. Bartholomew argues that Qohelet takes an orthodox statement and subverts it.

18. Fox, *Rereading Ecclesiastes*, 291.

know whether they will experience prosperity or adversity in the future.[19]

The uncertainty of how God will treat people in the future is reinforced in 9:2. It does not matter how a person lives their life, the same *'fate'* happens to everyone. This is emphasized in the opening statement of 9:2: *'everything is the same for everybody.'* It does not matter whether a person is *'righteous'* or *'wicked,'* *'clean'* or *'unclean,'* offers sacrifices or does not offer sacrifices, is *'good'* or is a *'sinner,'* *'swears an oath'* or *'fears an oath,'* the same *'fate'* comes to each one. It is clear that the word 'fate' (*miqreh*) refers in Ecclesiastes to death (2:14-17; 3:19-21), which is the common destiny of the different groups of people in 9:2.[20] It is used of both humans and animals (3:19). As was demonstrated in 2:14-17, and will also become apparent later in this text, death itself is not the major problem, but the timing of death and the finality of death are the problems with which Qohelet is wrestling. In 9:2 he argues that it does not matter how a person lives their life because it has absolutely no effect on how they are treated by God. The same destiny awaits everyone. The righteous is not treated any differently from the wicked. Both experience the finality of death, which is followed by nothing, neither reward nor punishment.[21] It does not matter whether someone worships God (offers sacrifices to God) or does not worship God (does not offer sacrifices). The good and the sinner are treated the same way. There is no distinction based on a moral standard concerning the way God treats different people.[22] This lack of distinction between the different groups of people explains why people do not know whether God's love or hate awaits them.

---

19. Ginsburg, *Coheleth*, 409.

20. See Ecclesiastes 2:14 for further discussion of the word 'fate' (*miqreh*).

21. A. Schüle, 'Qoheleth's Negative Anthropology,' in A. Berlejing and P. van Hecke (eds.), *The Language of Qoheleth in its Context: Essays in Honour of Prof. A. Schoors on the Occasion of His Seventieth Birthday* (Leuven: Peeters, 2007), 163.

22. Crenshaw (*Ecclesiastes*, 160) notes that 9:2 contradicts everything in Qohelet's heritage.

Qohelet demonstrates in 9:3 how *'one fate for all'* affects himself and other people. His sentiment is expressed at the beginning of 9:3, *'this is evil.'* Although the word *'evil'* (*raʿ*) can mean 'tragedy,'[23] the lack of a distinction between groups of people based on a moral standard in 9:2, along with the emphasis on death in these verses, favors the translation *'evil.'* However, not only is God's similar treatment of the righteous and the wise with *'one fate'* called evil, but it also fosters evil among people. The phrase *'and furthermore'* (*wĕḡam*) lays out a further implication for people when there is no relationship between how one lives and how one dies. When people realize that they gain nothing by doing good, the result is that *'the heart of people is full of evil and madness is in their hearts during their lives'* (a similar sentiment is expressed in 8:11). The common destiny for the righteous and the wicked leads people to living evil, irrational, and unprincipled lives because there is no reason to live a righteous life.[24] The end of 9:3 shows the outcome of death for those who live evil lives. However, the way 9:3 ends is itself making a statement about the kind of death that is in view. 9:3 ends abruptly, *'and afterwards—to the dead,'* which reflects the suddenness of death in the midst of life.[25] Thus the fate of those whose lives are *'full of evil'* is a sudden, unexpected, premature death. But since the same destiny awaits the wicked and the righteous (9:2), this is also describing the way the righteous die. This fact is what bothers Qohelet. There is *'one fate for all'* and there is no distinction in the way the righteous and the wicked die.

If such is the case, then what value is there to life? Would death be better than life? In the next several verses Qohelet is going to make several points about life. Qohelet offers a statement in 9:4 that seems positive toward life. This verse does not appear to be giving a reason for the statement in 9:3 that the common fate of all leads people to living evil lives,

---

23. Ogden, *Qohelet*, 159.
24. Fox, *Rereading Ecclesiastes*, 292; Gordis, *Koheleth*, 291.
25. Longman, *Ecclesiastes*, 227; Gordis, *Koheleth*, 292; Murphy, *Ecclesiastes*, 91.

which may quickly end in death.[26] Rather, 9:4 is highlighting life over against death, so the *kî* at the beginning of the verse should be translated *'indeed.'*[27] Qohelet states that *'there is hope for whoever is joined*[28] *to all the living.'* This sounds like a positive statement,[29] but the following verses show that this hope is a false hope. At the end of 9:4 Qohelet offers a proverb that begins to explain the hope that is connected to life: *'for a living dog is better than a dead lion.'* A *'lion'* is a fierce, majestic animal that is associated with royalty, but a *'dog'* is a despised animal that scavenges for food among garbage.[30] It is a term of contempt in that culture. Thus, although it is better to be alive than dead, this proverb is not a ringing endorsement of life. Living life in this world is compared to an unclean, contemptible animal.

In 9:5-6 Qohelet continues to offer his view of life, but now in comparison with death. At the beginning of 9:5 Qohelet gives a reason for the hope of 9:4a and why he compares life to a contemptible dog: *'for the living know that they will die, but the dead do not know anything.'* The advantage the living have over the dead is consciousness, because the dead do not know anything. However, this consciousness is not that great an

---

26. Ginsburg, *Coheleth*, 412.

27. Gordis, *Koheleth*, 294; Longman, *Ecclesiastes*, 225; Murphy, *Ecclesiastes*, 88. Ogden (*Qoheleth*, 160) argues that the *kî* emphasizes the inclusive sense of the pronoun *'whoever.'*

28. This verb could be *bāḥar* (the Ketiv, or what is written in the text) or *ḥābar* (the Qere, or what is read). The Ketiv could be pual ('chosen'), nifal ('exempted'), or qal ('choose'). Seow (*Ecclesiastes*, 300) opts for the qal, 'who is the one who chooses?,' but this does not make sense in the context (Bartholomew, *Ecclesiastes*, 297). Murphy (*Ecclesiastes*, 89, 91) accepts the translation, 'who is chosen,' with the meaning 'who is exempted from death?' Crenshaw (*Ecclesiastes*, 161) thinks the Qere reading is secondary and removes the sting of Qohelet's denial of reward and punishment in 9:3. However, all the versions read the Qere (Gordis, *Koheleth*, 294), which is also followed by many commentators (Longman, Delitzsch, Barton, Fox, Whybray, and Bartholomew), and is adopted here.

29. B. C. Davis ('Ecclesiastes 12:1-8—Death, an Impetus for Life,' *BibSac* 148 [1991]: 301) understands this hope as the possibility of finding meaning in life and success that will reach beyond the grave.

30. Longman, *Ecclesiastes*, 228.

advantage, because what the living are conscious of is that they will die. Their consciousness is a consciousness of death. Thus many understand the hope of 9:4a as ironic or sarcastic[31] because Qohelet demonstrates that the hope that the living have is no real hope at all. Or put in another way, the one thing the living are certain about is that they will die. The prospect of death dominates the lives of the living. What this prospect of death means is developed in 9:5b-6. Not only do the dead lack consciousness because they do not know anything, but *'there is no longer for them a reward because the memory of them is forgotten.'* There is a word play in this verse between the words *'reward'* (*śāḵār*) and *'memory'* (*zēḵer*).[32] The legacy or reputation of a person means little after they are gone because people forget all about them. The dead lack the one reward that could be theirs because they are no longer remembered. The dead are further described in 9:6. Their opportunity to participate in the experiences of life are gone because *'their love, their hate, their envy have already perished.'* Thus *'they will never again have a portion in anything that is done under the sun.'* The word *'portion'* (*ḥēleq*) here probably includes participation in all the experiences of life,[33] but it also brings to mind the more specific use of this word in Qohelet to refer to the limited enjoyment that is available to people even though there is no profit (*yitrôn*) in labor. Thus he anticipates his advice in 9:7-10, which further comments on this portion (9:9). Qohelet's comments on death in these verses demonstrate clearly that although being alive is better than being dead, life is not necessarily a positive experience in light of the consciousness of death. Death is a major problem because Qohelet takes away any thought that

---

31. The following take the hope as ironic: Crenshaw, *Ecclesiastes*, 161; Loader, *Ecclesiastes*, 109; Murphy, *Ecclesiastes*, 92; among others. Longman (*Ecclesiastes*, 228) calls it sarcastic. Whybray (*Ecclesiastes*, 142) argues against this view of hope because he thinks that the calls to enjoyment (9:7-10) are Qohelet's positive conclusions concerning life. But if the calls to enjoyment are limited, resigned conclusions, offering the best that one can hope for in this senseless world, then Whybray's analysis is undermined.

32. Gordis, *Koheleth*, 295; Crenshaw, *Ecclesiastes*, 161, n. 130; Longman, *Ecclesiastes*, 226; Murphy, *Ecclesiastes*, 92.

33. Fox, *Rereading Ecclesiastes*, 293.

death will be where people get what they really deserve. On the contrary, the dead do not know anything.

It seems that in 9:7-10 Qohelet offers a more positive view of life in another call to enjoyment. There are clear connections between this passage and the other calls to enjoyment (2:24-26; 3:12, 22; 5:18; 8:15), such as the exhortation to eat, drink, and enjoy life.[34] However, the way the call to enjoyment is set forth is different. The formula 'there is nothing better than' is not used in 9:7. Also, this call to enjoyment uses imperatives, it is longer and more specific than previous calls to enjoyments, and there is an emphasis on the festivity of the enjoyment.[35] It is no surprise that many have taken these verses in a very positive sense. Eaton calls these verses 'the remedy of faith' and believes that in this section Qohelet comes close to justification by faith.[36] Hubbard comments that these verses are alive with notes of grace.[37] There are indications, on the other hand, that these verses are a resigned conclusion in light of the senseless world in which people live. For one thing the horizon of death frames 9:7-10, with 9:10 specifically mentioning Sheol, and 9:11-12 picking up again the subject of death from 9:1-6. There is also an emphasis on *hebel* and 'under the sun' in 9:7-10, which is a reminder of the senselessness of life and the limited earthly perspective of Qohelet. And finally, people are encouraged to enjoy their 'portion' (*ḥēleq*), which reminds readers that there is no real 'profit' to labor, but only the limited enjoyment of the 'portion' that comes from labor (2:10-11). In the final analysis, this call to enjoyment expresses an urgency to enjoy life while that enjoyment is possible because the finality of death looms large on the horizon.[38] When death comes all activity ceases (9:10).

---

34. Ogden and Zogbo, *Handbook on Ecclesiastes*, 329.

35. The length of this call to enjoyment is noted by Loader, *Ecclesiastes*, 109, its more specific nature is noted by Whybray, *Ecclesiastes*, 143, and its festivity is noted by Crenshaw, *Ecclesiastes*, 162 and Longman, *Ecclesiastes*, 230.

36. Eaton, *Ecclesiastes*, 127.

37. Hubbard, *Ecclesiastes*, 201–202. These notes of grace include acceptance by God, the festivity of joy, and the gracious gift of God as a person's portion.

38. Longman, *Ecclesiastes*, 229; Crenshaw, *Ecclesiastes*, 162.

In 9:7 Qohelet urges people to participate in those activities that have been associated with the calls to enjoyment: '*eat your bread*' and '*drink your wine.*' The urgency of his exhortation is seen in the use of imperatives, including the opening imperative, '*go,*' which is a call to begin the action expressed in the verbs that follow.[39] The emphasis on the enjoyment of these activities is expressed in the qualifying phrases and the motive clause of 9:7. One should eat '*with pleasure*' and drink '*with a merry heart.*' The reason given is '*because God has already approved your works.*' This motive clause has been understood in a number of ways. Leupold argues that this refers to God's approval of the righteous, who can be assured that God takes delight in their works done in righteousness.[40] Some have argued that this statement gives people a blank check or unlimited approval of their behavior.[41] Since Qohelet warns people against excessive wickedness (7:16), he probably does not have in mind unlimited approval of people's behavior. The best explanation in context is that God approves of the activities listed in 9:7-10. Although this enjoyment is a limited enjoyment, it does have God's approval; in fact, it is the portion He has given to people (5:18; 9:9).[42]

In 9:8-9 Qohelet expands this call to enjoyment to include activities not mentioned in earlier calls to enjoyment. The festive nature of the enjoyment comes out in verse 8, with the exhortation to '*let your garments be white all the time and let not the oil upon your head be lacking.*' Although white garments have been associated with purity, the best explanation in this context is that they express joy and celebration. The use of white garments and oil can be very refreshing, especially in a hot climate.[43] The enjoyment of these things should be a continual experience in a person's life. Qohelet adds in 9:9

---

39. Ogden and Zogbo, *Handbook on Ecclesiastes*, 330.

40. Leupold, *Ecclesiastes*, 213.

41. Noted by Longman, *Ecclesiastes*, 230 and Towner, *Ecclesiastes*, 340, who seem disposed toward this view.

42. Murphy, *Ecclesiastes*, 92; Ogden and Zogbo, *Handbook on Ecclesiastes*, 331.

43. Crenshaw, *Ecclesiastes*, 162.

that this enjoyment should include *'the wife whom you love.'*[44] The fact that *'wife'* is used without the article has raised the possibility that Qohelet has in mind a woman rather than a wife because the word *'iššāh* can mean either one. In fact, Ginsburg specifically says that Qohelet does not have the marriage state in mind.[45] This could mean that Qohelet is encouraging promiscuous behavior. However, the fact that his search for meaning, which focused on pleasure, including concubines (2:8), came up empty leads one to think that Qohelet is not exhorting the enjoyment of life with just any woman. The word *'iššāh* can be used without the article to refer to a wife (Gen. 30:4, 9; 1 Sam. 25:43; Deut. 22:22).[46] In light of the unpredictable way the article is used in Ecclesiastes and the emphasis in wisdom literature on marriage,[47] it is better to understand marriage here as one of the limited gifts of God, which is included in the portion of life one may enjoy (9:9). The fact that Qohelet is negative toward women in 7:25-29 does not destroy this argument, because he is not here putting forth marriage as an answer to the problem. Marriage partakes of the character of the portion, which means it offers limited benefits. One might as well make the most of it regardless of the kind of woman to whom one is married.

The bright, positive nature of this call to enjoyment at the beginning of 9:7-10 begins to get cloudy and dark as one moves toward 9:9-10. This is seen in several ways. First, the use of the word *'portion'* in reference to *'your labour which you labour'* reminds the reader that labor does not bring a profit (1:3; 2:11), so one must be content with a portion. Second, the phrase *'under the sun'* occurs twice in 9:9, which emphasizes the limited, earthly horizon in which this call to enjoyment operates. Third, the word *'senseless'* (*hebel*) also occurs twice in

---

44. Seow (*Ecclesiastes*, 305) notes that the same matters are also found in the Gilgamesh Epic. For a discussion of the Gilgamesh Epic in its general relationship to Ecclesiastes see the discussion of genre in the Introduction to this commentary and Brown, *Ecclesiastes*, 2–7. There is no way to know whether Qohelet knew of the Gilgamesh Epic.

45. Ginsburg, *Coheleth*, 416–417.

46. Seow, *Ecclesiastes*, 301.

47. Longman, *Ecclesiastes*, 230–231.

9:9. Enjoying life with the wife is characterized as '*all the days of your senseless life which he has given to you under the sun all your senseless days.*' Although there is some evidence that the second phrase using '*senseless*' should be omitted, it is better to retain it.[48] The added *hebel* phrase sounds a note of quiet melancholy and resigned finality.[49] Finally, the march toward darkness climaxes in 9:10 with a strong statement on the finality of death. The beginning of 9:10, however, encourages people to make use of every opportunity: '*whatever your hand finds to do, do it with your might.*'[50] Here one is encouraged to use all one's energies in order to work wholeheartedly in whatever activities are available in this life.[51] This statement at first appears to be an enthusiastic endorsement of life and its activities.[52] However, the prospects of this life are bright because the looming certainty of death is so dark. Death ends all activity as Qohelet affirms that '*there is no work, or planning, or knowledge, or wisdom in Sheol to which you are going.*' The concept '*Sheol*' represents the realm of the dead and it is

---

48. Seow (*Ecclesiastes*, 302) and Murphy (*Ecclesiastes*, 89) argue that the second *hebel* phrase should be omitted based on the fact that it is omitted in some Greek manuscripts, the Targum, and seven Hebrew manuscripts, but the phrase is contained in some Greek manuscripts (Rahlfs *Septuaginta*). It is better to retain the phrase.

49. Fox, *Rereading Ecclesiastes*, 295. Gordis (*Koheleth*, 296) argues that the second *hebel* phrase is a shortened form of the first phrase, which gives the verse a haunting effect. This haunting effect can be heard if one reads 9:9 out loud in a translation that has both *hebel* phrases, such as the NIV.

50. The accents of the Masoretic text would lead to the translation 'whatever you are able to do in your strength, do,' but several Hebrew manuscripts, the Syriac, and the Vulgate do not follow the Masoretic accents (Bartholomew, *Ecclesiastes*, 298; Crenshaw, *Ecclesiastes*, 163; Seow, *Ecclesiastes*, 302).

51. Ogden and Zogbo (*Handbook on Ecclesiastes*, 334) take the 'whatever' in 9:10 as describing every activity available, but Fox (*Rereading Ecclesiastes*, 259–260) understands 9:10 to refer to activities engaged in according to ability based on the use of 'hand.' Longman (*Ecclesiastes*, 231) correctly points out that the issue is opportunity. If someone has the opportunity to do something, action must be taken now because the future is uncertain.

52. Whybray, *Ecclesiastes*, 145; Ogden, *Qoheleth*, 166–167. Brown (*Ecclesiastes*, 95) also comments that here the toil of work is turned into the celebration of life.

presented here as the destiny of everyone.[53] The darkness of Sheol is seen in the fact that there is no activity of any kind in that place.[54] There is no mental or physical activity in the realm of the dead. Death brings to a final end all our activity, which makes the exhortation in 9:10a all the more urgent. It is imperative that people make use of their opportunities in the present (9:10a) *'because'* death ends all such opportunities and activities (9:10b). If this is an endorsement of life, it is because this life is all there is from an 'under the sun' perspective.

There is some debate as to whether 9:11-12 begins a new unit, whether it stands alone as an independent piece,[55] or whether it goes with what comes before in 9:1-10. The opening phrase in 9:11, *'I turned and I observed under the sun,'* could signal a new unit as an almost identical phrase serves to begin a new unit in 4:1.[56] However, if 9:11 begins a new section, it is not clear where the section ends. Eaton takes 9:11–10:20 as a unit dealing with the themes of wisdom and folly.[57] Seow understands 9:11–10:15 to be a unit held together by the common thread that everything in life is precarious.[58] The thematic connections are stronger between 9:11-12 and the section that comes before than they are with the section that comes after them. Thus it is better to take 9:1-12 as a unit.[59]

In 9:11 Qohelet again observes that life does not turn out the way one would expect. As in 9:1-2 he severs the normal

---

53. Philip S. Johnston, *Shades of Sheol: Death and Afterlife in the Old Testament* (Downers Grove, IL: InterVarsity Press, 2002), 79–83. Johnson points out that *Sheol* is normally reserved for those under divine judgment and only in a few places in the Old Testament is it presented as the destiny of everyone. One of those places is Ecclesiastes 9:10, where Qohelet observes the absurdity of life.

54. Although some try to avoid the implication of these words that Qohelet does not believe in an afterlife (Kaiser, *Ecclesiastes*, 103), if all mental processes come to an end it would seem that the natural meaning of these words is that death is the final end (Longman, *Ecclesiastes*, 231).

55. Whybray, *Ecclesiastes*, 145.

56. Longman, *Ecclesiastes*, 232 and Seow, *Ecclesiastes*, 307.

57. Eaton, *Ecclesiastes*, 129–130.

58. Seow, *Ecclesiastes*, 320.

59. Bartholomew, *Ecclesiastes*, 296.

connection between deed and consequence. One would expect that *'the race'* would *'belong to the swift,'* that *'the battle'* would *'belong to the strong,'* that *'the wise'* would have *'food,'* that *'those who are perceptive'* would have *'wealth,'* and that *'those who have knowledge'* would enjoy *'favour.'* The three terms *'wise'* (ḥāḵām), *'those who are perceptive'* (bîn), and *'those who have knowledge'* (yd‘) are commonly found in wisdom emphasizing the competence of human ability. A wise industrious life should provide a livelihood[60] (Prov. 20:13; 28:19) and lead to wealth (Prov. 3:16; 8:18). A person who 'knows' should receive favor (Prov. 13:15).[61] But as Qohelet observes life he negates these connections with a strong negative (lō’). The expected results do not occur even for wisdom, which demonstrates the ineffectiveness of wisdom.

The reason Qohelet gives for this breakdown of effort and result is that *'a time of misfortune happens to all of them.'* The phrase *'a time of misfortune'* is translated by many as 'time and chance.'[62] This understands the phrase as a hendiadys, a grammatical construction where two concepts are joined by the conjunction 'and' but the two words describe one thing. The word *'time'* (‘ēṯ) reminds the reader of the poem in 3:1-8 where the appropriate time for every event is presented. The problem is that people are not able to discover what God is doing in the world, so the appropriate times are not discernible to people. This leaves a wise person vulnerable to the events of time. The 'time' of 9:11 is characterized by 'chance,' which may give the impression of a random event without purpose. However, the term 'chance' (peḡa‘) may mean 'incident' or 'accident' in the sense that something happens randomly.[63]

---

60. The term 'bread' can have a broader meaning, such as *'food,'* or even livelihood (Hubbard, *Ecclesiastes*, 204).

61. Although Proverbs 13:15 does not use the verb 'know' (yāḏa‘), it does use another wisdom term that is similar in meaning. The noun *śeḵel* refers to insight or understanding and is used of competent and successful persons in 1 Samuel 25:3; Ezra 8:18; and 1 Chronicles 26:14 (M.Sæbo, שׂכל, *TLOT*, 3:1271).

62. Longman, *Ecclesiastes*, 232; Delitzsch, 'Ecclesiastes,' 6:365; Bartholomew, *Ecclesiastes*, 305; Krüger, *Qoheleth*, 166.

63. This term is also used in 1 Kings 5:4, where it occurs with ra‘ ('evil'

This does not necessarily rule out the role of God in the events of human life (3:14-15; 9:1-2), but since no one knows the time of events, the incidents from a human standpoint 'under the sun' (9:11) appear as chance events. Human beings have no control over these things. Thus, from a human standpoint these times of calamity appear as random and they are the cause of the unexpected outcomes earlier in the verse.

The random, unexpected nature of such times is further explained in 9:12, where Qohelet notes, *'For indeed, people do not know their time.'* It is impossible for people to know when such a 'time of misfortune' will come into their lives. There is some debate as to what *'their time'* means. Some limit it to times of misfortune that occur in this life.[64] Although such times of misfortune are certainly in view, one cannot omit from the discussion the time of death. In fact, it is possible to argue that Qohelet is emphasizing the aspect of death in 9:12. Certainly death has been a major part of the discussion in 9:1-6. Even the urgent call to enjoyment in 9:7-10 ends with the subject of death in 9:10. Then 9:11 comments on the unexpected outcomes that may occur in life because times of misfortune will befall people. It makes sense that 9:12 would then move again to the subject of death, which is the ultimate time of misfortune when it occurs unexpectedly and suddenly. Qohelet follows up the statement *'people do not know their time'* with two illustrations which would normally signify death for the animals involved.[65] People are compared to *'fish caught in a cruel net'* and *'birds caught in a snare.'* The point is the unexpected and sudden nature of these events, which can also happen to people: *'so people are ensnared in an evil time*

---

or 'tragedy'). According to Bartholomew (*Ecclesiastes*, 298) it refers to some kind of misfortune or disaster ('an evil incident'). Ginsburg (*Coheleth*, p. 418) notes that the use of 'evil time' ('*ēṯ rā'āh*) in 9:12 shows that the concept *peḡa'* in 9:11 denotes misfortune.

64. Ginsburg, *Coheleth*, 418.

65. Crenshaw, *Ecclesiastes*, 165; Fox, *Rereading Ecclesiastes*, 297; Longman, *Ecclesiastes*, 233; Ogden, *Qoheleth*, 170. Those who do not understand 9:12 as speaking primarily of death understand the comparisons with the animals to be expressions of hopelessness (Murphy, *Ecclesiastes*, 94) or helplessness (Whybray, *Ecclesiastes*, 146) in the time of misfortune.

when it falls suddenly upon them.' Although this *'evil time'* may entail times of misfortune that do not include death, it is hard to eliminate death from the discussion. Ultimately it is death that clouds Qohelet's thinking, and not just any death, but the unexpected, sudden, premature death that takes people in the prime of their lives, just as a net can fall suddenly on a fish or a bird. This comparison seems to support Qohelet's contention in 3:19-20 that human beings have no advantage over the animals because they both experience death in the same way.[66] Thus the future, which includes times of sudden, unexpected misfortune, is uncertain. This answers the question that was raised at 6:12, 'who can tell mankind what will be after him under the sun?' The answer is that no one knows what the future may bring. Qohelet's perspective is that the future will include times of misfortune, including sudden, expected death. This fact explains the unexpected results in 9:11, reminds one of the ineffectiveness of wisdom, and is part of the problem as to why human beings cannot understand the way life works.

Homiletical Implications

Qohelet describes a dreary, drab world dominated by the finality of death. Such a world is not easy to present to people, but it is like living in a society where everything you do is watched by others. It is similar to the description of a trip to North Korea, where the government watches a person's every move and where visitors have government people follow them around.[67] At the border, government agents confiscated coffee mugs which were going to be given away because they were too bright and colorful. Newspapers, cell phones, and recording devices were prohibited. Everyone who lived there tried to blend in with everyone else so as not to stand out in any way. People wore gray and black and were reluctant to make eye contact. When the visitors at one point laughed too loudly a government man came over and reproached

---

66. Krüger, *Qoheleth*, 175.

67. This account of a trip to North Korea is found in *World Magazine*, April 28, 2007.

the group for being too loud. They demanded silence and a more somber mood. Everything was dour and bland. A fog hung over everything because of the fear of saying or doing something wrong. In the same way, death dominates Qohelet's perspective in this passage and it affects the way he observes life. It does not matter if you are in the hand of God (9:2) or if you are wise or righteous because death destroys all such distinctions. The sudden, unexpected nature of death happens to both animals and human beings. Even the call to enjoyment ends with the final destiny of everyone in Sheol, the realm of the dead (9:10). This explains the urgency of this call to enjoyment because the small pleasures of life (the 'portion') are to be enjoyed as the opportunity arises before death comes and it is too late. This 'under the sun' perspective does not offer any possibility of a future reward beyond death because death is final. Such a sentiment is expressed in the following:

> An agnostic compared himself to his dog.
> The dog barks and plays, has all he wants to eat.
> He never works and has no trouble in business.
> In a little while he dies, and that is all.
> I work with all my strength and have no time to play.
> I have trouble every day.
> In a little while I will die—I wish I had been my dog.

The fog of the finality of death must be penetrated by the light of the rest of Scripture. There are numerous ways this can be done. A couple of proverbs could be used to give the 'above the sun' view. For example, Proverbs 15:24 states that 'The path of life leads upward for the prudent, that he may turn away from Sheol beneath' (ESV). Sheol in this passage is not the destiny of everyone, because a prudent life can escape it. Also, Proverbs 12:28 states, 'In the path of righteousness is life, and in its pathway there is no death' (ESV). Certainly this proverb is not denying the reality of physical death, but it is pointing to a life beyond physical death. Psalm 49 is an interesting psalm that sounds very much like Qohelet but comes to a different conclusion concerning death. The psalmist recognizes the common death of the wise and the fool in that they must die and leave their wealth to others (vv. 10-11). There is even a comparison between human beings in their pomp and beasts that perish (v. 12), but the psalmist clearly makes a distinction between the righteous and the wicked in their death. The wicked end up in Sheol where they are consumed, but the righteous are ransomed from the power of Sheol and are received by God (vv. 14-15). Thus our response to death and the times of misfortune in life should be different from Qohelet's response. There is hope because God's people are in the hand of God. Difficult times of misfortune may come, but they do not have the last word. In Psalm 66:11-12 the psalmist says the following to God: 'You brought us into the net; you laid a crushing burden on our backs; you let men ride over our heads; we went through fire and through water; yet you have brought us out to a place of abundance' (ESV).

God is able to bring His people to a place of abundance. Even in the Old Testament, death does not have the final word, a perspective that shines even brighter in the resurrection of Jesus Christ.

Insignificant things have grave consequences (Eccles. 9:13–10:20)

9:13 *I have also observed this concerning wisdom under the sun, and it was important to me.*

9:14 *There was a small city with few men in it, and a great king came against it, surrounded it, and built great siege works against it.*

9:15 *And there was found[68] in it a poor[69] wise man, and he*

---

68. Fox (*Rereading Ecclesiastes*, 299) argues that the king himself found or captured the wise man, who then persuaded the king to spare the city. Although it is possible to take the king as the subject of the first verb in 9:15, almost all translations and commentaries understand the verb at the beginning of 9:15 to be an impersonal verb that should be translated *'there was found,'* as in Genesis 2:20 (Crenshaw, *Ecclesiastes*, 167; GKC 144d).

69. Seow (*Ecclesiastes*, 310) argues that the term *miskēn*, translated 'poor,' does not really mean 'poor' because it is used in contrast with rulers and nobles. Thus the term refers to someone who is not among the elite, a 'commoner.' Ogden and Zogbo (*Handbook on Ecclesiastes*, 172) describe this person as an insignificant member of the community. Thus the social status

delivered[70] *the city by his wisdom, yet no one remembered that poor man.*

9:16 *And I said, 'Wisdom is better than might, but the poor man's wisdom is despised and his words are not heard.'*

9:17 *The words of the wise in calmness*[71] *are heard*[72] *more than the shouting of a ruler among fools.*[73]

9:18 *Wisdom is better than weapons of war, but one offender destroys much good.*

10:1 *Dead flies*[74] *cause the perfumer's oil to*

---

of this individual makes it very unlikely that this person would ever be consulted in the situation described, even though they had wisdom.

70. Some argue that the point is wasted wisdom in the sense that the poor man could have delivered the city but he was never asked to do so (see Crenshaw, *Ecclesiastes*, 167); in other words, no one remembered or thought to ask him to deliver the city (Seow, *Ecclesiastes*, 310). This view takes the Hebrew perfects as expressing potential (Murphy, *Ecclesiastes*, 96–97). However, it is better to take the verbs as regular perfects describing what actually took place, because this is something that Qohelet has himself observed, it is illustrating the principle of 9:11, and the saying in 9:16 assumes that wisdom is victorious; otherwise the condition it offers is not convincing (Bartholomew, *Ecclesiastes*, 312; Ogden and Zogbo, *Handbook on Ecclesiastes*, 347).

71. There is debate concerning whether *'calmness'* (*naḥaṯ*) goes with how the words are spoken or with how the words are heard. Longman (*Ecclesiastes*, 235) takes it with how the words are spoken because of the parallel with the shouting of a ruler. He translates the verse as 'the quiet words of the wise' (see also Murphy, *Ecclesiastes*, 97; Fox, *Rereading Ecclesiastes*, 300). The accents of the Hebrew text puts 'calmness' with how the words are heard (see Seow, *Ecclesiastes*, 311; Ogden and Zogbo, *Handbook on Ecclesiastes*, 352), which the translation above follows.

72. Many point out the tension between the end of 9:16, where the words of the wise are not heard, and 9:17, where the words of the wise are heard. Seow (*Ecclesiastes*, 322) argues that the tension is a deliberate contradiction because the reality of life (9:16b) does not match up to the general principle (9:17a).

73. There is ambiguity concerning whether the ruler speaks to fools (Ogden and Zogbo, *Handbook on Ecclesiastes*, 353) or whether the ruler is one of the fools, even the chief fool (Seow, *Ecclesiastes*, 322). Qohelet's point is made either way it is understood.

74. There is much discussion concerning the phrase *'dead flies'* (*zĕḇûḇê mawet*). Does it refer to flies that are dead, flies that are dying, or flies that cause death? Some argue for flies that cause death, poisonous flies, because of the analogy with the phrase 'snares of death' (Ps. 18:5; 116:3). This refers to snares that cause death (Ginsburg, *Coheleth*, 423; Barton, *Ecclesiastes*,

stink,[75] *so a little folly is more precious than wisdom and honour.*

10:2 *A wise man's heart directs*[76] *him to his right, but a fool's heart to his left.*

10:3 *Even when the fool walks on the road he lacks sense, and he says to everyone that he is a fool.*

10:4 *If the anger of the ruler rises against you do not leave your place, for calmness lays great sins to rest.*

10:5 *There is a tragedy I have observed under the sun, indeed*[77] *an error which proceeds from the ruler.*

233, followed by the Septuagint and the Targums). However, others argue for 'dead flies' based on the context (see Longman, *Ecclesiastes*, 238; Bartholomew, *Ecclesiastes*, 317). Ginsburg (*Coheleth*, 423) even lists phrases that would support this view, although they do not use the word 'death' (Prov. 17:8; 5:19). There is also the problem that the subject 'flies' is plural and the verbs are singular. Both Fox (*Rereading Ecclesiastes*, 301) and Seow (*Ecclesiastes*, 312) argue for a redivision of the consonants (from *zbwby mwt* to *zbwb ymwt*) to read 'a dead fly,' which they argue fits the context better by making a stronger contrast with '*a little folly.*' On the other hand, Ogden and Zogbo (*Handbook on Ecclesiastes*, 356) argue for keeping the plural 'flies' as a collective singular noun. Plus, in other places of Ecclesiastes there is non-agreement between subject and verb (1:16; 2:7).

75. Two hifil imperfect 3ms verbs occur back to back without a conjunction (called asyndeton). The meaning of the first verb (*bā'aš*) is 'to stink' and the meaning of the second verb (*nāba'*) is 'to bubble.' Some argue that the second verb does not make sense in context and suggest the emendation of the verb *yby'* to the noun *gby'* ('cup'), which yields the translation 'a bowl of perfumer's oil.' This is followed by the Syriac (the Septuagint has the noun 'preparation' and the verb is omitted in Symmachus and the Vulgate). On the other hand, Longman (*Ecclesiastes*, 238) argues that the meaning 'bubble' in the sense of 'ferment' (an extension of the verb's basic meaning) is appropriate to the context. He translates the two verbs 'stink and ferment' (see also Murphy, *Ecclesiastes*, 96–97). The translation offered above combines the two ideas into one phrase, which could literally be translated 'to give off a stench.' This has been simplified to the basic idea '*to stink.*'

76. There is no verb expressed in this proverb, but the *lamed* preposition can signify direction (Delitzsch, 'Ecclesiastes,' 6:373).

77. The *kaph* in this clause gives emphasis to what follows and so should probably not be translated with 'as' or 'like' (Seow, *Ecclesiastes*, 314). Perhaps this is the *kaph veritatis*, which is defined as giving a certain emphasis, which may signify equivalent to something in every respect (*GKC*, 118x). It could be identified as an asseverative *kaph*, which expresses

10:6 *Folly is set in many high places and the wealthy sit in a low place.*

10:7 *I have seen slaves on horses, and princes walking on foot[78] as slaves.*

10:8 *One who digs a pit may fall into it and a snake may bite one who breaks down a stone wall.*

10:9 *One who quarries stones may be injured by them and one who splits logs may be endangered by them.*

10:10 *If the axe[79] becomes dull and one does not sharpen the blade,[80] one must exert strength, but wisdom helps one to succeed.*

10:11 *If the snake bites before[81] it is charmed there is no advantage to the charmer.*

---

identity (Williams, *Hebrew Syntax*, 47). The translation '*indeed*' stresses emphasis.

78. The Hebrew reads walking 'on the ground,' but almost everyone translates the phrase '*on foot*' to bring out the contrast with riding a horse.

79. The Hebrew literally reads 'iron' (*barzel*), which in other parts of Scripture (Deut. 19:5; 2 Kings 6:5-6; Isa. 10:34) and in this context clearly refers to some kind of iron tool used to cut wood (Seow, *Ecclesiastes*, 317), like an '*axe.*'

80. There are several difficulties related to this clause. It begins with the pronoun *hû*', so the question is whether the reference is to the immediate antecedent of the dull axe or the antecedent in 9:9 of the person who wields the axe. The negative *lō*' precedes a noun rather than the normal construction of preceding a verb. The noun *pānîm* ('*blade*') does not usually refer to the edge of something but normally means 'face(s).' The normal way to refer to the edge of something, like a sword, is to use the Hebrew *peh* ('mouth'). Because of these difficulties, many emend the phrase *lō*'-*pānîm* to the adverbial use of *pānîm* preceded by a *lamed* preposition, which means 'previously,' yielding the translation 'one does not sharpen it first' (Seow, *Ecclesiastes*, 317; see also Gordis, Ogden, and Zogbo). Ogden (*Ecclesiastes*, 184), however, points out that this emendation lacks manuscript support. The translation above has followed more closely the Hebrew text (also Longman, Fox). Ultimately, the meaning is not affected either way.

81. The Hebrew phrase begins with a *bet* preposition followed by the negative (*bĕlō*'). Seow (*Ecclesiastes*, 318) disregards the Hebrew accents and takes the phrase to mean 'without charm,' which stresses that the snake is not able to be charmed ('a snake without charm'). It is better to follow the Hebrew accents and take the prepositional phrase in the temporal sense of '*before*,' as in Ecclesiastes 7:17 (Murphy, *Ecclesiastes*, 98; Crenshaw, *Ecclesiastes*, 173; Bartholomew, *Ecclesiastes*, 319).

10:12 *The words of the mouth of a wise man win favour, but the lips of a fool destroy him.*

10:13 *The beginning of the words of his mouth is foolishness and the end of* the words of [82] *his mouth is evil delusion.*

10:14 *The fool multiplies words. No one knows what will be and who can tell him what will be after him?*

10:15 *The labour*[83] *of fools*[84] *wearies them because they do not know how to go to the city.*

10:16 *Woe to you, O land, when your king is inexperienced and your princes feast in the morning.*

10:17 *Blessed are you, O land, when your king is the son of nobility and your princes feast at the proper time, for strength, and not for drunkenness.*

10:18 *Through laziness the roof sags and through inactivity the house leaks.*

10:19 *One prepares a meal for laughter and wine makes life joyful and money answers everything.*

10:20 *Even*[85] *in your thoughts do not curse the king and in your bedroom do not curse the wealthy, for a bird of the heavens may carry your voice and a winged creature may declare the matter.*

---

82. The parallelism between the two clauses suggests the elllipsis of '*the words of*' (*diḇrê*) in the second clause.

83. The word '*labour*' (*'āmāl*) is masculine but the verb is feminine. This lack of agreement is explained in a number of ways, including the fact that Ecclesiastes is a book of anomalous grammar (Longman, *Ecclesiastes*, 246). It is also possible that '*āmāl* should be treated as a feminine noun (Seow, *Ecclesiastes*, 320 and Gordis, *Koheleth*, 314, who points to the same thing with the word *kāḇōḏ* in Gen. 49:6).

84. The singular 'fool' is reflected in Greek manuscripts and the Targum. The singular would also agree with the singular suffix on the verb '*wearies*.' Some take the *mem* on the end of '*fools*' to be an enclitic *mem* added to the *yod* of an old genitive case ending (mentioned by Murphy and Longman). The singular suffix on the verb could be distributive, which could refer to something plural (*GKC* 145m; Gordis, *Koheleth*, 314).

85. The *gam* is emphatic (Seow, *Ecclesiastes*, 333).

Qohelet introduces a new section in 9:13 with something he has observed. He presents an example story (9:13-15)[86] followed by his reflections on the story (9:16-18), which offer Qohelet's conclusions to the story. Chapter 10 then follows with a group of proverbs, except for a reflection in 10:5-7.[87] There is no agreement as to where the section ends.[88] One option is to take 9:13–10:20 as a unit emphasizing the theme of 9:18. Thus the example story with Qohelet's comments (9:13-18) is followed by a group of proverbs in chapter 10 that emphasize the theme that something insignificant can do great damage. The proverb in 10:20 shows that even someone's thoughts can do great harm. In chapter 11 the theme changes to how one should respond in light of the uncertainty of the future. Thus the topic in this section is the great damage that one sinner can do (9:18), which supports the general theme of the uncertainty of the future.

Qohelet presents something that he has observed *'concerning wisdom under the sun.'* A few commentators use the phrase 'an example of wisdom' in translating the verse.[89] In light of the story that follows Fox wonders how it is an example of wisdom, since wisdom seems ultimately to fail.[90] However, it

---

86. Murphy (*Ecclesiastes*, 100) and Longman (*Ecclesiastes*, 233) call the story an example story. It is a story which Qohelet has observed, so it really took place (contra Shields, *End of Wisdom*, who calls it a parable); however, attempts to identify the story historically are fruitless.

87. Murphy, *Wisdom Literature*, 146.

88. Gordis (*Koheleth*, p. 299) takes 9:13–10:1 as a unit dealing with the inadequacies of wisdom. Fox (*Rereading Ecclesiastes*, 297, 303, 311) takes 9:13–10:3 as a unit, which is followed by a grouped collection of miscellaneous maxims ending at 11:7. J. A. Loader (*Polar Structures in the Book of Qohelet* [Berlin: Walter de Gruyter, 1979], p. 56) ends the unit at 10:11, with 10:12 introducing a different theme of talk and silence. Seow (*Ecclesiastes*, 320, 328) ends the unit at 10:15 (see also Delitzsch), which deals with the theme of the precariousness of life, followed by 10:16–11:6, which has the theme of the uncertainty of risk. Murphy (*Ecclesiastes*, 99) divides the text at 10:18 based on the phrase 'not know.' Others end the unit at 11:6 (Towner; Ogden and Zogbo). For the justification of taking 9:13–10:20 as a unit see the discussion above.

89. Murphy, *Ecclesiastes*, 100 and Longman, *Ecclesiastes*, 233 use 'example of wisdom,' perhaps due to the fact that Qohelet presents an example story.

90. Fox, *Rereading Ecclesiastes*, 298. He also suggests that the word *'wisdom'* (*ḥokmāh*) be omitted because it is superfluous, but in light of Qohelet's comments in 9:16-18, the story is about wisdom and so the term should be kept.

is possible to take *'wisdom'* as an accusative of specification, with the idea that what is observed has to do with wisdom.[91] Qohelet observes an incident that concerns wisdom. It is obvious that this story has a great impact on Qohelet, for he goes on to say *'it was important to me.'* The significance of the story to Qohelet and the impression it makes on him will be seen in the comments that Qohelet makes following the story.

The story is set forth in 9:14-15. In 9:14 two contrasting elements of the story are given. Qohelet observes *'a small city with a few men in it.'* In contrast to this *'a great king came against it, surrounded it, and built great siege works against it.'* The *'small city'* is contrasted with *'a great king.'* The *'few men'* in the city shows that the city is not able to defend itself very well. This aspect is contrasted with the fact that the king builds *'great siege works'*[92] against the city. The city is doomed, with little hope of surviving. A time of misfortune has befallen the city just like fish caught in a net (9:12). One expects that the powerful king will conquer this defenseless city. However, there is a twist to the story that exemplifies the principle in 9:11 that the battle is not always to the more powerful. In 9:15 *'a poor wise man'* is introduced who *'delivered the city by his wisdom.'* When the situation seemed hopeless, an insignificant wise man used his wisdom to deliver the city. Although Qohelet does not specify how wisdom delivered the city, the point is that wisdom is more beneficial than military might (see Prov. 21:22). However, a further twist to the story is that *'no one remembered that poor man.'* It seems incredible that this poor wise man would not be remembered for delivering

---

91. Seow, *Ecclesiastes*, 309. Bartholomew (*Ecclesiastes*, 312) uses the term 'accusative of limitation,' which expresses a very similar idea.

92. There is a great deal of discussion concerning the Hebrew word translated *'siege works'* (*mĕṣôdîm*). Seow (*Ecclesiastes*, 309) argues that this term normally refers to a defensive weapon, which an invader would not make. He opts for the term *māṣôr* because it refers to an offensive weapon that a king would use to besiege a city (Deut. 20:20). This latter term has the support of the ancient versions (Murphy, *Ecclesiastes*, 97). However, Bartholomew (*Ecclesiastes*, 312) argues for keeping the term in the Masoretic text, which is also used in Eccles. 9:12 to mean 'nets.' He sees a word play between 9:12 and 9:14, with the term 'nets' as an image for siege works. It is a reminder that this is a time of misfortune for this city (9:12).

the city when the odds seemed so stacked against the city. However, this also illustrates the principle of 9:11 that 'food does not belong to the wise, nor wealth to those who are perceptive, nor favour to those who have knowledge.' The poor wise man does not receive the proper recognition or reward that he should receive, which is contrary to the expectations of Proverbs 10:7.[93]

Qohelet reflects (*'And I said'*) on the example story and draws some conclusions in 9:16-18. He basically concludes that wisdom can give a person a relative advantage but cannot guarantee success. The basic advantage of wisdom is stated twice in these verses: *'wisdom is better than might'* (9:16) and *'wisdom is better than weapons of war'* (9:18). These sayings are an obvious conclusion from the example story (9:13-15) and are in line with other proverbs (Prov. 21:22). The saying in 9:17 also supports this conclusion: *'the words of the wise in calmness are heard more than the shouting of a ruler among fools.'* Although there is ambiguity in this verse on several issues (see the notes on the translation), there is a clear contrast drawn between *'the wise'* and *'a ruler,'* and between *'calmness'* and *'shouting.'* A ruler is in a position of authority, so his words would seem to carry weight without shouting. But, *'the shouting of a ruler'* gets more attention than the *'calmness'* in which *'the words of the wise are heard.'* However, the value of wisdom is in the content, not in the volume of the speaking.[94] Thus it should be clear to everyone that wisdom has great advantage.

However, it should also be clear that the advantage of wisdom is only a relative advantage which does not guarantee success.[95] This fact was evident in the example story when the

---

93. Farmer, *Ecclesiastes*, 186.

94. Longman, *Ecclesiastes*, 236.

95. A few commentators take a very positive view of wisdom in these verses. For example, Ogden (*Qohelet*, 173–174) argues that wisdom is presented as having inestimable value, with the problem being human nature, not wisdom. Wisdom allows one to transcend the pain of the present enigmas of life and provides the possibility of meaning both now and in the future beyond death; in other words, wisdom offers a profit. Although the positive nature of wisdom is toned down a bit in Ogden and Zogbo, they

poor wise man was not remembered (9:15). Wisdom may give an advantage to people, but the benefit of wisdom is quickly forgotten. This aspect is brought out twice in 9:16-18. First, 9:16b restates what was said in 9:15b: '*but the poor man's wisdom is despised and his words are not heard.*' Even when wisdom shows its advantage, it can be '*despised*' and '*not heard.*' Perhaps the problem is the social status of the one who has demonstrated wisdom. If wisdom is despised because the man is '*poor,*' then it shows that no matter how beneficial wisdom may be, there are other factors that can hinder its effectiveness. Wisdom spoken by a poor man may not be heard because it is spoken by someone who is considered by others to be socially inferior. Thus, something like social status can thwart wisdom.[96] The main point of Qohelet's conclusion is stated in 9:18b: '*but one offender destroys much good.*' It does not take very much to destroy the benefit and the effectiveness of wisdom. It just takes one person to take away wisdom's advantage. The word '*offender*' (*ḥôṭe'*) should be understood to have moral connotations, so that one 'sinner' in his sin can destroy the good that wisdom has accomplished. But this word can also be used in contexts where it stresses that someone has erred in a non-theological way (Judg. 20:16; Prov. 8:36; 19:2), so that the thought is that one small mistake can also hinder the effectiveness of wisdom.[97] This aspect is brought out in the proverbs at the beginning of chapter 10.

Thus Qohelet argues in 9:13-18 that in some situations the advantages of wisdom are clearly seen by others, such as when wisdom shows itself better than might, or when the calmness of wisdom is set over against the shouting of a ruler among fools. In the latter situation, foolishness demonstrates chaos, which is contrasted with the calmness of wisdom.

---

still understand the passage as an endorsement of wisdom. Part of the purpose is that Qohelet is calling on the wise to be vigilant and not to commit even the smallest indiscretion (*Handbook on Ecclesiastes*, 354).

96. The use of participles shows that despising and not hearing the poor man's wisdom is not a one-time thing but a continuous problem (Barton, *Ecclesiastes*, 168).

97. Luc, חטא, *NIDOTTE*, 2:87-88. Also, see Ecclesiastes 2:26 for the discussion of whether certain terms in Ecclesiastes have moral connotations.

But Qohelet's ultimate conclusion is that the advantages of wisdom can easily be taken away and that it does not take very much to destroy what wisdom has accomplished. Wisdom may be better in principle, but it does not always work out in reality.[98] Just one offender or just one mistake can destroy much good. This conclusion by Qohelet is exemplified in the proverbs of chapter 10.

The idea that something small can destroy much good is specifically stated in the proverb in 10:1; in fact, the connection is thought to be so strong that many take 10:1 to go with 9:18.[99] There is no doubt that there is a connection with 9:18, but 10:1 also introduces the theme of the next several proverbs in 10:2-4. Although there are numerous problems related to 10:1 (see the notes on the translation), the basic idea of the verse is clear enough: something that is small can cause great damage. The first part of 10:1 uses the example of the effect of *'dead flies'* in *'perfumer's oil.'* Flies are very small creatures and yet if they get caught in perfume and die they will ruin the whole batch of perfume because they will cause it *'to stink.'* The point is that something valuable, like perfume, can be destroyed by something small, which illustrates the principle that something small can destroy what is good. The second part of 10:1 drives home the point in relationship to folly and wisdom: *'a little folly is more precious than wisdom and honour.'* There is debate concerning the meaning of the word translated *'precious'* (*yāqār*). Some do not think that the idea of precious fits this context well, so the meaning 'outweighs,' which is derived from Aramaic, is preferred.[100] Ultimately, both meanings work to make the point, but the concept 'precious' does fit the context. Perfumer's oil is something that would have been precious to people, but it is destroyed by something small. In the same way, wisdom should be something that is precious to people, but just a little folly can destroy the value of wisdom because people see folly as

---

98. Seow, *Ecclesiastes*, 323.

99. Ogden and Zogbo, *Handbook on Ecclesiastes*, 355 and Bartholomew, *Ecclesiastes*, 323.

100. Seow, *Ecclesiastes*, 312.

more precious than wisdom itself.[101] The basic point stands either way. It does not take very much folly to undo the great benefits of wisdom. Something that is small, such as a little folly, can destroy much good.

In 10:1 the subject of folly has been introduced, and it is the main theme in 10:2-4. In 10:2 an antithetical proverb is used to draw a basic contrast between the *'wise man'* and the *'fool.'* The contrast centers on the *'heart'* of each. The heart refers to the core of a person that directs the understanding, the will, and the emotions. The proverb states that the heart of a wise man *'directs him to his right, but a fool's heart to his left.'* At a basic minimum this proverb is teaching that the wise and fools are headed in opposite directions. However, it is also likely that the terms *'right'* and *'left'* carry moral connotations.[102] The right hand is associated with power and strength (Ps. 110:1) and the right side is the side of honor and position (Gen. 48:14; Matt. 25:33). This does not mean that the left hand or side is always negative (Judg. 3:15),[103] but when it is contrasted with the right hand or side a negative connotation follows. In Jonah 4:11 the inhabitants of Nineveh are described as not knowing their right hand from their left, which means that they were not able to tell the difference between what was right and wrong.[104] The point of the proverb is that wisdom and folly are headed in different directions.[105]

The negative direction in which folly is headed is demonstrated in 10:3. Qohelet presents the example of a *'fool'* who *'walks on the road.'* The word *'road'* (*derek*) can refer to a

---

101. Bartholomew, *Ecclesiastes*, 321.

102. Murphy, *Ecclesiastes*, 101.

103. Some over-interpret the negative connotations associated with the left side, connecting it with injury (Gordis, *Koheleth*, 307) or misfortune (Krüger, *Ecclesiastes*, 180) or ineptness and perversity (Crenshaw, *Ecclesiastes*, 169). Shields (*End of Wisdom*, 210–211) offers a good counterbalance when he argues that sometimes one is exhorted not to go to the right or the left, but to go straight ahead. However, contrary to Shields, the idea in 10:2 is more than just that the wise and fool are going in opposite directions, which becomes evident in 10:3.

104. Bartholomew, *Ecclesiastes*, 321; Seow, *Ecclesiastes*, 313.

105. Longman, *Ecclesiastes*, 240.

literal road, which would emphasize the conduct of a fool in a normal activity of life in a public place.[106] The word *derek*, however, can also be used metaphorically to refer to the general conduct of a fool's life. It could then be translated 'goes on the way.' Perhaps both are in view,[107] but either way the meaning is basically the same. As one observes a fool, several things become obvious. First, *'he lacks sense.'* This phrase literally reads 'his heart is lacking.' If heart refers to that inner core that gives direction to the mind, will, and emotions, then the idea is that there is nothing substantial in the heart of a fool to give proper direction. Another way of saying this is that the fool lacks sense, which is the way 'heart' is used in Proverbs 6:32; 7:7; 9:4, 16; 10:13; 11:12; 15:21; 24:30. The second thing that is obvious is that the folly of a fool is evident to everyone. The second part of verse 3 is ambiguous. The phrase *'he is a fool'* is either referring to what the fool *'says to everyone'* by his conduct, or it is referring to what the fool says of everyone he meets.[108] Either way, the folly of the fool is evident by his conduct or by what he thinks about everyone else. Everybody sees his foolishness even if the fool does not see it. The point is that it does not take much to see the evidence of foolishness because it is on display in a fool in the normal conduct of life. The fact that foolishness is so apparent in the life of a fool heightens the possibility that even just a little of that foolishness may destroy much good.

Having highlighted the folly of the fool in 10:3, Qohelet gives in 10:4 an example of the benefit of wisdom. He envisions a situation where *'the anger of the ruler rises against you.'* He does not give any details of the situation, but he does offer the following advice: *'do not leave your place.'* The reason (*'for'*) Qohelet offers this advice is that *'calmness*

---

106. Murphy (*Ecclesiastes*, 101) limits the meaning to a literal meaning and Ogden and Zogbo (*Handbook on Ecclesiastes*, 359) emphasize the public place of the road.

107. The metaphorical use would be more likely if *derek* had the 3ms suffix 'his' referring to the way that the fool lives.

108. Crenshaw (*Ecclesiastes*, 170) notes that the Septuagint, the Peshitta, and the Vulgate support the reading that the fool thinks that everyone else is a fool, but that the other view is expressed in Proverbs 12:23 and 13:16.

lays great sins to rest.' When confronted with the delicate situation of the anger[109] of the ruler, the temptation is to run away from the situation, but the proper response can do a lot to alleviate the situation. It is unclear if the '*great sins*' are referring to the actions of the ruler or not,[110] but it shows how serious the situation is. A calm response is able to defuse the situation and bring peace. Although the words 'wise' and 'wisdom' are not used, it is clear that this is an example of the benefit of wisdom (Prov. 16:14). The point in context, however, is not that wisdom should be followed because it is better than folly, but that even though wisdom has great benefit it can be messed up by folly. Wisdom does have a relative advantage over folly, but it is also very vulnerable to the effects of folly.

Qohelet further demonstrates in 10:5-7 the principle that a little folly can destroy much good. In 10:4 the emphasis was how a calm response could appease the anger of a ruler and effectively deal with great offenses. 10:5-7 also deals with a ruler,[111] but this time it is clear that the offense stems from the ruler himself, which leads to the triumph of folly. Qohelet introduces this section with the formula '*there is a tragedy I have observed under the sun*' (5:13; 6:1). This '*tragedy*' is specifically identified as '*an error which proceeds from the ruler.*' The term '*error*' (*šĕgāgāh*) is the term used in Leviticus 4 to refer to unintentional sins. It refers to things which are done inadvertently or by accident. Someone may commit an unintentional sin and not even know that they have committed the error (Lev. 5:2). So even though wisdom can deal with 'great offences,' it only takes an inadvertent error by a ruler to cause great harm.

---

109. The word for '*anger*' is *rûaḥ*, which means 'spirit' but can have the idea of anger (Judg. 8:3).

110. Ogden and Zogbo (*Handbook on Ecclesiastes*, 362) argue that the offending party is the king and that the point is that wise action is more powerful than a ruler's anger.

111. Two different terms are used for ruler in 10:4-5. In 10:4 the participal form of the verb *māšal* is used as a noun and in 10:5 the noun *šallîṭ* is used. It does not seem helpful to make a distinction between the two terms as they both have the meaning to rule over or to have power over.

The great harm caused by the inadvertent error of the ruler is described in 10:6-7. The error of the ruler allows *'folly'* to triumph, which is described as a reversal of the right order of society. The reversal consists of the fact that *'folly is set in many high places and the wealthy sit in a low place.'* The *'high places'* refer to important, influential places in society.[112] Fools occupy these positions of authority and responsibility. The *'wealthy,'* on the other hand, occupy positions that are not very influential or important. Qohelet has also *'observed slaves on horses, and princes walking on foot as slaves.'* The term *'princes'* does not normally refer to the Israelite king but to advisers to the king, such as city officials, royal officials, and military officials.[113] The mention of *'horses'* supports the idea of military officials, because horses were used for military purposes (Prov. 21:31). They were also status symbols of wealth and power (Esther 6:8-9).[114] *'Slaves,'* who usually have no status in society, occupy an important place of leadership, and *'princes,'* who usually occupy important positions of leadership, are functioning as servants. This reversal of order describes a world upside down (Prov. 19:10), which is a sign of the collapse of a society.[115]

Most of the contrasts in 10:6-7 are expected. For example, high places are contrasted with low places, princes are contrasted with servants, and riding a horse is contrasted with walking on foot; however, the contrast between folly and the wealthy is thought to be a little unusual. Not only is folly an abstract noun,[116] but the normal contrast would be between folly and wisdom. Some argue that the issue is not wealth but social status, and that Qohelet favors the privileged class.[117] However,

---

112. Ogden and Zogbo, *Handbook on Ecclesiastes*, 364.
113. Baker/Nel, שַׂר, *NIDOTTE*, 3:1295.
114. Seow, *Ecclesiastes*, 315.
115. Whybray, *Ecclesiastes*, 152.
116. This verse has *sekel* (*'folly'*) when normally in Ecclesiastes the term used is *sākāl* (*'fool'*), so many translate the abstract as the concrete noun 'fool,' based on the ancient versions and the context (Longman, *Ecclesiastes*, 242; also Murphy, Gordis, Fox, Whybray). However, Crenshaw (*Ecclesiastes*, 171) favors *'folly'* because it is the more difficult reading.
117. Seow, *Ecclesiastes*, 315; Longman, *Ecclesiastes*, 242.

Human limitations concerning knowledge 349

the focus may not be on class as much as on competence. The wealthy would have more experience at managing money and estates. This is supported not only by the contrast between the wealthy and folly, but also by the contrast between princes and slaves. Slaves normally lack the experience of filling a position of authority in government or as a leader in the military. To make military leaders serve as foot soldiers is a waste of ability.[118] If the issue is competence, then such a reversal has very negative consequences for a society. Incompetent people who have power and authority can do a lot of damage (Prov. 30:21-22 notes that the earth trembles when a servant rules). The point Qohelet is making is that the inadvertent error of a ruler that allows incompetent people to have positions of responsibility can cause serious, negative consequences for a society. Thus, 10:5-7 illustrates the principle of 9:18 that something small like an inadvertent error from a ruler can destroy much good.

The next subsection consists of 10:8-11, which is another series of proverbs. The use of 'serpent' (*nāḥāš*) and the verb 'bite' (*nāšak*) in verses 8 and 11 acts as an inclusio and sets this section apart.[119] Also, 10:8 and 10:9 are connected by their common use of participles, and 10:10 and 10:11 are connected by form, as each is a conditional sentence introduced by 'if' (*ʾim*). This section also continues the theme of this chapter that something small can cause great damage.

The proverbs of 10:8-9 set forth certain disasters that can occur in life which could be termed occupational hazards for those who work in these areas. Those who hunt animals have to be careful, because '*one who digs a pit may fall into it.*' Even the breaking down of a '*stone wall*' can conceal the hidden danger of '*a snake*' that bites. These particular walls are stone fences made up of unhewn stones piled on top of each other (Prov. 24:31; Num. 22:24). Snakes may easily lurk between the stones.[120] In

---

118. Hubbard, *Ecclesiastes*, 214.

119. Ogden, *Qoheleth*, 183.

120. Seow (*Ecclesiastes*, 316) notes that normally these walls do not use mortar between the stones (contra Murphy, *Ecclesiastes*, 102). Ogden and Zogbo (*Handbook on Ecclesiastes*, 367) also note that these walls were not the walls of a house but were stone walls that protected fields and vineyards, or were along roadsides.

10:9 two activities are mentioned that require caution when someone is participating in them: '*one who quarries stones may be injured by them and one who splits logs may be endangered by them.*' These situations have built in dangers that can make life very difficult.

The main question surrounding 10:8 is whether Qohelet is setting forth the traditional deed-consequence relationship so that there is an element of punishment involved in the consequence stated. In other words, did the person who dug the pit mean for someone else to fall into the pit, but instead he himself fell into it? Also, was the person breaking down the wall trying to steal something, but instead was bitten by a snake?[121] If so, then these proverbs would be teaching that evildoers get their just desserts. In this view, the verbs are not translated with a modal meaning ('may fall into the pit') but are understood as statements of fact ('will fall into the pit'). The strongest argument in support of this view is that other passages use the same image to teach the deed-consequence relationship.[122] For example, Psalm 7:15-16 states, 'He makes a pit, digging it out, and falls into the hole that he has made. His mischief returns upon his own head, and on his own skull his violence descends.' Clearly, the image of a pit is used in this passage to teach that evil intentions and actions have destructive consequences for the person who seeks to do evil. However, there is nothing in the context of Ecclesiastes 10 to suggest that Qohelet is affirming or struggling with the deed-consequence relationship. Usually Qohelet struggles with the fact that the proper consequences do not follow either wicked deeds or righteous deeds (3:16; 8:11-14; 9:11-12). It is better to understand 10:8-9 as setting forth accidents that can occur in life.[123] There is no indication that the people involved in these activities are wise or foolish or that the

---

121. Barton, *Ecclesiastes*, 171 and Crenshaw, *Ecclesiastes*, 172.

122. Bartholomew (*Ecclesiastes*, 323, 327) has the most extensive defense of this view. He argues that Qohelet is stating the teaching of traditional wisdom concerning the deed-consequence relationship, but then Qohelet 'problematizes' it. The view in the present commentary is that Qohelet is showing the problems of wisdom, but through the theme of 9:18.

123. Murphy, *Ecclesiastes*, 101–102; Longman, *Ecclesiastes*, 244.

disastrous consequences could have been avoided.[124] The focus on accident also supports the theme that any activity that produces good results can be hindered by an unexpected and uncertain event, such as an accident.[125]

The two proverbs of 10:10-11 are united by form and they also teach something specific concerning wisdom. 10:10 is full of linguistic difficulties; in fact, some have stated that 10:10 is the most difficult verse in the whole book.[126] Although there are problems with 10:10, the basic idea of the verse seems fairly clear. If a person uses an *'axe'* that *'becomes dull'* and he *'does not sharpen the blade,'* then he *'must exert strength'* in order to accomplish the work. A sharp axe will accomplish the work more efficiently than a dull axe. The use of a dull axe takes much more effort and time, and perhaps even increases the possibility of accident because one becomes more tired. The last clause of 10:10 drives home the benefit of wisdom in this situation: *'wisdom helps one to succeed.'*[127] In this situation, wisdom helps a person recognize the problem of the dull blade so that the blade can be sharpened and the work done more efficiently. It is also possible that in context the meaning includes the idea that wisdom can help a person avoid some of the accidental events in life.[128]

---

124. Shields, *End of Wisdom*, 213.

125. Bartholomew (*Ecclesiastes*, 323–324) does not carry over the deed-consequence relationship that is the focus of 10:8 into 10:9. He understands 10:9 as setting forth accidental happenings and so translates the verbs in 10:9 with 'may.' Thus it only takes one unpredictable, uncontrollable accident in life to shatter traditional wisdom. His understanding of 10:9 is correct, and this should also be the way 10:8 is understood.

126. Longman (*Ecclesiastes*, 244) quotes Wright, *The Book of Koheleth*, 423. Murphy (*Ecclesiastes*, 98) notes that the ancient versions are confused regarding Ecclesiastes 10:5 (see Longman for the various ways this verse has been translated and Gordis for the various ways this verse has been interpreted).

127. The word *'succeed'* is the word for 'profit' ($yit̲rôn$) and here could be translated 'advantage,' 'benefit,' or 'profit.' The advantage that wisdom gives in this situation does lead to success, which explains the translation *'succeed.'* However, this 'profit' does not rise to the level of answering the original question in 1:3 in a positive way, as becomes clear in 10:11.

128. Seow, *Ecclesiastes*, 326–327.

There is no doubt that 10:10 sets forth the advantage that wisdom gives to help one succeed in various situations of life, but as in other places of the first-person discourse, wisdom only gives someone a relative advantage (2:13-17). There is always the difficulty that wisdom is vulnerable in some way and its effects can be hindered. Even in 10:10 one must apply wisdom to the situation by sharpening the axe so that the advantage of wisdom can be demonstrated. In other words, for wisdom to succeed it must be applied. This is the point of 10:11: '*if the snake bites before it is charmed there is no advantage to the charmer.*' The word '*charmer*' is literally the phrase 'master of the tongue' (*baʿal hallāšôn*) and refers to those who are experts in this area.[129] Any '*advantage*' (*yitrôn*)[130] or benefit that comes with having a charmer is gone if the snake has already bitten its victim. Unless the charmer does his work before the snake bites, he is useless. Wisdom must be applied at the right time in order for there to be success. Something as small as timing, even if it is just a few seconds or minutes, can cause great damage to the person who is bitten by the snake.

In 10:12-15 there is a series of proverbs that deal primarily with the words of the fool. This section may be anticipated by the phrase 'master of the tongue' that was used to designate the snake charmer (10:10).[131] The theme that something small can destroy much good continues in this section that shows a progression from the negative damage of the words of a fool to the total

---

129. *ibid.*, 318. Other passages of Scripture that mention the charming of snakes include Jerermiah 8:17 and Psalm 58:4-5.

130. It is possible that *yitrôn* ('profit') refers to the profit that would come to the charmer for his work of charming the snake, which is lost if the snake has already struck. Perhaps this could reinforce Qohelet's view that there is no profit to labor (1:3; 2:10-11). However, *yitrôn* also has the meaning '*advantage*,' and here would refer to the advantage of having a charmer, which is lost if the snake has already struck.

131. Seow, *Ecclesiastes*, 327. However, the word 'tongue' is not used in 10:12-15, so it is hard to see a tight connection between the two sections. Also, it is hard to tell whether there is a contrast between the effectiveness of the charmer and the ineffectiveness of the words of the fool or, whether it is better to draw a comparison between the ineffectiveness of the charmer, who charms too late, and the ineffectiveness of the words of the fool. Perhaps not too much should be made of this connection.

incompetence of the fool. In 10:12 Qohelet contrasts the words of the wise man and the fool. There is an emphasis not just on the words that are spoken, but on the instrument that speaks the words, which presents a more graphic picture.[132] Thus Qohelet does not just say 'the words of a wise man' but he says '*the words of the mouth of a wise man.*' The characteristic of the words of the wise man is that they '*win favour.*' The Hebrew word is 'gracious' (*ḥēn*), and the contrast that Qohelet draws with the words of the fool leads to the translation '*win favour.*' These gracious words have positive benefits in the lives of other people. In contrast to this, the proverb goes on to state that '*the lips of a fool destroy him.*' The word '*destroy*' (*bālaʿ*) means 'to swallow up,' which fits well with the focus on lips and mouths. In contrast to the beneficial words of the wise man, the words of the fool bring great harm to himself (Prov. 14:3; 18:7). Thus, something as small as words which come from a person's lips can cause destruction. The damage, however, does not just stop with a few words, but grows even greater. The proverb in 10:13 sets forth both the beginning and the end of the words of the fool. '*The beginning of the words of his mouth is foolishness.*' There is nothing positive about the words of the fool, for even at the start they are characterized as foolish. However, the words of the fool progressively get worse, so that '*the end of the words of his mouth is evil delusion.*' Although the phrase '*evil delusion*' could be translated 'tragic delusion,' the delusion of a fool causes so much damage to himself and others that it is appropriate to see it as 'evil' (*rāʿāh*). The fool progresses in his words from mere foolishness to a way of thinking and talking about life that expresses opinions and views that are completely misguided and out of accord with the way life really works. Such '*evil delusion*' is harmful to the fool because he is not able to deal with the reality of life, and it is harmful to any who follow him because it can only bring negative consequences into a person's life. The fool's speech is nonsense, but it is dangerous nonsense (Prov. 18:7).[133]

---

132. Ogden and Zogbo, *Handbook on Ecclesiastes*, 375.

133. Murphy (*Ecclesiastes*, 97) uses the phrase 'dangerous nonsense.' Bartholomew (*Ecclesiastes*, 325) notes that folly never stands still, but it develops and deteriorates.

The next proverb in 10:14 gives some insight into the 'evil delusion' of a fool. The first part of the verse obviously refers to the fool's speech, but there is some discussion concerning the relationship of 10:14b to 10:14a.[134] However, 10:14b is preceded and followed by material that denigrates folly, so it is appropriate to understand it in relationship to the fool.[135] The beginning of 10:14 states what is obvious from 10:13: *'the fool multiplies words.'* The rest of 10:14 is a statement about the inability of anyone to know the future. Not only does *'no one know what will be'* in the future, but also no one can *'tell him what will be after him.'*[136] The last statement of 10:14 is in the form of a question that expects a negative answer. It is in line with other statements by Qohelet concerning the inability of anyone to know the future (8:7). The fool, however, never stops talking, and he talks about things he knows nothing about. In this way the fool demonstrates the evil delusion of his words.

The proverb in 10:15 continues the progression of the fool into foolishness by moving beyond the speech of the fool to his actions. Specifically, the labor (*'āmāl*) of the fool is in view in the statement, *'the labour of fools wearies them.'* Not only are there grammatical difficulties with 10:15a (see the notes on the translation), but there are also questions concerning how to understand 10:15b. These questions focus on how to translate the relative pronoun *'ăšer* and how to understand the statement *'they do not know how to go to the city.'* Garrett understands *'ăšer* as a true relative pronoun with the translation, 'the effort of fools wearies him who does not know the way to the city.' The idea is that the fool cannot even give simple directions to the city. His long-winded explanation wears out the weary traveler.[137] Others

---

134. Murphy (*Ecclesiastes*, 103) calls the connection tenuous.

135. Shields, *End of Wisdom*, 216.

136. Some limit the future to events in this life because death is not mentioned in this section (Fox, *Rereading Ecclesiastes*, 307), but others include the future aspect of what happens after death (Ogden and Zogbo, *Handbook on Ecclesiastes*, 377 and Whybray, *Ecclesiastes*, 156). The former view is correct, but either way, the point is made that the fool does not know the future.

137. Garrett, *Ecclesiastes*, 336.

understand *'ăšer* in a causal sense, giving the reason for why '*the labour of fools wearies them.*' Longman comments that the reason fools are so tired after a long day at work is that they get lost and so have to walk a longer distance than necessary to return to their home in the city.[138] The statement in 10:15b could just be a statement illustrating the stupidity of fools to explain that they get weary in their labor because of their stupidity. It is also possible that 10:15b is an idiomatic expression that demonstrates the incompetence of the fool.[139] The fool does not accomplish what he sets out to accomplish even in his labor. What starts out so small, just words and lips, progresses to speech characterized by evil delusions, and then labor marked by total incompetence. Just one offender who is a fool can destroy much good (9:18).

Many commentators take 10:16-20 as a unit, but argue that 10:16 begins the next section of the book. Murphy divides the section into 10:16–11:2 based on the phrase 'not know' and titles it 'A Collection of Sayings.'[140] Seow's division is 10:16–11:6, entitled 'Living with Risks.' He argues that a new unit begins in 10:16 marked by a shift of mood from the author's reflection (9:11–10:15) to a direct address of the audience (10:16–11:6). However, the theme that everything in life is precarious continues into this section.[141] Thus it is better to take 11:1 as beginning the next section (see the discussion there) and to understand 10:16-20 as continuing and completing the idea that one offender can cause great damage (9:18).

Although 10:16-20 is seen as a unit, there is no agreement concerning the relationship of the proverbs in this section to each other. Some argue that all the proverbs of 10:16-20 relate to the topic of politics and the character of those who govern, which is supported by the fact that 10:16-20 is framed by

---

138. Longman, *Ecclesiastes*, 248.
139. Seow, *Ecclesiastes*, 320; Fox, *Rereading Ecclesiastes*, 308. The latter points to an Egyptian phrase of not reaching the city which means to fail to attain the goal.
140. Murphy, *Ecclesiastes*, 105.
141. Seow, *Ecclesiastes*, 328, 338.

references to political rule.¹⁴² Others find the royal theme in 10:16-17 and 10:20, but take 10:18-19 as independent sayings that do not relate to the royal theme.¹⁴³ This raises the question of how proverbs, which are short sayings, function. Although they are meant to stand alone and to be used in different situations, they also become part of a literary context when they are gathered together in a collection.¹⁴⁴ Thus it is not necessarily inappropriate to connect 10:18-19 to the concept of the quality of those who govern, but that connection is not absolutely necessary if one keeps in mind the broader theme of this section that one offender can destroy much good.

Generally, verses 16-17 are taken together as showing a contrast between an immature, inexperienced ruler and a mature, competent ruler. The contrasts between the two verses include '*Woe*' versus '*Blessed*,' '*the king*' as '*inexperienced*' versus '*the king*' as '*a son of nobility*,' and '*princes*' that '*feast in the morning*' versus '*princes*' that '*feast at the proper time*.' These contrasts favor taking the Hebrew word *naʿar*, which can mean 'boy, youth, or child' to mean 'servant'¹⁴⁵ but translated as '*inexperienced*.' In many of the passages where *naʿar* refers to a 'servant' it is still translated 'young man' (Gen. 22:3; 1 Sam. 14:1; 21:3-6). There is also an interesting parallel between this passage and 1 Kings 3:7, where Solomon uses *naʿar* to refer to himself as inexperienced. He even refers to himself as one who 'does not know how to go out and come in,' which is very close to the statement concerning the fool in Ecclesiastes 10:15 that 'they do not know how to go to the city.'

---

142. Seow (*Ecclesiastes*, 338) notes the framing of 10:16-20 by political rule. Farmer (*Ecclesiastes*, 188–189) interprets the whole section of 10:16-20 as referring to political rule.

143. Longman, *Ecclesiastes*, 248.

144. See the two very different approaches to the composition of the book of Proverbs by Bruce Waltke, *The Book of Proverbs*, 2 vols. (Grand Rapids: Eerdmans, 2004; 2005) and Tremper Longman, *Proverbs* (Grand Rapids: Baker, 2006). Waltke understands the proverbs as having literary relationships with each other in the context of the sections where they appear, whereas Longman understands the proverbs as individual sayings which have virtually no relationship to each other in the sections of the book where they appear.

145. Fox, *Rereading Ecclesiastes*, p. 308.

There is a fine line between inexperience and incompetence. Solomon calls himself a *naʿar*, which stresses inexperience. Such inexperience could lead to the incompetence of the fool. Of course, that does not happen during the early stages of Solomon's reign because he asks wisdom from God. The king in Ecclesiastes 10:16, however, is not only *'inexperienced,'* but is incompetent, which is demonstrated by the *'Woe'* that begins the verse and by the conduct of his *'princes'* who *'feast in the morning.'* The Hebrew verb *'ākal* means 'to eat' or 'to consume' and the context supports the idea of feasting. There is not a problem with eating in the morning, but feasting in the morning would be debauchery,[146] which is inappropriate, as the contrast with 10:17 demonstrates (eating *'for*[147] *strength and not for drunkenness'*). Thus the function of 10:17 is to show the blessing that a competent ruler brings to a land, which stands in stark contrast to 10:16. Woe is pronounced on a *'land'* where the inexperience of the king leads to foolish and incompetent behavior by the other leaders of the land. One offender, here represented by the inexperienced king, can cause great damage in a land.

It is debated whether the proverbs of 10:18-19 should be interpreted as independent sayings or whether they should be understood in relationship to the topic of political rulers. It is not even clear whether these two proverbs should be interpreted in relationship to each other. The proverb in 10:18 states that *'through laziness the roof sags and through inactivity the house leaks.'* The roofs were flat and covered with material, such as lime, that needed constant attention to keep them from leaking.[148] The concept of *'inactivity'* is a phrase that literally means 'the lowering of the hands.' It reminds one of the proverbs in Proverbs 24:33-34: 'A little sleep, a little slumber, a little folding of the hands to rest, and poverty will come upon you like a robber.' It is amazing how quickly

---

146. Murphy, *Ecclesiastes*, 105; Ogden and Zogbo, *Handbook on Ecclesiastes*, 381.

147. The *lamed* preposition signifies the purpose of eating, which is for physical nourishment to sustain them through the day (Longman, *Ecclesiastes*, 250; Whybray, *Ecclesiastes*, 156).

148. Fox, *Rereading Ecclesiastes*, 309.

things can deteriorate through lack of attention. Just a little laziness, which results in inactivity, can cause great damage to a house.[149]

The proverb in 10:19 seems to deal with a completely different subject from 10:18. It is not even obvious what the connection of 10:19 is to 10:18 or to the rest of 10:16-20.[150] Part of the problem of 10:19 is that it can be understood either positively or negatively and the last clause of the verse can be understood in a number of ways. A positive view of 10:19 understands *'one prepares a meal'*[151] and the use of *'wine'* as positive gifts from God that bring laughter and pleasure into people's lives. Some who take a positive view of the verse would understand the verb *'ānāh* to mean 'answer,' with the idea that money is the means to provide for the enjoyment of life.[152] Others understand the verb *'ānāh* to mean 'preoccupy,' with the similar idea that if one does not have enough money for food and wine then life loses some of its basic pleasures.[153]

A negative view of 10:19 understands *'one prepares a meal'* and the use of *'wine'* to be for the purpose of one's self-indulgent *'laughter'* and pleasure.[154] The *lamed* preposition on *'laughter'* would set forth the purpose of the meal and

---

149. Some connect the proverb to the political situation of 10:16-17 so that the house refers to the dynasty and the proverbs warns that negligence of duty will lead to the danger of the collapse of the kingdom (see Seow, Fox, Delitzsch, Ginsburg).

150. There are numerous ways people understand 10:19 based on whether it is seen as an independent saying or as related to the context of political rulers. The meaning of 10:19 is also affected by which verse it is compared with or contrasted to in 10:16-18. The explanation above tries to understand the verse first as an independent saying and then seeks to understand its relationship to the context.

151. The Hebrew literally reads 'making bread,' which refers to the preparation of a meal in Ezekiel 4:15.

152. Seow (*Ecclesiastes*, 332) mentions this as a possibility.

153. Ogden and Zogbo, *Handbook on Ecclesiastes*, 386.

154. Longman (*Ecclesiastes*, 251) states that 10:19 encourages a sensual lifestyle to satisfy one's needs and luxuries. Others take 10:19 to be referring to the banquets of the wealthy (Fox, *Rereading Ecclesiastes*, 309; Shields, *End of Wisdom*, 220).

would contrast with the princes of 10:17, where feasting is not for laughter but for strength.[155] Bartholomew takes a negative view of 10:19 and understands the verb ʻānāh to mean 'answer,' with the idea that money enables one to feast. This is a statement against traditional wisdom, which would stress hard work.[156] Others understand the verb ʻānāh to mean 'preoccupy' or 'keep busy,' with the negative meaning that money enables people to keep busy with food and wine.[157]

It is difficult to choose between the positive and the negative views of 10:19. Based upon the parallel of moving from the negative to the positive in both 10:16-17 and 10:18-19, the positive view is more likely. Thus, in 10:16 the negative consequences of an inexperienced ruler are laid out, which are then contrasted with the positive effects of competent rulers in 10:17. In 10:18 the negative consequences of laziness are laid out, which are then contrasted with the positive effects of having money in 10:19. Laziness leads to the destruction of a house, but money allows one to enjoy life.

The proverb in 10:20 clearly deals with the king. As the concluding proverb in this section it reinforces the major theme of the section that something small can cause a lot of damage. This verse warns against even thinking bad things about the king and the wealthy: *'Even in your thoughts do not curse the king and in your bedroom do not curse the wealthy.'* Something as small and hidden as a bad thought about the king or something as small as a bad word spoken in secret in the bedroom against the rich can get a person in a lot of trouble. The proverb does not specify how the thought or word spoken in secret might get to the king or the wealthy, but uses proverbial sayings as the justification for the warning: *'for a bird of the heavens may carry your voice and a winged creature may declare the matter.'* The point is not how the thought or word gets out, but that in some way it very

---

155. Seow (*Ecclesiastes*, 386) and Fox (*Rereading Ecclesiastes*, 309) note the contrast to the rulers of 10:16-17.
156. Bartholomew, *Ecclesiastes*, 320.
157. Fox, *Rereading Ecclesiastes*, 310.

likely will get out.[158] Thus one needs to be careful in what one thinks and what one says in secret against those who are more powerful than they are. Something small, like a thought or a secret word, can cause great damage.

Homiletical Implications

Although there is an emphasis in 9:13–10:20 on the benefits of wisdom, the dominant thought is that it does not take very much to hinder the advantages of wisdom. The great benefits of wisdom are demonstrated in the story of the poor wise man who saved the city (9:13-16). The quiet words of the wise which have great power and wisdom are better than weapons of war, but one offender destroys much good (9:18). This is the theme of the section. The positive statements concerning wisdom in the proverbs of chapter 10 are negated by the effects of folly. Wisdom may be able through calmness to lay great sins to rest, but it is extremely vulnerable to the effects of folly (10:1-5). Wisdom can help one succeed in the daily tasks of life, but wisdom can be thwarted if it is not applied and it cannot anticipate the unexpected and uncertain events of life, such as accidents (10:6-11). The damage that the words of a fool can do is laid out in 10:12-15. The usual things that accompany foolishness, such as inexperience and laziness, come into view in 10:16-19, with 10:20 demonstrating the damage that something as small as a thought or secret word can do. A modern day example might be a grain of sand, which as an irritant in the right place can produce a great pearl; but if it is in the wrong place, like a person's eye, it can cause great pain. In Qohelet's world, the grain of sand always lands in the eye! This fits Qohelet's limited, 'under the sun,' perspective. Although it is true that one offender can do much damage, a broader perspective understands that foolishness will not win the day. God is able to work out His purposes even in the midst of the foolishness of life. He is able to use the weak, small things in life to accomplish His purposes (Ps. 8:2). Even though the wisdom of the poor wise man was forgotten,

---

158. These warnings are stated in a hyperbolic way and are similar to the saying 'a little bird told me' (Murphy, *Ecclesiastes*, 106).

another poor wise man's wisdom was rejected at first, but then later won the day. The One who is the wisdom of God (1 Cor. 1:30; Col. 2:3) appeared weak and was despised, but through His death and resurrection He won our victory. He is our guarantee that God's wisdom will triumph over the foolishness of the world. Although the word of a fool can do great damage, we are reminded of Christ's victory in the hymn, 'A Mighty Fortress Is Our God,' in the phrase 'one little word shall fell him.' Just one word from Jesus Christ will defeat all the powers of foolishness and darkness. Thus the future is not uncertain because of foolishness, but it is certain because of the power and victory of Christ.

7.
Living with the uncertainty of the future (Eccles. 11:1–12:8)

There is no agreement that 11:1 begins a new section. Murphy understands 10:16–11:2 to be a unit based on the phrase 'not know.'[1] Those who think 11:1 starts a new section are not agreed where the section ends. Some see 11:1-6 as a unit and others end the section with 11:7-8.[2] There is good reason, however, to see 11:1–12:8 as the closing section of the first-person discourse.[3] This section is characterized by imperatives which exhort people concerning how they are to live even though the future is uncertain, and in some ways, very dark. The imperatives occur in 11:1, 2, 6, 9, and 10, and 12:1, with jussives in 11:8. The use of imperatives and the common theme of the nature of the future bind together 11:1–12:8. The smaller sections support the common theme of how to live with the uncertainty of the future.

---

1. In Murphy's book on genre analysis (*Wisdom Literature*, 147) he divides the text at 11:6, but in his commentary (*Ecclesiastes*, 105) he divides the text at 11:2. Both are based on the phrase 'not know.'

2. The most common view is to see 11:1-6 as a unit, but a few, such as Delitzsch ('Ecclesiastes,' 6:391) and Provan (*Ecclesiastes*, 206), end the section at 11:8.

3. Krüger (*Ecclesiastes*, 191) calls this section the closing summary of the teachings of the book and Barton (*Ecclesiastes*, 179) entitles it 'Final Advice.' These final exhortations, however, should not be understood as a call to faith in the God Who controls all things (Eaton, *Ecclesiastes*, 139).

Take action even if the future is uncertain (Eccles. 11:1-6)

11:1 Release[4] *your bread upon the surface of the waters, for in many days you may find it.*

11:2 *Give a portion to seven or even to eight, for you do not know what disaster may occur on the earth.*

11:3 *If the clouds are full of rain they will empty themselves on the earth, and if a tree falls to the south or to the north, in the place where the tree falls there it will lie.*

11:4 *One who observes the wind will not sow and one who regards the clouds will not reap.*

11:5 *Just as you do not know what is the way of the wind nor how the bones are formed in the womb of the mother with child, so you do not know the work of God who makes everything.*

11:6 *In the morning sow your seed and at evening do not rest your hand, because you do not know which will succeed, this or that, or whether the second one as the first one will be good.*

This section is a collection of loose sayings that encourage people to take action even as it describes a future that is unpredictable. The key to the section is the closing, summary exhortation in 11:6, which brings together both the encouragement for action and the unknowability of the future. The imperatives of verses 1 and 6 also act as an inclusio. The two aspects of exhortation and comments concerning the future dominate 11:1-6.

The first two verses of this section are usually taken together because of the subject matter and the similar structure (imperative followed by a motive clause). The meaning of these two verses, however, is greatly debated. The difficulty is how to understand the opening clause of 11:1 and whether 11:2 should determine how 11:1 is understood.

---

4. Although many translations translate the verb *šālaḥ* as 'cast,' such a meaning is not attested for the piel of this verb. The translations 'send' or '*release*' are better translations of this verb (Longman, *Ecclesiastes*, 254).

The basic views will be briefly laid out. The traditional view, going all the way back to Jerome and the Targums, is that 11:1-2 is encouraging liberality in giving to the poor. 11:2 has the imperative *'give'* and the phrase 'release your bread on the waters' in 11:1 has parallels in the ancient Near East that support the view of doing good deeds. For example, the Egyptian wisdom book *The Instruction of Onchsheshonqy* has the following counsel, 'Do a good deed and throw it in the water; when it dries up you will find it.'[5] The basic meaning of this view is that if one is generous in giving to many others (*'to seven, or even to eight'*),[6] then that generosity will come back to the person when hard times come into their life.[7] However, the idea of releasing bread upon the water does not suggest almsgiving and charitable giving is not in keeping with Qohelet's general outlook.[8]

Another prominent view of 11:1-2 is that these verses are encouraging people to take risks in business ventures. In this view the word *'bread'* refers to grain (Isa. 28:28) or merchandise (Prov. 31:14), *'the waters'* refers to the sea (as in Isa. 18:2), and the verb *'find'* can mean 'to acquire wealth' (Hosea 12:8; Job 31:25).[9] Thus 11:1 is encouraging taking risks that come from foreign trade because those risks will be worth the effort. 11:2 then encourages the distribution of

---

5. Fox, *Rereading Ecclesiastes*, 312. This Egyptian instruction comes from around the fourth or fifth century B.C., which some would argue makes it a contemporary of Qohelet (see the Introduction for a discussion of the date of Ecclesiastes). Fox also quotes from a few other Egyptian works that have a similar theme but are not as close in wording as Onchsheshonqy is to Ecclesiastes 11:1. There is also an Arabic proverb that is very similar to Ecclesiastes 11:1, but it is likely that this proverb is influenced by the view that Ecclesiastes 11:1 refers to charity (Gordis, *Koheleth*, 320).

6. Many commentators point out that this numerical saying refers to a large though indefinite number (Longman, *Ecclesiastes*, 256; Seow, *Ecclesiastes*, 335, among many others).

7. Commentators who take this view include Ginsburg, Fox, Seow, and Krüger.

8. Murphy (*Ecclesiastes*, 106) argues the first and Gordis (*Ecclesiastes*, 320) argues the second.

9. Whybray (*Ecclesiastes*, 159) points out the possibility that the verb *'find'* can mean 'to acquire wealth.'

risk so that if a tragedy strikes everything will not be lost.[10] Although the terms 'bread,' 'waters,' and the verb 'find' can have the meanings attributed to them in this view, they are not the regular meanings of these terms; plus, the idea of taking risks in business ventures is not the obvious meaning of these verses. Also, if these verses are talking about business ventures, one would expect that an investment would produce more in return than just acquiring what was sent out, as 11:1 implies. In other words, a profit is expected for a business venture to be successful.[11]

Another approach understands the idea of releasing *'bread upon the surface of the waters'* to be referring to a senseless act, because in water bread merely dissolves, but then unexpectedly this senseless act results in a successful result. The uncertainty of the future leaves open the possibility that even senseless acts might turn out well. Murphy argues that this view fits Qohelet's mentality.[12] In this view the motivational clauses of 11:1-2 introduced by *kî* must be understood in an adversative sense ('yet,' 'but,' or 'however'), which makes for an awkward translation.

It is clear that 11:1-6 are encouraging people to be active in light of an uncertain future. No matter how 11:1-2 is understood, the activities in which Qohelet exhorts people to engage should be understood in a broad sense in light of 11:6. The question is, what activity is in view in 11:1-2? There are several key terms in Ecclesiastes that occur in 11:1-2. The terms *'bread'* (11:1) and *'portion'* (11:2) both occur in the calls to enjoyment. The word 'bread' (*leḥem*) is found in the most recent and most urgent call to enjoyment (9:7) and is implied in the other calls to enjoyment which encourage eating and drinking (2:24; 3:13; 5:18 [Heb. 5:17]; 8:15). The word 'portion' (*ḥēleq*) occurs in 3:22; 5:18 [Heb. 5:17]; and 9:9. Qohelet's point has been that because there is no profit to labor (2:11), one should at least enjoy the limited benefit that comes from labor,

---

10. Commentators who take this view include Delitzsch, Gordis, Longman, and Bartholomew.

11. Seow, *Ecclesiastes*, 335.

12. Murphy, *Ecclesiastes*, 106.

which is one's portion (2:10), consisting of eating, drinking, and enjoying other benefits in life. The use of these terms in 11:1-2 connects these verses to the calls to enjoyment. What is different in 11:1-2 is that Qohelet is not just encouraging a person to enjoy the limited benefits of labor (the portion), but he is encouraging people to use the limited benefits of labor in a way that might bring further benefit to themselves. If a person only enjoys the portion from labor, the danger is that a disaster may strike and that portion could be lost. However, by using the portion in a certain way, one can prepare to face the uncertainty of future disaster.

Qohelet is trying to encourage certain activities that may benefit a person. The phrase in 11:2, *'Give a portion,'* helps explain the parallel phrase in 11:1, *'Release your bread upon the surface of the waters.'* Also, the parallels between releasing bread upon the water and throwing a good deed on the water in *The Instruction of Onchsheshonqy* supports the view that Qohelet is encouraging using the limited benefits from labor on behalf of others. However, the point is not charitable giving itself, but what benefit giving to others will bring to a person. In other words, the emphasis should not be that Qohelet is encouraging charitable giving *per se*, but that Qohelet is encouraging giving to others because of the benefit one might receive from such activity. One gives to others because one is preparing for an uncertain future where disaster may strike. If disaster does strike, one's giving to others may then come back to a person so that the disaster does not destroy one's life. Thus if one releases bread upon the surface of the waters, it is likely that *'in many days you may find it.'* The act of releasing results in the possibility of receiving again whatever was released. The reason one would give to seven or to eight is *'for you do not know what disaster may occur on the earth.'* The reason for giving to others is that the future is uncertain. Giving to others attempts to ensure that if a disaster does strike, a person may receive help from others.

The next three verses describe certain characteristics of life which make it difficult for people to take action. Certain things in life are inevitable. So *'if the clouds are full of rain they will empty themselves on the earth'* (11:3). Human beings are not able to stop a coming storm because it is beyond the control and power of human beings. There are also certain events that happen randomly.[13] Thus, *'if a tree falls to the south or to the north, in the place where the tree falls there it will lie'* (v. 3). The point is not that a tree cannot be moved after it falls, but that one cannot decide ahead of time which way the tree will fall. The direction a tree falls is totally random and cannot be determined before the tree actually falls. Certain events are inevitable and certain events are random and one cannot control either type of event. These types of events could cause a person to be cautious in taking action. This is the point of 11:4, which states, *'One who observes the wind will not sow and one who regards the clouds will not reap.'* Clouds and wind are unpredictable, which makes taking action difficult because a person cannot be sure what is going to happen.[14] If a person waits for the best time to act he may hesitate and not act at all. Thus the right time to act always remains uncertain from the human standpoint. One must act even when there is uncertainty.[15] In 11:5 Qohelet emphasizes human ignorance not only in regard to the way the world works, but also in regard to the work of God. There is much discussion concerning what is compared to the work of God, but ultimately the meaning of the verse is not affected whichever view one takes. The debate hinges on the meaning of *rûaḥ*, the legitimacy of the preposition *kaph* and its role, and the meaning of *'eṣem* ('bone'). Many understand *rûaḥ* to mean life-breath or spirit, emend the *kaph* ('as') to a *bet* ('in'), and understand *'eṣem* to refer to the embryo in the womb.[16]

---

13. Whybray (*Ecclesiastes*, 159) comments that the first part of 11:3 emphasizes inevitability and the second part emphasizes randomness, which demonstrate the ignorance and helplessness of human beings.

14. Seow, *Ecclesiastes*, 344.

15. Murphy, *Ecclesiastes*, 109. With the mention of the work of God in 11:5 these verses are a subtle critique of the poem on time, which states that there is a time for every activity, but only God really knows the appropriate times. Thus the view of Ogden and Zogbo (*Handbook on Ecclesiastes*, 398) that if a person watches the weather carefully they can be successful is untenable.

16. Commentators who take this view include Murphy, Seow, Gordis, Fox, and Bartholomew.

The point is that just as human beings do not know how the life-breath enlivens an embryo in the womb, so human beings do not understand the work of God. Others see two comparisons with the work of God at the beginning of 11:5. The *kaph* is understood to be a comparison, the word *rûaḥ* refers to the wind as it does in the previous verse, and *'eṣem* refers to the developing embryo in the womb.[17] There is a lack of human knowledge concerning *'the way of the wind'* and concerning *'how the bones are formed in the womb of the mother with child.'* The course that the wind takes is unpredictable, and thus unknowable, and how an embryo forms is also beyond the realm of human knowledge. These two things are then compared with the lack of knowledge humans have concerning the work of God. The way that God works in the world is just as beyond human understanding and comprehension as the blowing of the wind and the formation of the embryo. Uncertainty concerning the way God governs the world makes it difficult for human beings to make good, timely decisions, a point already made in Ecclesiastes 3:9-15; 7:13; and 8:17.

Qohelet's advice in 11:6 is similar to his advice in 11:1-2. The uncertainty of the future does not mean that one should be cautious in one's approach to life. Certain things may be beyond human control because they are inevitable or random (11:3). Certain things may be beyond human knowledge (11:5). Human beings may not be able to comprehend the way that God works in the world (11:5). Disaster could strike anyone at any time (11:2b). The uncertainty of the future could cause a person to be overly cautious and observant trying to find the right time to act (11:4); however, such an approach can be crippling if a person never takes action. Qohelet's advice in 11:6 is to take action even if the future is uncertain. There is a sense that a person should always be ready to take action both *'in the morning'* and *'at evening.'* The action that Qohelet advises is to *'sow your seed'* and *'do not rest your hand.'*

---

17. This view follows the Masoretic text more closely and is supported by the Septuagint and the Vulgate. Commentators who take this view include Longman, Delitzsch, Ginsburg, Barton, and Krüger.

Although *'sow your seed'* refers specifically to agricultural activity, Qohelet's advice would apply to any kind of work or activity.[18] The reason a person should take action in the morning and at evening is because no one is certain which activity will be successful. The point seems to be that a person should be engaged in several activities because there is no way to know which activity will prosper. If a person is involved in only one activity and it fails, then that person is left with nothing; however, if a person is involved in many activities, the failure of one activity is not a disaster because there are other activities that might succeed. This advice fits in with the basic thrust of 11:1-6 that even though the future is uncertain, a person should not be afraid to act and even should be willing to act in a variety of situations.

Homiletical Implications

The phrase 'the paralysis of analysis' describes the problem that Qohelet faces in 11:1-6. The way life works 'under the sun' could cause someone to be timid and afraid to take action. Qohelet's observation about life has led him to the conclusion that life does not work well. A person's labor does not produce a profit (2:11). The righteous suffer and the wicked prosper (3:16; 8:11-14). The strong do not win the battle and the swift do not win the race because time and chance happen to them all (9:11-12). Wisdom is helpful but it can be easily destroyed by one offender. Something small can do such great damage (9:18). Even in 11:1-6 Qohelet sets forth the problems of life that make the future uncertain. Life is beyond human control because certain events are inevitable and certain events are random. Certain things are beyond human knowledge and disaster can strike a person at any time. Plus, the way God governs the world is incomprehensible. The inability to figure out the way life works, including the work of God in the world, could lead to an attitude that withdraws from such a confusing world. Why not just sit back and do nothing? Even Qohelet, in his 'under the sun' perspective, argues that a

---

18. Longman, *Ecclesiastes*, 258; Whybray, *Ecclesiastes*, 160; and Crenshaw, *Ecclesiastes*, 181.

person should take action and make use of every opportunity that comes along. The reason such action is necessary is that otherwise a person will miss out on the little that life has to offer (the portion). The exhortation to give to others (11:1-2) is based on the fact that hard times will probably come to your life and by giving to others you are trying to ensure that others will then help you. A similar principle may be found in Jesus' parable of the dishonest manager in Luke 16:1-9, although Jesus applies it in a much broader way to include 'eternal dwellings' (Luke 16:9). The exhortation to be active in a variety of activities (11:6) is based on the fact that if one activity fails you will not be left without anything. Qohelet is still operating from an 'under the sun' perspective because if one does not take these actions one could miss out on the little that life does offer. An 'above the sun' perspective would agree that a person should avoid the paralysis of analysis and take action even though the future is uncertain. Such action has consequences not just for this life but for the next life. Plus, there is much in this world that human beings cannot understand, including how God governs the world. However, our motivation for acting is different. We give to others not just so that we may be helped in a time of trouble, but because we have been blessed by God and to be gracious to others honors him. We try to make use of every opportunity, not just to ensure that some of the activities will be successful so that we are not left without anything, but as a way to bring glory to Jesus Christ. And even though there are many things about life that we do not understand and there are many things that make the future uncertain, we have confidence to take action because we know that God holds the future in His hands.

Enjoy life before the dark days come (Eccles. 11:7–12:8)

11:7 *Light[19] is sweet and it is good for the eyes to see the sun.*

---

19. 11:7 begins with the conjunction *waw*, which Longman (*Ecclesiastes*, 258) and Bartholomew (*Ecclesiastes*, 339) translate in an emphatic sense ('truly'), but others leave it untranslated (Murphy, Seow, Fox). Murphy (*Ecclesiastes*, 112) points out that a *waw* ('and') does not need to indicate the

11:8   Indeed, if a person lives many years let him enjoy all of them, but let him remember the days of darkness because they will be many. All that is coming is senseless.

11:9   Enjoy life, young man,[20] while[21] you are young and let your heart cheer you in the days of your youth. Walk in the ways of your heart and in the sight of your eyes but know that concerning all these things God may bring you into judgment.

11:10 Remove grief from your heart and banish misery from your body, for youth and vitality[22] are fleeting.

12:1   Remember your Creator in the days of your youth before the days of misfortune come and the years which you say, 'I have no pleasure in them';

12:2   before the sun and the light and the moon and the stars become dark and the dark clouds return after the rain;

12:3   on the day when the keepers of the house tremble and the strong men are bent over and the grinders cease because they are few and those who look through the windows grow dark;

12:4   the doors in the street are closed when the sound of the mill decreases, but the sound of the birds rise and the daughters of song are brought low;

12:5   they are also afraid of heights and terrors on the way; the almond tree blossoms, the grasshopper is laden, and the

---

continuation of the preceding section but can introduce a new section (3:16). Seow (*Ecclesiastes*, 347) calls it a disjunctive *waw*.

20. The vocative can be expressed without the article when reference is to persons not present or to persons who are more or less imaginary (Waltke and O'Connor, *Biblical Hebrew Syntax*, 427). Of course, Qohelet's use of the article is inconsistent throughout the book.

21. The preposition *bet* does not introduce the object of '*enjoy life*' but is temporal (Gordis, *Koheleth*, 325 and Longman, *Ecclesiastes*, 259, n. 27), which is supported by the parallel phrase '*in* (*bet*) *the days of your youth*' (Delitzsch, 'Ecclesiastes,' 6:400).

22. The word '*vitality*' (*saḥărût*) is only used here in the Hebrew Bible. The root *šḥr* means 'black' (Longman, *Ecclesiastes*, 259) and some have taken it to refer to the 'black hair' of youth in contrast to the white hair of the elderly (Leupold, *Ecclesiastes*, 272; Murphy, *Ecclesiastes*, 112). This root is also associated with the dawn (1 Sam. 9:26) and so could refer to the early period of a person's life. Seow (*Ecclesiastes*, 346) translates it as 'the dawn of life,' Fox (*Rereading Ecclesiastes*, 316) as 'juvenescence,' and Longman (*Ecclesiastes*, 259) as 'vitality,' which is followed here.

> caperberry bursts forth, but a human being goes to his eternal home and the mourners go about the streets;

12:6 before the silver cord is snapped,[23] and the golden bowl is smashed, and the pitcher is shattered, and the wheel at the well is broken,

12:7 and the dust returns to the earth as it was and the spirit returns to God who gave it.

12:8 'Utterly senseless!' says Qohelet, 'Everything is senseless.'

There is a fairly broad consensus among commentators that 11:9–12:7 is a distinct unit. The questions center on 11:7-8 and whether they are the conclusion to 11:1-6[24] or whether they are an independent unit.[25] It is clear that 11:7-8 have strong vocabulary and thematic ties with the section that follows. Two key verbs are introduced in 11:8, 'enjoy' and 'remember,' which are then used as exhortations (imperatives) in the following two sections.[26] The verb 'enjoy' sets the tone for 11:9-10 and the verb 'remember' sets the tone for 12:1-7. Also, themes of light and darkness (11:7-8 and 12:2), as well as expressions of time (11:7-8 and 12:1), connect 11:7-8 with 11:9–12:7.[27] The preceding passage, 11:1-6, has only a general connection to 11:7–12:7. The former passage encourages people to take action even though the future is uncertain, whereas the latter section encourages young people to make

---

23. This verb is difficult because neither the Ketiv (what is written) nor the Qere (what is read) makes a lot of sense. The Ketiv is Qal imperfect of *rāḥaq* which means 'to be distant.' The Qere is nifal imperfect of *rātaq*, which means 'bound' or 'joined.' Most commentators understand the verb to be describing destruction of some kind in parallel with the other verbs in 12:6. Seow (*Ecclesiastes*, 365) finds a connection with the Aramaic verb *rtq*, which means 'to break or crush.' Murphy (*Ecclesiastes*, 113) suggests the verb *ntq* ('torn'), which is followed by the Septuagint and the Syriac (Krüger, *Qoheleth*, 191) and is also used in Ecclesiastes 4:12.

24. Ginsburg (*Coheleth*, 454) uses the word conclusion for 11:8 and Lohfink (*Qoheleth*, 134) connects 11:7-8 with 11:1-6.

25. Whybray (*Ecclesiastes*, 161) argues that 11:7-8 is an independent unit because these verses are stylistically different and are not addressed to the youth.

26. Seow, *Ecclesiastes*, 368.

27. Murphy, *Ecclesiastes*, 116.

use of every opportunity during the time of youth because the future is full of darkness. Both sections deal with living in the present in light of a difficult future. Although 11:7–12:7 starts with light, the darkness slowly begins to dominate and puts a damper on the whole section.

In 11:7-8 Qohelet sets the stage for the rest of this unit, which is the final section of the first-person discourse (11:7–12:7).[28] He begins with a positive statement that stresses the value of being alive. The statement *'light is sweet'* expresses delight in life. The benefit of light hardly needs any comment, but Qohelet calls it *'sweet,'* a term used in Judges 14:14 to refer to honey, which is not only delightful but also very beneficial (see also Eccles. 5:12). Qohelet also states that *'it is good for the eyes to see the sun.'* This statement asserts that it is good to be alive. Life has its good moments, and it is these good moments that Qohelet is going to encourage people to enjoy as long as they can, because something else is on the horizon of life which will not be as pleasant or as delightful. The dark horizon comes into view in 11:8, but the beginning of 11:8 also encourages people to enjoy life. The verse begins with an emphatic *kî*, translated *'indeed,'* which is followed by the conditional clause, *'if a person lives many years.'*[29] Qohelet does not focus on the fact that a long life is a blessing from God, but he emphasizes how a person should respond to a long life with the exhortation *'let him enjoy all of them.'* The emphasis is on the enjoyment of life throughout a person's many years of living. However, a somber note is struck in the second part of 11:8, introduced by a *waw* of contrast, translated *'but.'* A person who lives many years must enjoy those years of life, *'but let him remember*[30] *the days of darkness because they will be*

---

28. For the role of Eccles. 12:8 see the discussion at the end of this section.

29. 11:8 begins with *kî 'im*, which could be understood in a concessive sense with the meaning 'even though,' but here it is best to take the two words separately. Bartholomew (*Ecclesiastes*, 339) understands *kî* to be a weakened asseverative and leaves it untranslated. It is better to understand the word *kî* to connect this verse to the preceding (Seow, *Ecclesiastes*, 346) and to translate it here as emphatic, *'indeed.'*

30. The first verb is commonly understood as a jussive (*'let him enjoy'*). Longman (*Ecclesiastes*, 260) argues that the second verb *'remember'* should

many.'³¹ The enjoyment of life comes with the full recognition that there will also be many *'days of darkness.'* No doubt these days of darkness include days of misery and gloom on this earth. Thus the future looks very dark, which is expressed in the statement, *'All that is coming is senseless.'* Here the word *hebel* (*'senseless'*) shows up again in Qohelet's thought. One must enjoy life with the recognition that there are meaningless days of darkness that one will experience. Thus the future looks bleak because what is coming in the future has the character of *hebel*. This certainly focuses on events in this life, and as will become clear in the next section, old age and death particularly become prominent. The phrase *'All that is coming'* could also include life after death, because in Qohelet's 'under the sun' view there is no activity after death (9:10). Thus death itself takes on the character of *hebel*.³² The future is extremely dark, which makes it all the more important that a person enjoy the years of life while the opportunity to enjoy them is a possibility.

In 11:8 Qohelet introduces two key verbs that are used as exhortations in the following sections. The verb 'enjoy' (*śāmaḥ*) becomes the exhortation in 11:9-10 and the verb 'remember' (*zākar*) becomes the exhortation in 12:1-7. Instead of a general exhortation to everyone as in 11:8, in 11:9 Qohelet exhorts a *'young man'* to *'enjoy life ... while you are young and*

---

not be taken as a jussive because then Qohelet would be giving contradictory advice to enjoy life and to remember that one is going to die. However, in light of the fact that both verbs are used later in this section as imperatives, the two verbs in 11:8 should be understood as jussives (Seow, *Ecclesiastes*, 346). It is not necessarily contradictory to enjoy something while at the same time knowing that such enjoyment may come to an end in the future.

31. It is possible to translate the *kî* as 'that' (Murphy, Seow) instead of causal (Longman). The causal sense gives the reason why the days of darkness should be remembered. Such days are not just a small part of life, but they will dominate life, which becomes clearer in the next few verses.

32. Seow (*Ecclesiastes*, 260) denies that Qohelet has death in view in 11:8. He also understands *'all that is coming'* to refer to human beings or generations that come into existence based on the use of this phrase in 5:16-17 and 6:4. However, Gordis (*Koheleth*, 325) points out that *'darkness'* refers primarily to death as this section unfolds and Towner (*Ecclesiastes*, 5:353) includes Sheol's oblivion as a part of the darkness.

let your heart cheer you in the days of your youth.' It is clear that the verb *śāmaḥ* in the imperative means '*enjoy life*' rather than 'rejoice.'[33] The parallel phrase to 'enjoy life' is '*let your heart cheer you.*' This is a difficult phrase because the heart is personified and it is represented as bringing happiness (*ṭôḇ* literally means 'good') to a person. Its meaning can be seen in the next phrase, '*walk in the ways of your heart and in the sight of your eyes.*' The '*heart*' and the '*eyes*' are the organs of desire.[34] Simply put, Qohelet encourages a young person to pursue a path that their heart desires and to follow what they can see with their eyes in their pursuit of the enjoyment of life. This advice seems problematic because it seems to contradict Numbers 15:39 and to go against the advice to young people in the book of Proverbs. It has produced many explanations to try to ensure that the advice falls within orthodox boundaries. Some versions of the Greek add 'blamelessly' to the phrase 'walk in the ways of your heart.'[35] Hengstenberg comments that Numbers 15 speaks concerning things which are forbidden and that Qohelet recommends the enjoyment of things that are permitted.[36] Some limit the enjoyment in this verse to the things that Qohelet has already recommended in the calls to enjoyment.[37] Many point to the last clause of 11:9 as that which keeps this advice within the realm of what is permitted, because there Qohelet mentions the judgment of God.[38]

It makes sense, on the one hand, that Qohelet is not advocating that young people pursue hedonism, for that has never been his advice up to this point. The calls to enjoyment are limited benefits from labor because there is no profit to labor (2:10-11)

---

33. The problem with the translation 'rejoice' is that it is too easy to read religious connotations into the word which are not part of Qohelet's 'under the sun' perspective. For example, Ogden and Zogbo (*Handbook on Ecclesiastes*, 411–412) define this joy as not mere entertainment but a joy that satisfies the intellect as well as other aspects of life.

34. Longman, *Ecclesiastes*, 261.

35. Longman (*Ecclesiastes*, 261) cites the Greek codex Vaticanus.

36. Hengstenberg, *Ecclesiastes*, 242; Ginsburg, *Coheleth*, 455.

37. Murphy, *Ecclesiastes*, 117.

38. Eaton, *Ecclesiastes*, 145; Garrett, *Ecclesiastes*, 340; Ginsburg, *Coheleth*, 454.

and God does approve of the enjoyment of those benefits (9:7). However, on the other hand, Qohelet does leave himself open to pushing his advice beyond permissible limits because of the way he states his exhortation. He has already questioned the clear distinction of the two ways (7:15-18) and there is no mention in the first-person discourse of the commandments of God. Thus his advice is not as clear as the instruction in other parts of Scripture. In Numbers 15:39 the commandments of God are set over against following after one's own heart and eyes, a path which is identified with spiritual whoredom. Thus there is a clear admonition in Numbers *not* to follow one's heart and eyes.[39] In the book of Proverbs the two ways are so clearly laid out that it is obvious that the path a wise person follows is the way of wisdom. In fact, the period of youth is a time of decision where guidance is needed because youth are open to being led astray down the path of foolishness (Prov. 1:8-19). Thus the son is exhorted to give his heart to the wisdom of the parents and to 'let your eyes' observe the ways of wisdom (Prov. 23:26). But wisdom in Qohelet has only possessed a relative advantage and is vulnerable to the effects of one offender (9:18). It is not clear in Qohelet's advice where the boundaries lie.

But what about the last clause in 11:9? Does not the mention of God's judgment keep things in proper perspective? Some argue that the judgment of 11:9 is a judgment that will come to a person if they do not enjoy the pleasures of life. Gordis understands the conjunction *waw* on the verb '*know*' as consecutive ('and') instead of adversative ('*but*'). Qohelet encourages young people to 'rejoice ... be happy ... walk ... and know.' What is the young person to know? God will bring them to account if they do not enjoy life to its full capacity.[40]

---

39. Seow (*Ecclesiastes*, 349–350) compares the phrase '*walk in the ways of your heart*' in 11:9 with a similar Egyptian saying that means 'enjoy.' He does not believe that it has anything to do with how one makes ethical decisions, so that a comparison with Num. 15:39 is not warranted. However, in light of Qohelet's epistemology based on experience and observation, and the fact that there is no mention of the law in the first-person discourse, a comparison with Num. 15:39 is not out of the question.

40. Gordis, *Koheleth*, 326. Towner ('Ecclesiastes,' 5:353) comments that God holds people responsible to follow the inclinations of their heart.

The admonition is still a warning, but it is not a warning against the perils of pleasure but a warning against not pursuing the enjoyment of life. However, an adversative *waw*, which would represent a stronger warning, fits the context better. A pattern is established in 11:7-8 of encouraging the enjoyment of life (11:7) followed by warnings concerning the future.[41] This pattern is continued in the following verses with the exhortations in 11:9a; 11:10a; and 12:1a followed by the warnings about the future in 11:9b; 11:10b; and 12:1b-7.

Others argue that the judgment in 11:9 refers to the future event of the final judgment, which would keep the exhortation to follow heart and sight within proper boundaries.[42] However, there are good reasons to argue that the judgment in 11:9 is not the final judgment. The other warnings in this passage refer to events that will happen in this life. The coming days of darkness and misfortune refer to difficulties that occur in this life (11:8), and then to old age and death (12:1-7). Here is where a consistent application of the 'under the sun' perspective and taking seriously what Qohelet says in 9:10 is important. Nowhere in the first-person discourse does Qohelet appeal to a final judgment as a solution to the problem of all the instances of injustice he has observed on this earth. His thinking is continually limited to this earthly horizon. The judgment in view is the judgment that might befall a person in this life (see the results related to living overly righteous or overly wicked in 7:15-18). However, one can never be certain whether righteousness will be rewarded and wickedness will receive the negative consequences it deserves, so Qohelet's warning is not that God *will* bring a person to judgment, but that '*God may bring you to judgment*.' No one can really be sure how God governs the world so Qohelet modifies his encouragement of pursuing the heart's desire by holding out the possibility of divine retribution in this life.

What was stated positively in 11:9, '*enjoy life*,' is stated negatively in 11:10, with a negative evaluation of the time

---

41. Longman, *Ecclesiastes*, 260.
42. Leupold, *Ecclesiastes*, 271; Eaton, *Ecclesiastes*, 145.

of youth added at the end of the verse. For one to enjoy life one must also *'remove grief from your heart and banish misery from your body.'* Here Qohelet focuses on both the inner and physical life of a person. To enjoy life the inner life, or *'heart,'* needs to be free from *'grief.'* This word (*kaʿas*) was used earlier in the book (1:18) with the sense of anger produced by distress, but here the general idea of grief seems to fit better (Pss. 6:7; 31:9; Eccles. 7:3). The word *'misery'* is the word *rāʿāh*, which can mean 'evil,' but here 'misery' fits well. Qohelet advises a young person to be proactive to *'remove'* anything that will cause a negative disturbance to their inner life and to *'banish'* anything that will cause physical pain. These things will hinder a young person from the enjoyment of life. The reason a young person needs to be proactive in removing negative things so that life can be enjoyed is given at the end of 11:10: *'for youth and vitality are fleeting.'* A young person must be sure to enjoy the period of youth because it will not last very long. The opportunity for enjoyment is limited. The word *'fleeting'* is the word *hebel*, and this is one place where the meaning is clearly to be understood on the level of time, because it refers to a period of life. However, in light of the dark days that are coming, including death which ends everything, the meaning of 'senseless' is not that far removed from the word, especially because that has been the major meaning of the word in the book. The fleeting time of youth makes the enjoyment of life to be urgent.[43]

The final exhortation of the first-person discourse is given in 12:1 by the imperative *'remember.'* Beyond that simple imperative are many questions which surround 12:1-7. One major question is who or what is to be remembered. The traditional view is that a person is to *'remember your Creator in the days of your youth.'* Some have argued that mentioning God as Creator at this point in the book does not fit the context.[44] Plus, the word for Creator is in the plural (*bôrĕʾeykā*), which has led to other suggestions for this word. One possibility is the word 'cistern' (*bĕʾērĕkā*), which in Proverbs 5:15 is a

---

43. Fox, *Rereading Ecclesiastes*, 319.
44. Crenshaw, *Ecclesiastes*, 184.

reference to one's wife. In this view 12:1 would be exhorting the young man to remember his wife before dark and difficult days come, which is similar to the exhortation in 9:7.[45] Others suggest that the word is 'pit' (*bôrĕkā*), which is a reference to death and fits the context of 12:1-7 that emphasizes death. During the period of youth one must remember that death is coming.[46] There is no need, however, for these changes because one can make sense of both the form and the reference to Creator at this point in the book. The plural form of Creator can be explained as a plural of majesty or as a *lamed aleph* verb vocalized as a *lamed he* verb. It is interesting that God is referred to as Maker by the plural participle of the verb 'to make' (*'āsāh*) in Job 35:10 and Isaiah 54:5, so it is not unusual for plural forms to be used in reference to God. The reason why Qohelet appeals to God as Creator in 12:1 will be examined in the explanation of the passage below.

The other major issue in 12:1-7 relates to what Qohelet is describing and how his description should be understood. Everyone agrees that 12:6-7 describe death, but there is no agreement on how 12:2-5 should be understood. Some argue that Qohelet is describing the onset of old age before death, but others think the emphasis is on death itself. There are also major discussions on how Qohelet describes old age or death in these verses. The major views will be briefly set forth here. Some argue for an allegorical approach where the descriptions are painting a picture of the debilitations that come to a person in old age. For example, when 12:3 mentions that the grinders cease because they are few, it is a reference to the trouble old people have in chewing their food because their teeth are few. The next phrase in the verse that speaks of the darkening of those who look through the window is a reference to the dimming of the eyesight in old age. The blossoming of the almond tree (12:5) is a reference to the white hair of older people. Although there are a few who argue for a

---

45. Crenshaw, *Ecclesiastes*, 185.

46. This view is mentioned by Murphy (*Ecclesiastes*, 111), but not accepted by him. Seow (*Ecclesiastes*, 375) argues that there is a word play going on in 12:1 and that it is possible that all three meanings are in view (see also Gordis, *Koheleth*, 331), but this seems unlikely.

full allegorical approach,[47] most recognize that many phrases do not fit well into the allegorical view. For example, being afraid of heights and terrors on the way in 12:5 seems to be a literal description, not an allegorical description.[48] Also, there is no agreement on what the allegorical meaning should be on many of the descriptions (see the discussion below). The problem with allegory is that the interpretation easily becomes arbitrary.

Although only a few argue for a full allegory, several commentators argue for a partial allegory so that some of the phrases in 12:1-7 are allegorical descriptions of old age. Instead of looking for a unifying metaphor that would explain the whole passage, Whybray argues that each image must be looked at separately to try to ascertain its meaning. He does believe that the passage is about old age and that most of the descriptions are to be understood in an allegorical way.[49] Even among some who interpret 12:1-7 in a way other than allegory, there is a tendency to accept the legitimacy of taking some of the phrases as allegorical; for example, by using the metaphor of a declining house facing a devastating storm Qohelet is able to set forth the negative effects of old age in an allegorical way.[50] The allegorical view continues to have adherents because it is difficult to make one metaphor explain the whole poem and because some of the phrases lend themselves very readily to an allegorical description. Although it is possible for a text to mix figurative and literal elements,[51] the allegorical approach should be the last resort after other approaches have failed. There is nothing in the text itself to indicate that this passage should be taken in an allegorical way except our propensity to see certain connections between phrases in the poem and old age.

---

47. Those who argue for a full allegory include the Targums, the Midrash, Delitzsch, and Garrett.

48. Murphy, *Ecclesiastes*, 119.

49. Whybray, *Ecclesiastes*, 163–164.

50. Longman, *Ecclesiastes*, 270.

51. Fox ('Aging and Death in Qohelet 12,' *JSOT* 42 [1988]: 69) quotes a portion of a Sumerian poem that mixes literal and metaphorical elements.

Other approaches seek to find a unifying metaphor that can be used to explain this passage, especially 12:3-5. Most approaches have difficulty making one unifying metaphor explain all the verses. The first thing that comes to mind in reading 12:2 is some kind of storm. Some have used the picture of an approaching storm to describe the fear, gloom, and desolation which grips the members of the household when one from among them is about to die or has just died. The object is to portray the hour of death. In this view 12:3-4a describes the fear of the household and the closing up of the activities of the house in light of the approaching storm. In 12:4b the song of the bird is hardly heard and the merrymakers are terrorized into silence. 12:5 describes the fear of the heavens from which the storm rages and the response of people who are afraid to go outside. In the wake of the storm the earth lies battered, with the almond tree thrust aside, the caper-shrub broken, and even the small grasshopper feels the power of the storm.[52]

John Sawyer argues that Qohelet uses the figure of the collapse of a house in 12:3-5 to describe the failure of human achievement. In wisdom literature human achievement and success are presented in terms of domestic security and contentment. Failure is also represented in terms of the collapse of a house (Prov. 9; 14:1; Ps. 127), with the ruin and disintegration of family and property. The focus of the poem is not a description of old age, because old age is predictable. Instead, the focus is the failure of human effort, which is not predictable because misfortune and death can occur at any time. The parable of the house consists of two parts. In 12:3-4a the subject is humanity and in 12:4b-5b the subject is the sights and sounds of nature, which is unmoved by the death of a human being. The first part (12:3-4a) describes man's downfall by depicting the reactions of four groups connected to the house. These groups should be taken literally as the male and female servants of the house. Their lack of activity

---

[52]. Michael Leahy, 'The Meaning of Ecclesiastes 12:1-5,' in Roy B. Zuck (ed.), *Reflecting with Solomon* (Grand Rapids: Baker Book House, 1994), 378 (also see Ginsburg, *Coheleth*, 457–458). The article by Leahy was originally published in *ITQ* 19 (1952): 297–300.

pictures the shutting down of the house, which is then contrasted with the continuing sounds of nature in 12:4b-5b. The birds can be heard singing as they look down from the sky on the fading human activity, the almond trees blossom, the locusts eat their fill, and the caper-berries grow. Nature thrives even though human beings die. This is a picture of the failure of human effort, which is as unpredictable as death itself.[53]

Fox argues for several levels of meaning in 12:1-7. The literal meaning takes its cue from the mourners and the description of death in 12:5. The events described in 12:3-5 take place when a person dies. All the events in these verses occur at the same time in reference to the funeral and thus do not describe the slow aging process of death. The mood of the village is fearful and dark because death has taken place. Doors are shut and the normal activities of life cease. The women mourn and people are afraid. In contrast to the human reaction, nature itself thrives, but without cheer. Rather, nature mocks the finality of our end. Fox also argues that there is a symbolic meaning to these verses which is beyond the literal meaning. This symbolic meaning is based on the fact that this is not a description of a normal funeral. The communal grief that is described is extreme and pervasive and suggests a disaster of cosmic proportions. Connections can be made between 12:1-7 and the way the prophets describe the crisis of coming cosmic events. The poem describes universal death and darkness in 12:2, much like Ezekiel 32:7-8; Joel 2:2; and Isaiah 13:9-10. The emotional reaction of the people in 12:3 seems to go beyond normal grief and reflects the quaking and writhing in eschatological scenes like Isaiah 13:7 and 21:3. Also, the statement that the grinders cease because they are few may call to mind the inactivity that follows depopulation (Isa. 13:12; Jer. 25:10).[54] The fear and terror of 12:5 is a reference to the emotions of those involved in the funeral procession. Nature is reborn in spring, but a

---

53. John F. A. Sawyer, 'The Ruined House in Ecclesiastes 12: A Reconstruction of the Original Parable,' *JBL* 94 (1976): 519–531.

54. Fox, 'Aging and Death,' 55–67.

human being is helpless in the face of death.⁵⁵ Fox argues that this eschatological symbolism is restrained because the focus is on individual death and not on the day of judgment or the world's end.⁵⁶ In fact, the real focus of the mourning is for the 'you' of 12:1. It is your fate they are mourning. Fox also argues that there is a legitimate allegorical level of meaning for 12:1-7. Certain phrases, especially the women looking through the window and the grinders ceasing their work, lend themselves naturally to an allegorical view. However, he also says that the allegorical approach is generally inadequate.⁵⁷

Seow argues that 12:1-7 is not about old age but that it is about death and that it portrays the permanent end of human life and existence entirely in eschatological terms. Cosmic disaster is described in 12:2 with the picture of all-encompassing darkness. The people in 12:3 are described with verbs that always describe fear or excitement and never physical weakness. The keepers of the house are themselves too terrified to be vigilant and the strong men crouch in fear. Women who grind at the mill stop because suddenly some of their number have disappeared, which reminds one of Matthew 24:40-41. Those who look through the windows become dim because their hopes are dashed, like Sisera's mother who looked out the window for her son to return (Judg. 5:28). In 12:4 normal life routines are interrupted and there is an increase of the sound of unsavory birds because the population has decreased (Rev. 18:2). The birds come down low because they see the devastation of the land from on high (12:5a). Nature itself languishes as the almond tree is diseased and revolting to behold, the locust tree droops because it is dead, and the caper plant is defoliated.⁵⁸ Seow argues that Qohelet is not speaking about the woes of old age or the death of the individual *per se*, but he is painting a picture of cosmic and universal destruction.⁵⁹

---

55. Fox, *Rereading Ecclesiastes*, 327–328.
56. Fox, *Rereading Ecclesiastes*, 76.
57. Fox, 'Aging and Death,' 55, 67–71.
58. C. L. Seow, 'Qohelet's Eschatological Poem,' *JBL* 118 (1999): 209–234.
59. Seow, *Ecclesiastes*, 353.

This general overview of the various approaches does not deal with the details of the passage, which are very important for how one understands it. The way certain verbs are understood, or whether emendations are accepted, make a big difference in the way the passage is understood. Opposite positions are even taken on certain elements in the passage. For example, some views take the description of the almond tree, the locust, and the caperberry as setting forth the rejuvenation of nature and others as setting forth the destruction of nature. Some attention will have to be given to these details in the discussion of the text.

The view which best explains 12:1-7 is the approach of Fox, because it is based on the literal meaning of the text and it best explains all the details. The figure of an approaching storm (Leahy) or a collapsing house (Sawyer) does not adequately explain the terror of the people in the passage (see Sawyer's translation).[60] Plus, Sawyer's view of the collapsing house changes the focus to the failure of human effort when the passage is more about enjoying life before death comes.[61] Seow's view of the eschatological demise of human life makes too much of the eschatological aspect, which takes one away from the primary focus of individual human death. Fox sees the eschatological dimension as a part of the symbolic meaning, which has connections with prophetic descriptions of eschatological destruction. However, he keeps the focus on individual human death, which is where Qohelet keeps the focus. Although Fox argues that the allegorical approach is valid, he also sees it to be generally inadequate because the basis for the allegorical reading is not secure. There is too much hermeneutical flexibility, which is demonstrated in the many different ways the individual clauses have been understood to refer to old age.

Qohelet exhorts the young man in 12:1 to '*Remember your Creator.*' The period of time in which the young man is to remember the Creator is '*in the days of your youth.*' The period of

---

60. Fox ('Aging and Death,' 58) argues that Sawyer depends on emendations and strained translations to support his view of the poem.

61. Fox ('Aging and Death,' 58) notes that the poem, as explained by Sawyer, does not really warn against unexpected disasters but complains of the indifference of nature in light of humanity's demise.

'*youth*' is the time in which one should remember the Creator because there is coming a time in the future when things will be difficult. This future time of difficulty is set out by three clauses that begin with the phrase '*aḏ 'ăšer lō*', which literally means 'until when not'[62] but is translated '*before.*' This Hebrew phrase marks the transition from one subject to another.[63] Thus the text can be broken down into 12:1b; 12:2-5; and 12:6-7 on the basis of this phrase. Ogden and Zogbo specifically argue that only death is in view in all three of these sections.[64] However, others argue that 12:1b-5 refers to old age and that death does not come into view until the end of 12:5 (before the last phrase translated '*before*').[65] It is hard to omit old age from 12:1b. The '*days of youth*' come '*before days of misfortune come*' where the typical response will be '*I have no pleasure in them.*' Both the period of '*youth*' and the period of '*misfortune*' are described with the use of the word '*days,*' so they both refer to a period of time. Thus the '*days of misfortune*' must refer to the period of time before death, which means it refers to the days of old age. The period of youth and the period of old age are contrasted with each other. The period of youth is the time to remember the Creator because the coming days of old age will not be very pleasant. Life will not be very enjoyable then.

What does Qohelet mean when he exhorts the young man to remember his Creator? The answer to that question depends to some degree on how one has understood Qohelet's message up to this point, but also how one understands the function of 12:1-7. Some argue that the exhortation to enjoy life in 11:7 makes 11:7–12:7 the final call to enjoyment of the book;[66] however, commentators have understood the calls to enjoyment in

---

62. Seow, *Ecclesiastes*, 351.

63. Ginsburg, *Coheleth*, 457.

64. See Ogden and Zogbo, *Handbook on Ecclesiastes*, 419 and Ogden, *Qoheleth*, 213. It is argued that death is in view in 12:1b based on the use of the word *rā'āh* (translated 'evil,' but the word can have other connotations such as misfortune or tragedy).

65. Murphy, *Ecclesiastes*, 113. Those who take an allegorical view of the descriptions in 12:2-5 understand these verses to be referring to old age.

66. Ogden (*Qoheleth*, 208) argues that the call to enjoyment here is fully consistent with the positive advice already given throughout Qohelet.

different ways. Those differences are also reflected in the way this last section of Qohelet is understood. Some have argued that the calls to enjoyment are the answer to the problems that Qohelet sets forth, and they take a very positive view of the exhortations in 11:7–12:7, especially the encouragement to remember the Creator. Kaiser argues that 'remember' calls for decisive action based on reflections of who God is and what He has done for human beings so that service for God will not diminish.[67] Kidner argues that 'remember' is a call to drop our pretense of self-sufficiency and commit ourselves to God.[68] The emphasis on God the Creator may also connect with 12:7, where in death the spirits of human beings return to God.[69] Bartholomew sees significance in the fact that although darkness and enigma are strongly present in 11:7–12:7, for the first time the enigma of life is set in the context of joy and remembrance rather than the other way around. The section begins in 11:7 with the affirmation of life, which signals a major shift in Qohelet's perspective. In 12:1 the object of remember is no longer the days of darkness, as in 11:8, but is God the Creator, which points to a possible resolution of Qohelet's struggle.[70] However, others argue that the exhortation to remember the Creator is not necessarily positive and it does not represent a resolution to the struggles of Qohelet. Longman argues that the use of the word Creator to refer to God is a more impersonal and objective reference to God.[71] Fox argues that in light of 12:7, the exhortation to remember the Creator in 12:1 is really an exhortation to remember a person's upcoming death.[72]

Although this last section of the book appears to be more positive, so that it could be offering a solution, the

---

67. Kaiser, *Ecclesiastes*, 118.
68. Kidner, *Ecclesiastes*, 100.
69. Murphy, *Ecclesiastes*, 117.
70. Bartholomew, *Ecclesiastes*, 354–355. Bartholomew notes that it is only a possible resolution because the fragility of life is still prominent in the juxtaposition of light and darkness, which produces a gap that needs to be filled. The gap is filled by the exhortation to remember the Creator.
71. Longman, *Ecclesiastes*, 268.
72. Fox, *Rereading Ecclesiastes*, 322.

positive aspect quickly disappears in the coming onslaught of darkness. If the calls to enjoyment are becoming more urgent in their exhortations to enjoy life, it is because the darkness of death is getting closer (9:10; 12:6-7). The fact that there is a limited time to remember the Creator is significant. It parallels the fact that there is a limited time to enjoy life. This implies that there is coming a time when life will not be enjoyed and the Creator will not be remembered. Life should be enjoyed before the difficult days of old age (12:1b) come when it will be difficult to enjoy life. Life should also be enjoyed before death comes (12:2-6) because it will be impossible to enjoy life once death arrives. Enjoyment of life here must refer to the pleasures of life because nothing is said of having joy in the midst of the trials of old age, or the joy of seeing God at death. There is also a limited time to remember the Creator before death comes. There is no clear mention of life after death, so the opportunity to remember the Creator is limted to this life in the period of youth. This limited period to remember the Creator stands before the onslaught of the darkness of death, which will be permanent.

One may wonder why Qohelet mentions the Creator at all and how this view fits in with the statement in 12:7 that the spirit returns to God Who gave it. The argument has been made in previous passages that although God is in the horizon of Qohelet's thinking, God is never brought in to solve the problems with which he is wrestling (this is especially clear in 9:1). In fact, it is impossible to understand the work of God in this world (3:11). One can never be sure whether justice will prevail because there are too many cases of injustice (3:16; 8:11-14). Qohelet is not quite sure whether wisdom and righteousness will make any difference in a person's life, but he also knows the possibility of God's judgment on foolishness and wisdom. He has already taken a cautious approach to God (5:1-7) and to the way one lives life (7:15-18). The Creator is mentioned in 12:1 because Qohelet has just encouraged the young person to pursue the ways of the heart and the sight of the eyes with the warning of the possibility of the judgment of God (11:8). The mention of the Creator is also a warning to youth not to get carried away in the time of youth.⁷³ The fact that the spirit returns to the God who gave it in 12:7 recognizes God's role, much as the calls to enjoyment recognize that the pleasures of life are the gift of God. But just as in the rest of the first-person discourse, God is not brought in as a solution to the problem, which here is the problem of death. The darkness and permanence of death is too overwhelming. Also, 12:7 is immediately followed by 12:8, which affirms again the main message of Qohelet that everything in life is *hebel*.

The next section introduced by *'before'* (*'ad̠ 'ăšer lō'*) is 12:2-5. Qohelet moves from a description of old age in 12:1b to a description of death and its devastating results. An important person in the community has died and the effects of his death are shown in the community. 12:2 would seem to be describing a thunderstorm in its description of the darkening of *'the sun and the light and the moon and the stars'* and especially in stating that *'the clouds return after the rain.'* However, this section (12:2-5) ends with mourning and death, so the best approach is to understand these verses as describing the effects of the death, mourning, and funeral of an important member of the community. The emphasis on darkness in the heavens in 12:2 is a way to describe the onslaught of gloom and despair that comes with death.⁷⁴ This darkness can be contrasted with the light in 11:7, where light represents life and seeing the sun pictures the enjoyment of life. In 12:2 that enjoyment comes to an end in darkness, which turns out to be the darkness of death.

The days of darkness in 12:2 cannot be separated from the events of 12:3-5, because 12:3 connects 12:2 with the

---

73. Shields (*End of Wisdom*, 233) notes that mentioning the Creator may be no more than a reminder of one's mortality. Life is in God's hands and is beyond our control.

74. The allegorical interpretation does not work well with 12:2. The Targum takes the sun to refer to the stately brightness of the countenance, the light to the light of the eyes, the moon to the ornament of the cheeks, and the stars to the apple of the eye. Delitzsch ('Ecclesiastes,' 6:404) understands the sun to be the male spirit, the light to be the activity of the spirit, the moon to be the soul, and the stars to be the five planets which represent the five senses. In a more general way, Barton (*Ecclesiastes*, 186) argues that 12:2 describes the failing of the eyesight as old age advances.

following verses by the temporal clause *'on the day when.'* This connection means that the days of darkness cannot be referring to old age but are related to the events of the following verses. This connection also supports the idea that 12:2-5 should be understood as a section which is governed by the mourning and death at the end of 12:5. In 12:3 the effects of the death of the owner of the house are described for four different groups of people. There are two groups of men and two groups of women who have different responsibilities for the household. First, two groups of men are described as *'the keepers of the house'* and *'the strong men.'*[75] The word *'keepers'* (participle of *šāmar*) is a word that means 'to watch' or 'to guard,' so this may refer to servants of the house who watch over certain aspects of the running of the house, including guarding the premises.[76] Their reaction to death is that they *'tremble'* (*zwʿ*). This verb is not used very often, but it has the connotation of fear (Esther 5:9) or terror (Hab. 2:7 and the related noun in Deut. 28:25 and Isa. 28:19). The word for *'strong'* (*ḥayil*) is an important word that has a variety of nuances, including military strength, wealth, or some kind of power. It probably refers here to the men who have authority over others in the house.[77] They are described as *'bent over'* (*ʿāwat*) in their reaction to the death. The meaning of this verb is best understood in its parallel relationship to *'terror,'* so that to be bent over is to cower or crouch in fear.[78] Then two

---

75. Delitzsch ('Ecclesiastes,' 6:406) points out that the Midrash understands the *'keepers of the house'* to refer to the knees of the old man and the *'strong men'* to refer to the ribs or arms of the old man. He basically agrees with these connections. For the different ways these phrases are understood allegorically see Barton, *Ecclesiastes*, 188.

76. Fox (*Rereading Ecclesiastes*, 323) notes that the word *'keepers'* is a broad term that includes concubines in 2 Samuel 20:3.

77. Although Longman (*Ecclesiastes*, 264) takes the Hebrew word *'strong'* as referring to landowners or owners of the house, it is more likely that it refers to servants who have authority over others in the house. He identifies groups one and three as lower-class servants and groups two and four as upper-class. Perhaps the latter should be upper-class servants.

78. Seow, *Ecclesiastes*, 355. He translates the verb as 'convulse.' Fox (*Rereading Ecclesiastes*, 323) understands this to be a reference to a posture of mourning and translates it 'writhe.'

groups of women are described as *'the grinders'* and *'those who look through the windows.'* The women who grind are female servants who are involved in the daily grinding of bread. They are said to *'cease because they are few.'* In other words, the work of grinding grain has slowed down because some workers have been lost. Perhaps some have been lost to other activities in preparation for the funeral, or maybe some have become mourners.[79] The second group of women is thought to be higher on the social scale because it is not clear what work they do in the household. Perhaps they are female members of the family who look out of the window in despair because of the death of the owner of the house. Perhaps they are in shock over what has happened. As they look, their view grows *'dark'* through grief (Lam. 5:17).[80]

In 12:4 the normal activities of life come to a halt. The focus expands from the household to the community in that *'the doors in the street are closed when the sound of the mill decreases.'*[81] The whole community is affected by this death. The word *'doors'* is a dual form which points to double doors. Although it is possible that some houses had double doors (Job 31:32) the reference here may be to doors in the community, such as the doors of an inn (Josh. 2:19). Seow understands the word *'street'* (*šûq*) to refer to a vibrant center of commercial and social

---

79. Some argue that it is strange that there would be a stoppage of the work of the grinders because they are few, because a numerical decrease of the grinders should increase the work of those who are left (Longman, *Ecclesiastes*, 270; Murphy, *Ecclesiastes*, 118). This difficulty with the literal view has led to the allegorical meaning that this refers to the the loss of teeth in old age so that chewing becomes more difficult. The Midrash also takes the women at the mill to be referring to the digestive organs (Delitzsch, 'Ecclesiastes,' 6:406). A literal view does make sense in the context of a funeral and the *shutting down* of the activities of the house because of the death of the owner.

80. Seow, *Ecclesiastes*, 357. The allegorical approach sees this as a reference to the eyes growing dim in old age.

81. The allegorical approach understands *'the doors,'* which is a dual form, to be referring to the lips, which are closed and drawn in because the teeth have disappeared. This idea is connected to the low sound of the mill because the old man has no teeth with which to grind (Delitzsch, 'Ecclesiastes,' 6:408-409); also see Barton, *Ecclesiastes*, 188–189 for a list of different ways that 12:4a has been understood allegorically.

activity based partly on the Akkadian *sūqu* ('marketplace'). This meaning is reflected in the Septuagint translation 'in the marketplace' (ἐν ἀγορᾷ). Thus the center of commercial and social activity in the community has shut down, including '*the mill*' where bread was baked daily.[82]

The next few clauses of 12:4 are difficult no matter what view one takes of this passage. It begins with the statement '*the doors in the street are closed*,' followed by the temporal clause[83] '*when the sound of the mill decreases*,' which is followed by two clauses joined by the conjunction *waw*. These three clauses refer to sound either decreasing or increasing with the movement of the verbs from '*decreases*' to '*rises*' to '*brought low.*' Because of this movement, the first *waw* after the temporal clause has been translated with '*but*' and the second *waw* with '*and*,' which yields the translation '*when the sound of the mill decreases, but the sound of the birds rise and the daughters of song are brought low.*'[84] The meaning of '*the sound of the birds*' is unclear, including what the increase of the sound means. There are also questions concerning the meaning of the '*daughters of song*' and what is meant by the statement that their activity is '*brought low.*' The first part of 12:4 describes the shutting down of the activity of the community, with the doors being shut and the work at the mill decreasing. The second part of 12:4 contrasts the rise of the sound of birds with the bringing low of the daughters of song. The parallel with birds might lead to the conclusion that daughters of

---

82. Seow, *Ecclesiastes*, 378.

83. The temporal clause is introduced by the preposition *bet* on an infinitive construct (Longman, *Ecclesiastes*, 265).

84. The phrase '*the sound of the birds*' is unusual in that the word '*sound*' (*qôl*) has the preposition *lamed* attached. It is possible that the *lamed* is marking the subject or is used for the sake of emphasis (Seow, *Ecclesiastes*, 358). The allegorical approach takes the verb to be impersonal followed by the object, which is translated 'he rises to the sound of the birds,' which either means that the old person is a light sleeper and so he wakes up because of the sound of the birds, or that the old person rises early at the same time as the birds sing (Delitzsch, 'Ecclesiastes,' 6:410). The other phrase, '*the daughters of song are brought low*' is understood to mean either the failure of the singing voice of the old person or the deafness of old age (Barton, *Ecclesiastes*, 189).

song also refers to birds, but the contrast between the sound rising and being brought low argues against the view that the two terms refer to the same thing.[85] It is possible in light of the context that the *'daughters of song'* refer to the women mourners, with the verb *'brought low'* expressing the posture of mourning, which would include sitting on the ground and prostrating oneself.[86] However, the word 'song' (*šîr*) is not used to refer to songs of lament or mourning[87] and it is hard to connect mourners with the beginning of 12:5. Perhaps the daughters of song refer to those who sing more festive songs, which would not be appropriate in a time of mourning.[88] Thus 12:4 describes normal, everyday activities that have ceased. Buying and selling stops, the work at the mill ceases, and the singing of festival, joyous songs also comes to an end. In the eerie quiet that results the sound of birds can be heard.

The first part of 12:5 is the most difficult part to fit into a unified picture of 12:3-5 and seems to make more sense as a description of old age: *'they are also afraid of heights and terrors on the way.'* It is unclear who or what the subject is in 12:5a, but the closest antecedent would be 12:4, so the meaning of 12:5a is dependent on how one understands its relationship to what has gone before. Those who understand these verses as referring to old age understand 12:5a to be a literal description of the difficulty that old people have in moving around and the fears they face in the normal movement and activities of life outside the home.[89] Some take it as referring specifically

---

85. Seow (*Ecclesiastes*, 357) argues that both clauses refer to birds and that the second clause refers to birds that swoop down to their new haunt in face of the depopulation of the human habitat. He also understands 12:1-7 to be describing an eschatological, cosmic disaster.

86. Fox, *Rereading Ecclesiastes*, 326.

87. Brown, *Ecclesiastes*, 112.

88. Ogden and Zogbo (*Handbook on Ecclesiastes*, 424) offer the possibility that the daughters of song are dancing women. Fox (*Rereading Ecclesiastes*, 326) argues against this view because the verb *'brought low'* means to 'bow low' and not cease, but in Isaiah 29:4 the verb does refer to speech which is low. Leahy ('Ecclesiastes 12:1-5,' 378), who argues for the overall picture of an approaching storm, also understands the daughters of song to be those who sing joyous songs. They are merrymakers who are terrorized into silence.

89. Delitzsch, 'Ecclesiastes,' 6:411.

to the shortness of breath that makes it difficult to walk up a hill and the stiffness of limbs that makes movement hard for older people.[90] Those who argue for the general picture of an approaching storm understand 12:5a to be referring to the fear people have of the raging storm.[91] The fear of what is high refers to the lightning and thunder in the skies and the terrors on the way refers to the problems one would have in being outside in the wind and the blowing rain. Seow, who understands the poem to be an eschatological description of cosmic demise, argues that the subject of 12:5a is the birds from 12:4. He understands the 'daughters of song' to be parallel with the birds, so that both are a reference to birds. He also argues that the verb is not the verb that means 'to fear' (*yārē'*) but is the verb that means 'to see' (*rā'āh*), which yields the translation 'from on high the birds see terrors are in the way.' The birds themselves see the panic of the community facing death.[92] Fox understands the daughters of song in 12:4 to be a reference to the female mourners, who are also the subject of 12:5a, which describes the fear and dismay of the mourners in the funeral procession. As they bow low they dread the power lurking over their heads and the scenes of dismay, which are vivid descriptions of the outpouring of emotions that mark the funeral procession.[93] 12:5a seems to be describing the terror and dismay that surrounds people from all sides when death occurs, but the specifics of the verse are more difficult to nail down. What is the subject of 12:5a? The word *also* (*gam*) certainly connects 12:5 to what has gone before, but instead of 12:5a being connected to the immediately preceding clause, the verse could be referring to the reaction of all the groups of people who have been mentioned in 12:3-4. The whole community experiences dread, dismay, and terror that accompany death. The mentioning of *'what is high'* seems unusual, but it could be a veiled reference to God. Fox argues that the term *gābōah* can refer to God, who is 'high in the

---

90. Barton, *Ecclesiastes*, 189.
91. Leahy, 'Ecclesiastes 12:1-5,' 378.
92. Seow, *Ecclesiastes*, 360.
93. Fox, *Rereading Ecclesiastes*, 327.

heavens' (Job 22:12).[94] The preposition *min* ('*from*') expresses the source of the fear. Certainly death reminds people of the frailty of life and the source of life. A veiled reference to God would fit the way God has been presented by Qohelet as distant (5:1-7) and not immediately involved in solving the problems of life (9:1).

There is much discussion concerning the meaning and the function of three short clauses in the middle of 12:5. The description of old-age-approach must revert to allegory to connect these clauses to old age. The first clause refers to the blossoming of the almond tree, whose white blossoms picture the white hair of the elderly. The grasshopper dragging itself along would refer to the difficulty old people have of walking or that the smallest weight is a burden.[95] The final clause about the caperberry is usually taken to refer to the decline of the appetite in old age, perhaps including sexual desire.[96] Others understand the three clauses in the middle of 12:5 to describe the decline of nature. Seow argues that the verb used with the almond tree is not *nṣṣ* ('to blossom) but *n'ṣ* ('to revile or be repulsed'), which results in the translation 'the almond tree becomes revolting.' He also takes the locust to be some kind of plant and the verb to mean 'drag,' 'droop,' or 'be weighed down.' The idea is that the locust tree is dead, so it droops from the weight of the pods. Finally, the caper bush is described as falling off or shedding, which refers to becoming defoliated. Thus all three clauses refer to the death of the plants in the description of the eschatological crisis.[97] Others argue that the three clauses in the middle of 12:5 refer to the rejuvenation of nature.[98] The choice between the rejuvenation of nature and the decline of nature is a tough choice. The

---

94. Fox (*Rereading Ecclesiastes*, 327) recognizes, however, that the word *gāḇōah* without the article is not a recognizable epithet for God.

95. Delitzsch ('Ecclesiastes,' 6:414) argues the first and Barton (*Ecclesiastes*, 189) the second (also see Barton for a listing of the various ways these clauses are understood in reference to old age).

96. Barton, *Ecclesiastes*, 190–191.

97. Seow, *Ecclesiastes*, 362–363.

98. Fox, *Rereading Ecclesiastes*, 327–328 and Sawyer, 'The Ruined House,' 529–530.

verbs that are used are not very common verbs and each view must either slightly emend the text or make adjustments to the meaning of the verbs. Which view one adopts, however, does not change the overall meaning of the passage.

The view that best fits in with the flow of verse 5 is the view of the rejuvenation of nature. Although the demise of nature would work well as a description of *'the terrors on the way,'* the three clauses seem to be describing the flourishing of nature. There is a great contrast when someone dies between the dismay and despair of death and the blossoming of even a small flower. Thus the first clause should be translated *'the almond tree blossoms.'* It is difficult to determine whether the second clause refers to a locust tree or a locust insect. The more common use of the noun is the locust insect. The verb $sābal$ in the hitpael can mean 'to grow fat,' which would refer to the locust eating well on the abundance of vegetation. Not only the plants but the insects are thriving. If the reference is to a locust plant, then the idea is that the plant is laden with growth. The translation *'the grasshopper is laden'* is ambiguous, which leaves open the possibility of referring to either the plant or the insect. Finally, the last clause is translated *'the caperberry bursts forth.'* The verb prr in the hifil has the meaning 'to break' in reference to the covenant, the commandments, or a vow. It can also be used in the sense of frustrating the purposes of someone. The Septuagint translates the clause 'the caperberry will be scattered.' In light of the fact that the Septuagint translates the other clauses as 'the almond tree shall blossom and the locust shall increase,' the idea of scattering probably refers to the scattering of seeds in fruitfulness. Fox suggests a slight emendation of the verb from prr to the verb $prḥ$, which means 'to blossom.'[99] This verb is used in Song of Solomon 7:12 in parallel to the verb $nāṣaṣ$ ('bloom'), which is the verb used earlier in Ecclesiastes 12:5. The inclination that the verb used with caperberry parallels the other verbs in meaning is correct, but an emendation is not necessary if the idea here is that the caperberry breaks or bursts forth in new growth.

---

99. Fox, *Rereading Ecclesiastes*, 328.

The end of 12:5 clearly refers to death. The transition to death is made by the Hebrew word *kî*. Those who understand the three clauses in the middle of 12:5 to refer to a description of old age usually translate the *kî* in a causal sense, showing the connection between old age and death.[100] Seow, who understands the three clauses in the middle of 12:5 to be describing the decline of nature, translates the *kî* with 'yea,' which is an affirmation that decline and death also comes to human beings.[101] If the three clauses in the middle of 12:5 refer to the rejuvenation of nature, then the transition to death at the end of 12:5 requires an adversative idea, such as '*but*,' or a temporal clause, such as 'when,' which brings together the rejuvenation of nature with the death of a human being.[102] Death is described as '*goes to his eternal home*' while '*the mourners go about the streets.*' The '*eternal home*' is a reference to the grave,[103] so this may have in view the funeral procession to the place of burial. Thus 12:2-5 describes the effect of death on the household of the owner who dies and on the community at large. Although nature is reborn every year, human beings have no such hope because only death awaits them.

The final section of the poem on death (12:1-7) occurs in 12:6-7, which is also introduced by '*before*' ('*ad̪ 'ăšer lō'*). The emphasis in this section is on the dissolution that comes to the human being at death. Four metaphors are used to describe death. There are questions concerning the relationship of the metaphors to each other and the meaning of some of

---

100. Longman, *Ecclesiastes*, 266; Delitzsch, 'Ecclesiastes,' 6:417; Ginsburg, *Coheleth*, 463.

101. Seow, *Ecclesiastes*, 347.

102. Although Fox (*Rereading Ecclesiastes*, 329) understands 12:5 to be referring to the rejuvenation of nature, he translates *kî* as 'for' because he understands it as giving the reason for the entire complex of occurrences of 12:3-5a.

103. Seow (*Ecclesiastes*, 364) argues that '*eternal home*' is equivalent to the Egyptian phrase 'house of eternity,' which refers to the grave, and that the sense of the finality of death is expressed in the Deir 'Allā inscription where the 'house of eternity' is a description of a place from which one does not return. There is little evidence that Qohelet affirms life after death (9:10), and he does not offer life after death as a hope in the face of death in these verses.

the verbs. The four metaphors are *'the silver cord,'* *'the golden bowl,'* *'the pitcher,'* and *'the wheel at the well.'* The four verbs used with these metaphors describe some kind of negative action that emphasizes destruction. Gordis argues that the four metaphors are part of one figure of a well worked by a cord tied to a wheel. At one end of the cord is a pitcher and at the other end of the cord is a metal ball as a counterweight. When the cord is torn, the ball, pitcher, and wheel all fall to the bottom of the well and are broken.[104] Seow understands the metaphors as referring to things that were commonly associated with tombs and burial. The word *'cord'* (*ḥebel*) refers to what is thin and elongated and can be used of various parts of a plant, such as the stalk, shoot, or branch. The *'golden bowl'* is used as a receptacle for oil (Zech. 4:2), so these two figures together refer to a lampstand. The silver cord could refer to a branch of the lampstand or the whole lampstand which contains bowls to receive the oil. Lamps were commonly found at tombs and were placed there to symbolically help the dead cope with the darkness of the netherworld. The destruction of the lampstand signifies the extinguishing of the light of life and the absolute darkness of death. The final two metaphors, according to Seow, both refer to some kind of vessel or pot. The term for wheel (*galgal*) is better understood as some kind of vessel (*golgōl*) because of the parallel with 'pitcher' and because wheels at wells were limited to palaces. They were also large and sturdy contraptions that were unlikely to be crushed.[105] The term *'well'* (*bôr*) can refer to a cistern or well as a source of water or to a pit, which can refer to the grave. The destruction of these pots refers to a funerary custom of smashing pots at a tomb, which is an action which symbolizes death.[106] The allegorical

---

104. Gordis, *Koheleth*, 338 (see Ginsburg, *Coheleth*, 466 for arguments against taking the whole verse as referring to one figure of a well).

105. Seow (*Ecclesiastes*, 367) and others refer to Mitchell Dahood's argument that the Hebrew term does not refer to a wheel but to some kind of globular vessel on the basis of Ugaritic *gl*, which refers to a drinking vessel, and Akkadian *gullu*, which can be used for cooking pots (M. Dahood, 'Canaanite-Phoenecian Influence in Qoheleth,' *Bib* 33 [1952]: 227–232).

106. Seow, *Ecclesiastes*, 381–382.

approach takes each metaphor as an individual reference to death.¹⁰⁷ The silver cord is understood as the spinal column, the soul directing the body, or a description that one's hold on life is severed. The golden bowl is understood as a reference to the brain or the physical body. The pitcher broken at the fountain is understood as the failing heart. Also, the wheel is understood as the system of veins and arteries that carry blood or the breathing organ that expands and contracts. Finally, a common view is to take the four metaphors to be describing two images.¹⁰⁸ The golden bowl is a lamp with the bowl holding the oil (Zech. 4:2-3). The silver cord is either a cord that holds the bowl in suspension or a part of the lampstand. When *'the silver cord is snapped'* then *'the golden bowl is smashed'* so that the light of the lamp, which symbolizes life, is gone. The other two metaphors are understood to describe a well with a broken pitcher and a wheel that no longer works so that water cannot be taken out of the well. Fox sees this as a picture of an old cistern, dry and neglected, with its wheel apparatus having fallen into disrepair and lying broken at the bottom of the well.¹⁰⁹ No matter which view one holds, the point of 12:6 is to describe the destruction of human life at death.

In 12:7 the end of human life is described in terms that refer to the origin of human life in Genesis 2:7, which states 'God formed the man of dust from the ground and breathed into his nostrils the breath of life, and the man became a living creature.' Both use the term *'dust'* (*'āpār*), with Qohelet stating that *'the dust returns to the earth as it was.'* Here dust is a reference to the body, which originated from the dust and becomes dust again at death. Genesis 2:7 uses 'breath (*nĕšāmāh*) of life' and 'living creature,' while Qohelet uses *'spirit'* (*rûaḥ*). The terms 'breath' and 'spirit' are basically interchangeable in these two contexts, as both refer to the

---

107. For the allegorical approach see Kaiser (*Ecclesiastes*, 121), who has a chart which shows each verse and the allegorical meaning of the clauses; Delitzsch, 'Ecclesiastes,' 6:421-425; and Fox in the JPS commentary (*Commentary*, 81) where he lays out the allegorical meaning of 12:6.

108. See Murphy, Ginsburg, Whybray, and Crenshaw.

109. Fox, *Rereading Ecclesiastes*, 330.

breath that is associated with life and when the breath departs there is death.[110] Qohelet states that *'the spirit returns to God who gave it.'* There is much discussion concerning the meaning of this statement and its relationship to Ecclesiastes 3:21. Some understand 12:7 to be stating that there is continued life after death, a consciousness in the presence of God.[111] Thus death is not the end, because the spirit does not perish with the body.[112] Others argue that Qohelet does not here affirm life after death but only affirms that God is the source of life.[113] Fox even argues that 12:7 is more pessimistic than 3:21 because 12:7 affirms that the spirit does return to God but that fact does not really change anything.[114] It is difficult to argue for life after death in this one statement of Qohelet when such a view seems to be denied in other places of the first-person discourse (3:21; 9:10). The whole point of this section is to enjoy life before death comes because when death does arrive the opportunity for the enjoyment of life will be over. The focus of 3:21 is whether there is any distinction between the manner of death and the destiny of human beings and animals in death. Qohelet denies in 3:21 that there is a distinction between human beings and animals in death; yet, both human beings and animals possess breath that comes from God (Gen. 2:7; Ps. 104:29). Thus, one can affirm that God is the giver of life to both human beings and animals and also deny that there is any difference between the two in death. Ecclesiastes 12:7 is merely affirming that breath comes from God, so God is the source of life, which could also be affirmed about animals without suggesting that Qohelet believes in a life after death for animals. In the final analysis, there is no reason to understand 12:7 as

---

110. Van Pelt/Kaiser/Block, רוּחַ, *NIDOTTE*, 3:1072.

111. Kaiser, *Ecclesiastes*, 122; Eaton, *Ecclesiastes*, 151.

112. Bartholomew, *Ecclesiastes*, 357; Ginsburg (*Coheleth*, 467) even speaks of immortality.

113. Murphy, *Ecclesiastes*, 120; Gordis, *Koheleth*, 339; and Fox, *Rereading Ecclesiastes*, 331. Longman (*Ecclesiastes*, 273) notes that in 12:7 there is simply a return to a pre-life situation.

114. Fox, *Rereading Ecclesiastes*, 332.

contradicting 3:21 and there is no reason to understand 12:7 as affirming life after death.

The meaning and function of the refrain in 12:8 has a bearing on the way one understands 12:7. The refrain of 12:8 is translated *'Utterly senseless!'* says Qohelet, *'Everything is senseless.'* This refrain reverts to third person, so it naturally goes with 12:9-14, which is part of the third-person narration (1:1-11 and 12:8-14) that frames the first-person discourse (1:12–12:7).[115] However, the refrain of 12:8 forms an inclusio with the similar refrain of 1:2.[116] Thus everything from 1:2 to 12:8 falls under the judgment of *hebel*. Although a distinction has been made between the first-person discourse and the third-person frame (see the Introduction), Ecclesiastes 1:1-11 expresses the same ideas that are found in the first-person discourse, so an argument can be made that everything from 1:2–12:8 would fall under the judgment that everything is *'senseless.'* It is also understandable why the refrain of 12:8 would be connected to the first-person discourse as a summary statement of the message of Qohelet even though the refrain is third-person and could be placed with 12:9-14.

Not everyone understands 12:8 to be Qohelet's summary conclusion which cements his negative, under the sun, view of life.[117] The meaning of *hebel* is very significant to how one understands the message of Qohelet. If *hebel* means fleeting or enigmatic or mysterious, then the message of Qohelet is not necessarily negative because his struggles do not dominate

---

115. Commentators vary as to whether they discuss 12:8 with 11:7–12:7 or with 12:9-14. Sometimes no explanation is given concerning where 12:8 is discussed. Longman (*Ecclesiastes*, 274) discusses it with the epilogue because it reverts to third person (see also Ginsburg, *Coheleth*, 470 for reasons why 12:8 should be taken with 12:9-14 and not 11:7–12:7). Fox (*Rereading Ecclesiastes*, 332), on the other hand, notes that the reader does not suddenly stop at 12:7, but reads 12:8, which acts as a summary of the book. Thus, 12:8 is a more natural stopping point than 12:7.

116. Ecclesiastes 12:8 is a shortened version of 1:2, which has an extra *hăḇēl hăḇālim*. Qohelet also has the definite article in 12:8 but not in 1:2.

117. Some commentators view 12:8 as the summary thesis of the book, but they understand *hebel* to mean fleeting or enigmatic, so the closing refrain is not as negative and the message of the first-person discourse is more positive (see Ogden and Zogbo, as well as Eaton).

his perspective. There is room for an answer to his struggles in God or in the calls to enjoyment as expressions of faith.[118] Some view 12:8 as an oversimplification of the message of the book because a more dominant thematization of the book is found in 12:13-14.[119] Bartholomew argues that 1:2 and 12:8 are merely entrance and exit points, like the covers of a book, so that 12:8 is not Qohelet's conclusion because it does not do justice to the complexity of the book. He also argues that 11:7–12:7 suggests the possibility of a resolution to the problems with which Qohelet wrestles because the structure of this final section is different. Instead of ending with the call to enjoyment, it begins with the call to enjoyment, with the Creator being the bridge between the *hebel* statements and the call to enjoyment. God as Creator is now brought into the picture to help one handle life's enigmas, which is tantamount to making the fear of God foundational for Qohelet's search for wisdom.[120] However, Qohelet never calls on God to solve the problems in life even though God is very much a part of the horizon of Qohelet's thinking (3:19-21; 9:1). The different structure of 11:7–12:7 can be explained by the fact that the calls to enjoyment are becoming more urgent in the book and that 11:7–12:7 is going to end with the finality of death, so the call to enjoyment cannot come last. Rather, it comes first to highlight the limited amount of time the youth has to enjoy life before it is too late. Thus 12:8 appropriately brings to a close the message of Qohelet that everything in life is senseless.

Homiletical Implications
Driving in a thick fog is miserable. One cannot see very far whichever way one looks. One is nervous about running into the back of another vehicle because one cannot see very far ahead. One is also worried that a large truck will come up

---

118. Eaton specifically argues that there are expressions of faith made by Qohelet. Farmer (*Ecclesiastes*, 195) also notes that if *hebel* means 'fleeting' then the refrain of 12:8 expresses a word of comfort.

119. G. Sheppard, *Wisdom as a Hermeneutical Construct* (Berlin: de Gruyter, 1980), pp.120-129.

120. Bartholomew, *Ecclesiastes*, 354–361.

quickly from behind and smash into one's vehicle. One thus drives very cautiously in a thick fog. Qohelet has been living in a thick fog which has affected his view of life. However, he recognizes that there is a time of life which is not as affected by the fog but is characterized as a time of light. The time of youth is such a period of life when the light shines before the darkness of the fog descends, which Qohelet identifies as the onslaught of old age and death. It is urgent that this period of light be enjoyed while such enjoyment is possible, because there is coming a time of life when the fog of darkness will descend and the light will be gone. Yet the fog of the future even affects the present time of youth. While one is enjoying the years of youth one must also remember that many days of darkness are on the horizon. While one pursues the sight of one's eyes and walks in the way of one's heart, one must not forget that there are consequences to the way one lives life. While one should remove pain and frustration from one's life, one must not forget that the period of youth takes on the character of *hebel*. It is either fleeting, which means it will not last very long, or it is senseless, which means that the pursuit of the enjoyment of life is itself frustrating and falls short of one's expectations. One should also remember one's Creator during this limited, senseless time of the enjoyment of life because days are coming when life will be miserable. There is nothing here of facing old age and death with dignity and wisdom because God can sustain one even in old age and death. The coming days of darkness overshadow the light of the time of youth because eventually life will end in the fog of darkness. A young person who spoke at a high school graduation told her classmates to enjoy life while they are young: live life to the fullest, take chances, cross the yellow line (a line in the middle of American roads that separates two lanes of traffic going in opposite directions). But then someone mentions that crossing the yellow line can have negative consequences. Qohelet's motivation behind his advice to make use of every opportunity to enjoy life is flawed because it comes from an 'under the sun' perspective. If the time of youth is the only window of opportunity to enjoy life, then you must do it while you can because this is it. If one misses this opportunity one misses it all. What a difference it would make if Qohelet could see beyond the darkness of the fog to the glory of the pleasures which are at God's right hand (Ps. 16:11). Psalm 16 is used in the New Testament to speak of the glory of the resurrection of Jesus Christ, who dispels the fog of darkness and shines the light of life on the dark events of this world. The knowledge that Jesus is coming again should motivate us to live our lives now in a way that is pleasing to Him. We want to follow His way to hear Him say, 'well done.' Knowing that He has won our victory, we make use of every opportunity, including the time of youth, to live in a way that brings glory to Him. Even old age does not have to be dominated by days of darkness but can be lived for the glory of Christ. Death is not just a dark hole that ends everything. The senselessness of life will not get the final word because we know that 'death is now but my entrance into glory.'[121]

---

121. From the hymn, 'Jesus lives, and so shall I' by Christian F. Gellert, translated by J. D. Lang.

8.
The epilogue: an evaluation of Qohelet's message (Eccles. 12:9-14)

There are several questions concerning the origin, function, and purpose of Ecclesiastes 12:9-14, which has been called the epilogue.[1] These verses shift from first person to third person and seem to be comments about Qohelet and his work. In fact, only a few modern commentators argue that these verses were written by Qohelet himself.[2] The shift in narrative voice to third person signals a new speaker who comments on the work of Qohelet.[3] The use of 'my son' gives these verses a didactic tone.[4] Although 'my son' is common in Proverbs, it is not found in Ecclesiastes apart from the epilogue. The use

---

1. Murphy (*Ecclesiastes*, 127) prefers the term epilogue or postscript with a broad sense of containing information about the author and the writing of his work. He argues that the term colophon has a technical meaning that does not quite fit Ecclesiastes (for a discussion of colophons see Michael Fishbane, *Biblical Interpretation in Ancient Israel* [Oxford: Clarendon, 1985], 29–31).

2. The following commentators argue that the same person who wrote the book also wrote the epilogue: Garrett, *Ecclesiastes*, 254–267; Kaiser, *Ecclesiastes*, 12–15; Delitzsch, 'Ecclesiastes,' 6:428–430; Ginsburg, *Coheleth*, 470–472. Delitzsch argues that in the book the author puts on the mask of Koheleth-Solomon, but in the epilogue the mask falls off and only Koheleth speaks.

3. Longman, *Ecclesiastes*, 274; Gordis, *Koheleth*, 341; Seow, *Ecclesiastes*, 391, among others.

4. Fox, *Rereading Ecclesiastes*, 363.

405

of 'my son' supports the view that someone is presenting the words of Qohelet as instruction and warning to others.

The simple truth: fear God and keep His commandments (Eccles. 12:9-14)

12:9 And furthermore, Qohelet was a wise man. He also taught the people knowledge. He listened and searched; he edited many proverbs.

12:10 Qohelet sought to find words of delight and to write correct words of truth.

12:11 The words of the wise men are like goads and the masters of collections are like firmly planted nails set[5] by a[6] shepherd.

12:12 And furthermore, my son, among these be warned: there is no end to the making of many books and much study wearies the body.

12:13 The end of the matter when all has been heard: fear God and keep his commandments, for this concerns every person.

12:14 For God will bring every deed into judgment, including[7] every hidden thing, whether good or evil.

---

5. The verb *nātan* can go with either '*masters of collections*' or with '*nails.*' Based on the use of the metaphor in this verse it is better to take it with '*nails,*' with the meaning '*set*' as used in Deuteronomy 15:17 (Fox, *Rereading Ecclesiastes*, 355).

6. Fox (*Rereading Ecclesiastes*, 355–356) points out that the modifier *'eḥād* does not mean 'one' in this context, because a declaration of monotheism would be out of place, and that this meaning would shift the weight of the verse to the idea of 'one' rather than the metaphor of goads. Instead, the modifier *'eḥād* functions here as an indefinite article (1 Sam. 24:14; 26:20; 1 Kings 19:4, 5; Ezek. 8:8). Bartholomew (*Ecclesiastes*, 368) argues that the Scripture references listed by Fox do not really support the view that *'eḥād* is an indefinite article because it means 'single,' 'solitary,' or 'another' in the specified verses. However, Bartholomew recognizes the possible use of *'eḥād* as an indefinite article and many English translations do translate *'eḥād* in the verses listed above with the indefinite article 'a.'

7. The preposition *'al* ('*including*') is a preposition of specification (Williams, *Hebrew Syntax*, 51) which introduces the basis for the judgment (Seow, *Ecclesiastes*, 391).

The epilogue is very much like the rest of Ecclesiastes in that there are a variety of views concerning the function and meaning of the epilogue. It is helpful to review the basic approaches to the epilogue in order to grasp some of the issues involved. Commentators differ concerning the meaning and purpose of this section. Some argue that the epilogue is a good summary of what Qohelet himself taught. Ogden argues that the epilogue is fully in line with orthodox teaching and that it shows that Qohelet never really cast doubt on the fundamentals of Israelite faith and practice.[8] Kaiser writes that the epilogue is where the real theme of the book is stated.[9] Garrett notes that the epilogue affirms what has already been stated in the book, namely, that the meaninglessness of life is an incentive to piety.[10] This approach stresses that the same concepts are found in the book and in the epilogue. For example, the notion of the 'fear of God' is found in the book (3:14; 5:6; 7:18; 8:12-13; 9:2) and in the epilogue (12:13), and this view argues that the meaning is the same in both places. In fact, Delitzsch argues that the fear of God is the kernel and star of the whole book and that it stands over against the pessimism of the book.[11] Also, the judgment of God is mentioned in the body of the book (3:17; 11:9) and in the epilogue (12:14). It is the certainty of the judgment of God that brings Qohelet out of his skepticism.[12] In this approach, the epilogue confirms the teaching of Qohelet in the first-person discourse. A variation of this view is argued by Bartholomew, who recognizes the struggle of Qohelet and that his wisdom approach is ironic because it leads him to Dame Folly; however, he argues that Qohelet was ultimately successful in his search, so he did come to a resolution of his struggles and arrived at a point of agreement with traditional wisdom. Thus 12:13-14 is a summary of Qohelet's journey.[13]

---

8. Ogden, *Qoheleth*, 212; see also Eaton, *Ecclesiastes*, 22, 40–41.
9. Kaiser, *Ecclesiastes*, 13–14; also Leupold, *Ecclesiastes*, 299.
10. Garrett, *Ecclesiastes*, 345.
11. Delitzsch, 'Ecclesiastes,' 6:438.
12. Delitzsch, 'Ecclesiastes,' 6:438, 441.
13. Bartholomew, *Ecclesiastes*, 274. Much of Bartholomew's argument is against Fox's approach. Seow (*Ecclesiastes*, 392) argues that the original

These approaches do not recognize the differences between the statements by Qohelet in the first-person discourse and the statements in 12:13-14. If Qohelet is orthodox, why is an epilogue needed? The work of an orthodox Qohelet could stand on its own two feet. In addition, Bartholomew correctly argues that the epistemology of Qohelet is not the epistemology of the wisdom of Proverbs (see the discussion of this point in the Introduction); however, he also argues that the resolution of this problem comes in 11:7–12:14.[14] In other words, he includes the epilogue in the resolution of the epistemological problem, but this ignores the change from the first-person speech of Qohelet to the third-person speech of the epilogist. It is agreed that a resolution comes in 12:13-14, but it is not clear that Qohelet himself comes to a resolution of this problem in 11:7–12:7. Although Qohelet mentions the Creator, he does not address the foundation of a proper epistemology in this section, which is the fear of God defined as the beginning of wisdom.

Shields also argues that Qohelet and the epilogist agree, but what they agree on is that wisdom is not able to answer the fundamental questions of life because it is undone by folly and is obliterated by death. Qohelet's approach in the first-person discourse is incompatible with the teaching of the Hebrew Bible. Qohelet reports his observations and conclusions openly and honestly. The epilogist draws out the implications of Qohelet's words for the wisdom movement by using the offensiveness of Qohelet's message to serve as a powerful warning against the wisdom movement. The way of the sages is not in accord with the way of God revealed

---

epilogue (12:9-13a) urges the reader to pay attention to the words of Qohelet because he was a learned sage whose words had been carefully crafted and carefully written. The final verses of the book (12:13b-14) are not contradictory to the rest of the book, but they do put a different spin on Qohelet's work by associating the fear of God with obedience to the commandments Thus, skeptical wisdom is not contradictory to the fear of God and the call to obedience (see also Seow, '"Beyond Them My Son, Be Warned": The Epilogue of Qohelet Revisited,' in M. L. Barre [ed.], *Wisdom, You Are My Sister* [Washington, D. C.: Catholic Biblical Association of America], 125–141).

14. Bartholomew, *Ecclesiastes*, 79.

through Moses and the prophets. This approach assumes the existence of a wisdom movement that is at odds with the orthodox teaching of the Hebrew Bible along the lines of a naïve, mechanistic view of the world that is evident in the friends of Job. Ecclesiastes thus marks an end of speculative wisdom in Israel. The epilogist points people to an alternative form of wisdom founded in the fear of God and obedience to His commands.[15] Shields' view is dependent on the existence of a wisdom movement within Israel that is opposed to the way of the law, but the existence of such an historical movement is based on too much speculation (see further comments below).

Fox argues that the speaker in the epilogue, called the frame narrator, transmits the teachings of Qohelet in order to mediate the words of Qohelet to the reader. There is no ideological conflict between the teachings of Qohelet and the epilogue; however, the narrator places distance between the epilogue and the words of Qohelet in a protective rather than a polemical way. The purpose of the epilogue is to make the teachings of Qohelet more plausible and tolerable to a more conservative reader who may align himself more with the stance of the epilogue. In reality, there is no real difference between the epilogue and the views of Qohelet. The probing of Qohelet is not dangerous because his conclusions fall within the proper boundaries of belief. Thus 12:13-14 is not contrary to Qohelet's thought. Fox argues that although Qohelet may not advocate legal piety, he does not contradict it either. He simply does not deal with this aspect of religion. Placing a boundary on wisdom allows the freedom of exploration demonstrated in Qohelet.[16] It is hard to see how Qohelet's conclusions fall within the proper boundaries of belief when he denies the differences between human beings and beasts (3:19-21), when he denies the existence of the two ways (7:15-18), or when he questions the deed-consequence relationship (8:11-14). These statements

---

15. Shields, *End of Wisdom*, 234–239.

16. Fox, *Rereading Ecclesiastes*, 363–374; see also Fox, 'Frame Narrative and Composition in the Book of Qohelet,' *HUCA* 48 (1977): 83–106.

are not just nuances of what other Scriptures teach, but raise major questions concerning these doctrines. The book of Proverbs, for example, would not encourage a person to explore pleasure (Eccles. 2:1), or to seek what the eyes desire (Eccles. 11:9), or not be committed to the way of righteousness and wisdom (Eccles. 7:16). It is also doubtful whether Qohelet himself comes to the right conclusions within the first-person discourse.

Others argue that the epilogue is contrary to Qohelet's thinking. The perspective of 12:13-14 is in line with the rest of the Old Testament, but does not coincide with the message of Qohelet. The narrator provides a frame around Qohelet's work and provides a perspective through which Qohelet should be read. Qohelet is in the canon to provide a teaching device in order to instruct others concerning the dangers of speculative, doubting wisdom in Israel.[17] Some go further and argue that there are two editors involved in the epilogue. The first editor may have been a student of Qohelet who praises the work and activity of Qohelet (12:9-11). The second editor does not agree with Qohelet's views and so adds 12:12-14 to dissuade readers from the heretical consequences of the book and to point people to a more orthodox view.[18] The view of two editors is not tenable. It assumes there are two different viewpoints in the first-person discourse, which leaves the reader not knowing where to really find Qohelet's thoughts. The supposed pious glosses do not fulfill the purpose ascribed to them because the negative view seems to always get the last word, as in 8:11-14.[19] Murphy notes that if the editor was trying to tone down the message of the book to make it more acceptable, he was a total failure.[20]

A few scholars stress broader connections between Ecclesiastes and other wisdom literature, especially in 12:11-12 where the 'words of the wise' are mentioned. Gerald Wilson

---

17. Longman, *Ecclesiastes*, 274 and Gordis, *Koheleth*, 339–340.

18. Barton, *Ecclesiastes*, 45; Crenshaw, *Ecclesiastes*, 189–190; Towner, 'Ecclesiastes,' 5:359, and Whybray, *Ecclesiastes*, 169.

19. Fox, *Rereading Ecclesiastes*, 19.

20. Murphy, *Ecclesiastes*, 130.

compares the epilogue to both Qohelet and the book of Proverbs. In fact, he argues that there are links that associate Qohelet to Proverbs, including a connection to Solomon and similarities between the superscription of Ecclesiastes and the superscriptions of Proverbs. Both the prologue of Proverbs and the epilogue of Ecclesiastes direct the reader to a collection of wisdom sayings that will guide people to proper conduct in life. There are also close associations between Proverbs and Deuteronomy. Proverbs 1–9 offers a reevaluation of wisdom and is added to earlier collections to make the book of Proverbs. Deuteronomy offers a new context in which to interpret the wisdom process. Ecclesiastes, apart from the epilogue, shows critical tendencies of later wisdom. Canonical editors added the superscriptions to both Proverbs and Ecclesiastes and they also added 12:9-14, making explicit connections with Proverbs 1–9. Thus Ecclesiastes and Proverbs are so bound together that each must be read in the context of the other and in light of the hermeneutical principles laid down in each superscription and epilogue. The fear of God and keeping His commandments is the proper context in which to evaluate the wisdom endeavor, which also shows that Proverbs and Ecclesiastes are bound together with the law.[21]

Gerald Sheppard also sees larger theological implications to the epilogue that go beyond the work of Qohelet. He argues that there are more connections between the epilogue of Ecclesiastes and the message of Qohelet than there are between the epilogue and the book of Proverbs. The epilogue provides a broad summary of the theme of Qohelet, which is not a comprehensive summary but an oversimplification of the message of Qohelet because it only highlights certain elements of his message. However, the summary theme of the epilogue does offer a synopsis of wisdom that is broader than Qohelet and very different from Proverbs. The focus in 12:13-14 sounds very much like the wisdom in Sirach, a wisdom book from the

---

21. Gerald H. Wilson, '"The word of the wise": the Intent and Significance of Qohelet 12:9-14,' *JBL* 103 (1984): 174–192. Wilson's article shows many more connections between Ecclesiastes and Proverbs than can be given in this summary. Also, Wilson argues against Sheppard's view (see the discussion to follow).

second century B.C. Thus the epilogue of Ecclesiastes offers a glimpse into a comprehensive, canon-conscious formulation related to the purpose of biblical wisdom.[22]

It is difficult to connect the epilogue of Ecclesiastes to broader movements of thought because it involves too much speculation concerning historical developments within Israel. Wilson, and also Sheppard to some extent, attempt to connect Ecclesiastes to developments and movements related to the law and to the wisdom literature. Assumptions concerning the dates of Ecclesiastes, Deuteronomy, and Proverbs come into play, as well as speculation concerning how wisdom and law developed in Israel. There does appear to be a relationship between some of the proverbs in the book of Proverbs, which can easily be *misunderstood* to teach a mechanical view of the deed-consequence relationship, and the debate in Job and the struggles of Qohelet. But this relationship does not support an historical development in wisdom because such issues can arise any time and any place in relationship to any person who has to wrestle with trying to come to grips with the tragedies of life.[23]

The purpose, function, and meaning of the epilogue, including its relationship to the message of Qohelet, are related to a person's overall approach to the book. Whether one understands the message of Qohelet as positive or negative also affects how certain verses of the epilogue are translated, which leads the reader of the epilogue to a certain view of Qohelet and his message. Some of these issues will be worked out in the comments that follow, but the approach taken in this commentary is that a wise man presents the words of Qohelet as warning and instruction to his son, and others, of

---

22. Gerald T. Sheppard, 'The Epilogue of Qohelet as Theological Commentary,' *CBQ* 39 (1977): 182–189.

23. Raymond C. Van Leeuwen, 'Wealth and Poverty: System and Contradiction in Proverbs,' *HS* 33 (1992): 25–32 argues that Proverbs does not represent a simplistic dogmatism concerning the deed-consequence relationship. For the relationship between Proverbs and the law see David A. Hubbard, 'The Wisdom Movement and Israel's Covenant Faith,' *TynBul* 17 (1966): 3–33 and Richard L. Schultz, 'Unity or Diversity in Wisdom Theology?' *TynBul* 48.2 (1997): 271–306.

the danger of speculative wisdom. When wisdom is not rooted in the right foundation of the fear of Yahweh as the beginning of wisdom, or when proverbs are misunderstood as teaching a mechanical relationship between deed and consequences (also a problem in Job's friends), a person can easily draw the wrong conclusions concerning life and concerning God. Such speculative wisdom does not represent a movement within Israel, but is a problem that can arise within the thoughts of any person. Eaton raises a good question when he asks why an orthodox writer would produce such a skeptical work if he were unhappy with the contents of the work.[24] Would it not be better to let such a work recede into the oblivion of history by not commenting on it? Such a view ignores the real dangers connected with wisdom and how one can easily become enamored of a speculative wisdom that is removed from the proper foundation. Plus, there is good reason to present this work because it is difficult to explain how someone as wise as Solomon could become so unwise in the living of his life.[25] If it could happen to Solomon, it could happen to anyone. The dangers of speculative wisdom are real.

The third-person epilogue can be divided into two sections. In 12:9-11 the work of Qohelet is described and evaluated, and in 12:12-14 there is an instructional warning with an emphasis on what is most important to know in order to avoid speculative wisdom.[26] Each section begins with the word *wĕyōṯēr*.[27] In 12:12 this word is set apart from the rest

---

24. Eaton, *Ecclesiastes*, 40–41.

25. The argument of the danger of speculative wisdom is not necessarily tied to Solomon being the author of the first-person discourse (see Longman and Shields as examples), but if Solomon is the author it provides a solid reason why someone would want to present his words as a warning of what can happen to someone as wise as Solomon (see the Introduction for the arguments related to Solomonic authorship).

26. The difference between these two sections can be seen in that the verses that describe the work of Qohelet (12:9-11) are in the indicative and the verses that are instruction and warning (12:12-14) use the imperative (Hubbard, *Ecclesiastes*, 247).

27. Seow (*Ecclesiastes*, 383) argues that the *waw* at the beginning of the epilogue does not necessarily mean that this verse or section is connected to the preceding because *waw* can also be used to introduce a new subject.

of the verse by the Masoretic accents, which suggests a translation of '*and furthermore.*'[28] This use suggests something 'in addition' and refers to the additional information given concerning Qohelet in these verses. Qohelet is described as '*a wise man*' (*ḥāḵām*). Some translations translate this word as 'wise,' which sets a positive tone for how people view Qohelet and the description of his work. However, *ḥāḵām* can mean 'wise man' and refer to people who work in the area of wisdom. In Jeremiah 8:9 the plural of *ḥāḵām* is used in parallel with the scribes, and in Jeremiah 18:18 the priest, the prophet, and the *ḥāḵām* are used together, suggesting that *ḥāḵām* refers to an official position.[29] Although some argue that *ḥāḵām* does not refer to a member of a professional class but rather to a person possessing the virtue of wisdom, the use of *ḥāḵām* in the Jeremiah passages does refer to a group standing alongside other officials.[30] Plus, the description of the work of Qohelet in 12:9 supports the view that *ḥāḵām*

---

28. Some translations ignore the Masoretic accents which set *wĕyōṯēr* off from the rest of the verse and translate it with what follows, which yields something like 'Not only was the teacher wise, but he also taught the people knowledge' (NIV; NASB; ESV). Gordis (*Koheleth*, 341–342) argues for this translation based on the comparison with a Mishnaic phrase, but see Fox (*Rereading Ecclesiastes*, 350) for an argument against this relationship. The function of the relative pronoun *šĕ* after *wĕyōṯēr* does raise some questions. Seow (*Ecclesiastes*, 382–383) translates it as 'because,' yielding the translation 'because Qohelet was a wise man he constantly taught the people knowledge.' Fox (*Rereading Ecclesiastes*, 350) takes the *šĕ* as meaning 'that,' with the translation 'and something remaining is (the fact) that Qohelet was a sage.' In this approach the *šĕ* does not need to be translated.

29. The word *ḥāḵām* is also used of the Babylonians in parallel with 'officials' (*śar*) in Jeremiah 50:35 and officials, governors (*peḥāh*), and 'commanders' (*seḡen*) in Jeremiah 51:57. Longman (*Ecclesiastes*, 277) also notes that there were both good and evil sages (2 Sam. 13:3; 16:15–17:29).

30. Whybray (*Ecclesiastes*, 170) specifically argues the point that *ḥāḵām* does not refer to a professional group (see also *The Intellectual Tradition of the Old Testament* [New York: De Gruyter, 1974]). Fox, in the earlier work *Qohelet and His Contradictions* (Sheffield: Almond, 1989), states that Whybray goes too far based on the passages in Jeremiah, as well as the use of *ḥāḵām* as a professional designation when applied to diviners (Gen. 41:8; Exod. 7:11). However, in the later work *Rereading Ecclesiastes* he does not even mention Whybray's view. It is interesting that in Whybray's commentary on Ecclesiastes (1989) he does not list his own 1974 work in the Bibliography.

means 'wise man' because it describes the work that a wise man would do. As a wise man Qohelet *'taught the people knowledge.'* He also *'listened*[31] *and searched; he edited many proverbs.'* The last three verbs specifically describe the work of collecting and evaluating proverbs. The wise man would listen to the wisdom of others and carefully search out or test such wisdom. He would also edit, in the sense of arrange or assemble such wisdom material as proverbs. This description applies to the work of Qohelet in the book of Ecclesiastes because he carefully listened, examined, and tested wisdom (2:1-17). He also used proverbs (1:15; 1:18; 4:5-6; 8:1-2) and grouped together proverbial sayings in chapters 7 and 10.

The description of the work of Qohelet as a wise man continues in 12:10, which is also a comment on what Qohelet tried to accomplish in the first-person discourse: *'Qohelet sought to find words of delight and to write correct words of truth.'* The second clause of this verse is difficult, because the Hebrew verb is presented as a passive participle, which has the sense of 'what was written.' If one takes *yōšer* as 'upright,' the translation that results is something like 'what was written were upright words of truth' (KJV; NIV). This translation easily leads to the conclusion that Qohelet's words are words of truth in line with the other wisdom writings of the Old Testament, such as Proverbs. However, 12:10 is not seeking to draw a conclusion concerning the results of Qohelet's work, but is trying to set forth what Qohelet attempted to accomplish in his writing. In this view the verb *'sought'* governs the rest of the verse (as in the ancient versions[32] and the NASB). Qohelet sought to do two things. He *'sought to finds words of delight'*

---

31. Many understand the verb *'izzēn* to be related to the word meaning 'scales' (*m'zn*), with the meaning 'weigh' or 'test' (Barton, *Ecclesiastes*, 199 and Whybray, *Ecclesiastes*, 170), but this would be the only time that this word means 'weigh' (F. C. Whitley, *Koheleth: His Language and Thought* [Berlin: De Gruyter, 1979], 102). It is better to understand this verb to be a denominative (a verb derived from a noun) from the word 'ear' (*'ōzzen*), which is attested by almost all ancient versions (Fox, *Rereading Ecclesiastes*, 352; Longman, *Ecclesiastes*, 275; Seow, *Ecclesiastes*, 384).

32. Murphy, *Ecclesiastes*, 123.

and he sought *'to write*[33] *correct*[34] *words of truth.'* The question is whether he succeeded in what he sought to do. The phrase *'words of delight'* is understood by commentators to refer to both the literary form of the words and their content. Concerning the literary form, Qohelet sought to write words that were aesthetically pleasing, which would bring delight to those who heard them.[35] Some argue that he also sought to write words that brought comfort, words that were deep and satisfying in their meaning, and words that were apt and timely.[36] One can legitimately question how delightful Qohelet's words really are, because the content is at times very disturbing.[37] His words do not bring comfort, they are not satisfying in their meaning, and they are not apt and timely. Rather, they are hard-hitting and blunt concerning the problems of wisdom and the way the world works. It has been shown throughout the commentary that the problems of life rather than solutions to those problems dominate Qohelet's thinking. Concerning whether Qohelet succeeded in writing correct words of truth, he himself answers this question earlier in the book. He is very clear in 7:23 that he did not attain wisdom and in 7:28 that his attempt to find the explanation of how the world works

---

33. Longman (*Ecclesiastes*, 275) notes that the passive participle is awkward in context and that it is better to read an infinitive absolute which is in parallel with the infinitive construct 'to find' and acts as a second verbal complement to the main verb *'sought.'* The change from passive participle to infinitive absolute only requires the change of one vowel (Fox and Seow also accept this reading).

34. Some translate *yōšer* as 'honestly' (Longman, *Ecclesiastes*, 275; Gordis, *Koheleth*, 190), but that would go against the idea that Qohelet failed in what he sought to do, because he did succeed in writing in an honest way in his description of the problems of wisdom. On the other hand, if he sought *'to write correct words of truth,'* then one can argue that he failed to accomplish that goal. It is also possible to acknowledge that Qohelet wrote *'correct words of truth,'* not in the sense that his words were in agreement with the truth of other biblical wisdom literature, but in the sense that his words were true to his starting point of a limited earthly horizon of 'under the sun' (see the Hermeneutical Keys to Ecclesiastes in the Introduction).

35. Seow, *Ecclesiastes*, 385; Crenshaw, *Ecclesiastes*, 191.

36. Leupold, *Ecclesiastes*, 294; Ogden, *Ecclesiastes*, 209; Seow, *Ecclesiastes*, 385.

37. Longman (*Ecclesiastes*, 278) argues that Qohelet's words do not get high literary marks and that they are not necessarily pleasant or delightful.

failed. He specifically says that he *sought* it repeatedly but did not find it. He also notes in chapter 8 that it is impossible to understand God's work in the world. No matter how much a person *seeks* to understand it, the explanation will not be found. Not even a wise man is able to figure it out (8:1, 16-17). If Qohelet denies that he has succeeded in what he sought to do, then the epilogue should not be read as overriding Qohelet's own words.

In 12:11 the epilogist continues his evaluation of the words of Qohelet by emphasizing a characteristic of wisdom writings in general which is also exhibited in Qohelet: '*the words of the wise men*[38] *are like goads and the masters of collections are like firmly planted nails set by a shepherd.*' Most commentators who argue that the epilogist is offering a positive evaluation of Qohelet recognize that goads can be painful, but see another metaphor concerning nails which is expressing something very positive. The nails refer to stakes, possibly tent spikes, which are driven into the ground and signify strength, firmness, or a basis for a responsible lifestyle.[39] In this approach many would understand the shepherd to be a reference to God, Who is the source of the wisdom sayings.[40] However, the chiastic relationship of the clauses of 12:11a leads to the view that there is only one metaphor and not two. A literal reading of the verse which shows the chiasm is given here: 'the words of the wise men are like goads and like nails firmly fixed are the owners of the collection.' Here the words of the wise men and the owners of the collection are parallel, which helps to solve the meaning of 'the owners of the collection.' It is possible that this phrase refers to the wise men themselves, whose special concern was to collect wise sayings,[41] but its parallel with the words of the

---

38. The exact Hebrew phrase, '*the words of the wise men,*' occurs in Proverbs 1:6 and 22:17. The former is part of the prologue to the book and the latter is a title to a section of wisdom sayings (Murphy, *Ecclesiastes*, 125).

39. Ginsburg, *Coheleth*, 474; Murphy, *Ecclesiastes*, 125; Bartholomew, *Ecclesiastes*, 360.

40. Murphy, *Ecclesiastes*, 125; Barton, *Ecclesiastes*, 198; Delitzsch, 'Ecclesiastes,' 6:435; Eaton, *Ecclesiastes*, 154, who even says that there is here a doctrine of inspiration.

41. Ogden and Zogbo, *Handbook on Ecclesiastes*, 438.

wise men leads to the conclusion that it refers to the collection of wise sayings, thus leading to the translation 'the collected sayings' (NIV; ESV).[42] The goads and the nails are also parallel in 12:11, which leads to the conclusion that they also refer to the same metaphor and not two different metaphors. In other words, the nails do not refer to stakes and they do not stand alone as a symbol of strength, but they reinforce the concept of the goads. Goads were nails firmly fixed at the end of a stick, which were used to move cattle. They were painful as they were used to prod cattle to get them to move.[43] Thus the emphasis is on the painful aspect of wisdom sayings, which fits well the words of Qohelet. Also, the shepherd is not a reference to God as the source of the wisdom sayings, but is continuing the reference to the metaphor of goads which are used by shepherds.[44]

The final section of the epilogue in 12:12-14 gives a warning against speculative wisdom and points to what is most important as the foundation for life. It also begins with *wĕyōṯēr*, which is translated *'and furthermore.'* The additional thing here is a command given to *'my son'* which reads *'among these be warned.'* The warning has to do with the work related to being a wise man: *'there is no end to the making of many*

---

42. Delitzsch ('Ecclesiastes,' 6:434) explains the word *'masters'* (*baʿălê*) as denoting masters not in the sense of leaders but in the sense of possessors, as in Genesis 14:13 and Nehemiah 6:18. The meaning 'possessors of collections' would refer to the words of the wise which constitute the collection. Longman (*Ecclesiastes*, 276) argues that parallelism is not a good way to argue that 'masters of collections' refers to the sayings because in parallelism the second line advances the thought of the first line in some way. Although that is true, there is also overlap between the parallel terms in the two lines. If there was a complete disjunction between the two then there would not be parallelism.

43. Fox, *Rereading Ecclesiastes*, 354–355. Both Fox and Longman (*Ecclesiastes*, 280) emphasize the painful and dangerous aspect of the wisdom teaching which they relate to the teaching of Qohelet. Longman argues that positive images associated with the shepherd would be the rod and staff (Ps. 23:4).

44. Fox (*Rereading Ecclesiastes*, 355–356) points out that when God is referred to as shepherd it refers to His capacity as keeper and protector, which is not relevant here. Plus, shepherds do not normally give words or commands (*Ecclesiastes*, 84).

books and much study wearies the body.' The 'making of many books' could refer to the writing and compilation of written texts or it could refer to the collection process of selecting and arranging proverbs.⁴⁵ The fact that 'there is no end' to this activity is a negative comment stressing that making many books is a process that can consume a person or that it is an activity that has no purpose.⁴⁶ The other warning stresses the physical effects that can overtake someone if this activity begins to consume them: 'much study wearies the body.' The key to the meaning of 12:12 is found in the meaning of *mēhē mmāh*. Some argue that *wĕyōṯēr*, which begins the verse, plus the preposition *min* on *hēmmāh*, should be understood to mean 'more than these' or 'beyond these.' The word *hēmmāh* ('*these*') is understood to refer back to the wisdom sayings of the previous verse so that the warning is not to go beyond the sayings of the wise men, including the work of Qohelet. In other words, there is no reason to add to or go outside the previous collections of wisdom writings because the sages have given their instruction and it is sufficient.⁴⁷ This view is positive toward Qohelet because it praises his work, which is part of the wisdom collections. Some argue that the reference of 'beyond these' is to pagan literature, but such a warning comes without preparation and the reader would need more information concerning the identity of the books in order to avoid them.⁴⁸ Another option is to translate *mēhēmmāh* as 'from these' or '*among these*,' with the warning being directed toward wisdom works which exhibit the character expressed in 12:11. Even among some of the words of the wise the son needs to be warned because wisdom can easily lose its way

---

45. Seow (*Ecclesiastes*, 389) argues the former view and Wilson ('The Significance of Qohelet 12:9-14,' 177) the latter view.

46. Fox (*Rereading Ecclesiastes*, 357) argues that the activity has no purpose. Ogden (*Qoheleth*, 212), on the other hand, sees this comment as a positive exhortation to be committed to the all-consuming task of wisdom because pure wisdom only comes at the end of a demanding, consuming search.

47. Murphy, *Ecclesiastes*, 126; Seow, *Ecclesiastes*, 388; Bartholomew, *Ecclesiastes*, 369.

48. Barton (*Ecclesiastes*, 198) and Eaton (*Ecclesiastes*, 155) mention the possibility of pagan literature.

and become speculative.[49] This understanding is the better option of the two; however, there may be a third possibility. The two views above understand *mēhēmmāh* as referring to the works mentioned in 12:11, but the *wĕyōtēr* ('*and furthermore*') at the beginning of 12:12 directs one's thinking forward so that the pronoun '*these*' (*hēmmāh*) in 12:12 is focusing the warning on the activities associated with wisdom, which include '*the making of many books*' and '*much study*.'[50] This view still sees 12:12 as a warning against speculative wisdom and the activities connected with it, without having to specifically define the content of 'the words of the wise men.' The wisdom pursuit can easily become a consuming task of much study and making many books. If one operates with an empirical method of observation and limits the search to 'under the sun,' as Qohelet does, one will struggle to find words of truth and to discover how everything fits together. A person can get caught up in always learning but never coming to an acceptance of the truth. There comes a point where wearying study and endless writing must cease and give way to something else, which is described in 12:13-14.

The epilogist moves the reader beyond speculative wisdom toward the real foundation of wisdom with a closing formula which many take as a conclusion: '*the end of the matter when all has been heard.*'[51] After wrestling with the words of Qohelet, the true conclusion is now given. It is composed of two imperatives followed by two motive clauses. The first imperative is '*fear God.*' The main question is whether this means the same thing as Qohelet's use of the fear of God in the first-person discourse. It has been argued in the course of this commentary that Qohelet's use of the fear of God stresses a caution before God because no one can figure out the work of God in this world, which means that no one is sure how

---

49. Longman, *Ecclesiastes*, 281.

50. Gordis, *Koheleth*, 344. Ogden and Zogbo (*Handbook on Ecclesiastes*, 440) mention this as a possibility.

51. Murphy, *Ecclesiastes*, 126; Ginsburg, *Coheleth*, 477; and Seow, *Ecclesiastes*, 390. Longman (*Ecclesiastes*, 282) comments that the abruptness of the last two verses may reflect the impatience of the frame narrator (the epilogist), who wants to get on with what is really important.

God will respond to different life situations. This explains why Qohelet struggles with injustice and the fact that the wicked instead of the righteous prosper. The exhortation *'fear God'* in the epilogue is used with concepts that are not found in the first-person discourse, which demonstrates that it is in line with traditional wisdom teaching, such as Proverbs 1:7 and Job 28:28. The second imperative is *'keep his commandments,'* which does not occur in the body of the book. It brings an additional dimension to what is found in Qohelet's teaching.[52] Instead of the emphasis on observation and the limited 'under the sun' perspective, the epilogue brings in the aspect of divine revelation. Here the epilogue goes beyond what Qohelet has said and even provides a critique of his empirical approach.[53]

The two motive clauses give a reason why someone should *'fear God and keep his commandments.'* The first one occurs at the end of 12:13: *'for this concerns every person.'* There is some discussion concerning the translation and meaning of this phrase. Garrett argues that the Hebrew *kōl* followed by a definite, singular noun means the whole of X (Gen. 2:2, 13; Exod. 14:20; Deut. 4:29), which would lead to the idea that to obey God is truly human.[54] However, most commentators translate the phrase in a way that expresses that *everyone* should be concerned with the fear of God and the keeping of His commandments as the most important things in their lives.[55] The next motive clause in 12:14 reinforces the idea that everyone is responsible to fear God and keep His commandments: *'for God will bring every deed into judgment,*

---

52. Seow, *Ecclesiastes*, 394. Although Seow argues that 12:13-14 do not contradict the book, he does recognize that the perspective of the epilogue differs from the rest of the book, for Qohelet did not have a judgment day in view in his thinking.

53. Longman, *Ecclesiastes*, 282. Bartholomew does not reconcile how Qohelet can operate on the basis of an autonomous epistemology in order to deconstruct tradition (*Ecclesiastes*, 87) and how Qohelet can also be in basic agreement with the epilogue.

54. Garrett, *Ecclesiastes*, 344.

55. Murphy, *Ecclesiastes*, 123; Fox, *Rereading Ecclesiastes*, 349; Ginsburg, *Coheleth*, 478; among others. Eaton (*Ecclesiastes*, 156) points out that the phrase *kôl hā'āḏām* is an idiom for 'every man' in Ecclesiastes 3:13 and 5:19 (Heb. 5:18).

including every hidden thing, whether good or evil.' Although Qohelet had mentioned judgment in several places (3:17; 11:9), the judgment of 12:14 is different in character from the judgment about which Qohelet spoke. In 3:17 the judgment of God is stated by Qohelet, but he does not allow it to help solve the problem of injustice with which he is wrestling there. In 12:14 the judgment of God is given as the reason why someone must fear God and keep His commandments. The judgment of God is affirmed as an event that will take place, and thus it should affect the way people live their lives. This judgment is different from 11:9, where the young person is encouraged to walk in the ways of their heart and the sight of their eyes while at the same time realizing that God may bring them into judgment for these things (see the discussion at 11:9). Qohelet consistently struggled with the seeming arbitrariness of the judgment of God in this life. Nowhere does he affirm a future, final judgment (9:10). The focus in 12:14 is different in that it is related to the commandments of God and it includes things which are hidden. There is a certainty that this judgment will take place in the future and there is an effectiveness concerning this judgment because it is comprehensive. The mention of *'hidden'* things seems to place this judgment after death.[56] Thus the epilogue goes beyond the teaching of Qohelet concerning the arbitrariness of God's judgment in affirming a certain, final, future judgment related to the commands of God where God will make things right. No matter how much someone may struggle with trying to figure out the work of God in this world or with trying to understand the tragedies and injustices of life, the most important response is to fear God and to keep His commandments.

Homiletical Implications
In most situations there is a simple explanation and a complex explanation. The simple explanation is usually straight and to the point. The complex explanation includes exceptions,

---

56. Longman, *Ecclesiastes*, 283 and Ginsburg, *Coheleth*, 478. The difference between Qohelet and the epilogue in the understanding of judgment is more than just the aspect of delay in judgment.

anomalies, and possible problems, which can be used to stress ambiguity or doubt. The complex explanation can even obscure the simple explanation. For example, how would you answer the question, 'Is God good?' The simple explanation says, 'Yes, God is good,' and then goes on to offer an explanation of the evil and tragedies of life. The complex explanation might start with the problems in life which in turn could throw doubt on the view that God is good. The problems can become so large that the goodness of God is questioned. In the book of Ecclesiastes the problems have taken center stage. Qohelet has wrestled with the difficulties and anomalies of life, which have caused Qohelet to doubt many things, and in the process the simple answer has been obscured. The simple answer comes in 12:13-14. It has taken twelve chapters to get to the simple answer and the reader may wonder why one has to wade through twelve tough chapters to finally get to the simple explanation. Why not just give it at the beginning? Welcome to wisdom literature, where the process of struggling through problems is just as important at times as giving the simple explanation. Qohelet genuinely struggles with the problems he raises. The author of Psalm 73 struggles for sixteen verses until there is a solution. Job and his friends debate the issue of whether he has sinned because he is suffering for over twenty chapters! In Ecclesiastes the author struggles with the problems of life for almost twelve chapters and then in two verses the answer is given! This is the way life works. The struggles of life are not always easily resolved, even when the answer is staring us right in the face. Sometimes it takes time to work through an issue before a person is able to hear or understand the simple answer. The danger is that someone can get so involved in trying to solve the problems of life that the simple explanation is forgotten. The danger is that someone who is as wise as Solomon can leave the true foundation of wisdom and end up struggling to understand life from a wrong basis (1 Kings 11:1-8). Thus the epilogue stands as a warning not to get so caught up with analyzing life that one forgets the basic truths of Scripture. The simple answer is that one must submit to God by doing what is pleasing to Him.

Scripture Index

Genesis
1:26-28 122
1:31 .... 284, 286
2 201
2:2, 13 421
2:7 .... 160, 243, 399, 400
2:15 122
2:19 160
2:19-20 242
3:16 77
3:19 .... 160, 243
4:24 .... 241n6
5:24 166
6:5 .... 284, 285, 298
9:11 .... 226n234
9:12 80
11:3 .... 172n24
12:11 .... 90n4
14:13 .... 418n42
14:19 .... 211n169
15:1 268
15:16 80
17:7 80
20:6 .... 191n100
20:11, 18 .... 155n94
22:3 356
23:4 .... 83n56
24:60 229
25:8 62
26:9 .... 115n117
28:11 178
28:17 .... 189n94
28:18-22 198
30:4, 9 328
37:30 184
39:6 .... 144, 180n61
39:9, 23 .... 245n25
39:23 .... 211n172
40:1 130
40:7 .... 246n28
41:8 .... 293, 414n30
41:25 293
41:37-45 294
41:49 268
42:22 184
48:14 345

Exodus
1:10 267
2:6 .... 173n25
3:15 80
3:19 .... 191n100
7:11 .... 414n30
9:5 .... 154n93
12:14 86
12:48 .... 241n6
14:20 421
19:5 .... 105n75
19:12 193
21:14 .... 313n239

Leviticus
5:1-4 .... 198n128
5:2 347
25:6 .... 83n56

Numbers
12:6 196

14:41 294
15:39 .... 106, 376, 377
22:18 294
22:24 349
23:10 62
23:21 76
24:13 294
24:14 .... 141n38

Deuteronomy
1:32 .... 264n96
4:1-2 .... 142n42
4:21 .... 155n94
4:29 421
6:10-15 219
12:31 .... 136n10
12:32 .... 142n42
13:17 .... 211n172
15:17 406
17:15 .... 225n229
19:5 .... 338n79
20:5-7 300
20:20 .... 341n92
21:4 .... 203n140
22:22 328
23:21-23 192
23:22 199
25:18 84
26:7 77
28:25 390
28:26 .... 303n209
28:50 293
32:21 54
32:35 128
33:9 .... 180n61, 190n98

425

Joshua
2:19 391
4:7 86
24:13 84

Judges
3:15 345
5:28 384
6:29 .... 172n24
9:19 .... 182n71
12:1-6 24
14:14 374
18:31 .... 189n94
20:16 343
20:37 128

Ruth
2:19 .... 241n6

1 Samuel
1 .... 189n94, 198, 199
2:3 .... 202n137
4:15 .... 172n22
12:5 .... 211n172
13 295
14:1 356
16:21 268
18:16 .... 181n69
18:23 .... 182n75
19:11 206
20:3 77
20:38 128
21:3-6 356
24:14 .... 406n6
25:3 .... 331n61
25:43 328
26:20 .... 406n6

2 Samuel
1:4 268
1:5 .... 115n117
1:19 .... 115n117
3 18
3:33 .... 115n119
7:12 84
8:8 268
11:16 206
12 296
12:22 .... 119n131
13:3 .... 414n29
13:5 266
13:32 .... 154n93
16:15-17:29 .... 414n29
20:3 .... 390n76

21:16 .... 313n239
23:10 84

1 Kings
1:21 130
2:43 .... 289n169
3:7 356
3:10-14 67
3:12 .... 17, 96, 290n171
4:29-30 112
4:29-34 .... 96, 292
4:33-34 .... 243n13
5:4 .... 331n63
7:1-12 104
8:31 .... 112n108, 130
8:57 209
10:5 104
10:10 268
10:12 105
10:14-27 104
10:23-24 96
10:23-25 112
11:1-8 423
11:3 106
11:4-8 67
11:9 11
12 .... 120n132
12:6 .... 115n117
12:8 184
12:14 18
14:9 17
14:11 .... 303n209
16:13 54
16:13, 26 54
16:25, 30 17
17:17 218
19:4 .... 406n6
20 .... 202n136
20:14-19 20
21:23-24 .... 303n209

2 Kings
1:2 218
2:1, 9 166
3:19, 25 140
6:5-6 .... 338n79
10:18 268
17:15 54
20:13 250

1 Chronicles
4:9-10 77
26:14 .... 331n61
29:3 .... 105n75

2 Chronicles
1:10 .... 181n69
1:11-12 .... 225n228
6:22 .... 112n108
10:7 .... 292n179
13:8 .... 313n239
31:5 .... 210n165

Ezra
2:55 26
2:63 .... 181n68
3:8 .... 189n94
6:22 .... 189n94
7:25 243
8:18 .... 331n61
8:36 .... 189n94
10:1, 6, 9 .... 189n94
10:2 .... 225n229
10:14 .... 181n68

Nehemiah
2:2 .... 246n28
5:7 .... 183n76
6:18 .... 418n42
7:57 26

Esther
1:20 306
4:14 .... 119n131
5:9 390
6:8-9 348

Job
3 251
3:11-19 171
4:8 76
7:2 80
7:7 102
7:16 .... 54, 55
8:3 .... 95n33, 261
9:12 .... 296n188
9:21 .... 180n61
9:29 54
19:6 .... 95n33, 261
19:14 .... 303n209
20:2 128
21:34 54
22:12 394-5
27:12 54
28 .... 278n141
28:21 145
28:28 421
31:5 128
31:25 365

31:32 391	78:33 54	3:1 37
34:12 .... 95n33, 261	78:40 77	3:2, 16 266
34:23 .... 154n93	90:3 160	3:7 .... 267n109
35:10 380	90:11 .... 119n131	3:9-10 .... 219, 223n221
35:16 54	91:1 259	3:13-18 98
40:2 243	91:16 62	3:14 .... 210n165, 260
42:3 145	94:11 54	3:16 ... 62, 116, 229, 233, 331
	96:1 86	3:16-18 115
Psalms	97:12 .... 182n71	3:18 117
1 98	102:11 260	3:33 321
6:6 84	103:6 170	4:10 .... 229, 266
6:7 .... 97, 379	104:3-4 82	4:27 194
7:15-16 350	104:10-11 82	5:1 37
8:2 360	104:29 400	5:4 281
8:4 111	104:29-30 160	5:15 379-80
10:4 .... 202n137	106:47 171	5:19 .... 337n74
10:12 321	107:12 77	6:1 37
11 54	107:37 .... 210n165	6:10 174
14:5a 158	109:23 260	6:12-15 62
15:22 185	110:1 345	6:23-24 281
16:11 404	110:4 .... 289n169	6:26 280
17:8 259	112:6 114	6:32 346
18:5 .... 336n74	112:10 97	7:1 37
19:5 82	115 195-6	7:4-5 281
20:18 185	116:3 .... 336n74	7:6-23 51
21:4 62	119:37 106	7:7 346
23:4 .... 418n42	119:65 .... 141n38	7:13 293
24:6 185	119:78 .... 95n33, 261	7:13-20 301
31:6 54	119:131 80	7:23 281
31:9 .... 97, 379	121:4 .... 90n4	7:24-27 266
32:11 .... 182n71	126:1 .... 197n124	8:11, 19 260
34:10 .... 184n81	127 382	8:18 .... 229, 331
34:12 102	127:3, 5 229	8:18-21 219
37 64	144:3 111	8:34-36 62
37:3, 27 .... 141n38	144:4 .... 54, 55	8:35 116
39:4-5, 11 55	145:1 .... 254n62	8:36 343
39:5 54	145:14 .... 177n48	9 382
42:4 .... 189n94	146:7 170	9:2 .... 103n66
49 .... 64, 166, 334-5	146:9 .... 95n33, 261	9:4, 16 346
52:8 .... 189n94		9:10 .... 62, 153
55:14 .... 189n94	**Proverbs**	9:13-18 280
58:4-5 .... 352n129	1:1 .... 15n7, 66-7n186, 71	10 .... 65n183
61:6 62	1:2-6 292	10:2 266
62:8 196	1:6 .... 417n38	10:4 174
62:9 54	1:7 .... 64, 421	10:4-5 .... 137, 296
62:10 54	1:8 37	10:7 .... 114, 342
63:4 171	1:8-19 377	10:13 346
66:11-12 335	1:11-13 301	10:16 .... 210n165
69:5 .... 190n98	1:15-16 194	10:19 196
72:2 243	1-9 .... 65n183, 411	10:21, 27 62
72:5 .... 80n41	2:1 37	10:22 .... 262, 263
73 .... 64, 65-6, 423	2:5 .... 153, 201	10:27 .... 62, 201, 266
73:13-16 165	2:10 98	11:4 266
73:23-28 201	2:87 .... 188n90	11:4, 28 287

11:5 266	19:10 .... 105, 348	31:30 .... 54, 55
11:12 346	19:15 174	
11:14 185	19:21 .... 65n184, 287	**Song of Solomon**
11:19 62	19:25 254	1:3 250
11:31 .... 159n112	20:2 130	7:6 106
12:1 254	20:13 .... 174, 331	7:12 396
12:11 76	20:18 137	8:2 .... 103n66
12:16 .... 97, 258	20:25 199	
12:21 .... 65, 266	21:6 54	**Isaiah**
12:23 .... 346n108	21:16 62	5:2 140
12:28 334	21:19 97	10:34 .... 338n79
13:1, 18 254	21:22 .... 341, 342	13:9-10 383
13:11 54	21:23 196	13:12 383
13:14 115	21:25 174	14:3 77
13:15 331	21:30-31 .... 65n184, 287	18:2 365
13:16 .... 346n108	21:31 348	28:16 128
13:22 ...... 129, 130, 131, 217	22:1 250-1	28:19 390
13:23 .... 65n184, 287	22:3 .... 113, 253	28:28 365
14:1 382	22:4 233	30:7 54
14:3 353	22:17 .... 417n38	41:4 .... 80n41
14:6 292	22:17-18 262	42:10 .... 254n62
14:8, 15 253	23:4 84	42:14 81
14:21 130	23:26 377	43:22 84
14:23 76-7	24:2 76	44:9 .... 226n236
14:26 201	24:5-6 274-5	45:7 261
14:27 .... 62, 115	24:21 .... 205, 294	45:20 .... 226n236
14:28 186	24:22 .... 119n131	48:16 .... 154n93
14:30 173	24:30 346	49:4 54
14:31 .... 65n184, 287	24:30-34 51	49:14 .... 303n209
14:32 .... 115, 117	24:31 349	50:2 321
14:35 294	24:33-34 357	51:9 .... 80n41
15:6 .... 210n165	25:2 .... 243n13	54:5 380
15:7 292	25:6 294	57:13 .... 53, 54
15:21 346	25:11 .... 137, 143	63:10 77
15:23 .... 137, 143	25:16 .... 215n195	65:11 .... 303n209
15:24 .... 115, 117, 334	26:4-5 .... 139, 262	65:16-17 87
15:27 256	26:12 .... 267n109	65:17 86
16:8 .... 210n165, 247n33	26:27 178	
16:8, 19 287	27:3 97	**Jeremiah**
16:9 .... 65n184	27:5 254	1:1 71
16:14 .... 294, 295, 347	27:12 253	2:5 54
16:16 260	28:8 129	2:24 81
16:16, 22 98	28:10 178	3:13 .... 190n98
16:18 266	28:11 .... 267n109	6:7 .... 218n209
16:23 .... 290n171	28:16 229	7:33 .... 303n209
17:1 .... 65n184	28:19 331	8:9 .... 292, 414
17:8 .... 337n74	29:15 254	8:17 .... 352n129
17:10 254	29:19 .... 221n216	8:19 54
17:24 .... 197n124	30:1 71	10:3, 15 54
18:7 353	30:7-31 .... 133n1	10:8 54
18:22 286	30:21-22 349	10:19 .... 218n209
18:24 188	31:1 71	14:22 54
19:1 .... 65n184	31:10 286	16:17 55
19:2 .... 130, 343	31:14 365	16:19 54

Scripture Index

18:18 .... 292, 414
20 251
20:14-18 171
20:18 76
23:16 54
25:10 383
25:34 .... 135n8
30:14 .... 303n209
31:31 86
44:23 .... 303n211
50:35 .... 414n29
51:57 .... 414n29

Lamentations
4:17 54
5:5 151
5:17 391

Ezekiel
8:8 .... 406n6
32:7-8 383
36:9, 34 .... 203n140
40:25 .... 292n179
47:22 .... 292n179

Daniel
11:35 159
12:10 159

Hosea
2:7 .... 181n67
11:4 .... 100n54
12:1 56
12:8 365
13:13 .... 137n14

Joel
2:2 383

2:14 .... 119n131, 161

Amos
1:1 71
3:6 261

Jonah
2:6 54
2:9 .... 198, 199
3:9 .... 119n131, 161
4:11 345

Micah
1:16 105
2:9 105
4:11 .... 172n22
7:8 .... 177n48

Habakkuk
1:13   76
2:7   390

Haggai
1:6, 9   268

Zechariah
4:2   398
4:2-3   399
10:2   54, 55

Malachi
2:7   191n102

Sirach
6:32   267n110
10:26   267n110

Matthew
6:7-8   192

6:19-21, 24 219
24:40-41 384
25:33 345

Luke
16:1-9 371

John
1:14 209
9:2 66

Romans
8:18-25 87
8:20 86-7
8:28 122
8:32 209

1 Corinthians
1:24 117
1:30 361
10:31 .... 132, 236
15:58 122

2 Corinthians
11:24-28 287
12:9-10 287

Colossians
2:2-3 117
2:3 361

1 Timothy
4:4-5 236
6:10 .... 219, 235

James
1:2-4 314

Revelation
18:2 384

Subject Index

A

'A Mighty Fortress Is Our
    God' hymn 361
Abner 115
'above the sun' perspective 68, 122,
    134, 164, 237, 263,
    287, 314, 334, 371
Abraham 62
Adam 110-11, 201, 242, 284
advice when life does not
    make sense 123-32
agnostics 334
Agur 71
Ahab 20, 202n136
Akkadian language 24, 105n80,
    105n81, 128, 184n84,
    295n187, 392, 398n105
Akkadian literature 33-5
allegory 380-1, 384, 385, 389,
    391-2, 393-4, 395, 397,
    398-9
Amenophis II 106n81
Amos 71
anger 199-200, 257-8, 346-7
animals, man has no
    advantage over 154-66, 333,
    334-5, 400
approaches, different 37-51
    the heterodox Qohelet 38-41
    the orthodox Qohelet 41-5
    the struggling Qohelet 45-51
Aquila 127n156, 304n213
Arabic 127n156, 241n5, 365n5
Aramaic language 21-2, 23, 24, 57,
    105n78, 202n136,
    344, 373n23
Archer, Gleason 14, 15n8
Assurbanipal 32
Assyrians 25, 32-3
authorship 14-29
    character of the Hebrew 21-5
    historical setting 18-21
    the term Qohelet 25-9
    autobiography 23, 27, 33-4, 35-6

B

Babylonians 18, 20n31, 414n29
Balaam 62
Bartholomew, Craig 46-7, 49-50,
    52-3, 125, 162-3, 205,
    308, 321, 359, 387,
    402, 407, 408
Barton, George 39
beasts see animals
Boaz 113n114
Bridges, Charles 25-6
Brown, William P. 30

C

Canaan 24
Canaanite language 106n81
Charles, R. H. 28
Christ see Jesus Christ
Christianson, Eric S. 54
companionship 169-89

431

concubines 105-6, 328
consequences, insignificant
    things have grave 335-61
corruption, among government
    officials 202-9
cosmic destruction 383, 384, 385, 394
creation 51-2, 84, 87, 145, 242,
                      261n90, 379-80,
                      385-9, 402, 408
Crenshaw, James L. 20, 130, 152,
                                157, 167
Cuthean Legend of
    Naram-Sin 33-4, 36n92

D

Dame Folly 280-1, 407
dark days 380-404
David 17-18, 115, 182, 296
'son of' 14-15, 66, 71, 72
death
    cosmic destruction 383, 384,
                                  385, 394
    as dark days 380-404
    day of 299-300, 301
    dishonorable 229
    failure of wisdom in light
        of folly and 109-16
    funerals 251-2, 383-4, 389,
                       391, 393, 394, 397
    hebel and 53, 375
    hour of 382
    of humans and animals 159-62,
                                  163, 164
    life after 115, 160, 166, 245, 375, 388
    living under the cloud of 317-35
    metaphors 397-9
    in the Old Testament 62
    praise for the dead 171
    premature 62, 161, 265-6, 269-70,
                   279, 283, 300, 301, 323
    reactions to 390-2, 394, 397
    of Sarah Ann Longstreet 116-17
    see also old age
deed-consequence relationship 38n97,
                    39, 41, 42, 47, 49, 50, 61-3,
                    75, 125-6, 129-30, 158,
                  265-70, 307-8, 310-11, 331,
                350-1, 378, 412, 413
Delitzsch, F. 14, 18, 20, 21, 36, 68,
                  205, 206, 207, 214, 407
determinism 136-7, 143, 242
Deuteronomy 411, 412
disasters 349-51, 367, 369,
                      383, 384, 385, 395

divine government, arbitrary
    nature of 302-13
divine retribution
    see deed-consequence relationship
dreams 190, 191n103, 194,
                      196-8, 200, 293-4
dust, returning to 160, 243, 399

E

Early Biblical Hebrew (EBH)
    see Standard Biblical Hebrew
Eaton, Michael 43-4, 63, 186, 192,
                  206, 207, 326, 330, 413
Eden, Garden of 108, 109n89, 201
Egypt 19
Egyptian literature 31-2, 35, 365, 367
Egyptian phrases 355n139, 377n39,
                              397n103
Elamites 58
Elijah 166
Ellermeier, F. 128
Elohim (God) 133, 201
enjoyment, calls to 13-14, 38, 60-1,
                   89, 149, 151, 152n84, 217,
                   222, 309, 311, 325-9, 334,
                     358-9, 366-7, 371-404
Enoch 28n62, 166
envy 173-4, 175, 187
epilogue 405-23
eschatological perspective 158, 383-4,
                      385, 394, 395
Eshmunazor 58
Eve 201, 284
evolution 165
expectations, frustration of
    unfulfilled 167-237
Ezekiel 22n39

F

Fall, the 93, 122
Farmer, Kathleen A 59
fictional autobiographies 27, 31, 33-4
folly 109-16, 344-9, 353-5, 360
    Dame Folly 280-1, 407
foolishness *see* folly
Fox, Michael 19, 27, 37, 40-1, 47-8,
            50, 51, 54, 57, 59, 61, 68-9, 69-70,
            73, 74-5, 79, 92, 111, 120, 130,
            137-8, 139, 145, 146, 148, 150,
            167, 168, 177, 183, 193-4, 197-8,
            205, 256, 279, 284, 287-8, 309,
            340, 383-4, 385, 387, 394-5, 396,
                            399, 409

Subject Index 433

Fredericks, Daniel 23, 24, 53, 56, 125, 214
funerals 251-2, 383-4, 389, 391, 393, 394, 397
future, uncertainty of the 317-61, 363-404

G

'gain' 60-1
Garden of Eden 108, 109n89, 201
Garrett, Duane 14, 36-7, 110, 151, 158, 354, 407, 421
Genesis 284-5
genre 29-37
Gilgamesh Epic 20n31, 30, 35, 179n55, 328n44
Ginsburg, Christian D. 139, 206-7, 242, 328
God
  anger of 199-200
  arbitrary nature of
    divine government 302-13
  blessings from 62, 125, 161, 229, 231, 236, 262, 263, 311, 374
  calling home 117
  caution in approaching 189-202, 208-9, 263-71, 420-1
  commandments 40, 41, 45n122, 47, 48, 50, 64, 377, 406-23
  creation 51-2, 84, 87, 145, 242, 261n90, 379-80, 385-9, 402, 408
  as determinist 136-7, 143, 242
  domain 58
  as Elohim 133, 201
  Enoch's relationship with 28n62
  faith in 43-4, 48
  fear of 40n105, 41, 44-5n122, 47, 64, 94, 152-3, 166, 192-3, 200-1, 202, 208-9, 267-8, 270, 306, 307-8, 406-23
  freedom of 42
  gifts from 60, 108, 124-5, 128-9, 130-1, 149, 193, 222-4, 227-8, 236, 327, 358
  glory of 209, 237
  goodness of 65, 66, 263, 423
  Job's relationship with 243
  judgment of 50, 63, 64, 158-9, 162, 163, 164, 376, 377-8, 388, 407
  justice of 38n97, 42, 43, 48, 51, 52, 95n33, 158, 163, 261, 308
  labor and 122, 127, 130, 142-3, 144, 153
  majesty of 192
  oaths made to 198-9, 294-5
  the oppressed and 170
  pleasing 423
  power of 66, 86, 195, 321-2
  providence of 136-7
  punishment from 38n97, 93
  purposes 117, 360
  Qohelet's relationship
    with 39, 59, 65-6, 76, 127, 152-3, 195, 201-2, 270, 388, 395
  return of the spirit to 388-9, 400
  the role of human
    beings and 133-66
  Solomon's relationship
    with 67, 96, 357
  as the source of life 395, 400
  sovereignty of 42, 65n184, 113n114, 117, 195, 262n93, 286, 287
  strength of 243-4
  trust in 48, 66, 160, 166, 271, 315
  wisdom of 361
  work of 31, 52, 53, 69, 75, 85, 93, 140-54, 193, 200, 261, 265-6, 286-7, 306, 312-13, 313, 331-2, 368-9, 371, 417, 420-1
  see also deed-consequence
    relationship; Yahweh
good
  proverbial sayings on 'what
    is good' 245-63
  who knows what is good? 239-315
Gordis, Robert 39-40, 41, 127, 145-6, 206, 214-15, 398
government, arbitrary nature
  of divine 302-13
government officials,
  corruption among 202-9
grain of sand example 360
Greek language 25, 109n89, 127, 304n213
Greek manuscripts 127, 304n213, 329n48, 339n84, 376
Greek period 19, 20, 21, 113n114, 202n136
Gregory Thaumaturgos 41-2

H

Habakkuk 64
Hannah 198
Harrison, R. K. 14

hebel
  importance of statement............50, 63
  meaning of.....43, 53-7, 72-5, 86-7, 379
  numerical value of.................... 68n190
  statements................50, 63, 69, 89, 102,
    108, 110, 120, 124, 125, 126,
    129-30, 131, 156n99, 162,
    175, 193, 213, 254-5, 256,
    305, 375, 389, 401-2
Hebrew, character of the.................... 21-5
Hebrew Bible 13, 210n168, 226n236,
    372n22, 408-9
Hengstenberg, E. W. 14, 160, 376
hermeneutical keys............................ 51-63
  the breakdown of the deed-
    consequence relationship 61-3
  the meaning of *hebel* 53-7
  the phrase 'under the sun' 57-9
  Qohelet's epistemology............... 51-3
  the question of 'gain' and
    the calls to enjoyment 60-1
Hertzberg, Hans Wilhelm....................46
historical setting...............................18-21
Holy Spirit..87, 189
homiletical implications
  prologue...86-7
  1:12-2:26 108-9, 116-17, 122, 131-2
  3:1-22 164-6
  4:1-6:9 187-9, 208-9, 219-20, 235-7
  6:10-8:17 262-3, 270-1, 286-7, 313-15
  9:1-10:20 333-5, 360-1
  11:1-12:8 370-1, 402-4
  epilogue 422-3
house, parable of the 382-3, 385
Hubbard, David A. 56, 84, 97, 152,
    160, 326
Hughes, Howard........................... 219-20
human beings, search for
  understanding the role of........ 133-66
human government, arbitrary
  nature of................................... 289-302
human limitations
  concerning knowledge........... 239-315,
    317-61
  as the essence of humanity 240-5
human world, futility of 82-6

I

injustice, Qohelet's
  reflections on............................ 154-66
*The Instruction of
  Onchscheshonqy*.......................365, 367
Instructions, for Egyptian
  kings................................ 31-2, 35, 96

Isaksson, Bo................. 23, 23-4, 35, 75n20
Isin..34
Israel................... 14-18, 20, 24, 65, 66, 86,
    105n75, 409, 410, 412
Israelites....................................... 193, 267

J

Jacob..189n94, 198
Jeremiah.....................................64, 71, 171
Jeroboam 17
Jerome.................... 123n143, 179n57, 365
Jerusalem...................... 14-18, 23, 66, 72
Jesus Christ
  faith in.................................. 117, 314-15
  as Immanuel....................................209
  kingdom and glory of............... 108-9
  parable of the dishonest
    manager 371
  power of................................... 287, 361
  on prayer..192
  resurrection 87, 122, 335, 404
  return..263
  suffering of 287
  as the ultimate companion........ 188-9
  as the wisdom of God 361
Joab...18, 62
Job..........................64, 65, 95n33, 171, 243,
    265, 409, 412, 423
Jonah 198
Joseph..................... 182-3, 184, 293-4
Joüon, Paul 75n20
Judah........................15n7, 18, 22, 25

K

Kaiser, Walter 14, 387, 407
Kidner, Derek 14, 97, 387
kings
  attributes.................................... 104-5
  authority 342
  behavior in the presence
    of.................................... 295-6, 346-7
  behavior of......................................170
  corruption of 206-7
  errors made by 347-9
  example story............................ 341-2
  experienced and
    inexperienced 356-7
  foolish................................. 183-5, 186
  not thinking bad
    things about........................ 359-60
  obedience to 289n169, 294-5, 296
  power 295-6
  responsibilities....................................243

Subject Index

knowledge, human
    limitations concerning 239-315
Koh, Y. V. 32, 34, 36
Krüger, Thomas 77, 186, 249, 288
Kushner, Rabbi Harold 66

L

labor
    benefits from 142-3, 144, 311
    failure of the
        results of 117-22, 126-7, 153,
        217-18, 250, 326,
        328, 366-7, 376
    frustrations of alleviated
        through companionship 171-80
    God and 122, 127, 130,
        142-3, 144, 153
    sleep of the laborer 215
Late Biblical Hebrew (LBH) 22, 23, 24
Lauha, Aare .... $39n100$, 193
laziness 174, 187, 287, 357-8, 359, 360
Leahy, Michael 385
Lemuel 71
Leupold, H. C. 14, 59, 327
life
    advice when life does not
        make sense 123-32
    a cautious approach to
        life and God 263-71
    enjoy life before the
        dark days come 371-404
Loader, J. A. 138
Lohfink, Norbert .... 71-$2n2$, 74, 78, 85
loneliness, frustration of
    met in companionship 169-89
Longman, Tremper, III 14, 27, 33-4,
    35, 47, 50, 54-5, 56-7,
    97, 125, 152, 160, 173,
    186, 214, 256, 355, 387
Longstreet, Sarah Ann 116-17
Lys, D. 124

M

Maccabean revolt .... $19n27$
man, no advantage over beasts ... 154-66
mankind, misfortune of 298-9
marriage 173, 178, 328-9
Masoretic Text .... $91n9$, 92, $155n98$,
    $215n193$, $247n37$, $304n213$,
    $329n50$, $369n17$, 414
Mishnaic Hebrew (MH) .... 21, 23, $414n28$
Moses 409

Murphy, Roland 40, 77, 130, 134,
    205, 264, 279, 355, 363, 366, 410

N

Naram-Sin .... 33-4, $36n92$
Nathan 295
nature
    futility of the natural world 79-82
    laws of 165
    parallel with human life 78, 84-5
    rejuvenation or death of 382-3,
    384-5, 395-6, 397
Nebuchadnezzar .... $104n74$
Nineveh 345
North Korea 333-4
numerical patterns 68

O

oaths, made to God 198-9, 294-5
Ogden, Graham 14, 43, 56, 59,
    84, 95, 116, 121, 125, 146,
    151, 162, 173, 182-3, 207,
    214-15, 255, 284, 386, 407
old age .... $95n33$, 380-1, 386, 388,
    $389n74$, $391n79$, $392n84$,
    393-4, 395, 397, 403, 404

P

pagan literature 419
Palestine 19, 23
paradise 109
Paul 122, 235, 287
Persian language .... 22, 25, $100n55$,
    $109n89$, $306n222$
Persians 18, 20-1, 21-2, 25,
    $202n136$, 300
Peshitta .... $248n38$, $346n108$
Pharaoh 267, 293-4
Philistines 24
Phoenician language .... 58, $124n143$,
    $211n173$
pleasure, failure of 99-109
poetry
    in Ecclesiastes 77-87
    Hebrew 77
    poem on time 135-40, 296, 297
    Qohelet's reflections
        on the poem on time 140-54
political power
    fleeting nature of 180-7
    oppresses with no one
        to comfort 169-71

preaching and teaching
   Ecclesiastes 67-70
   see also homiletical implications
prologue 71-87
   futility of the human world 82-6
   futility of the natural world 79-82
   homiletical implications 86-7
   introductory poem 77-87
   key question of the book 75-7
   motto 72-5
   superscription 71-2
Provan, Ian 14, 159-60
Proverbs 40, 41, 47, 51-2, 62,
        64-5, 94, 98, 104, 116, 152, 153,
        159n112, 192, 200-2, 253, 260,
        265-6n104, 270-1, 277n139, 279,
        280-1, 287, 292, 307n224, 376, 377,
        405, 408, 410, 411, 412, 415
proverbs, function of 356
Psalms 64, 195, 201
pseudepigraphy 27-8, 31, 34
pseudo-autobiography 34
Ptolemaic dynasty ... 19, 181n64, 202n136
purification 159-60

Q

Qohelet
   epistemology 51-3
   as heterodox 38-41
   identity 19, 63-7, 71-2
   as king 15-16
   as orthodox 41-5
   reflections on injustice 154-66
   reflections on the poem
        on time 140-54
   search for meaning 276-86, 312-13
   as struggling 45-51
   Targum of 41, 81, 123n43, 140n29,
        160, 264n98, 304n213,
        329n48, 339n84, 389n74
   use of the term 25-9
   as a wise man 414-16, 417-18, 419
   see also deed-consequence
        relationship

R

rabbis...139
random events 113, 115, 125, 165,
        331-2, 368, 369
Rehoboam 120n132, 184
Royal Inscriptions 32-3, 35
Royal Testaments, Egyptian 31-2, 35
rulers see kings

Ruth..113n114

S

Salyer, Gary D. 239
Samuel 295
Sargon 34
Sargon II 32
Sartre, Jean Paul, *Nausea* 314
Saul 62, 182n75, 295
Sawyer, John F. A. 382, 385
Schoors, A. 21
scientists 165
self-righteousness 266-7
Semites........................... 20n31, 113n114
Semitic language .. 16-17, 32, 35, 229n249
Sennacherib 32
Seow, C. L. 18, 20, 26, 32-3, 74,
        94, 96, 127-8, 130, 151, 159,
        184, 185, 196, 204-5, 214, 256,
        259, 300, 355, 384, 385, 391-2,
        394, 395, 398
Septuagint 54, 56n151, 76n22, 81,
        83n54, 86, 91n9, 93, 105, 110n99,
        113n114, 123n143, 154n92,
        155n96, 156n101, 170n8, 180n64,
        181n69, 191n102, 212nn176,
        177, 215n193, 221n216, 240n5,
        247n37, 248n39, 264n98, 282n150,
        292, 300n201, 303nn208, 209,
        304n213, 307n223, 318nn2, 3, 5,
        337nn74, 75, 346n108, 369n17,
        373n23, 392, 396
sexual desire 139-40, 178, 395
Sheol 166, 227n240, 326,
        329-30, 334, 335, 375n32
shepherds 417-18
Sheppard, Gerald T 411-12, 412
Shields, Martin A. 408-9
Shiloh 189n94
sin 38, 47, 49, 65, 87, 129-31,
        198n128, 199, 209, 263, 274, 275-6,
        281, 285, 322, 340, 347, 360, 423
Singer, Peter 165
Sirach 411-12
Sisera's mother 384
snakes 349, 350, 352
Solomon
   as a builder 104
   dedication of the temple 209
   disputed authorship of
        Ecclesiastes 14-18, 19-20n29,
        25-6, 26-7, 28, 66-7, 71-2,
        405n2, 411, 413n25

Subject Index

as inexperienced 356-7
proverbs 71
relationship with God 67, 96, 357
unwise in living of life ... 108, 413, 423
wealth of 15, 17, 104, 108
wisdom of 15, 16, 17, 28, 67, 96,
112, 292, 413, 423
Song of Solomon 24n45
Standard Biblical
Hebrew (SBH) 22-3, 23-4, 25, 67
stillborn children 225n231, 226n235,
226n236, 226n237, 230-1
storms 367-8, 381, 382, 385, 389, 394
the sum of things, searching for ... 271-87
Sumerian poem 381n51
sun
as good to see 374, 389
movement of 79, 80-1, 82
see also 'above the sun'
perspective; 'under the sun'
perspective
Symmachus 156n127, 304n213, 337n75
Syriac version 123n143, 155n96,
170n8, 181n69, 191n102, 247n37,
248n39, 304n213, 318n5, 329n50,
337n75, 373n23

T

Tabnit 58
Targums 105, 337n74, 365, 381n47
Targum of Qohelet 41, 81, 123n143,
140n29, 160, 264n98, 304n213,
329n48, 339n84, 389n74
teaching Ecclesiastes 67-70
Theodotion 127n155, 304n213
time
poem on 135-40, 296, 297
the proper time 296-9, 301
Qohelet's reflections on
the poem on time 140-54
truth 51n133, 415-16, 420, 423

U

Ugaritic language 105-6n81, 127n155,
145, 211n173, 295n187,
398n105
'under heaven' 57, 92-3, 94, 158
'under the sun' perspective 67-8, 74,
75-7, 87, 144, 146-7, 150, 152,
170, 171, 208, 236, 244-5, 252,
259, 271, 287, 311, 313, 314,
328-9, 360, 370-1, 375, 378,
401, 420, 421

meaning of phrase 57-9, 85-6
Qohelet's search for
meaning 89-132
unfulfilled expectations,
frustration of 167-237
United Monarchy 24
Untashgal 58
'upon the earth' 57

V

Vidal, Gore 173n31
vows, to God 198-9, 294-5
Vulgate 54, 105, 123n143, 135n8,
151, 154n92, 155n96, 156n101, 160,
181n69, 203n140, 221n216, 248n39,
329n50, 337n75, 346n108, 369n17

W

Waltke, Bruce 28, 44, 63
wealth
advice in light of the
dissatisfaction of 220-4
general dissatisfaction with 209-19
tragedy of not enjoying
one's wealth 224-37
unfulfilled expectations
related to 209-37
Whybray, R. N. 16, 40, 41, 42-3, 78,
78-9, 81, 83-4, 85, 120, 124,
138-9, 139, 150, 152, 159, 167,
175, 204, 266-7, 300, 381
Williams, Willie 'Pete' 313-15
Wilson, Gerald H 410-11, 412
wisdom
benefits of 259-60, 274-5,
293-4, 342-3, 346-7,
351-2, 360
the danger of
speculative 11, 47, 63-7,
99, 408-9, 410,
412-13, 418-20
failure of 90-9, 109-17, 186,
233, 249, 255-7, 259-60,
274, 277, 331, 344-5, 352
and folly 253-6, 259, 267-9,
344-6, 347, 352-3, 360
Lady Wisdom 283n153, 285n159
of the poor youth 183-6
Qohelet as a wise man 414-16,
417-18, 419
of Solomon 15, 16, 17, 28, 67,
96, 112, 292, 413, 423

traditional............. 38-9, 39-40, 47, 137, 143, 159, 161*n*124, 258-9, 281, 285, 377, 407-8, 421
wisdom literature........... 19, 23, 24, 32, 63, 76, 94, 95-6, 114, 173*n*29, 251, 382, 410-12, 423
of the wise man........ 291-3, 296-7, 301, 302, 313, 341-2, 343, 353, 360-1
women, Qohelet on..... 279-81, 285-6, 328
world, arbitrary nature of the 287-315
Wright, George Addison................. 68, 69

Y

Yahweh
    command of 294
    fear of 52, 53, 64, 152, 153, 201, 413
    Solomon and 67
Young, E. J. 14
Young, Ian... 24, 25

Z

Zogbo, Lynell................ 173, 207, 284, 386

Christian Focus Publications

Our mission statement –

STAYING FAITHFUL

In dependence upon God we seek to impact the world through literature faithful to His infallible Word, the Bible. Our aim is to ensure that the Lord Jesus Christ is presented as the only hope to obtain forgiveness of sin, live a useful life and look forward to heaven with Him.

Our books are published in four imprints:

CHRISTIAN FOCUS

Popular works including biographies, commentaries, basic doctrine and Christian living.

CHRISTIAN HERITAGE

Books representing some of the best material from the rich heritage of the church.

MENTOR

Books written at a level suitable for Bible College and seminary students, pastors, and other serious readers. The imprint includes commentaries, doctrinal studies, examination of current issues and church history.

CF4•K

Children's books for quality Bible teaching and for all age groups: Sunday school curriculum, puzzle and activity books; personal and family devotional titles, biographies and inspirational stories – because you are never too young to know Jesus!

Christian Focus Publications Ltd,
Geanies House, Fearn, Ross-shire,
IV20 1TW, Scotland, United Kingdom.
www.christianfocus.com
blog.christianfocus.com